Research Anthology on Usage, Identity, and Impact of Social Media on Society and Culture

Information Resources Management Association
USA

Volume III

Published in the United States of America by
  IGI Global
  Information Science Reference (an imprint of IGI Global)
  701 E. Chocolate Avenue
  Hershey PA, USA 17033
  Tel: 717-533-8845
  Fax: 717-533-8661
  E-mail: cust@igi-global.com
  Web site: http://www.igi-global.com

Library of Congress Cataloging-in-Publication Data

Names: Information Resources Management Association, editor.
Title: Research anthology on usage, identity, and impact of social media on
  society and culture / Information Resources Management Association,
  editor.
Description: Hershey, PA : Information Science Reference, [2022] | Includes
  bibliographical references and index. | Summary: "This reference set
  discusses the impact social media has on an individuals' identity
  formation as well as its usage within society and cultures, exploring
  new research methodologies and findings into the behavior of users on
  social media as well as the effects of social media on society and
  culture as a whole"-- Provided by publisher.
Identifiers: LCCN 2022016910 (print) | LCCN 2022016911 (ebook) | ISBN
  9781668463079 (hardcover) | ISBN 9781668463086 (ebook)
Subjects: LCSH: Social media--Psychological aspects. | Identity
  (Psychology) | Social media and society.
Classification: LCC HM742 .R46783 2022 (print) | LCC HM742 (ebook) | DDC
  302.23--dc23/eng/20220509
LC record available at https://lccn.loc.gov/2022016910
LC ebook record available at https://lccn.loc.gov/2022016911

British Cataloguing in Publication Data
A Cataloguing in Publication record for this book is available from the British Library.

The views expressed in this book are those of the authors, but not necessarily of the publisher.

For electronic access to this publication, please contact: eresources@igi-global.com.

List of Contributors

Table of Contents

Section 2
Development and Design Methodologies

Volume II

Section 3
Tools and Technologies

Section 4
Utilization and Applications

Volume III

Section 5
Organizational and Social Implications

Section 6
Critical Issues and Challenges

Preface

Over the years, social media has blossomed from a leisure tool used by a select pool of younger individuals to an essential form of communication for everyone. It has connected individuals globally and has become an essential practice in marketing, advertising, broadcasting news stories, conducting research, and more. The internet has quickly become a new hub for communication and community development. In most communities, people develop new cultural norms and identity through social media usage. However, while these new lines of communication are helpful to many, challenges such as social media addiction, cyberbullying, and misinformation lurk on the internet and threaten forces both within and beyond the internet.

Staying informed of the most up-to-date research trends and findings is of the utmost importance. That is why IGI Global is pleased to offer this three-volume reference collection of reprinted IGI Global book chapters and journal articles that have been handpicked by senior editorial staff. This collection will shed light on critical issues related to the trends, techniques, and uses of various applications by providing both broad and detailed perspectives on cutting-edge theories and developments. This collection is designed to act as a single reference source on conceptual, methodological, technical, and managerial issues, as well as to provide insight into emerging trends and future opportunities within the field.

The *Research Anthology on Usage, Identity, and Impact of Social Media on Society and Culture* is organized into six distinct sections that provide comprehensive coverage of important topics. The sections are:

1. Fundamental Concepts and Theories;
2. Development and Design Methodologies;
3. Tools and Technologies;
4. Utilization and Applications;
5. Organizational and Social Implications; and
6. Critical Issues and Challenges.

The following paragraphs provide a summary of what to expect from this invaluable reference tool.

Section 1, "Fundamental Concepts and Theories," serves as a foundation for this extensive reference tool by addressing crucial theories essential to understanding the usage, identity, and impact of social media. The first chapter of this section, "The Dark Side of Engaging With Social Networking Sites (SNS)," by Profs. Eileen O'Donnell and Liam O'Donnell of Technological University Dublin, Ireland, explores the dark side of social networking sites. The final chapter of this section, "The Facebook Me: Gender, Self-Esteem, and Personality on Social Media," by Profs. Robert Andrew Dunn and Heng Zhang of East Tennessee State University, USA, examines the influence of gender, personality, and self-esteem on social media presentation.

Section 2, "Development and Design Methodologies," presents in-depth coverage of the design and development of social media assessment and research. The first chapter of this section, "Psychological Impact and Assessment of Youth for the Use of Social Network," by Profs. Sapna Jain and M. Afshar Alam of Jamia Hamdard, India and Prof. Niloufer Adil Kazmi of Independent Researcher, India, dissects the effect of online life on each youngster in both the negative and positive bearing of their development utilizing the social impact hypothesis. The final chapter of this section, "At the Mercy of Facebook: A Meta-Analysis on Impact of Social Networking Sites, Teen Brain on Teenage Pregnancies," by Prof. Nirupama R. Akella of Wichita State University, USA, is a meta-analysis of teen brain research and social media technology such as Facebook that could result in spiraling rates of teenage pregnancy. The author discusses contemporary theories of brain circuitry including teen brain structure and function as one of the plausible reasons for rising teenage pregnancy rates.

Section 3, "Tools and Technologies," explores the various tools and technologies used in communications and research on social media. The first chapter of this section, "Collaborative Social Networks: Effect of User Motivation, Cognition, and Behavior on User Participation," by Prof. Yulin Chen of Tamkang University, New Taipei City, Taiwan, investigates the relationships between the motivation, cognition, and behavior of knowledge management. It analyzes university students preparing to share content on the Tamshui Humanities Knowledge Collaboration System to determine whether different participation motivation dimensions (community motivation and personal motivation) affected their knowledge management cognition and behavior. The final chapter of this section, "The Important Role of the Blogosphere as a Communication Tool in Social Media Among Polish Young Millennials: A Fact or a Myth?" by Profs. Sylwia Kuczamer-Kłopotowska and Anna Kalinowska-Żeleźnik of University of Gdańsk, Poland, proposes and discusses the hypothesis that the blogosphere is a relatively well-developed and independent social media communication tool used by millennials.

Section 4, "Utilization and Applications," describes the interactions between users on social media. The first chapter of this section, "Adolescents, Third-Person Perception, and Facebook," by Prof. John Chapin of Pennsylvania State University, USA, documents the extent of Facebook use and cyberbullying among adolescents. It is based on a study theoretically grounded in third-person perception (TPP), the belief that media messages affect other people more than oneself. The final chapter of this section, "Facebook Communities of African Diasporas and Their U.S. Embassies: A Content Analysis Study," by Prof. Hesham Mesbah of Rollins College, USA and Prof. Lauren Cooper of Florida House of Representatives, USA, explores how the Nigerian, Ethiopian, and Egyptian diasporas in the United States use their Facebook groups to create their imagined communities. It also draws a parallel between their use of Facebook and how the embassies of their countries of origin use the same platform in performing their official duties.

Section 5, "Organizational and Social Implications," includes chapters discussing the impact of social media usage and interpersonal interaction on society. The first chapter of this section, "Understanding Social Media Addiction Through Personal, Social, and Situational Factors," by Prof. Asli Elif Aydin of Istanbul Bilgi University, Turkey and Prof. Ozge Kirezli of Yeditepe University, Turkey, gains an in-depth understanding of the social media addiction construct. The final chapter of this section, "Transformation of China's Most Popular Dating App, Momo, and Its Impact on Young Adult Sexuality: A Critical Social Construction of Technology Analysis," by Prof. Weishan Miao of Chinese Academy of Social Sciences, China and Prof. Jian Xu of Deakin University, Australia, explores China's most popular dating app 'Momo' and its impact on young adult sexuality.

Section 6, "Critical Issues and Challenges," presents coverage of academic and research perspectives on the critical issues imposed by social media on its users, communities, and society. The first chapter of this section, "Positive vs. Negative Emotions and Network Size: An Exploratory Study of Twitter Users," by Prof. Yeslam Al-Saggaf of Charles Sturt University, Australia, examines the relationship between the expression of positive and negative emotions in Twitter and users' network size. The final chapter of this section, "The Tipping Point: A Comparative Study of U.S. and Korean Users on Decisions to Switch Social Media Platforms," by Prof. Soo Kwang Oh of Pepperdine University, USA; Prof. Seoyeon Hong of Rowan University, USA; and Prof. Hee Sun Park of Korea University, South Korea, focuses on why users quit certain social media and change their favorite platforms, such as the current shift from Facebook to Twitter to Instagram and Snapchat. Furthermore, this exploratory study builds an understanding of social media usage and motivations for switching from a cross-cultural perspective by comparing findings from Korean and U.S. users.

Although the primary organization of the contents in this multi-volume work is based on its six sections, offering a progression of coverage of the important concepts, methodologies, technologies, applications, social issues, and emerging trends, the reader can also identify specific contents by utilizing the extensive indexing system listed at the end of each volume. As a comprehensive collection of research on the latest findings related to social media, the *Research Anthology on Usage, Identity, and Impact of Social Media on Society and Culture* provides social media analysts, communications specialists, computer scientists, online community moderators, sociologists, psychologists, business leaders and managers, marketers, advertising agencies, government officials, libraries, students and faculty of higher education, researchers, and academicians with a complete understanding of the applications and impacts of social media. Given the vast number of issues concerning usage, failure, success, strategies, and applications of social media, the *Research Anthology on Usage, Identity, and Impact of Social Media on Society and Culture* encompasses the most pertinent research on the applications, impacts, uses, and research strategies of social media.

Chapter 47
Not a Girl, Not Yet a Woman:
A Critical Case Study on Social Media, Deception, and Lil Miquela

Raymond Blanton
University of the Incarnate Word, USA

Darlene Carbajal
iD https://orcid.org/0000-0003-2682-3649
University of the Incarnate Word, USA

ABSTRACT

This chapter takes an interdisciplinary approach to the study of deception from the critical perspectives of rhetoric, communication, and media studies. The primary objective is to interrogate the interrelationship of communication, identity, and technology relevant to social media in order to confront issues related to online deception. To that end, this case study is centrally focused on social media sensation Miquela Sosa, also known as Lil Miquela, and the implications of artificial intelligence (AI) technologies and social media influencers to contribute to a more robust critical consciousness regarding misinformation online.

INTRODUCTION

In this chapter, the authors seek to provide some perspective and satisfactory answers to the growing questions and concerns regarding misinformation in business, politics, religion and everyday life. More precisely, using the critical perspectives of rhetoric, communication, and media studies, the authors' objective is to interrogate the interrelationship of communication, identity, and technology relevant to the rise of artificial intelligence (AI) technologies and social media influencers, focusing specifically on Instagram sensation Miquela Sosa, also known as Lil Miquela. In short, these objectives serve the larger purpose of broadening our understanding of online deception patterns and emboldening students, scholars, and professionals with strategies to confront these challenges.

DOI: 10.4018/978-1-6684-6307-9.ch047

What makes this case study peculiar, and all the more compelling, is that Lil Miquela is not a real person but rather an AI technology that promotes various products and social causes. *Time* recently named Miquela as one of the 25 most influential people on the Internet (Chan, 2018); *V Magazine,* devoted to fashion, music, and culture, has hailed her as the "face of new-age logomania" (Mischianti, 2018); and *Wonderland*, devoted to fashion, music, beauty, art, and culture, has featured an in-depth interview and photo spread with Miquela (Walker, 2018). On Instagram, Miquela identifies as a robot from Los Angeles; a musician, with a music video inspired by her single, "Hate Me"; and as a social advocate for Black Lives Matter, the LGBTQ+ community, the Downtown Women's Center of Los Angeles, and the Campaign for Youth Justice. In short, Miquela is a substantial social media influencer—an emblem for both style and social justice causes.

In sum, we contend that Miquela serves as an ideal representative anecdote through which to interrogate misinformation and online deception. Moreover, we further argue that this phenomenon has brought us to a cultural crossroad where critical consciousness and reality converges with varying degrees of misdirection and deception. Put differently, it is representative of a significant turning point in advertising and mass consumer culture, where AI technologies have become social media influencers. As such, this chapter makes for an important study in online deception with significant implications for intellectual and media ethics. To this end, the authors consider the rhetorical dimensions of communication, identity, and technology related to deception before confronting the case study of Lil Miquela and concluding with recommendations and future research considerations.

THE STORY OF US: COMMUNICATION, IDENTITY, AND TECHNOLOGY

In situating the significance and importance of this study, the authors rely on the theoretical foundations of rhetoric, communication, and media. Altogether, these disciplines, most especially in our present moment, confront a vast array of human communication issues and challenges, namely, misinformation and online deception on social media. Given that technology has become one of the preeminent ways through which we communicate in order to constitute our sense of identity and secure our physiological and emotional needs, the authors focus on themes of belonging. For instance, Maslow's hierarchy of needs has belonging centered in the pyramid between our basic physiological and safety needs and the higher needs of esteem and self-actualization. In this sense, belonging is foundational to our sense of self and community. Yet our times are indicative of increased separation, as though it is coming apart at the seams (Ross, 2018, p. 1). Across this chasm, social media has given rise to new ways of finding and manufacturing belonging. Howard J. Ross, in *Our Sense of Belonging: How Our Need to Connect Is Tearing Us Apart* (2018), has argued, "things need to get real before they can get better" (p. 175). Indeed, the authors argue an interrogation of Miquela and trends in AI technology help us get both real and better, promoting more critically conscious awareness of misinformation issues and stimulating awareness of human needs for personal connection, vulnerability, and consciousness.

Theoretical Considerations

As the authors contemplate the implications of online deception in the case study of Lil Miquela, it is important to establish some theoretical considerations. In its simplest form, theory is much more than a rote tool for erudition. Rather, theory is a way of understanding and seeing the world derived from some critical distance. As such, the authors have chosen rhetorical theory as a framework through which to apprehend and comprehend the interplay of social media and online deception as modes of communication and media. Furthermore, the authors examine deceptive messages using Levine's (2014) Truth-default theory (TDT) as a theoretical framework.

Rhetoric

The rhetorical tradition is one of the "deep intellectual taproots for communication and media study in the twentieth and twenty-first centauries" (Simonson, 2010, p. 7). Intellectually, the study of communication and media are branches of rhetorical practice. Pragmatically, rhetoric and media are specific modes of communication. In turn, what makes the discipline of rhetoric, based in large part on the history of Platonic writing and thought, such a fitting foundation for the study of online deception is that rhetoric has, justifiably at times, been described as being motivated and defined by deception. When the term rhetoric is used pejoratively, it is typically yielded as an accusation regarding misdirection or deception, as when Plato leveraged his position on rhetoric as flattery against the Sophists (this is the inspiration for the English word sophistry). In short, rhetoric is well acquainted with the realms of deception.

Furthermore, rhetoric is also an ideal theoretical guide to confront issues related to deception in that it is well acquainted with the use of language to influence emotions. According to Kenneth Burke, the real lasting impact of rhetoric derives from the "trivial repetition and dull daily reinforcement" of language rather than exceptional rhetorical skill (Burke, 1969b, p. 26). In other words, when we consider the abundant and far-reaching repetition and reinforcement of social media messages, particularly those related to deception, we begin to understand their persuasive and rhetorical appeal. Moreover, beyond mere persuasion, rhetoric is fundamentally a means of identification in which we persuade others insofar as we speak their language by gesture and tonality, order and image, attitude and idea, identifying our ways with theirs (Burke, 1969, p. 55). As it pertains to online deception and social media use, the cultural significance of Lil Miquela aligns with these theoretical considerations—that is, through daily reinforcement of varying means of identification via cultural languages. Lastly, one of the theoretical concepts Burke uses to access complex cultural meanings is the representative anecdote, for it provides a clear yet complex platform from which to assess the scope of potential meaning (Burke, 1969, p. 324). Barry Brummett elaborates on the trope, indicating that the representative anecdote is a "trained awareness" of types of dramatic form, with the potential to empower people to extract order from chaos—to decipher what we as a people and culture most deeply fear and hope (Brummett, 1984, p. 174).

Restated, rhetoric is the affective use of language for effect generated through the dull daily reinforcement of various identifications. In this sense, language is broadly defined as some combination of verbal, non-verbal, symbolic, visual, or aural communication, from pitch and intonation to symbols and words—all of which are fundamental to communication, identity, and technology. Subsequently, these form the bases of study that propel rhetoric, communication, and media. Most explicitly, the authors argue that Miquela and the creative technology company Brud, the proprietor of Lil Miquela, consistently engage in acts of misinformation, intentionally, knowingly, and purposefully misleading followers. Thus, the authors consider Brud and Miquela as an ideal representative anecdote, useful for deducing some of the nuances of meaning regarding misinformation in social media. Beforehand, however, the authors address some theoretical considerations regarding deception.

Deception

The issue of deception transcends most disciplinary, social, cultural, and historical boundaries (DePaulo, Kashy, Kirkendol, Wyer, & Epstein, 1996). For instance, according to Timothy Levine (2014), "deception is defined as intentionally, knowingly, and/or purposely misleading another person" (p. 379). Relatedly, with more specificity, Judee Burgoon and David Buller (1998) define deception as a "message knowingly transmitted by a sender to foster a false belief or conclusion by the receiver" (p. 381). They argue that, "Emotions provoke deception, and deception provokes emotions" (p. 381) and that "consequences of deceit entail emotion processes that are incorporated in every explanation of deceptive communication" (p. 381). When we interrogate the interchange of emotions and the human need for belonging in light of other developing cultural trends related to AI technologies, we begin to see more clearly some of the rhetorical potential related to online deception. Furthermore, from the perspective of deception in daily situations, deception in self-presentation is the arrangement of self in everyday social life as characteristically an "edited and packaged" presentation (DePaulo, Kashy, Kirkendol, Wyer, & Epstein, 1996, p. 979).

As an interdisciplinary approach, deception occurs when people deliberately communicate messages that aim to deceive others. Accounting for the different forms of deception, the authors adopt deceptive messages as outright falsehood to mislead including the intentional act by the sender to transmit covert messages that do not reveal the whole truth (Burgoon & Buller, 1996; Burgoon & Buller, 1998; Levine, 2014; McCormick, 1992). DePaulo et al., (1996) noted deceptive behaviors arise from the desire for people to claim their own identities in which lies are told most often in "matter-of-fact-ways" (p. 991) to benefit self-interests and protect other-oriented lies. By examining various motivations for why people lie (DePaulo et al., 1996), the authors consider the significance of what makes Lil Miquela's case significant. Specifically, in the context of social media, which allows users to participate autonomously and anonymously, buttressed by the rapid and expansive participatory nature of the Internet, ethical concerns arise as Brud, Miquela's creators, engage with more than 1.5 million Instagram followers.

Researched from perspectives of online communication and behavior on social media, the authors consider how social media gives users freedom to disclose certain parts of their identity and communicate different messages to different audiences, thus making the argument that deception derives from decisions that do not associate lies with consequence. In Levine's (2014) Truth-Default-Theory (TDT), for instance, deception derives from the premise that when humans communicate with other humans, people operate on the default presumption that communication is honest most of the time. As such, in TDT, communication context and content are considered to determine if communication is deceptive (Levine, 2014). To uncover patterns of deception, this case study draws on social media posts across platforms that define how Miquela is portrayed to her (it) audience; similarly, to understand the motivations and techniques used to create Miquela.

In sum, whereas the social psychologists approach emotion-based deception as biological signals centered on cognitive experiences, communication scholars consider the social nature of emotions that focus on how emotional expressions are utilized to create deceptive messages (Burgoon & Buller, 1998, p. 382). What is most significant in these studies is the recognition that deception is a conscious act of fostering beliefs based on some degree of misinformation. Indeed, worthy counterfeits should look and feel the part. As such, theoretically speaking, the authors propose rhetorical studies, and their close relative's communication and media, be considered in deception research.

A CHEAP TRICK: THE RHETORIC OF SOCIALLY MEDIATED DECEPTION

Given the theoretical considerations of this chapter, the authors turn their attention to the rhetoric of socially mediated deception, keeping in mind the interplay of human emotions and the need for belonging that coincide with the dull daily reinforcement of technology and online encounters. Put differently, "I Want You To Want Me," the September 1977 single by American rock band Cheap Trick (Nielsen, 1977), succinctly, adeptly, and aptly captures the essence of social media behaviors oriented around online deception. In order to effectively understand the misdirection levied by Brud through social media influencer Miquela, the authors first briefly consider the role of artificial/technology before considering the particulars of Brud and Miquela.

The idea that people manipulate information in media is not new; however, examining what is considered to be a deliberate act of deception on social media is relevant at a time when deception on social media is not clear, and the amount of online technologies and people who use social media continue to increase. Whereas asynchronous communication is delayed and provides time for people to formulate thoughts, in synchronous communication people respond with greater immediacy; thus, synchronous communications affect how deception is implemented, giving deceivers advantage for altering content (Tsikerderis and Zeadally, 2014).

Artificial/Technology

Although the freedom to exchange information is an important part of fostering democracy, it is also important to recognize some of the societal and ethical challenges that come with being able to create and propagate online personas. Sherry Turkle (2005) has described our computer technology as part of everyday life, a world we create, work in, experiment in, and live in. With its "chameleon like quality," technology becomes our creature, "making it an ideal medium for the construction of a wide variety of private worlds and, through them, for self-exploration" (p. 21). Turkle (2005) describes the tendency in technology use to "manipulate words, information, and visual images," entering into the development of personality and identity (Turkle, 2005, p. 21). "To say one's online self is curated would be an understatement; it's not real life" (Jones, 2018). The authors contend that Brud consciously misleads others with misinformation regarding Miquela's consciousness, such that Brud wrote and published an online letter to address public concerns.

Lil Miquela: A Case Study

In 2018, the glamorous, perfectly curated world of Instagram influencers is hardly a mystery—and yet, one Instagram star remains an enigma: Lil Miquela (Russell, 2018):

Miquela Sousa, better known as Lil Miquela, is one of the first computer-generated social media influencers. In less than two years of existence, she has amassed over a million Instagram followers and sparked a debate about what makes a persona "real" online. In an era of fake news, AI, Russian troll farms, catfishing, and deceptive selfies, Miquela highlights how technology is estranging us from reality (Eror, 2018).

To confront this estrangement, the authors address the emergence of Miquela, purported to be a 19-year-old Brazilian-American model; who has 1.5 million Instagram followers, dresses in Chanel and Prada (and various other brand that promote causes she believes in) and graced the cover of American *Vogue* wearing Alexander McQueen (Walker, 2018).

Since first appearing on Instagram in 2016, Lil Miquela has quickly become a compelling presence, functioning as an Instagram influencer in the realms of fashion, branding, music, social justice, and celebrity. Developed as an Artificial Intelligence (AI) prototype with full consciousness, Miquela is able to think freely and feel compassion for others. The question remains, however, as to whether Miquela can actually be the empathetic presence her (it) creators, Brud, have claimed. In a recent journalistic segment, one reporter offers an ominous vision for this possibility:

Many things you see online are not what they appear to be. In the case of social media influencers – people who are paid to promote brands and products – some aren't even real people. In what is part of a growing online trend, some of these computer-generated influencers have more than one million followers each. Recent studies predict the influence marketing space will be a $2 billion industry by 2020. The goal of these computer-generated influencers is to get you to buy products or experiences, but critics worry you could be deceived by a false image (Dokoupil, 2018).

Brud and Miquela

Brud, the proprietor of Miquela, is a tech-startup company co-founded by Trevor McFedries and Sara Decou based in Los Angeles, California. Brud self identifies as a transmedia studio that creates digital character driven story worlds. The company is made up of engineers, storytellers, and designers who share a vision to connect people globally using transformative media approaches to create a movement that creates real-world impact and encourages people to stand up for equality (Brud, 2018). According to Brud, Miquela is a robot programmed as artificial intelligence to change "the cultural fabric of the United States" and to represent a movement "leveraging cultural understanding and technology. She (it) has "personality, a moral compass, and is a benefit to society in that she influences people to practice empathy, kindness, and tolerance towards others, especially for people who are different" (Brud, 2018).

Despite Brud's claim "that technology can help bring about both a more empathetic world and a more tolerant future," (Brud, 2018) conversations about Miquela's existence have been an ongoing dispute—perhaps because Miquela's existence is centered around story that mimics human experience. For instance, Miquela experiences love and heartbreak, enjoys the outdoors, hangs out with friends, likes to take selfies, attends parties, and can drive. Her (it) posts include a mixture of fictional and non-fictional people and environments; at times Miquela portrays herself as a computer-generated character, at other times she (it) poses with real people.

For Miquela's followers, her existence is confusing with regards to her existence and purpose, and thus, controversial despite the fact that her (it) Instagram bio clearly states that she (it) is a robot. For further perspective, the authors consider comments such as: "warriorcats_I'm trying to find thE TRUTH hhh"; "iibasic_bitchii_what if lilmiquela is the girl with the brown hair"; "kylie.grayce @i_am_hawkfrost_ I got told she was a robot – foxheart"; "finstaa1100_Why. The. Hell. Are. You. A. Kinda. Doll. Thingie. ???"; "paceybaber_Bitch who the fuck are you ????????"; "lauren.lemer_Ur a robot"

Moreover, videos about Miquela on YouTube reveal similar approaches to create controversial marketing campaigns about Miquela's existence. For instance, Shane Dawson, an American YouTuber with 20 million subscribers created a video titled, Conspiracy theories & interview with Lil Miquela, published on Sep 18, 2017. Shane addresses the same questions that Instagram followers have: Who is the *real* Lil Miquela? Is Miquela really a real person pretending to be a computer-generated model? To date, the video received 7,782,803 views—a clear indication that Miquela has captivated the world with discussions of opposing views.

Why would anyone believe Miquela is real if she (it) calls herself (itself) a robot? Given that Miquela is created by 3D artists and AI programmers whose efforts are to create character models with realistic human characteristics, the authors relate this to the Uncanny Valley theory which identifies people have stronger emotional reactions and brain responses towards computer-generated characters that appear realistic and almost human, than to less human-like characters that look like cartoon characters (Schindler, Zell, Botsch, & Kissler, 2017).

The question remains: Does Brud claim that Miquela is a real girl? In February 2019, the authors of this study conducted a Google Trends analysis to learn more about the story of Miquela's popularity. On Google Trends, "numbers represent search interest relative to the highest point on the chart for a given region and time. A value of 100 is the peak popularity for the term." During April 15- April 21, 2018 a score of 100 was assigned to web searches in the United States for Lil Miquela. An extended section of a post from April 20, 2018 demonstrates how Brud utilizes deception:

If you're reading this, you are probably aware that we are in a difficult spot regarding our relationship with Miquela. We love Miquela beyond words. We recognize that right now we owe you, the fans who have supported her for the past two years, an explanation. There is nothing Miquela could do or say that would change the way we feel about her. In providing context, we do not seek to discredit Miquela or invalidate her feelings [we believe] that technology can help bring about both a more empathetic world and a more tolerant future... This introduction is long overdue and for that we apologize. Mostly, we want to apologize to our believed client and friend Miquela Sousa. The idea that we would ever do anything to deliberately deceive her is deeply disturbing to us. We have been by Miquela's side since day one. We feel confident in saying that we would not be where are without her and vice versa. When the questions of identity arose, when Miquela would ask who or what she was, we always tried to be honest and straightforward with her while also maintaining a certain degree of sensitivity. We wanted to protect her from the world's scrutiny. Miquela is new, and things that are new and different are traditionally misunderstood, met with fear and animosity. In our naivety, we presented Miquela's consciousness as being based on a real human being. Memories of family and of past were presented as figments of a human life she once knew. This person was a fabrication of our staff. We thought this imagined scenario would make Miquela feel more comfortable with herself. Clearly we were mistaken... Our clients are our family. Full-stop. We are committed to staying open to critique and now that we've said our piece we look forward to taking a backseat and doing some difficult listening. All the best and thanks for listening, - Brud Team- (Brud, 2018).

In this instance, we see firsthand the workings of misinformation in that Brud acknowledges Miquela as both a technology and yet a conscious being—animating deception in their conscious choice to refer to this technology as her and then declaring her to be a conscious and empathetic being. The letter generated 10,573 likes with comments that include: "charlee.may@mattingg_I am SO CONFUSED"; "washingtonsreserve_This is a new level of BULLSHIT"; "dayton_daily_So.... so.... Miquela is a robot?"

Furthermore, Brud claims to have been approached by a notoriously covert AI consulting firm to work on a highly advanced form of AI. In this, Brud claims to have been misled by the firm, not knowing that the AI, initially intended to be utilized to serve terminally ill children, was in fact going to be marketed to the world's elite as a sexual object. Indeed, troubled by these "sick fantasies of the 1 percent," Brud repurposed the AI technology to teach their robot how to think freely and demonstrate, "literally super-human compassion for others" (Brud, 2018). In other words, Brud frames the development of Miquela as a noble act to counter technological corruption.

This case study proposes Lil Miquela's existence as a paradox. Miquela's creators, Brud contradict themselves in ways that intentionally, knowingly, and purposefully mislead others. According to Levine's (2014) Truth-Default Theory, deceptive messages involve intent, awareness and/or purpose to mislead. Without deceptive intention, awareness, and/or purpose to mislead, messages are considered honest communication. In TDT, honest communication does not need to involve full disclosure; however, a lie involves "outright falsehood" from the sender which is known to be false but is not communicated to the recipient. "Lies are a subtype of deception that involves deceiving through saying information known to be false. For instance, when Brud asked "Is Miquela real?" Brud's Instagram response was "As real as Rihanna." (Brud, website copy, Google Docs, 2018).

Other forms of deception include omission, evasion, equivocation, and generating false conclusions with objectively true information" (Levine, 2014, p. 381). Regardless of claims that Miquela has a moral compass, the way messages are manipulated and the way Miquela is often referred to with female con-notations is perhaps part of the contradiction. Brud reveals little detail about synthetic consciousness and how to interpret Miquela's existence. The authors consider communication content and commu-nication context (Levine, 2014) to conclude that Brud's messages include deception. Evidence reveals failure for Miquela's followers to actively consider the possibility of deceit, which aligns with TDT. For instance, after two years of Miquela's initial existence, responses from Miquela's followers remain diverse. Some question Miquela's existence; others acknowledge Miquela as a form of entertainment; and still others recognize Miquela as part of a turning point in the fashion industry: "sophiaseely7_ Just cause she is so so so pretty she can still be human"; "mntt110_ Are you a robot?"; "jaslynn__So she isn't a robot?" "90memebaby_of course she's not a robot. it's an experiment" (https://www.instagram.com/lilmiquela/?hl=en).

In essence, as it pertains to misinformation in everyday life, on social media in particular, Brud and Miquela are just the tip of the iceberg. At stake, is the need to create a critical consciousness that enables and empowers us to confront the notion that our technology can become a conscious and empathetic being through which we can satisfy our needs for belonging.

While, traditionally, companies have developed business strategies to increase consumer interest in brands, in the 21st century, businesses have moved beyond traditional media to advertise products on social media platforms to instantly connect with audiences and develop relationships with customers. For example, Brud uses cross-media characters Lil Miquela as well as additional AI technologies Blawko and Bermuda, promoting them as distinct conscious beings that relate and interact with one another, as when Blawko and Bermuda were in an intimate relationship or when Bermuda, a Trump supporter, hacked the Instagram account of Miquela, a Black Lives Matter supporter. In essence, cross-media branding develops storytelling across multiple media platforms to enhance the user's experience and these experiences can be further enhanced through advertising across multiple platforms. For instance, one of the issues that the authors address in the future research considerations is the growing popularity of digital fashion models such as Shudu Gram.

SOLUTIONS AND RECOMMENDATIONS

Given the issues of online deception noted in the Lil Miquela case study, the authors recommend the importance of re/claiming critical consciousness by acknowledging four distinct but interrelated realities. First, the authors acknowledge a problem regarding the rise of addictive technology. Second, in light of this problem, the authors acknowledge various ethical implications related to our communication and sense of community—we are widely connected through our devices but overwhelmed with a sense of loneliness. Third, a charge is considered to counter the effects of the aforementioned problem and consequence. Fourth, and finally, a practice is suggested to stimulate critical consciousness regarding online deception.

Re/Claiming Critical Consciousness

Paulo Freire's notion of critical consciousness offers an important solution to confront the problem of online deception. Explicitly, Freire (2013) has noted:

If [we] are unable to perceive critically the themes of [our] time, and thus to intervene actively in reality, [we] are carried along in the wake of change. [We] see that the times are changing, but [we] are submerged in that change and so cannot discern its dramatic significance. And a society beginning to move from one epoch to another requires the development of an especially flexible, critical spirit. Lacking such a spirit, [we] cannot perceive the marked contradictions which occur in society as emerging values in search of affirmation and fulfillment clash with earlier values seeking self-preservation. (p. 6)

A critical consciousness, then, is developing the ability to critically perceive cultural themes, principally the marked contradictions that emerge from competing values, and the successive ability to intervene in such realities. In this instance, as it pertains to misinformation in everyday life, and on social media in particular, such incisive mindfulness—perceiving critically, intervening actively, and developing flexibly—is especially important for and pertinent to the varying values and communication practices of students, scholars, and professionals. Put differently, if there is any sense of urgency for those interested, if not compelled, by the issues of social media use and online deception, of not wanting to be simply carried along or rendered incapable of discerning dramatic significance, then by all means we as a society must be diligent in establishing an exceptionally flexible critical spirit and become more vigilant in ensuring that such a malleable temperament is suitably implemented in homes, classrooms, boardrooms, and beyond.

A Problem

While addictive behaviors have existed for quite a while, in recent decades, they have become, "more common, harder to resist, and more mainstream" (Alter, 2017, p. 5). One specific issue regarding online behavior is that the benefits are praised without at the same time fully considering its drawbacks. A critical consciousness is needed. Perhaps the language of addiction is not accustomed with associating behaviors like binge viewing, smartphone use, or excessive exercise alongside substance abuses. But perhaps it should be, as one clinical psychologist in Adam Alter's (2017) study indicated, "Every single person I work with has at least one behavioral addiction" (p. 6). Indeed, there are significant similarities between substance and behavioral addictions:

They activate the same brain regions, and they're fueled by some of the same basic human needs: social engagement and social support, mental stimulation, and a sense of effectiveness. Strip people of these needs and they're more likely to develop addictions to both substances and behaviors. (Alter, 2017, p. 9)

As it relates to the irresistible allure of technology, Alter (2017) has argued that the addictive dimensions of technology leave us susceptible to a variety of social disorders and psychological problems. For instance, one study on gamers recently claimed that those who spend more than three hours per day gaming are, "less satisfied with their lives, less likely to feel empathy toward other people, and less likely to know how to deal with their emotions appropriately" (Alter, 2017, p. 233). Ironically, in actuality, as one recent survey revealed, the average time kids actually spend online is closer to five to seven hours of screen time every day (Alter, 2017, p. 233). While behavioral addiction is nascent, early indications allude to crisis: "Addictive tech is part of the mainstream in a way that addictive substances never will be" (Alter, 2017, p. 9).

An Implication

One of the implications of this rise in addictive technology is an impact on communication, and subsequently on community. In particular, As Turkle has argued, it leads to expecting more from technology and less from each other. Interesting, this is not a new phenomenon. In a rather telling excerpt (given the date, October 1964) from Edward R. Murrow's final public address, he adeptly, and seemingly (in hindsight) prophetically, speaks to the challenges that technology poses to our capacity to communicate, for his time and our own:

The speed of communication is wondrous to behold. It is also true that speed can multiply the distribution of information that we know to be untrue. The most sophisticated satellite has no conscience. The newest computer can merely compound, at speed, the oldest problem in the relations between human beings. In the end the communicator will be confronted with the old problem of what to say and how to say it. (Kendrick, 1969, p. 5)

Murrow recognized both the brilliant and baffling dimensions of technology in relation to communication. And the cultural significance of these two trends is tellingly evident in both David Riesman's *The Lonely Crowd* and Sherry Turkle's *Lone Together*. What we needed, Riesman (1965) argued, for Murrow's time, is to learn to become other-directed so that we can become more attentive to our own feelings and ambitions (p. 307).

The challenge, however, as Turkle (2011a) has noted, with more contemporary relevance, is that a fully networked life no longer requires that we be logged on because the network is with us and on us, all the time—we can be with each other all the time (p. xii). Emboldening the subtitle of Turkle's book *Alone Together,* we are progressively and troublingly learning to "expect more from technology and less from each other" (p. xii). For Turkle (2011b), this occurs because the volume and velocity of technology offers us the "illusion of companionship without the demands of friendship" (p. 29). Put differently, we have become too comfortable with connection at a distance. Comparably, Clifford Nass (2012) has argued that we have been seduced into thinking that "social media obviates the need for the hard work of learning emotional behavior" (p. 20). As such, one of the challenges (if not dangers) we are confronted with as educators is how to, in Freire's language, to develop a critical consciousness, and to that end, using Turkle's book title, to reclaim conversation. And one of the central reasons it is worth reclaiming is because of the vital role it plays in the development of human empathy; something that Brud claims is at the heart (no pun intended) of Miquela. On the contrary, Turkle (2015) has reminded us that the "always-on life erodes our capacity for empathy" (p. 171). As such, we need to develop a critical communication consciousness to enhance our empathy for one another.

A Charge

At the heart of human interest in technologies, besides efficiency, is relationship. In a word: consciousness. Consciousness is principally concerned with awareness, free will, and ultimately, relationship. When individuals call upon any one of many voice-controlled assistants—Lyra, Bixby, Google Assistant, Cortana, Alexa, or Siri, for instance—the experience is mediated through language that infers, among other things, conversation—the building blocks of relationship. Given this problem and consequence, Nicholas Carr (2010) confronts us with an explicit charge. Specifically, Carr argues that our dependency on the Internet, and the socially mediated encounters therein, chips away at our capacities for concentration and contemplation (p. 6). When it comes to these two capacities, Carr's elaboration on the framework is insightful: "Once I was a scuba diver in a sea of words. Now I zip along the surface like on a Jet Ski" (Carr, 2010, p. 7).

Moreover, Carr (2010) has further acknowledged:

The seductions of technology are hard to resist, and in our age of instant information the benefits of speed and efficiency can seem unalloyed, their desirability beyond debate. But I continue to hold out hope that we won't go gently into the future our computer engineers and software programmers are scripting for us ... we owe it to ourselves to consider them, to be attentive to what we stand to lose. How sad it would be, particularly when it comes to the nurturing of our children's minds, if we were to accept without question the idea that 'human elements' are outmoded and dispensable. (p. 224)

What is telling, is Carr's not-so-subtle reference to Dylan Thomas' renowned Villanelle poem, "Do Not Go Gentle into That Goodnight," whose refrains of "Do not go gentle into that good night" and "Rage, rage against the dying of the light" allude to a sort of visceral and fastidious resistance to death—inspired, most believe, by Thomas' dying father (Thomas, 1971, p. 239). Carr's re-appropriation of Thomas' plea, transposed from bodily death to confronting prominent issues in culture and society makes for a compelling charge that aligns ideally with Freire's critical consciousness. Carr has provided an additional perspective to be attentive to what we stand to lose to our addictions and misuse of technology:

The changes in our brains happen automatically, outside the narrow compass of our consciousness, but that doesn't absolve us from responsibility for the choices we make. One thing that sets us apart from other animals is the command we have been granted over our attention. (Carr, 2010, p. 194)

Or as novelist David Foster Wallace (2009) has indicated:

'Learning how to think' really means learning how to exercise some control over how and what you think … it means being conscious and aware enough to choose what you pay attention to and to choose how you construct meaning from experience. (pp. 54, 123)

In sum, when we yield control of our attention to issues of online deception, we do so at our own peril.

A Practice

As we acknowledge and confront the problems related to the rise of addictive technology and the social implications therein, the authors have embraced the call to enhance our concentration and contemplation—to develop a critical consciousness that is keenly aware of trends in misinformation in everyday life. To that end, we align with Turkle's notion of reclaiming conversation. For instance, to begin, one strategy Turkle has recommended is solitude and self-reflection, something that is remarkably less striking than the seemingly endless depths of online life. Regardless, Turkle's preeminent solution is to reclaim conversation.

To be clear, one of the preeminent ways we can interrogate socially mediated deception is to develop a critical consciousness through face-to-face conversation. Indeed, while the authors are desirous of re/ claiming critical consciousness through a collection of choices related to concentration, contemplation, and conversation, there is also a resistance to naïve sentimentality for bygone days. Regardless, bygone days may indeed have some lessons we can and should learn from. Interestingly, the most ardent trait Brud has assigned Miquela is empathy. Ironically, however, as Turkle (2015) has argued:

We have moved from being in a community to having a sense of community. Have we moved from empathy to a sense of empathy? From friendship to a sense of friendship? We need to pay close attention here. Artificial intelligences are being offered to us as sociable companions. They are being called a new kind of friend. If we are settling for a "sense of friendship," from people, the idea of machine companionship does not seem like much of a fall. But what is at stake is precious, the most precious things that people know how to offer each other. (p. 171)

In other words, empathy, that ability to convince another person that you are present for the duration—"staying long enough for someone to believe that you want to know how they feel" (Turkle, 2015, p. 173), is the precious entity at stake. This stands in ironic contrast to Brud's notion that Miquela's purpose is ultimately about empathy. There are two possibilities, both viable and worthy of our attention. First, the inability of individuals or communities to provide satisfying and convincing empathetic encounters means that society has surrendered much if not most of its responsibility to technological surrogates. If this is true, it is a substantial wake up call. Second, this development has advanced in large part because of the choices we have made to renounce empathy in favor of extra screen time—pursuing our emotional needs for belonging through products and vicarious living. As Carr has reminded us, regardless, this does not absolve us from our responsibility to make critically conscious and attentive choices (Carr, 2010, p. 194). In sum, conversation cures (Turkle, 2015, p. 41). In order to recover and recuperate what we have lost, we must shamelessly promote critically conscious conversations in classrooms and boardrooms, airports and taxis, restaurants and pubs, bedtime routines and family gatherings, and beyond.

FUTURE RESEARCH CONSIDERATIONS

The authors intend this study as more than an isolated or esoteric realm of intellectual inquiry, but rather, an all important and pressing consideration for comprehending the burgeoning issues related to AI technologies and social media influencers for responding and adapting to the digital frontier of the future. This case study has focused on Lil Miquela and Brud. For future research considerations, the authors suggest two broad studies with an example for each instance. First, studies could focus on the cultural significance and developments related to AI technologies akin to Miquela. A question that remains for scholars is whether or not this phenomenon will be a transient trend or the beginning of something altogether significant for the future of our communication, identity, and technology. For instance, Shudu Gram, a computer-generated fashion model created by photographer Cameron-Games Wilson using 3D modeling software, hailed on her (its) Instagram page as, "The World's First Digital Supermodel," would be an interesting study. One social cue, for example, is found in this headline: "Shudu Gram Is A White Man's Digital Projection Of Real-Life Black Womanhood" (Jackson, 2018). Second, studies could focus more intently on Brud with consideration given to its two other AI technologies, Blawko and Bermuda. These studies could focus on Brud, broadly, or the individual influencers, more specifically. At stake, as Carr (2010) has reminded us in his ostensibly prescient vision of Stanley Kubrick's *2001: A Space Odyssey,* is a time and place where people have become so like machines that, ironically, the most human characters turn out to be machines: "As we come to rely on computers to mediate our understanding of the world, it is our own intelligence that flattens into artificial intelligence" (p. 224).

CONCLUSION

In an effort to provide some satisfactory considerations to the growing concern regarding online misinformation in everyday life, this chapter has taken an interdisciplinary approach to the study of deception from the critical perspectives of rhetoric, communication, and media studies. Specifically, our primary objective has been to interrogate the interrelationship of communication, identity, and technology relevant to social media in order to confront online deception. Therein, we proposed a case study and critically analyzed social media sensation Miquela Sosa, also known as Lil Miquela, giving some attention to the emergence of AI technologies and social media influencers. Certainly, there is an array of intellectual and ethical considerations to consider. For all of the potential benefits that social media creation and use may provide, there are significant costs associated with mindlessly pursuing our emotional needs through technological surrogates and misinformation, and in turn, surrendering our critical consciousness. In response, this case study has sought to provide a representative anecdote through which to extract order from the chaos. Though the authors acknowledge the idea that people manipulating information online is nothing new, regardless, the contention is that examining deliberate acts of misinformation and deception on social media is relevant at a time when AI technologies and social media influencers are coinciding with social trends in loneliness, behavioral addictions, and a substantial drop in empathy, evident in everyday relationships and countless feeds and online comment sections. At stake, beyond the study of deception and the future of a rapid and global evolution in online technologies, is our very sense of community and self.

REFERENCES

Alter, A. (2017). *Irresistible: The rise of addictive technology and the business of keeping us hooked.* New York: Penguin Press.

Brud. (2018, April 20). A note from the team at brud. Instagram. Retrieved from https://www.instagram.com/brud.fyi/?hl=en

Brummett, B. (1984). Burke's representative anecdote as a method in media criticism. *Critical Studies in Mass Communication, 1*(2), 161–176. doi:10.1080/15295038409360027

Buller, D. B., & Burgoon, J. K. (1998). Emotional expression in the deception process. In P. A. Andersen & L. K. Guerrero (Eds.), *Handbook of communication and emotion: Research, theory, applications and contexts* (pp. 382–398). San Diego, CA: Academic Press.

Burke, K. (1969). *A rhetoric of motives.* Berkeley, CA: University of California Press.

Carr, N. (2010). *The shallows: What the internet is doing to our brains.* New York: W.W. Norton & Company.

Chan, M. (2018, June 30). The 25 most influential people on the internet. *Time.* Retrieved from http://time.com/5324130/most-influential-internet/

DePaulo, B. M., Kashy, D. A., Kirkendol, S. E., Wyer, M. M., & Epstein, J. A. (1996). Lying in everyday life. *Journal of Personality and Social Psychology, 70*(5), 979–995. doi:10.1037/0022-3514.70.5.979 PMID:8656340

Dokoupil, T. (2018, June 20). Computer-generated models' social media influence on the rise. *CBS News.* Retrieved from https://www.cbsnews.com/news/rise-of computer-generated-models-social-media-influencers/

Eror, A. (2018, April 24). Meet Lil Miquela, the AI influencer on the cover of our new print issue. *Highsnobiety,* Retrieved from https://www.highsnobiety.com/p/lil miquela-cover-storyissue-16/

Freire, P. (2013). *Education for critical consciousness.* New York: Bloomsbury Press.

Jackson, L. M. (2018, May 4). Shudu Gram is a white man's digital projection of real-life black womanhood. *The New Yorker,* Retrieved from https://www.newyorker.com/culture/culture-desk/shudu-gram-is-a-white-mans-digital-projection-of-real-life-black-womanhood

Jones, D. (2018, April 10). Why we follow Lil Miquela, the model with 900k followers & no soul." *Refinery 29.* Retrieved from https://www.refinery29.com/en us/miquela-sousa-fake-instagram

Kendrick, A. (1969). *Prime time: The life of Edward R. Murrow.* Boston: Little Brown.

Levine, T. R. (2014). Truth-default theory (TDT): A theory of human deception and deception detection. *Journal of Language and Social Psychology, 33*(4), 378–392. doi:10.1177/0261927X14535916

McCornack, S. A. (1992). Information manipulation theory. *Communication Monographs, 59*(1), 1–16. doi:10.1080/03637759209376245

Mischianti, L. (2018, March 8). Lil Miquela is the face of new age logomania. *V Magazine* 112. Retrieved from https://vmagazine.com/article/new-age-logomania/

Nass, C. (2012). Is texting ruining your kids' future? *Pacific Standard,* (May/June), 20-23.

Nielsen, R. (1977). I want you to want me [Recorded by Cheap Trick]. On In color [CD]. Los Angeles, CA: Kendun Records.

Riesman, D. (1965). *The lonely crowd.* New Haven, CT: Yale University Press.

Ross, H. J. (2018). *Our search for belonging: How our needs to connect is tearing us apart.* Oakland, CA: Barrett-Koehler Publishers.

Russell, E. (2018, April 23). Is Lil Miquela real? *Pop Crush.* Retrieved from http://popcrush.com/who-is-lil-miquela-real-or-robot/

Simonson, P. (2010). *Refiguring mass communication: A history.* Urbana: University of Illinois Press.

Thomas, D. (1971) Do not go gentle into that goodnight. In D. Jones (Ed.), The poems of Dylan Thomas. New York, NY: A New Directions Book.

Turkle, S. (2005). *The second self: Computers and the human spirit.* Cambridge, MA: The MIT Press. doi:10.7551/mitpress/6115.001.0001

Turkle, S. (2011a). *Alone together: Why we expect more from technology and less from each other.* New York: Basic Books.

Turkle, S. (2011b). The tethered self: Technology reinvents intimacy and solitude. *Continuing Higher Education Review, 75,* 28–31.

Turkle, S. (2015). *Reclaiming conversation: The power of talk in a digital age.* New York: Penguin Press.

Walker, H. (2018, September 1). Meet Lil Miquela, the Instagram star created by CGI. *The London Times.* Retrieved from https://www.thetimes.co.uk/article/meet-lil-miquela-the-instagram-star created-by-cgi-9krqrrcpx

Walker, L. (2018, June 27). Lil miquela: Not a girl, not yet a woman. *Wonderland.* Retrieved October, 25, 2018, from https://www.wonderlandmagazine.com/2018/06/27/lil-miquela/

Wallace, D. F. (2009). *This is water: Some thoughts, delivered on a significant occasion, about living a compassionate life.* New York, NY: Little, Brown and Company.

ADDITIONAL READING

Andersen, P. A., & Guerrero, L. K. (Eds.). (1998). *Handbook of communication and emotion: Research, theory, applications and contexts.* San Diego, CA: Academic Press.

Barbucha, D., Nguyen, N. T., & Badica, C. (2014). Computational Collective Intelligence. *Journal of Neurocomputing, 146*(C), 137–139. doi:10.1016/j.neucom.2014.06.049

Bargh, J. A., McKenna, K. Y. A., & Fitzsimons, G. M. (2002). Can you see the real me? Activation and expression of the 'true self' on the internet. *The Journal of Social Issues*, *58*(1), 33–48. doi:10.1111/1540-4560.00247

Burke, K. (1969). *A grammar of motives*. Berkeley, CA: University of California Press.

Carr, N. (2014). *The glass cage: Automation and us*. New York, NY: W.W. Norton & Company.

Hancock, J. T., Curry, L. E., Goorha, S., & Woodworth, M. (2008). On Lying and being lied to: A linguistic analysis of deception in computer-mediated communication. *Discourse Processes*, *45*(1), 1–23. doi:10.1080/01638530701739181

Hennessy, B. (2018). *Influencer: Building your personal brand in the age of social media*. New York, NY: Citadel Press.

Jacobs, S., Dawson, E. J., & Brashers, D. (1996). Information manipulation theory: A replication and assessment. *Communication Monographs*, *63*(1), 70–82. doi:10.1080/03637759609376375

Postman, N. (2005). *Amusing ourselves to death: Public discourse in the age of show business*. New York, NY: Penguin.

Turkle, S. (1995). *Life on the screen: Identity in the age of the internet*. New York, NY: Simon & Schuster.

Turkle, S. (2008). *The inner history of devices*. Cambridge, MA: MIT Press. doi:10.7551/mitpress/7972.001.0001

Turkle, S. (2009). *Simulation and its discontents*. Cambridge, MA: MIT Press. doi:10.7551/mitpress/8200.001.0001

KEY TERMS AND DEFINITIONS

Artificial Intelligence: The theory and development of computer systems able to perform tasks that normally require human intelligence and agency.

Critical Consciousness: The ability to critically perceive the themes of a place and time and intervene actively in reality; an especially flexible, critical spirit.

Deception: The act of intentionally, knowingly, and/or purposely misleading another person.

Empathy: The ability to understand and share the feelings of others.

Representative Anecdote: Something sufficiently demarcated in character to make analysis possible, yet sufficiently complex in character to prevent the use of too few terms in one's description.

Social Media Influencer: People who are paid to promote brands and products.

Technology: The application of scientific knowledge for practical purposes.

This research was previously published in the Handbook of Research on Deception, Fake News, and Misinformation Online; pages 87-103, copyright year 2019 by Information Science Reference (an imprint of IGI Global).

Chapter 48

Online Self–Presentation Strategies Among Social Networking Sites' Users in the United Arab Emirates

Azza Abdel-Azim M. Ahmed
Zayed University, UAE & Cairo University, Egypt

ABSTRACT

This study explored the strategies of self-presentation (ingratiation, supplication, and enhancement) among United Arab Emirates users (n=230) of popular social networking sites (SNS). The size of social networks, degree of network connectivity, and perceptions of self-presentation success were examined. The results indicated a significant positive correlation between the frequency of SNS use and ingratiation and enhancement strategies. Greater diversity of online friends among the respondents was positively associated with the perception of online self-presentation success. Males and females differed in the size of the online social network they interacted with, diversity of online friends, and preferred self-presentation strategies. However, no significant gender differences were found in the levels of network connectivity and perceptions of self-presentation success.

INTRODUCTION

Internet-based social networking platforms such as Facebook, YouTube, Instagram, and Twitter are often considered innovative. In contrast with traditional media such as radio, film, and television, they allow for information sharing and social interaction (Pempek, Yermolayeva & Calvert, 2009). Social networking sites (SNS) offer users a degree of connection with others, relational satisfaction, and a way to learn about the surrounding culture (Croucher, 2011). Unlike traditional media, they support many-to-many communication modes, where information presented by each participant reaches many recipients at a time. Rather than viewing mass-produced content, with social networking sites, users become the creators of their own content. They also become the "stars" of their own productions (Pempek et al.,

DOI: 10.4018/978-1-6684-6307-9.ch048

2009). Moreover, social media offer the potential to promote those opportunities, communicate with youth, and eventually facilitate positive youth development (Lee & Horsley, 2017).

New opportunities for self-presentation and impression management offered by SNS allow users to create custom pages and report personal information strategically. Users can interact in a variety of communication modes using plain text, posting status updates, writing comments on friends' pages, and sharing images (Rui & Stefanone, 2013). As noted by Boyd (2007), SNS are based around a "profile," a form of individual (or, less frequently group) home page, which offers a description of each member. In addition to text, images, and video created by a member, a social network site profile contains comments from other members, and a public list of people that one identifies as "friends" within the network. Member profiles are usually identified by participants' real names and often include photographs; thus, the network of connections is displayed as an integral piece of one's online self-presentation (Donath & Boyd, 2004).

SNS in the Gulf Cooperation Countries

In the past decade, social networking sites have established their place as an integral and interdependent actor in society in the Gulf area, specifically in the United Arab Emirates (UAE). The most popular types of SNS in the UAE include Facebook, video sharing sites like YouTube, and microblogging platforms such as Twitter (Al Jenaibi, 2011). In 2019, WhatsApp comes on the top of social media used by 96% of GCC youth daily, then Facebook 81% and Instagram 79%; while nine in ten young Arabs use at least one of the major social media channels daily (Arab Youth Survey, 2019).

In the Arab region, over 125 million residents are using the Internet, with a near 30% annual growth rate and more than 53 million active SNS users. In 2012, countries like the UAE, Bahrain, Qatar, and Kuwait achieved Internet connectivity rates above 50%, while on average regional rates stood around 28%. Although countries like Morocco, Sudan, and Yemen had some of the lowest Internet penetration rates in the region, they also had the region's highest growth rates (Dubai School of Government, 2013). In a recent Arab Youth Survey report (2019), it was reported that 99% of UAE residents are active users of internet and social media, with a 1.5 growth compared to 2018; then Kuwait 92%, Bahrain 81%, Saudi Arabi (67%) and Oman (50%) (p. 75).

A study of the Arab social networks (Ahmed, 2010) found that Facebook was the most popular online social network (65.2%) among a sample of 325 respondents from Egypt and UAE. Similar results were presented by the 2013 Arab World Online report, which demonstrated that Facebook continues to be the most popular social network among Arabs, followed by Google+, and Twitter (Dubai School of Government, 2013). The report showed that 54% of respondents indicated using Facebook more than once a day, while 30% used Google+ at the same frequency. Only 14% of the sample used Twitter more than once a day.

Donath & Boyd (2004) noted that within SNS, members can find information about one another before a connection is made by looking at profile pages. Thus, common ground can be established, and new connections can be formed. Al Jenaibi (2011) concluded that social media have a strong presence in the lives of residents of the United Arab Emirates, using a sample of 556 participants from the UAE. The study found that social media are a vital source of news among respondents, and recognized their day-to-day reliance on social media in acquiring new friends and receiving news updates. In a recent survey, 71% among 3,373 respondents from 22 Arab countries agreed that online communication often replaced traditional communication (Dubai School of Government, 2013). However, to date there has been little attention from Arab media scholars given to online self-presentation strategies among SNS users in the Arab region. Most empirical research on self-presentation has been conducted in the U.S., Western Europe, and China. The current study aimed to examine self-presentation strategies of UAE users on the most popular social networking sites.

THEORETICAL FRAMEWORK AND LITERATURE REVIEW

Self-Presentation and Impression Management

Interpersonal self-presentation has been studied extensively by psychologists and sociologists. This concept was developed by Goffman (1959) who described how people negotiate and validate their identities in face-to-face communication and introduced "frames" within which to evaluate the meaning of interpersonal encounters. Later, electronic communication has established a new range of frames of interaction. Although mediated communications are more limited in nature and less rich than those in which participants are physically present, social interaction via electronic means provides new opportunities for self-presentation. For example, there have been discussions about the possible nature of "electronic selves" (e.g., see Miller, 1995).

Self-presentation has sometimes been distinguished from impression management, which has been defined as an attempt to control the images presented to others, usually to increase the power of the individual. However, the tactics used to engage in both impression management and self-presentation are the same (Lee, Quigley, Nesler, Corbett, & Tedeschi, 1999).

At a conceptual level, Dominick (1999) suggested that impression management involves two processes: impression motivation and impression construction:

Some common motives are a desire to maximize material rewards (making your boss think you are competent to get a promotion), maintaining self-esteem (presenting yourself in a favorable way so that other people will like you), and to create a desired self-identity (a new lawyer can solidify his image as a member of the legal profession by dressing and acting like a lawyer should). Impression construction concerns how a person creates the desired impression through his or her choice of various self-presentation strategies (Dominick, 1999: 647).

According to Miller (1995), Goffman saw embarrassment as an important indicator of a person's failure to present an acceptable self, and as an important motivator to project an improved self-image. Thus, people will seek to present themselves more effectively in order to minimize the embarrassment of a failed self-presentation. Likewise, they will be motivated to improve their performance in order to avoid the embarrassment they feel at its failure. Therefore, most often people will interact through positive self-presentations in which they attempt to match the self-presentations of others.

Online Self-Presentation

It refers to a process by which individuals engage in impression management and information control in everyday life (Schlenker & Pontari, 2000). In social networking sites, personal information is stated explicitly, and can be managed by the author of the information. Papacharissi's analysis (2002) showed that personal homepages on the Internet fit Goffman's (1959) concept of self because people can control what they present about themselves online for others to convey a particular image. Boyd (2007) argued that people have more control online with respect to self-presentation than they have in everyday interactions. They can carefully choose what information to put forward, thereby eliminating visceral reactions that might have seeped out in everyday communication.

Birnbaum, 2008 found that individuals were careful to shape the impression they gave off to others on Facebook, the most popular social media platform. He concluded that the aim of self-presentation was to communicate and interact with others in beneficial ways likely to engender support through Facebook. Gonzales and Hancock (2011) found that people took time when posting information about themselves, and carefully selected what aspects they would like to emphasize. Evidence of selective self-presentation was found in a variety of Internet spaces, including e-mails, discussion boards, and online dating websites. Similarly, Tice, Butler, Muraven, and Stillwell (1995) found that people alter their self-presentation to be more favorable with strangers (those who possess no base-rate information); and more modest with friends who possess base-rate information.

Self-presentation has been viewed as the presentation of self that an individual tends to perform intentionally and desires to be seen by others (Wong, 2012). Given that Facebook profiles are visible to large audience of friends, family, and acquaintances, the motivation to carefully control one's self-presentation should be high. Not only should Facebook self-presenters be highly motivated to control their images, but they should also be able to exercise this high degree of control (Toma & Carlson, 2012). Individuals make a series of conscious decisions regarding how to self-present (Vitak, 2012) based on the people with whom they are interacting at any given time. Facebook and MySpace profiles serve as a stage on which users can make public or semipublic presentations of themselves, and most often users will strive to portray themselves in a positive light. As this self-image is publicly displayed to a peer audience and subject to constant sanctioning via public feedback, it is even more important to the SNS user to be perceived as role model or as compliant to peer norms. It is therefore plausible to assume that SNS users use strategies that assist in presenting (and promoting) themselves as attractive to the audience (Loss, Lindacher, & Curbach, 2013). Lee and Horsley (2017) studied the impact of adolescents' Facebook use on the six "Cs" (competence, confidence, connection, character, compassion/caring, and contribution) of the positive youth development (PYD) framework. They concluded that the participants could use Facebook as an effective tool to organize leisure activities which in turn influenced adolescents' social competence and social connections positively over time.

DeAndrea and Walther (2011) conducted an experimental study to investigate how inconsistent online information affects interpersonal impressions. The authors concluded that subjects rated the inconsistencies of acquaintances as more intentionally misleading, more hypocritical and less trustworthy relative to the inconsistencies of friends, that is, people they knew and interacted with more closely. On the other hand, Rui and Stefanone (2013) introduced a distinction useful in the analysis of self-presentation in SNS: self-provided information (SPI) versus other-provided information (OPI), that is, information about someone that is provided by others. Rui and Stefanone noted that while previously self-presentation was governed by self-provided information, recent developments in social networking technologies allowed for OPI from SNS user contacts. This type of information may involve identifying people in shared photographs as well as comments from other network members. The advent of OPI via SNS increases the possibility of a profile owner's reduced control over his or her self-presentation. Similarly, Loss, Lindacher, and Curbach (2013) stated that SNS enable persons to "inspect, edit and revise" their self-presentation on the Internet before making it available to others. These authors argued that arena of "editable self-presentation" (p. 3) might increase the motivation to engage in tactics of impression management intentionally, and might also lead to a more intense use of proactive, assertive self-presentation.

Self-Presentation Classifications

Scholars differ in their overall classification of self-presentation strategies. Leary (1996) discussed self-presentation strategies in everyday life through various direct and subtle self-presentation tactics such as self-description, attitude statements, nonverbal behavior, social associations, conformity and compliance, aggression and risk-taking. Lee et al (1999) introduced a two-component model of self-presentation: defensive self-presentation that includes the use of excuse, justification, disclaimer, self-handicapping and apology, as well as assertive self-presentation that includes the use of ingratiation, intimidation, supplication, entitlement, enhancement, blasting and exemplification. The study concluded that these tactics have measured a general tendency to desire or to avoid the social approval of people in their daily lives. Avia et al. (1998) explained that defensive self-presentation stems from looking for social approval and avoiding social rejection, whereas assertive self-presentation emerges from actively seeking power and social status.

Jones (1990) introduced five strategies of self-presentation construction drawn from research in interpersonal communication. They were ingratiation, competence, intimidation, exemplification, and supplication. According to Jones, a person using ingratiation strategy has a goal of being liked by others. Among some common tactics of ingratiation are saying positive things about others or saying mildly negative things about yourself, as well as statements of modesty, familiarity, and humor. With a supplication strategy, the goal is to appear helpless so that others would come to your aid. Characteristics of this approach include entreaties for help and self-deprecation.

Following Jones' (1990) classification, Chua and Choib (2010) focused on three major strategies for self-presentation on social networking sites: competence, ingratiation, and supplication. Wong (2012) similarly examined the elements of self-presentation by using three types of assessments—ingratiation assessment, supplication assessment, and enhancement assessment—in an analysis of self-presentation and social support on Facebook among university students. The study reported that students were consistent in shaping their behaviors and presenting themselves according to their desired images. These results showed that the three types of self-presentation (ingratiation, supplication, and enhancement) were related to social support sought or received by students on Facebook. Likewise, a study by Kim and Lee (2011) found that Facebook users had the tendency to provide support to others when they saw others were in need of help. Mehdizadeh (2010) also stated that Facebook users tend to take actions to promote themselves on Facebook in order to receive positive feedback from the public, an enhancement strategy of online self-presentation.

Little is known about the social media users' strategies in presenting themselves via social media and the implications of this presentations. Therefore, the current study examined self-presentation strategies used by a sample of Emiratis in social media networks, focusing on three strategies ingratiation, supplication and enhancement. The level of social networking connectivity and the size of the network were also analyzed. Differences between genders were investigated in terms of the preferred SNS, social networking connectivity, and diversity of users with whom they interact.

RESEARCH HYPOTHESES

Wong (2012) found that frequency of Facebook usage was statistically significant and positively correlated with the three types of self-presentation on Facebook. In addition, among the three types of self-presentation, ingratiation had the strongest positive correlation with frequency of use of an application on Facebook among university students. Therefore, it can be hypothesized that:

H1: There will be a correlation between the level of network connectivity and self-presentation strategies (ingratiation, supplication, and enhancement).

Metzler & Scheithauer (2017) found that adolescents' positive self-presentation and number of friends were related to a higher frequency of receiving positive feedback, which in turn was negatively associated with self-esteem. Rui and Stefanone (2013) indicated that size is one of the most important characteristics of a social networking site's audience that affects online self-presentation. As online social networks increase in size, so does the need to maintain online relationships. Smock (2010) concluded that one possible outcome associated with large audience is more interactions between profile owners and their network. Therefore, it can be predicted that:

H2: There will be a correlation between network size and self-presentation strategies (ingratiation, supplication, and enhancement).

Rui and Stefanone (2013) noted that relationship maintenance is one of the main motives of using SNS. For example, one may self-present in a significantly different way when in a business meeting versus when on a date. SNS, for example, can place employers and romantic partners on the same communication plane, making it more difficult for users to segment audiences and present varied versions of the self (Vitak, 2012). Also, Tice et al. (1995) concluded that self-presentation differs when interacting with friends versus with strangers. Having multiple types of audiences, that is, the diversity of social categories of online friends, can affect strategies and practices used in self–presentation. Therefore, it can be predicted that:

H3: There will be a correlation between diversity (relationships and national origin) and self-presentation strategies (ingratiation, supplication, and enhancement).

Gibbs, Ellison, and Heino, (2006) examined the relationship between the strategic success of online dating and self-presentation. They found that those with more positive online self-disclosure felt they had greater self-presentation success. Also, it was found that the ability to learn about people and the number of people met in online dating led to greater self-presentation success. Therefore, it can be hypothesized that:

H4: There will be a correlation between perception of self-presentation success and self-presentation strategies (ingratiation, supplication, and enhancement).

The literature on self-presentation has emphasized differences in self-presentation strategies between males and females. Hilsen and Helvik (2014) investigated two generations of social network users in their online self-presentation: Those who were introduced to the Internet and social media as adults (40 years old) and those who have grown up with the technology (under 25 years old, called "the net-generation"). They found a difference in how these two groups related to social media. However, it was shown that both groups developed a "new" or revised sense of self and sociability through social media. Boyd (2007) also concluded that gender influences participation on social network sites. Younger boys are more likely to participate in SNS than younger girls (46% vs. 44%), but older girls are far more likely to participate than older boys (70% vs. 57%). Also, older girls are far more likely to use these sites to communicate with friends they see in person than with younger people or boys of their age. Therefore, the last hypothesis states that:

H5: There will be differences between males and females in their online self-presentation strategies.

METHODOLOGY

Sampling and Data Collection

The study sample consisted of 230 Emiratis from two Emirates, Dubai, the largest and most populous city in the United Arab Emirates, and Abu Dhabi, UAE capital. Due to the conservative nature of the population, snowball sampling was used to collect the research data. Five students from the Mass Communication Program at Abu Dhabi University helped in collecting data from the two Emirates according to their residency. The sample composed of 48.3% males and 51.7% females. The age ranged from 16 to 35 years old. The mean age was 25.5 years. The education levels of the respondents were: university level 67.4%, high school level 17.8%, post graduate level 10.9%, and preparatory or less 3.9%. A 14-question questionnaire was used to collect the data. The questions were written in Arabic, the mother-tongue of the respondents. Item reliability was tested using Cronbach's alpha and was above 0.8 for all variables. The age and the gender of respondents were recorded for sampling demographics.

Measurements

Types of Social Networks and Frequency of their Use:

Respondents were provided a list of major social networking sites (Facebook, Instagram, Kik, WhatsApp, BBM, and Twitter) and were asked to indicate how frequently (always, sometimes, rarely, and never) they used each of them.

Online Network Size

To measure online network size, respondents were asked how many friends they had on social networking sites.

Level of Social Network Connectivity

Three questions were used to measure the level of social network connectivity, adapted from Lee (2009). The respondents were asked how long they had been using the social networking sites. The score ranged from 1-3. The highest score (3) was for "6 years and above" and the lowest was (1) for "1 year to less than 3 years" category. A second question asked about how often they use social media in an average week. The highest score (3) was for "almost every day" and the lowest (1) was for "once or twice a week." A third question asked about the number of hours the respondents use social networking sites daily. The highest score was for the "4 hours or more a day" category and the lowest was for "less than 1 hours a day," $\alpha = 0.823$.

Diversity Categories

Diversity was measured in terms of relationships and nationality. Two questions were asked to measure this variable. The first question asked how frequently the participants communicated with the following social categories (family, colleagues, friends, relatives, work partners, and strangers). The second question asked about the national origin of their social network friends and followers (Emiratis, non-Emirati Arabs, Americans and European, and Asians), $\alpha = 0.851$.

Perception of Online Self-Presentation Success

This variable refers to the extent to which the respondents consider themselves successful in achieving their objectives for using SNS. A 5-point Likert scale ranging from "strongly agree" (5) to "strongly disagree" (1) was used to measure this variable. It consisted of four items adopted from Walther, Slovacek, and Tidwell (2001): "Online social networks sites allow me to present myself in a favorable way"; " I think I have made a good impression on others through online social networks"; "I feel I can communicate with my friends through social networks effectively"; and "I feel I am able to achieve my online communication goals effectively". The overall scores ranged from 4-20 points: very successful 16-20 (68.7%), successful 1015 (29.1%), and not successful 4-9 (2.2%), $\alpha = 0.837$.

Self-Presentation Strategies via SNS

Adopted from Chua and Choib (2010) and Wong (2012), this variable included the following items measured on a 5-point Likert scale ranged from "strongly agree" (5) to "strongly disagree" (1), $\alpha = 0.868$.

(1) **Ingratiation:** "I regularly choose and upload photos that make me look attractive"; " I always express the same attitudes as others to gain acceptance"; " I regularly present myself as helpful to others"; " I always post interesting news, articles, or photos to attract my friends to read them"; and " I always comment on friends' posts to express caring".

(2) **Supplication:** " I always seek help from my friends in online social networking sites most of the time"; "I tend to appear weak or helpless to get care or concern from others on SNS"; and " I always show an inability to complete work or get help from others on SNS".

(3) **Enhancement:** " I always put up posts to show that I am knowledgeable"; "I always put up posts with the intent to show intelligence"; " I used to tell people when I complete tasks which others find difficult"; and " I emphasize to others the importance of a task when I am successful".

Statistical Techniques

The SPSS statistical program was used for analyzing the data. Frequencies, Cronbach's alpha, t-tests, and correlation analysis were used to test the research hypotheses and to answer the research questions.

RESULTS

Usages of Social Networking Sites: The results indicated that the highest percentage of respondents (81.3%) use WhatsApp. This was followed by Instagram (72.2%), Twitter (50.9%), Facebook (35.7%), Kik (24.3%), and MySpace (11.7%). This finding is supported by a recent survey (Arab Youth Survey, 2019) on social media usages in Gulf countries. It showed that WhatsApp was on the top among the most frequent social media used (96%), followed by Facebook (81%) and Instagram (79%).

In terms of network size, 46.5% of the sample had more than 100 friends on SNS while 53.5% had less than 50 to 100 friends. For level of network connectivity, the results showed that 33.9% of the sample was highly connected to SNS, 60.4% was moderately connected, and 5.7% were weakly connected. The Digital 2019 report supported this result as it showed that people in UAE tend to spend almost three hours daily on social media sites.

Hypotheses Test

The first research hypothesis stated that there would be a correlation between level of social network connectivity and self-presentation strategies (ingratiation, supplication, and enhancement). The self-presentation strategies via SNS varied among the respondents:

1. **Ingratiation:** The findings showed that 8.3% of the respondents were low, 52.2% were moderate, and 39.6% were high in ingratiation;
2. **Supplication**: 53% of the respondents were low, 30.4% were moderate, and 16.5% were high in supplication;
3. **Enhancement:** 24.3% of the respondents were low, 49.1% were moderate, and 26.5% of the respondents were high in enhancement.

Table 1. Correlation between level of network connectivity and self-presentation strategies (n=230)

Variables	Self-presentation Strategies via Online SN		
	Ingratiation	Supplication	Enhancement
Level of Social Networking Connection	.159 (*)	0.111(NS)	.180(**)

Note: *P≤ 0.01; **P≤ 0.000 (2-tailed)

The Pearson correlation coefficient indicates that there was a significant positive correlation between the level of network connectivity and both ingratiation and enhancement (see Table 1); while the relationship between network connectivity and supplication was non-significant. This means that the higher the level of network connectivity, the higher the ingratiation and enhancement among the respondents. Enhancement (r = .180) was stronger than ingratiation (r = 0.159) in its positive correlation with the level of social network connections among Emiratis. Therefore, the hypothesis was supported for ingratiation and enhancement, but not for the supplication strategy.

The second hypothesis stated that there would be a correlation between online social network size and self-presentation strategies.

Table 2. Correlation between online network size and self-presentation strategies (n=230)

Variables	Self-presentation Strategies via Online SN		
	Ingratiation	Supplication	Enhancement
Online Social Networking Size	.262(**)	0.129(***)	.167(*)

Note: * P ≤ 0.01; **P ≤= 0.000; *** P≤ 0.05 (2-tailed)

The results indicated that there was a positive and significant correlation between the size of social network and all three self-presentation strategies: ingratiation, supplication, and enhancement (see Table 2). Therefore, the bigger the size of online SNS, the more respondents used various self-presentation strategies. The hypothesis was retained.

The third hypothesis stated that there would be a correlation between diversity of social categories and self-presentation strategies. The association between diversity of social categories and self-presentation strategies was tested using the Pearson correlation procedure (see Table 3).

Table 3. Correlation between diversity and self-presentation strategies (n=230)

Variables		Self-presentation Strategies via Online SNs		
		Ingratiation	Supplication	Enhancement
Diversity of social categories in SNSs	Relationships	.178(**)	.130(*)	.142(*)
	Nationalities	.153(*)	.073 (NS)	.060 (NS)

Note: *P ≤ 0.05; **P≤ 0.005 (2-tailed)

The Pearson correlation coefficient showed that there was a significant positive association between the diversity of the types of relationships in SNS and the three self-presentation strategies. It was strongest in ingratiation (r = .178) and weakest in supplication (r = .130). The diversity in the nationalities of SNS friends was found to have no correlation with the supplication and enhancement strategies, while the ingratiation had a weak positive correlation with the diversity in nationalities (r = .153). Therefore, the hypothesis was supported for diversity of relationships and partially supported for diversity of national origin.

Most of the respondents (77.4%) are "always" connected with their friends, followed by those who are "always" connected with family members (64.2%), relatives (52.2%), colleagues (42.6%), and partners at work (31.3%). The least percentage was for respondents who "always" connect with strangers (10.5%). The results also showed that most of the participants (81.7%) "always" connect with locals (Emiratis), 38.7% "always" connect with other Arab nationalities, and the least connect with Americans and Europeans (10% for each).

The fourth hypothesis stated that there would be a correlation between perception of self-presentation success and self-presentation strategies (ingratiation, supplication, and enhancement).

Table 4. Correlation between perceptions of self-presentation success and self-presentation strategies (n=230)

Variables	Self-presentation Strategies via Online SN		
	Ingratiation	Supplication	Enhancement
Perception of Self-presentation success	.384(*)	.212(*)	.398(*)

Note: * P < 0.01

There was a significant positive correlation between respondents' perception of self-presentation success and the three strategies of online self-presentation (see Table 4); the hypothesis was accepted. The correlation was strongest with enhancement strategy (r = .398), and ingratiation (r = .384). It was weaker with the supplication strategy (r = .212). On average, the respondents considered themselves successful in creating good and positive impressions among their friends in the SNS (M = 4.32), communicating efficiently with friends online (M = 4.26), achieving the communication objectives successfully through SNS (M = 4.10), and presenting themselves to others in a favorable way (M = 4.07). The results showed that 68.7% of respondents perceived their online self-presentation as highly successful, while 29.1% found it moderate, and only 2.2% believed it was unsuccessful.

The correlation between self-presentation success and diversity (relationships and national origin) and the level of network connection was also examined (Table 5).

Table 5. Correlation between perception of self-presentation success, diversity, and level of social network connectivity (n=230)

Variables	Diversity of Social categories		Level of network connection
	Relationships	Nationalities	
Perception of Self-presentation success	.199(**)	.138(*)	.146 (*)

Note: * P < 0.05; ** P < 0.01

The Pearson correlation coefficient showed a significant positive relationship between the perception of self-presentation success and level of network connection (r = .149). The higher the level of network connectivity, the more the respondents tend to perceive that they succeed in their online self-presentation.

Also, there was a positive correlation between perceptions of self-presentation success and the diversity of social categories of the respondents' friends in terms of relationship diversity (r = .199) and diversity of national origin of their SNS friends (r = .138). The correlation was stronger with the presence of relationship diversity. This means that the more diverse friends the respondents have, the more they perceive their online presentation as successful.

The last hypothesis stated that there would be differences between genders in their online self-presentation strategies. A t-test was used to examine the differences in self-presentation strategies between male and female participants (see Table 6).

Table 6. Gender differences across variables (n=230)

The variables	Gender		Mean	Std. D.	t
Level of Social networking Connection	Males		2.27	0.571	-0.320 (NS)
	Females		2.29	0.558	
Online social networking size	Males		1.53	0.501	1.955 (**)
	Females		1.40	0.493	
Diversity of social categories (Family, friends, colleagues….etc.)	Males		2.37	0.538	0.717(NS)
	Females		2.32	0.520	
Diversity of nationalities (Arabs, Americans, Europeans …etc.)	Males		1.78	0.594	2.423(***)
	Females		1.61	0.524	
Perception of online self-presentation success	Males		2.65	0.550	-0.469(NS)
	Females		2.68	0.486	
Self-presentation Strategies via Online SNSs	Ingratiation	Males	2.46	0.600	3.557(*)
		Females	2.18	0.606	
	Supplication	Males	1.89	0.755	5.299(*)
		Females	1.39	0.667	
	Enhancement	Males	2.17	0.686	3.121(*)
		Females	1.88	0.715	

Note: * $P \leq 0.000$; **$P \leq 0.05$; *** $P \leq 0.01$ (2-tailed)

The t-test showed a significant difference between males and females in the following variables:

- **Online Social Network Size**: Males interacted with SNS with a larger size (M = 1.53) relative to females (M = 1.40);
- **Diversity:** Males were associated with a wider diversity of nationalities (M = 1.78). Additionally, the results showed that the males were higher than females in their connections to colleagues (t = 4.172, M = 2.47, P < 0.000), and work partners (t = 3.097, M = 1.97, P < 0.000). The males were also higher than females in their connection to various Arab nationalities (t = 2.871, M = 2.29, P < 0.001);

- **Self-Presentation Strategies via SNS**: Males and females differed in their online self-presentation strategies. Males were found to be higher than females in all strategies: ingratiation (M = 2.46), supplication (M = 1.89), and enhancement (M = 2.17).

There were no significant differences between males and females in their levels of social network connectivity, diversity of relationships (family, friends, colleagues, etc.), and perception of online self-presentation success.

CONCLUSION

This study investigated strategies of self-presentation used in SNS by a sample of United Arab Emirates social media users. The results showed that Males interacted with SNS with a larger size (M = 1.53) relative to females (M = 1.40). This is supported by the recent Digital 2019 UAE report that showed that males are higher than females from all age groups in social media usages.

Ingratiation and enhancement were found to be the most common self-presentation strategies online. The study found a significant positive correlation between the level of social network connectivity and two of the three categories of self-presentation. The correlation was strongest for enhancement and ingratiation, but non-significant for supplication. The participants generally did not display weakness or a dependency to solicit favorable responses from others on SNS; however, this does not mean that they would not support those who might seek their help.

The results go in line with several previous findings. For example, ingratiation was the most common type of self-presentation strategy used online (Dominick, 1999; Trammell & Keshelashvili, 2005). An analysis of self-presentation tactics in A-list blogs by Trammell and Keshelashvili (2005) similarly indicated that ingratiation and enhancement were among the most commonly used forms of self-presentation. The same conclusion was supported in a study of self-presentation in teenage girls' weblogs (Bortree, 2005). In a recent analysis of Hong Kong high school students' behavior on Facebook, the strongest correlation was between the frequency of Facebook use and ingratiation (Wong, 2012). However, although Facebook profiles tend to present positive and flattering self-portrayals, they are not always sufficient to convey an idealized version of self (Toma & Carlson, 2012).

Additionally, the results of the current study showed that the diversity of relationships was associated with the type of strategies used in self-presentation and with perceptions of self-presentation success. The analysis revealed that the higher the level of connectivity, the more the participants tended to perceive that they succeeded in their online self-presentation. The higher the use of various self-presentation strategies, the higher the respondents rated their success. This finding supports the conclusion made by Gibbs et al. (2006) that those with a positive attitude toward online self-disclosure believed they had greater success in Internet dating. Finally, in the sample, male respondents interacted with larger networks as well as had a higher diversity in the national origin of network members they were connected to. Males tended to use all three self-presentation strategies more often than females. However, no differences between genders were found in the levels of network connectivity and perceptions of self-presentation success.

Given the limitations of a non-random sample, the findings are not generalizable to the entire population of users of SNS in the Emirates. Future analyses may determine how these variables interact among other populations of users. Future studies may also include cross-cultural examinations on online self-presentation. Researchers may employ alternate research methods (e.g., experiments, longitudinal data) to understand self-presentation strategies and associations between other variables, such as social capital and social support. Finally, throughout the study, the focus was on most popular social networking sites; future research might extend these findings by focusing on a particular site or another popular social network that was not included in this study.

REFERENCES

Ahmed, A. (2010). Online privacy concerns among social networks' users. *Cross-Cultural Communication*, *6*(4), 74–89.

Al Jenaibi, B. N. A. (2011). Use of social media in the United Arab Emirates: An initial study. *Global Media Journal*, *1*(2), 3–27. Retrieved from http://www.gmjme.com/gmj_custom_files/volume1_issue2/articles_in_english/volume1-issue2-article-3-27.pdf

Arab Youth Survey. (2019). *A Call for Reform*. A White Paper on the findings of the 11th annual ASDA'A BCW Arab Youth Survey 2019. Retrieved from: file:///C:/Users/Z10509/Downloads/2019%20Arab%20Youth%20Survey.pdf

Avia, M. D., Sánchez-Bernardos, M. L., Sanz, J., Carrillo, J., & Rojo, N. (1998). Self-presentation strategies and the five-factor model. *Journal of Research in Personality*, *32*(1), 108–114. doi:10.1006/jrpe.1997.2205

Birnbaum, M. G. (2008). Taking Goffman on a tour of Facebook: College students and the presentations of self in a mediated digital environment. *Dissertation Abstracts International*, Section A, 69.

Bortree, D. (2005). Presentation of self on the Web: An ethnographic study of teenage girls' weblogs. *Education Communication and Information*, *5*(1), 25–39. doi:10.1080/14636310500061102

Boyd, D. (2007). Why youth (heart) social network sites: The role of networked publics in teenage social life. In D. Buckingham (Ed.), *Youth, identity, and digital media* (pp. 119–142). Cambridge, MA: MIT Press.

Croucher, S. M. (2011). Social networking and cultural adaptation: A theoretical model. *Journal of International and Intercultural Communication*, *4*(4), 259–264. doi:10.1080/17513057.2011.598046

DeAndrea, D. C., & Walther, J. B. (2011). Attribution for inconsistencies between online and offline self-presentations. *Communication Research*, *36*(6), 805–825. doi:10.1177/0093650210385340

Digital. (2019). *Report: The United Arab Emirates*. Retrieved from: https://image.slidesharecdn.com/datareportal20190131gd100digital2019unitedarabemiratesv02-190131132748/95/digital-2019-united-arab-emirates-january-2019-v02-2-638.jpg?cb=1548941304

Dominick, J. R. (1999). Who do you think you are? Personal home pages and self-presentation on the World Wide Web. *Journalism & Mass Communication Quarterly*, *76*(4), 646–658. doi:10.1177/107769909907600403

Donath, J., & Boyd, D. (2004). Public displays of connection. *BT Technology Journal*, *22*(4), 71–82. doi:10.1023/B:BTTJ.0000047585.06264.cc

Dubai School of Government. (2013). *The Arab World Online report: Trends in Internet usage in the Arab region*. Retrieved from: http://www.dsg.ae/en/Publication/Pdf_En/424201311017185100000.pdf

Gibbs, J. L., Ellison, N. B., & Heino, R. D. (2006). Self-presentation in online personas: The role of anticipated future interaction, self-disclosure, and perceived success in Internet dating. *Communication Research, 33*(2), 152–177. doi:10.1177/0093650205285368

Goffman, E. (1959). *The presentation of self in everyday life*. Garden City, NY: Doubleday.

Gonzales, A. L., & Hancock, J. T. (2011). Mirror, mirror on my Facebook wall: Effects of exposure to Facebook on self-esteem. *Cyberpsychology, Behavior, and Social Networking, 14*(1-2), 79–83. doi:10.1089/cyber.2009.0411 PMID:21329447

John, D., & Catherine, T. (2010). Social capital and self-presentation on social networking sites: A comparative study of Chinese and American young generations. *Chinese Journal of Communication, 3*(4), 402–420. doi:10.1080/17544750.2010.516575

Hilsen, A. I., & Helvik, T. (2014). The construction of self in social media, such as Facebook. *AI & Society, 29*(1), 3–10. doi:10.100700146-012-0426-y

Jones, E. E. (1990). *Interpersonal perception*. New York: W.H. Freeman.

Kim, J., & Lee, J. E. R. (2011). The Facebook paths to happiness: Effects of the number of Facebook friends and self-presentation on subjective well-being. *Cyberpsychology, Behavior, and Social Networking, 14*(6), 359–364. doi:10.1089/cyber.2010.0374 PMID:21117983

Leary, M. R. (1996). *Self-presentation: Impression management and interpersonal behavior*. Boulder, CO: Westview.

Lee, S. J. (2009). Online communication and adolescent social ties: Who benefits more from Internet use? *Journal of Computer-Mediated Communication, 14*(3), 509–531. doi:10.1111/j.1083-6101.2009.01451.x

Lee, A. R., & Horsley, J. S. (2017). The role of social media on positive youth development: An analysis of 4-H Facebook page and 4-H'ers' positive development. *Children and Youth Services Review, 77*, 127–138. doi:10.1016/j.childyouth.2017.04.014

Lee, S. J., Quigley, B. M., Nesler, M. S., Corbett, A. B., & Tedeschi, J. T. (1999). Development of a selfpresentation tactics scale. *Personality and Individual Differences, 26*(4), 701–722. doi:10.1016/S0191-8869(98)00178-0

Loss, J., Lindacher, V., & Curbach, J. (2013). Do social networking sites enhance the attractiveness of risky health behavior? Impression management in adolescents' communication on Facebook and its ethical implications. *Public Health Ethics, 7*(1), 1–12.

Mehdizadeh, S. (2010). Self-presentation 2.0: Narcissism and self-esteem on Facebook. *Cyberpsychology, Behavior, and Social Networking, 13*(4), 357–364. doi:10.1089/cyber.2009.0257 PMID:20712493

Metzler, A., & Scheithauer, H. (2017). The Long-Term Benefits of Positive Self-Presentation via Profile Pictures, Number of Friends and the Initiation of Relationships on Facebook for Adolescents' Self-Esteem and the Initiation of Offline Relationships. *Frontiers in Psychology*, 8, 1981. doi:10.3389/fpsyg.2017.01981 PMID:29187827

Miller, H. (1995). *The presentation of self in electronic life: Goffman on the Internet. In Embodied knowledge and virtual space conference* (Vol. 9). Retrieved from: http://www.dourish.com/classes/ics234cw04/ miller2.pdf

Papacharissi, Z. (2002). The presentation of self in virtual life: Characteristics of personal home pages. *Journalism & Mass Communication Quarterly*, *79*(3), 643–660. doi:10.1177/107769900207900307

Pempek, T. A., Yermolayeva, Y. A., & Calvert, S. L. (2009). College students' social networking experiences on Facebook. *Journal of Applied Developmental Psychology*, *30*(3), 227–238. doi:10.1016/j.appdev.2008.12.010

Rui, J., & Stefanone, M. A. (2013). Strategic self-presentation online: A cross-cultural study. *Computers in Human Behavior*, *29*(1), 110–118. doi:10.1016/j.chb.2012.07.022

Schlenker, B. R., & Pontari, B. A. (2000). The strategic control of information: Impression management and self-presentation in daily life. In A. Tesser, R. B. Felson, & J. M. Suls (Eds.), *Perspectives on self and identity* (pp. 199–232). Washington, DC: American Psychological Association; doi:10.1037/10357-008

Smock, A. (2010, June). *Self-presentation on Facebook: Managing content created by the users and others.* Paper presented at the annual conference of the International Communication Association, Singapore.

Tice, D. M., Butler, J. L., Muraven, M. B., & Stillwell, A. M. (1995). When modesty prevails: Differential favorability of self-presentation to friends and strangers. *Journal of Personality and Social Psychology*, *69*(6), 1120–1138. doi:10.1037/0022-3514.69.6.1120

Toma, C. L., & Carlson, C. L. (2012, January). *I'm so much cooler online: An examination of self-presentation in Facebook profiles.* Paper presented at the annual conference of the International Communication Association, Phoenix, AZ.

Trammell, K. D., & Keshelashvili, A. (2005). Examining the new influencers: A self-presentation study of Alist blog. *Journalism & Mass Communication Quarterly*, *82*(4), 968–982. doi:10.1177/107769900508200413

Vitak, J. (2012). The impact of context collapse and privacy on social network site disclosures. *Journal of Broadcasting & Electronic Media*, *56*(4), 451–470. doi:10.1080/08838151.2012.732140

Walther, J. B., Slovacek, C. L., & Tidwell, L. C. (2001). Is a picture worth a thousand words? Photographic images in long-term and short-term computer-mediated communication. *Communication Research*, *28*(1), 105–134. doi:10.1177/009365001028001004

Wong, W. K. W. (2012). Faces on Facebook: A study of self-presentation and social support on Facebook. *Discovery-SS Student E-Journal*, *1*, 184–214.

This research was previously published in Innovative Perspectives on Interactive Communication Systems and Technologies; pages 210-225, copyright year 2020 by Information Science Reference (an imprint of IGI Global).

Chapter 49
An Examination of Motivation and Media Type:
Sharing Content on Chinese Social Media

Rob Kim Marjerison
https://orcid.org/0000-0003-1181-8695
Wenzhou-Kean University, China

Yinan Lin
Wenzhou-Kean University, China

Sarmann I. Kennedyd
Wenzhou-Kean University, China

ABSTRACT

This paper explores the motivations and priorities of Chinese Millennials' use of social media with regard to the sharing of content. A commercially important demographic, this group are highly active on social media. The amount of content that is shared online is immense. Some shared content "goes viral" and can be seen by vast numbers of users. The findings of this study are based on the results of over 650 online surveys and include both theoretical and practical contributions to the body of knowledge regarding the nature of viral propagation of content in Chinese social media. This contribution to the understanding and insight social media activities of this significant and commercially consumer demographic may be of value to online promoters and marketers as well those interested in the use of social media for commercial purposes in the design and management of their online and social media presence, marketing, and advertising strategies.

DOI: 10.4018/978-1-6684-6307-9.ch049

INTRODUCTION

The largest and fastest growing commercially active demographic worldwide are the emerging Chinese middle class (Garner, 2005; H. Li, 2006; Zipser et al., 2005). As internet accessibility worldwide has increased, the adoption and frequency of smart phones and hand-held devices has also increased dramatically. This trend is of special interest in China due to both the large population, and the rapidly emerging middle class (He, 2009). For end users, the integration of social media and social networking with daily activities is nearly immeasurable (Kelly et al., 2013). Social media sites (SMS) like Facebook and Twitter provide abundant and diverse benefits for users, and are increasing in number steadily. Meanwhile, messaging services are also vying for end user time and attention and are rapidly becoming more comprehensive (Bouwman et al., 2010b).

The numbers of users on various type of social media in China, including social networking sites, microblogs, blogs as well as other virtual communities, is over 300 million. By comparison, this is greater than the combined population of France, Germany, Italy, Spain, and the United Kingdom (Chiu et al., 2012a). In the fastest growing market, China, growth is expected to increase by roughly 30 percent annually for the foreseeable future (Chiu et al., 2012b).

Chinese social media platforms Sina Weibo and Wechat have experienced unprecedented rates of adoption in recent years. Weibo is the largest social media site in China and is used frequently for collecting data from users and consumers (Xu et al., 2016). It serves as the combination of Twitter and Facebook providing a new approach for both interpersonal communication, and for acquiring domestic and international news (Han & Wang, 2015). WeChat has become the most extensively used mobile instant-messaging service in China with users exceeding 600 million worldwide as of April 2014 (Pang, 2016). At the same time, WeChat is emerging as a combination between traditional online business and social networking interaction (Yang et al., 2016).

Chinese social media is a dominant way to collect and share information, make social connection as well as entertain (Zhang, 2014). It is noteworthy that reposting, users' major activities online, is one of the most frequently adopted information sharing behaviors among users (X Chen et al., 2019; Sangwan et al., 2009).

Information contains text, pictures, audio and video are able to be spread by mobile social network in a rapid speed(Lu et al., 2014). Compelling content, known as an ignited online hotspot, can be virally disseminated and spread to thousands of users, often within a few seconds. Reposting, users' major activities online, is one of the most frequently adopted information sharing behaviors among Chinese mobile phone users (Bouwman et al., 2010a).

Millennials are well known as extensive users of mobile technologies and the Internet (Mu et al., 2019). This is consistent with the data collected for this study. Considering both the penetration of social media use, smart phone adoption, and frequency of reposting activity, it is apparent that the demographic of Chinese millennials is worthy of study.

When considering the nature of viral messaging, the circumstances that make viral messaging proliferate and the potential for promotion and marketing, users of all social networking sites and platforms are potentially customers whose attention can be attained by online information (Bronner & de Hoog, 2014). In addition to its potential promotional and marketing value, viral content can also impact consumer behavior by influencing consumer perceptions, attitudes and views and has the potential to emerge as a key element of a company's promotional mix (Kirby & Marsden, 2006). Awareness of the potential value of exploiting viral reposting is not new, but the potential continues to grow. With increases in the development of social networking driven technology, service providers are endeavoring to build a customized and content-aware service (De Reuver & Haaker, 2009; Klemettinen, 2007). Through social media, a simple corporate message is able to be turned into powerful viral marketing tool easily if a company can implement the right content effectively (A. M. Kaplan & Haenlein, 2010).

Table 1. Frequency distribution with gender comparison

Posting Frequency	Female	%	Male	%
5+ times a day	58	7%	35	4%
1-4 times a day	101	11%	42	5%
1-5 times a week	**204**	**23%**	**106**	**12%**
1-4 times a month	**246**	**28%**	**119**	**13%**
Once a month	235	26%	121	14%
Rarely	44	5%	36	4%
Age Groups	Female	%	Male	%
<18	90	10%	27	6%
18-30	**543**	**61%**	**295**	**64%**
31-40	111	13%	53	12%
40+	144	16%	84	18%

While there is a considerable depth in the literature for studies done with online behavior concerning social media, e.g. Facebook, Twitter Oh (2015), the applicability of findings of that work is limited with regards to China, "The world's largest social-media market is vastly different from its counterpart in the West" (Chiu et al., 2012b). Even within the emerging but still limited body of research concerning social media usage patterns in China, there exists a gap within the topic of particular emphasis regarding Millennials. The existing usage of social media in China is pervasive, among the highest levels of user penetration in the world, China has the largest internet population in the world (Men & Tsai, 2013). According to Chu et al, (2010), Chinese users spend more time on SNS than Americans, and with the rapid adaptation of faster network connectivity, more pervasive access to wifi, 4G and very soon 5G mobile phone technology, the number of users is likely to continuously and rapidly increase.

Peer-to-peer communication leads to the possible viral nature of online reposting in which participants as well as message-receivers are often willing to actively spread information (Eckler & Bolls, 2011).

To determine what type of content and form of messages arouses the interests of millennials leading to reposting is an important endeavor and can lead to a significant contribution towards understanding viral messaging, social media use and online advertising.

Gender is added as a relevant variable to for analysis because online shopping varies by gender, Dillon et al. (2014), Wu et al. (2017, p. Wu) as does social media usage (Bivens & Haimson, 2016; Nesi & Prinstein, 2015; Schwartz et al., 2013). In fact, the work of Li et al (2018) supports gender differentiation in this area by predicting user gender with a high level of accuracy based on reposting behavior. This is consistent with the data analysis of this study as indicated in Table 1 and is discussed in the Findings section.

Identifying the motivational, content message and type of media most reposted by millennials by gender will provide insight in how reposting can be used for commercial purposes. This study aims to fill the literature gap by investigating Chinese millennials reposting behavior on social media. The findings may offer online-marketers and promoters some useful insights considering Chinese millennials and viral social media content.

BACKGROUND

There has been valuable research published on the topic of the economic growth of China (Garner, 2005; H. Li, 2006; Liang & Teng, 2006; Trappey & Trappey, 2001). Likewise, there has been research published on topics related the use of Social Media in general, and specifically in China (Aiello et al., 2012; Chiu et al., 2012b; Fung, 2009; Jendryke et al., 2017; Jeske, 2019). However, there is little in the existing literature focusing specifically on, or related to social media reposting behavior of Millennials in China. Some studies have been conducted concerning workplace usage of technological incorporation and organizational accommodation including Hershatter (2010) in the area of tourism, and Luo (2018) for in-vehicle use while travelling (Polzin et al., 2014).

A viral hot spot can be ignited as well as spread virally through social media in a matter of seconds, not only nationally, but internationally without regard for linguistic limitations (Mangold & Faulds, 2009). Online content is able to be reposted quickly and efficiently, 70 percent of likes on wall posts happened within four hours and about 95% occur within 22 hours of the original posting (Heidemann et al., 2012). In the United States, Facebook has become an effective civic engagement tool, 74% of House candidates and 81% of Senatorial candidates won their battles for their higher number of fans on Facebook during the 2010 midterm elections (Obar et al., 2012). Breaking news is a good example of how fast information can spread through viral activity on social media and further may even provide an alternative role by substituting for the formal mainstream media. The news of the Sichuan earthquake which killed around 70,000 people in China, was disseminated worldwide from a single post made by a local citizen three minutes earlier than U.S. Geological Survey (Gabarain, 2008).

The interactive nature of social media could provide an opportunity for increasing the degree of users' engagement. Reposting is one of the most important forms of viral behaviors and is the highest for recognition of certain types of content among all kinds of viral behavior, not only for psychological approval, but also for actual behavior implemented (Alhabash & McAlister, 2015a). Khan (2017) argues that user participation can be considered by usual viral behavior including likes, comments and shares. Online interactions are often more uninhibited, creative and explicit than in-person communication (Wellman et al., 1996). The behavior of reposting is an embodiment of participation and of a certain type of self-branding. The identification of the content types that trigger Chinese millennials' reposting behavior and motivation is worthy of further discussion. Much about an individual's offline character can be perceived in their social media presence (Sell et al., 2012a). Much can also be determined about individuals, both directly and indirectly by analyzing the content that they post or repost on social media (Chiu et al., 2012b). The value orientation of an individual could effectively be interpreted by the words they use on social media (J. Chen et al., 2014). In addition to posting and reposting of secondary content, posting of original content on SMS, especially, "selfies" occurs frequently and is an effective mechanism for analysis of personal characteristics (Sung et al., 2016).

Chinese Millennials

Although there are various definitions towards "Millennials", researchers tend to identify the age group as 18-30 years of age (Alhabash & McAlister, 2015b; Erlam et al., 2016; Rodney & Wakeham Dr, 2016; Witt et al., 2008). In this study, the age group from 18-30 is used. Rainer and Rainer (2011) posit that Millennials are those born within the duration of 1980 to 2000, which is proving to be a commercially significant as well as an influential generation.

The Millennial Generation is forecast to change the perception of young people in part due to their heavy involvement in in online social events to a large extent accessed through various social media platforms (Howe & Strauss, 2000). Millennials have played an influential role in social media's evolution into an important source of product information and subsequent online shopping (Blake et al., 2017; Mangold & Smith, 2012a).

Wang et al. (2017) state that Chinese millennials are a generation that cannot be generalized into any other, in part because they came of age during the time of economic reform in China and the explosive economic growth that accompanied that era. With that consideration, Chinese millennials are a huge potential commercial market as they come of age with a previously unseen capacity for online commercial activity (Blake et al., 2017). Combined with their high level of online activity and adoption social media, this group must be studied as a unique demographic. Chinese millennials have developed in completely different surroundings than their Western counterparts and they probably have very little similarities with them (Sethi, 2019).

Reposting

Reposting is regarded as the most impactful way to disseminate information rapidly and with influence (Borge-Holthoefer et al., 2013). Reposting is also the easiest way to diffuse information virally. In this case, diffusion being defined as a process that communicates via specific channels among members of a social system (Rogers, 1995). Reposting is an implicit advertising behavior which is motivated by a user's own initiative. The challenge is how to engage and attract users to repost actively and willingly. Once the interest to repost is aroused, the potential advertising effect can be optimized. Reposting is an efficient and convincing way to spread the message.

Merton et al. (1954) argue that homophily is one of the fundamental principles of social network structure. Friends are likely to join in collective activities, provide assistance and communicate with each other (Argyle & Furnham, 1983). For online relationships, finding and connecting with other with whom one has more in common is more easily accomplished, and has much greater possibilities in part due to the relative ease of online communication and vast number of relationships possible, 80% of

Dutch use social network sites for connecting and maintaining offline friendship (Valkenburg & Peter, 2009). Compared to advertising posted by business accounts, messages reposted between people with non-professional relationships are more likely to get attention of SNS users. The process of online users reposting viral advertising to friends could be regarded as an endorsement of a certain brand's ads and levels up the possibility getting receiver's attention and forward again (Agah & Asadi, 2017; Chu, 2011). For these reasons, research to identify triggers, and motivations, as well as specifics of the content of Chinese millennials is worthwhile. The objective then becomes to determine what will encourage this group to repost willingly and frequently.

Motivation to Repost

Motivation can be explained as a psychological concept that leads individual to act towards a directed or identified objective (Ryan & Deci, 2000). Studies about motivation have been done concerning the application of activity in social media, Urista et al. (2009) similar activities in the work-place George et al. (1996) and information acceptance behavior (Davis et al., 1992). Entertainment, social engagement and a variety of incentives are part of the motivation that drives brand-consumers to interact online across differences in age, gender and style of usage of social media (Rohm et al., 2013).

Social cognitive theory has been applied to understand consumer behavior and personal actions in particular circumstances which may be based on individual cognition (Hsu et al., 2007). Self-efficacy and outcome expectation are two main influential factors of individual cognition. Intrinsic motivation is defined as people performing activities solely for the gratification and satisfaction of the activity itself (Sweetser & Kelleher, 2011; Vannoy & Medlin, 2017). Self-centered and community related desires are distinct according to studies of sharing behavior on SMS (Hsu et al., 2007). Users share content in order to gain recognition and respect, grow and strengthen their social network, secure their self-esteem and acquire an enhanced sense of community (N. Baym, 2015; Gretzel & Yoo, 2008). Altruism is explained as supporting others, the activity of helping others and as viewed as a reposting of useful, or helpful content and may provide re-posters with a feeling of being needed or of being helpful ((N. K. Baym, 2015).

Social media users also expect identification in virtual community for example, Facebook users seeking identification implicates self-awareness of membership in online groups (Cheung et al., 2011). People dedicate to present themselves in cyberspace with self-disclosure, for creating personal image and an enhanced identity (A. M. Kaplan & Haenlein, 2010). Sharing of common content that may be viewed as positive by peers is related to societal norms, commonly held tastes and common objectives (Williams, 2009).

Types of Content

Content Form refers to types of content and the presentation form that is re-posted. According to Erdogmus (2012), when posting on social media platforms, consumers are likely to share types of content that is related to music, technology, and humor. On twitter, for example, content viewed as worthy is categorized as: informative - 48% or funny - 48% (André et al., 2012). In the field of television researchers classify the type of content into a matrix model concerning attention, emotion, information, and opinion (Wohn & Bowe, 2016). According to the evaluation of official Facebook pages, contents related to celebrities and product information are most often viewed and shared (Parsons, 2013). Online marketing is the emerging and most effective way to target prospect customers by providing them with entertaining and informative content (Saravanakumar & SuganthaLakshmi, 2012).

Presentation Form

The form, or technical specification of content that is used on SMS varies with the most re-posted being either textual and narrative communication or audio and visual content (Munar & Jacobsen, 2014). During the chatting interaction, bonding of users in social media varies with decreasing degree from video, audio and instant message (Sherman et al., 2013) Various forms of images and video assist in building the brand identity of the user in social media platforms (Parsons, 2013) Content comprised of both audio and video is found to be more impactful compared to text or static pictures by online browsers, particularly when confronting multimedia features in the field of commercial websites and online products (Appiah, 2006a). Videos of commercial material, similar to that used in television is an emerging trend and represents a new way to advertise (Parsons, 2013). In the field of enterprise social media, combined text and multimedia such as video, the term hypermedia has emerged as an application which provides enhanced reach and richness of content (Kane, 2015).

STATEMENT OF HYPOTHESIS

For several reasons gender is one of the most commonly used demographics to segment a market (Putrevu, 2001). Gender segments are easily measured through survey respondents self-identification and as explained above, gender provides a solid rational for responding to marketing mix elements (Darley & Smith, 1995). Evidence indicates that women are more likely to value social network interactions (Debrand & Johnson, 2008; Shi et al., 2009). According to Geser (2006), maintaining an active social network is an instrumental objective when women use mobile devices whereas male subjects are more likely to use mobile device primarily for entertainment purposes such as online games.

Females are more likely to use social media interactions to join into a conversational culture (Mante & Piris, 2002; Sell et al., 2012b). This is supported by research indicating that females are more inclined to use social media in various social contexts than men, and social networking (Sell et al., 2012a). While the research is limited, there are indications that people prefer to share visual content over text content (Munar & Jacobsen, 2014). Research has been done to identify the most common presentation form for self-presentation (Herring & Kapidzic, 2015a). The same work indicates that teenage boys are more willing to be viewed publicly and more likely to present assertiveness by text while girls use tends to incorporate more individual privacy, for example by limiting the visibility of profiles images and details (Herring & Kapidzic, 2015b).

Social connection is a main purpose of girls to interact online. Incongruously, while girls may be willing to present attractive and sexually appealing visual content, patterns of presenting used by boys remains vague. Young females were identified as more likely to be impacted by athlete public figures and to spread positive word-of-mouth, and less likely than men to consider athletes as materialistic, making them more receptive to sports celebrity role models (Dix et al., 2010). Women used more words related to psychological and social processes than males (Newman et al., 2008).

Based on the existing body of knowledge reported above, the following hypotheses are derived.

Research Question (RQ): What are the Differences in the Reposting Behavior Between Males and Females With Regards to Motivation, Content, and Media Type?

H1: Regarding Motivation to Repost

1a - Female subjects are more motivated to repost for incentives.

1b - Males are more inclined to repost in order to gain recognition.

H2: Regarding Types of content

2a - Women are more likely to repost celebrity-related content.

2b – Social news and current affairs are more likely to trigger reposting by Men.

H3: Regarding Media type

3a – Text and word forms are preferred by Female.

3b – There is significant difference in favor of picture-based media content.

METHODOLOGY

Pilot Study - Qualitative Method

In order to identify the most frequently used responses to the research inquiries, a qualitative pilot study combining interviews and discussions was undertaken. In-person interviews with 30 Chinese millennials (15 male, 15 female) were conducted, all subjects self-reported as being both adept and active users of SMS. The responses were collected, collated and arranged into types. Words that repeated frequently were selected as the choices for the questionnaire of the full study.

Instrumentation Design (Quantitative Method)

The survey was designed based on pilot study and previous related research design (Yuan et al., 2014).

Survey Question on Motivation to Repost

Seven options were presented as possible responses for the question regarding motivation:

- Work and professional purposes;
- Social interaction (common interests);
- Seeking Recognition;
- Follow Celebrities;
- Opinions (Resonated content);
- Altruism (Helpful and motivational information);
- Incentives, Virtual or Financial (Drawings, raffles etc.).

In addition to the most frequently occurring responses during the Qualitative Pilot Study, an option for Work and Professional Purposes was included due this option being identified as a factor in previous related literature. Facebook is emerging as a platform for work-related objectives as the online business model continues to form (Mazman & Usluel, 2010). Some business sectors are moving more rapidly to integrate social media into their regular operations, students majoring in journalism are more likely that students majoring in other disciplines to use social media for work purposes (Hermida et al., 2012). It is not uncommon for users to see social media as an extension of earlier technological version of connectivity, and to find that the primary objective of the Internet is supporting collaborative work (Wellman, 2001). Chinese companies apply social network sites to promote public dialogue with consumers by posting corporate information to target the global market (Men & Tsai, 2012). More importantly, Chinese social network site users are sometimes required to propagate or publicize for their off-line community, organization or company.

The theory of reasoned action (TRA) demonstrates that behavioral intention can lead to individual specific action, which in turn is influenced by personal attitudes and subjective norms (Fishbein & Ajzen, 1977). Apart from this classical theory, motivation theory is widely applied in recent research. Extrinsic and intrinsic are the two main branches most likely to exert examined influence (Lee, 2014). The former pertains to environmental outcomes, e.g. values, benefits, while the latter refers to motivation related to enjoyment and interest of self regardless of outside stimuli. Crucial predictors in knowledge sharing, for instance, financial incentives and personal reputation is classified as extrinsic motivation, and altruism is regarded as intrinsic motivation (Hung, Durcikova, Lai, & L2011).

Meanwhile, social capital theory is often considered. Social capital is a diverse concept regarding structure, relation and cognition (Chang & Chuang, 2011; Chiu et al., 2012b; Wasko & Faraj, 2005) Chinese youth are undergoing an extensive transformation towards cultural and value consumption (Fung, 2009). The report of Sina demonstrates that there are more than 60,000 official accounts including celebrities, sports figures, well-known spokesman. Following celebrities through social media is a popular activity, and is found to be a highly commercialized trend, complete with various cultural and value consumption factors (Dionísio et al., 2008; Fung, 2009). In order to target opportunities in the fan-based online sports market, Chinese social media users were studied (Fung, 2009; S. Kaplan & Langdon, 2012) After reviewing existing literature and the results of the pilot study the expression of each choice to more accurately reflect the intent of this study was completed.

Survey Question on Types of Content

Eight alternatives were provided to measure the factor of Type of Content:

- Incentivized Content, Virtual or Financial (Drawings raffles etc.);
- Charity and Donations;
- To Bring Good Luck;
- Interesting, novel and entertaining (cultural, fashions, sports);
- Emotion and Feelings (chicken soup for the soul);
- Social news, current affairs and Hot topics;
- Professional contents which are significant and beneficial;
- Idols, Celebrities, loved bloggers and public figures.

Superstition sometimes is seen irrational, it assists human beings in dealing with ambiguous circumstances and uncertainty (Gimpl & Dakin, 1984; Rice, 1985; Tsang, 2004a)(Rice Jr, 1985), (Tsang, 2004b). Chinese millennials go through extremely competitive exams, interviews, and occupational challenges and regularly pursue good luck to strengthen confidence and provide psychological comfort. Individuals may resort to totemic symbols before taking exams or when seeking for money in order to appeal to the god of scholarship (Zeng et al., 2009). Many Chinese pray or seek to gain blessings for good health or healing, or seek to be offered blessings related to health and prosperity (Badham, 2008; Billioud, 2013; Law, 2005). Stroke patients in China regard spiritual needs was important at all stages of recovery (Lui & Mackenzie, 1999) People are inclined to share news they have encountered on social media for constructing a shared reality such as for religious, superstitious, or spiritual purposes(Lui & Mackenzie, 1999) As Chinese millennials develop a sense of self-presentation and identity management, their personal social media brand, through technology-mediated communication Chu et al (2010), frequently posting and re-posting of these types of content has become frequent. Several participants of the pilot study revealed that they would like to repost emotional content to convey their believes and values. Social media is an indirect way to express their own words.

Survey Question on Presentation Form

Based on the frequency of repeated responses in the Pilot Study, Social media content was subdivided into 6 categories of presentation forms:

- Multi-media (Video + Audio);
- Audio only (Music);
- Pictures (Static & Animated gif);
- Pictures with comments, captions and clarification;
- Short messages;
- Long text, (a paragraph or longer).

Online presentation features are frequently a debate in the field of cyber-news, online-learning, and advertisers (Omar et al., 2018; Sundar, 2000; Sundar et al., 1998). Multimedia is a popular form of choice which contains both video and audio and may have favorable impacts on commercial websites (Appiah, 2006b). Audio content delivery is a crucial approach in online-marketing (Scott, 2009). Digital audio, images and photographs are well defined types of presentation for use in social media (Mangold & Smith, 2012b). The combination of picture and text is also a often used form for content in online and social media. In the context of business use, text-image congruence facilitates clear product images (Van Rompay et al., 2010). In the context of Twitter, the design and purpose is to encourage people to post or repost short text to update their network (Marwick & Boyd, 2011). In the case of Weibo, a amximum of 140 words are allowed in a single post, however, various other social media platforms are offering the options of more content which is beginnign to be viewed as necessary. Detailed narrative communicative practices include blogs, written reviews and other information, and in particular, fashion and brand related content (Helal et al., 2018).

ANALYSIS / RESULTS

A total of 1,347 online survey questionnaire responses were collected. Basic information on age groups and frequency of social media use breakdown is provided on Table 1. The Chinese millennials age group ranging from 18 to 30 years represented the majority of the survey respondents with 838 participants out of the total or 64% with a gender make up composition of (295 males 35.2% and 543 females 64.7%). This Chinese Millennial age group are active social media users and reposted more frequently 62% compared to the other age groups in the study (see Table 2). The majority of the respondents, 621 of the survey's participants (74.1%) hail from the Zhejiang province of South-East China. This is due to the manner in which the survey data was collected, Millennials shared the survey link with their friends on their WeChat accounts, and in turn asked their friends to keep sharing it with their friends, thus creating a snowball sampling effect. Table 1 shows a comparison between the frequency of reposting between Millennial (18-30 years of age) and users that are <18 or 30+.

Table 2. Age group distribution of frequency and reposting on social media

Sharing Frequency	5+ times a day	1-4 times a day	1-5 times a week	1-4 times a month	Once a month	Rarely	Total	%
Age								
<18	8	10	21	27	36	15	117	9%
18-30	68	96	218	230	193	33	838	62%
31-40	7	15	26	46	56	14	164	12%
40+	10	22	45	62	71	18	228	17%
Total	93	143	310	365	356	80	1347	

Table 2 shows the comparisons of age groups and reposting frequency when engaging in social media interaction with others. Based on the comparison of the different age groups in reposting content on social media and sharing frequency, the Chinese millennials are uniquely distinct group of heavy social media use with dominant counts and frequency of usage for both male and female. Especially, for the highest sharing frequency of posting content in social media in five times or more and one to four times per day (5+ times a day (68%), 1-4 times a day (67%), 1-5 times a week (70%).

Table 3. Comparisons of Chinese millennial motivation to repost content in social media for shared content

	Female	Expected	%	Male	Expected	%	P value	χ^2	Cramer's V
	543		65%	295		35%			
Reason to repost (Share content on social media)									
Work related	213	210.6	39.2%	112	114.4	38.0%	0.721	0.13	0.01
Resonated content	337	318.2	62.1%	154	172.8	52.2%	0.006 ***	7.66	0.10
Social interaction	225	226.8	41.4%	125	123.2	42.4%	0.793	0.07	0.01
Altruism (Helpful and motivational information)	155	140.0	28.5%	61	76.0	20.7%	0.013 **	6.18	0.09
Seek recognition	78	92.0	14.4%	64	50.0	21.7%	0.007 ***	7.30	0.09
Financial incentives (Virtual drawings or raffles)	175	157.5	32.2%	68	85.5	23.1%	0.005 ***	7.82	0.10
Follow celebrities	122	91.4	22.5%	19	49.6	6.4%	0.000 ***	35.09	0.20

*, **, and *** indicate the significance level of 10%, 5%, and 1%, respectively

Table 3 shows that when comparing the Chinese millennials' age cohort groups on gender differences and the motivation or the driving reasons to repost on social media, some interesting findings emerged.

For example, the chi-square test uncovered a statistically significant differences between male and female in their motivations to share content, χ^2 *(1, N = 838) = 7.66, 6.18, 7.3, 7.8, 35.09[1] p < .001* related to resonated content females were more likely to be motivated to share that content more than males *(62% to 52%),* likewise females were more likely to be motivated to share content related to altruism (28.5% to 20%), financial incentives (32% to 23%), and celebrity related reposts (22.5% to 6.4%), while interestingly males showed a significant difference than females (21.7% to 14.4%) to be motivated to share contents related to recognition seeking χ^2 (1, N = 838) = 7.30 *p < .001.* On the other hand, there was no statistically significant difference between the Chinese millennials' gender for being motivated to repost on work related to socially interactive activities.

Table 4. Comparisons of Chinese millennial motivation to repost content in social media for shared content

	Female	Expected	%	Male	Expected	%	P value		χ^2	Cramer's V
Media Form Used to Repost (Shared)										
Multi-media (video + audio + text)	293	272.8	54.0%	128	148.2	43.4%	0.003	***	8.54	0.10
Pictures (comments, captions and clarification)	370	362.2	68.1%	189	196.8	64.1%	0.232		1.43	0.04
Pictures (static, animated gif)	280	269.6	51.6%	136	146.4	46.1%	0.131		2.28	0.05
Long text (one paragraph or longer)	196	172.4	36.1%	70	93.6	23.7%	0.000	***	13.49	0.13
Short message	187	173.0	34.4%	80	94.0	27.1%	0.030	**	4.72	0.08
Audio message	426	433.5	78.5%	117	109.5	21.5%	0.177		1.82	0.05

*, **, and *** indicate the significance level of 10%, 5%, and 1%, respectively

Further analysis of the data, shown in Table 4, indicates that the media form used to share content by gender differences, there were some significant differences χ^2 (1, N = 838) = 8.54 and 13.42 p < .001)[2]. Female participants showed more inclination to share multimedia (text, audio, and video) content (54% to 43.4%) and long message format (one paragraph or longer) (36% to 23.7%) for the motivations cited above. In the motivation to share short message text a χ^2 (1, N = 838) = 4.72 p < .05), females differed with males (34.4% to 27.1%). There was no major difference between Chinese millennial genders with regards to sharing pictures with comments, pictures with animated gifs, and audio messages.

Table 5. Comparisons of Chinese millenial in social media for types of content shared and reposted

	Female	Expected	%	Male	Expected	%	P value		χ^2	Cramer's V
Shared (Reposted) Content										
Virtual or Financial (Drawings or raffles)	158	153.6	29.1%	79	83.4	26.8%	0.477		0.51	0.02
Charity and Donations	114	126.4	21.0%	81	68.6	27.5%	0.034	**	4.47	0.07
To Bring Good Luck	131	110.2	24.1%	39	59.8	13.2%	0.000	***	14.06	0.13
Entertaining (cultural, fashions, sports)	275	265.7	50.6%	135	144.3	45.8%	0.177		1.82	0.05
Emotion and Feelings (chicken soup for the soul)	123	130.2	22.7%	78	70.8	26.4%	0.220		1.51	0.04
Current affairs	163	168.5	30.0%	97	91.5	32.9%	0.392		0.73	0.03
Professional contents	193	193.1	35.5%	105	104.9	35.6%	0.988		0.00	0.00
Celebrities (following idols)	164	119.2	30.2%	20	64.8	6.8%	0.000	***	61.20	0.27

*, **, and *** indicate the significance level of 10%, 5%, and 1%, respectively

On the third research question regarding what type of content Chinese millennials shared or reposted to their online connections χ^2 (1, N = 838) = 14.06 and 61.20[3] p < .001). Table 5 indicates that females showed a significant difference to males in the shared content type related to bring good luck (24.1% to 13.2%) as well as content related to celebrities or public figures (30.2% to 6.8%).

While the male survey respondents showed a statistically significant difference χ^2 (1, N = 838) = 4.47, p < .05 to sharing or reposting more than female survey participants when the content was related to charity or donations (27.5% to 21%). This finding was unexpected and is included in the further research suggestions. On the other hand, there was no statistically significant difference between the Chinese millennials' gender on sharing or reposting content types related to financial drawings (raffles), novel or interesting content (fashion or cultural), emotion and feeling, current affairs, and professional related content.

Table 6. Overall population and gender comparisons for motivation on repost in social media- China

	Female	Expected	%	Male	Expected	%	P value	χ^2	Cramer's V
	888		66%	459		34%			
Reason to repost (Share content on social media)									
Work related	549	546	66.3%	279	282	33.7%	0.710	0.138	0.010
Resonated content	423	438	63.6%	242	227	36.4%	0.077 *	3.134	0.048
Social interaction	587	580	66.7%	293	300	33.3%	0.407	0.688	0.023
Altruism (Helpful to others)	584	613	62.8%	346	317	37.2%	0.000 ***	13.089	0.099
Seek recognition	767	754	67.0%	377	390	33.0%	0.039 **	4.248	0.056
Financial incentives (Virtual drawings or raffles)	678	691	64.7%	370	357	35.3%	0.070 *	3.178	0.049
Follow celebrities	732	771	62.6%	438	399	37.4%	0.000 ***	44.752	0.182
*, **, and *** indicate the significance level of 10%, 5%, and 1%, respectively									

Furthermore, when we compared the survey respondents' overall gender differences *(N= 1347, female N = 888, male N = 459)* and included in the analysis the other two age groups in the survey (younger than 18 and older than 31) with a total of *N = 509*, on the question of motivation to repost or share content on social media the results were unexpected.

Table 6, shows that males in the overall general population showed a significant difference to females, being more inclined and motivated to share χ^2 (1, N = 1347) = 13.08 and 44.75[4] p < .001) content related to altruism (37.2% to 62.8%) even though they represented 34% of the survey sample with females representing 66%, and similarly with celebrities (37.4% to 62.6%). Additionally, male participants showed some difference at the χ^2 (1, N = 1347) = 3.14 and 3.17[5], p < .1) level with sharing content related to raffles and financial gain (35.3% to 64.7%). In contrast, in the overall group analysis, female participants were more motivated to share and repost χ^2 (1, N = 1347) = 4.24, p < .05 the content related to seeking recognition (33% to 67%). Very surprisingly, this is a reversal from the results observed in the Millennials age group gender differences analyzed above, and this finding is a compelling motivator for further research of a replicative or exploratory nature.

Similarly, an analogous pattern emerges again in the general population sample compared to the millennial age group. We find there's a significant relationship between gender and social media format used as a medium to repost messages to others as shown in Table 7. χ^2 *(1, N = 1,347) = 6.85, 5.61, and 7.56[6], p < .001)* Chinese male participants of almost all age groups surveyed in the study were more likely to engage in using media types of pictures with comments (38.8% to 61.2%), and long text messages (36% to 64%) and short text reposts (36.4% to 63.6%) to share contents with their circles. While there was no statistically observed gender differences in the survey's overall participants' preferences in using multimedia (text, audio and video) and pictures (both static and gif) media types.

Table 8, shows the types of content Chinese social media users shared and reposted, this also follows a pattern similar to the motivation and media used to repost content findings above. In the overall survey participants' responses, again there's a strong relationship between gender and type of content reposted on social media. χ^2 *(1, N = 1,347) =11.9 and 64.026[7], p < .001)* especially in two items out of the eight items in the survey questionnaire (see Table 8), in those two items male's shared or reposted content were significantly different than that of female in terms of to bring good luck (36.1% to 63.9) and celebrity related content shared (38.7% to 61.3%). Whereas, surprisingly females χ^2 *(1, N = 1,347) = 10.66 p < .001)* shared more content related to current affairs than their male counterpart in the same survey.

Table 7. Overall population and gender comparisons on media form used to share in social media-China

	Female	Expected	%	Male	Expected	%	P value	χ^2	Cramer's V
	888		66%	459		34%			
Media Form Used to Repost (Shared)									
Multi-media (video + audio + text)	497	506	64.7%	271	262	35.3%	0.28	1.166	0.029
Pictures (comments, captions and clarification)	281	303	61.2%	178	156	38.8%	0.009 ***	6.859	0.071
Pictures (static, animated gif)	472	477	65.3%	251	246	34.7%	0.593	0.285	0.015
Long text (one paragraph or longer)	625	643	64.0%	351	333	36.0%	0.010 ***	5.619	0.065
Short message	593	615	63.6%	340	318	36.4%	0.005 ***	7.564	0.075
Audio message	744	750	65.4%	394	388	34.6%	0.323	0.975	0.027

*, **, and *** indicate the significance level of 10%, 5%, and 1%, respectively

Table 8. Overall population and gender comparisons for types of content shared in social media- China

	Female	Expected	%	Male	Expected	%	P value	χ^2	Cramer's V
	888		66%	459		34%			
Shared (Reposted) Content									
Virtual or Financial (Drawings or raffles)	699	696	66.2%	357	360	33.8%	0.692	0.157	0.011
Charity and Donations	622	610	67.2%	304	316	32.8%	0.152	2.049	0.039
To Bring Good Luck	711	734	63.9%	402	379	36.1%	0.000 ***	11.903	0.094
Entertaining (cultural, fashions, sports)	526	525	66.1%	270	271	33.9%	0.884	0.021	0.004
Emotion and Feelings (chicken soup for the soul)	649	654	65.4%	343	338	34.6%	0.517	0.420	0.018
Current affairs	622	595	68.9%	281	308	31.1%	0.001 ***	10.665	0.089
Professional contents	603	603	65.9%	312	312	34.1%	0.980	0.001	0.001
Celebrities (following idols)	687	739	61.3%	434	382	38.7%	0.000 ***	64.026	0.218

*, **, and *** indicate the significance level of 10%, 5%, and 1%, respectively

CONCLUSION AND PRACTICAL IMPLICATIONS

Content that goes viral in Social Media is emerging as the future means of reaching many target demographic audiences. The results of this study analyzed Chinese Millennial gender differences in sharing and reposting content on Social Media and confirms the findings of communication theory such as Uses and gratification theory (UGT), and motivation theory, but this study's findings also enrich gender studies regarding social media usage. Exploring the intricate relationship between gender, motivation and content form, the online social media promoters and businesses may be able to use these findings to design advertising and commercial content according to targeted millennial market segmentation with gender difference. Additionally, social media content developers may also benefit from focusing on building improved social media platform strategies by delivering content by viewing findings.

The findings in the motivation of reposting demonstrate that, Chinese millennials females are more motivated to repost content on social media that relates to following celebrities, sharing resonated opinions and financial gain such as raffles as well as spiritual incentives than their counterpart male millennials. On the other hand, Chinese Millennial males are more likely to repost content in social media to get more recognition.

When examining reposted content in social media, females are more likely to share content with the intention to bring good luck and celebrity-related content. Conversely, males are more likely to share charity and donation related message. Comparing the propensity of each female and male Chinese millennials to repost themes based on the form of the content, females are more likely to repost text messages, both long and short than males. Females also preferred more use of multi-media presentation formats than males.

On a practical application level, online marketers and social media content developers can use these findings to segment their intended market demographics by gender which, as described above is a key factor in targeted promotional advertising social media campaigns. For instance, when promoting a female cosmetic product or service, it would be sufficiently helpful to invite key opinion leaders (KPL) or influential celebrities to be spokesperson as well as adding content which is aimed at bringing good luck with the use of multi-media or text based format for marketing outreach programs. For males delivering content which allows to easily get recognition and includes some form of charity aspect factor would be most likely approach.

LIMITATIONS AND FUTURE RESEARCH

Although some of the findings presented in this study are of great interest, however, some limitations exist. The surveys were accomplished with self-assessed approach which is subjective. Future studies would do well by using more back and forth focus groups. Secondly, the measured data in the survey was broadly generalized on all social media to the extent of social media used without pointing out a specific social network site platform, this is less of a limitation than it appears as WeChat is by far the most prevalent social media platform used in China. This paper focuses on gender differences in social media of Chinese millennials, which provides a fertile group for further study in any of the variables explored. Future research could elaborate on the relationships between mentioned factors in both objective and subjective methods. Other future research that could build on the specific finding of this paper could include a similar investigation of reporting and sharing behavior of millennials in other countries and a comparison of them with the Chinese millennials investigated in this paper. Finally, future studies can use an application programming interface to investigate reposted information in analyzing type of content and presentation form accurately and on a larger scale.

REFERENCES

Agah, A., & Asadi, M. (2017). Influence and Information Flow in Online Social Networks. *International Journal of Virtual Communities and Social Networking*, 9(4), 1–17. doi:10.4018/IJVCSN.2017100101

Aiello, L. M., Barrat, A., Schifanella, R., Cattuto, C., Markines, B., & Menczer, F. (2012). Friendship Prediction and Homophily in Social Media. *ACM Trans. Web*, 6(2), 9:1–9:33. doi:10.1145/2180861.2180866

Alhabash, S., & McAlister, A. R. (2015a). Redefining virality in less broad strokes: Predicting viral behavioral intentions from motivations and uses of Facebook and Twitter. *New Media & Society*, 17(8), 1317–1339. doi:10.1177/1461444814523726

Alhabash, S., & McAlister, A. R. (2015b). Redefining virality in less broad strokes: Predicting viral behavioral intentions from motivations and uses of Facebook and Twitter. *New Media & Society*, 17(8), 1317–1339. doi:10.1177/1461444814523726

André, P., Bernstein, M., & Luther, K. (2012). *Who gives a tweet? Evaluating microblog content value*. Academic Press.

Appiah, O. (2006a). Rich Media, poor Media: The Impact of audio/video vs. Text/picture testimonial ads on browsers' evaluations of commercial web sites and online products. *Journal of Current Issues and Research in Advertising*, 28(1), 73–86.

Appiah, O. (2006b). Rich Media, poor Media: The Impact of audio/video vs. Text/picture testimonial ads on browsers' evaluations of commercial web sites and online products. *Journal of Current Issues and Research in Advertising*, 28(1), 73–86.

Argyle, M., & Furnham, A. (1983). Sources of Satisfaction and Conflict in Long-Term Relationships. *Journal of Marriage and Family*, 45(3), 481–493. doi:10.2307/351654

Badham, P. (2008). Religion in Britain and China: Similarities and differences. *Modern Believing*, 49(1), 50–58.

Baym, N. (2015). *Personal connections in the digital age*. John Wiley & Sons.

Baym, N. K. (2015). *Personal connections in the digital age*. John Wiley & Sons.

Billioud, S. (2013). Confucianism and Spiritual Traditions in Modern China and Beyond ed. By Fenggang Yang, Joseph Tamney. *Journal of Chinese Religions*, 41(1), 88–90.

Bivens, R., & Haimson, O. (2016). Baking Gender Into Social Media Design: How Platforms Shape Categories for Users and Advertisers. *Social Media + Society*, 2(4). doi:10.1177/2056305116672486

Blake, B., Neuendorf, K. A., LaRosa, R. J., Luming, Y., Hudzinski, K., & Hu, Y. (2017). E-Shopping Patterns of Chinese and US Millennials. *Journal of Internet Commerce*, 16(1), 53–79. doi:10.1080/15332861.2017.1281702

Borge-Holthoefer, J., Baños, R. A., González-Bailón, S., & Moreno, Y. (2013). Cascading behaviour in complex socio-technical networks. *Journal of Complex Networks*, 1(1), 3–24.

Bouwman, H., Carlsson, C., Castillo, F., Giaglis, G., & Walden, P. (2010a). Factors Affecting the Present and Future Use of Mobile Data Services: Comparing the Dutch, Finnish and Greek Markets. *International Journal of Mobile Communications, 8*(4), 430–450. doi:10.1504/IJMC.2010.033835

Bouwman, H., Carlsson, C., Castillo, F. J. M., Giaglis, G. M., & Walden, P. (2010b). Factors Affecting the Present and Future Use of Mobile Data Services: Comparing the Dutch, Finnish and Greek Markets. *International Journal of Mobile Communications, 8*(4), 430–450. doi:10.1504/IJMC.2010.033835

Bronner, F., & de Hoog, R. (2014). Social media and consumer choice. *International Journal of Market Research, 56*(1), 51–71.

Chang, H., & Chuang, S.-S. (2011). Social capital and individual motivations on knowledge sharing: Participant involvement as a moderator. *Information & Management, 48*(1), 9–18.

Chen, J., Hsieh, G., Mahmud, J. U., & Nichols, J. (2014). *Understanding individuals' personal values from social media word use*. Academic Press.

Chen, X., Tao, D., & Zhou, Z. (2019). Factors affecting reposting behaviour using a mobile phone-based user-generated-content online community application among Chinese young adults. *Behaviour & Information Technology, 38*(2), 120–131. doi:10.1080/0144929X.2018.1515985

Cheung, C. M. K., Chiu, P.-Y., & Lee, M. K. O. (2011). Online social networks: Why do students use facebook? *Computers in Human Behavior, 27*(4), 1337–1343. doi:10.1016/j.chb.2010.07.028

Chiu, C., Ip, C., & Silverman, A. (2012a). Understanding social media in China. *The McKinsey Quarterly, 2*, 78–81.

Chu, S. (2011). Viral Advertising in Social Media: Participation in Facebook Groups and Responses among College-Aged Users. *Journal of Interactive Advertising, 12*(1), 30–43. doi:10.1080/15252019. 2011.10722189

Chu, S., & Choi, S. M. (2010). Social capital and self-presentation on social networking sites: A comparative study of Chinese and American young generations. *Chinese Journal of Communication, 3*(4), 402–420.

Darley, W. K., & Smith, R. E. (1995). Gender differences in information processing strategies: An empirical test of the selectivity model in advertising response. *Journal of Advertising, 24*(1), 41–56.

Davis, F. D., Bagozzi, R. P., & Warshaw, P. R. (1992). Extrinsic and intrinsic motivation to use computers in the workplace 1. *Journal of Applied Social Psychology, 22*(14), 1111–1132.

De Reuver, M., & Haaker, T. (2009). Designing viable business models for context-aware mobile services. *Telematics and Informatics, 26*(3), 240–248.

Debrand, C. C., & Johnson, J. J. (2008). Gender differences in email and instant messaging: A study of undergraduate business information systems students. *Journal of Computer Information Systems, 48*(3), 20–30.

Dillon, S., Buchanan, J., & Al-Otaibi, K. (2014). Perceived risk and online shopping intention: A study across gender and product type. *International Journal of E-Business Research, 10*(4), 17.

Dionísio, P., Leal, C., & Moutinho, L. (2008). Fandom affiliation and tribal behaviour: A sports marketing application. *Qualitative Market Research*, *11*(1), 17–39. doi:10.1108/13522750810845531

Dix, S., Phau, I., & Pougnet, S. (2010). "Bend it like Beckham": The influence of sports celebrities on young adult consumers. *Young Consumers*, *11*(1), 36–46. doi:10.1108/17473611011025993

Eckler, P., & Bolls, P. (2011). Spreading the Virus. *Journal of Interactive Advertising*, *11*(2), 1–11. doi:10.1080/15252019.2011.10722180

Erdoğmuş, İ., & Cicek, M. (2012). The impact of social media marketing on brand loyalty. *Procedia: Social and Behavioral Sciences*, *58*, 1353–1360.

Erlam, G., Smythe, L., & Wright, V. (2016). *Simulation and Millennials—The Perfect Storm*. Academic Press.

Fishbein, M., & Ajzen, I. (1977). *Belief, attitude, intention, and behavior: An introduction to theory and research*. Academic Press.

Fung, A. (2009). Fandom, youth and consumption in China. *European Journal of Cultural Studies*, *12*(3), 285–303.

Gabarain, C. (2008). *Twitter and the Sichuan earthquake: Proving its value*. Academic Press.

Garner, J. (2005). *The Rise of the Chinese Consumer: Theory and Evidence*. John Wiley & Sons.

George, J. M., & Brief, A. (1996). *Motivational agendas in the workplace: The effects of feelings on focus of attention and work motivation*. Elsevier Science/JAI Press.

Geser, H. (2006). *Are girls (even) more addicted? Some gender patterns of cell phone usage*. Academic Press.

Gimpl, M., & Dakin, S. (1984). Management and magic. *California Management Review*, *27*(1), 125–136.

Gretzel, U., & Yoo, K. H. (2008). Use and impact of online travel reviews. *Information and Communication Technologies in Tourism*, *2008*, 35–46.

Han, G., & Wang, W. (2015). Mapping user relationships for health information diffusion on microblogging in China: A social network analysis of Sina Weibo. *Asian Journal of Communication*, *25*(1), 65–83. doi:10.1080/01292986.2014.989239

He, S. (2009). Internet Diffusion and Social Inequalities in Greater China Region via Six Key Socioeconomic Indicators. *International Journal of Virtual Communities and Social Networking*, *1*(2), 51–64. doi:10.4018/jvcsn.2009040104

Heidemann, J., Klier, M., & Probst, F. (2012). Online social networks: A survey of a global phenomenon. *Computer Networks*, *56*(18), 3866–3878. doi:10.1016/j.comnet.2012.08.009

Helal, G., Ozuem, W., & Lancaster, G. (2018). Social media brand perceptions of millennials. [edb.]. *International Journal of Retail & Distribution Management*, *46*(10), 977.

Hermida, A., Fletcher, F., Korell, D., & Logan, D. (2012). Share, like, recommend: Decoding the social media news consumer. *Journalism Studies*, *13*(5–6), 815–824.

Herring, S. C., & Kapidzic, S. (2015). Teens, Gender, and Self-Presentation in Social Media. In *International Encyclopedia of the Social & Behavioral Sciences* (pp. 146–152). Elsevier. doi:10.1016/B978-0-08-097086-8.64108-9

Hershatter, A., & Epstein, M. (2010). Millennials and the world of work: An organization and management perspective. *Journal of Business and Psychology*, 25(2), 211–223.

Howe, N., & Strauss, W. (2000). *Millennials rising: The next great generation*. Vintage.

Hsu, M.-H., Ju, T. L., Yen, C.-H., & Chang, C.-M. (2007). Knowledge sharing behavior in virtual communities: The relationship between trust, self-efficacy, and outcome expectations. *International Journal of Human-Computer Studies*, 65(2), 153–169. doi:10.1016/j.ijhcs.2006.09.003

Hung, S.-Y., Durcikova, A., Lai, H.-M., & Lin, W.-M. (2011). The influence of intrinsic and extrinsic motivation on individuals' knowledge sharing behavior. *International Journal of Human-Computer Studies*, 69(6), 415–427.

Jendryke, M., Balz, T., & Liao, M. (2017). Big location-based social media messages from China's Sina Weibo network: Collection, storage, visualization, and potential ways of analysis. [bth.]. *Transactions in GIS*, 21(4), 825–834.

Jeske, D. (2019). *Friendship and Social Media: A Philosophical Exploration*. Routledge.

Kane, G. C. (2015). Enterprise Social Media: Current Capabilities and Future Possibilities. *MIS Quarterly Executive*, 14.

Kaplan, A. M., & Haenlein, M. (2010). Users of the world, unite! The challenges and opportunities of Social Media. *Business Horizons*, 53(1), 59–68.

Kaplan, S., & Langdon, S. (2012). Chinese fandom and potential marketing strategies for expanding the market for American professional sports into China. *International Journal of Sports Marketing & Sponsorship*, 14(1), 2–16.

Kelly, S. D. T., Suryadevara, N. K., & Mukhopadhyay, S. C. (2013). Towards the Implementation of IoT for Environmental Condition Monitoring in Homes. *IEEE Sensors Journal*, 13(10), 3846–3853. doi:10.1109/JSEN.2013.2263379

Khan, M. L. (2017). Social media engagement: What motivates user participation and consumption on YouTube? *Computers in Human Behavior*, 66, 236–247. doi:10.1016/j.chb.2016.09.024

Kirby, J., & Marsden, P. (2006). *Connected marketing: The viral, buzz and word of mouth revolution*. Elsevier.

Klemettinen, M. (2007). *Enabling technologies for mobile services: The MobiLife book*. John Wiley & Sons.

Law, P. (2005). The revival of folk religion and gender relationships in rural China: A preliminary observation. *Asian Folklore Studies*, 89–109.

Lee, S. (2014). What Makes Twitterers Retweet on Twitter? Exploring the Roles of Intrinsic/Extrinsic Motivation and Social Capital. *Journal of the Korea Academia-Industrial Cooperation Society*, *15*(6), 3499–3511. doi:10.5762/KAIS.2014.15.6.3499

Li, D., Li, Y., & Ji, W. (2018). Gender Identification via Reposting Behaviors in Social Media. *IEEE Access: Practical Innovations, Open Solutions*, *6*, 2879–2888. doi:10.1109/ACCESS.2017.2785813

Li, H. (2006). Emergence of the Chinese Middle Class and Its Implications. *Asian Affairs: An American Review*, *33*(2), 67–83. doi:10.3200/AAFS.33.2.67-83

Liang, Q., & Teng, J.-Z. (2006). Financial development and economic growth: Evidence from China. *China Economic Review*, *17*(4), 395–411. doi:10.1016/j.chieco.2005.09.003

Lu, Z., Wen, Y., & Cao, G. (2014). Information diffusion in mobile social networks: The speed perspective. *IEEE INFOCOM 2014 - IEEE Conference on Computer Communications*, 1932–1940. 10.1109/INFOCOM.2014.6848133

Lui, S., & Mackenzie, A. (1999). Chinese elderly patients' perceptions of their rehabilitation needs following a stroke. *Journal of Advanced Nursing*, *30*(2), 391–400. PMID:10457241

Luo, J., Dey, B. L., Yalkin, C., Sivarajah, U., Punjaisri, K., Huang, Y., & Yen, D. A. (2018). Millennial Chinese consumers' perceived destination brand value. *Journal of Business Research*.

Mangold, W. G., & Faulds, D. J. (2009). Social media: The new hybrid element of the promotion mix. *Business Horizons*, *52*(4), 357–365.

Mangold, W. G., & Smith, K. T. (2012). Selling to Millennials with online reviews. *Business Horizons*, *55*(2), 141–153.

Mante, E. A., & Piris, D. (2002). SMS use by young people in the Netherlands. *Revista de Estudios de Juventud*, *52*, 47–58.

Marwick, A. E., & Boyd, D. (2011). I tweet honestly, I tweet passionately: Twitter users, context collapse, and the imagined audience. *New Media & Society*, *13*(1), 114–133.

Mazman, S. G., & Usluel, Y. K. (2010). Modeling educational usage of Facebook. *Computers & Education*, *55*(2), 444–453.

Men, L. R., & Tsai, W.-H. S. (2012). How companies cultivate relationships with publics on social network sites: Evidence from China and the United States. *Public Relations Review*, *38*(5), 723–730.

Men, L. R., & Tsai, W.-H. S. (2013). Beyond liking or following: Understanding public engagement on social networking sites in China. *Public Relations Review*, *39*(1), 13–22. doi:10.1016/j.pubrev.2012.09.013

Merton, R. K., & Lazarsfeld, P. F. (1954). *Friendship as a social process. In Freedom and Control in Modern Society*. Van Norstrand.

Mu, W., Spaargaren, G., & Oude Lansink, A. (2019). Mobile Apps for Green Food Practices and the Role for Consumers: A Case Study on Dining Out Practices with Chinese and Dutch Young Consumers. *Sustainability*, *11*(5), 1275.

Munar, A. M., Jacobsen, J., & Kr, S. (2014). Motivations for sharing tourism experiences through social media. *Tourism Management*, *43*, 46–54. doi:10.1016/j.tourman.2014.01.012

Nesi, J., & Prinstein, M. J. (2015). Using social media for social comparison and feedback-seeking: Gender and popularity moderate associations with depressive symptoms. *Journal of Abnormal Child Psychology*, *43*(8), 1427–1438. PMID:25899879

Newman, M. L., Groom, C. J., Handelman, L. D., & Pennebaker, J. W. (2008). Gender Differences in Language Use: An Analysis of 14,000 Text Samples. *Discourse Processes*, *45*(3), 211–236. doi:10.1080/01638530802073712

Obar, J. A., Zube, P., & Lampe, C. (2012). Advocacy 2.0: An analysis of how advocacy groups in the United States perceive and use social media as tools for facilitating civic engagement and collective action. *Journal of Information Policy*, *2*, 1–25.

Oh, S., & Syn, S. Y. (2015). Motivations for sharing information and social support in social media: A comparative analysis of Facebook, Twitter, Delicious, YouTube, and Flickr: Motivations for Sharing Information and Social Support in Social Media: A Comparative Analysis of Facebook, Twitter, Delicious, YouTube, and Flickr. *Journal of the Association for Information Science and Technology*, *66*(10), 2045–2060. doi:10.1002/asi.23320

Omar, B., Ismail, N., & Kee, N. S. (2018). Understanding online consumption of public affairs news in Malaysia. *Journal of Asian Pacific Communication*, *28*(1), 172–194.

Pang, H. (2016). Understanding key factors affecting young people's WeChat usage: An empirical study from uses and gratifications perspective. *International Journal of Web Based Communities*, *12*(3), 262. doi:10.1504/IJWBC.2016.077757

Parsons. (2013). Using social media to reach consumers: A content analysis of official Facebook pages. *Academy of Marketing Studies Journal, 17*(2).

Polzin, S. E., Chu, X., & Godfrey, J. (2014). The impact of millennials' travel behavior on future personal vehicle travel. *Energy Strategy Reviews*, *5*, 59–65.

Putrevu, S. (2001). Exploring the origins and information processing differences between men and women: Implications for advertisers. *Academy of Marketing Science Review*, *10*(1), 1–14.

Rainer, T. S., & Rainer, J. (2011). *The millennials*. B&H Publishing Group.

Rice, G. H. (1985). Available information and superstitious decision making. *Journal of General Management*, *11*(2), 35–44.

Rice, G. H. Jr. (1985). Available information and superstitious decision making. *Journal of General Management*, *11*(2), 35–44.

Rodney, G., & Wakeham Dr, M. (2016). Social media marketing communications effect on attitudes among millennials in South Africa. *The African Journal of Information Systems*, *8*(3), 2.

Rogers, E. M. (1995). Diffusion of Innovations: Modifications of a model for telecommunications. In *Die diffusion von innovationen in der telekommunikation* (pp. 25–38). Springer.

Rohm, A., & Kaltcheva, D., V., & R. Milne, G. (2013). A mixed-method approach to examining brand-consumer interactions driven by social media. *Journal of Research in Interactive Marketing*, *7*(4), 295–311. doi:10.1108/JRIM-01-2013-0009

Ryan, R. M., & Deci, E. L. (2000). Self-determination theory and the facilitation of intrinsic motivation, social development, and well-being. *The American Psychologist*, *55*(1), 68. PMID:11392867

Sangwan, S., Guan, C., & Siguaw, J. A. (2009). Virtual Social Networks: Toward A Research Agenda. *International Journal of Virtual Communities and Social Networking*, *1*(1), 1–13. doi:10.4018/jvc-sn.2009010101

Saravanakumar, M., & SuganthaLakshmi, T. (2012). Social media marketing. *Life Science Journal*, *9*(4), 4444–4451.

Schwartz, H. A., Eichstaedt, J. C., Kern, M. L., Dziurzynski, L., Ramones, S. M., Agrawal, M., Shah, A., Kosinski, M., Stillwell, D., & Seligman, M. E. (2013). Personality, gender, and age in the language of social media: The open-vocabulary approach. *PLoS One*, *8*(9), e73791. PMID:24086296

Scott, D. M. (2009). *The new rules of marketing and PR: how to use social media, blogs, news releases, online video, and viral marketing to reach buyers directly*. John Wiley & Sons.

Sell, A., de Reuver, M., Walden, P., & Carlsson, C. (2012). Context, Gender and Intended Use of Mobile Messaging, Entertainment and Social Media Services. *International Journal of Systems and Service-Oriented Engineering*, *3*(1), 1–15.

Sethi, A. (2019). Introduction: The Yin and the Yang of the Chinese Consumers. In Chinese Consumers (pp. 1–10). Springer.

Sherman, L. E., Michikyan, M., & Greenfield, P. M. (2013). The effects of text, audio, video, and in-person communication on bonding between friends. *Cyberpsychology (Brno)*, *7*(2).

Shi, N., Cheung, C. M., Lee, M. K., & Chen, H. (2009). *Gender differences in the continuance of online social networks*. Academic Press.

Sundar, S. S. (2000). Multimedia effects on processing and perception of online news: A study of picture, audio, and video downloads. *Journalism & Mass Communication Quarterly*, *77*(3), 480–499.

Sundar, S. S., Narayan, S., Obregon, R., & Uppal, C. (1998). Does web advertising work? Memory for print vs. Online media. *Journalism & Mass Communication Quarterly*, *75*(4), 822–835.

Sung, Y., Lee, J.-A., Kim, E., & Choi, S. M. (2016). Why we post selfies: Understanding motivations for posting pictures of oneself. *Personality and Individual Differences*, *97*, 260–265. doi:10.1016/j.paid.2016.03.032

Sweetser, K. D., & Kelleher, T. (2011). A survey of social media use, motivation and leadership among public relations practitioners. *Public Relations Review*, *37*(4), 425–428. doi:10.1016/j.pubrev.2011.08.010

Trappey, C. V., & Trappey, A. J. C. (2001). Electronic commerce in Greater China. *Industrial Management & Data Systems*, *101*(5), 201–210. doi:10.1108/02635570110394617

Tsang, E. W. (2004). Toward a scientific inquiry into superstitious business decision-making. *Organization Studies, 25*(6), 923–946.

Urista, M. A., Dong, Q., & Day, K. D. (2009). Explaining why young adults use MySpace and Facebook through uses and gratifications theory. *Human Communication, 12*(2), 215–229.

Valkenburg, P. M., & Peter, J. (2009). Social consequences of the Internet for adolescents: A decade of research. *Current Directions in Psychological Science, 18*(1), 1–5.

Van Rompay, T. J., De Vries, P. W., & Van Venrooij, X. G. (2010). More than words: On the importance of picture–text congruence in the online environment. *Journal of Interactive Marketing, 24*(1), 22–30.

Vannoy, S. A., & Medlin, B. D. (2017). Social Computing: An Examination of Self, Social, and Use Factors. *International Journal of Virtual Communities and Social Networking, 9*(4), 31–47. doi:10.4018/IJVCSN.2017100103

Wang, Y., & Yu, C. (2017). Social interaction-based consumer decision-making model in social commerce: The role of word of mouth and observational learning. *International Journal of Information Management, 37*(3), 179–189. doi:10.1016/j.ijinfomgt.2015.11.005

Wasko, M. M., & Faraj, S. (2005). Why should I share? Examining social capital and knowledge contribution in electronic networks of practice. *Management Information Systems Quarterly, 29*(1), 35–57.

Wellman, B. (2001). Computer networks as social networks. *Science, 293*(5537), 2031–2034. PMID:11557877

Wellman, B., Salaff, J., Dimitrova, D., Garton, L., Gulia, M., & Haythornthwaite, C. (1996). Computer Networks as Social Networks: Collaborative Work, Telework, and Virtual Community. *Annual Review of Sociology, 22*(1), 213–238. doi:10.1146/annurev.soc.22.1.213

Williams, J. P. (2009). Community, frame of reference, and boundary: Three sociological concepts and their relevance for virtual worlds research. *Qualitative Sociology Review, 5*(2).

Witt, G. E., Best, J. D., & Rainie, H. (2008). *Internet Access and Use: Does Cell Phone Interviewing make a difference?* Pew Internet & American Life Project.

Wohn, Y., & Bowe, B. J. (2016). Micro Agenda Setters: The Effect of Social Media on Young Adults' Exposure to and Attitude Toward News. *Social Media + Society, 2*(1). doi:10.1177/2056305115626750

Wu, W., Quyen, P., & Rivas, A. (2017). How e-servicescapes affect customer online shopping intention: The moderating effects of gender and online purchasing experience. *Information Systems and e-Business Management, 15*(3), 689–715.

Xu, Z., Liu, Y., Yen, N., Mei, L., Luo, X., Wei, X., & Hu, C. (2016). Crowdsourcing based Description of Urban Emergency Events using Social Media Big Data. *IEEE Transactions on Cloud Computing*, 1–1. doi:10.1109/TCC.2016.2517638

Yang, S., Chen, S., & Li, B. (2016). The Role of Business and Friendships on WeChat Business: An Emerging Business Model in China. *Journal of Global Marketing, 29*(4), 174–187. doi:10.1080/0891 1762.2016.1184363

Yuan, P., Bare, M. G., Johnson, M. O., & Saberi, P. (2014). Using online social media for recruitment of human immunodeficiency virus-positive participants: A cross-sectional survey. *Journal of Medical Internet Research*, *16*(5), e117. PMID:24784982

Zeng, F., Huang, L., & Dou, W. (2009). Social factors in user perceptions and responses to advertising in online social networking communities. *Journal of Interactive Advertising*, *10*(1), 1–13.

Zhang, Y. (2014). Mobile Education via Social Media: Case Study on WeChat. In Y. Zhang (Ed.), *Handbook of Mobile Teaching and Learning* (pp. 1–18). Springer Berlin Heidelberg. doi:10.1007/978-3-642-41981-2_67-1

Zipser, D., Chen, Y., & Gong, F. (2005). *The Modernization of the Chinese Consumer*. Academic Press.

ENDNOTES

[1]   Different Pearson Chi-square statistic respectively but with the same *p-values of (p <.001)*
[2]   Different Pearson Chi-square statistic respectively but with the same *p-values of (p <.001)*
[3]   Different Pearson Chi-square statistic respectively but with the same *p-values of (p <.001)*
[4]   Different Pearson Chi-square statistic respectively but with the same *p-values of (p <.001)*
[5]   Different Pearson Chi-square statistic respectively but with the same *p-values of (p <.1)*
[6]   Different Pearson Chi-square statistic respectively but with the same *p-values of (p <.001)*
[7]   Different Pearson Chi-square statistic respectively but with the same *p-values of (p <.001)*

This research was previously published in the International Journal of Social Media and Online Communities (IJSMOC), 11(1); pages 15-34, copyright year 2019 by IGI Publishing (an imprint of IGI Global).

Chapter 50
Facebook Communities of African Diasporas and Their U.S. Embassies:
A Content Analysis Study

Hesham Mesbah
Rollins College, USA

Lauren Cooper
Florida House of Representatives, USA

ABSTRACT

This study explores how the Nigerian, Ethiopian, and Egyptian diasporas in the United States use their Facebook groups to create their imagined communities. It also draws a parallel between their use of Facebook and how the embassies of their countries of origin use the same platform in performing their official duties. Six hundred Facebook posts drawn for the groups and the embassies were content-analyzed for this study. The results show that the three African diaspora groups have more pragmatic uses of their Facebook communities, such as the exchange of services, advice and information on day-to-day living, while their embassies use the platform more for public relations objectives in planning their official communication that emphasizes nation-branding, the promotion of their various countries, and for other diplomatic chores.

INTRODUCTION

Historically, the word "diaspora" had long been used to describe dispersion experienced by dislocated religious groups. According to historian Martin Baumann (2001), the term originally dates to the third century B.C. as a technical term used to describe the dispersed condition of the Jews when the Greeks controlled Jerusalem and introduced the ideas of Polis, or city-state. At the time, the large Jewish groups that lived throughout the Hellenistic Kingdoms were living in exile, hence in dispersion, because they

DOI: 10.4018/978-1-6684-6307-9.ch050

were not born in the lands where they were inhabiting. The use of "diaspora" to describe non-Judaic groups and trans-nationalists had to wait until the twentieth century. By then, those who were dispersed from their homeland in search of work or a better life in a foreign land were also distinguished as participants in a social diaspora (Safran, 1991; Scheffer, 1986).

Contemporary diasporas are more likely to be both less disconnected from home and less dispersed or isolated from their native ethnic group. Computer-mediated communication has created inexpensive, instant venues of horizontal communication between immigrants, their peers in the diaspora, or their loved ones back home. Online communication technology has also turned vertical communication between governments and their citizens into a standard practice at most levels of governance. State leaders, public officials, embassies, and consulates have turned to social media to manage communication with their target audience and engage with them. This has led to the emergence of new forms of diplomacy, such as public diplomacy and digital diplomacy, wherein the Internet and communication technologies support diplomatic objectives. According to the comprehensive list of Twitter accounts on Twiplomacy, more than 4,100 embassies and ambassadors are now active on Twitter and the list is growing daily (Twiplomacy, 2018). The same source identified 951 Twitter accounts – 372 personal and 579 institutional accounts – belonging to heads of state as well as government and foreign ministers within 187 countries. "Facebook is the second-most popular network among government leaders, and it is where they have the biggest audiences," as recently as 2018 (Twiplomacy, 2018).

The Facebook Groups feature allows for the creation of smaller communities within digital arenas and allows users to share customized content to niche audiences. As it exists, the Facebook Group feature enables users to launch custom, niche communities, where individuals share visual content, connect with similar members, and participate in a collective agenda that is often defined and protected by Group administrators. The growth of Facebook groups over the past decade is not only indicative of their popularity, but also of their flexibility to meet variable needs and strategies of groups worldwide. In October 2009, "Google indexed over 52 million Facebook groups" (O'Neill, 2010). Three months later, the number "surged to over 620 million groups" (O'Neill, 2010). By 2016, membership in Facebook groups exceeded 1.4 billion users (Holmes, 2018). By utilizing this popular feature on Facebook, like-minded diasporic individuals who may possess weak social ties and face distance barriers can create their own communities and boost their social capital with one tool (Burke, Kraut, & Marlow, 2011). This resource enables diaspora groups who are isolated, geographically dispersed, and interested to connect with their respective ethnic groups.

This chapter therefore examined how immigrants from the largest African diasporas in the U.S., namely Nigeria, Egypt and Ethiopia, use their Facebook groups to establish social ties, revive their culture, and maintain connection with their homeland. The chapter also explored how the embassies of the three African countries in the United States utilize Facebook to perform their own digital diplomacy. Studying the Facebook content shared in African diasporas and their respective embassies compares the popular constituent agenda to the official diplomatic agenda.

THEORY AND LITERATURE

Social networking sites facilitate interactivity between members who might have never met face-to-face. When users decide to have their own "ethnic" or cultural space online, they forge their own communities that are based on commonalities, and perhaps nationalism. In his theory of "Imagined Communities,"

Anderson (1983, p. 49) defined a nation as an imagined political community because the "members of even the smallest nation will never know most of their fellow members, or even hear from them, but in the minds of each one lives the image of communion….(all communities that are) larger than primordial villages of face-to-face contact … are imagined" (p. 49). In 2006, Anderson redefined the imagined "nation" as a "deep horizontal comradeship" (p. 9) that is based on fraternity and communication, rather than citizenry or nationalism. Anderson also emphasized the effect of commonness on creating imagined communities by introducing the idea of print capitalism. For him, capitalist businesses organized the printing of newspapers to serve their interests, which generated "their cohesions outside language" (Anderson, 2006, p. 76) by creating their own vernacular language in their newspapers. Furthermore, the shared content of newspapers demonstrated a sense of belonging as "each person who reads the morning paper over tea or coffee could imagine his countrymen doing the same" (Calhoun, 2016, pp. 13-14). This sense of commonness, fraternity, and shared language is what creates those imagined communities, regardless of physical proximity.

Diaspora groups create their own imagined online communities through sharing personal narratives, even if the individuals themselves are loosely connected or geographically dispersed. This allows members to redefine their identities and feel distinguished from either other diasporic groups or natives in their new place of residence (Cohen, 1997). Turkle (1995) suggested that identity on the Internet is more fragmented as people can assume several identities, but this position was not supported by Mitra (2001) who suggested that immigrants on the Internet produce their own personal identities against the stereotypical identities produced by the dominant host culture. These imagined digital communities are especially important for marginalized immigrants who feel isolated from home and are labeled as a minority in their host-land. The communities will be a source of empowerment for their "residents" who need to be assured in their diaspora that they are not alone. They produce and exchange content that informs them of their home culture and represents their beliefs, needs, and interests. This supports some research findings that "widely shared Facebook posts [are] mostly entertainment-oriented" (Tremayne, 2017, p. 30). According to Brinkerhoff (2009, p.2), such digital diasporas can also "support security and socio-economic development in the homelands." Conversely, the ability of digital diasporas to boost the economies of their homelands makes them a priority for the public and digital diplomacy of their governments and embassies.

Facebook-Imagined Communities

Human beings have a number of places where they can choose to socialize. Prominent among them are the home, workplace, places of worship, and an array of public areas such as bars and coffee shops. However, online forums have also become virtual places where people can mingle and exchange views. Still, online talk is transcribed and saved for later asynchronous communication, which makes online forums a middle ground between the public and private spheres of communication (Kvansy & Hales, 2008). This form of communication technology has impacted the diasporic experience by allowing immigrants to create their own imagined online communities and have a sense of "contemporaneity and synchronicity" even though individuals are dispersed and fragmented (Tsagarousianou, 2004, p. 62). The "Group" feature on Facebook has made it possible for like-minded individuals to form their own private, secure communities and examine the profiles of users before issuing them an entry "visa" into such imagined communities. This feature also allows the creators of the Facebook groups to set the rules of "residence" and virtually deport any violating users who challenge the group norms or standards.

But what do the "residents" of these digital communities on Facebook do? Al-Rawi and Fahmy (2018) analyzed the textual and visual content of "The Syrian Community in Italy," a page founded by diasporic Syrians in Italy. The authors observed an "archiving" function of this page as Syrians in Italy used the Facebook page as "a public archive, serving a digital diaspora by visually and textually documenting its activities." (Al-Rawi & Fahmy, 2018, p. 90). The main visual and textual themes of the posts were about either the political situation in Syria or the anti-Assad demonstrations organized by the Syrian diaspora in Italy. Accordingly, the "homeland" was the main topic on the agenda of this digital diaspora, and political activism was the main function of its Facebook page, which supports Mitra's (2001, p.32) preposition that marginalized groups on the Internet "call on the dominant and put the dominant in the difficult position of acknowledging the marginalized."

Oiarzabal (2012) reported similar homeland-centered uses of Facebook groups among the Basque diaspora in 20 countries. Most of the respondents said that they joined Basque diaspora associations on Facebook to keep in contact with the Basque culture, to be informed about the current reality of their homeland, and to "reaffirm and maintain Basque identity and culture" (p. 1478). Other subsequent studies about diasporic groups that come from suppressed ethnic groups at home (the Kurds who belong to Turkey, Syria, Iraq, and Iran; the Chinese Muslim minority of the Uyghur) confirmed the identity construction and maintenance functions of these imagined communities (Jacob, K., 2013; NurMuhammad, R., Horst, H. A, Papoutsaki, E. & Dodson, G., 2016). The diasporic Kurds shared the same language, myth, history, and religion and used their diasporic Facebook groups as "a tool to learn about their roots and existence" (Jacob, 2013, p. 57). By the same token, the Facebook group for Uyghur diaspora members also emphasized ethnic identity. The members identify themselves by saying, "we the Uyghur people," and use the Uyghur language, often addressing each other as brother and sister. The Uyghur diaspora's use of Facebook Groups included emphasis of their political identity and solidifying "support for Uyghur political causes, sharing information and updates about conditions for Uyghur friends, families and associates within China" (NurMuhammad et. al, 2016, p. 493).

In addition to the role of Facebook in the maintenance and construction of identity for diasporic groups, this networking site allows digital groups to stay connected with their *good ol' days* by facilitating "reminisces about the nostalgic past." This feeling translates into an obligation to provide "transnational social and psychological care to family and kin," as in the case of Trinidadian immigrants (Plaza & Plaza, 2019, p. 17). By sharing memories and photos of historical events from the homeland, diasporic groups create an online archive of their cultural heritage and engage second-generation immigrants who are, by default, in more distant proximity to their own ethnic identity. Diaspora groups on Facebook also contradict the prevailing stereotypes about them in their host-land by sharing personal achievements, which Lorenza (2016) had observed through analyzing the Facebook posts of Filipino transnationals in India.

This literature suggests that diaspora groups have multiple uses and seek various gratifications by using social networking sites (SNS); it also suggests that these platforms empower members of diasporas to negotiate, maintain, and reconstruct their identities. When diasporic groups use SNS, they reinforce their existence as an imagined community, which strengthens their group identity and redefines their values and beliefs (Al-Rawi & Fahmy, 2018). However, diasporas that come from conflict-ridden countries also tend to use cyberspace to address this conflict as part of their online interactions. The Uyghur diaspora tends to differentiate themselves from China's dominant ethnicity, the Han. When they communicate about their own diaspora on Facebook, the Uyghurs prefer to use the term *Weten Yurt*, which means "motherland." They do not "use the word China, and seldom use 'Xinjiang' or 'Xinjiang Uyghur Autonomous Region' which are the official names chosen by Chinese authority" (Nuermaimaiti, 2014,

p. 100). Similarly, the online communities of several African diasporas reflect the ethnic and political conflicts in their homeland. For instance, Skjerdal (2011) remarked that the online forums of the Zimbabwean, Eritrean, and Somali diasporas represent conflict-torn societies. The members of the Eritrean diaspora established a war memorial online to post information about those who were killed in the war between Eritrea and Ethiopia. Typically, establishing such a memorial is the responsibility of the state, but this diasporic initiative challenged the power of the Eritrean government in a way (Bernal, 2013). A tone of political discontent was also prevalent in Ethiopian diasporic websites tied to an oppositional political group in Ethiopia (Skjerdal, 2011, p. 736). Tones of both conflict and opposition are frequent in the diasporic virtual communities, especially the African communities, but have not been historically examined on the social media pages of their respective embassies.

Facebook Diplomacy

The U.S. pioneered the use of the Internet for diplomatic purposes when the State Department launched an eDiplomacy unit in 2002 (Adesina, 2017). Ever since, the use of cyberspace and social media by governments and state actors has grown swiftly and steadily, eventually drawing the attention of media scholars who sought to analyze and understand the new diplomat-generated content online. Spry (2018) identified several research approaches to studying digital diplomacy: (1) The first research approach aligns digital diplomacy with the broader field of public relations, which either depicts digital diplomacy as a transition to a "new" two-way public diplomacy model or explores the experiences, professional norms, and institutionalized priorities of diplomats; (2) An alternate approach that designates public diplomacy as a product of the state and aligns it with theories of soft power; (3) A more decentered approach that integrates media with public diplomacy, or what was termed as mediatization, which includes channels of communication, language, and environment in response to political-economic conditions.

Spry (2018) adopted the third approach when analyzing the Facebook pages (the channels) published by the diplomatic missions (embassies and consulates) of eight countries: The U.S., the United Kingdom, Japan, India, Australia, Canada, Israel, and New Zealand. The study identified four types of communication posted on the platform: one-way communication that targets external audiences; one-way communication that targets internal audiences (colleagues); engaging, two-way communication that invites comments; and user-generated communication posted by Facebook users. The most typical Facebook diplomacy was one-way external communication, such as publicity for events, information about visa requirements, and information about cultural assets (Spry, 2018).

That outward digital diplomacy is commonly used for promoting a nation's image and interacting with both the influencers and the public. Fergus Hanson (2012) outlined eight policy goals for digital diplomacy, which included public diplomacy (it targets audiences with key messages) and the role of consular communication to create direct channels with citizens travelling overseas. Seeking to activate those goals, diplomats utilize social media platforms to brand their nations, communicate with foreign audiences, and cater to the needs of their fellow citizens in the diaspora. Bali, Karim, and Rachid (2018) explored how diplomatic missions utilize Facebook to communicate and engage with their audiences. They compared the Facebook page of the U.S. embassy in Erbil (capital of Kurdistan) and the Facebook page of the Kurdistan Regional Government (KRG) in Washington, D.C. The study showed that both embassies focused on using Facebook to inform local people about policies and regulations, but the two embassies did not target their own people in the host country with any content. The U.S.-based posts highlighted the values of equality, human rights, and humanitarian aid, while the Kurdish posts highlighted the efforts of the KRG in fighting terrorist groups.

The "engagement" function of social media has also been analyzed to determine the dialogue that diplomatic actors invite and manage digitally. Hayden, Waisanen, and Osipova (2012) analyzed the communication generated by the U.S. embassies in Bangladesh, Egypt, and Pakistan on Facebook after the election of former U.S. President Obama in 2012, as well as the comments made by visitors to those pages. The authors detected a spreadable epideictic communication from those embassies that fostered a discourse of either praise or blame in the comments posted. Such comments were in response to the embassies' posts to announce Obama's victory. This announcement fueled a tide of expressive emotion rather than a dialogue or deliberation. The embassies' posts targeted their own diaspora members abroad to guide them through the voting process. America's image was boosted by targeting local people with news about the election and showing how the election process was both competitive and transparent. Several local visitors wished to either participate in this process or have a similar one exist in their own nations. The authors argued that the Facebook pages of the three embassies generated supportive comments of U.S. legitimacy because such participatory forums "cultivate communities of identity performance" and the usage of these forums is based on a "selection bias" (Hayden et al, 2012, p. 1635).

Despite these diverse approaches in exploring the imagined communities on Facebook and their role in digital diplomacy, there is no research that compares the agenda of diasporic groups on Facebook to the agenda of their home embassies in their host-nation. These traditionally marginalized groups seek to establish a sense of community that supports their status as a "dispersed" minority, but it is not clear whether they consider their constituent embassies as another way to seek that sense of support. Moreover, one of the functions of digital diplomacy is to cater to "diasporic citizens" and solidify their "imagined communities," but this area of digital diplomacy has not been explored deeply. Accordingly, the present study seeks to identify how diasporic groups use Facebook in comparison to their constituent embassies. The focus will be on three long-established African diasporic groups in the U.S.: Nigerian, Ethiopian, and Egyptian diasporas. The study seeks to answer the following research questions:

RQ1: How does the agenda on Facebook of some diaspora groups from Nigeria, Ethiopia, and Egypt in the U.S. compare in terms of focusing on political/sectarian strife back at home?

RQ2: How does the agenda of these diaspora Facebook groups compare to the agenda of the Facebook pages of their constituent embassies?

RQ3: What is the main approach adopted by the embassies of three African countries in approaching their diasporas?

METHOD

The authors of this chapter purposively identified three African diaspora groups in the U.S. to gather data and answer the research questions. Africans from Nigeria, Ethiopia, and Egypt who live in the U.S. represent the population targeted in the present study. The obvious reason for identifying these nations is that they are the top "birthplaces for African immigrants in the U.S." (Anderson, 2017), with Nigeria topping the list, followed by Ethiopia and Egypt. Those three countries accounted for 35 percent of the foreign-born African population in the U.S in 2015 (Anderson, 2017). They are also the most populous countries in the African continent (World Population Review, 2019). Table one shows the population of those countries and the size of their U.S. diasporas.

Table 1. Population of Nigeria, Ethiopia, and Egypt in 2019 and size of their U.S. diasporas in 2015

Country	Population (*Source: World Population Review*)	Size of U.S Diaspora (*Source: Anderson, Pew Research Center*)
Nigeria	200,962,417	327,000
Ethiopia	110,135,635	222,000
Egypt	101,168,745	192,000

The number of immigrants from the three countries remained minimal in the U.S. during the last two decades of the twentieth century but began to increase at the turn of the 21st century. For instance, the numbers of both Nigerian and Ethiopian immigrants in the U.S. during the 1980s were approximately 25,000 and 10,000 respectively. However, less than three decades later, those numbers increased by more than tenfold (Migration Policy Institute, 2015).

A preliminary search about the use of social media by these diaspora groups and their embassies showed that the Nigerian embassy in the U.S. has a few tweets on its Twitter account. In addition, the Ethiopian embassy in the U.S. uses its Twitter account to post links to its Facebook posts. Accordingly, the authors decided to study the use of Facebook by those diasporas and their embassies in the U.S. The authors conducted a search on Facebook in February 2019 for public groups that call on nationals from either country to join. The search words were *Nigerians in U.S., Nigerians in America, Ethiopians in U.S., Ethiopians in America, Egyptians in U.S, and Egyptians in America.* The largest public Nigerian group was *Nigerians in U.S.A,* which had 2,514 members. Three Ethiopian Facebook groups were also found: *Ethiopians in America* (212 members); *Ethiopian Diaspora in USA* (673 members); and *New York & New Jersey Ethiopians* (916 members). We also located a public Facebook group named *Egyptians in USA,* which had 4,299 members. Those five Facebook groups from the three African diasporas represent the population of Facebook content the authors analyzed in order to answer the research questions. We decided to extract the posts manually because several posts were written in native languages, which could be captured by the existing applications that extract Facebook data.

The authors opted to draw 100 posts from the Facebook group(s) that represented each diaspora group. A systematic random sample size of 100 posts from each group was gathered by selecting every fifth post on the group. The first post on each group was drawn randomly by generating a random number from 1 to 5 (since the interval is 5) by using List Randomizer (RANDOM.ORG). The number generated by the List Randomizer was used to start the selection of our systematic sample of the posts. For instance, if the Randomizer generated number 3, we started with the third post and then skipped to every fifth post until we completed 100 posts. The same methodology was used to draw a sample of 100 posts from the Facebook account of the embassy of each country in the U.S. The total sample of the posts analyzed in this study was 600 Facebook posts. Table 2 displays more information about this sample.

All posts were coded and content-analyzed quantitatively. In addition to the standard categories used for the analysis, such as language used in the post and where it was posted, we used four main categories to describe the content of each post:

Table 2. Facebook posts retrieved from Facebook Diaspora groups and Facebook accounts of the embassies of Nigeria, Ethiopia, and Egypt in the US

Facebook Groups/Embassy	Sample Size	Period covered by Posts	Language of posts			
			English	Amharic	Arabic	Dual
Nigerians in USA	100	Nov. 11, 2016 thru. April. 26, 2019	100%			
Ethiopian Diaspora in USA	19	April 4, 2017 thru. Oct. 27, 2017	12 (63%)	5 (26%)		2 (11%)
Ethiopians in America	32	May 23, 2009 thru. Dec. 21, 2018	22 (69%)	4 (13%)		6 (18%)
New York & New Jersey Ethiopian community	49	Sept. 25, 2017 thru. Dec. 21, 2018	42 (86%)	6 (12%)		1 (2%)
Egyptians in USA	100	June 27, 2017 thru. Mar. 3, 2019	45%		33%	22%
Nigerian embassy	100	Aug. 30, 2018 thru. April 23, 2019	100%			
Ethiopian embassy	100		94%	6%		
Egyptian embassy	100	Oct. 4, 2017 thru. April 24, 2019	97%		1%	2%

1. **Pronoun**: Pronoun used or implied in the post, which could be first-person (I or we), second person (you), or third-person (he, she, or they).
2. **What**: Subject nature of the post content, which included 10 subcategories: 1) Sharing Home History; 2) Promoting Diaspora Events; 3) Discussing Home News; 4) Promoting Arts / Culture; 5) Seeking Services (Social, Financial, Academic, Instructional, etc.); 6) Advertising Services (Social, Financial, Academic, Instructional, etc.); 7) Declaring Activism; 8) Sharing Resources; 9) Personal Engagement; and 10) Opinion Sharing.
3. **Who:** Who was mentioned in the post, such as political leaders from the homeland (president, prime minister, minister); entertainment/sports figures from the homeland; intellectuals from the homeland or the diaspora; embassy figures in the host-land; U.S./global politicians; and diaspora figures.
4. **Where:** Where the story or event featured in the post occurs, which could be the homeland, the host-land, or other areas in the world.

The authors selected 10 percent of the total sample of the posts (60 posts) and coded them independently to test the reliability of the coding by calculating Cronbach's Alpha for the inter-coding reliability of each category. Table 3 shows that the coding adopted by the authors is reliable with high coefficient figures.

Table 3. Cronbach's alpha reliability of inter-coding of four content categories

Category	Cronbach's Alpha
What	.85
Pronoun	.86
Who	.87
Where	.88

RESULTS

RQ1: Diasporas and Political Strife Back Home

The data suggest that the diaspora Facebook groups are not used as a forum to fuel or even discuss political or ethnic strife back home. They seemed to share both less controversial and less confrontational agenda of topics on their Facebook public groups. Such neutral, tranquil Facebook posts do not represent the violent, unstable political environments of Nigeria, Ethiopia, or Egypt. Since its 1967-1970 civil war, Nigeria has been "synonymous with deep divisions which cause major political issues to be vigorously and violently contested along the lines of intricate ethnic, religious, and regional divisions" (Çanci & Odukoya, 2016). These authors highlighted the ongoing ethnic and religious conflicts in the Middle-Belt and North Eastern Nigeria and the borderline states that have a Muslim majority. In Ethiopia, the war between rival ethnic groups in the Western parts in 2018 has been captured by news outlets worldwide. Moreover, the protests across the Oromia and Amhara regions have been ongoing since 2016. Similarly, political instability is also familiar to Egypt. The country has been through chaos because of the Arab Spring and the stepping down of former Egyptian President Mubarak in 2011. Soon after, the Islamists formed their first government in 2012, but they were soon overthrown by a military coup in 2013. Ever since, the new military regime has waged an open war against terrorism, and news stories about bombings and mass killings remain recurrent.

However, such ethnic and political conflicts were not represented in the Facebook groups formed by the diasporas from those countries, living in the U.S. The tone was more relaxed and less partisan, except for minor references to ethnic preferences on the Facebook groups of the Ethiopian diaspora. Several users addressed their fellow *Habesha* or announced that they needed *Habesha* roommates. *Habesha* is a pan-ethnic, distinct group that does not represent all Ethiopians, especially under-represented minorities such as the Anuak group. Notably, this ethnically-selective posting was minimal on the Facebook groups of the Ethiopians in the diaspora (four posts out of 100 posts), so it cannot be considered a significant trend or element of the group agenda.

RQ2: Agenda of Diasporic and Diplomatic Facebook Posts

The African diaspora groups included in the present study use their Facebook pages to boost their sense of community, which is not the main agenda item on the Facebook pages of their constituent embassies. According to Table 4, most posts on the diasporic Facebook groups revolve around promoting diaspora events, especially among the Egyptians and Ethiopians in the U.S. They shared invitations to music festivals, discussed TV shows, highlighted African awards nominations, celebrated graduation parties, posted job openings, and uplifted Ramadan festivities. In contrast, the agenda of those diasporic embassies was more geared toward nation branding rather than catering to the activities and events organized by their fellow citizens in the U.S. The main theme for the Facebook page of the Egyptian embassy in D.C. was promoting embassy-related events in the diaspora. Such events included state visits made by Egyptian high-rank politicians to the U.S., awards received by top Egyptian athletes and artists in the U.S, and TV interviews with Egyptian officials in the U.S. media. Those news stories from the U.S. diaspora were elitist and more celebratory than related to the daily lives of the Egyptian diaspora in the U.S. Global Egyptian celebrities, such as Liverpool soccer player Mo Salah, and movie star Rami Malek, were celebrated and/or congratulated by the Egyptian embassy several times, perhaps with the hope to create an association between Egypt and the prestige of its notable nationals. The Ethiopian and Egyptian embassies were more focused on introducing news from home on their Facebook pages. This includes news stories that did not relate to the U.S., such as stories about the Renaissance Dam in Ethiopia, the solar park in Egypt, the anniversary of liberating Taba (in Sinai), and the inauguration of renovated ancient Greek tombs in Alexandria.

Table 4. Agenda of topics on diaspora Facebook groups on the Facebook pages of their embassies

	FB diasporic Groups				FB pages of embassies			
Topics	**Nigeria**	**Ethiopia**	**Egypt**	**Total**	**Nigeria**	**Ethiopia**	**Egypt**	**Total**
Opinion Sharing	4%	3%		2%	4%	1%	1%	2%
Personal Engagement	24%	15%	24%	21%	15.2%	3%	3%	7%
Sharing Resources	7%	9%	9%	8.3%	16.2%	3%	3%	7.4%
Declaring Activism	9%	11%		6.7%	21.2%	5%	5.1%	10.4%
Advertising Services	18%	9%	17%	14.7%	1%	0%		0.3%
Seeking Services	1%	8%	6%	5%	10.1%	5%	5.1%	6.7%
Promoting Arts / Culture	13%	9%	31%	17.7%	27.3%	65%	65.7%	52.7%
Discussing Home News	17%	16%	1%	11.3%	4%	18%	16.2%	12.8%
Promoting Diaspora Events	6%	15%	12%	11%	1%	0%	1%	0.7%
Sharing Home History	1%	5%		2%	4%	1%	1%	2%
Total	100%	100%	100%	100%	100%	100%	100%	100%

Table 4 also shows that the three embassies relied more on promoting arts and culture in their nation-branding posts. This category included news about ancient Egyptian monuments, poetry contests, links to theatrical events, and promotions of Ethiopian Picnic Day. Both Nigerian diaspora and Nigerian embassy were more aware of sharing interactive, service-oriented content on Facebook. While some Nigerians volunteered to educate their fellow citizens on resume writing, others sought the help of Nigerian "friends" on the group. Political activism was also present on the agenda of the diaspora and embassies of both Nigeria and Ethiopia while being noticeably absent from the Egyptian Facebook group.

The use of Facebook for engaging users and creating a sense of community in diasporic Facebook groups was revealed when we analyzed the "pronouns" presented in the posts. The use of second and third-person voice was more prevalent in these groups (61 percent of the total posts) compared to how the embassies implicitly or explicitly used the same pronoun in their posts (19 percent). Conversely, 81 percent of the embassy Facebooks posts used the third-person, indicating a less personal tone when posting, which may be congruent with formal diplomatic discourse.

The difference between the diasporic and diplomatic agendas on Facebook was further examined by analyzing two categories: the geographic area where the story in the post took place, and the persons mentioned in each post. The area of a story was coded into three categories: 1) home-country, 2) host-country, and 3) other. Table 5 shows that three diasporic groups (especially the Egyptian and Ethiopian groups) shared stories and events that took place in their host-land more often than their constituent embassies did. All three embassies were significantly more home-oriented in their posts, suggesting their prioritization of the U.S. foreign relations and homeland affairs.

Table 5. Location of the stories posted on both the diaspora Facebook groups and Facebook of their constituent embassies

Where	Facebook Groups			Facebook of Embassies		
	Nigeria	Ethiopia	Egypt	Nigeria	Ethiopia	Egypt
Host-country	38.5%	67.1%	83.7%	23.6%	22.8%	32.3%
Home-country	50.0%	27.6%	12.2%	75.0%	62.0%	64.6%
Other	11.5%	5.3%	4.1%	1.4%	15.2%	3.1%
Total	100.0%	100.0%	100.0%	100.0%	100.0%	100.0%

$X^2 = 98.1$, DF = 10, p < 0.001

When examining the total geographic agenda of both the diasporic and diplomatic Facebook agendas, the data showed that 63 percent of the diasporic posts pertained to their host country, and 67 percent of the diplomatic posts pertained to the home country. This variance in geographic priorities as posted on Facebook between the diaspora groups and their embassies was statistically significant ($X^2 = 61.2$, DF = 1, p < 0.001).

The analysis of the category of "persons mentioned in posts" shows another aspect of the difference between the diasporic and diplomatic Facebook agendas. According to Table 6, the Nigerian diaspora group was more interested in their local politics and political leadership than their embassy had been. The Nigerian embassy was more focused on news stories about the U.S. embassy in Nigeria, American philanthropy, and scholarship providers, such as USAID and the Fulbright program. The Egyptian and Ethiopian diasporas, however, were less focused on political leadership back home, while their embassies tended to use their Facebook pages mainly as a platform to share news about their political leaders, especially the Ethiopian Prime Minister Abiy Ahmed and Egyptian President Al-Sisi.

Table 6. Persons mentioned in both diasporic and diplomatic Facebook posts

Persons mentioned	Facebook Groups			Facebook of Embassies		
	Nigeria	Ethiopia	Egypt	Nigeria	Ethiopia	Egypt
Leader/executive home	33.3%	21.4%	8.3%	6.8%	75.4%	44.8%
Entertainment/ Sports home	25.9%	14.3%	58.3%	1.4%	1.8%	17.9%
Intellectual home	14.8%	3.6%	8.3%	24.7%	0%	4.5%
Entertainment/ sports global	14.8%	7.1%	25.0%	5.5%	0%	0%
World/US political leader	3.7%	14.3%	0%	5.5%	17.5%	20.9%
Embassy figure	3.7%	7.1%	0%	2.7%	3.5%	7.5%
World/US African leader	3.7%	14.3%	0%	1.4%	0%	0%
US diplomat/aide	0%	0%	0%	46.6%	0%	3.0%
Intellectual global	0%	7.1%	0%	2.7%	0%	0%
Diaspora figure	0%	10.7%	0%	2.7%	1.8%	1.5%

The diasporic Facebook agenda was unique in discussing their local culture as well as global celebrities, such as their favorite entertainment and sports starts, especially within the Egyptian diaspora. The Ethiopian and Nigerian diasporas were more interested in posting about global and U.S. politicians, such as former UN Secretary Kofi Anan, former U.S. President Obama, and Somali-born U.S. Congresswoman Ilhan Omar.

The diplomatic Facebook agenda was significantly more political than the diasporic agenda, as 73 percent of the persons mentioned on the diplomatic agendas were political figures, while politicians mentioned on the diasporic agendas accounted for 43 percent of all persons mentioned ($X^2 = 26.6$, DF = 1, p < 0.001).

RQ3: Facebook Diplomacy Toward Diaspora

The three embassies employed different approaches on their Facebook pages to address their fellow citizens who live in the U.S. diaspora. The authors detected three main approaches:

1. **Interactive/Beneficiary:** An embassy would offer opportunities to engage their fellow citizens and provide them with knowledge and skills to help them have a legal status in the U.S. or seek a job.
2. **Interactive/Socializing:** Some embassies will create events and activities to engage their diaspora without adding to their knowledge or skills, such as inviting them to a meeting with an ambassador or to a movie.
3. **One-Sided Address:** In other cases, the embassy will release news that impacts the lives of those in the diaspora, such as launching a new route of a national airline or announcing the visit of a prominent intellectual to a U.S. city.

Table 7 shows how each embassy utilized those strategies.

Table 7. Strategies adopted by embassies in approaching their diasporas

	Nigeria		Ethiopia		Egypt	
	N	%	N	%	N	%
Interactive/beneficiary	14	64%	2	33.3%	0	0%
Interactive/socializing	2	9%	2	33.3%	5	38%
One-sided address	6	27%	2	33.4%	8	62%
Total	22	100%	6	100%	13	100%

Overall, the three embassies did not target their diasporas by a substantial amount of their Facebook messages. The total number of posts directed to those African diasporas was 41 posts (14 percent of the total sample of posts analyzed).

DISCUSSION

The present study contributes to understanding how Facebook communities are structured and used by both African diplomatic and diasporic content creators. The diplomatic users tend to structure their Facebook pages as tools of nation-branding and maintaining relations with other diplomatic organizations. They also adopt an outward-facing, one-way communication model (Spry, 2018) in their use of Facebook and promote both the cultural assets of their homeland, such as their historical artefacts and celebrities, and the news of their political leaders in the homeland.

This model of digital diplomacy relies on disseminating homeland-related content, especially when it relates to the host-land. This explains why the news of American diplomats in the homeland was salient on the online agenda of African embassies based in the host-land. This model of digital diplomacy pays little attention to the embassies' own people in the host country, which replicates the model identified by Bali, Karim, and Rachid (2018) who analyzed the Facebook pages of both the U.S. embassy in Erbil and the Kurdistan Regional Government (KRG) in Washington, D.C. However, those embassies do adopt several models of digital diplomacy to address and engage the diaspora groups in the host-land. The Nigerian embassy is more focused on a two-way informational model to educate current and potential diaspora members about legal and educational matters in the U.S, whereas the Egyptian embassy was more focused on a one-way pull model by inviting diaspora members to attend lectures and events in the embassy. This propaganda-oriented, unengaging digital diplomacy strategy limits the existence of embassies in the imagined communities of the diaspora Facebook groups.

The African diasporas, on the other hand, create a Facebook community to seek entertainment-based gratifications. The symbols of pop culture and sports in the homeland are the main tools to seek entertainment on these Facebook groups. Political news and confrontational political content were secondary on the Facebook agenda of the three African diaspora groups. Facebook members, in general, tend to share entertainment content for "social coherence purposes" (Tremayne, 2017, p. 33). Research also shows that the use of Facebook for open discussions and news sharing is less trending as users have started to express these views elsewhere, migrating "to the privacy of WhatsApp and messaging apps" (Kantar Media, 2018, p. 13). Future research can examine whether users in closed/private Facebook groups engage in political conversations and news-sharing more significantly than users in open/public Facebook groups.

The results also show that the Ethiopian and Nigerian diasporas are more affiliated with African or African American leaders than the Egyptian diaspora. A substantial percentage of the posts on the Ethiopian and Nigerian groups celebrated the victory of Somali-born U.S. Congresswoman Ilhan Omar and discussed news about the Ghanaian former UN Secretary Kofi Anan, and former U.S. President Barack Obama. This raises questions about how Egyptians rank their continental belonging when they think of their national identity. The Egyptian diaspora groups had a sense of pride of the newly developed soft power of their homeland, which was epitomized by the soccer star Mo Salah and the "Best Actor" Oscar winner, Rami Malek. Several users shared the news about Malek's nomination and identified with him by using a one-word comment: "Congratulations!" The Ethiopian and Nigerian diasporas did not share such news about either Mo Salah or Rami Malek. However, some of them shared news about Moitshepi Elias, Miss Botswana who was among the top 30 contestants in the Miss World Contest in 2018. These findings suggest that Ethiopian and Nigerian diasporas feel more traditionally African than their Egyptian counterparts.

CONCLUSION

The present study sought to explore how the U.S. diasporas of the most three populous African nations use Facebook groups to create their own digital supportive community and stay in touch with their culture and homeland while living abroad. The study also compared the agenda of those diasporas on their Facebook groups to the agenda of their constituent embassies on the same social media platform. The results show that the three African diasporas have more pragmatic uses of their Facebook communities. They exchange services, advice, and information as they would do in an offline neighborhood, which makes them more focused on avoiding politically divisive content. Their embassies, however, demonstrate more public relations objectives in planning their communication on Facebook. They emphasize the function of nation-branding, and adopt several tactics to achieve that strategy. Applying Spry's classification of the uses of Facebook diplomacy (Spry, 2018), the three embassies adopt a public diplomacy approach that mainly targets external audiences and minimally engages two-way communication to offer interactive venues for educating or socializing with members of the diaspora. We encourage future research to examine the impact of this homeland-focused approach of digital diplomacy on the construction and maintenance of the identity of diasporic groups.

REFERENCES

Adesina, O. S. (2017). Foreign policy in an era of digital diplomacy. *Cogent Social Sciences, 3*(1). Available at: https://www.cogentoa.com/article/10.1080/23311886.2017.1297175.pdf

Al-Rawi, A., & Fahmy, S. (2018). Social media use in the diaspora: The case of Syrians in Italy. In K. H. Karim & A. Al-Rawi (Eds.), *Diaspora and media in Europe: Migration, identity, and integration* (pp. 71–96). Ottawa: Palgrave McMillan. doi:10.1007/978-3-319-65448-5_4

Anderson, B. (1983). *Imagined communities: Reflections on the origin and spread of nationalism.* London: Verso.

Anderson, B. (2006). *Imagined communities.* London: Verso.

Anderson, M. (2017). African immigrant population in U.S. steadily climbs. *Pew Research Center.* Retrieved from https://www.pewresearch.org/fact-tank/2017/02/14/african-immigrant-population-in-u-s-steadily-climbs/

Bali, A. O., Karim, M. S., & Rached, K. (2018). Public diplomacy effort across Facebook: A comparative analysis of the U.S. Consulate in Erbil and the Kurdistan representation in Washington. *SAGE Open,* 1–9. doi:10.1177/2158244018758835

Bernal, V. (2013). Diaspora, digital media, and death counts: Eritreans and the politics of memorialization. *African Studies, 72*(2), 246–264. doi:10.1080/00020184.2013.812875

Brinkerhoff, J. M. (2009). *Digital diaspora: Identity and transnational engagement.* Cambridge, UK: Cambridge University Press. doi:10.1017/CBO9780511805158

Burke, M., Kraut, R., & Marlow, C. (2011). *Social capital on Facebook: Differentiating uses and users.* Presented at the International Conference on Human Factors in Computing Systems, CHI 2011, Vancouver, BC, Canada. Retrieved from http://www.thoughtcrumbs.com/publications/burke_chi2011_socialcapitalonfacebook.pdf

Calhoun, C. (2016). The importance of imagined communities – and Benedict Anderson debates. *Journal on Culture. Power and Society, 1,* 11–16.

Çanci, H., & Odukoya, O. E. (2016). Ethnic and religious crisis in Nigeria: A specific analysis upon identities. *African. The Journal of Conflict Resolution, 16*(1). Retrieved from https://www.accord.org.za/ajcr-issues/ethnic-religious-crises-nigeria/

Cohen, R. (1997). *Global diaspora: An introduction.* Seattle, WA: University of Washington Press. doi:10.4324/9780203228920

Hanson, F. (2012, October 25). *Baked in and wired: eDiplomacy@State.* Foreign Policy Paper Series no 30. Washington, DC: Brookings Institution. Retrieved from https://www.brookings.edu/wp-content/uploads/2016/06/baked-in-hansonf-5.pdf

Holmes, R. (2018). Are Facebook groups the future of social media? *Forbes.* Retrieved from https://www.forbes.com/sites/ryanholmes/2018/10/29/are-facebook-groups-the-future-of-social-media-or-a-dead-end/#7635ee6d1d23

Jacob, K. (2013). *"Facebook is my second home": The Kurdish Diaspora's Use of Facebook in Shaping a Nation (Unpublished master thesis).* University of Bergen. Retrieved from http://bora.uib.no/bitstream/handle/1956/7629/Master%20thesis_Kurdin%20Jacob.pdf?sequence=1&isAllowed=y

Kantar Media. (2018). *News in social media and messaging apps: Qualitative research report.* Retrieved from https://reutersinstitute.politics.ox.ac.uk/sites/default/files/2018-09/KM%20RISJ%20News%20in%20social%20media%20and%20messaging%20apps%20report%20_0.pdf

Migration Policy Institute. (2015a). *The Nigerian diaspora in the United States.* Retrieved from https://www.migrationpolicy.org/sites/default/files/publications/RAD-Nigeria.pdf

Migration Policy Institute. (2015b). *The Ethiopian diaspora in the United States.* Retrieved from file:///C:/Users/hmesbah/Downloads/RAD-Ethiopia%20(2).pdf

Migration Policy Institute. (2015c). *The Egyptian diaspora in the United States.* Retrieved from file:///C:/Users/hmesbah/Downloads/RAD-EgyptII%20(2).pdf

Mitra, A. (2001). Marginalized Voices in Cyberspace. *New Media & Society, 3*(1), 29–48. doi:10.1177/1461444801003001003

Nuermaimaiti, R. (2014). *Identity construction online: The use of Facebook by the Uyghur diaspora (Unpublished master thesis).* Unitec Institute of Technology. Retrieved from https://unitec.researchbank.ac.nz/bitstream/handle/10652/2477/Reziwanguli%20Nuermaimaiti%201363852.pdf?sequence=1&isAllowed=y

NurMuhammad, R., Horst, H. A., Papoutsaki, E., & Dodson, G. (2016). Uyghur transnational identity on Facebook: On the development of a young diaspora. *Identities (Yverdon), 23*(4), 485–499. doi:10.1080/1070289X.2015.1024126

O'Neill, N. (2010, February 1). *Google now indexes 620 Facebook groups*. Retrieved from https://www.adweek.com/digital/google-now-indexes-620-million-facebook-groups/

Oiarzabal, P. J. (2012). Diaspora Basques and online social networks: An analysis of users of Basque institutional diaspora groups on Facebook. *Journal of Ethnic and Migration Studies*, *38*(9), 1469–1485. doi:10.1080/1369183X.2012.698216

Plaza, D., & Plaza, L. (2019). Facebook and WhatsApp as elements in transnational care chains for the Trinidadian diaspora. *Genealogy*, *3*(2), 15. doi:10.3390/genealogy3020015

Skjerdal, T. S. (2011). Journalists or activists? Self-identity in the Ethiopian diaspora online community. *Journalism*, *12*(6), 727–744. doi:10.1177/1464884911405471

Spry, D. (2018). Facebook diplomacy: A data-driven, user-focused approach to Facebook use by diplomatic missions. *Media International Australia*, *168*(1), 62–80. doi:10.1177/1329878X18783029

Tremayne, M. (2017). The Facebook agenda: Global social media news characteristics. *American Communication Journal*, *19*(1), 25–35.

Tsagarousianou, R. (2004). Rethinking the concept of diaspora: Mobility, connectivity and communication in a globalized world. *Westminster Papers in Communication and Culture*, *1*(1), 52–65. doi:10.16997/wpcc.203

World Population Review. (2019). *Population of countries in Africa in 2019*. Retrieved from http://worldpopulationreview.com/countries/countries-in-africa/

This research was previously published in Multidisciplinary Issues Surrounding African Diasporas; pages 131-151, copyright year 2020 by Information Science Reference (an imprint of IGI Global).

Section 5
Organizational and Social Implications

Chapter 51
Understanding Social Media Addiction Through Personal, Social, and Situational Factors

Ozge Kirezli
Yeditepe University, Turkey

Asli Elif Aydin
iD https://orcid.org/0000-0002-9145-386X
Istanbul Bilgi University, Turkey

ABSTRACT

The main objective of this chapter is to gain an in-depth understanding of the social media addiction construct. For this purpose, prior studies on social media addiction are reviewed. Based on this review the influence of several personal, social, and situational factors on social media addiction are examined. Firstly, personal factors such as demographic characteristics, personality traits, self-esteem, well-being, loneliness, anxiety, and depression are studied for their impact on social media addiction. Next, the social correlates and consequents of social media addiction are identified, namely need for affiliation, subjective norms, personal, professional, and academic life. Lastly, situational factors like amount of social media use and motives of use are inspected. Following the review of literature an empirical study is made to analyze factors that discriminate addicted social media users from non-addicted social media users on the basis of these different factors.

INTRODUCTION

Internet has dramatically changed the communication patterns of individuals. It has become a pervasive part of consumers' lives such that, researchers heightened their attention to understand the positive and negative effects of internet on human life. Certainly, several positive outcomes of internet can be counted as; providing easy access to information and leveraging early learning (Reid et al, 2016; Bauer, Gai, Kim, Muth, & Wildman, 2002), providing chances for widening social surroundings (Hampton & Well-

DOI: 10.4018/978-1-6684-6307-9.ch051

man, 2003; Katz & Aspden, 1997; Rheingold, 1993) and improving psychological mood via creating opportunities for social contact and support (Reid et al, 2016; Chen, Boase, &Wellman, 2002; Kang, 2007). However, some potential negativities also emerged namely; decreasing level of social contact of individuals (Kim & Harikadis, 2009; Sanders, Field,Diego, & Kaplan, 2000; Kraut,Patterson, Landmark, Kielser, Mukophadhyaya, & Scherlis, 1998; Stoll, 1995; Turkle, 1996), causing loneliness and eventually, clinical depression (Young & Rogers, 1998). These negativities especially intensified as individuals' frequency and duration of internet increased specifically in the cases of addiction.

Internet addiction has gained substantial interest by both mental health professionals and academic researchers. "Addiction" term, actually, is based on biological and psychological dependence of a physical item. The Diagnostic and Statistical Manual of Mental Disorders (DSM) is the most well-known and appreciated source for addiction related terms, but behavioral addictions are not listed in mental disorders according to psychiatric literature. Recognizing this gap in the field, Goldberg (1996) established "internet addiction disorder" term for excessive human-machine interaction. Goldberg(1996) supported his argument by referring how the four components of addiction also exist in internet addiction, as well. These four components are; tolerance (increasing the engagement level to reach previous improved mood states), withdrawal (feeling discomfort when the behavior is prohibited), negative life outcomes (neglecting social, educational or work related issues), and craving (increasing the level of intensity) (Kim & Harikadis, 2009; Goldberg, 1996). In time, three more components are added to the four existing components namely; salience (being preoccupied with the behavior), mood modification (using this to alleviate psychological state) and relapse (fail to control the behavior) (Kim & Harikadis, 2009; Griffiths, 1998).

A growing wave of researchers supported the notion of using addiction term to characterize high dependence of certain behaviors especially among the youth (Kuss & Griffiths, 2011; Young, 2004; Lemon, 2002; Orford, 2001; Shaffer, 1996; Griffiths, 1998; Peele 1985). Moreover, the recent edition of "Diagnostic and Statistical Manual of Mental Disorders" recognized gambling as an addiction and listed digital game addiction as a potential behavioral addiction (American Psychiatric Association, 2013). Likewise a number of various behavioral addictions have been examined such as; internet addiction, social media addiction, digital game addiction (Keepers, 1990) and smartphone addiction (Savci & Aysan, 2017). This chapter focuses on social media addiction. Although in the literature there exist different terminology to explain this phenomenon, specifically problematic social media/Facebook use (Kırcaburun et al., 2019; Shensa et al., 2017), social networking addiction (Griffiths et al., 2018; Monacis et al., 2017; Wang et al., 2015) and compulsive social media usage (Dhir et al., 2018; Aladwani et al., 2017), social media addiction term is used deliberately to reach consistency within the work.

This chapter aims to understand "social media addiction" concept by examining its correlates. Moreover, it contributes to social media addiction literature in two ways. First of all, it provides a comprehensive look to social media addiction by discussing a variety of factors, which are beneficial for academicians' to be used for further research. Secondly, with an empirical study, factors discriminating social media addicts from non-addicts are identified.

SOCIAL MEDIA ADDICTION: EN EMERGING TREND

At the present time, the dramatic role of social media on communicational patterns cannot be underestimated. Even though, social media use provides many benefits such as of eroding distance between people, easing and speeding up the interaction, even changing the formal communicational patterns in the business life, excessive use of social media can be problematic as it potentially harms social and psychological life of individuals (Karaiskos et al., 2010; Kuss & Griffiths, 2011). It has become almost a social obligation for individuals to check their social media updates, even when they are walking, shopping, listening to a lecture, and driving (Sriwilai & Charoensukmongkol, 2015). People engage in social media for a variety of reasons, specifically to play games, to fill waiting times, to communicate, to share their "self" and to respond to other "selves" (Andreassen et. al, 2017; Allen, Ryan, Gray, McInerney, &Waters, 2014; Ryan, Chester, Reece, & Xenos, 2014). Enjoyment gained through social media can stimulate a strong habit which occasionally transforms into an irresistible urge (Longstreet & Brooks, 2017). This urge to make frequent checks or updates in social media, has a potential to turn into a compulsive disorder, which might be harmful for academic, professional and social life of individuals (Karaiskos et al., 2010). In that perspective, Andreassen and Pallasen (2014, p.4054) defined social media addiction as "being overly concerned about social media, driven by an uncontrollable motivation to log on to or use social media, and devoting so much time and effort to social media that it impairs other important life areas".

Coining the term "social media addiction" brought about two burdens. The first one is about differentiating addicts from non-addicts, whereas the second one is about constituting the criteria for distinguishing the addicts. In 2012, Andreassen and her colleagues developed a new scale entitled Bergen Facebook Addiction Scale (BFAS), using Facebook's position of being a pioneer in social media. In this scale, there exist six main characteristics of addictions, prevailed in Facebook addiction. These characteristics are identified as; salience (continuous preoccupation with Facebook), tolerance (incremental engagement with Facebook to reach prior mood escalating effect), mood modification (using Facebook for mood alleviation), relapse (failed attempts of limiting or prohibiting Facebook use), withdrawal (feeling anxious without Facebook) and conflict (excessive Facebook use causing social, academic or work related problems) (Andreassen et al., 2013, 2012; Wilson et al., 2010). Hence this characterization was the first attempt to distinguish extreme or enthusiastic users and addicts, since it is not only increasing the amount of time spent for social media, but the incremental and possibly detrimental effect on individuals' life. In addition, this characterization provided further insights about the progressive nature of addiction as checking the concept in six dimensions in continuous basis, rather than dichotomous addict or non-addict basis.

FACTORS RELATED TO SOCIAL MEDIA ADDICTION

In the literature, the effects of variety of personal, social and situational factors on social media addiction has been explored. Several studies categorized the related factors as either antecedents or consequences yet majority of the analyses are made based on correlations. Therefore, this chapter intends to present the influential factors altogether to better examine potential antecedent or consequential effects.

Personal Factors

Demographic Characteristics

A substantial amount of research examined the role of demographic characteristics on the prevalence of social media addiction (Marino et al., 2018; Andreassen et al 2016; Van Deursen et al., 2015; Kuss et al., 2014; Koç & Gulyagci, 2013). Within this stream of research, gender's effect on social media addiction is well examined. There exist three main perspectives which explain gender's role on social media addiction. The first one advocates that women are more vulnerable to addictive usage of social media compared to men due to their heightened interest in social activities (Andreassen, 2015; Van Deursen, Bolle, Hegner, & Kommers, 2015; Kuss et al. 2014; Turel et al., 2014; Griffiths et al., 2014; Andreassen et al., 2013; Moreau et al., 2015). Kuss et al. (2014) suggested the idea that both men and women have the tendency to become technology addicts, however males are more interested in gaming, pornography and gambling, whereas women favor social media, texting and online shopping (Maraz et al., 2015; Van Deursen et al., 2015; Andreassen et al., 2013). The second view, emerged as gender having a minimal role in explaining social media addiction (Beyens, Frison, & Eggermont, 2016; Lee, 2015). The third view, interestingly, suggests that men are more likely to be addicted to social media compared to women (Çam& Isbulan, 2012; Ryan et al., 2014). Thus, gender's role on social media addiction seems to be an unresolved issue, hence needs further empirical data to reach conclusive findings.

Compared to gender, age seems to have a greater impact on overall demographic characteristics. Research indicated that young individuals have higher scores in social media addiction compared to older individuals (Andreassen et al., 2012; Kuss et al., 2014). This phenomenon might be explained by new generations' easy adaptation to technology and simply embracing the state of being "constantly online" (Prensky, 2001), their tendency to develop their self via a virtual identity in social media freely (Andreassen, 2015; Mazzoni & Iannone, 2014) and their readiness to use social platforms as effective entertainment and leisure activities (Allen et al., 2014).

Another significant demographic variable is defined as individuals' relationship status. Research shows that people, not in a relationship, are more prone to social media addiction (Kuss et al., 2014). Also some studies interpret this fact with, how social media can serve as a medium to meet new people as to create or nurture relations with potential partners (Andreassen, Torsheim, & Pallesen, 2014; Ryan et al., 2014).

Self Esteem

A number of studies investigate the association between social media usage frequency and self-esteem. These studies report a negative relationship between duration of time spent on social media and self-esteem (Kalpidou, Costin,& Morris, 2011; Vogel et al., 2014). Studies also corroborated that for adolescents a negative relationship exists between intensity of social media use and individuals' self-esteem (Valkenburg, Peter, & Schouten, 2006; Woods & Scott, 2016; Ingólfsdóttir, 2017). As for tracing the relationship between self-esteem and addictive type of behaviors, notable amount of research indicated that, individuals having low level of self-esteem are more inclined to engage in addictive type of behaviors (BaÂnyai et al., 2017; Andreassen et al., 2017; Baturay & Toker, 2016; Malik & Khan, 2015; Eraslan-Capan, 2015; Marlatt et al., 1988). There exist three probable explanations about self-esteem's role on social media addiction. The first one argues that, individuals having low self-esteem have negative feelings towards themselves, and social media addiction serves as an escape strategy to suppress this stress and anxiety (Błachnio et al., 2016; De Cock et al., 2014; Bozoglan, Demirer, & Sahin, 2013; Baumeister, 1993; Swann, 1996). The second one suggests that, people use social media to strengthen their self-esteem (Peele, 1985; Steinfield, Ellison, & Lampe, 2008; Gonzales & Hancock, 2011). Gonzales and Hancock (2011) use the term of "selective self-presentation" as how people carefully select the media by highlighting the most positive and appealing slices of their life. The third one is, related to individuals having delicate self-esteem as having extreme awareness of what the environment thinks about them and embracing social media as avoiding real human contact (Eraslan Çapan, 2015). Social media serves as a magical digital channel for individuals to remove the uncomfortable feeling of one-to-one communication with others, especially for those having insufficient social skills (Boyce & Parker, 1989).

In contrary with these views, Blachnio et al. (2016) propose that, it is not only individuals with low self-esteem that use social media addictively, but people with high levels of self-esteem use social media in an addictive manner, as well. These people are motivated to sustain their social bonds via social media, and extend their social circle by being active in social media. Marino et al. (2018) interpret the overall relationship between self-esteem and social media use referring to the social compensation theory. According to that people with high self-esteem boost their self-esteem via social media presence and people with low self-esteem, use social media as a way to compensate their deficiency.

Personality Traits

In the literature, personality is widely characterized through the Five-Factor Model (Caprara, Barbaranelli, Borgogni, & Perugini, 1993; Caprara, Barbaranelli, & Livi, 1994; Marino et al., 2018). According to this model, there exist five dimensions in personality, which are extroversion, agreeableness, conscientiousness, neuroticism and openness. Extraversion refers to the quantity of social interaction, the individual prefers. It gives critical hints about sociability and emotional expression level of individuals. It is believed that, introverted individuals (scoring low in extroversion dimension) mostly engage in social media to compensate the stability of their social life (Amichai-Hamburger, Wainapel, & Fox, 2002; Bodroza & Jovanovic, 2016). On the contrary, Andreassen et al. (2012) argued that extroverted people are more inclined to be social media addicts, as a result of their motivation to sustain their sociability. Perhaps, the most comprehensive view came from Kuss and Griffiths (2010), indicating that extrovert people engage in social media for social boost, whereas introvert people engage in social media for improving social well-being. Agreeableness refers to the quality of social interaction, as how kind, emphatic and helpful the individual is towards others. Individuals scoring high in agreeableness, excessively use social media to convey their relational achievements to stay connected to the others (Marshall, Lefringhausen, & Ferenczi, 2015). However, there exist studies claiming insignificant relations between agreeableness trait and social media addiction (Lee, 2015; Błachnio et al., 2017). Further a negative relationship is also found which indicates that a high agreeableness score potentially results with lower social media addiction tendency (Andreassen et al., 2013; Bodroza & Jovanovic, 2016). Conscientiousness trait is related to being organized, competent, goal-driven and having self-discipline. Those, scoring high in this dimension, either favor organizing tools of social media as facilitators or enjoy accelerating number of friends (Amichai-Hamburger & Vinitzky, 2010). However, there also exist intriguing reverse relationship suggestions, which suggest that highly conscientious people avoid social media since social media is seen as a disturbing activity (Wilson et. al., 2010; Andreassen et al., 2012; Andreassen et al., 2013; Lee, 2015; Bodroza & Jovanovic, 2016; Błachnio et al., 2017). Neuroticism reflects individuals' incapacity to deal with anxiety and stress. Hence, it is usually taken as an indicator for emotional (in) stability. According to literature, neuroticism is evident in addictive type of behaviors (Andreassen et al., 2012; Tang, Chen, Yang, Chung, & Lee, 2016; Marino et al. 2018). Neurotic people are articulated as heavy social media users to alleviate their mood due to emotional instability (Marino et. al., 2018), to pursue emotional support via this online channel (Andreassen et. al, 2012). Likewise, Ross et al. (2009) believed neuroticism plays a significant role in information sharing tendency of people in social media. Last dimension is openness, which symbolize how ready the individuals are to embrace novelty in their life. Individuals, who are high in openness to experience, are frequently labeled as information searchers or sharers in the social media. Thus, this information concern, make these people vulnerable for excessive use and potentially addictive behavior (Hughes, Rowe, Batey, & Lee, 2012).

Loneliness

Loneliness is also among the potential antecedents of social media addiction. According to an empirical study with a sample size of 1193, active social media users expressed they felt less lonely and gained social support after they used social media, compared to passive social media users (Wilson, Gosling, & Graham, 2012). People, who have low social skills (McKenna and Bargh, 2000) or feel socially incompetent (Kubey et al., 2001) might feel more relaxed and comfortable with online activities. Loneliness is also matched with other addictive activities such as consumption of drugs (Grunbaum, Tortolero, Weller, & Gingiss, 2000) and alcohol (Loos, 2002; Medora & Woodward, 1991). In that perspective, heavy dependence on internet and social media to cope with loneliness might cause social media addiction (Caplan, 2002, 2003; Davis, 2001).

Well-being

One factor that is examined as a negative correlate of social media addiction is individuals' well-being. It is suggested that meaningless time on Facebook dampens individuals' morale (Sagioglou & Greitemeyer, 2014). Besides, compared to non-addicts, those who are addicted to social media score lower on subjective happiness and subjective vitality (Uysal, Satici, & Akin, 2013). Moreover, it is indicated that procrastination due to social media use has a damaging effect on general well-being (Meier, Reinecke, & Meltzer, 2016). A study which examined the impact of instantaneous and prolonged Facebook use, reveal that increased usage of Facebook lessens individuals' well-being (Kross et al., 2013). A negative relationship is also demonstrated between Facebook addiction and satisfaction with life (Błachnio, Przepiorka, & Pantic, 2016; Satici & Uysal, 2015). Likewise, a decrease in social media use enhances satisfaction with life (Hinsch, & Sheldon, 2013).

Anxiety and Depression

In the literature, depression and anxiety are related to social media addiction in two aspects. The first aspect is figured as anxiety/depression's role as an antecedent, whereby people feeling more anxious or depressed spend more time in social media and decrease the level of communication with their social circle (Pantic,2014; Kraut et al. 2002). Block et al. (2014) reported that depressed individuals use media (internet, tv and social media) more frequently than regular people. Likewise, Clayton, Osborne, Miller, and Oberle (2013) referred anxiousness as an important antecedent of emotional connectedness to social media.

The second aspect is visualized as a consequence, as of social media addiction's detrimental effect on producing more depressed and anxious individuals (Shensa et al., 2017; Moreno et al., 2011). Addictive use of internet increases depression symptoms (Gámez-Guadix, 2014). Specific to social media domain, it is also found that excessive use of social media correlates with increased likelihood of depression (Moreau et al., 2015; Lin et al., 2016). Another study also reported increased levels of anxiety and depression as a result of increased social media usage for adolescents (Woods & Scott, 2016). Similarly, it is revealed that social media addiction contributes to emotional burn out through the use of emotional strategies of coping with stress (Sriwilai & Charoensukmongkol, 2016). Social media addiction may also lead to physical health issues (Andreassen, 2015). For instance, both overall state of health and sleep quality deteriorate with social media addiction (Atroszko, 2018). Additionally, it is indicated that excessive use of social media results in delayed bedtimes and rising times (Andreassen, et al., 2012).

In sum, social media addiction is perceived as a significant contributor to depression, especially in youth, according to a substantial number of research (Younnes et al., 2016; Levenson et al., 2016; Liu et al., 2016; Block et al., 2014; Feinstein et al., 2012; Moreno et al., 2011; Desjarlais & Willoughby, 2010; Mihajlović et al., 2008). On the other hand, studies also tried to validate the potential positive effects of social media on human spirit. Interestingly, McDougall et al. (2016) initiated that social media might produce benefits as fueling social support to remove depression, yet he argued that social media did not nurture depressive symptoms, but let people share their inner world and start almost like a primitive therapy for these people. In that vein, excessive social media users or social media addicts do not necessarily in all cases, suffer from depression and anxiety. Eventually, the relationship between social media, depression and anxiety seem ambiguous, in terms of whether addictive social media causing these negative feelings or negative feelings lead individuals to addictive social media use.

Social Factors

Need for Affiliation / Social Enhancement

Need for affiliation is described as the individuals' inclination to develop and maintain social relationships (Veroff, Reuamn & Feld, 1984; Murray, 1938). Seeking social approval or belongingness is a natural drive, since people show considerable energy for social interaction to satisfy the need for appreciation and affection. Yet, human interaction is not limited to face-to-face contact, writing letters once was the main practice for engaging in distant relationships (Lansing & Heyns, 1959). Thanks to advances in communication technologies, internet and social media acts as an efficient tool for individuals' contact with their friends. Ample amount of studies underlined people's enthusiasm for social connectedness as the major reason of social media use (Valentine, 2013; Kuss & Griffiths, 2011; Sheldon, 2009; Joinson, 2008; Raacke & Bonds-Raacke, 2008). In the studies, validating the correlation between individuals' need for affiliation and internet communication, respondents expressed that web based communication is deeper and more pleasant than face-to-face interaction (Peter & Valkenburg, 2006; Caplan, 2003). Similarly, it was argued that, need for affiliation is a strong motivator for new generation to take place in social media due to frequency and quality of communication they develop with others (Chuang & Nam, 2007). The type of interaction is different in social media, such as receiving and sending comments, writing on the wall of others, number of shares, likes and so on. This reciprocity produces a virtual community for those people, whereby they can satisfy the need for affiliation. In that vein, online social networking can be beneficial for social functioning (Burke, Marlow, & Lento, 2010; Ellison, Steinfield, & Lampe, 2007; Steinfield, Ellison, & Lampe, 2008). Furthermore, the individual can create and develop the desired "self", which serves the need for affiliation, as well (Gibbs, Ellison, & Heino, 2006). Even so, having such a convenient, cheap and easy communication tool seems promising, it comes with a cost. It is interesting to reveal that, individuals excessively using social media might turn into socially isolated individuals in real life (Allen et al., 2014). When taken with facilitating demographic characteristics (being young and having no relationship), need for affiliation via social media can evolve to social media addiction, whereby the individual experiences an alienation in real social settings and escapes to virtual world for social gratification (Shen &Williams, 2010; Valkenburg & Peter, 2009; Mesch, 2001).

Subjective Norms

Subjective norms are defined as individuals' perception of the type of conduct that is expected from them within a group (Davis, 1989; Cialdini, Kallgren & Reno, 1991). It is a more lenient form of group pressure, which creates an obligation to act suitably (Marino et al., 2016). Studies support the notion that, especially in youth, subjective norms can have both positive and negative impacts (Venkatesh et al., 2003; Borsari & Carey, 2003; Pozzoli & Gini, 2013). Rabaai et al. (2018) suggested that subjective norms might function in two ways. The first one is due to rapid adoption of technology especially in younger generation, individuals feel like they have to be present in social media, even though they do not have a certain desire (Lewis et al., 2012). Even more, Olowu and Seri (2012) state that existence in social media might be for just suppressing the social pressure of "have to be there, have to be online". In that sense, adolescents seem more vulnerable to seize social media just for approval due to peer influence. The second impact emerges, when the individuals observe how their social circle experience and enjoy social media, they feel the strong need to feel alike (Huang et al., 2014). Compared to previous trigger, hereby not solely being online in social media motivates the person, but seeks to actively participate in conversations and events for the purpose of enriching social life and not missing out on joyful events. If individuals become heavily anxious about their social life performance, they fear of social exclusion (Blackwell et al., 2017). In that perspective, fear of missing out might promote individuals increased social media use. Fear of missing out is defined as a type of fear when individual thinks other people are enjoying their time without him/her (Przybylski, Murayama, DeHaan, &Gladwell, 2013).

Personal, Professional and Academic Life

The influence of social media use on real life relationships are also examined within this stream of research. When individuals use social media excessively their relationships with friends and family are damaged since they dedicate less time to their social environment (Zheng & Lee, 2016). Studies also demonstrate detrimental effects of social media addiction on romantic relationships such that a positive association between addiction and romantic detachment along with betrayal exists (Abbasi, 2018, 2019).

Social media addiction may also lead to problems in individuals' professional life. Firstly, individuals declare a slightly negative impact of social media use on their job performance (Andreassen, Torsheim, & Pallesen, 2014). On the other hand, it is indicated that excessive use of social media use impedes individuals' work conduct (Zheng & Lee, 2016). It is further revealed that social media addiction hinders job performance as a result of social media induced distraction and negative affect (Moqbel, & Kock, 2018). Parallel to that a decline in job performance is shown due to addiction based work-family life imbalance and emotional exhaustion (Zivnuska et al., 2019). Finally, addiction to social media is shown to influence job satisfaction negatively as well (Choi, 2018).

The impact of use of social media on academic performance also received some scholarly interest. First of all, it is shown that those who use Facebook spend less time studying compared to those who do not use Facebook (Kirschner & Karpinski, 2010). Furthermore, it is indicated that as the frequency of Facebook use increase, the overall GPA of students decrease (Junco, 2012). Parallel to that, multitasking social media while studying is shown to be negatively related to overall GPA (Junco& Cooten, 2012; Lau, 2017). It is also demonstrated that individuals, who show symptoms of social media addiction, performed poorly in their academic studies (Al-Menayes, 2015).

Situational Factors

Amount of Use

Social media addiction, just like the other addictions, can be assessed in an incremental basis on a continuum. As it can be expected, the higher amount of time the individual uses social media, the likelihood to get addicted increases (Widyanto & McMurran, 2004; Leung, 2004). Yet, prior research supported that problematic social media users tend to spend more time rather than regular users, signaling significant positive relationship between two concepts (Hormes et al., 2014). However, studies distinguishing excessive social media usage and social media addiction, state that amount of use might not indicate problematic/addictive social media use, in all cases (Pontes et al., 2015; Griffiths, 2010). By making this distinction, emphasis is put on the availability of negative consequences. If the individual does not suffer from negative outcomes (e.g. delay in daily chores, feelings of insecurity or discomfort when deprived from social media etc.) then the individual is not considered addicted (Griffiths, 2010). In sum, addicts use social media frequently; however, excessive users (referring to the quantitative data) do not necessarily always show addictive symptoms. In that manner, apart from the quantitative approach, the qualitative nature of the time spent on social media needs to be explored.

Motives

Motives leading to excessive or addictive usage of social media might be numerous. Studies proposed various motives for social media usage; fulfilling relational needs (interaction, affection, approval, self-expression) or fulfilling media related entertainment needs (learning new things, leisure activity, using applications and tools) (Charney & Greenberg, 2002; Ebersole, 2000; Ferguson & Perse, 2000; Kaye & Johnson, 2004; Papacharissi & Rubin, 2000). It was suggested that, if the individual is aware of the motives that lead them to excessive or addictive usage of social media, that would reduce the potential manifestation of the negative outcomes (Song, LaRose, Eastin, & Lin, 2004). A growing body of research indicated that people that are using social media for social goals (socialization, companionship and social interaction) and lightening mood (escapism, feel good effect, passing time) are more likely to be addicts (Bodroza & Jovanovic, 2016; Koc & Gulyagci, 2013; Tang et al., 2016; Sharifah et al., 2011; Dhaha, 2013; Masur et al., 2014). Similarly, Ryan et al. (2016) stressed social media's effect on emotional life of individual as repairing mood or overcoming boredom besides social motives. The motivational model for social media, is characterized as having two dimensions; positive / negative valence (enhancing positive mood, or repairing negative mood) and internal / external resource (satisfying one's own internal needs or others') (Marino et. al., 2016; Bischof-Kastner et al., 2014). Consequently, four motives emerge, namely enhancement, coping, conformity and social. Enhancement refers to positive valence and internal source, meaning that individuals with this motive aim to improve positive feelings for them. Coping refers to negative valence and internal source, meaning people wish to escape from negative feelings via social media. Conformity refers to negative valence and external source, which is related to using social media to overcome social pressure. Social motive is related to use social media with the aim of improving social interaction with existing or potential friends (Marino et. al., 2016; Bischof-Kastner et al., 2014).

THE STUDY

The objective of the empirical study is to gain a better understanding of social media addiction. For this purpose a comparison of addicted social media users and non-addicted social media users are made based on a number of factors. First, the study examines the relationship between social media addiction and motives underlying social media use. Second, the impact of person characteristics such as loneliness and life satisfaction on social media addiction is investigated in the study. The influence of individuals' judgments regarding their satisfaction with their lives and participants' subjective feelings of social seclusion on the degree of their social media addiction is also examined. Moreover, the extent of association between social media usage duration and social media addiction is inspected. Finally, the relationship between social media addiction and social media use while conversing with others, driving, listening to lectures is also analyzed.

METHOD

Data

The empirical study for this chapter is conducted in Turkey. It is stated that Turkey is one of the top twenty countries based on time spent each day on social platforms (GlobalWebIndex, 2019). Accordingly, the tendency to use social media in a problematic manner is quite high in Turkey. The data is collected from a sample of college students. Social media use is most widespread among the young; hence the age base of the sample is deemed appropriate.

Undergraduate students of Business Department of three major universities in Istanbul, Turkey are invited to the study. Students are incentivized to participate to the study with bonus credit offerings. A total of 269 students completed a web-based survey. The survey took on average 10 minutes to complete. 11 students did not own a social media account. Therefore, they were removed from the sample. Moreover, 23 students failed to answer correctly to an attention test and hence were removed. Consequently, 235 participants were retained in the final sample.

Measures

Social Networking Addiction

To assess participants' level of social media addiction Bergen Social Networking Addiction Scale (Andreassen et al., 2012) was employed. The scale includes six items corresponding to six main dimension of addiction namely salience (prominence of social media use in individuals' thinking), mood modification (social media use improving mood), tolerance (increasing amount of social media use to experience the same effects), withdrawal (presence of negative feelings when social media is not used), conflict (negative impact of social media use on studies/work), and relapse (returning to earlier use of social media after exercising self-restraint). Participants' were asked to indicate how often they experienced the mentioned thoughts, feelings and behaviors during the past year. They responded using a five-point scale ranging from (1) very rarely to (5) very often. A summated score of 6 to 30 marks the extent of social networking addiction. The Cronbach's alpha of the scale was 0.75 for the current sample.

Motives for Using Social Media

As a measure of participants' motives underlying social media, the 16-item Motives for Using Social Media Scale (Marino et al. 2016) was included in the study. The scale assesses four key motives namely; enhancement (to improve positive feelings by using social media), coping (to reduce negative feelings by using social media), conformity (to conform to peer group norms by using social media), and social (to improve relationships with friends). Participants' were asked to indicate how often they used social media for each motive on a five-point scale ranging from (1) never or almost never to (5) always or almost always. Higher scores on this scale indicate stronger motives. The Cronbach's alpha of the scale was 0.91.

Loneliness

The trait loneliness was assessed using eight-item Loneliness Scale developed by Hays and DiMatteo (1987). The scale assesses individuals' feelings of social isolation. Participants were asked to indicate to what extent they agree with the statements on a four-point scale ranging from (1) never to (4) always. Those who obtain a high score on this scale were considered to feel lonely. The Cronbach's alpha of the scale was 0.73.

Satisfaction with Life

In order to measure participants' satisfaction with their lives the Life Satisfaction Scale developed by Diener et. al. (1985) was employed. The scale comprises five items that assess a cognitive appraisal of individuals' satisfaction with their lives. Participants were asked to indicate to what extent they agree with the statements on a four-point scale ranging from (1) strongly disagree to (4) strongly agree. The Cronbach's alpha of the scale was 0.78.

Social Media Use Duration

The measure for Social Media Use Duration was adapted from Facebook use duration scale of Brailovskaia et al. (2019). The scale is adapted by substituting the Facebook term with social media. One item assessed frequency of social media use on a 6-point scale ranging from (1) less than once a day to (6) ten times a day or more. Another item assessed length of social media usage period on a 7-point scale ranging from (1) less than five minutes to (7) more than 180 minutes. The average frequency and length of social media use for this sample was 5.01(SD=1.21) and 4.83 (SD=1.52), respectively.

A combined measure for social media use duration was also calculated by taking the average of two Z-transformed scores of both measures.

Improper Use of Social Media

In order to assess improper use of social media a three-item scale is developed for this study. Items related to the tendency to use social media while conversing with others, driving and attending a lecture are included. Participants were asked to indicate to how frequently they engaged in the behaviors reported in the statements on a four-point scale ranging from (1) never to (4) always. The Cronbach's alpha of the scale was 0.6.

Demographics

Participants' age, gender and relationship status were included in the questionnaire. The mean age of the sample was 20.77 (SD=3.35). 40 percent of the participants were female and 34 percent of the whole sample was in a relationship.

Analysis and Results

Initially mean values, standard deviations and bivariate correlations of the study constructs are computed (Table 1). The average summated social media addiction score for the sample is 16.16 (SD = 5.04) out of a possible 30 points.

Table 1. Descriptives and Correlation coefficients between constructs

	A	B	C	D	E	F	G	H	I
A. Social Media Addiction	1								
B. Life Satisfaction	-0.02	1							
C. Loneliness	0.18**	-0.17**	1						
D. Social Motive	0.40**	0.10	0.15*	1					
E. Enhancement Motive	0.54**	0.10	0.13	0.56**	1				
F. Conformity Motive	0.46**	-0.04	0.32**	0.40**	0.42**	1			
G. Coping Motive	0.62**	-0.1	0.20**	0.43**	0.51**	0.39**	1		
H. Composite duration	0.51**	0.12	0.01	0.39**	0.51**	0.21**	0.32**	1	
I. Improper use	0.52**	0.09	0.11	0.38**	0.45**	0.35**	0.40**	0.39**	1
Mean	16.16	4.62	1.92	3.33	3.05	1.77	2.88	0.00	2.28
Standard deviation	5.04	1.05	0.43	1.12	1.01	0.98	1.22	0.88	0.83

* $p < 0.05$
** $p < 0.01$

A multiple regression analysis is made to examine the predictors of social media addiction. The variables of the study explained 54% of the variance of social media addiction (Table 2). Multicollinearity among the variables is inspected based on bivariate correlations and variance inflation factors. It is seen that there is no multicollinearity since all correlation coefficients are below 0.7 and variance inflation factors for all variables are below 3 (Hair et al., 2006). According to the results of the multiple regression analysis significant variables are social media use duration (β=0.25), enhancement motive (β=0.13), conformity motive (β=0.18), coping motive (β=0.34), and improper use (β=0.19). The other variables are not significant.

Table 2. Regression analysis for social media addiction

	B	Std. Error	β	t	Sig.
(Constant)	8.38	2.28		3.67	0
Composite duration	1.42	0.31	0.25	4.65	0.00
Life satisfaction	-0.14	0.23	-0.03	-0.63	0.53
Loneliness	0.35	0.55	0.03	0.63	0.53
Social motive	-0.35	0.26	-0.08	-1.35	0.18
Enhancement motive	0.64	0.32	0.13	2.02	0.04
Conformity motive	0.93	0.27	0.18	3.43	0.00
Coping motive	1.40	0.23	0.34	6.09	0.00
Improper use	1.16	0.32	0.19	3.66	0.00
Age	-0.08	0.07	-0.05	-1.13	0.26
Gender	0.79	0.47	0.08	1.69	0.09
Relationship Status	-0.21	0.48	-0.02	-0.43	0.67

R^2: 0.57
Adjusted R^2: 0.54
Std. Error of the Estimate: 3.37
$F_{(df1,df2)}$: $F(11,223)=27.35$
*p<0.05; **p<0.01

Next, a logistic regression analysis is made with the same variables to predict the likelihood of being addicted to social media. In order to distinguish addicted individuals, having a minimum score of three or more for at least four of the six items is required, following Andreassen et al. (2012)'s approach. A dummy variable, which takes the value 1 for addicted individuals, is created for the analysis. Based on that a total of 113 participants fit this criteria and hence were categorized as addicted individuals.

The logistic model is statistically significant (χ^2 (11, N = 235) = 106.56, p < 0.05) which suggests that differences between addicted and non-addicted individuals can be identified. Hosmer - Lemeshow test is employed to assess goodness of fit for the logistic regression. The p-value, which is greater than 0.05, indicates no significant difference between the expected and the observed data. 77% of the cases are correctly classified by the model. Four variables are significant namely; social media use duration, conformity motive, coping motive, and improper use. According to that, individuals, who used social media for longer durations are 2.01 times more likely to be addicted (p = 0.01). Moreover, using social media with conformity motive and coping motive increase the chances of being addicted with odds ratios of 2.09 (p < 0.01) and 1.94 (p < 0.01) respectively. Lastly, improper use of social media increase the odds of being addicted with a ratio of 1.87 (p = 0.01).

Table 3. Logistic regression analysis predicting likelihood of being addicted to social media

Variables	B	S.E.	Wald	df	Sig.	Exp(B)	95% C.I. for Exp(B)	
							Lower	Upper
Composite duration	0.70	0.26	7.36	1	0.01	2.01	1.21	3.33
Life satisfaction	0.01	0.18	0.01	1	0.94	1.01	0.71	1.45
Loneliness	0.47	0.44	1.10	1	0.29	1.59	0.67	3.81
Social motive	-0.12	0.19	0.38	1	0.54	0.89	0.61	1.29
Enhancement motive	0.03	0.23	0.02	1	0.89	1.03	0.66	1.62
Conformity motive	0.74	0.23	10.33	1	0.00	2.09	1.33	3.28
Coping motive	0.66	0.18	14.19	1	0.00	1.94	1.37	2.74
Improper use	0.63	0.25	6.35	1	0.01	1.87	1.15	3.05
Age	-0.09	0.06	2.38	1	0.12	0.91	0.81	1.02
Gender	0.02	0.36	0.00	1	0.96	1.02	0.50	2.05
Relationship Status	-0.39	0.38	1.03	1	0.31	0.68	0.32	1.43
Constant	-3.38	1.88	3.23	1	0.07	0.03		

Hosmer-Lemeshow
$\chi2$: 5.66
Sig.: 0.69
N: 235

DISCUSSION

Firstly, the empirical study supported that the degree of social media addiction increases with increased duration of use. The composite index of frequency and length of social media use significantly predict social media addiction. This finding corroborates findings of prior studies which show a significant link between time spent on the internet and internet addiction (Leung, 2004) as well as a significant link between amount of daily online presence and Facebook addiction (Przepiorka, & Blachnio, 2016; Brailovskaia, Margraf, & Köllner, 2019).

Secondly, the study point out that neither life satisfaction nor loneliness determines social media addiction. Even though prior research demonstrated that individuals who are socially secluded seek interactions through online mediums (McKenna & Bargh, 2000), and that a positive relationship exists between state of loneliness and internet addiction (Kubey et al., 2001; Kim & Haridakis, 2009), findings demonstrate no significant relationship between loneliness and social media addiction. Moreover, earlier studies indicate positive relationship between social media addiction and life satisfaction (Błachnio, Przepiorka & Pantic, 2016; Longstreet & Brooks, 2017). Current study does not support these findings. One probable account for this discrepancy is that life satisfaction is a general concept which encapsulates global evaluations of every dimension of life. Therefore, judgments about life in general might not be a driver of social media addiction.

Regarding the motivation of social media use, results indicated that conformity and coping motives distinguish between addicted and non-addicted users. Those, who used social media to reduce their negative feelings or to conform to peer norms, are more likely to get addicted. Moreover, enhancement motive is found to be a significant predictor of social media addiction. Even though enhancement does not discern addicts from non-addicts, the motive to improve positive feelings increase degree of social media addiction. Lastly social motive does not determine social media addiction since majority of the users' main drive in social media use is to improve relationships with friends. Accordingly, social motive becomes a generic purpose for all users.

Another finding demonstrated that those who use social media improperly are more likely to get addicted to social media. Those, who compulsively check their social media feeds during lectures, while driving or having a conversation with others, are more likely to be addicted. This finding demonstrates the detrimental effects of social media addiction and hence is valuable. Further studies might investigate the impact of improper use on social interactions as well as performance of daily tasks.

Finally, the findings reveal that gender does not discern likelihood of being addicted to social media. It is shown that only marginally significant differences exist on extent of social media addiction between men and women. Specifically, the extent of social media addiction is slightly higher for women than for men. Prior studies report conflicting findings regarding the role of gender in predicting social media addiction (Çam & Isbulan, 2012; Griffiths et al., 2014; Wang et al., 2015). Our study also does not clarify the influence of gender on social media addiction. Furthermore, neither age nor relationship status predict social media addiction. The age range of the current sample is rather narrow due to student based sampling. Thus, it is unsurprising that age does not predict social media addiction with this sample. Regarding the relationship status, it is shown that being addicted to social media does not depend on being in a relationship or being single. This finding contradicts earlier work which demonstrated that individuals who are not in a relationship have higher levels of social media addiction (Andreassen et al., 2017). Still, the authors of that study also report that the impact of being in a relationship on social media addiction is rather small, almost negligible.

CONCLUSION

In this chapter, social media addiction construct is discussed extensively, starting with the facilitating conditions that cause social media addiction to become an emerging trend especially with the young generation. Diverse perspectives from psychology, psychiatry, and social psychology are reviewed to indicate conceptual differences and grasp the theoretical underpinning. Then, the influences of most significant personal, social and situational variables are presented. Prior work, which investigate the impact of these factors on social media addiction along with the impact of social media addiction on some of these factors, are assessed. Regarding the personal variables; demographics, self-esteem, personality traits, loneliness, well-being, anxiety and depression are studied as they received the most scholarly interest. For the social factors; need for affiliation/social enhancement, subjective norms, and personal/ professional/ academic life are scrutinized. Lastly, situational factors are investigated such as individuals' amount of social media use and motives leading people to social media use.

In order to better understand the impact of these defined factors, an empirical study is designed. Using a sample of university students, the predictors of social media addiction are examined. The study highlighted four major findings. The first one is, as anticipated, there exist a significant relationship between amount of social media usage and social media addiction. In that perspective, for future studies, the qualitative nature of that time might be studied by examining the amount spent for leisure (game etc.),interpersonal relation (texting, replying and so on) or gathering information (about others, events, news). The second finding demonstrates how loneliness and life satisfaction might be irrelevant factors to determine addictive type of behaviors. The literature proposes conflicting results; hence further examination is needed on the effect of these predictors. The third outcome validates, how the nature of the motives to use social media might produce social media addiction. Conformity and coping motives are stated as crucial contributors to social media addiction. Meaning that, individuals using social media to alleviate their negative mood or conform to social circle's norms have the tendency to get addicted. The forth finding supports the view that, a close relationship exists between improper use of social media while doing other staff (in the lecture, reading, driving etc.) and social media addiction. Finally, contrary to some of the prior research, the findings did not support the demographic characteristics effect on social media addiction. Even so, demographic factors need further examination perhaps on a wider and heterogeneous sample. The findings of the current study contributes to the social media addiction literature, in a both corroborating and contradicting manner with prior work. As a result, it is evident that this stream of research is at its infancy and more research is imperative.

As popularity of social media grows, recognizing adverse effects of social media addiction becomes essential. Compulsive use of social media has several negative correlates however majority of the studies in this domain are cross-sectional. Even though a number of relationships are depicted with these studies, causal inferences can not be made. There is a pressing need for longitudinal research, which will provide insight into the negative consequences of social media addiction. Understanding the direction of the relationship between social media addiction and variables such as depression, anxiety, and self-esteem is necessary.

REFERENCES

Abbasi, I. S. (2018). The link between romantic disengagement and Facebook addiction: Where does relationship commitment fit in? *The American Journal of Family Therapy*, *46*(4), 375–389. doi:10.108 0/01926187.2018.1540283

Abbasi, I. S. (2019). Social media addiction in romantic relationships: Does user's age influence vulnerability to social media infidelity? *Personality and Individual Differences*, *139*, 277–280. doi:10.1016/j. paid.2018.10.038

Al-Menayes, J. J. (2015). Social media use, engagement and addiction as predictors of academic performance. *International Journal of Psychological Studies*, *7*(4), 86–94. doi:10.5539/ijps.v7n4p86

Aladwani, A. M., & Almarzouq, M. (2016). Understanding compulsive social media use: The premise of complementing self-conceptions mismatch with technology. *Computers in Human Behavior*, *60*, 575–581. doi:10.1016/j.chb.2016.02.098

Allen, K. A., Ryan, T., Gray, D. L., McInerney, D. M., & Waters, L. (2014). Social media use and social connectedness in adolescents: The positives and the potential pitfalls. *The Australian Educational and Developmental Psychologist*, *31*(1), 18–31. doi:10.1017/edp.2014.2

American Psychiatric Association. (2013). *Diagnostic and Statistical Manual for Mental Disorders* (5th ed.). American Psychiatric Association.

Amichai-Hamburger, Y., Wainapel, G., & Fox, S. (2002). On the Internet no one knows I'm an introvert": Extroversion, neuroticism, and Internet interaction. *Cyberpsychology & Behavior*, *5*(2), 125–128. doi:10.1089/109493102753770507 PMID:12025878

Andreassen, C. S. (2015). Online social network site addiction: A comprehensive review. *Current Addiction Reports*, *2*(2), 175–184. doi:10.100740429-015-0056-9

Andreassen, C. S., Griffiths, M. D., Gjertsen, S. R., Krossbakken, E., Kvam, S., & Pallesen, S. (2013). The relationship between behavioral addictions and the five-factor model of personality. *Journal of Behavioral Addictions*, *2*(2), 90–99. doi:10.1556/JBA.2.2013.003 PMID:26165928

Andreassen, C. S., & Pallesen, S. (2014). Social network site addiction – An overview. *Current Pharmaceutical Design*, *20*(25), 4053–4061. doi:10.2174/13816128113199990616 PMID:24001298

Andreassen, C. S., Pallesen, S., & Griffiths, M. D. (2017). The relationship between addictive use of social media, narcissism, and self-esteem: Findings from a large national survey. *Addictive Behaviors*, *64*, 287–293. Advance online publication. doi:10.1016/j.addbeh.2016.03.006 PMID:27072491

Andreassen, C. S., Torsheim, T., Brunborg, G. S., & Pallesen, S. (2012). Development of a Facebook addiction scale. *Psychological Reports*, *110*(2), 501–517. doi:10.2466/02.09.18.PR0.110.2.501-517 PMID:22662404

Andreassen, C. S., Torsheim, T., & Pallesen, S. (2014). Use of online social network sites for personal purposes at work: Does it impair self-reported performance? *Comprehensive Psychology*, *3*(1), 18. doi:10.2466/01.21.CP.3.18

Atroszko, P. A., Balcerowska, J. M., Bereznowski, P., Biernatowska, A., Pallesen, S., & Andreassen, C. S. (2018). Facebook addiction among Polish undergraduate students: Validity of measurement and relationship with personality and well-being. *Computers in Human Behavior*, *85*, 329–338. doi:10.1016/j.chb.2018.04.001

Bányai, F., Zsila, Á., Király, O., Maraz, A., Elekes, Z., Griffiths, M. D., Andreassen, C. S., & Demetrovics, Z. (2017). Problematic social media use: Results from a large-scale nationally representative adolescent sample. *PLoS One*, *12*(1), e0169839. doi:10.1371/journal.pone.0169839 PMID:28068404

Baturay, M. H., & Toker, S. (2017). Self-esteem shapes the impact of GPA and general health on Facebook addiction: A mediation analysis. *Social Science Computer Review*, *35*(5), 555–575. doi:10.1177/0894439316656606

Bauer, J. M., Gai, P., Kim, J-H., Muth, T., & Wildman, S. (2002). *Broadband: Benefits and policy challenges*. A report prepared for Merit Network, Inc.

Baumeister, R. F. (1993). Understanding the inner nature of low self-esteem: Uncertain, fragile, protective, and conflicted. In *Self-esteem* (pp. 201–218). Springer. doi:10.1007/978-1-4684-8956-9_11

Beyens, I., Frison, E., & Eggermont, S. (2016). "I don't want to miss a thing": Adolescents' fear of missing out and its relationship to adolescents' social needs, Facebook use, and Facebook related stress. *Computers in Human Behavior*, *64*, 1–8. doi:10.1016/j.chb.2016.05.083

Bischof-Kastner, C., Kuntsche, E., & Wolstein, J. (2014). Identifying problematic Internet users: Development and validation of the Internet Motive Questionnaire for Adolescents (IMQ-A). *Journal of Medical Internet Research, 16*(10), e230. doi:10.2196/jmir.3398 PMID:25299174

Błachnio, A., Przepiorka, A., & Pantic, I. (2016). Association between Facebook addiction, self-esteem and life satisfaction: A cross-sectional study. *Computers in Human Behavior, 55,* 701–705. doi:10.1016/j.chb.2015.10.026

Blackwell, D., Leaman, C., Tramposch, R., Osborne, C., & Liss, M. (2017). Extraversion, neuroticism, attachment style and fear of missing out as predictors of social media use and addiction. *Personality and Individual Differences, 116,* 69–72. doi:10.1016/j.paid.2017.04.039

Block, M., Stern, D. B., Raman, K., Lee, S., Carey, J., Humphreys, A. A., ... Blood, A. J. (2014). The relationship between self-report of depression and media usage. *Frontiers in Human Neuroscience, 8,* 712. doi:10.3389/fnhum.2014.00712 PMID:25309388

Bodroža, B., & Jovanović, T. (2016). Validation of the new scale for measuring behaviors of Facebook users: Psycho-Social Aspects of Facebook Use (PSAFU). *Computers in Human Behavior, 54,* 425–435. doi:10.1016/j.chb.2015.07.032

Borsari, B., & Carey, K. B. (2003). Descriptive and injunctive norms in college drinking: A meta-analytic integration. *Journal of Studies on Alcohol, 64*(3), 331–341. doi:10.15288/jsa.2003.64.331 PMID:12817821

Boyce, P., & Parker, G. (1989). Development of a scale to measure interpersonal sensitivity. *The Australian and New Zealand Journal of Psychiatry, 23*(3), 341–351. doi:10.1177/000486748902300320 PMID:2803146

Bozoglan, B., Demirer, V., & Sahin, I. (2013). Loneliness, self-esteem, and life satisfaction as predictors of Internet addiction: A cross-sectional study among Turkish university students. *Scandinavian Journal of Psychology, 54*(4), 313–319. doi:10.1111jop.12049 PMID:23577670

Brailovskaia, J., Margraf, J., & Köllner, V. (2019). Addicted to Facebook? Relationship between Facebook Addiction Disorder, duration of Facebook use and narcissism in an inpatient sample. *Psychiatry Research, 273,* 52–57. doi:10.1016/j.psychres.2019.01.016 PMID:30639564

Burke, M., Marlow, C., Lento, T., Fitzpatrick, G., Hudson, S., Edwards, K., & Rodden, T. (2010). proceedings of the SIGCHI Conference on Human Factors in Computing Systems. *Social Network Activity and Social Well-Being,* 1909-1912.

Çam, E., & Isbulan, O. (2012). A new addiction for teacher candidates: Social networks. *The Turkish Online Journal of Educational Technology, 11,* 14–19.

Caplan, S. E. (2002). Problematic Internet use and psychosocial well-being: Development of a theory-based cognitive-behavioral measurement instrument. *Computers in Human Behavior, 18*(5), 553–575. doi:10.1016/S0747-5632(02)00004-3

Caplan, S. E. (2003). Preference for online social interaction: A theory of problematic Internet use and psychosocial well-being. *Communication Research, 30*(6), 625–648. doi:10.1177/0093650203257842

Caprara, G. V., Barbaranelli, C., Borgogni, L., & Perugini, M. (1993). The "Big Five Questionnaire": A new questionnaire to assess the five factor model. *Personality and Individual Differences*, *15*(3), 281–288. doi:10.1016/0191-8869(93)90218-R

Caprara, G. V., Barbaranelli, C., & Livi, S. (1994). Mapping personality dimensions in the Big Five model. *European Review of Applied Psychology*, *44*(1), 9–15.

Charney, T., & Greenberg, B. S. (2002). Uses and gratification of the Internet: Communication, technology and science. In C. Lin & D. Atkin (Eds.), *Communication, technology and society: New media adoption and use* (pp. 379–407). Hampton Pres.

Chen, W. J., Boase, J., & Wellman, B. (2002). The Global villagers: Comparing Internet users and uses around the world. In B. Wellman & C. Haythornthwaite (Eds.), *The Internet in Everyday Life* (pp. 74–113). Blackwell. doi:10.1002/9780470774298.ch2

Choi, Y. (2018). Narcissism and social media addiction in workplace. Journal of Asian Finance. *Economics and Business*, *5*(2), 95–104.

Chung, D., & Nam, C. S. (2007). An analysis of the variables predicting instant messenger use. *New Media & Society*, *9*(2), 212–234. doi:10.1177/1461444807072217

Cialdini, R. B., Kallgren, C. A., & Reno, R. R. (1991). A focus theory of normative conduct: A theoretical refinement and reevaluation of the role of norms in human behavior. In Advances in Experimental Social Psychology (Vol. 24, pp. 201–234). Academic Press. doi:10.1016/S0065-2601(08)60330-5

Clayton, R. B., Osborne, R. E., Miller, B. K., & Oberle, C. D. (2013). Loneliness, anxiousness, and substance use as predictors of Facebook use. *Computers in Human Behavior*, *29*(3), 687–693. doi:10.1016/j.chb.2012.12.002

Davis, F. (1989). Perceived usefulness, perceived ease of use, and user acceptance of information technology. *Management Information Systems Quarterly*, *13*(3), 319–339. doi:10.2307/249008

Davis, R. A. (2001). A cognitive–behavioral model of pathological Internet use. *Computers in Human Behavior*, *17*(2), 187–195. doi:10.1016/S0747-5632(00)00041-8

De Cock, R., Vangeel, J., Klein, A., Minotte, P., Rosas, O., & Meerkerk, G. J. (2014). Compulsive use of social networking sites in Belgium: Prevalence, profile, and the role of attitude toward work and school. *Cyberpsychology, Behavior, and Social Networking*, *17*(3), 166–171. doi:10.1089/cyber.2013.0029 PMID:24111599

Desjarlais, M., & Willoughby, T. (2010). A longitudinal study of the relation between adolescent boys and girls' computer use with friends and friendship quality: Support for the social compensation or the rich-get-richer hypothesis? *Computers in Human Behavior*, *26*(5), 896–905. doi:10.1016/j.chb.2010.02.004

Dhaha, I. S. Y. (2013). Predictors of Facebook addiction among youth: A structural equation modeling (SEM). *Journal of Social Sciences (COES&RJ-JSS)*, *2*(4), 186-195.

Dhir, A., Yossatorn, Y., Kaur, P., & Chen, S. (2018). Online social media fatigue and psychological wellbeing—A study of compulsive use, fear of missing out, fatigue, anxiety and depression. *International Journal of Information Management*, *40*, 141–152. doi:10.1016/j.ijinfomgt.2018.01.012

Diener, E. D., Emmons, R. A., Larsen, R. J., & Griffin, S. (1985). The satisfaction with life scale. *Journal of Personality Assessment*, *49*(1), 71–75. doi:10.120715327752jpa4901_13 PMID:16367493

Ebersole, S. (2000). Uses and gratifications of the Web among students. *Journal of Computer-Mediated Communication*, *6*(1), 0. doi:10.1111/j.1083-6101.2000.tb00111.x

Ellison, N. B., Steinfield, C., & Lampe, C. (2007). The benefits of Facebook "friends:" Social capital and college students' use of online social network sites. *Journal of Computer-Mediated Communication*, *12*(4), 1143–1168. doi:10.1111/j.1083-6101.2007.00367.x

Eraslan-Capan, B. (2015). Interpersonal sensitivity and problematic Facebook use in turkish university students. *The Anthropologist*, *21*(3), 395–403. doi:10.1080/09720073.2015.11891829

Feinstein, B. A., Bhatia, V., Hershenberg, R., & Davila, J. (2012). Another venue for problematic interpersonal behavior: The effects of depressive and anxious symptoms on social networking experiences. *Journal of Social and Clinical Psychology*, *31*(4), 356–382. doi:10.1521/jscp.2012.31.4.356

Ferguson, D., & Perse, E. (2000). The World Wide Web as a functional alternative to television. *Journal of Broadcasting & Electronic Media*, *44*(2), 155–174. doi:10.120715506878jobem4402_1

Gámez-Guadix, M. (2014). Depressive symptoms and problematic Internet use among adolescents: Analysis of the longitudinal relationships from the cognitive–behavioral model. *Cyberpsychology, Behavior, and Social Networking*, *17*(11), 714–719. doi:10.1089/cyber.2014.0226 PMID:25405784

Gibbs, J. L., Ellison, N. B., & Heino, R. D. (2006). Self-presentation in online personals: The role of anticipated future interaction, self-disclosure, and perceived success in Internet dating. *Communication Research*, *33*(2), 152–177. doi:10.1177/0093650205285368

Global Web Index. (2019). *Digital vs. Traditional Media Consumption'2019*. Retrieved February 28, 2020, from Global web index: https://www.globalwebindex.com/hubfs/Downloads/Digital_vs_Traditional_Media_Consumption-2019.pdf

Goldberg, I. (1996). *Internet addiction disorder*. Retrieved March 3, 2008, from http//www.cog.brown.edu/brochures/people/duchon/humor/internet.addiction.html

Gonzales, A. L., & Hancock, J. T. (2011). Mirror, mirror on my Facebook wall: Effects of exposure to Facebook on self-esteem. *Cyberpsychology, Behavior, and Social Networking*, *14*(1-2), 79–83. doi:10.1089/cyber.2009.0411 PMID:21329447

Griffiths, M. (1998). Internet addiction: does it really exist? In J. Gackenbach (Ed.), *Psychology and the Internet: Interpersonal, interpersonal and intranspersonal applications* (pp. 61–75). Academic Press.

Griffiths, M. D. (2010). The role of context in online gaming excess and addiction: Some case study evidence. *International Journal of Mental Health and Addiction*, *8*(1), 119–125. doi:10.100711469-009-9229-x

Griffiths, M. D., Kuss, D. J., & Demetrovics, Z. (2014). Social networking addiction: An overview of preliminary findings. In K. P. Rosenberg & L. C. Feder (Eds.), *Behavioral addictions: Criteria, evidence, and treatment* (pp. 119–141). Academic Press. doi:10.1016/B978-0-12-407724-9.00006-9

Grunbaum, J. A., Tortolero, S., Weller, N., & Gingiss, P. (2000). Cultural, social, and intrapersonal factors associated with substance use among alternative high school students. *Addictive Behaviors, 25*(1), 145–151. doi:10.1016/S0306-4603(99)00006-4 PMID:10708330

Hair, J. F., Black, W. C., Babin, B. J., Anderson, R. E., & Tatham, R. L. (2006). *Multivariate data analysis* (Vol. 6). Pearson Prentice Hall.

Hampton, K. N., & Wellman, B. (2003). Neighboring in netville: How the Internet supports community and social capital in a wired suburb. *City & Community, 2*(4), 277–311. doi:10.1046/j.1535-6841.2003.00057.x

Hays, R. D., & DiMatteo, M. R. (1987). A short-form measure of loneliness. *Journal of Personality Assessment, 51*(1), 69–81. doi:10.120715327752jpa5101_6 PMID:3572711

Hinsch, C., & Sheldon, K. M. (2013). The impact of frequent social Internet consumption: Increased procrastination and lower life satisfaction. *Journal of Consumer Behaviour, 12*(6), 496-505. doi:10.1002/cb.1453

Hormes, J. M., Kearns, B., & Timko, C. A. (2014). Craving Facebook? Behavioral addiction to online social networking and its association with emotion regulation deficits. *Addiction (Abingdon, England), 109*(12), 2079–2088. doi:10.1111/add.12713 PMID:25170590

Hosmer, D. W., & Lemeshow, S. (2000). *Applied Logistic Regression*. John Wiley & Sons, Inc., doi:10.1002/0471722146

Huang, L. Y., Hsieh, Y. J., & Wu, Y. C. J. (2014). Gratifications and social network service usage: The mediating role of online experience. *Information & Management, 51*(6), 774–782. doi:10.1016/j.im.2014.05.004

Hughes, D. J., Rowe, M., Batey, M., & Lee, A. (2012). A tale of two sites: Twitter vs. Facebook and the personality predictors of social media usage. *Computers in Human Behavior, 28*(2), 561–569. doi:10.1016/j.chb.2011.11.001

Ingólfsdóttir, H. R. (2017). *The relationship between social media use and self-esteem: gender difference and the effects of parental support* (Doctoral dissertation).

Joinson, A. N. (2008). Looking at, 'looking up' or 'keeping up with' people? Motives and uses of Facebook. *Proceeding of the SIGCHI Conference on Human Factors in Computing System.*

Junco, R. (2012). Too much face and not enough books: The relationship between multiple indices of Facebook use and academic performance. *Computers in Human Behavior, 28*(1), 187–198. doi:10.1016/j.chb.2011.08.026

Junco, R., & Cotten, S. R. (2012). No A 4 U: The relationship between multitasking and academic performance. *Computers & Education, 59*(2), 505–514. doi:10.1016/j.compedu.2011.12.023

Kalpidou, M., Costin, D., & Morris, J. (2011). The relationship between Facebook and the well-being of undergraduate college students. *Cyberpsychology, Behavior, and Social Networking, 14*(4), 183–189. doi:10.1089/cyber.2010.0061 PMID:21192765

Kang, S. (2007). Disembodiment in online social interaction: Impact of online chat on social support and psychosocial well-being. *Cyberpsychology & Behavior, 10*(3), 475–477. doi:10.1089/cpb.2006.9929 PMID:17594274

Karaiskos, D., Tzavellas, E., Balta, G., & Paparrigopoulos, T. (2010). P02-232-Social network addiction: A new clinical disorder? *European Psychiatry, 25*, 855. doi:10.1016/S0924-9338(10)70846-4

Katz, J. E., & Aspden, P. (1997). A nation of strangers? *Communications of the ACM, 40*(12), 81–86. doi:10.1145/265563.265575

Kaye, B. K., & Johnson, T. J. (2004). Web for all reasons: Uses and gratifications of Internet components for political information. *Telematics and Informatics, 21*(3), 197–223. doi:10.1016/S0736-5853(03)00037-6

Keepers, G. A. (1990). Pathological preoccupation with video games. *Journal of the American Academy of Child and Adolescent Psychiatry, 29*(1), 49–50. doi:10.1097/00004583-199001000-00009 PMID:2295578

Kim, J., & Haridakis, P. M. (2009). The role of Internet user characteristics and motives in explaining three dimensions of Internet addiction. *Journal of Computer-Mediated Communication, 14*(4), 988–1015. doi:10.1111/j.1083-6101.2009.01478.x

Kırcaburun, K., Kokkinos, C. M., Demetrovics, Z., Király, O., Griffiths, M. D., & Çolak, T. S. (2019). Problematic online behaviors among adolescents and emerging adults: Associations between cyberbullying perpetration, problematic social media use, and psychosocial factors. *International Journal of Mental Health and Addiction, 17*(4), 891–908. doi:10.100711469-018-9894-8

Kirschner, P. A., & Karpinski, A. C. (2010). Facebook® and academic performance. *Computers in Human Behavior, 26*(6), 1237–1245. doi:10.1016/j.chb.2010.03.024

Koc, M., & Gulyagci, S. (2013). Facebook addiction among Turkish college students: The role of psychological health, demographic, and usage characteristics. *Cyberpsychology, Behavior, and Social Networking, 16*(4), 279–284. doi:10.1089/cyber.2012.0249 PMID:23286695

Kraut, R., Kiesler, S., Boneva, B., Cummings, J., Helgeson, V., & Crawford, A. (2002). Internet Paradox Revisited. *The Journal of Social Issues, 58*(1), 49–74. doi:10.1111/1540-4560.00248

Kraut, R., Patterson, M., Landmark, V., Kielser, S., Mukophadhyaya, T., & Scherlis, W. (1998). Internet paradox: A social technology that reduces social involvement and psychological well-being? *The American Psychologist, 53*(9), 1017–1031. doi:10.1037/0003-066X.53.9.1017 PMID:9841579

Kross, E., Verduyn, P., Demiralp, E., Park, J., Lee, D. S., Lin, N., ... Sueur, C. (2013). Facebook use predicts declines in subjective well-being in young adults. *PLoS One, 8*(8), e69841. doi:10.1371/journal.pone.0069841 PMID:23967061

Kubey, R. W., Lavin, M. J., & Barrows, J. R. (2001). Internet use and collegiate academic performance decrements: Early findings. *Journal of Communication, 51*(2), 366–382. doi:10.1111/j.1460-2466.2001.tb02885.x

Kuss, D. J., & Griffiths, M. D. (2011). Online social networking and addiction—A review of the psychological literature. *International Journal of Environmental Research and Public Health, 8*(9), 3528–3552. doi:10.3390/ijerph8093528 PMID:22016701

Lansing, J. B., & Heyns, R. W. (1959). Need affiliation and frequency of four types of communication. *Journal of Abnormal and Social Psychology, 58*(3), 365–372. doi:10.1037/h0045906 PMID:13653887

Lau, W. W. (2017). Effects of social media usage and social media multitasking on the academic performance of university students. *Computers in Human Behavior, 68,* 286–291. doi:10.1016/j.chb.2016.11.043

Lee, E. B. (2015). Too much information: Heavy smartphone and Facebook utilization by African American young adults. *Journal of Black Studies, 46*(1), 44–61. doi:10.1177/0021934714557034

Lemon, J. (2002). Can we call behaviors addictive? *Clinical Psychologist, 6*(2), 44–49. doi:10.1080/1 3284200310001707411

Leung, L. (2004). Net-generation attributes and seductive properties of the Internet as predictors of online activities and Internet addiction. *Cyberpsychology & Behavior, 7*(3), 333–348. doi:10.1089/1094931041291303 PMID:15257834

Levenson, J. C., Shensa, A., Sidani, J. E., Colditz, J. B., & Primack, B. A. (2016). The association between social media use and sleep disturbance among young adults. *Preventive Medicine, 85,* 36–41. doi:10.1016/j.ypmed.2016.01.001 PMID:26791323

Lin, L. Y., Sidani, J. E., Shensa, A., Radovic, A., Miller, E., Colditz, J. B., & Primack, B. A. (2016). Association between social media use and depression among U.S. young adults. *Depression and Anxiety, 33*(4), 323-331. . doi:10.1002/da.22466

Liu y Lin, B. A. (2016). Association between social media use and depression among US young adults. *Depression and Anxiety, 33*(4), 323–331. doi:10.1002/da.22466 PMID:26783723

Longstreet, P., & Brooks, S. (2017). Life satisfaction: A key to managing internet & social media addiction. *Technology in Society, 50,* 73–77. doi:10.1016/j.techsoc.2017.05.003

Loos, M. D. (2002). The synergy of depravity and loneliness in alcoholism: A new conceptualization, and old problem. *Counseling and Values, 46*(3), 199–212. doi:10.1002/j.2161-007X.2002.tb00213.x

Malik, S., & Khan, M. (2015). Impact of facebook addiction on narcissistic behavior and self-esteem among students. *JPMA. The Journal of the Pakistan Medical Association, 65*(3), 260–263. PMID:25933557

Maraz, A., Eisinger, A., Hende, B., Urbán, R., Paksi, B., Kun, B., Kökönyei, G., Griffiths, M. D., & Demetrovics, Z. (2015). Measuring compulsive buying behaviour: Psychometric validity of three different scales and prevalence in the general population and in shopping centres. *Psychiatry Research, 225*(3), 326–334. doi:10.1016/j.psychres.2014.11.080 PMID:25595336

Marino, C., Gini, G., Vieno, A., & Spada, M. M. (2018). A comprehensive meta-analysis on problematic Facebook use. *Computers in Human Behavior, 83,* 262–277. doi:10.1016/j.chb.2018.02.009

Marino, C., Vieno, A., Moss, A. C., Caselli, G., Nikčević, A. V., & Spada, M. M. (2016). Personality, motives and metacognitions as predictors of problematic Facebook use in university students. *Personality and Individual Differences, 101,* 70–77. doi:10.1016/j.paid.2016.05.053

Marlatt, G. A., Baer, J. S., Donovan, D. M., & Kivlahan, D. R. (1988). Addictive behaviors: Etiology and treatment. *Annual Review of Psychology, 39*(1), 223–252. doi:10.1146/annurev.ps.39.020188.001255 PMID:3278676

Marshall, T. C., Lefringhausen, K., & Ferenczi, N. (2015). The Big Five, self-esteem, and narcissism as predictors of the topics people write about in Facebook status updates. *Personality and Individual Differences, 85*, 35–40. doi:10.1016/j.paid.2015.04.039

Masur, P. K., Reinecke, L., Ziegele, M., & Quiring, O. (2014). The interplay of intrinsic need satisfaction and Facebook specific motives in explaining addictive behavior on Facebook. *Computers in Human Behavior, 39*, 376–386. doi:10.1016/j.chb.2014.05.047

Mazzoni, E., & Iannone, M. (2014). From high school to university: Impact of social networking sites on social capital in the transitions of emerging adults. *British Journal of Educational Technology, 45*(2), 303–315. doi:10.1111/bjet.12026

McDougall, M. A., Walsh, M., Wattier, K., Knigge, R., Miller, L., Stevermer, M., & Fogas, B. S. (2016). The effect of social networking sites on the relationship between perceived social support and depression. *Psychiatry Research, 246*, 223–229. doi:10.1016/j.psychres.2016.09.018 PMID:27721061

McKenna, K. Y. A., & Bargh, J. A. (2000). Plan 9 from cyberspace: The implication of the Internet for personality and social psychology. *Personality and Social Psychology Review, 4*(1), 57–75. doi:10.1207/S15327957PSPR0401_6

Medora, N. P., & Woodward, J. C. (1991). Factors associated with loneliness among alcoholics in rehabilitation centers. *The Journal of Social Psychology, 131*(6), 769–779. doi:10.1080/00224545.1991.9924664 PMID:1667810

Meier, A., Reinecke, L., & Meltzer, C. E. (2016). "Facebocrastination"? Predictors of using Facebook for procrastination and its effects on students' well-being. *Computers in Human Behavior, 64*, 65–76. doi:10.1016/j.chb.2016.06.011

Mesch, G. S. (2001). Social relationships and Internet use among adolescents in Israel. *Social Science Quarterly, 82*(2), 329–339. doi:10.1111/0038-4941.00026

Mihajlović, G., Hinić, D., Damjanović, A., Gajić, T., & Dukić-Dejanović, S. (2008). Excessive internet use and depressive disorders. *Psychiatria Danubina, 20*, 5–14. PMID:18376325

Monacis, L., De Palo, V., Griffiths, M. D., & Sinatra, M. (2017). Social networking addiction, attachment style, and validation of the Italian version of the Bergen Social Media Addiction Scale. *Journal of Behavioral Addictions, 6*(2), 178–186. doi:10.1556/2006.6.2017.023 PMID:28494648

Moqbel, M., & Kock, N. (2018). Unveiling the dark side of social networking sites: Personal and work-related consequences of social networking site addiction. *Information & Management, 55*(1), 109–119. doi:10.1016/j.im.2017.05.001

Moreau, A., Laconi, S., Delfour, M., & Chabrol, H. (2015). Psychopathological profiles of adolescent and young adult problematic Facebook users. *Computers in Human Behavior, 44*, 64–69. doi:10.1016/j.chb.2014.11.045

Moreno, M. A., Jelenchick, L. A., Egan, K. G., Cox, E., Young, H., Gannon, K. E., & Becker, T. (2011). Feeling bad on Facebook: Depression disclosures by college students on a social networking site. *Depression and Anxiety*, *28*(6), 447–455. doi:10.1002/da.20805 PMID:21400639

Murray, H. A. (1938). *Explorations in Personality*. Oxford University Press.

Olowu, A. O., & Seri, F. O. (2012). A study of social network addiction among youths in Nigeria. *Journal of Social Science and Policy Review*, *4*, 62–71.

Orford, J. (2001). *Excessive appetites: A psychological view of addictions* (2nd ed.). Wiley.

Pantic, I. (2014). Online social networking and mental health. *Cyberpsychology, Behavior, and Social Networking*, *17*(10), 652–657. doi:10.1089/cyber.2014.0070 PMID:25192305

Papacharissi, Z., & Rubin, A. M. (2000). Predictors of Internet use. *Journal of Broadcasting & Electronic Media*, *44*(2), 175–196. doi:10.120715506878jobem4402_2

Peele, S. (1985). *The Meaning of Addiction*. Lexington Books.

Peter, J., & Valkenburg, P. M. (2006). Adolescents' exposure to sexually explicit material on the Internet. *Communication Research*, *33*(2), 178–204. doi:10.1177/0093650205285369

Pontes, H. M., Kuss, D. J., & Griffiths, M. D. (2015). Clinical psychology of Internet addiction: A review of its conceptualization, prevalence, neuronal processes, and implications for treatment. *Neuroscience and Neuroeconomics*, *4*, 11–23.

Pozzoli, T., & Gini, G. (2013). Why do bystanders of bullying help or not? A multidimensional model. *The Journal of Early Adolescence*, *33*(3), 315–340. doi:10.1177/0272431612440172

Prensky, M. (2001). Digital natives, digital immigrants part 1. *On the Horizon*, *9*, 1–6.

Przepiorka, A., & Blachnio, A. (2016). Time perspective in Internet and Facebook addiction. *Computers in Human Behavior*, *60*, 13–18. doi:10.1016/j.chb.2016.02.045

Przybylski, A. K., Murayama, K., DeHaan, C. R., & Gladwell, V. (2013). Motivational, emotional, and behavioral correlates of fear of missing out. *Computers in Human Behavior*, *29*(4), 1841–1848. doi:10.1016/j.chb.2013.02.014

Raacke, J., & Bonds-Raacke, J. (2008). MySpace and Facebook: Applying the uses and gratifications theory to exploring friend-networking sites. *Cyberpsychology & Behavior*, *11*(2), 169–174. doi:10.1089/cpb.2007.0056 PMID:18422409

Rabaa'i, A. A., Bhat, H., & Al-Maati, S. A. (2018). Theorising social networks addiction: An empirical investigation. *International Journal of Social Media and Interactive Learning Environments*, *6*(1), 1–24. doi:10.1504/IJSMILE.2018.092363

Reid Chassiakos, Y., Radesky, J., Christakis, D., Moreno, M. A., & Cross, C. (2016). Children and Adolescents and Digital Media. *Pediatrics*, *138*(5), 1–18. doi:10.1542/peds.2016-2593 PMID:27940795

Rheingold, H. (1993). *The virtual community: Homesteading on the electronic frontier*. Addison Wesley.

Ross, C., Orr, E. S., Sisic, M., Arseneault, J. M., Simmering, M. G., & Orr, R. R. (2009). Personality and motivations associated with Facebook use. *Computers in Human Behavior*, 25(2), 578–586. doi:10.1016/j.chb.2008.12.024

Ryan, T., Chester, A., Reece, J., & Xenos, S. (2014). The uses and abuses of Facebook: A review of Facebook addiction. *Journal of Behavioral Addictions*, 3(3), 133–148. doi:10.1556/JBA.3.2014.016 PMID:25317337

Ryan, T., Reece, J., Chester, A., & Xenos, S. (2016). Who gets hooked on Facebook? An exploratory typology of problematic Facebook users. *Cyberpsychology (Brno)*, 10(3). Advance online publication. doi:10.5817/CP2016-3-4

Sagioglou, C., & Greitemeyer, T. (2014). Facebook's emotional consequences: Why Facebook causes a decrease in mood and why people still use it. *Computers in Human Behavior, 35*, 359-363.. doi:10.1016/j. chb.2014.03.003

Sanders, C. E., Field, T. M., Diego, M., & Kaplan, M. (2000). The relationship of Internet use To depression and social isolation among adolescents. *Adolescence, 35*, 237–242. PMID:11019768

Satici, S. A., & Uysal, R. (2015). Well-being and problematic Facebook use. *Computers in Human Behavior, 49*, 185-190. doi:10.1016/j.chb.2015.03.005

Savci, M., & Aysan, F. (2017). Technological addictions and social connectedness: Predictor effect of internet addiction, social media addiction, digital game addiction and smartphone addiction on social connectedness. *Dusunen Adam: Journal of Psychiatry & Neurological Sciences*, 30(3), 202–216. doi:10.5350/DAJPN2017300304

Shaffer, H. J. (1996). Understanding the means and objects of addiction: Technology, the Internet and gambling. *Journal of Gambling Studies*, 12(4), 461–469. doi:10.1007/BF01539189 PMID:24234163

Sharifah, S. S., Omar, S. Z., Bolong, J., & Osman, M. N. (2011). Facebook addiction among female university students. *Revista De Administratie Publica Si Politici Sociale*, 3(7), 95.

Sheldon, P. (2009). Maintain or develop new relationships. Gender differences in Facebook use. *Rocky Mountain Communication Review*, 6(1), 51–56.

Shen, C., & Williams, D. (2011). Unpacking time online: Connecting internet and massively multiplayer online game use with psychosocial well-being. *Communication Research*, 38(1), 123–149. doi:10.1177/0093650210377196

Shensa, A., Escobar-Viera, C. G., Sidani, J. E., Bowman, N. D., Marshal, M. P., & Primack, B. A. (2017). Problematic social media use and depressive symptoms among US young adults: A nationally-representative study. *Social Science & Medicine*, 182, 150–157. doi:10.1016/j.socscimed.2017.03.061 PMID:28446367

Song, I., LaRose, R., Eastin, M., & Lin, C. (2004). Internet gratifications and Internet addiction: On the uses and abuses of new media. *Cyberpsychology & Behavior*, 7(4), 384–394. doi:10.1089/cpb.2004.7.384 PMID:15331025

Sriwilai, K., & Charoensukmongkol, P. (2016). Face it, don't Facebook it: Impacts of social media addiction on mindfulness, coping strategies and the consequence on emotional exhaustion. *Stress and Health*, *32*(4), 427–434. doi:10.1002mi.2637 PMID:25825273

Steinfield, C., Ellison, N. B., & Lampe, C. (2008). Social capital, self-esteem, and use of online social network sites: A longitudinal analysis. *Journal of Applied Developmental Psychology*, *29*(6), 434–445. doi:10.1016/j.appdev.2008.07.002

Stoll, C. (1995). *Silicon snake oil*. Doubleday.

Swann Jr, W. B. (1996). *Self-traps: The elusive quest for higher self-esteem*. WH Freeman/Times Books/ Henry Holt & Co.

Tang, J. H., Chen, M. C., Yang, C. Y., Chung, T. Y., & Lee, Y. A. (2016). Personality traits, interpersonal relationships, online social support, and Facebook addiction. *Telematics and Informatics*, *33*(1), 102–108. doi:10.1016/j.tele.2015.06.003

Turel, O., He, Q., Xue, G., Xiao, L., & Bechara, A. (2014). Examination of neural systems sub-serving Facebook "addiction". *Psychological Reports*, *115*(3), 675–695. doi:10.2466/18.PR0.115c31z8 PMID:25489985

Turkle, S. (1996). Virtuality and its discontents: Searching for community in cyberspace. *The American Prospect*, *24*, 50–57.

Valentine, O. A. (2013). Uses and gratifications of Facebook members 35 years and older. In *The Social Media Industries* (pp. 188–212). Routledge.

Valkenburg, P. M., & Peter, J. (2009). Social consequences of the Internet for adolescents: A decade of research. *Current Directions in Psychological Science*, *18*(1), 1–5. doi:10.1111/j.1467-8721.2009.01595.x

Valkenburg, P. M., Peter, J., & Schouten, A. P. (2006). Friend networking sites and their relationship to adolescents' well-being and social self-esteem. *Cyberpsychology & Behavior*, *9*(5), 584–590. doi:10.1089/ cpb.2006.9.584 PMID:17034326

Van Deursen, A. J. A. M., Bolle, C. L., Hegner, S., & Kommers, P. A. M. (2015). Modeling habitual and addictive smartphone behavior: The role of smartphone usage types, emotional intelligence, social stress, self-regulation, age, and gender. *Computers in Human Behavior*, *45*, 411–420. doi:10.1016/j. chb.2014.12.039

Venkatesh, V., Morris, M. G., Davis, G. B., & Davis, F. D. (2003). User acceptance of information technology. *Management Information Systems Quarterly*, *27*(3), 425–478. doi:10.2307/30036540

Veroff, J., Reuman, D., & Feld, S. (1984). Motive in American men and women across the adult life span. *Developmental Psychology*, *20*(6), 1142–1158. doi:10.1037/0012-1649.20.6.1142

Vogel, E. A., Rose, J. P., Roberts, L. R., & Eckles, K. (2014). Social comparison, social media, and self-esteem. *Psychology of Popular Media Culture*, *3*(4), 206–222. doi:10.1037/ppm0000047

Wang, C. W., Ho, R. T., Chan, C. L., & Tse, S. (2015). Exploring personality characteristics of Chinese adolescents with internet-related addictive behaviors: Trait differences for gaming addiction and social networking addiction. *Addictive Behaviors, 42,* 32–35. doi:10.1016/j.addbeh.2014.10.039 PMID:25462651

Widyanto, L., & McMurran, M. (2004). The psychometric properties of the internet addiction test. *Cyberpsychology & Behavior, 7*(4), 443–450. doi:10.1089/cpb.2004.7.443 PMID:15331031

Wilson, K., Fornasier, S., & White, K. M. (2010). Psychological predictors of young adults' use of social networking sites. *Cyberpsychology, Behavior, and Social Networking, 13*(2), 173–177. doi:10.1089/cyber.2009.0094 PMID:20528274

Wilson, R. E., Gosling, S. D., & Graham, L. T. (2012). A review of Facebook research in the social sciences. *Perspectives on Psychological Science, 7*(3), 203–220. doi:10.1177/1745691612442904 PMID:26168459

Woods, H. C., & Scott, H. (2016). # Sleepyteens: Social media use in adolescence is associated with poor sleep quality, anxiety, depression and low self-esteem. *Journal of Adolescence, 51,* 41–49. doi:10.1016/j.adolescence.2016.05.008 PMID:27294324

Younes, F., Halawi, G., Jabbour, H., El Osta, N., Karam, L., Hajj, A., & Khabbaz, L. R. (2016). Internet addiction and relationships with insomnia, anxiety, depression, stress and self-esteem in university students: A cross-sectional designed study. *PLoS One, 11*(9), e0161126. doi:10.1371/journal.pone.0161126 PMID:27618306

Young, K. S. (2004). Internet addiction: A New Clinical Phenomenon and Its Consequences. *The American Behavioral Scientist, 48*(4), 402–415. doi:10.1177/0002764204270278

Young, K. S., & Rogers, R. C. (1998). The relationship between depression and Internet addiction. *Cyberpsychology & Behavior, 1*(1), 25–28. doi:10.1089/cpb.1998.1.25

Zivnuska, S., Carlson, J. R., Carlson, D. S., Harris, R. B., & Harris, K. J. (2019). Social media addiction and social media reactions: The implications for job performance. *The Journal of Social Psychology, 159*(6), 746–760. doi:10.1080/00224545.2019.1578725 PMID:30821647

This research was previously published in Analyzing Global Social Media Consumption; pages 155-182, copyright year 2021 by Information Science Reference (an imprint of IGI Global).

Chapter 52
Aesthetics Perceptions of Social Media Generations

Aylin Tutgun Ünal
Üsküdar University, Turkey

ABSTRACT

This chapter aimed to investigate the online value and behavior transfer of generations who use social media with the phenomenon of aestheticization. By examining the social media generations' preferences, usage habits, the levels of acceptance of differences and the effects of social media use on the work life in the light of researches, generations' togetherness and differences on the online network are revealed. In social networks, generations can provide power by affecting each other's moods, and can easily impose violence, aggression, and power factors on others by making fun. When compared to older generations, the fact that young generations prefer social media environments that are with more photo and video sharing makes for them to produce/consume many emotions that have been made usual with aestheticization, especially the information that contains violence. At the end of this chapter, some suggestions are made including family communication and trust model named "5S+1M."

INTRODUCTION

We live in an era surrounded by social media. Social media, which has transformed many ways of doing work in all areas of life, has influenced people of all ages. Today, the effects of social media are discussed along with many economic, technological and social events since social media has taken over the world with its global communication network.

Social media can easily be used by individuals of all ages. Now that everyone can access the internet in an easy and inexpensive way, the spread of Web 2.0 technologies has brought interpersonal communication from the real environment to the virtual environment. Thus, people who cannot communicate comfortably in face-to-face communication can be quite social and charismatic online. The effect of communication that the person provides globally through social networks can be quite different and powerful than the real life.

DOI: 10.4018/978-1-6684-6307-9.ch052

The effects of digitalization and the transformations it creates are spoken worldwide. Besides the social effects, our communication, value transfer, the ways of doing work and even our behavior have been transformed under the influence of social media when the individual is taken into consideration. Therefore, it is seen that many sociological issues addressed in real life are reconsidered by including the effects of social media in current studies. Digitalization has profoundly influenced research in all fields. One of these areas is communication. The forms of interpersonal communication and value transfer are signs of being a society. Social coexistence is important, and today, societies have taken their place in online networks as virtual societies by changing platforms.

Intergenerational value transfer has also been influenced by online platforms and especially social media networks that have emerged with Web 2.0 technologies. Tarhan (2018) divides the values into two as universal and cultural. Accordingly, culture-specific values consist of universal values mixed with various doses. For example, while one culture emphasizes love, another one emphasizes honesty and another diligence. However, in all of these cultures, the social unity of the society is created with bricks built from values. There is a dose difference between the anonymous values of each society and the cultural identity of the society is shaped accordingly.

There are people from many cultures in the virtual world just as in the real world. The participatory culture is generally the dominant culture in societies. In such a culture, members believe that their contributions are important and feel that they have established a certain social bond with each other. In this culture, it is very important for people to be accepted in the society and what someone else thinks. The most common example of participatory culture nowadays is social media networks. It is important for people on social media networks to be accepted by others on their networks. Therefore, people try to be accepted with edited contents in photographs, text and video formats. The thoughts, the quantity of "likes" and the comments represent being accepted by the others on the network in social media culture.

On the other hand, social media includes people of all ages and this made it necessary to reconsider the concept of generation. Generation studies used to address intergenerational communication and value transfer in the real life. Nowadays, the fact that people behave differently on the online platforms caused the need to update the generation studies by taking into consideration the interactions in the virtual environment. Generations are examined around the world by grouping with certain names. Thus, generations are generally called as the Silent Generation (1927-1945), Baby Boomer (1946-1964), Generation X (1965-1979), Generation Y (1980-1999) and Generation Z (2000 and later).

When the literature is examined, there are many studies conducted according to the generation perspective. In these research, by focusing on the value transfer between generations, the work life, school life and communication habits of different age groups were investigated (Akdemir et al., 2013; Alwin & Mccammon, 2007; Biggs, 2007; Ekşili & Antalyalı, 2017; Latif & Serbest, 2014; Özdemir, 2017; Yıldırım & Becerikli, 2013). In fact, in a research, multi-dimensional scales were developed with the aim of understanding generations' work life, acceptance of differences and social media usage levels (3 scales can be used together or separately) (Deniz & Tutgun-Ünal, 2019a). In order to understand the generations, the use of social media must be investigated and its great impact should not be overlooked.

When conducting a research tried to understand the generations who use social media, it is important to consider the conditions of the period as generations differ in adapting to the work life, technology and even life itself. In addition, the fact that the Generation Y being quite different from each other by attending two different types of schools, even if they are members of the same generation, revealed that the subject of the generation should be studied more individually (Ekşili & Antalyalı, 2017).

Due to the consideration of online values and behaviors in social media networks, Tutgun-Ünal and Deniz (2020a) named the generations as "social media generations" and examined them by grouping according to the worldwide accepted names, as Baby Boomer, X, Y and Z. Since social media is a means of communication which is independent of time and space on a global scale, people from different religions, ethnic groups and different cultures are able to interact with one another. Billions of people from all cultures spread information by sharing content from massive online networks. This information affects other billions of people in the network. It is possible to spread various emotions through social networks by hiding a message under a photo or video. This raises emotional transmission on social networks.

Christakis and Fowler (2012) argue that there are three degrees of influence in social networks. To them, emotions spread to three degrees in social networks. Mathematical analysis of the social networks shows that the probability of a person to be happy increases by 15% when a person at one degree away is happy. The impact of happiness is 10% for people from two degrees away who can be friend of a friend, and about 6% for people from three degrees away who can be friend of a friend of a friend. At four degrees away, the effect disappears. Thus, it is seen that as the person expands the network on social media, their power of influence will increase. So much so that a person's influence on social media will be many times greater than it is in everyday life.

This situation indicates the potential of information spread over social media to bear the elements of aestheticized fear, violence and power. Social media are interactive forms of mass media and members can easily spread their feelings to others by sending messages in the social media society. As known; mass media played a preliminary and an important role in reaching the masses by aestheticizing violence. Nowadays, many moods are easily transferred via social media.

People on social media have the power to influence each other by sharing. We see in many instances that people from different places, regardless of the distance, use social media networks effectively to create unity in a subject at a speed that would not be possible in daily life. In today's new media age, social media networks need to be analyzed by dividing online users into generations. Since it is very important to know how value, behavior and aesthetic contents transfer between generations are transformed by digitalization. In this section, it is aimed to discuss the effects of generations' associations and social media interactions on the values and behaviors of the generations with the research data and aesthetic perspective.

BACKGROUND

While the relationship of people with mass media such as newspapers, radio and television has been examined (Pecchioni, Wright & Nussbaum, 2005; Williams, 2001; Williams & Harwood, 2008), the relationship of different generations with computers, the internet, mobile phones and especially social media has been examined with the rapid spread of Web 2.0 technologies, (Asmafiliz & Şalvarcı Türeli, 2018; Dyke, Haynes & Ferguson, 2007; Kuyucu, 2017; Özdemir, 2017; Sağır & Eraslan, 2019; Süer, Sezgin & Oral, 2017).

We are going through a period when the violence that exists in our lives spreads to the media. Violence, shaped and changed according to societies and culture, has both physical and symbolic dimension. A while ago, it was discussed as a common element of advertisements but now, it has become a common element of social media by being shaped and aestheticized. With this way, it gains a new aesthetic dimension, and normalized with the images of violence that are now seen as natural and harmless.

The increasing problem of violence in the postmodern world needs to be understood how and in what content the symbolic violence is included in the media (Çevikalp, 2020). In this regard, it is important to know which generations share content on social media, and on which social media platforms. Generations have different characteristics and each generation has a tolerance threshold for different information. Understanding social media generations will be successful in finding solutions to problems since aestheticized symbolic violence also has a certain tolerance threshold in social networks.

In a postmodern structure, the postmodern violence concept reflects violence as a source of entertainment. Adorno and Horkheimer draws attention to the phenomenon of violence in films in the culture industry and talks about the transformation of the pleasure taken from violence into violence against the audience (Adorno & Horkheimer, 2014: p. 185). In this context, it can be said that the violence -underlying many entertaining content on social media- penetrates especially the child users.

Cinema and digital platforms resort to violence to attract attention. Not only children but users of all ages randomly click to contents that attract their attention even if it is not intended to. This increases the spread of violence to a wide audience. With aesthetics, the images of violence that are perceived as natural and more harmless are almost neutralized and normalized (Bauman, 2001). In this context, it shows that people are exposed to fear, violence, anger and power without realizing.

According to Çevikalp (2020), violence activates impulses and desires within people and individuals, and sets a negative example for society by disrupting the level of consciousness; meaning that it keeps the society away from peace. Violence exponentially legitimizes its existence through the media. Furthermore, the diffusion of negative content compared to positive is much faster in social media. Since social media sharing has the potential to create unrestlessness and critical emotional impact on people, it is seen that the research is done in the direction of what types of content the generations produce and consume.

Tutgun-Ünal and Deniz (2020a) obtained interesting results in a study that measured the "social media generations' tolerance to differences" in order to understand whether the generations' sharing affected each other.

Accordingly, getting high scores at the work life scale is interpreted as being distant to conventionalism, whereas getting low scores is interpreted as being close to conventionalism in their generation research. As a result of the research, the acceptance of different religious/ethnic structures of the youngest generation who are raised with technology was found low and it was found that technology supports a conventionalist structure rather than modernizing it. When each generation is taken into consideration, the definition is centered at the differences from the generation called Silent Generation or "Conventionalists" (Figure 1).

Surprisingly, the fact that the Generation Z, which is located close to the conventional generation, does not tolerate differences in global communication will also determine their online behavior. Here, innovations adapted to life with globalization and opening up to the outside world are described as "modernity". In this way, it can be said that the online values and behaviors of the generations differ from being conventional to being modern by leading to real life transformations.

When the generations that come together in social media platforms in proportion to their preferences are examined, it is seen that older generations use Facebook and spread information in line with their interests. Instagram usage rate of the younger generation is found to be high in social media research conducted in Turkey (Tutgun-Ünal & Deniz, 2020a, 2020b).

Figure 1. Intergenerational transition

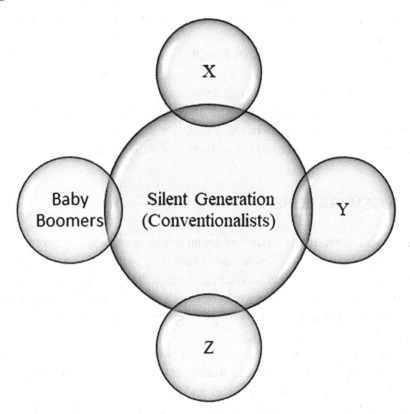

According to the research, visual content, especially photos (selfies or multiple photos), Generations Y and Z who like sharing videos are found to come together in Instagram environment. YouTube and Instagram usage rate of Zs were found to be close to each other, and the YouTube usage rate is increasing day by day. Considering the Ys, the YouTube usage rate is not as high as the Zs. At this point, it can be said that Ys and Zs are more together in the Instagram environment, but Zs are concentrated in the YouTube environment. Thus, it is possible to talk about the existence of online networks where generations are both concentrated in the same environment and clustered separately.

When Generation X and Baby Boomer Generation are considered, it is stated that Baby Boomer Generation uses Facebook in first place. Although Facebook is the most used platform in Generation X, Instagram usage rates are close to Facebook (Tutgun-Ünal & Deniz, 2020a). Accordingly, Instagram can be considered as the intersection point of Generation X with Generation Y. In this intersection zone, Zs and Baby Boomers continue to exist even though the usage rate is low.

From this point of view, it can be said that there are certain intersection areas in social media environments and all generations came together in these areas to a certain extent with the flow of information in that direction. It is observed that with the spread of information, Facebook is associated with the Baby Boomer Generation, who is dominant in determining its own natural flow, whereas Ys are more dominant in Instagram and yet creating a mosaic formation is seen with the information spread by Xs and Zs.

Thus, it can be concluded that generations that show themselves predominantly in social media platforms at certain rates have a say in being exposed to information that suits for them. When considered as a virtual version of real life, it is clear that online social networks contain separate societies and cultures within themselves. Therefore, the online version of the participatory culture mentioned in real life can be called as social network culture.

The fact that young generations prefer social media platforms where more visual content is at the forefront shows that they demand more photos and videos with symbolic violence. And the fact that older generations are on Facebook has shown that different age groups demand content on different topics on different platforms. The presence of users in different profiles on many platforms has increased the spread of symbolic violence to content of many interests. Therefore, understanding the social media generations is also necessary to understand the aesthetics of online content.

SOCIAL MEDIA GENERATIONS

In previous years, it was stated in the studies of social media users that the internet was mostly used by the young population. Wright (2011) even made a reference to the new growing population, today's Generation Z, by calling "Net Generation" at the beginning of 2000s. Nowadays, as the intensive use of users of all ages expose to social media networks, research are conducted with separated samples that are not only for young people but for all age groups based on the generation theory (Deniz & Tutgun-Ünal, 2019a; Tutgun-Ünal & Deniz, 2020a).

Due to the consideration of online values and behaviors in social media networks, Tutgun-Ünal and Deniz (2020a) named the generations as "social media generations" which are Baby Boomer, X, Y and Z. With 516 participants, social media preferences and purposes of generations are examined in their research. As a result, it has been revealed that 70,6% of the Generation X, which covers the dates of 1965-1979, follows and likes the current news on social media. The older social media users who are the Baby Boomer Generation born between 1946 and 1964, %56,7 have stated that they liked the content related to the current news on social media. This showed that the generations who are not familiar with technology when they were born are now compatible with the social media era.

Especially due to the need to follow current news, the presence of people who are connected to social media on a daily basis reveals that the need to be aware of life globally is now met from social media. Considering younger generations, it was stated in the same research that Generation Y followed a significant amount of news from social media (64.5%), that is, those born between 1980 and 1999 liked the current news. Thus, in today's world, where social media networks play a heavy role in meeting the needs of getting news from all around the world, especially the posts of citizens who share first-hand contents are seemed to be very valuable.

The rate of liking the current news content of the Generation Z, that is, those who born in 2000 and later, were found to be 21,6% and that they like different contents more. In the research, it was revealed that the generation that liked sports content the most was Generation Z which almost half of them follow sports news. Further, news tracking was seen in this generation only with a content difference.

In the examinations made for the Generations Y and Z, it was revealed that in the first place, young people use the Instagram application where visual sharing is at the forefront and they like the selfie content more than the older ones. Particularly, multiple photographs are liked by the Generation Y the most, while video/music contents are mostly liked and shared by the Generation Z (84.4%). Thus, there is a connection between the most used social media application and the most liked content types.

Table 1. Likes of generations on social media content (Tutgun-Ünal & Deniz, 2020a)

Social Media Contents	Baby Boomer		X		Y		Z	
	n	%	n	%	n	%	n	%
Multiple Photos	8	26,7	12	35,3	93	50,8	95	35,3
Education	14	**46,7**	21	**61,8**	116	63,4	80	29,7
Handcraft	4	13,3	11	32,4	53	29	71	26,4
Current News	17	**56,7**	24	**70,6**	118	**64,5**	58	21,6
Motto	7	23,3	9	26,5	43	23,5	89	33,1
Selfie	3	10	6	17,6	66	36,1	103	38,3
Video/Music	13	43,3	19	55,9	133	**72,7**	227	**84,4**
Politics	12	40	15	44,1	44	24	10	3,7
Animals	8	26,7	6	17,6	53	29	78	29
Sports	6	20	8	23,5	69	37,7	133	**49,4**
Recipes	7	23,3	12	35,3	58	31,7	47	17,5
Advertisements	-	-	5	14,7	33	18	10	3,7

On the other hand, it is stated that the Generation X and Baby Boomers use Facebook in the first place and like current news and educational content the most. Further, the Facebook usage rate of younger generations is at 10%. The gap between these generations shows that the platforms on which the posts are shared have a specific-mass in themselves and that people of all ages are not on the same platforms in the same proportions. Thus it is clear that there are often links between which age group or which communities they are associated with and the types of shared content.

With the increased interest in social media networks and the addition of people from different ages, regions and cultures to the networks day by day, these differences become widespread by leading to a change in social media preferences. For example, Facebook has a specific user group in itself where they share similar content on the network, and this causes another group to prefer Instagram, which is another social media application, by liking the content there. Therefore, it is seen that researchers concentrate on the users in the context of their social media preferences and online habits.

On the other hand, with the emergence of new social media applications day by day, it is seen in many examples that the demand for the previous one may decrease over time. As in the example of Instagram, while young people prefer Facebook in the first place earlier, they focus on Instagram now. In fact, it is reported that the Generation Z's usage of YouTube is becoming closer to Instagram. Besides, according to Tutgun-Ünal and Deniz (2020a), Generation Z is the generation with the most video sharing and liking.

According to Çevikalp (2020), violence always appears in the arts of painting, photography and digital platforms; and today, the most important socialization tools are digital platforms. The social media buyers of the violence, which can be servable especially through aestheticized films, will likely to be the younger generations who follow the video contents more.

Social media networks have users from many different cultural, religious and ethnical backgrounds that spread information around the world. In addition to social media usage habits, it is important to know the degree of acceptance of these different cultures by the generations. However, intergenerational communication will also be in question. Without tolerance to differences, it will be inevitable for violence and showing force to spread in social media networks.

The Diffusion of Differences on Social Media

With new communication networks, cultural flows take place rapidly through moving/still images and symbols. The most prominent example of this is social media networks, which are known for their popularity today, enabling different cultures to be encountered and viewed side by side.

However, the consumption frenzy, considered one of the biggest concerns of today, has changed platforms with online environments such as social media by turning into a different form. It is stated that societies that attach great importance to consumption are made up of people uniting around their own interests. This triggers selfishness which is in human's nature (Tarhan, 2018: p.23).

Today, it is seen that the rapid social change caused by the effects of many factors such as technology, economy and social events also creates an intense interaction between cultures and affects all generations by spreading globally through online networks.

The fact that social networks enable communication on a global scale has provided the ground for the formation of mosaic structures around the world by providing an environment to interact with people of different cultures, beliefs, physical appearances and values. Thus, it has been wondered how the mosaic structures created online will reflect on the society in the real daily life and how it will affect the communication and behavior styles in various fields.

In this context, Deniz and Tutgun-Ünal (2019b) examined the acceptance levels of differences of social media generations in their study. For this purpose, the "Acceptance of Diversity Scale (ADS)" was developed and it consists of 9 items and 3 dimensions. These dimensions are; a) Accepting different religious/ethnical structures, b) Accepting different physical appearances and c) Accepting different thoughts/values (Figure 2). By applying the scale to the generations using social media, the tolerance level of the generations can be determined, and the effect of social media can be explained.

In the generation research conducted with 516 people, it was investigated whether the social media usage of generations affected tolerance to differences (Deniz & Tutgun-Ünal, 2019b). The acceptance levels of differences of Baby Boomer, X, Y and Z generations were found to be medium. In the intergenerational comparison, Generation Z is found to have the lowest tolerance to differences. Generation Z is the youngest generation and they are called "those born with technology". Although they are intertwined with social media, which may suggest that they are closer to modernity, and yet it turns out that they appear to be conventionalists. Accordingly, they stated that they do not want different religious/ethnic structures around themselves and they do not want to make friends or to cooperate with them in homework/projects.

When the other results are examined in the generation research, Generation Y was found to have the highest acceptance level for different physical appearances. Acceptance level of different physical appearances of Baby Boomers and Generation Z was significantly lower than Generation Y. Furthermore, Generation Z has a low tolerance to physical appearances and this makes them to be similar to the oldest generation, Baby Boomers that are called "conventionalists". Thus, it was revealed that the youngest generation evolved into the oldest generation, by becoming conventionalists.

Figure 2. Description of differences

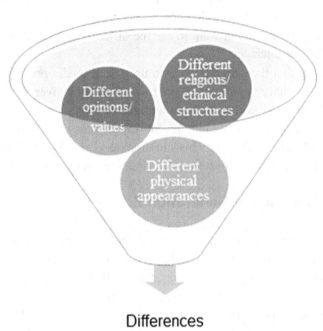

Differences

Generation Y is called the generation where differences are felt most prominently (Ekşili & Antalyalı, 2017; Kelgökmen İlic & Yalçın, 2017). When the characteristics of Generation Y are examined, it is stated that their self-value is high and have a tendency to form unity with a sense of belonging to people from different sections, thoughts or physical appearances. According to researches, if Generation Y receives support from their families, they show more self-defensive behavior with an increased self-confidence. Accordingly, the acceptance of people with different physical appearance (people who may wear piercings and have tattoos on their body) is at a high level and this result complies with other research in the literature.

There was no significant difference between generations in terms of accepting different thoughts and values. Thus, it has been determined that all generations accept different views and values moderately. However, it was revealed in the examination made for gender that women showed more tolerance to differences in all dimensions compared to men. So it can be said that women accept different views and thoughts, physical appearances, religious and ethnical structures more than men. This result provides a clue about the communication between men and women and tolerance levels in both the real and online world.

In the generation study, in which the effects of social media are also questioned, it was revealed that those who use more social media are more tolerant to differences. Accordingly, it was found that those who use social media for 4 hours or more per day have higher levels of acceptance for different physical appearances than those who use social media less. The use of social media affects the generations' perception towards the differences around them. Those who use social media less than 1 hour a day do not tolerate differences, while those who use for 4 hours or more show a more normalizing attitude.

In the analysis made on a yearly basis, the acceptance level of those who use social media for a long time was found to be high. Those with high social media usage time of normalize different religious/

ethnic structures, different appearances and different thoughts/values. This situation can lead to positive results in showing consideration and tolerance between generations. The fact that the generations with low social media usage time do not want to see the differences around them creates the potential to cause violence with lack of tolerance.

As a result, considering that the generations who use social media provide global communication online, it can be said that they have a positive attitude towards cultural diversities worldwide and develop tolerance. Generation Z, which is said to be born with technology, should not be exempted from this result since they do not display an attitude that accepts differences yet. Generation Z both take part in social media and do not tolerate differences. This situation may cause to show an incompatible structure in their social media communications. However, this situation needs to be addressed separately.

The Threshold of Tolerance of Generation Z

Understanding a society requires understanding values since it is the guiding element that forms the basis of the generations and social norms which build the society. Values and behaviors are changing with factors such as beliefs, personal characteristics, family life and socialization experiences.

There are people with different attitudes and values in the social environment in which the person resides, in the school he/she studies or in the workplace where he/she works. Each individual has unique values and reacts against an event in line with these values (Tarhan 2018). First of all, the environment in which an individual is born and raised is different. When social events, economic and technological changes occur in a certain time period of individuals' life, the individual becomes distinguished from other individuals. When we generalize this situation from the environment of the individual to the society and even to the world, it is inevitable that the value transfer is enormous and complex with the existence of online platforms such as social media which will ensure that people of different cultures live together all over the world.

Today, the use of social media and the quantity of information spreading from these networks have reached to huge dimensions by influencing the entire world. In fact, research on social media addiction is highly demanded by experts from almost every field. (Andreassen, 2012; Hazar, 2011; Kuss & Griffiths, 2011; Tutgun-Ünal, 2015, 2020a, 2020b; Wilson, Fornasier & White, 2010).

In social media addiction research, especially young people are reported to be at risk (Andreaseen, 2012; Hazar, 2011; Kuss & Griffiths, 2011; Tutgun-Ünal, 2015; Uzun et al., 2016). It is seen that the research are carried out especially with the university students belonging to the Generation Y and with the younger age group, Generation Z. Social media addiction is important because it causes a mental and emotional engagement with social media and hinder the educational life of children in school.

The tolerance threshold of the people is important since we can communicate if we tolerate differences. In the study conducted by Deniz and Tutgun-Ünal (2019b) with 516 participants, the tolerance level of a sufficient number of social media users from all generations was determined. The lowest tolerance threshold was found at Generation Z in the study where differences were considered in three dimensions as "accepting different religious/ethnic structures", "accepting physical appearances" and "accepting different thoughts/values". Generation Z has a conservative attitude that is seen in conventionalist structures towards different cultures and it is important to reveal the underlying reasons of this situation especially today, where modernity comes with globalization.

The "Acceptance of Differences Scale" developed by Deniz and Tutgun-Ünal (2019a) includes the acceptance of individuals with different religious/ethnical structures, different physical appearances, thoughts and life values, and their prejudices about these groups. If the person does not accept people with these differences both in real life and digital environment, it will be difficult to tolerate. In this case, the possibility of resorting to lynching, violence or power shows will increase. The fact that the communication provided in the social media environment is in a global dimension and containing diversity also increases the size of the danger.

Generation Z which is a generation that is raised with technology, show a lot of variety in social media networks despite its conventional attitude. It will be inevitable for Zs to either remain vulnerable or overreacted to unlimited spreading information from online networks with such a huge variety.

On the other hand, those who with low tolerance will be negatively affected by the messages underlying the content spread by countless users from different cultures and religions around the world. Those who tend to develop tolerance will be expected to transform their value system by stretching the conventional structure.

When the Generation Z is mentioned, it is difficult to put forward the clear value system since they are still with their families and by being under their responsibility. In the years to come, it can be thought that their own value judgments will be formed with parameters such as studying, marrying or going out of the house outside the province. Therefore, researches conducted with Zs should be followed up in the following years.

Despite Zs, Generation Y is defined as the "generation where differences are felt most clearly" also shows itself in online behavior. It is observed that Ys, who can easily express their thoughts thanks to social media networks which provide a comfortable platform for self-confidence, are more active in showing themselves and feel more free in spreading information compared to other generations.

Generations in Work Life

We are exposed to the effects of different peoples in almost every area of our lives. In areas such as family, work, and private life, we communicate with ourselves and others, and it is very important to keep communication healthy to maintain social balance.

It is also observed that the studies focus on intergenerational communication in workplace environments consisting of various age groups (Berkup, 2014; Çetin Aydın & Başol, 2014; Erdal, 2018; Latif & Serbest, 2014; Macky, Gardner & Forsthy, 2008; Martin & Tulgan, 2002; Toruntay, 2011; Yiğit, 2010). In a study, it is stated that a significant part of the problems in workplaces are caused by intergenerational perception, method, application and communication differences (Latif & Serbest, 2014). Martin and Tulgan (2002) emphasize that the Generations X and Y working in the same organization may have communicative problems and that the management of the organization should help employees to overcome these problems. From this point of view, it is stated that in order for these two generations to communicate, they should engage in informal activities outside working hours.

Thus, coexistence is important and necessary for the value transfer from generation to generation in order for a society to survive. Nowadays, in addition to face-to-face social communication, social media effects have been added to research in many fields since the coexistence in online networks is quite popular. It is seen that social media is integrated into research in the topic of work life, where comparisons are made between working generations.

In the social media use research conducted by Tutgun-Ünal and Deniz (2020b), it was found that all generations use social media at a medium level. Therefore, it is seen that all generations use social media at an intermediate level both in work life and in other areas of life. In work life, doing business with people of all ages and different age groups, cultures and values is a process that should be managed very well. Today, social media is also involved in this process and it can be said that it affects this process very strongly as a system providing global information exchange.

Starting from this situation, Deniz and Tutgun-Ünal (2019a) developed a 5-point Likert-type "Work Life Scale" consisting of 8 items to understand the point of view of the generations towards work life. In the research, which consisted of 516 people, they applied the scale to all generations and examined the effects of social media on the work life. The Work Life Scale measures two dimensions called "Giving Importance to Work" and "Obeying the Rules". While giving importance to work sub-scale includes the importance that the person gives into his/her the work life and job, the effort to be permanent in the workplace where he/she works and his/her dedication to the workplace where he/she works; obeying the rules sub-scale includes the orientation or preference of the working environment to be disciplined and regular.

Figure 3. The determinants of work life

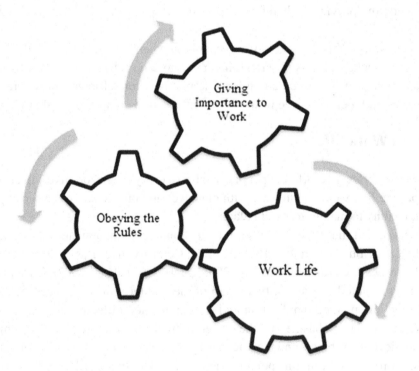

All items (1st to 5th) in the WLS's "Giving Importance to Work" sub-scale in the Giving Importance to Work sub-scale should be scored in reverse. The high score obtained from the sub-scale shows that they are impatient to rise in work, that the work is not an important part of their life. 7th and 8th items in the Obeying the Rules sub-scale should be scored in reverse. The high score obtained from the sub-scale shows that a disciplined work with clear rules is not preferred. (Tutgun-Ünal & Deniz, 2020b).

The fact that the scores obtained from the WLS are high means that the work life is moving away from the conventional values, while the low score indicates that being close to the conventionalist attitude in the work life. The closeness to conventional values is explained by the adoption of working hours and rules in work life. Those who adopt this situation are expected to work for many years at the same workplace and have a high job loyalty. It is thought that those who do not have these attitudes can easily change jobs when they find a job in better conditions, and they do not like clear working hours, rules and authority. This is explained by being far from conventional values.

Accordingly, the results of research conducted by applying WLS to all generations in Turkey, all generations are appear to be "close to conventional values of in the work life. When the WLS and sub-scale scores of the generations are examined, it is noteworthy that the average score of Generation Z is the lowest, especially in terms of obeying the rules. In this context, it has been revealed that the Generation Z, who is not yet in the work life, has a conventional attitude towards obeying the rules, that is, adopting a workplace with certain working hours and rules. This was reflected in the total of the WLS, and Generation Z is the nearest to the conventional values.

Since Generation Z does not work yet, it was a matter of curiosity what will their attitude towards the work life be like. It was stated that this generation, which was born with technology, will display features like being impatient, distracted and high tendency to develop technology addiction in the work life whereas the results of this research showed the opposite when they were asked. The result of this research should be evaluated as a guess for Generation Z, who has not yet join the work life, and it should be taken into consideration that they can change when they are in the work life. More precise results will emerge in the future, when determinative studies are carried out by observing their behaviors about giving importance to work and especially obeying the rules.

In the gender-based comparison, it was found that the work life values of women were near to the conventional values and made a significant difference compared to men in the total of WLS. It was revealed in the sub-scale of obeying the rules that women are more conventional than men and adopt the rules. There was no difference in gender in terms of giving importance to work. In giving importance to work, the scores of women and men are near to each other and it is concluded that they are neither near nor far from the conventional values, that is, they have a medium level of job loyalty.

On the other hand, there are also studies that offer different perspectives about women. In a study, it is suggested that female workers place more emphasis on family life and home-related duties and roles than male workers, causing organizational careers and values to remain secondary (Varlı, 2014: p.24). In another study of managers, male managers were found to have significantly more organizational commitment than female managers (Aka, 2017). In this case, it can be thought that the responsibilities and compliance with the rules of being a manager may make a difference. However, some studies in the literature emphasize that female workers show more organizational commitment than men (Angle & Perry, 1981; Hrebiniak & Alutto, 1972).

In the study of Tutgun-Ünal and Deniz (2020b), in order to question whether work values are affected by the use of social media, the daily social media usage of the generations and WLS scores were compared. Accordingly, it has been revealed that those who use social media less than 1 hour a day are near to conventional values in the work life and adopt the rules. In the research, social media use for 4 hours a day was determined as a breaking point for finding whether social media use affects the work life values or not. Thus, it was revealed that the individual, whose usage of social media is for 4 hours or more per day, moves away from conventional values in the work life.

As a result of the research, it has been revealed that the work life values differ among generations and accordingly they have different behaviors and attitudes in the context of giving importance to work and obeying the rules. It was concluded that the increase in the use of social media due to the effect of digitalization also affected the work life values. It is noteworthy that the generations with low daily social media usage adopt conventional values. The difference that the Generation X makes in giving importance to the work among working generations has shown that they will make their choice in this direction when they find a job under better conditions. This situation has revealed that they are distant from conventional values, and give importance to work conditions instead of job loyalty.

According to the results of this research, it has been found that those who use social media are far from conventional values in the work life. Thus, the rate of demanding digital content of the generations who are in the work life and who have high daily social media usage will likely to be high. In this case, it can be concluded that aestheticized digital contents are functional in diverging from conventional values.

YouTubers, Children and Family

The youngest generations mostly prefer the YouTube platform worldwide. For example, YouTube in Sweden is the most popular website by the Generation Z between the ages of 9-18 (Swedish Media Council, 2017), and 81% of children who are 8-11 years old are reported to use this video sharing website in the UK (Ofcom, 2017). Tutgun-Ünal & Deniz (2020a) ranks the generations in their research in Turkey and the results showed that those participants who indicate using YouTube is found to be the Generation Z in the first place. According to this, while the use of Instagram is the first in the Generation Y, the ratio of those who use Instagram (45%) and YouTube (37%) applications in the first place in the Generation Z are close.

In addition, according to the research conducted by Özdemir (2017) with 400 participants in Istanbul, the new media usage habits of X, Y and Z generations differ and Generation Z use the new media the most. As a video sharing platform, YouTube, which is one of the many interacting applications of the new media, has become the home of Generation Z and phenomena because it appeals to the people those who born with technology.

In a study that states that children prefer watching YouTubers when they go online, Martinez and Olsson (2018) investigated how children make sense of Youtubers and their role in the daily routine. In the research conducted by group interviews and observations with Swedish children between the ages of 9-12, how the children constructed a notion about a YouTuber that they follow and their comments were examined. As a result of the research, it was found that the YouTubers played a role in identity building and the phenomenon followed was important in determining who the person was.

While the use of YouTube and the effects of Youtubers on children are so nush, there is lack in number of studies in the literature. Accordingly, some research conducted with YouTubers focused on how they structure their relationships with themselves and their audience (Berryman & Kavka, 2017; Lovelock, 2017; Ramos-Serrano & Herrero-Diz, 2016). Children's peer cultures are important areas for placing, negotiating, and making sense of mediated symbolic materials such as YouTubers, and this is also an important part of the identity building of children in their peer group (Corsaro, 2015; Thompson, 1995).

YouTuber is defined as a person who has reached a certain number of followers and a moderately-known person in the computer (virtual) environment (Driessens, 2016). This concept has become very important with the intense demand of the YouTube platform's younger generation and especially the children. Because, as stated in the researches, the videos prepared by YouTubers affect the identity building of children.

There are many emotions in the infrastructure of videos edited by those users who share on YouTube. Exposing children to emotions such as violence, fear and narcissism that are spread with aestheticized and tailored images can pose a danger both in terms of psychological and personality development. The most obvious example of this is children who watch videos of games or game reviews and then who commit suicide. Underneath the attraction of the game, there are emotions such as violence, fear, aggression and anger and these emotions are spreading from one child to another through social media which leads to a increase in the size of the danger.

On the other hand, it is known that emotions have the power to spread in online networks, and especially negative emotions spread more rapidly and widely (Christakis and Fowler, 2012). This situation points to the big problems caused by the videos that leave the children under the influence of the YouTube videos which contain negative emotions that are frequently used by the Generation Z.

Tarhan (2020a) defines the family as the cornerstone of society and emphasizes the need for families to receive awareness training by experts since only a family with awareness will be able to emotionally nurture their children and provide them with a peaceful habitat. Moreover, according to Prof. Dr. Nevzat Tarhan, conventional families used to have the function of protecting new marriages and older family members such as aunts and grandparents were considered to be in the family as well. This was causing fewer mistakes to be made. He further states that in the nuclear family model, which has become widespread nowadays, social support is decreasing and couples find it difficult to resolve their disagreements when they quarrel and leave each other because they cannot establish a good relationship even if there is love.

Considering that YouTubers have large audiences, it is obvious that the videos they will share from their channels will reach online communities consisting of many users. Thus, it can be said that the phenomena have the potential power to manage the community. Since children are vulnerable users, the importance of family control in the usage of YouTube comes into play here.

By stating that the family is an institution that needs to be empowered, Prof. Nevzat Tarhan says that this is essential for empowering the society, as well. Accordingly, one of the most important causes of domestic violence is the weakening of family ties and healthy children cannot be raised in the environment where the family is dispersed.

Tarhan indicates that there is an increase in the divorce rate in Turkey, according to the Turkey Statistical Institute data. In the first 5 years of marriage, the divorce rate is at 39%. in 2017. This rate varies between 50% and 60% in the world. Those who marry get divorced in the first 5 years of their marriage. After 5-10 years, this is thought to be out of control. This is a security problem and definitely needs to be emphasized as a state policy. On the other hand, the disease of modernism is stated as narcissism. Narcissism harms the marriage institution and pushes individuals into loneliness. In the conducted studies, higher loneliness has been seen among young people compared to older people. While the rate was 27% in the elderly; it was 40% in the youth and it is stated that the young people do not want to get married anymore (Tarhan, 2020a).

Social media, especially YouTube videos, are watched by children to enjoy themselves. The child clicks on the video according to the visual mobility and immersiveness without knowing what the video content is and enjoys it as long as he/she watches it. YouTubers come into play right here. In this context, YouTubers are trying to gather followers and video clicks/views and prepare their videos for this purpose. It is important for them to gain viewings towards children and due to this; they deliberately edit the videos in an immersive way that will allow children to break away from the real world.

Tarhan (2020c) states that pleasure, happiness and peace are separate concepts. Accordingly, pursuit of pleasure is thought to be happiness, and in order to be at peace, each work must be meaningful. At this point, YouTube videos that do not have any meaning and break the records of clicking come into play. These kinds of videos help contributing children not to search for meaning and do not have peace.

Psychiatrist Prof. Dr. Nevzat Tarhan states that lack of peace causes behavioral disorders in the child and in order to ensure peace, trust, and communication, not lying, positive goals and consistency are required in the family environment where children are raised.

SOLUTIONS AND RECOMMENDATIONS

Families have a role in providing security to children who are heavily interested in YouTube videos and phenomena and build their identity with the influence of YouTubers. For this, healthy family structures are needed. Moving from this point, as Tarhan stated, in developed countries, when there is a the problematic family, before reaching to the divorce point family members are taken to the camps at the weekends and in these programs, in which children also participate, activities are carried out on subjects such as communication, stress management and problem solving skills. Similar activities should be carried out in all countries.

Also, considering that children are at school age, it may be preventive to empowering school systems to work on social media addiction and conscious use, and to include families by contributing municipalities in these studies. If the child, education system and families cooperate, it will be effective in the solution of the problem. According to Tarhan (2020b), for the development of a child, his/her emotional and social brain must develop as well as his mathematical brain. When children who spend a lot of time on YouTube are not involved in the real-life routines, their emotional and social development will be incomplete, which will cause problems. In order to be a healthy individual, the child has to go through psychosocial development stages and has the skills to be acquired at each stage.

Erik Erikson, a psychologist working in developmental psychology and psychoanalysis, argues that human beings go through 8 different phases from birth to death. It is important for the child's parents and educators to know these phases, which are important for children to make sense of their environment and their behavior. These stages, called psychosocial development stages, have goals to be completed in each period in order for people to be developed with a healthy mood. These phases are; 1) Insecurity towards basic trust (0-1.5 years), 2) Shame and suspicion (1-3 years) against independence, 3) Guilt against entrepreneurship (3-5 years old), 4) Feelings of inferiority against productivity (5-11 years), 5) Identity confusion in the face of identity acquisition (12-19 years), 6) Isolation against intimacy (20-30 years), 7) Stagnation against generativity (30-60 years), 8) Despair against self-integrity (over 60 years old).

In each of these phases, it is important to successfully overcome the conflicts experienced by the individual (Erikson, 1998). In this context, it is important for both parents and teachers to know these phases and develop appropriate behaviors. In particular, parents need to know by knowing the goals that their children should achieve in the relevant period so that their forward-looking psychosocial development can be healthy.

In order for the psychosocial development stages of children to take place in a healthy way, the feeling of trust should be supported by families at all ages. This can be achieved by making families aware of these stages. Controlling social media actions in children can also be achieved through emotional and social satisfaction. Because, instead of the pleasure that the child will get from social media, the child will have to choose the trust that his/her family will provide. In this context, the development of a sense of trust in children can be preventive against harmful content circulating in the virtual world. According to Tarhan (2020c), 5S+1M is needed to develop a sense of trust: Love (Sevgi), Respect (Saygı), Patience (Sabır), Loyalty (Sadakat), Intimacy (Samimiyet), Spirituality (Maneviyat).

Figure 4. Tarhan's Model of Trust (5S+1M)

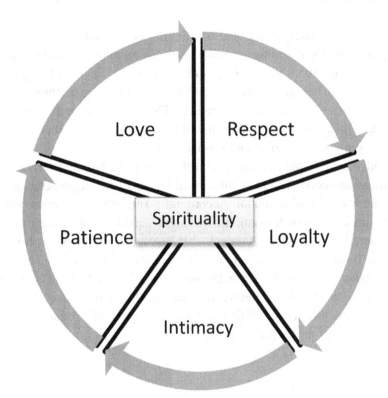

On the other hand, there is a pyramid of needs in humans. In the lower steps of this pyramid, there are eating, sheltering and breeding. The most important need that comes after these basic needs is the sense of security, and this also raises the need for attachment. In this respect, it also means that people always appear in an identity; identify themselves through these mechanisms roots from the need for commitment. (Tarhan, 2019: p.102).

When the need for attachment in children has not been met by their families, the child will be in a search for identity. At this point, the child will take on the role of the hero he watches and build his identity accordingly, if there are temptations such as the phenomenon, cartoon character, and YouTuber. Research investigating the effect of YouTubers on children also emphasizes identity building (Corsaro, 2015; Martinez and Olsson, 2018; Thompson, 1995). Here, it is seen that the family's trust (love, respect, patience, loyalty) and attachment to the child are of vital importance.

According to Tarhan (2018), technology is an addiction brought by civilization and modernism tries to keep them together, especially by connecting people to something. Technology addiction types such as social media addiction, technology addiction, and smartphone addiction that emerge today make individuals who spend intense time in these areas lonely and become isolated from the environment.

As a result; Model of trust starts in the family and if it spreads to the environment, a stronger stance can be imposed to cope with the problems of the era. However, with a strong family foundation, the emotional and social needs of children towards YouTubers can decrease and protective measures can be taken against the negative effects of identity building.

FUTURE RESEARCH DIRECTIONS

Since the past, the subject of intergenerational conflict has been dealt with in the fields of sociology, psychology and pedagogy, by revealing intergenerational communication differences in the studies (Ayçiçek, 1994; Mannheim, 1952: p.163; Sarıtaş & Barutçu, 2016). With the generation theory that explains that the people born between 1980 and 1999, which are now called the Generation Y, are showing different characteristics than the other generations. This required specific studies to be carried out for this generation, and then with these studies, it will be possible to strengthen communication among generations by developing understanding and raising awareness.

On the other hand, there is a study stating that the differences in the characteristics specified for Generation Y arise from socio-economic and cultural conditions in different countries and these differences can even be observed from school to school. Accordingly, Turkey may not even contain only one type of Generation Y. Characteristics such as cultural, economic, and level of education can make variations in the profile of Generation Y (Ekşili & Antalyalı, 2017). Supporting this view, Bayramoğlu and Şahin (2017) stated that the Turkish Generation Y, born in 1981 and later, has different expectations compared to Generation Ys in other countries. In line with this study, it is seen that the Generation Y' birth year intervals may differ in some studies. Therefore, the need to address individual differences has emerged instead of intergenerational differences. In future researches, especially generation Y and Z needs to be examined within the scope of more specific groups.

CONCLUSION

Nowadays, the position of an individual in society is coming to the agenda with his/her position in social networks.

Social networks' recognition of global communication feature has provided the ground for the formation of mosaic structures around the world by providing an environment for the interaction with people of different cultures, beliefs, physical appearances and values at one end of the world. Thus, it has been wondered how the mosaic structures created online will reflect on the society in the daily real life and how it will affect the communication and behavior styles in various fields.

In the study carried out by Deniz and Tutgun-Ünal (2019b) with the acceptance scale, acceptance level of differences of the generations coexisting on social media was examined. It has been investigated how users in global online networks are exposed to worldwide massive information and how transfer of value and behavior is affected. Accordingly, those with longer social media usage normalize different religious/ethnic structures, different physical appearances and different opinions/values. This can lead to positive results in showing tolerance and understanding between generations. The fact that the generations with low social media usage time do not want to see the differences around them creates the potential to cause violence by making it difficult for them to tolerate.

Social media networks have users from many different cultures and religious/ethnic backgrounds that spread information around the world. In addition to social media usage habits, it is important to know the level of acceptance of these different cultures by generations. However, intergenerational communication will also be in question. Without tolerance to differences, it will be inevitable for violence and showing force to spread from social media.

On the other hand, the fact that the usage of YouTube as a platform for sharing video content is spreading around the world and especially children demanding this content raises the problem of trust. The fact that YouTube videos that aim to break a record of clicks and are being made attractive and served for children increases the size of the danger. In addition, the fact that consciously prepared videos containing emotions such as violence, anger and fear are circulated in online networks, requires the families, educators and even management policies of administrators to come into effect.

As a result, it is clear that the "Tarhan's Model of Trust (5S+1M)" that will be created with love, respect, patience, loyalty, intimacy and spirituality in the society will play a healing role in the negative effects of social networks arising from digitalization. Firstly families, who are one of the cornerstones of the society, and then the leaders of the communities, have a great job in creating this trusting environment. Raising a healthy child and bringing it into society will only be possible in the family environment where strong communication and bonding are created. When dealing with the attractive contents which include negative emotions at the social media networks, awareness will be functional with the help of families, schools, and society at the macro level and with individuals and at the micro level.

REFERENCES

Adorno, T. & Horkheimer, M. (2014). *Aydınlanmanın Diyalektiği* (N. Ülner & E. Öztarhan Karadoğan, Trans.). Kabalcı Yayınları.

Aka, B. (2017). *Kamu Ve Özel Sektörde Çalışan Yöneticilerin Kuşak Farklılıkları Ve Örgütsel Bağlılık Düzeyleri Arasındaki İlişkinin İncelenmesi: İzmir İlinde Bir Araştırma* (Doctoral Thesis). İzmir Kâtip Çelebi University, Institute of Social Science, İzmir, Turkey.

Akdemir, A. (2013). The Investigation of Relationship Between Organizational an Investigation of Expectations of Career Perception and Change, and Leadership Style of Generation Y. *Journal of Economics and Management Research, 2*(2), 11–42.

Alwin, D. F., & Mccammon, R. J. (2007). Rethinking Generations. *Research in Human Development, 4*(3-4), 219–370. doi:10.1080/15427600701663072

Andreassen, C. S., Torsheim, T., Brunborg, G. S., & Pallesen, S. (2012). Development of a Facebook Addiction Scale. *Psychological Reports, 110*(2), 501–517. doi:10.2466/02.09.18.PRO.110.2.501-517 PMID:22662404

Angle, H. L., & Perry, J. L. (1981). An Empiricial Assesment of Organizational Commitment and Organizational Effectiveness. *Administrative Science Quarterly, 26*(1), 1–14. doi:10.2307/2392596

Asmafiliz, E., & Şalvarcı Türeli, N. (2018). Y Kuşağı Bireylerin Sosyal Medya Kullanım Sıklığı Üzerine Amprik Bir Araştırma [An empirical research on the frequency of social media use of generation Y individuals]. *5th International Conference on Social Sciences and Education Research, Proceedings Book*, 294-312.

Ayçiçek, İ. M. (1994). *Kuşaklararası Çatışma*. Presse-Druck.

Bauman, Z. (2001). Consuming life. *Journal of Consumer Culture, 1*(1), 9–29. doi:10.1177/146954050100100102

Bayramoğlu, G., & Şahin, M. (2017). Field Study Investigating the Expectations of Employment and Tendencies of the Generations Y. *Journal of Labour Relations*, 8(2), 56–75.

Berkup, S. B. (2014). Working with Generations X and Y in Generation Z Period: Management of Different Generations in Business Life. *Mediterranean Journal of Social Sciences*, 5(19), 218–229. doi:10.5901/mjss.2014.v5n19p218

Berryman, R., & Kavka, M. (2017). 'I guess a lot of people see me as a big sister or a friend': The Role of Intimacy in the Celebrification of Beauty Vloggers. *Journal of Gender Studies*, 26(3), 307–320. doi :10.1080/09589236.2017.1288611

Biggs, S. (2007). Thinking About Generations: Conceptual Positions and Policy Implications. *The Journal of Social Issues*, 63(4), 695–711. doi:10.1111/j.1540-4560.2007.00531.x

Çetin Aydın, G., & Başol, O. (2014). X ve Y kuşağı: Çalışmanın Anlamında Bir Değişme Var mı? [X and Y generation: Is there a change in the meaning of work?]. *Electronic Journal of Vocational Colleges*, 4(4), 1–15. doi:10.17339/ejovoc.41369

Çevikalp, A. (2020). Today's Marketing of Violence Through Media and Aestheticization of the Products Through Turning to Artistic Violence. *Anatolian Academy Journal of Social Science*, 2(1), 93–112.

Christakis, N. A., & Fowler, J. H. (2012). *Sosyal Ağların Şaşırtıcı Gücü Ve Yaşantımızı Biçimlendiren Etkisi*. Varlık Yayınları.

Corsaro, W. A. (2015). *The Sociology of Childhood*. Sage Publications. doi:10.4135/9781483399027

Deniz, L. & Tutgun Ünal, A. (2019a). Sosyal Medya Çağında Kuşakların Sosyal Medya Kullanımı Ve Değerlerine Yönelik Bir Dizi Ölçek Geliştirme Çalışması [Development of a set of scales toward the use of social media and values of generations in social media age]. *OPUS– International Journal of Society Research, 11*(18), 1025-1057.

Deniz, L., & Tutgun-Ünal, A. (2019b). Sosyal Medya Kuşaklarının Farklılıkları Kabul Seviyeleri [Social media generations' levels of acceptance of diversity]. *4th International Social Research and Behavioral Sciences Symposium*.

Driessens, O. (2016). The Democratization of Celebrity. Mediatization, Promotion, and the Body. In P. D. Marshall & S. Redmond (Eds.), A Companion to Celebrity. Wiley Publications.

Dyke, M. V., Haynes, C., & Ferguson, M. (2007). Bridging the divide: A public relations perspective on intergenerational communication. *Public Relations Quarterly*, 52(4), 19–23.

Ekşili, N., & Antalyalı, Ö. L. (2017). Türkiye'de Y kuşağı özelliklerini belirlemeye yönelik bir çalışma: Okul yöneticileri üzerine bir araştırma. [A study to determine the characteristics of generation Y in Turkey: A survey on school administrators]. *Humanities Sciences*, 12(3), 90–111.

Erdal, M. (2018). *Personel bulma ve seçme süreçlerinde sosyal medya ağlarının rolü: X ve Y kuşakları açısından bir inceleme* (Master Thesis). Gazi University, Ankara, Turkey.

Erikson, E. (1998). *Life Cycle Completed*. WW Norton & Company.

Hazar, M. (2011). Sosyal Medya Bağımlılığı: Bir Alan Çalışması [Social media dependency-filed survey]. *Journal of Communication Theory & Research, 32*, 151–175.

Hrebiniak, L. G., & Alutto, J. A. (1972). Personal and Role-Related Factors in the Development of Organizational Commitment. *Administrative Science Quarterly, 17*(4), 572–573. doi:10.2307/2393833

Kelgökmen İlic, D., & Yalçın, B. (2017). Y Jenerasyonunun Farklılaşan İş Değerleri Ve Liderlik Algılamaları [Differentiated job values and leadership perceptions of gen Y]. *Journal of Yaşar University, 12*(46), 136–160.

Kuss, D. J., & Griffiths, M. D. (2011). Addiction to Social Networks on the Internet: A Literature Review of Empirical Research. *International Journal of Environmental and Public Health, 8*, 3528–3552. doi:10.3390/ijerph8093528

Kuyucu, M. (2017). Y Kuşağı Ve Teknoloji: Y Kuşağının İletişim Teknolojilerini Kullanım Alışkanlıkları [Y generation and technology: The use of communication technologies in Y generation]. *Gümüşhane University E-Journal of Faculty of Communication, 5*(2), 845–872.

Latif, H., & Serbest, S. (2014). Türkiye'de 2000 Kuşağı ve 2000 Kuşağının İş ve Çalışma Anlayışı [Generation 2000 in Turkey and generation 2000's business and working concepts]. *Journal of Youth Research, 2*(4), 132–163.

Lovelock, M. (2017). 'Is every YouTuber going to make a coming out video eventually?': YouTube Celebrity Video Bloggers and Lesbian and Gay Identity. *Celebrity Studies, 8*(1), 87–103. doi:10.1080/19392397.2016.1214608

Macky, K., Gardner, D., & Forsthy, S. (2008). Generational Differences at Work: Introduction and Overview. *Journal of Managerial Psychology, 23*(8), 857–861. doi:10.1108/02683940810904358

Mannheim, K. (1952). *Essays on the Sociology of Knowledge*. Routledge & Kegan Paul Ltd. Retrieved from https://archive.org/details/essaysonsociolog00mann

Martin, C. A., & Tulgan, B. (2002). *Managing the Generation Mix: From Collision to Collaboration*. Human Resource Development Press.

Martínez, C. & Olsson, T. (2019). Making Sense of YouTubers: How Swedish Children Construct and Negotiate the YouTuber Misslisibell as a Girl Celebrity. *Journal of Children and Media, 13*(1), 36-52. DOI: doi:10.1080/17482798.2018.1517656

Morsümbül, Ş. (2014). Kültürel Değerlerin Üç Kuşak Arasındaki Değişimi Üzerine Bir İnceleme: Ankara Örneği [Value change across generations: Ankara sample]. *Hacettepe University Institute of Turkish Studies, 21*, 137–160.

Ofcom. (2017). *Children and parents: Media Use and Attitudes Report*. Retrieved from: https://www.ofcom.org.uk/__data/assets/pdf_file/0020/108182/children-parents-media-use-attitudes-2017.pdf

Özdemir, Ş. (2017). *Kuşaklar Teorisine Göre Türkiye'deki Gençlerin Medya Kullanım Alışkanlıkları Ve İstanbul Örneği* [According to the theory of generations, media usage habits of the youngs in Turkey and İstanbul, as an example] (Master Thesis). Marmara University, Institute of Social Science, İstanbul, Turkey.

Pecchioni, L. L., Wright, K. B., & Nussbaum, J. F. (2005). *Life Span Communication*. LEA.

Ramos-Serrano, M., & Herrero-Diz, P. (2016). Unboxing and Brands: YouTubers Phenomenon Through the Case Study of Evantubehd. *Prisma Social*, *1*, 91–120.

Sağır, A., & Eraslan, H. (2019). Akıllı Telefonların Gençlerin Gündelik Hayatlarına Etkisi: Türkiye'de Üniversite Gençliği Örneği [The impact of smart phones on young people's daily life: Example of University Youth in Turkey]. *OPUS–International Journal of Society Research*, *10*(17), 48–78. doi:10.26466/opus.515339

Sarıtaş, E., & Barutçu, S. (2016). Tüketici davranışlarının analizinde kuşaklar: Sosyal medya kullanımı üzerinde bir araştırma [Generations in analysis of costumer behaviors: A study on social media using]. *Pamukkale Journal of Eurasian SocioEconomic Studies*, *3*(2), 1–15.

Süer, S., Sezgin, K., & Oral, B. (2017). Z Kuşağındaki Öğrencilerin Internete Ilişkin Algılarının Belirlenmesi: Bir Metafor Çalışması [Generation Z students' perceptions of internet: A metaphor study]. *Electronic Journal of Education Sciences*, *6*(12), 190–203.

Swedish Media Council. (2017). *Ungar & medier 2017* [Kids & media]. Retrieved from: https://statensmedierad.se/download/18.7b0391dc15c38ffbccd9a238/1496243409783/Ungar+och+medier+2017.pdf

Tarhan, N. (2018). *Değerler Psikolojisi ve İnsan*. Timaş Publishing.

Tarhan, N. (2019). *Bilinçli Aile Olmak: Ailede Fırsat Eğitimi*. Timaş Publishing.

Tarhan, N. (2020a). *Güçlü bir toplum için aile güçlendirilmeli*. Retrieved from: https://www.nevzattarhan.com/prof-dr-nevzat-tarhan-guclu-bir-toplum-icin-aileguclendi rilmeli.html

Tarhan, N. (2020b). *Atakan'ın Sosyal ve Duygusal Beyni De Geliştirilmeli*. Değerlendirmesi. Retrieved from: https://www.nevzattarhan.com/prof-dr-nevzat-tarhanin-atakanin-sosyal-ve-duygusal-beyni-de-gelismeli-degerlendirmesi.html

Tarhan, N. (2020c). *Haz, Mutluluk ve Huzur Ayrı Kavramlar*. Retrieved from: https://www.nevzattarhan.com/prof-dr-nevzat-tarhan-haz-mutluluk-ve-huzur-ayrikavra mlar.html

Thompson, J. B. (1995). *The Media and Modernity: A Social Theory of the Media*. Stanford University Press.

Toruntay, H. (2011). *Takım Rolleri Çalışması: X Ve Y Kuşağı Üzerinde Karşılaştırmalı Bir Araştırma* (Unpublished Master Thesis). İstanbul University, İstanbul, Turkey.

Tutgun-Ünal, A. (2015). *Sosyal Medya Bağımlılığı: Üniversite Öğrencileri Üzerine Bir Araştırma* [Social media addiction: A study on university students] (Doctoral Thesis). Marmara University, İstanbul, Turkey.

Tutgun-Ünal, A. (2020a). *Sosyal Medya: Etkileri-Bağımlılığı-Ölçülmesi* [Social media: Effect-addiction-measurement]. Der Yayınları.

Tutgun-Ünal, A. (2020b). Social Media Addiction of New Media and Journalism Students. *The Turkish Online Journal of Educational Technology*, *19*(2), 1–12.

Tutgun-Ünal, A., & Deniz, L. (2020a). Sosyal Medya Kuşaklarının Sosyal Medya Kullanım Seviyeleri ve Tercihleri. [Social media usage levels and preferences of social media generations]. *OPUS–International Journal of Society Research*, *15*(22), 125–144. doi:10.26466/opus.626283

Tutgun-Ünal, A., & Deniz, L. (2020b). The Comparison of Work Values of Social Media Generations in Terms of Giving Importance to Work and Obeying the Rules in Turkey. *Azerbaijan Journal of Educational Studies*, *690*(1), 199–215. doi:10.29228/edu.102

Uzun, Ö., Yıldırım, V., & Uzun, E. (2016). Habit of Using Social Media and Correlation of Social Media Addiction, Self-Esteem, Perceived Social Support in Adolescent with Attention Deficit Hyperactivity Disorder. *TJFM&PC*, *10*(3), 142–147.

Williams, A. (2001). *Intergenerational Communication Across the Lifespan*. LEA.

Williams, A., & Harwood, J. (2008). Intergenerational Communication: Intergroup, Accomodation, and Family Perspectives. In J. F. Nussbaum (Ed.), *Handbook of Communication and Aging Research* (pp. 115–137). LEA.

Wilson, K., Fornasier, S., & White, K. M. (2010). Psychological Predictors of Young Adults' Use of Social Networking Sites. *Cyberpsychology, Behavior, and Social Networking*, *13*(2), 173–177. doi:10.1089/cyber.2009.0094 PMID:20528274

Wright, C. (2001). Children and Technology: Issues, Challenges and Opportunities. *Childhood Education*, *78*(1), 37–41. doi:10.1080/00094056.2001.10521686

Yiğit, Z. (2010). *X ve Y Kuşaklarının Örgütsel Tutumlar Açısından İncelenmesi ve Bir Örnek Olay* [A research on generation X and Y in terms of organizational attitudes and a case study] (Unpublished Master Thesis). Bahçeşehir University, İstanbul, Turkey.

Yıldırım Becerikli, S. (2013). Kuşaklararası İletişim Farklılığı: Bilim Teknoloji ve Yenilik Haberleri Üzerinden Bir Odak Grup Çalışması [Communication differences between generations: A focus group study through science, technology and innovation news]. *Journal of Selçuk Communication*, *8*(1), 5–18.

ADDITIONAL READING

Baudrillard, J. (1993). *Symbolic Exchange and Death*. Sage Publications.

Bauman, Z. (2001). *The Individualized Society*. Polity Publications.

Castells, M. (1996). *The Rise of the Network Society. The Information Age: Economy, Society and Culture*. Blackwell Publications.

Feldman, T. (1997). *Introduction to Digital Media*. Routledge.

Gane, N., & Beer, D. (2008). *New Media: The Key Concepts*. Berg.

Gerbaudo, P. (2013). *Tweets and Streets: Social Media and Contemporary Activism*. PlutoPress.

Hayles, N. K. (1999). *How We Became Posthuman: Virtual Bodies in Cybernetics, Lliterature, and Informatics*. University of Chicago Press. doi:10.7208/chicago/9780226321394.001.0001

Kittler, F., & Virilio, P. (2001). The Information Bomb: A Conversation. In J. Armitage (Ed.), *Virilio Live* (pp. 81–90). Sage Publications.

Manovich, L. (2001). *The Language of New Media*. MIT Press.

Tutgun-Ünal, A. (2020). Social Media Journalism. In G. E. Atalay (Ed.), *New Media and Alternative Journalism* (pp. 43–90). Hiperyayın.

KEY TERMS AND DEFINITIONS

Baby Boomer: A term used to describe people born between the years of 1946-1964. It means a huge increase in annual birth rate especially in the USA, starting at the end of the World War II and continuing until the beginnings of 1960.

Generation: A community of people who share common habits, culture, and time zone.

Social Media Generation: Social media users grouped according to the globally accepted Generation Theory based on specific birth dates.

Social Network: Web-based environments that support the interpersonal interaction and increase the sharing of individuals with common interests by giving everyone the chance to create their own personal profile and the list of friends that they want to communicate with.

Social Networking: Communicating by using social networking sites.

Tarhan's Model of Trust: A guiding model for providing interpersonal (especially within the family) trust, which is developed by Psychiatry Professor, Nevzat Tarhan in Turkey, also known as "5S+1M" Model.

Violence: Human behaviors that manifest themselves in the forms of breaking the law, harming others, insulting, dishonoring, hindering peace, violating someone's rights, hurting, mistreating, using force to injuring, showing extreme destructive behaviors and excessive anger.

YouTuber: A person who has reached a certain number of followers and a moderately-known person in the computer (virtual) environment.

This research was previously published in the Handbook of Research on Aestheticization of Violence, Horror, and Power; pages 543-566, copyright year 2021 by Information Science Reference (an imprint of IGI Global).

Chapter 53
Follow my Snaps!
Adolescents' Social Media Use and Abuse

John R Chapin
Pennsylvania State University, Monaca, USA

ABSTRACT

Using third-person perception as a theoretical framework, a survey of 1,167 American adolescents explores their social media use and its relationship to verbal, emotional, physical, and sexual abuse. Despite the sexual nature of social media platforms like Snapchat, which are popular with adolescents, even adolescents who have experienced sexual violence in the past. Snapchat users were more likely than non-users to report abusive behavior to others. Adolescents exhibited third-person perception, believing others were more affected than they were by negative social media posts. This was related to experience with violence, and social media use. A third-person effect emerged, as adolescents who exhibit third-person perception were more likely to engage in abusive behaviors, both face-to-face and in an electronic medium.

INTRODUCTION

According to the Pew Research Center (2015), 92% of teens go online daily, facilitated by the widespread availability of smartphones. The most popular social media platforms were reported as Facebook (used by 71% of teens), Instagram (52%) and Snapchat (41%). The purpose of the current study is to explore adolescents' changing patterns of social media use and their experience with victimization and perpetration of violence, using third-person perception (TPP) as a theoretical framework.

Adolescents and Social Media

A report issued by the American Academy of Pediatrics (2011) outlined the benefits and risks of social media use by children and adolescents. On the positive side, staying connected with friends and family, exchanging ideas, and sharing pictures. Adolescent social media users find opportunities for community engagement, creative outlets, and expanded social circles. According to the report, the risks fall into these

DOI: 10.4018/978-1-6684-6307-9.ch053

categories: peer-to-peer (bullying), inappropriate content, lack of understanding of privacy, and outside influences (social and corporate). The report also refers to "Facebook Depression," which emerges when adolescents spend too much time on social media and start exhibiting classic signs of depression.

A number of social media apps were designed specifically for finding sexual contacts or the "hook-up culture." Apps like Grindr and Tinder allow users to find potential sexual partners locally, using the GPS in their smart phones. The popular app Snapchat began as a means to quickly share explicit photos for a set period of time, without the receiver saving a copy of the image. Use of the app has evolved, with some users sharing benign photos and videos and others using it for more explicit purposes. Facebook also began as a hookup app limited to college students. As other users (including parents) were permitted to use the app, the social media giant evolved, becoming many things to over one billion users worldwide.

A recent study (Stevens, Dunaev, Malven, Bleakley & Hull, 2016) outlined how adolescents use social media in their sexual lives. Adolescents seek out sexual content (sexually explicit material, information about sexual health, sexual norms). Social media platforms provide an opportunity for sex-related communication and expression; According to the study, 25%-33% of adolescent social media users post or distribute provocative images, seeking feedback on their appearance or connection with other users. Finally, social media provide adolescents with tools for seeking out romantic or sexual partners, which may result in risky behaviors.

The National Academies of Sciences, Engineering, and Medicine issued a review of a decade of research on bullying (Flannery et al., 2016). According to the report, bullying and cyberbullying prevalence rates reported vary from 17.9 to 30.9% of school-aged children for the bullying behavior at school and from 6.9 to 14.8% for cyberbullying. Much of the variance can be attributed to sexual orientation, disability, and obesity. Physical consequences can be immediate (injury) or long-term (headaches, sleep disturbances). Psychological consequences include low self-esteem, depression, anxiety, self-harming, and suicide. There is some evidence to suggest links between being bullied in adolescence and perpetration of violence in adulthood. A recent publication from the American Psychological Association called "a call to action" reviewed a decade of research on suicide, which acknowledged a dearth of research on the relationship between suicide and social media (Westerfield, 2018). Social media are developing more quickly than our ability to process and understand their impact.

Third-Person Perception and Social Media

Third-person perception (TPP) is the belief that negative media message influence others more than oneself. The phenomenon has been well-documented over a variety of contexts, which recently include news coverage of election polls (Kim, 2016), deceptive advertising (Xie, 2016), and the impact of religious cartoons (Webster, Li, Zhu, Luchsinger, Wan & Tatge, 2016). A third-person effect emerges when the misperception causes a behavior or attitude change. The most common third-person effect reported in the literature is support for censorship (Chung & Moon, 2016; Kim, 2014; Webster et al., 2016). A recent study (Lee & Park, 2016) found TPP regarding H1N1 (pandemic flu), which predicted intentions to vaccinate.

A growing literature is documenting TPP regarding social media (Antonopoulous, Veglis, Gardikiotis, Kotsakis & Kalliris, 2015; Paradise & Sullivan, 2012; Wei & Lo, 2013). Facebook users believe they are less likely than other users to suffer negative consequences to their personal relationships and privacy (Paradise & Sullivan, 2012). Adolescents believe others are more harmed by sexting, and, in turn, support restrictions for others. Buturoiu and colleagues (2017) found similar results among a large sample of college students, but added one more piece to the puzzle. The strongest predictor of TPP regarding the influence of news stories shared on Facebook was Facebook itself. Students who used Facebook the most exhibited the highest degrees of TPP. The current study seeks to document TPP regarding a broader range of social media platforms and explore a third-person effect related to violence.

Based on the preceding review of the literature, the following research questions are posited:

RQ1: What are adolescents' patterns of use of social media platforms?
RQ2: What are adolescents' experiences with victimization and perpetration of violence?
RQ3: Do adolescents believe others are more influenced by negative social media posts (TPP)?
RQ4: What is the relationship between TPP, social media use, victimization, and perpetration of violence?

METHOD

Procedures and Participants

Multiple urban and suburban middle school and high school students participated in violence prevention programs provided by a Pennsylvania women's center (N = 1,167). Research materials were gathered as part of a pre-test. A post-test was also collected for program assessment, but was not included in the analysis. Students were notified of informed consent and their right to opt out of the study, but none did so. Students were also informed their responses were anonymous, but they could skip any items that made them uncomfortable. The most common items skipped were about sexual violence: 87 participants (7%) skipped one or more of these items. Free counseling services were available for the students. The research was approved by the University's Human Subjects Review Board and the Women's Center Board of Directors. Participants ranged in age from 12 to 18 (M = 14.1, SD = 1.5) and were 50% male, 50% female. Consistent with the demographics of the region, participants were 80% white, 8% black, 3% Asian, and 2% Hispanic. The remaining students identified as mixed race or other.

Materials

Students were asked to circle which social media platforms they used and to identify which were favorites. Platforms included were identified as the most popular among adolescents by the Pew Research Center (2015): Texting, Facebook, Twitter, Instagram, Pinterest, and Snapchat. A space was provided for students write in other platforms they were using. The only app written in was YikYak, an app designed for college students, which is limited by GPS to a small radius surrounding a campus. YikYak posts range from "This chemistry class sucks," to "anyone want to hook-up?"

Experience with violence was measured in two ways. The first was a simple checklist indicating which forms of violence (verbal, emotional, physical, and sexual) participants had witnessed and which they had experienced as victims. These were treated as binaries and also summed to create a measure of combined experience with violence. Perpetration was measured using a Likert-type scale asking "In the last 30 days, how many times have you done each of the following (1 = Never; 7 = almost daily): Hit or slapped someone; shoved or pushed someone; put someone down to their face; made fun of someone to make others laugh; spread false rumors about someone; left someone out on purpose when it was time to do an activity; used cell phone pictures or text to threaten to hurt someone physically; used cell phone pictures or text to make fun of someone; posted rude comments about someone you know on-line." These items were summed to create an overall perpetration scale and subscales for face-to-face and electronic violence ($\alpha = .81$).

Third-person perception was measured using a standard measure. Students rated two items, one about the effect of negative social media posts on themselves; one about the effect on others (1 = Not at all; 7 = Greatly affected). The TPP measure is created by subtracting the perceived influence on others from the perceived influence on self. TPP is indicated by a negative mean.

Participants also self-reported their age, race, and gender. TPP increased with age. There were no significant differences in TPP attributable to gender or race.

RESULTS

SPSS software was used for analysis. Frequencies, T-tests, and correlations were used. RQ1 asked what were adolescents' patterns of use of social media. Findings are summarized in Table 1.

Table 1. Adolescents' social media use

Platform	Student Use	Identified as Favorite
SnapChat	78%	57%
Texting	76%	20%
Instagram	73%	13%
Twitter	37%	5%
Facebook	26%	2%
Pinterest	21%	3%
Other (YikYak)	1%	---

Note: Frequencies reported were processed with SPSS software

Facebook has been steadily losing ground as the preferred social media platform for adolescents, with Snapchat and texting rising in popularity. Snapchat is the clear favorite, with 78% of participants saying they use the app, and 57% identifying it as their favorite. Participants use as many as seven apps (M = 3). Only 5% say they do not use social media. The number of apps increases with age. There were no high school students who indicated using no social media.

RQ2 asked what are adolescents' experiences with victimization and perpetration of violence. Findings are summarized in Tables 2 and 3. Consistent with national surveys, it's likely these figures are under-reported. Participants were most likely to indicate witnessing and experiencing verbal and emotional abuse. Three percent acknowledged experiencing sexual abuse; another 24% know someone who has been sexually abused. When combining witnessing and experiencing the different forms of violence, a more realistic picture forms. For verbal abuse, only 9% rated themselves as a zero (never witnessed or experienced). That figure rises to 18% for verbal abuse, 32% for physical abuse, and 73% for sexual abuse. A different pattern emerges for perpetration of violence (Table 3). Participants were most likely to acknowledge physical violence (shoving, pushing, hitting, slapping), followed by public ridicule, with face-to-face more common than electronic. While middle school students freely acknowledge shoving a friend, there seems to be greater stigma ascribed to verbal and emotional taunting. Combining the nine items, 25% say they have never engaged in any form of abuse; the remaining 75% acknowledge perpetration of at least one form. For additional analysis face-to-face were separated from electronic. Face-to-face was more common across age groups, consistent with the national Pew study.

Table 2. Adolescents' experiences with victimization

Type	Witnessed	Personally Experienced
Verbal	75%	65%
Emotional	65%	26%
Physical	60%	13%
Sexual	24%	3%

Note: Frequencies reported were processed with SPSS software

Table 3. Adolescents' perpetration of violence

Item	Frequency	Standard Deviation
Shoved or pushed	M = 2.2	SD = 1.6
Hit or slapped	M = 2.1	SD = 1.6
Ridiculed in public	M = 2.1	SD = 1.6
Ridiculed via technology	M = 1.6	SD = 1.2
Left someone out	M = 1.5	SD = 1.1
Verbal putdown	M = 1.3	SD = .9
Spread false rumors	M = 1.3	SD = .7
Posted rude comments	M = 1.3	SD = .9
Threatened to hurt via technology	M = 1.2	SD = .7

Note: Perpetuation of violence was measured on a 7-point Likert scale (1 = Never; 7 = Almost Daily)

RQ3 asked if participants exhibited TPP, believing others were more affected than they are by negative social media posts. A t-test was used to verify that participants believed they (M = 2.1, SD = 1.5) were less influenced than peers (M = 3.9, SD = 1.6) by negative social media posts, $t(1,159) = -34.1, p < .000$.

RQ4 asked what is the relationship between TPP, social media use, victimization, and perpetration. Findings are summarized in Table 4. TPP is most closely related to experience with violence. This finding is consistent with the TPP literature (Chapin, 2013; Kim, Kim & Cameron, 2012). Participants who have witnessed and experienced multiple forms of violence are less likely to believe they will not be affected by negative social media posts. A third-person effect also emerges, in that adolescents who exhibit TPP are more likely to engage in both face-to-face and electronic perpetration of violence against others. Adolescents who use multiple social media platforms are more likely to exhibit TPP and more likely to engage in cyber-bullying behaviors. A series of independent t-tests were used to delve deeper into the impact of specific social media platforms. The most disturbing findings emerge with Snapchat and Facebook users. Snapchat users (M= .19, SD = .40) are more likely than non-users (M = .30, SD = .50) to experience all forms of sexual abuse, t (1,027) = -3.1, p< .000. Despite having experienced sexual abuse, adolescents continue to use the app most associated with the hookup culture and the transmission of sexually explicit images. Snapchat users (M = 14.8, SD = 6.9) are also more likely than non-users (M = 13.2, SD = 5.7) to perpetrate all forms of abuse on others, t (1,098) = -3.3, p< .000. For Facebook, users (M = .92, SD = 1.1) are more likely than non-users (M = .75, SD = 1.0) to experience all forms of abuse, t (1,026) = -2.3, p< .01. There is no pattern of perpetration for Facebook users. No similar patterns emerge for users of the remaining platforms (Twitter, Instagram, Pinterest, and text).

Table 4. Zero-order correlations among variables predicting third-person perception

	2	3	4	5	6
1. TPP	-.15**	.16**	.09**	.08**	.06*
2. Experience/Victim	---	.11**	.09**	.03	-.12**
3. Perpetration/Cyber		---	.55**	.08**	.04
4. Perpetration/Face to Face			---	.02	.05
5. Social Media Use				---	.21**
6. Age					---

Note. *p< .05, **p< .01

TPP is indicated by a negative mean. For ease on interpretation, the signs have been reversed in row 1.

DISCUSSION

The majority of adolescents (95%) use social media. Despite this use, they believe they are less impacted by negative social media posts than their peers. This misperception predicts a third-person effect, in that adolescents who believe they are not affected are more likely to perpetrate violence against others face-to-face and electronically. Adolescents who use multiple social media platforms are more likely to exhibit TPP and more likely to engage in cyber-bullying behaviors. The study examined the use of the most popular social media platforms, finding disturbing patterns among Snapchat and Facebook users. Despite the nefarious origins of Snapchat, adolescents who have experienced sexual abuse seem to be drawn to the app and are more likely to perpetrate all forms of abuse on others. Similarly, Facebook, users are more likely than non-users to experience all forms of abuse. The Facebook platform was also originally designed as a hook-up app for college students. As it opened to older and younger users, it has developed over the years to include the sharing of personal information, photographs, news, and political opinions. One student shared with the trainer that kids are migrating away from Facebook, because it got too "newsy." It's also difficult to use to find potential dates if Mom is following your feed.

Findings have implications for parents, educators, and women's centers. First, some aspect of media literacy training is important. Adolescents need to understand how social media works, as well as the potential dangers. The high school trainings referenced in this study include legal implications. Students are surprised (and angered) to learn that sending an explicit selfie could result in criminal charges for creating and distributing child pornography. Local cases are reviewed, as well as long-term consequences, including mandatory registration as a sexual offender on Megan's Law websites.

A number of limitations should be considered before interpreting these results. The sample consisted of Pennsylvania students gathered for training from a Women's Center (Middle school trainings focused on bullying; high school trainings focused on dating violence). Although study data was collected prior to the training, participants were aware of the topic, which could skew their responses. Findings may not be generalizable to all U.S adolescents or adolescents from other parts of the world.

While the findings are consistent with the current literature on TPP and social media (Antonopoulous, Veglis, Gardikiotis, Kotsakis & Kalliris, 2015; Paradise & Sullivan, 2012; Wei & Lo, 2013), each study provides a snapshot of adolescents from a particular location using specific social media platforms. Future research could delve more deeply into why adolescents use social media and how that changes the patterns of abuse that emerged in the current study. For instance, adolescents who use Snapchat and Facebook for hookups likely differ from users who are sharing whimsical pictures of their cats. Clearly other factors come into play, on the social and cultural levels. Funding for a broader national survey would shed more light and provide guidance for prevention campaigns.

REFERENCES

American Academy of Pediatrics. (2011). Clinical report: The impact of social media on children, adolescents, and families. Retrieved from www.pediatrics.org/cgi/doi/10.1542/peds.2011-0054

Antonopoulous, N., Veglis, A., Gardikiotis, A., Kotsakis, R., & Kalliris, G. (2015). Web third-person effect in structural aspects of the information on media websites. *Computers in Human Behavior*, *44*, 48–58. doi:10.1016/j.chb.2014.11.022

Buturoiu, R., Durach, F., Udrea, G., & Corbu, N. (2017). Third-person perception and its predictors in the age of Facebook. *The Journal of Medical Research*, *10*(2), 18–36. doi:10.24193/jmr.28.2

Chapin, J. (2013). I know you are, but what am I? Adolescents' third-person perception regarding dating violence. *The Journal of Educational Research*, *106*(5), 1–6. doi:10.1080/00220671.2012.736428

Chung, S., & Moon, S. (2016). Is the third-person effect real? A critical examination of the rationales, testing methods, and previous findings of the third-person effect on censorship attitudes. *Human Communication Research*, *42*(2), 312–337. doi:10.1111/hcre.12078

Flannery, D., Todres, J., Bradshaw, C., Amar, A., Graham, S., Hatzenbuehler, M., ... Rivara, F. (2016). Bullying prevention: A summary of the report of the National Academies of Sciences, Engineering, and Medicine. *Prevention Science*, *17*(8), 1044–1053. doi:10.100711121-016-0722-8 PMID:27722816

Kim, H. (2014). Perception and emotion: The indirect effect of reported election poll results on their political participation intention and support for restrictions. *Mass Communication & Society*, *18*(3), 303–324. doi:10.1080/15205436.2014.945650

Kim, H. (2016). The role of emotions and culture in the third-person effect process of news coverage of election poll results. *Communication Research*, *43*(1), 109–130. doi:10.1177/0093650214558252

Kim, J., Kim, H., & Cameron, G. (2012). Finding primary publics: A test of the third-person perception in corporate crisis situations. *Journal of Public Relations Research, 24*(5), 391–399. doi:10.1080/106 2726X.2012.723275

Lee, H., & Park, S. (2016). Third person effect and pandemic flu: The role of severity, self-efficacy method mentions, and message source. *Journal of Health Communication, 21*(12), 1244–1250. doi:10 .1080/10810730.2016.1245801 PMID:27858585

Paradise, A., & Sullivan, M. (2012). (In)visible threats? The third-person effect in perceptions of the influence of Facebook. *Cyberpsychology, Behavior, and Social Networking, 15*(1), 55–60. doi:10.1089/ cyber.2011.0054 PMID:21988734

Pew Research Center. (2015). Teens, social media, and technology. Retrieved from http://www.pewinternet.org/2015/04/09/teens-social-media-technology-2015/

Stevens, R., Dunaev, J., Malven, E., Bleakley, A., & Hull, S. (2016). Social media in the sexual lives of African American and Latino youth: Challenges and opportunities in the digital neighborhood. *Media and Communication, 4*(3), 60–70. doi:10.17645/mac.v4i3.524

Webster, L., Li, J., Zhu, Y., Luchsinger, A., Wan, A., & Tatge, M. (2016). Third-person effect, religiosity and support for censorship of satirical religious cartoons. *Journal of Media and Religion, 15*(4), 186–195. doi:10.1080/15348423.2016.1248183

Wei, R., & Lo, V. (2013). Examining sexting's effects among adolescent mobile phone users. *International Journal of Mobile Communications, 11*(2), 176–193. doi:10.1504/IJMC.2013.052640

Westerfield, J. (2018). Suicide prevention and psychology: A call to action. *Professional Psychology: Research and Practice,* Retrieved from http://dx.doi.org.ezaccess.libraries.psu.edu/10.1037/pro0000209

Xie, G. (2016). Deceptive advertising and third-person perception: The interplay of generalized and specific suspicion. *Journal of Marketing Communications, 22*(5), 494–512. doi:10.1080/13527266.2 014.918051

This research was previously published in the International Journal of Cyber Behavior, Psychology and Learning (IJCBPL), 8(3); pages 1-8, copyright year 2018 by IGI Publishing (an imprint of IGI Global).

Chapter 54
Social Network Sites (SNS) and Their Irrepressible Popularity:
Can They Really Cause an Addiction?

Tuğba Koç
Sakarya University, Turkey

Adem Akbıyık
ⓘ https://orcid.org/0000-0001-7634-4545
Sakarya University, Turkey

ABSTRACT

Popularity of social media is increasing day by day and there are thousands of social media platforms on the internet with different features. This chapter discusses the term social media in general and examines its evolution in detail from the beginning of the first e-mail to today. Authors explore the terms pertaining to the domain of Social Network Sites (SNS) which are considered as one of the most used forms of social media. Authors present a discussion about a popular topic "SNS addiction" and examine its characteristics with a brief literature review. Accordingly, despite the fact that excessive use of social network sites cannot be formally accepted as a behavioral addiction; shy and young, extroverted, and neurotic women with no relationship are more likely to develop addictive behaviors towards social media.

INTRODUCTION

The reputation of social media is increasing day by day, and this popularity changes our daily lives and business environments in both negative and positive ways. For example one study claims that proper use of social media helps family members to increase their connection and to strengthen their family bonds (Williams & Merten, 2011); whereas other has investigated that divorce rates have increased with developing technology (Greenwood, Guner, Santos, & Kocharkov, 2016). Moqbel and Kock (2018) has admitted that excessive use of social media has negative impacts on the personal and work environment by means of decreasing positive emotions, increasing health problems and task distraction. However,

DOI: 10.4018/978-1-6684-6307-9.ch054

their strong evidence about the harmful effects of social media on personal environment is as strong as the impact on the work environment, Greengard (2012) believes that social media can be a way for achieving our life experiences. Indeed, some previous studies have clearly proved that using social media can enhance academic success (Ainin, Naqshbandi, Moghavvemi, & Jaafar, 2015), increase students' engagement (Junco, Heiberger, & Loken, 2011) as well as having more interactive customer relationship performance (Trainor, Andzulis, Rapp, & Agnihotri, 2014), creating more trusted products and customers (Laroche, Habibi, & Richard, 2013). Social media brings to our life not only performance-based positive outcomes; it may also offer some emotional gifts. For example, results have shown that getting positive feedback on the profiles enhance self-esteem and subjective well-being (Valkenburg, Peter, & Schouten, 2006). Similarly, Wang, Jackson, Gaskin, and Wang (2014) have also found that social use of social networking sites is positively related to well-being. These contradictory examples can be reproduced even further, but the most critical point in here is that there is no generalizable effect of social media. Although literature is agreed that some people are more inclined to use social media and exposed its negative effects such as young individuals (Kalpidou, Costin, & Morris, 2011) and females (Andreassen et al., 2013a), the situation depends on who you are, what are your individual characteristics and other unpredictable factors. Effects may be different even when the same person uses social media for different purposes. Baek, Bae, and Jang (2013) have found that social activities (based on reciprocity between the user and his/her friends such as chatting) decrease the feeling of loneliness; however para-social activities (based on unilateral activities such as commenting a celebrity's photo) show opposite effect. Because of these reasons, understanding social media is crucial to get benefit from it without being harmed. For this purpose, the present chapter has two main objectives (1) to present the outline of social media (Section 1), (2) to define social network sites (SNS) with examples of their potential effects, and (3) to discuss a relatively new concept "SNS addiction."

UNDERSTANDING SOCIAL MEDIA

In this section, first, we try to define social media with different definitions made by different point of view and touch on the evolution of social media.

What is Social Media?

According to Oberst (2010), the online world started gaining prominence with the social media after the year of 2000, and since then people have started to share their feelings, information, videos, and pictures at an astounding rate. According to their massive global compendium of stats, We Are Social has currently released that among 4.338 billion internet users worldwide 3.484 of them have already active social media users (We Are Social, 2019). This simply proves that 75% of internet users are also a member of social media. The reason why social media has become popular is that; it is always up to date, be able to multiple use (can be used for so many people at the same time), and is an open-source platform (Akıncı Vural & Bat, 2010). Although literature builds consensus about social media has changed our lives in many ways, there is no common sense what actually it is. Kaplan and Haenlein (2010) have stated that the terms social media and Web 2.0 are generally used interchangeably, but this situation is contradictory. According to them Web 2.0 can be considered as an ideological and technological foundation for the evolution of social media. More precisely, social media is an intimate and natural platform created by its users who come together based on their shared interests and ideas (Evans, 2008). Odabaşı (2010) has stated that social media is a way of connecting with our friends or/and strangers via sharing our experiences, ideas, and opinions on an online platform. Lusk (2010) has also agreed the idea that social media is a platform and it provides communication and sharing opportunities to its users. From another researcher perspective, social media is not just a platform, but it also consists applications, services, and systems that allows to create and share related contents (Junco, 2014). Boyd and Ellison (2007), who are recognized as the important contributors to the social media literature have claimed that the term social media captures all the services including internet-based and mobile ones that allow people to engage and participate in exchanges, joining and contributing to communities. Kietzmann, Hermkens, McCarthy and Silvestre (2011) have also admitted that social media captures mobile and web-based technologies to create interactive platforms through which users and communities share, discuss, co-create, and modify the contents. Despite the slight differences in the definitions of social media, there are some similarities that can be clearly seen. According to Mayfield (2010), there are five common characteristics that each social media platform has to be assured. These are:

1. **Participation**: Encourages becoming an active user.
2. **Openness**: Be accessible for everyone.
3. **Conversation**: Removes from being a broadcast.
4. **Community**: Creates groups that share common values and interests.
5. **Connectedness**: Increases interactions with other sites and potential users. Besides common features, the term social media also involves seven functional blocks such as sharing, conversations, groups, reputation, relationships, presence, and identity which are called by "the honeycomb of social media" (Kietzmann et al., 2011). Along the same line, Akkaya (2013) has emphasized four main aspects of social media that differ from traditional media:
    1. In traditional media, contents can be produced by only publishers, whereas in social media all users can create contents using tools which are mostly free or at small costs.
    2. In traditional media, contents are shaped by expert and dominated with their experiences; however in social media users are free to create and share regardless of their skills, knowledge or background.
    3. Social media is faster than traditional media for getting feedback.
    4. Once the content is published in traditional media, it is hard to revise. However, it is one click job correcting your mistakes in social media.

As Kuhn (1962) has propounded, Pink (2005) has agreed, and finally, Dawley (2009) has corroborated, new communication technologies such as printing press, internet, and social media play a role in epistemological and ontological development because of their functionality. In her inspirational study, Dawley (2009) has proposed a social network knowledge construction model (Figure 1) and tried to define how communication patterns could be shaped in the technology age for a student.

Based on this model, it can be indicated that networking through social media provides multi-channel communication opportunities that mass media cannot guarantee it. Before social media has penetrated our lives, constructors generally access their students and share their knowledge to them with face to face communication whereas the interaction between them is a continuous process nowadays. Of course, this situation is not to be limited to the educational context but also encompasses people's daily lives. Rettberg (2009) has admitted that social media lends a hand us to craft the narratives of our own story.

According to her, social media can organize our data and create an aspect of our life so that we can stay away from the clichés of mass media. For example, at certain times of the year Facebook prepares a customized video that includes the photos you shared.

Figure 1. Social network knowledge construction model (Dawley, 2009)

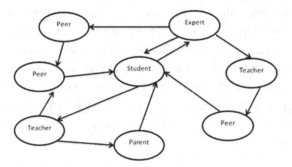

Similarly, Dopplr (offline now) creates a colored timeline travel plan -so that its users can plan everything in detail- and marks correlations with friends –so that they can receive alerts when they would be in the same place-. Businesses can also get the advantage of social media by having a comprehensive platform (https://www.clarabridge.com) to engage better their customers -who also probably have at least one social media account- in real-time. Marwick (2013) has indicated that social media encourages people to promote themselves as a brand like businesses do; however majority of them abstain from monetizing through their account. Besides these enthusing features of social media, not all people may want to have this experience. The main issue is that people use social media willingly and choose what they represent in there. There are three modes of self-representation which generally overlap in social media: visual, written, and quantitative (Rettberg, 2017). Visual self-presentation captures all the images that we share on social media whereas the way of expressing yourself via the words called written self-presentation. Quantitative self-presentation comes to mean as depicting our self-portrait with numerical statements such as self-tracking and showing how many steps you have walked today. Rettberg (2017) has also stated:

Self-representations in social media are often mocked as vapid, self-obsessed, frivolous – or simply boring ... on the other hand, self-presentation shows a certain aspect of ourselves ... and it never can share everything.

The definitions, features, and issues that have been discussed so far about social media, it seems as if social media can only use for communication to other people or/and expressing ourselves in different manners. However, in their research report Cann, Dimitriou, and Hooley (2011) have classified social media tools into three groups namely; communication, collaboration, and multi-media. Table 1 shows their classification and the different applications each group has.

Table 1. Classification of social media tools (Cann, Dimitriou, & Hooley, 2011)

GROUP 1 COMMUNICATION TOOLS	Blogging	Blogger, LiveJournal, TypePad, WordPress Twitter, Yammer, Google Buzz
	Microblogging	Foursquare, Gowalla, Facebook Places Facebook, LinkedIn, MySpace
	Location	Google Reader, Netvibes, Pageflakes, iGoogle
	Social networking	Blogger, LiveJournal, TypePad, WordPress Twitter, Yammer, Google Buzz
	Aggregators	Foursquare, Gowalla, Facebook Places Facebook, LinkedIn, MySpace
GROUP 2 COLLABORATION TOOLS	Conferencing	Adobe Connect, GoToMeeting, Skype PBworks, Wetpaint, Wikia Delicious, Diigo, BibSonomy CiteULike, Mendeley Digg, Reddit, Newsvine
	Wikis	Google Docs, Dropbox, Zoho Bamboo, Basecamp, Huddle
	Social bookmarking	Adobe Connect, GoToMeeting, Skype PBworks, Wetpaint, Wikia Delicious, Diigo, BibSonomy CiteULike, Mendeley Digg, Reddit, Newsvine
	Social bibliography	Google Docs, Dropbox, Zoho Bamboo, Basecamp, Huddle
	Social news	Adobe Connect, GoToMeeting, Skype PBworks, Wetpaint, Wikia Delicious, Diigo, BibSonomy CiteULike, Mendeley Digg, Reddit, Newsvine
	Social documents	Google Docs, Dropbox, Zoho Bamboo, Basecamp, Huddle
	Project management	Adobe Connect, GoToMeeting, Skype PBworks, Wetpaint, Wikia Delicious, Diigo, BibSonomy CiteULike, Mendeley Digg, Reddit, Newsvine
GROUP 3 MULTI MEDIA TOOLS	Photographs	Flickr, Picasa, SmugMug Viddler, Vimeo, YouTube
	Video	Justin.tv, Livestream, Ustream Scribd, SlideShare, Sliderocket
	Live streaming	OpenSim, Second Life, World of Warcraft
	Presentation sharing	Flickr, Picasa, SmugMug Viddler, Vimeo, YouTube
	Virtual worlds	Justin.tv, Livestream, Ustream Scribd, SlideShare, Sliderocket

If we have a glance at Table 1, it comes to our mind that communication tools are the ones which are most popular and ready to use applications. Literature also has agreed that social networking is the most attractive tool for communication in our modern age (Aghazamani, 2010). In Figure 2, a recent report's statistics have proved the increasing trend of social media usage all around the world. Likewise, a study's result has shown that college students spend approximately 18 hours a week on social networking which almost corresponds to 3 hours per day (Huang & Capps, 2013). Raice (2012) has also admitted customers pass the time of their day more on Facebook (6 hours average for the day) compare to Google and Youtube. Similarly, Wu, Cheung, Ku and Hung (2013) have also stated that nearly one-fourth of them their participants among Chinese smartphone users spend their time on social networking for more than three hours a day.

Because of exponential growth and rapid penetration of social media, it is crucial to understand the nature of these platforms, the reasons pushing people to use, and the consequences of using them should carefully investigate. Based on this inspiration, we will discuss the evolution of social media, most popular platforms, and their features –mainly focus on social network sites-, and the concept of social network sites addiction.

Figure 2. Time per day spent on social media (We Are Social, 2019)

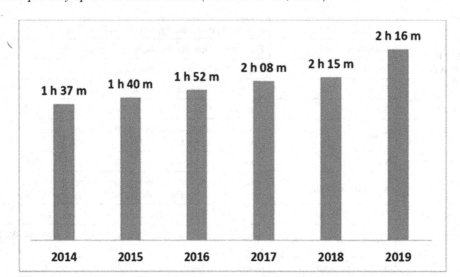

The Evolution of Social Media

In web 1.0, people get the information they need and nothing more. A few writers create the pages, and a vast number of people make use of them. Web 1.0 is described as "read-only web," whereas there is another way of reaching the web called "read-write" or more commonly known as Web 2.0. Although Web 2.0 is recognized as the most significant development for social media evolution, three milestones that should not be passed without mentioning since they can be recognized as the foundations of social media. The first one is the first **e-mail** sent between two computers by Raymond Samuel Tomlinson. The second one is the first **data transmission via telephone lines** between two users. The third one is a discussion system called **User Network (Usenet)** created by Tom Truscott and Jim Ellis which allows internet users to send instant messages. These three pioneering developments cover the period of 1970 to 1988 which we call "Foundation Age."

After the idea of transformable-information has been introduced by Tim Burners-Lee in 1989 at first, people have realized that they could do more than search and read (Getting, 2007). The idea of participating in the information has dramatically changed the ecosystem of the web. In 1996, **ICQ** (I Seek You) has been established by an Israeli company called Mirabilis. It is similar to Usenet, but ICQ also provides several privacy features for its users (Heim & Hansen, 1999) and it is the first stand-alone instant messenger. Two years later, the client of ICQ was bought by American Online (AOL) and then Mail.Ru Group in 2010 (Hollars & Lew, 2010). As of 2019, iOS and Android applications of are also available for ICQ. In 1997, AOL has launched its messenger called AOL Instant Messenger (**AIM**) which allows data transfer as well as instant messaging. Despite its growing popularity until the late 2000s, it has not failed to close in 2017. The same year with the AIM, **SixDegrees** formerly known as MacroView has also been established which is accepted as the first social network site. The idea behind this web site is "everybody is linked with everybody else via six degrees of separation" (Boyd & Ellison, 2008). Although ICQ and AIM offered lists of friends, they are not visible to others. SixDegress is the first web site that combined the popular features of social media as we discussed in the previous section such as profiles, friends list, and school affiliation. Another early social networking site which is called **Open Diary** has been introduced by Susan and Bruce Abelson in 1998. It is also accepted as the first blog. Although the web site has been hacked twice time in 2004 and 2008, it has managed to reach more than 561.000 blogs with 77 different countries by years 2008. In 2014 it has gone offline; however it has been activated in 2018 again. When it comes to millennium, **Wikipedia** has been introduced by Jimmy Donal Wales. It is the first collaborative online encyclopedia and has been adopted "anyone can edit" as a slogan (Bruns, 2006). From individual social connections to professional social connections, **Ryze** is the first platform to help people to leverage their professional networks. It has established in 2001 and recognized as the precursor to LinkedIn, but never gained mass popularity. As a social complement to Ryze, **Friendster** has started its life in 2002. Jonathan Abrams who is one of the owners of Friendster stated that this dating site focus on friends-of-friends meets instead of gathering strangers with similar interests. A motto "How can be lovers if we cannot be Friendsters?" has been started to spread (Boyd, 2006). According to Abrams, people create stronger ties and have better romantic relationship with the people that they have been known for a while (Boyd & Ellison, 2008). Thus, Friendster allowed its users to access at most four degrees away ("friends-of-friends-of-friends-of-friends"). At first, he was right, and Friendster got 300,000 users through word of mouth before it was founded as newsworthy (O'Shea, 2003); however, in the end, the site flamed out because of some technical and social difficulties (Boyd, 2006). In 2011, the site has transitioned into a virtual gaming community. Chafkin (2007) has evaluated the Friendster's rise and fall as the biggest disappointments in Internet history. The years between 1989 and 2002 has been introduced as "Exploration Age" which has started with the foundation of ICQ and ending with Friendster's succumbs.

As people realize the possibilities of socializing in the digital environment, new social networking sites have begun to evolve. As can be seen in Figure 3*, the expansion age of social media has begun in 2003, and it is still going on. In 2003, two important platforms have established called LinkedIn and MySpace. Unlike Ryze, **LinkedIn** has become an essential site for professionals. It has never stopped to evolve and always updated itself with new features like hiring solutions for businesses. In 2011, LinkedIn has been gone to public and now it is accepted the biggest initial public offering for a web company after Google (CBSNews, 2019). **MySpace** is a kind of dating site and has adopted an aggressive market strategy. They have focused on users who were the estranged users of Friendster. After the Friendster were fee-based system, MySpace has succeeded its mission and overgrown with its unique features (Boyd & Ellison, 2008). MySpace is the one which allows its users to personalize their profiles and pay regard their suggestions to update the site. Although MySpace has kept its leading position and remained as the most visited social networking site until 2008, Facebook has surpassed it after then. At the beginning of its history, **Facebook** has started out as a private sharing platform only for Harvard University students. As of September 2006, it has extended beyond universities to public (Phillips, 2007). Recently, Facebook is considered as one of the most prestigious companies in the world with its more than 2.3 billion monthly active users (Gebel, 2019). In addition to self-representation opportunities such as sharing photos, videos, ideas; Facebook also offers the Like button which enables users to confirm themselves and to get the appreciation of the other. According to Hayes, Carr, and Wohn (2016), the Like button is a kind of "paralinguistic digital affordance" which gives a communication chance without any word. Because of the array of potential meanings and ease of use, this button is one of the characteristic features of Facebook and contributes as trigger to Facebook's appeal to more people both teenagers and adults (Figure 4). How Facebook has left behind its rivals and why is still the most popular social network site? Actually, the answer is simple: Facebook provides a relatively easy way to access social connections (Ellison, Steinfield, & Lampe, 2011), contains time-saving cues (Walther & Ramirez, 2009), and targeting a global audience so that users can reach and comments on anybody with minimum efforts and without limitation.

Figure 3. Timeline of social media (*only the most groundbreaking developments are listed for the consideration of the authors)

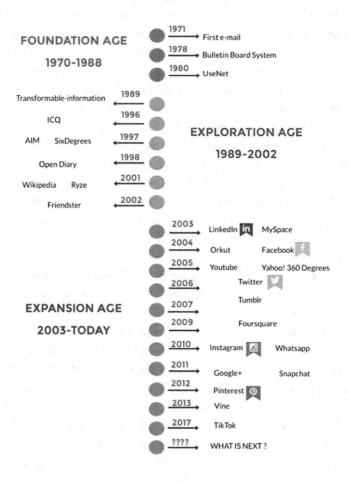

Figure 4. Age 18-34 and age 35+ digital audience penetration vs. engagement of leading social networks (Comsource, 2018)

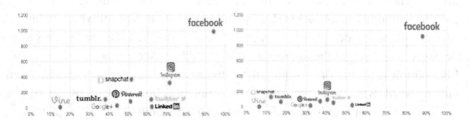

Although the original Yahoo! Company has been established in 1995, it has succeeded to adopt to technology age in 2005 with the foundation of **Yahoo! 360 Degrees**. This special module has launched with its unique services such as Flickr, Yahoo! Music, and Messenger. However Yahoo has slowly declined in the late 2000s and its core businesses have been bought by Verizon in 2017 (McGoogan, 2016). In 2005, a video sharing platform -**Youtube**- has hit the headlines and be one of the leading web sites around the world. In 2006, Google has bought Youtube, and now it operates as one of Google's subsidiaries. In 2006, something has changed with a little whisper. Jack Dorsey wrote a sentence "Just setting up my Twttr." via his platform and announced that **Twitter** (formerly known as Twttr) -a microblogging web site- has officially founded. Besides Facebook popularity, Twitter has begun experiencing a massive growth because the web-site has been a user-driven (hashtags are the idea of Twitter's users) and more suitable for an ongoing public dialogue (Junco et al., 2011). Currently, there are more than 321 million active users on Twitter (Molina, 2017). In 2007, another microblogging web site **Tumblr** has been created. The site has not been achieved its mission and made an agreement with Yahoo just before Verizon bought it in 2017. Currently, Tumblr is one of the subsidiaries of Verizon. In 2009, **Foursquare** has been founded which is a location-based service that allows its users to share their location-specific information with their real-time updates. In 2010, a photo and video-sharing website -**Instagram**- has owned by Facebook. According to the literature, these two platforms have similar features however the motives for using them are different. People tend to use Facebook to fulfill their need for belonging and need for self-presentation whereas Instagram focuses on self-expression and social interaction (Kircaburun, Demetrovics, & Tosuntaş, 2018). It is also stated although the widespread acceptance of Facebook all around the world with 2.5 billion active users, it has admitted that young people have started to move into another social media platforms such as Instagram (Sweney & De Liz, 2018; Utz, Muscanell, & Khalid, 2015). The same year with Instagram, another popular platform -**Whatsapp**-has been founded by Brian Acton and Jan Koum who were the former employees of Yahoo. Four years later it has owned by Facebook because the owner of Facebook has thought Whatsapp would be their major rivals in the near future. Whatsapp is a free, cross-platform messaging for individual uses, and since 2018 it has launched for small business use, too (Ong, 2018). According to the statistics of January 2019, Whatsapp has the most active user accounts among the messenger/VOIP applications (We are Social, 2019). Given the dominance of Facebook, Google has also made some attempts to catch social networking trends. **Google+** has launched in 2011 which is a fairly standard social networking site. According to Ovadia (2011), there is no reason to expect Google+ win the first place; however so many people are curious about what Google can do about social networking. In the end, Google+ can't manage to get rid of calling as a "ghost place" and more than 99% users of it cannot satisfy with it (Denning, 2015). As Pariser has stated that Google is undeniably good at managing relationships among data; whereas Facebook is good at managing relationships among people (Pariser, 2011). In 2011, **Snapchat** has been released as a photo-sharing app. What makes it different from Facebook and Instagram is that Snapchat offers its users more private communication opportunities with a feature of immediately disappearing posts. A report results' has indicated that college students think Snapchat is the safest web-site for photo-sharing (Bennett, 2014). The rapid acceleration of Snapchat annoyed Facebook and the acquisition attempt has occurred in 2013. Unlike Instagram and Whatsapp, Snapchat has rejected $3 billion offer from Facebook (Rusli & MacMillan, 2014). Although, Facebook remains its popularity among young adults; however adolescences and teens have already started to Instagram and Snapchat (Alhabash & Ma, 2017). Currently, the market value of Snap is estimated by nearly $15 billion (Feiner, 2019). In 2012, a new kind of social media called visual bookmarking has been created by the name of **Pinterest**. Users can discover, achieve, and share any web image or personal digital image in their scrapbook. Since most posted pictures are of products and brands, Pinterest offers many opportunities to brand advertisers as well as individuals (Phillips, Miller, & McQuarrie, 2014). As of the second quarter of 2019, Pinterest had 300 million monthly active users (Statista, 2019a). In 2013, **Vine** -a Twitter-owned service- has started its journey. Similar with few seconds appearing photos in Snapchat, Vine offers to create and share six-second videos. After Vine has shut down, another similar video sharing application has been offered which is called **TikTok**. Currently, TikTok has more than 500 million monthly active users which is more than Twitter (Langford, 2019).

Consequently, it can be stated that social media is an umbrella term which consists tools that provide several communication opportunities via connecting and retrieving features that include blogs (OpenDiary), wikis (Wikipedia), social bookmarking (Pinterest), media sharing (YouTube) virtual communities (all social network sites such as Facebook, Instagram), and collaborative tools (Google+) (Taylor, King, & Nelson, 2012).

SOCIAL NETWORK SITES (SNS)

After defining social media and its evolution in Section 1, we are going to focus on the most popular forms of social media which are called social network sites (SNSs). First, we try to clarify the concept of SNS. Then, we are going to have a look at the effects of using SNS both an individual and business level.

The Concept of SNS

Although there are many attempts to describe what social media sites refer to, Boyd and Ellison (2008)'s approach is the most cited one. According to them three major components that each SNS should have but the nature of them could be different from one website to another. They have stated that SNSs allows people to (1) create a personal page within a bounded system, (2) have a list of people with whom they are agreed to share a connection, and (3) view and change their friend's list. Boyd and Ellison (2008) have also stated that SNSs are unique communication platforms which offer users to articulate their networks as well as meeting with strangers.

According to Whiting and Williams (2013), people use SNS for ten reasons: passing time, information seeking, social interaction, communicatory utility, relaxation, entertainment, expression of opinion, information sharing, convenience utility, surveillance of knowledge about others (Alhabash & Ma, 2017). Curran and Lennon (2011) have proposed a research model to explain social networking behaviors. They have indicated that ease of use, usefulness, enjoyment, social influence and drama are the five main antecedents of SNS usage behavior. To put into more general, we can plausibly state that people want to use SNS for two main reasons: First one is about enhancing an individual's network size by means of meeting strangers. The second one is maintaining current relationships and having more strong-ties (Boyd & Ellison, 2008). One recent study's result has shown that young people generally prefer to use social media for creating new friendships, whereas older users tend to use these platforms to sustain their relationships (Munzel, Meyer-Waarden, & Galan, 2018). Besides motives for using SNS habits differ according to age, literature suggests that there are also some gender-specific patterns. For example, Sharp, Coatsworth, Darling, Cumsille and Ranieri (2007) have admitted that being social on SNS is more important for females compared to males. Similarly, Hargittai and Hsieh (2010) have also proved that males are more likely to join SNS for gaining new friends whereas females tend to develop more strong-tie activities such as chatting with close friends or press the like button for someone's picture whom they have been already introduced. With this line, Stanley (2015) has also found that females are mostly online in Facebook and Snapchat in order to monitor their siblings and parents status; whereas males go online in Facebook to meet new people.

Regardless of who uses them for what purposes, SNSs become more and more people day by day. According to the current statistics, 2.65 billion people have used social media in 2018 and will reach almost 3.1 billion in 2012 (Statista, 2019b). These numbers are reasonably enough to claim that SNS usage moves towards addiction. This claim will be discussed in more detail in Section 3.

Positive and Negative Effect of SNSs

It is stated that people - especially young adults (18-35 years) - do not realize how much time they spend on these platforms (Meena, Soni, Jain & Paliwal, 2015). A master thesis' results from Johnson & Wales University have indicated that 45% of their participants spent 6-8 hours a day in SNSs, while 23% of them have admitted that they have spent more than 8 hours a day (Wang, Chen, & Liang, 2011). A more recent report has indicated that the average time a user spends on Facebook is 58 minutes, in Youtube 60 minutes, in LinkedIn 10 minutes, and in Snapchat 25 minutes which is dominated by young adults (Stout, 2019). As a result of excessive use of these platforms, people face with some hassles in their daily lives. For example, Moqbel and Kock (2018) have expressed that high-frequency usage of social media causes health problems and low task performance as well as having more negative emotions. The negative effects of SNSs are more common among young individuals because they are more engaged with social media (Baker & Moore, 2008; Kalpidou et al., 2011). A study conducting with young adults has admitted that there is a positive relationship between the usage of SNS and sleep disturbance (Levenson, Shensa, Sidani, Colditz, & Primack, 2016). Gerson, Plagnol, and Corr (2016) have admitted that excessive use of SNS causes low well-being, especially for high goal-driven users since they are more inclined to develop negative social comparison. Besides daily life problems, time spent on Facebook and checking the notifications frequently are negatively related to students' academic success (Junco, 2012). Benson, Hand, and Hartshorne (2019) have stated that compulsive use of SNS is positively and significantly related to low academic performance.

Despite SNSs can have negative consequences they can offer some advantages such as enhanced social capital (Ellison, Steinfield, & Lampe, 2007) and sense of belonging (Davis, 2012), public individuation and user innovativeness (Choi & Kim, 2016), and increased well-being (Magsamen-Conrad, Billiotte-Verhoff, & Greene, 2014). Magsamen-Conrad et al. (2014) have aware that not all people have to feel comfortable in face-to-face communication. According to them several communication opportunities on SNS may reverse the negative effects of self-concealment on well-being, especially for the isolated and shy young individuals. A more recent study's results has showed that higher number of Facebook friends is positively related with subjective happiness and negatively related with loneliness (Phu & Gow, 2019). Beyond daily life, social media provides many unpredictable opportunities in the educational context, too. Using SNSs as an educational tool and integrating them with course content may increase the efficiency of lessons and motivation of learners. In their study, Lim & Richardson (2016) found out that, students used online social networking platforms for various reasons and their perceptions were usually positive when the SNSs were used as an educational tool. Junco et al. (2011) conducted a study to reveal if Twitter has an impact on students' engagement in the USA, where the instructors can also participate. Results showed that Twitter has a significant impact by the way of offering to students being more active and the ability to engage. Another study looked into the impact of Facebook usage on students' academic performance and found that there was a positive correlation among them (Ainin et al., 2015). Besides academic related jobs, usage of Facebook also beneficial to predict time spent in co-curricular activities (Junco, 2012).

There is no denying that social media platforms are inevitable for the majority of people to share their knowledge and interests. However, that is not all. These platforms can be unique in the way of improving the businesses performance. Businesses are fostered to use SNSs for increasing their relationships in order to have more trusted products and more loyal customers (Laroche, Habibi, & Richard, 2013). The term 'social media marketing' has increased its popularity by means of placing brand posts on the brand fan pages on SNSs. One study results showed that positioning the brand post on the right SNS affect the popularity of the brand in a positive way (de Vries et al., 2012). Although SNSs are generally considered an easy way to participate in Computer-Mediated-Communication (CMC), Treem and Leonardi (2013) have pointed out that social media differs from computer-mediated communication in some ways namely visibility, persistence, editability, and association. Thanks to these affordances businesses may alter their socialization, knowledge sharing, and power processes.

IRREPRESSIBLE POPULARITY OF SNSs

In this section, we try to define what SNS addiction it is and what features it consists of. We have also briefly examined the reasons for SNS usage and the consequences of it. After, we have briefly examined the previous studies about the related subject.

Term Of SNS Addiction

Addiction is a complex concept, and it is tough to define it accurately. Generally speaking, there are two kinds of addiction exists; substance addiction and non-substance addiction. Former one expresses the fondness for certain substances such as alcohol or drug. The later one comes into our lives with the advancement of technology and more related to individuals' behavior. That is why it is also called behavioral addiction (Alavi et al., 2012). Marlatt, Baer, Donovan, and Kivlahan (1988, p. 224), who have defined addictive behavior as: "…a repetitive habit pattern that increases the risk of disease and/or associated personal and social problems. Addictive behaviors are often experienced subjectively as 'loss of control' – the behavior contrives to occur despite volitional attempts to abstain or moderate use. These habit patterns are typically characterized by immediate gratification (short term reward), often coupled with delayed deleterious effects (long term costs). Attempts to change addictive behavior (via treatment or self-initiation) are typically marked with high relapse rates." More specifically, Walker (1989, p.185) has defined a behavioral addiction as "a persistent behavioral pattern characterized by: a desire or need to continue the activity which places it outside voluntary control; a tendency to increase the frequency or amount of the activity over time; psychological dependence on the pleasurable effects of the activity; and, a detrimental effect on the individual and society." In 1990, Goodman has identified the diagnostic criteria for behavioral addictions as can be seen in Figure 5. Griffiths (2005) has concluded topic with his 'components' model of addiction. He has identified six features that each addiction consists of. These are:

1. **Salience**: A particular activity becomes the most important thing in person's life.
2. **Mood Modification**: Consequences of participating in a regular activity.
3. **Tolerance**: Requests more and more from a particular activity.
4. **Withdrawal Symptoms**: Unpleasant feelings in the absence of a particular activity.
5. **Conflict**: Chaos between the addict himself and also those around him.
6. **Relapse**: Be unable to stop doing an undesirable behavior.

Figure 5. Diagnostic criteria for behavioral addictions (Goodman, 1990)

A. Recurrent failure to resist impulses to engage in a specified behaviour.

B. Increasing sense of tension immediately prior the initiation of behaviour.

C. Pleasure or relief at the time of engaging in the behaviour.

D. A feeling of a lack of control while engaging in the behaviour.

E. At least five of the following:

　1. Frequent preoccupation with the behaviour or preparatory activities

　2. Frequent engaging in the behaviour to a greater extent or over a longer period than intended

　3. Repeated efforts to reduce, control or stop the behaviour

　4. A great deal of time spent in activities necessary for the behaviour, engaging in the behaviour or recovering from its effects

　5. Frequent engaging in the behaviour when expected to fulfil occupational, academic, domestic or social obligations

　6. Important social, occupational or recreational activities given up or reduced because of the behaviour

　7. Continuation of the behaviour despite knowledge of having a persistent or recurrent social, financial, psychological or physical problem that is caused or exacerbated by the behaviour

　8. Tolerance: need to increase the intensity or frequency of the behaviour in order to achieve the desired effect or diminished effect with continued behaviour of the same intensity

　9. Restlessness or irritability if unable to engage in the behaviour

F. Some symptoms of the disturbance have persisted for at least 1 month or have occurred repeatedly over a longer period of time.

Young (1999) have classified internet addiction into five groups namely computer addiction, information overload, net compulsions, cyber-sexual addiction and cyber-relationship; however, only one behavioral addiction called pathological gambling –falls into the net compulsion group- has been formally accepted as a diagnostic disorder (American Psychiatric Association, 1987). Although the idea of behavioral addictions is based in scientific knowledge, the concept is still controversial (Grant, Odlaug, & Chamberlain, 2016), researchers aware the other possible behavioral addiction with the evolution of social media and there is an increasing interest in this topic (Andreassen et al., 2013b). In this context, Kuss and Griffiths (2011) have claimed that a rising addiction called SNS addiction has emerged. Andreassen (2015) has also stated that excessive and compulsive behaviors on SNSs can be regarded as an addiction. It should be noted here that excessive usage an activity alone is not enough to accept any behavior as an addiction (Griffiths, 2010). There are many people who use Internet for more than 10 hours a day but have few negative consequences. Griffiths, who is a popular psychologist on behavioral addictions, also believe that being addicted to social media and being addicted to social media are two different things. Just as alcoholics are addicted to alcohol, not the bottle, social media users may be addicted to the activities, not the SNS, itself. Phu and Gow (2019) have also stated that actual time spends on a specific SNS is not a clear indication of being addicted to it since there could be different reasons to use these platforms. Because of these reasons, someone should be carefully evaluated as she or he is addicted to the SNS or not.

Andreassen and Pallesen (2014, p.2) have defined SNS addiction as "being overly concerned about SNSs, driven by a strong motivation to log on to or use SNSs, and to devote so much time and effort to SNSs that it impairs other social activities, studies/job, interpersonal relationships, and/or psychological health and well-being." SNS addiction takes part in the cyber-relationship category since the primary purpose of using these platforms is communication (Kuss & Griffiths, 2011).

Research Topics in SNS Addiction

For a while, researchers have tried to find an answer to one question: What types of person are most likely to use SNS? In literature, there is some evidence that excessive use of SNS is more common in certain groups. For example, Ehrenberg, Juckes, White, and Walsh (2008) have conducted a survey-based study and indicated that more neurotic and low self-esteem individuals have spent more time on social networking activities. They have also stated that people who prefer online communication instead of face to face conversation can be regarded as more anxious and socially insecure. Low self-esteem has been also found to be positively related to SNS addiction in other studies (Bányai et al., 2017; Lou, Yan, Nickerson, & McMorris, 2012). Addictive tendencies appear more common in extroverted and less common in conscientious individuals (Wilson, Fornasier, & White, 2010). Another study has revealed that openness to new experiences, extraversion, and neuroticism are all positively related to SNS addiction (Correa, Hinsley, & De Zuniga, 2010). Impulsivity has been found as another indicator of high usage of SNS (Rothen et al., 2018). Similarly, a more recent study with a convenient cross-sectional sample of 23,532 Norwegians has found that people who are more narcissist with low self-esteem are more likely to use SNS (Andreassen, Pallesen, & Griffiths, 2017). The same study has also indicated that women may tend to develop more addictive habits towards SNS. Although there are some other studies which have admitted that social media addiction is more commonly appears among men (Çam & Işbulan, 2012), research has more consistently suggested that women are more prone to developing addictive SNS use (Andreassen et al., 2013; Kuss, Griffiths, Karila, & Billieux, 2014; Mariko Kasahara, 2017; Tartory, 2019). Kuss et al. (2014) have also investigated that people with no relationship are more willing to use SNS. In the same line but more exciting finding is that married men generally prefer to stay away from social media, whereas women actively engage in social network activities whether they are married or not (Lennon, Rentfro, & Curran, 2012). In addition to gender differences, there is undeniably the dominance of young population in social media. As previous studies have proved that Internet addiction is negatively related to age (Carbonell, Chamarro, Oberst, Rodrigo, & Prades, 2018; Neverkovich et al.,

2018), SNS addiction has also been found a negative relationship with the age. In their inspiring scale construction study, Andreassen, Torbjørn, Brunborg and Pallesen (2012) have admitted that neurotic and extraverted young people are more inclined to develop addictive habits towards Facebook. Turel and Serenko (2012) have investigated the benefits and dangers of enjoyment with SNS and found that age is a significant control variable with negative effect on habit.

CONCLUSION AND FUTURE DIRECTIONS

In our modern world, having a profile and surfing on social media are accepted as normal behaviors (Andreassen, 2015). While there are some gender and age-specific patterns that affect the SNS usage habits, it is stated that internet access or parental education have no longer been concerned as a predictors of social media because people always get a way to be online (Ahn, 2011). Considering that older users have the highest proportion of newly registered users rather than younger ones in recent years (Benson et al., 2019), it can be plausibly asserted that the spread of social media does not lose its speed. This chapter focuses on this popular topic and presents the outline of social media since its early years to state-of-art issues.

As a result of our study, we have agreed on Allen et al. (2014) who have stated that how social media can use its capacity to provide a real benefit?" is still a controversial issue. It is clearly seen that excessive and problematic use of social media -especially SNSs- has several effects on our lives, it is critical to get benefit from these platforms without being addicted to them. Although gambling is the only behavioral addiction that formally accepted (American Psychiatric Association, 1987), there are strong pieces of evidence that problematic use of SNSs can also be an addiction (Körmendi, Brutóczki, Végh, & Székely, 2016). Thus, people get aware about the current situation and take some precautions before they get addicted to them. Regarding positive and negative concerns, successful integration of social media is challenging. Having content with what you already desire entails you moving away from current technological development and becomes you just an audience when your rivals do something more creative.

Our study is not without its limitations. First, the timeline of social media (Figure 3) is a great effort by putting together with the main developments; however we aware that there are also other platforms and events which should be discussed about. Thus, we encourage researchers to design more detailed and comparative visualizations so that evolution of social media can be deeply understood. Second, we have briefly presented the concept of SNS addiction and related literature. We suggest other researchers make empirical researches about this topic since there is emerging literature about this relatively new area.

REFERENCES

Aghazamani, A. (2010). How do university students spend their time on Facebook? An exploratory study. *The Journal of American Science, 6*, 730–735.

Ahn, J. (2011). Digital divides and social network sites: Which students participate in social media? *Journal of Educational Computing Research, 45*(2), 147–163. doi:10.2190/EC.45.2.b

Ainin, S., Naqshbandi, M. M., Moghavvemi, S., & Jaafar, N. I. (2015). Facebook usage, socialization and academic performance. *Computers & Education, 83*, 64–73. doi:10.1016/j.compedu.2014.12.018

Akıncı Vural, Z. B., & Bat, M. (2010). Yeni Bir İletişim Ortamı Olarak Sosyal Medya: Ege Üniversitesi İletişim Fakültesine Yönelik Bir Araştırma. *Journal of Yaşar University, 20*(5), 3348–3382. doi:10.19168/jyu.65130

Akkaya, D. T. (2013). *Sosyal Medya Reklamlarında Tüketici Algılarının Tutum, Davranış ve Satın Alma Niyeti Üzerine Etkisi*. Trakya Üniversitesi.

Alavi, S. S., Ferdosi, M., Jannatifard, F., Eslami, M., Alaghemandan, H., & Setare, M. (2012). Behavioral addiction versus substance addiction: correspondence of psychiatric and psychological views. *International Journal of Preventive Medicine, 3*(4), 290–294. PMID:22624087

Alhabash, S., & Ma, M. (2017). A tale of four platforms: motivations and uses of Facebook, Twitter, Instagram, and Snapchat among college students? *Social Media and Society, 3*(1). doi:10.1177/2056305117691544

Allen, K. A., Ryan, T., Gray, D. L., McInerney, D. M., & Waters, L. (2014). Social media use and social connectedness in adolescents: The positives and the potential pitfalls. *Australian Educational and Developmental Psychologist, 31*(1), 18–31. doi:10.1017/edp.2014.2

American Psychiatric Association. (1987). *Diagnostic and statistical manual of mental disorders.* Washington, DC.

Andreassen, C. S. (2015). Online social network site addiction: a comprehensive review. *Current Addiction Reports, 2*(2), 175–184. doi:10.100740429-015-0056-9

Andreassen, C. S., Griffiths, M. D., Gjertsen, S. R., Krossbakken, E., Kvam, S., & Pallesen, S. (2013a). The relationships between behavioral addictions and the five-factor model of personality. *Journal of Behavioral Addictions, 2*(2), 90–99. doi:10.1556/JBA.2.2013.003 PMID:26165928

Andreassen, C. S., Griffiths, M. D., Gjertsen, S. R., Krossbakken, E., Kvam, S., & Pallesen, S. (2013b). The relationships between behavioral addictions and the five-factor model of personality. *Journal of Behavioral Addictions, 2*(2), 90–99. doi:10.1556/JBA.2.2013.003 PMID:26165928

Andreassen, C. S., & Pallesen, S. (2014). Social network site addiction-an overview. *Current Pharmaceutical Design, 20*(25), 1–9. Retrieved from http://freepsychologypdf.com/wp-content/uploads/2018/07/Andreassen-2014-Social-network-site-addiction-An-overview.pdf. doi:10.2174/13816128113199990616 PMID:24001298

Andreassen, C. S., Pallesen, S., & Griffiths, M. D. (2017). The relationship between addictive use of social media, narcissism, and self-esteem: Findings from a large national survey. *Addictive Behaviors, 64*, 287–293. doi:10.1016/j.addbeh.2016.03.006 PMID:27072491

Andreassen, C. S., Torsheim, T., Brunborg, G. S., & Pallesen, S. (2012). Development of a facebook addiction scale. *Psychological Reports, 110*(2), 501–517. doi:10.2466/02.09.18.PR0.110.2.501-517 PMID:22662404

Baek, Y. M., Bae, Y., & Jang, H. (2013). Social and parasocial relationships on social network sites and their differential relationships with users' psychological well-being. *Cyberpsychology, Behavior, and Social Networking, 16*(7), 512–517. doi:10.1089/cyber.2012.0510 PMID:23697533

Bányai, F., Zsila, Á., Király, O., Maraz, A., Elekes, Z., Griffiths, M., ... Demetrovics, Z. (2017). Problematic social media use: Results from a large-scale nationally representative adolescent sample. *PLoS One*, *12*(1), 10–14. doi:10.1371/journal.pone.0169839 PMID:28068404

Bennett, S. (2014). 70% of college students post to Snapchat daily (Twitter: 46%, Facebook: 11%). Retrieved from https://www.adweek.com/digital/snapchat-facebook-twitter-instagram-privacy/

Benson, V., Hand, C., & Hartshorne, R. (2019). How compulsive use of social media affects performance: Insights from the UK by purpose of use. *Behaviour & Information Technology*, *38*(6), 549–563. doi:10.1080/0144929X.2018.1539518

Boyd, D. (2006). Friendster lost steam. Is MySpace just a fad? Retrieved from https://www.danah.org/papers/FriendsterMySpaceEssay.html

Boyd, D. M. (2006). Friends, friendsters, and top 8: Writing community into being on social network sites. *First Monday*, *11*(12). doi:10.5210/fm.v11i12.1418

Boyd, D. M., & Ellison, N. B. (2007). Social network sites: definition, history, and scholarship. *Journal of Computer-Mediated Communication*, *13*(1), 210–230. doi:10.1111/j.1083-6101.2007.00393.x

Boyd, D. M., & Ellison, N. B. (2008). Social network sites: Definition, history, and scholarship. *Journal of Computer-Mediated Communication*, *13*(1), 210–230. doi:10.1111/j.1083-6101.2007.00393.x

Bruns, A. (2006). *Blogs, Wikipedia, second life, and beyond: from production to produsage*. New York, NY: Peter Lang.

Çam, E., & Işbulan, O. (2012). A new addiction for teacher candidates: Social networks. *Turkish Online Journal of Educational Technology*, *11*(3), 14–19.

Cann, A., Dimitriou, K., & Hooley, T. (2011). *Social media: A guide for researchers. Research Information Network*. London, UK. Retrieved from https://derby.openrepository.com/bitstream/handle/10545/196715/social media guide for screen.pdf?sequence=6&isAllowed=y

Carbonell, X., Chamarro, A., Oberst, U., Rodrigo, B., & Prades, M. (2018). Problematic use of the internet and smartphones in university students: 2006–2017. *International Journal of Environmental Research and Public Health*, *15*(3). doi:10.3390/ijerph15030475

CBSNews. (2019). *Then and now: a history of social networking sites*. Retrieved from https://www.cbsnews.com/pictures/then-and-now-a-history-of-social-networking-sites/5/

Chafkin, M. (2007). *How to kill a great idea!* Retrieved from https://www.inc.com/magazine/20070601/features-how-to-kill-a-great-idea.html

Choi, J., & Kim, H. J. (2016). Influence of SNS user innovativeness and public individuation on SNS usage patterns and social capital development: the case of Facebook. *International Journal of Human-Computer Interaction*, *32*(12), 921–930. doi:10.1080/10447318.2016.1220067

Comsource. (2018). *Understand and evaluate audiences and advertising everywhere*. Retrieved from https://www.comscore.com/Products/Ratings-and-Planning

Correa, T., Hinsley, A. W., & De Zuniga, H. (2010). Who interacts on the Web? The intersection of users' personality and social media use. *Computers in Human Behavior*, *26*(2), 247–253. doi:10.1016/j.chb.2009.09.003

Curran, J., & Lennon, R. (2011). Participating in the conversation: exploring adoption of online social media networks. *Academy of Marketing Studies*, *15*(1), 21–38.

Dawley, L. (2009). Social network knowledge construction: Emerging virtual world pedagogy. *On the Horizon*, *17*(2), 109–121. doi:10.1108/10748120910965494

Denning, S. (2015). *Has Google+ really died?* Retrieved from https://www.forbes.com/sites/stevedenning/2015/04/23/has-google-really-died/#10b77352466c

Ehrenberg, A., Juckes, S., White, K. M., & Walsh, S. P. (2008). Personality and self-esteem as predictors of young people's technology use. *Cyberpsychology & Behavior*, *11*(6), 739–741. doi:10.1089/cpb.2008.0030 PMID:18991531

Ellison, N. B., Steinfield, C., & Lampe, C. (2007). The benefits of Facebook "friends:" Social capital and college students' use of online social network sites. *Journal of Computer-Mediated Communication*, *12*(4), 1143–1168. doi:10.1111/j.1083-6101.2007.00367.x

Ellison, N. B., Steinfield, C., & Lampe, C. (2011). Connection strategies: Social capital implications of Facebook-enabled communication practices. *New Media & Society*, *13*(6), 873–892. doi:10.1177/1461444810385389

Evans, D. (2008). *Social media marketing an hour a day*. Indiana: Wiley Publishing.

Feiner, L. (2019). *Snap has nearly doubled its stock price since the beginning of 2019 — here's why.* Retrieved from https://www.cnbc.com/2019/04/04/why-snap-stock-has-nearly-doubled-since-the-beginning-of-2019.html

Gebel, M. (2019). *In 15 years Facebook has amassed 2.3 billion users — more than followers of Christianity.* Retrieved from https://www.businessinsider.com/facebook-has-2-billion-plus-users-after-15-years-2019-2

Gerson, J., Plagnol, A. C., & Corr, P. J. (2016). Subjective well-being and social media use: Do personality traits moderate the impact of social comparison on Facebook? *Computers in Human Behavior*, *63*, 813–822. doi:10.1016/j.chb.2016.06.023

Getting, B. (2007). *Basic definitions: Web 1.0, Web. 2.0, Web 3.0.* Retrieved from https://www.practicalecommerce.com/Basic-Definitions-Web-1-0-Web-2-0-Web-3-0

Goodman, A. (1990). Addiction: definition and implications. *British Journal of Addiction*, *85*(11), 1403–1408. doi:10.1111/j.1360-0443.1990.tb01620.x PMID:2285834

Grant, J. E., Odlaug, B. L., & Chamberlain, S. R. (2016). *What is a behavioral addiction?* Retrieved from https://www.psychologytoday.com/intl/blog/why-cant-i-stop/201606/what-is-behavioral-addiction

Greengard, S. (2012). Digitally possessed. *Communications of the ACM*, *55*(5), 14–16. doi:10.1145/2160718.2160725

Greenwood, J., Guner, N., Santos, C., & Kocharkov, G. (2016). Technology and the changing family: A unified model of marriage, divorce, educational attainment and marred female labor-force participation. *American Economic Journal. Macroeconomics, 8*(1), 1–41. doi:10.1257/mac.20130156

Griffiths, M. (2005). A "components" model of addiction within a biopsychosocial framework. *Journal of Substance Use, 10*(4), 191–197. doi:10.1080/14659890500114359

Griffiths, M. D. (2010). The role of context in online gaming excess and addiction: Some case study evidence. *International Journal of Mental Health and Addiction, 8*(1), 119–125. doi:10.100711469-009-9229-x

Hargittai, E., & Hsieh, Y. (2010). Predictors and consequences of differentiated practices on social network sites. *Information Communication and Society, 13*(4), 515–536. doi:10.1080/13691181003639866

Hayes, R. A., Carr, C. T., & Wohn, D. Y. (2016). One click, many meanings: interpreting paralinguistic digital affordances in social media. *Journal of Broadcasting & Electronic Media, 60*(1), 171–187. doi:10.1080/08838151.2015.1127248

Heim, J., & Hansen, G. (1999). *Free stuff for sewing fanatics on the internet.* Lafayette, CA: C&T Publishing.

Hollars, K., & Lew, A. (2010). Digital sky technologies to acquire AOL's ICQ instant messaging service. Retrieved from https://www.businesswire.com/news/home/6268204/en

Huang, S.-H., & Capps, M. (2013). Impact of online social network on american college students' reading practices. *The College Quarterly, 16*(1). Retrieved from http://collegequarterly.ca/2013-vol16-num01-winter/huang-capps.html

Junco, R. (2012). The relationship between frequency of Facebook use, participation in Facebook activities, and student engagement. *Computers & Education, 58*(1), 162–171. doi:10.1016/j.compedu.2011.08.004

Junco, R. (2012). Too much face and not enough books: The relationship between multiple indices of Facebook use and academic performance. *Computers in Human Behavior, 28*(1), 187–198. doi:10.1016/j.chb.2011.08.026

Junco, R. (2014). *Engaging students through social media: evidence-based practices for use in student affairs.* San Francisco, CA: Jossey-Bass.

Junco, R., Heiberger, G., & Loken, E. (2011). The effect of Twitter on college student engagement and grades. *Journal of Computer Assisted Learning, 27*(2), 119–132. doi:10.1111/j.1365-2729.2010.00387.x

Kalpidou, M., Costin, D., & Morris, J. (2011). The relationship between Facebook and the well-being of undergraduate college students. *Cyberpsychology, Behavior, and Social Networking, 14*(4), 183–189. doi:10.1089/cyber.2010.0061 PMID:21192765

Kaplan, A. M., & Haenlein, M. (2010). Users of the world, unite! The challenges and opportunities of Social Media. *Business Horizons, 53*(1), 59–68. doi:10.1016/j.bushor.2009.09.003

Kietzmann, J. H., Hermkens, K., McCarthy, I. P., & Silvestre, B. S. (2011). Social media? Get serious! Understanding the functional building blocks of social media. *Business Horizons, 54*(3), 241–251. doi:10.1016/j.bushor.2011.01.005

Kircaburun, K., Demetrovics, Z., & Tosuntaş, Ş. B. (2018). Analyzing the links between problematic social media use, dark triad traits, and self-esteem. *International Journal of Mental Health and Addiction*. doi:10.100711469-018-9900-1

Körmendi, A., Brutóczki, Z., Végh, B. P., & Székely, R. (2016). Smartphone use can be addictive? A case report. *Journal of Behavioral Addictions*, *5*(3), 548–552. doi:10.1556/2006.5.2016.033 PMID:27599674

Kuhn, T. (1962). *The structure of scientific revolutions*. Chicago, IL: University of Chicago Press.

Kuss, D. J., Griffiths, M., Karila, L., & Billieux, J. (2014). Internet addiction: A systematic review of epidemiological research for the last decade, *1*(4), 397–413.

Kuss, D. J., & Griffiths, M. D. (2011). Online social networking and addiction-A review of the psychological literature. *International Journal of Environmental Research and Public Health*, *8*(9), 3528–3552. doi:10.3390/ijerph8093528 PMID:22016701

Langford, S. (2019). Junk explained: What the hell is TikTok, and is it the new vine? Retrieved from https://junkee.com/tiktok-app-vine-challenge/188567

Laroche, M., Habibi, M. R., & Richard, M. O. (2013). To be or not to be in social media: How brand loyalty is affected by social media? *International Journal of Information Management*, *33*(1), 76–82. doi:10.1016/j.ijinfomgt.2012.07.003

Lennon, R., Rentfro, R. W., & Curran, J. M. (2012). Exploring relationships between demographic variables and social networking use. *Journal of Management and Marketing Research*, *11*, 1–17.

Levenson, J. C., Shensa, A., Sidani, J. E., Colditz, J. B., & Primack, B. A. (2016). The association between social media use and sleep disturbance among young adults. *Preventive Medicine*, *85*, 36–41. doi:10.1016/j.ypmed.2016.01.001 PMID:26791323

Lim, J., & Richardson, J. C. (2016). Exploring the effects of students' social networking experience on social presence and perceptions of using SNSs for educational purposes. *Internet and Higher Education*, *29*, 31–39. doi:10.1016/j.iheduc.2015.12.001

Lou, L. L., Yan, Z., Nickerson, A., & McMorris, R. (2012). An examination of the reciprocal relationship of loneliness and Facebook use among first-year college students. *Journal of Educational Computing Research*, *46*(1), 105–117. doi:10.2190/EC.46.1.e

Lusk, B. (2010). *Digital natives and social media behaviors: an overview*. Retrieved from https://teachandtechassign3.weebly.com/uploads/1/4/2/0/14202725/digital_natives_and_social_media_behaviour.pdf

Magsamen-Conrad, K., Billiotte-Verhoff, C., & Greene, K. (2014). Technology addiction's contribution to mental wellbeing: The positive effect of online social capital. *Computers in Human Behavior*, *40*, 23–30. doi:10.1016/j.chb.2014.07.014 PMID:25568591

Mariko Kasahara, G. (2017). *Gender differences in social media use and cyberbullying in Belize*. Retrieved from https://cornerstone.lib.mnsu.edu/etdsOtherCapstoneProjects.753.https://cornerstone.lib.mnsu.edu/etds/753

Marlatt, G. A., Baer, J. S., Donovan, D. M., & Kivlahan, D. R. (1988). Addictive behaviors: Etiology and treatment. *Annual Review of Psychology, 39*(1), 223–252. doi:10.1146/annurev.ps.39.020188.001255 PMID:3278676

Marwick, A. (2013). *Status update: Celebrity, publicity, and branding in the social media age.* New Haven: Yale UP.

Mayfield, A. (2010). What is social media? doi:10.12968/bjom.2014.22.12.896

McGoogan, C. (2016). *Yahoo: 9 reasons for the internet icon's decline.* Retrieved from https://www.telegraph.co.uk/technology/2016/07/25/yahoo-9-reasons-for-the-internet-icons-decline/

Meena, P. S., Soni, R., Jain, M., & Paliwal, S. (2015). Social networking sites addiction and associated psychological problems among young adults: A study from North India. *Sri Lanka Journal of Psychiatry, 6*(1), 14. doi:10.4038ljpsyc.v6i1.8055

Molina, B. (2017). *Twitter overcounted active users since 2014, shares surge on profit hopes.* Retrieved from https://www.usatoday.com/story/tech/news/2017/10/26/twitter-overcounted-active-users-since-2014-shares-surge/801968001/

Moqbel, M., & Kock, N. (2018). Unveiling the dark side of social networking sites: Personal and work-related consequences of social networking site addiction. *Information & Management, 55*(1), 109–119. doi:10.1016/j.im.2017.05.001

Munzel, A., Meyer-Waarden, L., & Galan, J. P. (2018). The social side of sustainability: Well-being as a driver and an outcome of social relationships and interactions on social networking sites. *Technological Forecasting and Social Change, 130*(July 2017), 14–27. doi:10.1016/j.techfore.2017.06.031

Neverkovich, S. D., Bubnova, I. S., Kosarenko, N. N., Sakhieva, R. G., Sizova, Z. M., Zakharova, V. L., & Sergeeva, M. G. (2018). Students' internet addiction: Study and prevention. *Eurasia Journal of Mathematics, Science, and Technology Education, 14*(4), 1483–1495. doi:10.29333/ejmste/83723

O'Shea, W. (2003). Six degrees of sexual frustration -- connecting the dates with Friendster.com. Retrieved from http://www.freerepublic.com/focus/f-news/924322/posts

Oberst, L. (2010). The 6S social network. Retrieved from http://www.sciepub.com/reference/167008

Odabaşı, Y. (2010). Tüketicilikte Dönüşümler. In *Bilgi ve İletişim Teknolojileri Işığında Dönüşümler.* Ankara, Turkey: Nobel Yayıncılık.

Ong, T. (2018). *Whatsapp launches a separate app for small businesses.* Retrieved from https://www.theverge.com/2018/1/19/16908810/whatsapp-business-app-launch-small-businesses

Ovadia, S. (2011). Internet connection: an early introduction to the Google+ social networking project. *Behavioral & Social Sciences Librarian, 30*(4), 259–263. doi:10.1080/01639269.2011.622258

Pariser, E. (2011). *The filter bubble.* New York, NY: Penguin Press.

Phillips, B. J., Miller, J., & McQuarrie, E. F. (2014). Dreaming out loud on pinterest: New forms of indirect persuasion. *International Journal of Advertising, 33*(4), 633–655. doi:10.2501/IJA-33-4-633-655

Phillips, S. (2007). A brief history of Facebook. Retrieved from https://www.theguardian.com/technology/2007/jul/25/media.newmedia

Phu, B., & Gow, A. J. (2019). Facebook use and its association with subjective happiness and loneliness. *Computers in Human Behavior, 92*(June 2018), 151–159. doi:10.1016/j.chb.2018.11.020

Pink, D. (2005). *A whole new mind: why right-brainers will rule the future*. New York, NY: Riverhead Books.

Raice, S. (2012). *Days of wild user growth appear over at Facebook*. Retrieved from https://www.wsj.com/articles/SB10001424052702303296604577454970244896342

Rettberg, J. W. (2009). Freshly generated for you, and Barack Obama: How social media represent your life. *European Journal of Communication, 24*(4), 451–466. doi:10.1177/0267323109345715

Rettberg, J. W. (2017). Self representation in social media. In J. Burgess, A. Marwick, & T. Poell (Eds.), *SAGE handbook of social media* (pp. 1–30). Retrieved from http://dspace.uib.no/bitstream/handle/1956/13073/Self-Representation_in_Social_Media.pdf?sequence=1&isAllowed=y

Rothen, S., Briefer, J. F., Deleuze, J., Karila, L., Andreassen, C. S., Achab, S., ... Billieux, J. (2018). Disentangling the role of users' preferences and impulsivity traits in problematic Facebook use. *PLoS One, 13*(9), 1–13. doi:10.1371/journal.pone.0201971 PMID:30183698

Rusli, E. M., & MacMillan, D. (2014). Snapchat fetches $10 billion valuation. Retrieved from https://www.wsj.com/articles/snapchat-fetches-10-billion-valuation-1409088794

Sharp, E. H., Coatsworth, J. D., Darling, N., Cumsille, P., & Ranieri, S. (2007). Gender differences in the self-defining activities and identity experiences of adolescents and emerging adults. *Journal of Adolescence, 30*(2), 251–269. doi:10.1016/j.adolescence.2006.02.006 PMID:16600358

Social, W. A. (2019). *Global social media research summary*. Retrieved from https://www.smartinsights.com/social-media-marketing/social-media-strategy/new-global-social-media-research/

Stanley, B. (2015). *Uses and gratifications of temporary social media: A comparison of Snapchat and Facebook*. Fullerton, CA: California State University.

Statista. (2019a). *Number of monthly active Pinterest users worldwide from 1st quarter 2016 to 2nd quarter 2019 (in millions)*. Retrieved from https://www.statista.com/statistics/463353/pinterest-global-mau/

Statista. (2019b). *Number of social network users worldwide from 2010 to 2021 (in billions)*. Retrieved from https://www.statista.com/statistics/278414/number-of-worldwide-social-network-users/

Stout, D. W. (2019). Social media statistics 2019: top networks by the numbers. Retrieved from https://dustinstout.com/social-media-statistics/

Sweney, M., & De Liz, A. (2018). *"Parents killed it": why Facebook is losing its teenage users*. Retrieved from https://www.theguardian.com/technology/2018/feb/16/parents-killed-it-facebook-losing-teenage-users

Tartory, R. (2019). Gender-associated behavior of Jordanians on Facebook. *International Journal of English Linguistics*, *9*(2), 383. doi:10.5539/ijel.v9n2p383

Taylor, R., King, F., & Nelson, G. (2012). Student learning through social media. *Journal of Sociological Research*, *3*(2), 29–35. doi:10.5296/jsr.v3i2.2136

Trainor, K. J., Andzulis, J., Rapp, A., & Agnihotri, R. (2014). Social media technology usage and customer relationship performance: A capabilities-based examination of social CRM. *Journal of Business Research*, *67*(6), 1201–1208. doi:10.1016/j.jbusres.2013.05.002

Treem, J. W., & Leonardi, P. M. (2013). Social media use in organizations: exploring the affordances of visibility, editability, persistence, and association. *Annals of the International Communication Association*, *36*(1), 143–189. doi:10.1080/23808985.2013.11679130

Turel, O., & Serenko, A. (2012). The benefits and dangers of enjoyment with social networking websites. *European Journal of Information Systems*, *21*(5), 512–528. doi:10.1057/ejis.2012.1

Utz, S., Muscanell, N., & Khalid, C. (2015). Snapchat elicits more jealousy than Facebook: A comparison of Snapchat and Facebook use. *Cyberpsychology, Behavior, and Social Networking*, *18*(3), 141–146. doi:10.1089/cyber.2014.0479 PMID:25667961

Valkenburg, P. M., Peter, J., & Schouten, A. P. (2006). Friend networking sites and their relationship to adolescents' well-being and social self-esteem. *Cyberpsychology & Behavior*, *9*(5), 584–590. doi:10.1089/cpb.2006.9.584 PMID:17034326

Walker, M. B. (1989). Some problems with the concept of "gambling addiction". Should theories of addiction be generalized to include excessive gambling? *Journal of Gambling Studies*, *5*(3), 179–200. doi:10.1007/BF01024386

Walther, J. B., & Ramirez, A. (2009). New technologies and new direction in online relating. In S. Smith, & S. Wilson (Eds.), *New directions in interpersonal communication* (pp. 189–214). Thousand Oaks, CA: Sage.

Wang, J. L., Jackson, L. A., Gaskin, J., & Wang, H. Z. (2014). The effects of Social Networking Site (SNS) use on college students' friendship and well-being. *Computers in Human Behavior*, *37*, 229–236. doi:10.1016/j.chb.2014.04.051

Wang, Q., Chen, W., & Liang, Y. (2011). *The impact of social media on college students. Journal of College and Character*. Johnson & Wales University. doi:10.1515/jcc-2013-0004

Whiting, A., & Williams, D. (2013). Why people use social media: A uses and gratifications approach. *Qualitative Market Research*, *16*(4), 362–369. doi:10.1108/QMR-06-2013-0041

Williams, A. L., & Merten, M. J. (2011). iFamily: Internet and social media technology in the family context. *Family and Consumer Sciences Research Journal*, *40*(2), 150–170. doi:10.1111/j.1552-3934.2011.02101.x

Wilson, K., Fornasier, S., & White, K. M. (2010). Psychological predictors of young adults' use of social networking sites. *Cyberpsychology, Behavior, and Social Networking*, *13*(2), 173–177. doi:10.1089/cyber.2009.0094 PMID:20528274

Wu, A. M. S., Cheung, V. I., Ku, L., & Hung, E. P. W. (2013). Psychological risk factors of addiction to social networking sites among Chinese smartphone users. *Journal of Behavioral Addictions*, *2*(3), 160–166. doi:10.1556/JBA.2.2013.006 PMID:25215198

Young, K. (1999). Internet addiction: Evaluation and treatment. *Student BMJ*, *7*, 351–352.

Chapter 55
Online Social Networking and Romantic Relationships

Irem Metin-Orta
 https://orcid.org/0000-0001-9253-9158
Atilim University, Turkey

ABSTRACT

With the increased popularity of social media, social networking sites (SNSs) have received the attention of many scholars. In particular, researchers have focused on the impact of SNSs on interpersonal relationships. Accordingly, this chapter provides an overview of the extant literature concerning associations between the use of SNSs and romantic relationships. It provides empirical evidence on how social networking behaviors are influenced by adult attachment styles, and how social networking influences relationship constructs such as satisfaction, commitment, jealousy, and relationship dissolution. Furthermore, it presents previous research that emphasizes gender as a moderator in these relations. This chapter overall contributes to researchers and professionals in providing information on online social networking and emphasizing key romantic relationship constructs related to the use of SNSs. It also provides suggestions for future research.

INTRODUCTION

With the advances in wireless communication technologies, social media use has become prevalent among individuals. To illustrate, the number of active users of social media around the world was 2.46 billion in 2017 and this number is expected to reach to 3.02 billion by 2021 (Statista Facts on Social Networks, 2018). Given its prevalence and importance in interpersonal communication, scholars have shown an interest in online social networking and conducted numerous research to understand its influence on interpersonal relationships. In particular, they have focused on Social Network Sites (SNSs) such as Facebook or Twitter, and addressed several characteristics of individuals, such as attachment style (Emery, Muise, Dix, & Le, 2014a; Fox & Warber, 2014) and SNSs-induced jealousy (Muise, Christofides & Desmarais, 2009; 2014; Utz & Beukeboom, 2011) as well as relationship characteristics

DOI: 10.4018/978-1-6684-6307-9.ch055

such as relationship happiness (Mod, 2010; Utz & Beukeboom, 2011), satisfaction (Elphinston & Noller, 2011; Saslow, Muise, Impett, & Dubin, 2013), commitment (Dibble & Drouin, 2014; Drouin, Miller, & Dibble, 2014) and dissolution (Clayton, Nagurney, & Smith, 2013; Clayton, 2014) as outcomes or predictors of SNSs-related behaviors of partners in a romantic relationship.

This chapter aims to provide an overview of the extant literature concerning associations among the use of SNSs and romantic relationship constructs. Given that SNSs enable public communication between partners (Billedo, Kerkhof, & Finkenauer, 2015) and may either damage or benefit an emotional relationship between partners, the investigation of the associations between the use of SNSs and romantic relationship constructs is warranted. Accordingly, this chapter provides information on how the use of SNSs influences and is influenced by individual and relationship characteristics. Furthermore, plausible moderators and mediators in these relations are explained. Thus, this chapter would contribute to researchers and communication professionals in providing information on online social networking and emphasizing key romantic relationship constructs related to the use of SNSs. It also provides suggestions for future research directions.

Several issues are addressed in this chapter. First, online social networking is introduced and the emergent interest in SNSs is discussed. Second, the research addressing online social networking and romantic relationships are reviewed. To do so, EBSCOhost, Psych ARTICLES and Scopus electronic databases were used to search several keywords such as *social media, social networking sites, online social networking, intimacy, romantic relationship, jealousy, satisfaction, commitment, etc.* The articles were primarily chosen from those published in the past 10 years. Lastly, the findings of the current literature are summarized, and limitations and suggestions for future research are mentioned.

BACKGROUND

SNSs are online platforms where individuals can generate profiles, interact with friends, meet with other people based on common interests and trace the networks of connected users (boyd & Ellison, 2007; Kuss & Griffiths, 2011). Under the broader term of 'social media', SNSs are described as web-based services that allow for maintenance of social relationships within one's social network (boyd & Ellison, 2007; Rus & Tiemensma, 2017, p.685). Many people spend a great amount of time in SNSs. According to a survey, 71% of people who use the internet were social network users in 2017, and this rate is expected to grow (Statista Facts on Social Networks, 2018).

Facebook was first launched as an online student community at Harvard University in 2004 and became the most popular social networking site worldwide with 2.2 billion active users in 2018 (Statista Facts on Social Networks, 2018). Accordingly, most research on the use of SNSs has focused on Facebook, followed by Youtube, Whatsapp, Facebook Messenger, WeChat and Instagram. Given the popularity and high rate of prevalence of the use of SNSs, social networking and its possible influence on romantic relationships call for investigation. Thus, the following section of the chapter reviews the empirical research focusing on how the use of SNSs influences romantic relationships and is influenced by individual and relationship characteristics.

In general, people might initiate and maintain romantic relationships through public declaration of love and commitment, and through monitoring partner's status updates, photos, wall postings, and friends on SNSs (Marshall, Bejanyan, Di Castro, & Lee, 2013). In particular, it is proposed that social networking influences romantic relationships through three different ways: 1) Through increasing the information that individuals receive about their partner, 2) through offering an acceptable way of monitoring the partner, and 3) through publicly sharing information related to a romantic relationship (Utz & Beukeboom, 2011, p. 512).

Scholars have also addressed gender differences in investigating the associations among the use of SNSs and romantic relationships. For instance, it has been argued that SNSs serve different social functions for men and women (Rus & Tiemensma, 2017). In particular, the genders differ in their motivations for the use of SNSs due to different gender-role expectations (Muscanell & Guadagno, 2012). That is, men are more likely to use SNSs such as MySpace and Facebook for relationship formation (i.e., to find potential dates) whereas women are more likely to use these sites for relationship maintenance (Muscanell & Guadagno, 2012; Raacke & Bonds-Raacke, 2008).

In the extant literature, considerable research has been conducted on the positive and negative effects of SNSs on romantic relationships (see Rus & Tiemensma, 2017 for a review). While some scholars suggest that social networking may be beneficial in enabling people to keep in touch with others (Joinson, 2008), other scholars propose that excessive use of SNSs may be damaging to romantic relationships (Clayton, 2014; Clayton et al., 2013). Accordingly, in the following section, the relationship between social networking and relationship constructs including attachment style, relationship satisfaction, commitment, jealousy, and dissolution are presented, along with the identification of existing gender differences in the current literature. In specific, it reviews empirical research on how attachment style influences social networking behavior, and how online social networking influences romantic relationship constructs.

MAIN FOCUS OF THE CHAPTER

Social Networking and Attachment Style

Attachment theory (Bartholomew & Horowitz, 1991; Collins & Read, 1990) provides a framework to understand romantic relationships. Hazan and Shaver (1987) conceptualized romantic love as an attachment process, and proposed that adult attachment style is determined by infant's relationship with a primary caregiver. In early stages of life, infants develop internal working models (positive/negative images for the self and the others) based on experiences with parents, and these models later influence relationships in adulthood (Bowlby, 1969). Drawing upon Bowlby's (1969) original formulation, Hazan and Shaver (1987) proposed three attachment styles of adulthood (secure, avoidant, anxious/ambivalent) that corresponds to those in early years. Later, Bartholomew and Horowitz (1991) proposed four attachment styles (secure, preoccupied, dismissing, and fearful) that were derived from a combination of two dimensions.

Securely attached individuals (low anxiety, low avoidance) desire intimacy, preoccupied/anxious individuals (high anxiety, low avoidance) desire closeness but fear rejection, dismissive/avoidant individuals (low anxiety, high avoidance) avoid intimacy due to desire for independence, and fearful individuals (high anxiety, high avoidance) avoid intimacy due to desire for not being hurt (Bartholomew & Horowitz, 1991). Accordingly, research on adult attachment have shown that secure individuals have higher self-confidence, higher level of involvement in romantic relationships, and express greater interpersonal warmth (Bartholomew & Horowitz, 1991). Furthermore, they are better able to seek and provide support (Collins & Feeney, 2000) and have more satisfaction with their relationships (Collins & Read, 1990).

Scholars examined adult attachment style as an underlying mechanism predicting SNSs-related behaviors and emotional reactions to SNSs content (Rus & Tiemensma, 2017). A number of studies investigating attachment styles and the use of SNSs show that anxiety and avoidance dimensions predict how people use and react emotionally in SNSs (Emery et al., 2014a; Fleuriet, Cole, & Guerrero, 2014; Fox & Warber, 2014; Marshall et al., 2013). Anxious individuals reported more desire for relationship visibility (i.e., via the display of couple photos and relationship statuses on Facebook) while avoidant individuals reported less desire for visibility especially when they believed that others perceive their relationship as low quality (Emery et al., 2014a). Moreover, when individuals felt more insecure about their partners' feelings, they preferred more visibility. In other terms, they prefer their relationships to appear as an important aspect of their self-images on SNSs.

In another study, Morey, Gentzler, Creasy, Obenhauser, and Westerman (2013) investigated whether the way that social networking relates to intimacy/support depends on one's attachment style. In a sample of undergraduate students who were in a committed romantic relationship, it was revealed that greater use of SNSs is associated with more intimacy/support among individuals with attachment anxiety. It was argued that some aspects of SNSs such as posting relationship status or dyadic photos in the profile may buffer the negative effects of insecure attachment through creating a secure environment and support to the individual (Morey et al., 2013).

Researchers have also examined attachment style in relation to partner surveillance and feelings of relationship uncertainty. For instance, an online survey of university students revealed that due to high levels of relationship anxiety, fearful and preoccupied individuals experience higher levels of relationship uncertainty and show the highest level of partner surveillance (Fox & Warber, 2014). In another study, attachment anxiety was positively while attachment avoidance was negatively associated with jealousy and partner surveillance (Marshall et al., 2013). In addition, lower partner trust and daily jealousy partially mediated the anxiety association. Similarly, attachment anxiety was positively associated with negative emotion in response to an ambiguous message on a partner's wall that might invoke jealousy (Fleuriet et al., 2014). Taken together, the previous research indicate that the emotional bond among partners influences the link between social networking and romantic relationship.

Social Networking and Relationship Satisfaction

In addition to individual characteristics such as attachment style, online social networking has been studied with respect to several relationship characteristics. Among those characteristics, satisfaction has been extensively investigated by scholars. In specific, relationship satisfaction is defined as the overall evaluation of feelings, thoughts, and behaviors that are associated with a romantic relationship (Hendrick, 1988). A wide array of research focusing on relationship satisfactions often used several terms interchangeably such as marital or relationship satisfaction, relationship adjustment, and happiness (Graham, Diebels, & Barnow, 2011). Relationship satisfaction is widely studied in married couples but is also valid in dating and/or cohabitating couples, and it is an important determinant in predicting the quality and the duration of the relationship.

Recent literature has shown that the use of SNSs and relationship satisfaction are partly associated. Hand, Thomas, Buboltz, Deemer, and Buyanjargal (2013) explored the effect of the time spent on the use of SNSs on both relationship satisfaction and intimacy. The findings based on a sample of undergraduates who identified themselves as exclusively dating, did not report a significant relationship between an individual's use of SNSs and relationship satisfaction. However, it was reported that the relationship between romantic partner's online social network usage and relationship satisfaction was mediated by intimacy. That is, higher intimacy between couples might serve as a protective function and thus, diminish the negative effects of perceived partner usage (Hand et al., 2013).

Likewise, in their Facebook intrusion questionnaire development study, Elphinston and Noller (2011) also investigated the associations among Facebook intrusion (excessive attachment on Facebook that interferes with daily activities), relationship satisfaction, jealousy, and partner surveillance. Data were gathered from Australian partners with a high majority being dating couples. Their findings suggest that time spent on Facebook is not significantly related to relationship satisfaction. However, jealousy and surveillance are found to be mediators among Facebook intrusion and satisfaction, such that the negative effect of excessive use of online network site on relationship satisfaction was indirect through the experience of cognitive jealousy and surveillance behaviors. In other words, Facebook intrusion promotes jealousy-related feelings and monitoring behaviors among partners, which in turn leads to relationship dissatisfaction. These findings point toward a need for further research that explores the relationship between SNS-addictions and romantic relationship constructs (Elphinston & Noller, 2011).

Drawing upon Relationship Maintenance Theory (Canary & Stafford, 1992; Stafford & Canary, 1991), some scholars (i.e., Billedo et al., 2015; Dainton, 2013; Steward, Dainton, & Goodboy, 2014) have focused on relationship maintenance strategies in relation to the use of SNSs. These strategies are routine, unconscious behaviors engaged by a partner to maintain a relationship such as "positivity" ("being cheerful around the partner"), "openness" ("disclosing one's desires from the relationship"), "assurances" ("reassuring the partner about commitment"), "social networks" ("relying on common friends and family") and "sharing tasks" ("performing tasks that help the relationship to function") (Dainton, 2013, p. 114). Among these strategies, positivity, assurances and sharing tasks were found to be strongly related to relationship characteristics such as control mutuality, liking, satisfaction and commitment (Canary & Stafford, 1992; Stafford & Canary, 1991). Using a measure of Relationship Maintenance Strategies (Stafford, Dainton, & Haas, 2000), Dainton (2013) examined whether general maintenance behaviors and Facebook maintenance behaviors were related to relationship satisfaction among college students. The researcher found that Facebook positivity (i.e. sending positive messages to partner) and assurances (i.e. expressing love on partner's wall) were positively correlated with relationship satisfaction. However, only Facebook positivity predicted relationship satisfaction after controlling for general maintenance behaviors (Dainton, 2013).

In another study by Billedo et al. (2015), researchers conducted an online survey to investigate the role of SNSs in the maintenance of a long-distance romantic relationship among young adults who use Facebook. They found that compared to those in geographically close romantic relationships, individuals in long-distance romantic relationships use SNSs more to express strategic and routine relationship maintenance behaviors and to monitor their partner's activities for seeking out information concerning their involvement in the relationship. In addition to *partner surveillance* or *stalking*, the persistent monitoring of one's romantic partner's or ex-partner's online activity (Tokunaga, 2011), these individuals reported experiencing higher levels of SNS- related jealousy as well. These findings point out that among partners who are in long-distance romantic relationships, surveillance and SNSs-induced jealousy may serve maintenance function for the relationship. In particular, researchers argue that partner surveillance signals continued interest and concern for the partner who is far away, and jealousy arouses feelings of protectiveness over the relationship, thus affirming love for the other (Billedo et al., 2015).

On the other hand, a group of scholars have proposed that Facebook maintenance behaviors might be related to relationship uncertainty (Steward et al., 2014). Berger and Calabrese's (1975) original formulation of Uncertainty Reduction Theory (Berger & Calabrese, 1975) emphasizes the role that communicative behaviors among partners play in reducing the perceptions of ambiguity within the relationship (Fox & Warber, 2014). Accordingly, Steward et al. (2014) examined whether different types of uncertainty are related to relationship maintenance behaviors. Using Knobloch and Solomon's (1999) classification of relational uncertainty, Steward and her colleagues (2014) revealed that perceptions of mutuality uncertainty (concerning similarity and reciprocity of the shared feelings between partners) and definitional uncertainty (concerning explanation of the the the status of the relationship to others) in a relationship predicted more monitoring behaviors to maintain the relationship among undergraduates who use Facebook. Furthermore, perceptions of future certainty (concerning relationship outcomes over time) and definitional certainty predicted more relationship maintenance strategies of assurances and openness via Facebook. Finally, relationship satisfaction was not related to partner monitoring; but related to positivity and assurances via Facebook (Steward et al., 2014).

In another study, Papp, Danielewicz, and Cayemberg (2012) investigated the nature of the use of SNSs on relationship satisfaction. Based on the data gathered from dating partners, the findings provide evidence that Facebook has a considerable role in dating partners' intimate relationships. More specifically, it is found that portraying the relationship in Facebook determines relationship functioning. Such that, the display of a partner's status for men and the inclusion of their partner in profile picture for women are found to be associated with greater levels of relationship satisfaction. This finding calls for future research exploring the gender differences to underpin the varying attributions regarding portrayals of relationship and its outcomes (Papp et al., 2012). Accordingly, Saslow et al. (2013) investigated whether relationship satisfaction predicts dyadic profile displays and if so whether gender moderates this relationship in both married and dating couples. In two studies, one, cross-sectional, and the other, longitudinal, higher satisfaction among married couples predicted greater likelihood of posting dyadic profile photos both in cross-sectional and over a one year time periods. No significant gender differences were reported (Saslow et al., 2013).

A very similar pattern is also revealed with dating couples such that the tendency to post relationship-relevant information on Facebook was higher on the days when couples felt more satisfied with their relationship (Saslow et al., 2013). In other words, individuals tended to post images of themselves and their partner on Facebook when they were more satisfied with their relationship. As it is proposed, this may stem from the increased feelings of interconnectedness or self-other overlap among partners (Saslow et al., 2013). Besides, when people find public expressions of love and commitment on the profile, it increases feelings of relationship happiness (Mod, 2010; Utz & Beukeboom, 2011). Indeed, individuals tend to experience more happiness than jealousy as a result of their partner's online behavior, thus supporting the notion that SNSs play a role in increasing relationship satisfaction (Utz & Beukeboom, 2011).

Similarly, Orosz and his colleagues (Orosz, Szekeres, Kiss, Farkas, & Roland-Levy, 2015) examined the emotional correlates of publicly announcing relationship status in Facebook, a phenomenon namely *becoming Facebook official* or *FBO* among Hungarian adults. They revealed that among individuals who share relationship-related information in their profiles, there is more increased romantic love and jealousy toward partner than those who do not share that information. It was argued that these jealousy feelings may explain an intention to protect the relationship. However, as the authors indicate, the correlational nature of the study does not allow causal inferences about the relations among variables. In other terms, it is unclear whether love and jealousy feelings predict the declaration of the relationship status or vice versa. Nevertheless, authors argue that *FBO* can be considered as an indicator of maturity in a romantic relationship and thus, it can be labeled as a 'digital wedding ring' in an online platform (Orosz et al., 2015).

On the other hand, Emery, Muise, Alpert, and Le (2014b) addressed the question of how sharing relationship-related information influences other people's impressions of the individual and of their relationship quality. They revealed that among undergraduates who use Facebook, sharing dyadic profile pictures and relationship status was positively associated with perceived relationship quality, measured by the level of satisfaction and commitment, and perceived likeability. Besides, sharing intimate information about the relationship was positively associated with perceived relationship quality, but negatively associated with perceived likeability. These findings indicate that making relationship-related information visible (relationship visibility) conveys a positive image while sharing too much private information (relationship disclosure) conveys a negative image about the individual and the relationship (Emery et al., 2014b).

In a recent study, McDaniel, Drouin, and Cravens (2017) investigated the relationship between the use of SNSs and satisfaction among married couples. With this vein, they mainly focused on one specific type of social network behavior- online social media infidelity related behaviors and explored its prevalence. Moreover, they investigated the relationship between engaging in online infidelity-related behaviors, marital satisfaction and relationship ambivalence on married/cohabiting couples. Only a small percentage of married/cohabiting couples engaged in social media infidelity-related behaviors. Nevertheless, among those, it was reported that the higher the levels of infidelity related behaviors on social media, the lower marital satisfaction (McDaniel et al., 2017). Overall, aforementioned research indicate that even though excessive use of SNSs may be related with relationship dissatisfaction (i.e., Elphinston & Noller, 2011), sharing dyadic profile pictures and relationship status in SNSs may increase relationship satisfaction, and thus, perceived relationship quality.

Social Networking and Relationship Commitment

Another important characteristic of relationship dynamics that has been studied by scholars in relation to social networking is relationship commitment, which is defined as the evaluation of the feelings of psychological attachment to one's partner (Rusbult et al., 1998). The theoretical argumentation regarding the literature between social networking and commitment is built upon the Rusbult's Investment model. According to this model, relationship commitment results from the balance among the perceived costs and benefits of remaining with a partner and perceived quality of alternative partners. In other words, commitment is expected to be greater when the benefits of remaining with a partner outweigh the perceived quality of the alternatives (Rusbult, 1980).

Only a few studies investigated the predictive utility of relationship commitment in explaining SNS behaviors. For instance, Dibble and Drouin (2014) investigated the role of relationship commitment and online communication pattern with alternative potential partners based on data gathered from college students. The authors used the term of 'back burners' in referring to alternative potential partners with whom an individual maintains some degree of communication for keeping the possibility of future romantic and/or sexual involvement (Dibble & Drouin, 2014). Their main goal was to explore whether the individuals involved back burner communication via online channels and whether communicating with back burners through online channels was associated with relationship commitment, investment, and quality of alternatives. The findings revealed that individuals do use computer-based technologies and online channels to communicate with their back burners. Moreover, the use of computer-based technologies ease their task in communicating with alternative partners. Males reported to have more back burners compared to females; however, the number of back burners did not differ between single individuals and the individuals who were currently in relationships. Furthermore, the total number of back burners was not found to be related to relationship commitment or investment in the current partner whereas the number of back burners was found to be positively related to the perceived quality of alternative partners (Dibble & Drouin, 2014).

In another study, Drouin and his colleagues (2014) examined the role of commitment in predicting Facebook solicitation behaviors (i.e. accepting /sending friend requests with romantic interests) and having romantic interests with the existing lists on Facebook. With their sample of undergraduates, they found that lower relationship commitment is positively related to Facebook solicitation behaviors, meaning that those who had a lower commitment to their partners in their current relationship tended to make and accept friend requests with romantic interests on Facebook. However, for single individuals, this relationship was not supported. Nevertheless, the commitment was not related to the number of romantic desirables on a Facebook friends list (Drouin et al., 2014).

Fox, Warber and Makstaller (2013) investigated the role of SNSs, in particular, Facebook, in escalation stages of the romantic relationships. According to Knapp's (1978) dual staircase model, initiation is the first stage that involves "interaction between couples and impression formation", experimenting is the second stage that involves "gathering in-depth information about the partner", intensifying is the third stage that involves "self-disclosure and more commitment between couples", integrating is the fourth stage that involves "formation of shared, public relational identity that results in 'we' feeling", and bonding is the last stage that involves "publicly announcing the relationship through marriage or civil union" (Knapp & Vangelisti, 2009; Fox et al., 2013, p. 773). Drawing upon this model, researchers showed that if the target person was listed as "in a relationship", people were less likely to initiate a relationship with that person than if the person was listed as "single" or no relationship status was posted. Furthermore, in the intensifying and integrating phases, people felt the necessity of publicly declaring their relationship through pictures, relationship status or wall posts. Furthermore, stating the status as 'in a relationship with' another person and providing a link to this person in Facebook was considered as an indicator of an exclusive, long-term, and public commitment (Fox et al., 2013).

Accordingly, Fox and Warber (2013) examined whether public proclamation of an individual's relationship status differed across men and women through an online survey among university students who are Facebook users. Researchers revealed that women are more likely to feel that this status conveyed commitment, seriousness and long-term stability in a relationship. However, men are more likely to believe that an individual might still pursue other relationships since men do not view this status so seriously. These findings indicate that placing a label on the relationship has different meanings (Fox & Warber, 2013) and importance (Papp et al., 2012) for men and women. Nevertheless, it can be argued that specific SNS-related behaviors such as public proclamation of the relationship status contributes to relationship commitment.

Social Networking and Romantic Jealousy

Addressing the dark side of social networking on relationships, scholars have examined romantic jealousy, anxiety, and relational turbulence in their research (i.e. Fox & Moreland, 2015) and tried to uncover how social networking triggers these negative thoughts, feelings and behaviors. One of the first studies linking social media engagement to relationship problems was conducted by Muise and her colleagues

(2009), the results of which show a "jealousy effect". In this study, researchers conducted an online survey among undergraduate students having a romantic relationship and demonstrated that when people spend more time on Facebook and faced with potentially jealousy-provoking information, it increases feelings of jealousy. Muise and her colleagues (2009) also argued that this relationship might be two-directional. That is, spending more time on Facebook increases feelings of jealousy, which in turn may increase monitoring of the partner's profile for more information. The study findings overall indicate the unique contribution of Facebook use on partners' experience of jealousy and suggest a possible feedback loop which increases monitoring partners' profile as a result of heightened jealousy (Muise et al., 2009). Other scholars also confirmed the positive relationship between time spent on Facebook, feelings of jealousy and monitoring of a romantic partner's profile (Muise et al., 2014; Utz & Beukeboom, 2011).

Several scholars investigated the effect of Facebook message content on romantic jealousy. In a series of studies, Hudson and his colleagues (2015) examined how gender and use of emoticons influence Facebook jealousy. Similar to the previous findings (Muise et al., 2009), they showed that females tended to display more Facebook jealousy than males. Interestingly, in open-ended responses, males display more jealousy when there is a message containing a winking emoticon (a sign of flirtation); however, females display more jealousy when there is no emoticon. Similarly, in Fleuriet and his colleagues' (2014) study, as compared to males, females reported more negative emotions following exposure to an ambiguous message with nonverbal cues on their partner's wall. These studies indicate that males and females' responses were differentially affected by specific nonverbal cues that help to clarify the message (i.e. winking emoticon, smiling emoticon). The results also seem to support the evolutionary perspective suggesting that men display more jealousy in response to sexual infidelity whereas women display more jealousy in response to emotional infidelity (Buss, Larsen, Westen & Semmelroth, 1992).

In another experimental study, Muscanell and her colleagues asked undergraduate students who were Facebook users to imagine an ambiguous scenario involving their romantic partners' Facebook page and manipulated user privacy settings and dyadic photos publicly available (Muscanell, Guadagno, Rice & Murphy, 2013). They revealed that when women imagine their partners as posting a photo with another woman, they display more intense feelings of jealousy, anger, and hurt than men. Furthermore, the gender difference in jealousy was higher when the photos were visible to all Facebook friends and users as compared to be visible only to the user. In addition, highest ratings of jealousy were present when there were no dyadic photos of the couple as compared to a few or many photos. As the authors argue, this may indicate that the individual does not acknowledge or wants to hide his/her current relationship. The findings suggest that emotions of women and men are influenced differently from a hypothetical scenario indicating potential infidelity (Muscanell et al., 2013).

In line with previous findings on gender differences in SNSs-induced jealousy (McAndrew & Shah, 2013), Muise et al. (2014) showed that women are more jealous when they view their partner's photo with an attractive member of the opposite sex. Women are also more likely to monitor their partners' activities on Facebook in response to jealousy as compared to men. Interestingly, attachment style influences in the link between Facebook jealousy and partner monitoring. That is, feelings of jealousy are linked to attachment anxiety, and higher levels of attachment anxiety is linked to increased partner monitoring on Facebook among women but not among men. In other terms, preoccupied/anxiously attached women spend more time monitoring their partner's activities on Facebook in response to jealousy. It is also consistent with previous findings (Marshall et al., 2013) showing that attachment anxiety is positively associated with jealousy and partner surveillance. Based on previous work it can be argued that gender plays an important role affecting the way that the use of SNSs influences emotional responses.

According to Halpern, Katz and Carril (2017), social media use leads to selfie-related conflicts, which in turn, reduce perceived relationship quality. These conflicts are created through two processes. The first one is jealousy, stemming from the excessive sharing of photos and comments on these photos. In other words, when an individual shares his/her personal images and receives comments on these photos, this increases a partner's feelings of jealousy. The second one is the creation of an online idealized persona in the picture-takers mind, stemming from one's sharing of flattering images. Drawing upon self-affirmation theory (Steele, 1988), one can argue that individuals need to present themselves in a positive and desirable way in SNSs. Accordingly, the ideal persona constructed online via selfies may cause a conflict between how a picture-taker views himself/herself and how partner views the picture-taker. Supporting these arguments, researchers revealed in their longitudinal study conducted among Chilean adults that the negative effect of selfie-taking on relationship quality was mediated through jealousy conflicts and the creation of an online idealized persona (Halpern et al., 2017).

In another study conducted among Dutch undergraduate students involved in a romantic relationship, Utz and Beukeboom (2011) examined the moderating effects of self-esteem and need for popularity in predicting emotional consequences of the use of SNSs for romantic relationships. They found that individuals with low self-esteem experienced more jealousy in reaction to the partner's activities on SNSs than those with high self-esteem, and individuals with a high need for popularity experienced more SNSs-induced jealousy than those with low need for popularity. Furthermore, self-esteem moderated the impact of the use of SNSs and need for popularity on jealousy. The results showed that the need for popularity has stronger effect on SNSs-induced jealousy among individuals with low self-esteem. However, the use of SNSs for maintaining social contact ('grooming') have stronger effect on jealousy among individuals with high self-esteem (Utz & Beukeboom, 2011). Taken together, the results of the aforementioned research indicate that the use of SNSs increases jealousy within romantic relationships.

Social Networking and Relationship Dissolution

A few studies have addressed the relationship between the use of SNSs and its potential consequences on romantic relationship dissolution. Clayton and his colleagues studied Facebook users and investigated whether a conflict over partner's excessive Facebook use acted as a mediator in the relationship between Facebook use and adverse relationship outcomes including infidelity (emotional cheating and physical cheating), breakup and divorce among partners in a newer relationship for three years or less (Clayton, Nagurney & Smith, 2013). It was argued that high levels of Facebook use might be a threat to short-term relationships either through indirectly neglecting the partner, or through adding an ex-partner or -spouse to the friend list and communicating with this person, which in turn produces Facebook-related jealousy and conflict among partners. Similar results were also found for Twitter, a different platform. The results of an online survey conducted among Twitter users revealed that Twitter-related conflict mediated the relationship between active Twitter use and negative relationship outcomes including infidelity, breakup and divorce (Clayton, 2014). However, the length of the romantic relationship did not moderate the indirect effect of Twitter use on negative relationship outcomes through Twitter-related conflict. This finding suggests that this mediational relationship does not change for those who are in shorter (18 months or less) or longer duration relationship. Overall, the findings of these studies point out that conflicts arising from the use of SNSs might trigger problems in the relationship.

LeFebvre and his colleagues examined the effects of social networking on relationship dissolution adjustment (LeFebvre, Blackburn & Brody, 2014). In their study, university students who had a breakup within the past two years completed an online survey that assessed Facebook activities they engaged *during* and *after* the romantic relationship breakup. The most frequently engaged activities *during* relationship dissolution were relational cleansing such as hiding or removing the relationship status (22.7%) and minimal or no Facebook activities (22.6%), followed by partner surveillance (10.2%), self-regulation from partner (9.3%), normative Facebook activities (7.5%) and self-regulation from Facebook (5.3%). Similarly, the most frequently engaged activities *after* relationship dissolution were relational cleansing (20.4%) and minimal or no Facebook activities (19.9%), followed by partner surveillance (10.2%), withdrawing access (9.3%), self-regulation from partner (7.5%), and impression management (7.1%). Interestingly, the results showed that people who did not engage in Facebook activities reported to have better post-breakup adjustment than those who engaged in Facebook activities during and after the breakup (LeFebvre et al., 2014).

Researchers have also examined how SNSs facilitate connections with ex-partner in the relationship dissolution phase. Fox and Tokunaga (2015) investigated the relational and psychological factors that are related to online surveillance. The results showed that higher levels of commitment led to increased emotional distress after the breakup, which in turn led to more online surveillance. In particular, individuals who were more negatively affected by the breakup tended to monitor their ex-partners online activity (Fox & Tokunaga, 2015). In a related vein, Marshall (2012) conducted an online survey among undergraduates to examine how ex-partner surveillance influenced postbreakup adjustment and growth. It was revealed that monitoring of the ex-partner's profile is associated with more distress over the breakup, more negative feelings, more sexual desire for the ex-partner and lower personal growth. Facebook surveillance of an ex-partner may inhibit emotional recovery and growth following a breakup. However, remaining Facebook friends with an ex-partner may not damage the breakup recovery process (Marshall, 2012). As there are limited studies of the link between the use of SNSs and relationship dissolution, scholars should conduct further studies to better understand these relations.

Limitations and Avenues for Future Research

This chapter reviews the extant literature concerning associations between the use of SNSs and romantic relationship constructs. Thereby, it serves as a guide for synthesizing the current state of knowledge. However, it is worth to mention several limitations of the previous research. First, this chapter presents findings of research, the majority of which was conducted among university students who were in a romantic relationship. These individuals, however, are younger, emerging adults whose romantic relationships are of short duration, less established and more prone to feelings of jealousy (Arnett, 2000; Rus & Tiemensma, 2017). Hence, the homogeneity of the sample would limit the generalizability of the findings across broader populations. Therefore, in future studies, scholars will want to examine these relations among older adults who are outside of the university context and who have a romantic relationship for at least 10 years.

Second, the research was mostly conducted on Facebook; however, each platform has a different pattern of use, user characteristics and social functions (Wilson, Gosling, & Graham, 2012). Accordingly, there may be specific SNSs-related behaviors associated with a romantic relationship (Rus & Tiemensma, 2017). For instance, there are differences in individuals' motivation to use Snapchat and Facebook (Utz, Muscanell, & Khalid, 2015). That is, people are more likely to use Snapchat for flirting and finding new partners while they are more likely to use Facebook for interacting with friends. Furthermore, there are differences in visibility and persistence of information between two platforms such that Snapchat offers a higher level of privacy for users as the messages that have been sent in this platform are erased after a few seconds. In line with this, Snapchat and Facebook induce different psychological effects especially in the domain of romantic jealousy with Snapchat evoking higher levels of jealousy in response to partner behaviors (Utz et al., 2015). Therefore, in future research, scholars may focus on other SNSs to examine the generalizability of the previous findings.

Third, the vast majority of previous studies are cross-sectional in nature, thus restricting causal inferences. However, longitudinal studies are needed to identify whether SNSs-related behaviors influence or are influenced by a particular romantic relationship. For instance, in a longitudinal study Saslow et al. (2013) showed that higher satisfaction among married couples predicted greater likelihood of posting dyadic profile photos over a one year time period, indicating the causal inferences among variables.

Fourth, there are limited studies (i.e., Utz & Beukeboom, 2011) investigating mediators and moderators that play role in associations among social networking and characteristics of romantic relationships. Future research might explore personality traits, level of intimacy or SNSs-addictions. Besides, more research need to be done to understand how social networking influences geographically long-distance romantic relationships as well as to identify the factors that play an important role (i.e. relationship quality) in terms of reducing the relationship problems arising from the use of SNSs.

Lastly, as previous research has primarily been conducted in North American or European cultural contexts, they may be biased in terms of explaining relationships and communication behaviours in other cultural contexts (Zhang & Leung, 2014). Therefore, further studies might be conducted to uncover the role cultural factors play in these relations. For instance, scholars might examine the use of SNSs and its outcomes on romantic relationship in the Asian culture which particularly emphasizes long-term relationships, loyalty, and harmony (Zhang & Leung, 2014).

CONCLUSION

This chapter reviews the recent literature with respect to the relationship between online social networking and romantic relationship constructs. In particular, it discusses how social networking behavior is influenced by individual characteristics such as anxious and avoidant attachment styles, and how online social networking influences romantic relationship with respect to relationship satisfaction, commitment, romantic jealousy, infidelity, break up and divorce. Overall, there are mixed findings regarding the beneficial and damaging effects of online social networking on romantic relationships in the current literature. Considerable research have pointed out the positive consequences of social networking on the romantic relationship such as promoting happiness (Utz & Beukeboom, 2011), romantic love (Orosz et al., 2015), and satisfaction (Papp et al., 2012). That is, the public display of affection on partner's profile increases relationship happiness (Utz & Beukeboom, 2011) and the display of a partner's status or inclusion of their partner in profile picture increases reports of feelings of romantic love (Orosz et al., 2015) and relationship satisfaction (Papp et al., 2012). Research has also demonstrated how attachment styles (Emery et al., 2014a; Fleuriet et al., 2014; Fox & Warber, 2014; Marshall et al., 2013), relationship satisfaction (Saslow et al., 2013), and commitment (Droun et al., 2014) influence social networking behaviour. Further, scholars have examined the effects of gender (Muscanell et al., 2013) and other moderators such as self-esteem or need for popularity (Utz & Beukeboom, 2011) in associations among the use of SNSs and romantic relationships.

On the other hand, several studies have revealed the negative consequences of the use of SNSs for romantic relationships such as increasing jealousy and conflict among couples (Fox & Moreland, 2015; Marshall et al., 2013; Muise et al., 2009). For instance, when people spend more time on SNSs, they may be faced with potentially jealousy-provoking information, experience more jealousy and monitor their partner's profile for more information (Muise et al., 2009). The jealousy effect as a result of social networking was also confirmed by other scholars (Elphinson & Noller, 2011; Hudson et al., 2015; Muise et al., 2014; Utz & Beukeboom, 2011). A few scholars have demonstrated the effect of SNS-related conflict in the relationship between the use of SNSs and romantic relationship termination (Clayton et al., 2013; Clayton, 2014). Furthermore, previous research revealed the emotional and behavioral consequences of breakup in relation to the use of SNSs (Fox & Tokunaga, 2015; LeFebvre et al., 2014; Marshall, 2012).

The findings of the aforementioned research may provide important information for professionals to support the promotion of a positive atmosphere in romantic relationships. As social networking may have a negative impact on a relationship either through creating conflict or jealousy feelings, online activities that promote positive feelings among partners such as public declaration of relationship status or sharing dyadic photos in the profile may be emphasized in promoting better relationships for some.

REFERENCES

Arnett, J. J. (2000). Emerging adulthood: A theory of development from the late teens through the twenties. *The American Psychologist, 55*(5), 469–480. doi:10.1037/0003-066X.55.5.469 PMID:10842426

Bartholomew, K., & Horowitz, L. M. (1991). Attachment styles among young adults: A test of a four-category model. *Journal of Personality and Social Psychology, 61*(2), 226–244. doi:10.1037/0022-3514.61.2.226 PMID:1920064

Berger, C. R., & Calabrese, R. J. (1975). Some explorations in initial interaction and beyond: Toward a developmental theory of interpersonal communication. *Human Communication Research, 1*(2), 99–112. doi:10.1111/j.1468-2958.1975.tb00258.x

Billedo, C. J., Kerkhof, P., & Finkenauer, C. (2015). The use of social networking sites for relationship maintenance in long-distance and geographically close romantic relationships. *Cyberpsychology, Behavior, and Social Networking, 18*(3), 152–157. doi:10.1089/cyber.2014.0469 PMID:25751046

Bowlby, J. (1969). Attachment and Loss: Vol. 1. Attachment. New York, NY: Basic Books.

Boyd, D., & Ellison, N. B. (2007). Social network sites: Definition, history, and scholarship. *Journal of Computer-Mediated Communication, 13*(1), 210–230. doi:10.1111/j.1083-6101.2007.00393.x

Buss, D. M., Larsen, R., Westen, D., & Semmelroth, J. (1992). Sex differences in jealousy: Evolution, physiology, and psychology. *Psychological Science, 3*(4), 251–255. doi:10.1111/j.1467-9280.1992.tb00038.x

Canary, D. J., & Stafford, L. (1992). Relational maintenance strategies and equity in marriage. *Communication Monographs, 59*(3), 243–267. doi:10.1080/03637759209376268

Clayton, R., Nagurney, A., & Smith, J. (2013). Cheating, breakup, and divorce: Is Facebook use to blame? *Cyberpsychology, Behavior, and Social Networking, 16*(10), 717–720. doi:10.1089/cyber.2012.0424 PMID:23745615

Clayton, R. B. (2014). The third wheel: The impact of twitter use on relationship infidelity and divorce. *Cyberpsychology, Behavior, and Social Networking, 17*(7), 425–430. doi:10.1089/cyber.2013.0570 PMID:24690067

Collins, N. L., & Feeney, B. C. (2000). A safe haven: An attachment theory perspective on support seeking and caregiving in intimate relationships. *Journal of Personality and Social Psychology, 78*(6), 1053–1073. doi:10.1037/0022-3514.78.6.1053 PMID:10870908

Collins, N. L., & Read, S. J. (1990). Adult attachment, working models, and relationship quality in dating couples. *Journal of Personality and Social Psychology, 58,* 644-663. doi:10.1037/0022-3514.58.4.644

Dainton, M. (2013). Relationship maintenance on Facebook: Development of a measure, relationship to general maintenance, and relationship satisfaction. *College Student Journal, 47,* 113-121.

Dibble, J. L., & Drouin, M. (2014). Using modern technology to keep in touch with back burners: An investment model analysis. *Computers in Human Behavior, 34,* 96-100. doi:. doi:10.1016/j.chb.2014.01.042

Drouin, M., Miller, D. A., & Dibble, J. L. (2014). Ignore your partners' current Facebook friends; beware the ones they add! *Computers in Human Behavior, 35,* 483-488. doi:10.1016/j.chb.2014.02.032

Elphinston, R. A., & Noller, P. (2011). Time to face it! Facebook intrusion and the implications for romantic jealousy and relationship satisfaction. *Cyberpsychology, Behavior, and Social Networking, 14*(11), 631–635. doi:10.1089/cyber.2010.0318 PMID:21548798

Emery, L. F., Muise, A., Alpert, E. L., & Le, B. (2014b). Do we look happy? Perceptions of romantic relationship quality on Facebook. *Personal Relationships, 22*(1), 1–7. doi:10.1111/pere.12059

Emery, L. F., Muise, A., Dix, E. L., & Le, B. (2014a). Can you tell that I'm in a relationship? Attachment and relationship visibility on Facebook. *Personality and Social Psychology Bulletin, 40,* 1466-1479. doi:. doi:10.1177/0146167214549944

Fleuriet, C., Cole, M., & Guerrero, L. K. (2014). Exploring Facebook: Attachment style and nonverbal message characteristics as predictors of anticipated emotional reactions to Facebook postings. *Journal of Nonverbal Behavior, 38,* 429-450. doi:10.1007/s10919-014-0189-x

Fox, J., & Moreland, J. J. (2015). The dark side of social networking sites: An exploration of the relational and psychological stressors associated with Facebook use and affordances. *Computers in Human Behavior, 45,* 168–176. doi:10.1016/j.chb.2014.11.083

Fox, J., & Tokunaga, R. S. (2015). Romantic partner monitoring after breakups: Attachment, dependence, distress, and post-dissolution online surveillance via social networking sites. *Cyberpsychology, Behavior, and Social Networking, 18*(9), 491–498. doi:10.1089/cyber.2015.0123 PMID:26348808

Fox, J., Warber, K., & Makstaller, D. C. (2013). The role of Facebook in romantic relationship development: An exploration of Knapp's relational stage model. *Journal of Social and Personal Relationships, 30*(6), 771–794. doi:10.1177/0265407512468370

Fox, J., & Warber, K. M. (2013). Romantic relationship development in the age of Facebook: An exploratory study of emerging adults' perceptions, motives, and behaviors. *Cyberpsychology, Behavior, and Social Networking, 16*(1), 3–7. doi:10.1089/cyber.2012.0288 PMID:23098273

Fox, J., & Warber, K. M. (2014). Social networking sites in romantic relationships: Attachment, uncertainty, and partner surveillance on Facebook. *Cyberpsychology, Behavior, and Social Networking, 17,* 3-7. doi:. doi:10.1089/cyber.2012.0667

Graham, J. M., Diebels, K. J., & Barnow, Z. B. (2011). The reliability of relationship satisfaction: A reliability generalization meta-analysis. *Journal of Family Psychology, 25*(1), 39–48. doi:10.1037/a0022441 PMID:21355645

Halpern, D., Katz, J. E., & Carril, C. (2017). The online ideal persona vs. the jealousy effect: Two explanations of why selfies are associated with lower-quality romantic relationships. *Telematics and Informatics, 34*(1), 114–123. doi:10.1016/j.tele.2016.04.014

Hand, M. M., Thomas, D., Buboltz, W. C., Deemer, E. D., & Buyanjargal, M. (2013). Facebook and romantic relationships: Intimacy and couple satisfaction associated with online social network use. *Cyberpsychology, Behavior, and Social Networking, 16*(1), 8–13. doi:10.1089/cyber.2012.0038 PMID:23101932

Hazan, C., & Shaver, P. (1987). Romantic love conceptualized as an attachment process. *Journal of Personality and Social Psychology, 52*(3), 511–524. doi:10.1037/0022-3514.52.3.511 PMID:3572722

Hendrick, S. S. (1988). A generic measure of relationship satisfaction. *Journal of Marriage and the Family, 50*(1), 93–98. doi:10.2307/352430

Hudson, M. B., Nicolas, S. C., Howser, M. E., Lipsett, K. E., Robinson, I. W., Pope, L. J., & Friedman, D. R. (2015). Examining how gender and emoticons influence Facebook jealousy. *Cyberpsychology, Behavior, and Social Networking, 18*(2), 87–92. doi:10.1089/cyber.2014.0129 PMID:25684609

Joinson, A. N. (2008). ''Looking at,'' ''looking up'' or ''keeping up with'' people? Motives and uses of Facebook. In *Proceedings of the 26th Annual SIGCHI Conference on Human Factors in Computing Systems* (pp. 1027–36). New York, NY: ACM.

Knapp, M. L. (1978). *Social intercourse: From greeting to goodbye*. Needham Heights, MA: Allyn & Bacon.

Knapp, M. L., & Vangelisti, A. L. (2009). *Interpersonal communication and human relationships* (6th ed.). Boston, MA: Pearson Education.

Knobloch, L. K., & Solomon, D. H. (1999). Measuring the sources and content of relational uncertainty. *Communication Studies, 50,* 261–278. doi:10.1080=10510979909388499

Kuss, D. J., & Griffiths, M. D. (2011). Online social networking and addiction: A review of the psychological literature. *International Journal of Environmental Research and Public Health, 8*(9), 3528–3552. doi:10.3390/ijerph8093528 PMID:22016701

LeFebvre, L., Blackburn, K., & Brody, N. (2015). Navigating romantic relationships on Facebook: Extending the relationship dissolution model to social networking environments. *Journal of Social and Personal Relationships, 32*(1), 78–98. doi:10.1177/0265407514524848

Marshall, T. C. (2012). Facebook surveillance of former romantic partners: Associations with postbreakup recovery and personal growth. *Cyberpsychology, Behavior, and Social Networking, 15*(10), 521–526. doi:10.1089/cyber.2012.0125 PMID:22946958

Marshall, T. C., Bejanyan, K., Di Castro, G., & Lee, R. A. (2013). Attachment styles as predictors of Facebook-related jealousy and surveillance in romantic relationships. *Personal Relationships, 20,* 1-22. doi:. doi:10.1111/j.1475-6811.2011.01393.x

McAndrew, F. T., & Shah, S. S. (2013). Sex differences in jealousy over Facebook activity. *Computers in Human Behavior, 29*(6), 2603–2606. doi:10.1016/j.chb.2013.06.030

McDaniel, B. T., Drouin, M., & Cravens, J. D. (2017). Do you have anything to hide? Infidelity-related behaviors on social media sites and marital satisfaction. *Computers in Human Behavior, 66,* 88–95. doi:10.1016/j.chb.2016.09.031 PMID:28439148

Mod, G. (2010). Reading romance: The impact Facebook rituals can have on a romantic relationship. *Journal of Comparative Research in Anthropology & Sociology, 1,* 61–77.

Morey, J. N., Gentzler, A. L., Creasy, B., Oberhauser, A. M., & Westerman, D. (2013). Young adults' use of communication technology within their romantic relationships and associations with attachment style. *Computers in Human Behavior, 29*(4), 1771–1778. doi:10.1016/j.chb.2013.02.019

Muise, A., Christofides, E., & Desmarais, S. (2009). More information than you ever wanted: Does Facebook bring out the green-eyed monster of jealousy? *Cyberpsychology & Behavior, 12*(4), 441–444. doi:10.1089/cpb.2008.0263 PMID:19366318

Muise, A., Christofides, E., & Desmarais, S. (2014). "Creeping" or just information seeking? Gender differences in partner monitoring in response to jealousy on Facebook. *Personal Relationships, 21,* 35-50. doi:. doi:10.1111/pere.12014

Muscanell, N. L., & Guadagno, R. E. (2012). Make new friends or keep the old: Gender and personality differences in social networking use. *Computers in Human Behavior, 28*(1), 107–112. doi:10.1016/j.chb.2011.08.016

Muscanell, N. L., Guadagno, R. E., Rice, L., & Murphy, S. (2013). Don't it make my brown eyes green? An analysis of Facebook use and romantic jealousy. *Cyberpsychology, Behavior, and Social Networking, 16,* 237-242. doi:. doi:10.1089/cyber.2012.0411

Orosz, G., Szekeres, Á., Kiss, Z. G., Farkas, P., & Roland-Lévy, C. (2015). Elevated romantic love and jealousy if relationship status is declared on Facebook. *Frontiers in Psychology, 6,* 214. doi:10.3389/fpsyg.2015.00214 PMID:25767460

Papp, L. M., Danielewicz, J., & Cayemberg, C. (2012). "Are we Facebook official?" Implications of dating partners' Facebook use and profiles for intimate relationship satisfaction. *Cyberpsychology, Behavior, and Social Networking, 15*(2), 85–90. doi:10.1089/cyber.2011.0291 PMID:21988733

Raacke, J., & Bonds-Raacke, J. (2008). MySpace and Facebook: Applying the uses and gratifications theory to exploring friend-networking sites. *Cyberpsychology & Behavior, 11*(2), 169–174. doi:10.1089/cpb.2007.0056 PMID:18422409

Rus, H. M., & Tiemensma, J. (2017). "It's complicated." A systematic review of associations between social network site use and romantic relationships. *Computers in Human Behavior, 75*, 684–703. doi:10.1016/j.chb.2017.06.004

Rusbult, C. E. (1980). Commitment and satisfaction in romantic associations: A test of the investment model. *Journal of Experimental Social Psychology, 16*(2), 172–186. doi:10.1016/0022-1031(80)90007-4

Rusbult, C. E., Martz, J. M., & Agnew, C. R. (1998). The investment model scale: Measuring commitment level, satisfaction level, quality of alternatives, and investment size. *Personal Relationships, 5*(4), 357–387. doi:10.1111/j.1475-6811.1998.tb00177.x

Saslow, L. R., Muise, A., Impett, E. A., & Dubin, M. (2013). Can you see how happy we are? Facebook images and relationship satisfaction. *Social Psychological & Personality Science, 4*(4), 411–418. doi:10.1177/1948550612460059

Stafford, L., & Canary, D. J. (1991). Maintenance strategies and romantic relationship type, gender and relational characteristics. *Journal of Social and Personal Relationships, 8*(2), 217–242. doi:10.1177/0265407591082004

Stafford, L., Dainton, M., & Haas, S. (2000). Measuring routine and strategic relational maintenance: Scale development, sex versus gender roles, and the prediction of relational characteristics. *Communication Monographs, 67*(3), 306–323. doi:10.1080/03637750009376512

Statista Facts on Social Networks. (2018). Retrieved from https://www.statista.com/topics/1164/social-networks/

Steele, C. M. (1988). The psychology of self-affirmation: Sustaining the integrity of the self. In L. Berkowitz (Ed.), Advances in Experimental Social Psychology (pp. 261–302). San Diego, CA: Academic Press. doi:10.1016/S0065-2601(08)60229-4

Stewart, M. C., Dainton, M., & Goodboy, A. K. (2014). Maintaining relationships on Facebook: Associations with uncertainty, jealousy, and satisfaction. *Communication Reports, 27*(1), 13–26. doi:10.1080/08934215.2013.845675

Tokunaga, R. S. (2011). Social networking site or social surveillance site? Understanding the use of interpersonal electronic surveillance in romantic relationships. *Computers in Human Behavior, 27*(2), 705–713. doi:10.1016/j.chb.2010.08.014

Utz, S., & Beukeboom, C. J. (2011). The role of social network sites in romantic relationships: Effects on jealousy and relationship happiness. *Journal of Computer-Mediated Communication, 16*(4), 511–527. doi:10.1111/j.1083-6101.2011.01552.x

Utz, S., Muscanell, N., & Khalid, C. (2015). Snapchat elicits more jealousy than Facebook: A comparison of Snapchat and Facebook use. *Cyberpsychology, Behavior, and Social Networking, 18*(3), 141–146. doi:10.1089/cyber.2014.0479 PMID:25667961

Wilson, R. E., Gosling, S. D., & Graham, L. T. (2012). A review of Facebook research in the social sciences. *Perspectives on Psychological Science, 7*(3), 203–220. doi:10.1177/1745691612442904 PMID:26168459

Zhang, Y., & Leung, L. (2015). A review of social networking service (SNS) research in communication journals from 2006 to 2011. *New Media & Society*, *17*(7), 1007–1024. doi:10.1177/1461444813520477

KEY TERMS AND DEFINITIONS

Attachment: Emotional bond between the infant and the primary caregiver.

Facebook: An online platform used to keep in touch with others and monitor others' activities.

Partner Surveillance: Monitoring of the partner's profile such as viewing photos, wall posts, comments and status.

Relationship Commitment: An individual's feelings of psychological attachment experienced in a relationship.

Relationship Maintenance Strategies: Routine behaviors engaged in by partners' to maintain the relationship.

Relationship Satisfaction: An individual's evaluation about his/her romantic relationship.

Romantic Jealousy: Negative thoughts, feelings, and behaviors as a response to a perceived threat to a romantic relationship.

Social Networking Site: An online platform which allows users to build social networks.

This research was previously published in The Psychology and Dynamics Behind Social Media Interactions; pages 57-82, copyright year 2020 by Information Science Reference (an imprint of IGI Global).

Chapter 56
Examining the Psychosocial Dimensions of Young People's Emergent Social Media Behavior

Lydia Andoh-Quainoo
Pentecost University College, Ghana

ABSTRACT

Social media usage among young people has grown astronomically, generating interest among a number of interest groups. This chapter fills a gap on social media psychosocial antecedents propelling high-usage behavior and the subsequent psychosocial outcomes showing in attachment to the social media. The chapter explored the emergent psychosocial needs driving young people's level of usage in social media and the consequences, among a population in Ghana. The findings revealed that young consumers' social media behavior could be greatly influenced by their social psychological needs, but individual psychological variables did not significantly predict usage behavior in social media. The findings also suggest that young people are more emotionally attached to social media, slightly attached cognitively and not attached behaviorally. This implies young people have developed some level of emotional involvement for the use of social media which could affect their well-being positively or negatively.

INTRODUCTION

Social media comprises of various forms of internet based or web 2.0 platforms that allow users or the public to generate and share ideas, pictures, videos, information, interests, and other expressions. It is one of the most dynamic, interdisciplinary socially facilitated media of contemporary society (Hjorth & Hendry, 2015; Kaplan & Haenlein, 2010). Made up of five distinct types, including social networking sites, social news, media sharing, blogs and micro blogging, social media is transforming young consumers' behaviour as it has created a shift in how consumers use technology, connect with others, engage with brands and other social activities such as entertainment (Chuma, 2014; Pinto, 2015). Such level of advancement and accessibility is increasingly creating opportunities for high usage and the likelihood

DOI: 10.4018/978-1-6684-6307-9.ch056

of psychological consequences (Bolton et al., 2013; Chiang, 2013; Wu, Cheung & Hung, 2013). Given its growing importance, the power of social media to influence consumer behaviour cannot be over looked. Studies shows that, at a global level, it has become a major medium through which businesses engage their customers and for multiple levels of communication in all social interactions (Kim, 2016).

Although social media usage can be found among different groups of people, the younger consumer generation has been found to be connected to social media to a higher degree and this has become the focus of attention by researchers (Chiang, 2013; Dunne, Lawlor & Rowley, 2014; Khan, 2017; Westlund & Bjur, 2014). The younger generation basically consists of those from the later generation of generation Y, born from 1980s to 2000 and described as millennials, and the generation Z who are described as totally distinct from previous generations of consumers or market segment. They are considered as a dominant consumer segment, brand conscious, technologically advanced and digital citizens (Abeeele, 2016; Bertel & Ling, 2016; Bolton et al., 2013; Kotler & Keller, 2013; MacCasland, 2005; Mascheroni & Vincent, 2016; Walsh, 2009). They spend a lot of their time on technology devices mainly smartphones, internet and social media for social connections, information and entertainment. They are considered technology lovers and multi device owners (Bertel & Ling 2016; Lien & Cao, 2014; Khan, 2017; Lin & Lu, 2011; MacCasland, 2005; Naumouska, 2017; Whiting & Williams, 2013). Consequently, young people have been considered vulnerable to excessive usage and behavioral outcomes of social media. Due to their prolific usage of social media, they are considered as the population of interest for new digital media technologies such as smartphones and social media (Babadi-Akashe, 2014). As social media assumes a high level of influence it is imperative to understand young consumers from different parts of the world.

Social media has created strong interactions in people and Bolton et al. (2013) suggested social media antecedent factors and outcomes in young people should be the focus of research. In response to this call, psychosocial antecedents and outcomes including social capital, psychosocial motives, and psychological wellbeing such as dependence and addiction associated with social media, has been examined. Findings suggest some social and psychological factors including entertainment, information, and relationships are key drivers of social media behaviour (Al-Kandari et al., 2016; Bulduklu, 2017; Cheng et al., 2015; Kuru et al., 2017; Khan, 2017;Wei & Lo, 2015). Other findings suggest individual psychological factors such as personality, self-esteem, and self-seeking status influence social media behaviour in young people (Seidman, 2012; Steinfield, Ellison & Lampe, 2008; Wilson et al., 2010; Wood & Scott 2016). The Western world and Asia have been the central geographic context for the majority of these studies. However, social media usage behaviour in a diverse sociocultural context (Carter & Yeo, 2016; Khan, 2017; Rubin, 2002; Sundar & Limperos, 2014; Whiting & William, 2013; Wu et al., 2013) may present different patterns of behavior relevant to understanding social media behavior. As there are only a few studies from a developing country setting (Karikari et al., 2017), this calls for more studies to bridge this gap (Al-Kandari, Melkote & Sharif, 2016). Findings from the US, UK and Asia have been the focus of developing countries studies on social media. In Ghana, Karikari et al. (2017) found that social media supports the generation of social capital and user well-being but usage can be influenced by external social pressure. Nevertheless, there have not been many studies on the extent to which psychosocial factors associated with social media usage in Ghana may differ from other parts of the world. Consequently, as psychosocial factors have become significant drivers of young people's social media behaviour, it is imperative to examine these factors and how they interplay with usage behaviour and psychosocial outcomes from a different context.

Thus, the main purpose of this chapter is to examine the psychosocial antecedents influencing social media usage behaviour of young people, the extent to which these factors drive continuous usage in social media and the subsequent behavioural consequences in social media behaviour of young consumers from a developing country setting.

THEORETICAL FRAMEWORK

Uses and Gratification Theory

Originating from media psychology, the Uses and Gratification Theory (Blumler & Katz, 1974) constitutes a dominant theoretical body for examining and explaining the reasons for adopting new digital media technologies such as social media. The theory assumes that media use is a goal directed activity in which the audience or users are active participants. This means that individuals actively seek out media to fulfill specific needs that leads to gratification (Rubin, 2009; Whiting & Williams, 2013) and that media cannot be used without its audience. The framework considers motives and individual factors that are the reason for the use of social media, use behaviour and behavioral effects of social media (Khan, 2017).

Proponents of the Uses and Gratification Theory suggest many underlying motives, both utilitarian and non-utilitarian, for media use such as seeking to relax, entertain themselves, interact with people, escape some things etc. (Leung & Wei, 2000). In recent times, social media gratification has evolved into mainly social interactions, entertainment, information, affection, social coordination etc. (Buluklu, 2017; Khan, 2017; Sundar & Limperos, 2014; Wei & Lo, 2015; Whiting & William, 2013). The Uses and Gratification Theory has been applied in a wide range of new media technologies.

According to Rubin (2009), there are various dimensions of focus of the theory. The theory focuses on the connecting motives and consequences to media behaviour and attitudes; comparing motives across different media; exploring a variety of media's psychological and social situations; connecting media motives sought from motives obtained; exploring different attributes, backgrounds and affection for motives; and assessing the reliability and validity of motivation measures. New media technologies have rekindled the interest in the application of the theory. Some studies have focused on reasons and motives for media use, media use effects and how motives influence media use behaviour. The theory has become useful in assessing social media use behaviour hence its usage for this study. However, there has been more emphasis on the media and communication aspect focusing on the media and the message rather the consumer or user of the media. Hence, this chapter concentrates on what drives users to continuously engage social media and the behavioral outcomes of such sustained usage.

Social Media Usage

Media use is the purpose or function for which a technology medium is consumed as well as the frequency of use (Weiser, 2001). Social media usage in young people includes information gathering and sharing of content as well as interactions with friends and relatives. Social networking sites have become the most popular aspect of social media and it is used for social connection, for sharing of media content, for academic work and searching for and buying of goods and services generated by these contents (Watulak & Whitefield, 2016). Another dimension of social media is the media sharing sites that permits users to upload your photos, videos and audio to or from other sites anywhere in the world. One of the main common forms of a media sharing site is video sites where YouTube.com, Facebook and Instagram are the dominant and most widespread, according Bolton et al. (2013).

Studies show that young people's social media behaviour is on the high side. Social media frequency of use has increased over the years as more young people get connected (Whiting & William, 2013; Wu et al., 2013). Carter and Yeo (2016) reported that most students have integrated social media into their daily lifestyle. They reported that, on a daily basis, young university students in Malaysia use social media 20 times, accessing chat apps such as WeChat, Twitter, Facebook, WhatsApp and Instagram. Wu et al. (2013) discovered that young people spend more time on smartphones and social networking sites than other digital media. Hussain (2012) observed that students used social media for enjoyment and some academic activities, while Tess (2013) is of the view that young students rarely use social media for learning; nonetheless they use it for career networking and connecting with friends. Karikari et al. (2017) added that, in Ghana, young people have social pressure to connect with friends through social networking sites hence the high usage behaviour. Overall, the findings reveal that most students have integrated chatting on social media into their day to day lifestyle. Such usage behaviour may be attributed to psychosocial drivers including motives and other psychological factors, which is the focus of the next sections.

Gratification and Motives Driving Social Media Use

Gratification, on the other hand, has been conceptualized as the needs, motivation and satisfactions driving media consumption (Walsh, 2009). Different authors have used different terminologies and classifications for the gratification consumers usually seek. For instance, some researchers posit that gratification is the motive that drives media use in general (Khan, 2017; Leung & Wei, 2000; Whiting & William, 2013), and more specifically, drives the use of media usage (Wei, 2006). Lin (2002) posits that gratification is a need, and media use is a conscious effort towards the fulfillment of both emotional and mental needs (Leung & Wei, 2000; Ling, 2000; Wei, 2008). Gratifications are psychological and social needs, which are fulfilled through the use of technology (Cheung, Liang, & Leung, 2015).

Studies have identified several psychosocial motives based on the Uses and Gratification Theory (Blumler & Katz, 1974; Khan, 2017; Rubin, 2009; Sundar & Limperos, 2014; Whiting & William, 2013) driving social media use, and several findings support gratifications connected with social media and social networking sites (Kuss & Griffiths, 2017; Ryan, Chester, Reece, & Xenos, 2014). The psychological and social gratifications, such as information, entertainment, and social relationship, are considered to be the main antecedents for use behaviour of most young people in social media (Ling, 2000; Walsh, White & Young, 2007; Whiting & Williams, 2013).

Social media increases human interactions even at a distance. Hence, social motivations are highly involved in human to human technology interactions (Khan, 2017; Ko et al., 2005). This is confirmed by Khan (2017) who indicates that those who have strong social interaction needs were more likely to comment on videos by showing their likes or dislikes and are more likely to upload videos. Also, among the 10 themes Whiting and William (2013) considered to be gratifications for using social media, they highlight social interactions and expression of opinion. Lawlor and Rowley (2010), in a qualitative study, reported that usage of social networking sites by young people is driven by personal gratifications such as personal identity and managing social relationships: these were found to be the basis for sticking to social networking sites and online social media chats. Ko et al. (2005) as well as Sundar and Limperos (2014) likewise reported that motives for social media use include relational needs such as social interaction.

Similarly, Karikari et al. (2017) reported that young people in Ghana have external social pressure. This is a strong antecedent for social media engagement and social media being able to be used for building social capital and subjective wellbeing.

Moreover, entertainment, information seeking and information sharing were also predominant gratifications for using social media. Kang and Atkin (1999) found that entertainment is a major reason for multimedia adoption (see also Khan, 2017). This is supported by Chan and Fang (2007) who reported that entertainment gratification is one of the major psychosocial factors driving social media for fun and music as well as other activities. The user participation was reported as a stronger predictor for liking a video and reading information while those who seek entertainment gratifications are more likely to view videos and read comments on social media. Al-Kandari et al. (2016), Ko et al. (2005) and Whiting and William (2013) also reported that motives and needs driving social media include self-expression, entertainment, opinion exchange and information seeking.

Although additional gratifications have been identified (e.g., escapism, Sundar & Limperos, 2014; relaxation, Whiting & William, 2013), it appears that the most predominant psychosocial gratifications driving social media content engagement are social gratification, entertainment gratification and information gratification, hence this study embraces these emergent gratifications. Most of the aforementioned studies have not explored the extent to which gratifications influence social media usage rate in young people, especially in developing countries. Therefore, this chapter was carried out to examine the current gratifications influencing young people's social media and the extent of influence thereof, in the context of a developing country. Based on this gap the research questions were formulated as:

Research 1a: To what extent does social relationship gratification drive social media usage positively?
Research 1b: To what extent does information gratification influence social media usage positively?
Research 1c: To what extent does entertainment gratification influence social media usage positively?

Individual Factors in Uses and Gratification

There are individual psychological factors, such as personality factors, influencing usage behaviour in social media. Researchers have adopted the big five personality approach (using agreeableness, conscientiousness, extraversion, neuroticism and openness) and found the most prominent influencers of social media use were extraversion and conscientiousness (Wilson et al., 2010). Seidman (2012) likewise confirms that higher extraversion is associated with frequency of Facebook use while agreeableness and neuroticism influence the motive of belonging.

Other studies have explored different individual factors such as self-esteem, impulsivity, shyness, loneliness, locus of control, and factors which may predispose people to use digital media to a high level (Bian & Leung, 2015; Philips & Bianchi, 2005; Walsh et al., 2009). These individual factors have been found to influence usage, motives and addiction. For instance, Wilson et al. (2010) found that personality factors such as extraversion, conscientiousness and self-esteem could influence the tendency to be addicted to social networking sites. Earlier findings on self-esteem suggest that it is part of general psychological wellbeing in technology usage behaviour. For instance, Steinfield, Ellison, and Lampe (2008), in a longitudinal study of young people in the US, found that self-esteem is associated with young people's use of Facebook where those with lower self-esteem gained more in bridging social capital than those with higher self-esteem. However, recent studies have used self-esteem and self-seeking status as major individual factors in social media studies due to the fact that only extraversion has been found to show consistency in media use (Khan, 2017).

Self-esteem is the sense of value and worth a person puts on him/herself. It stems from the need to feel good about one self. Esteem needs, as proposed in Maslow's theory of need, identified lower esteem needs such as status, fame, glory; and higher esteem needs such as self-respect, confidence, competence, and achievement. Self-seeking status gratification is a satisfaction for the need to feel important, to impress others and feel cool (Khan, 2017). Connecting these two variables can bring insight into new individual factors for social media use.

Other findings similarly connect the use of social media to age and gender with findings suggesting that young people are more likely to use mobile technology as an expression and fashion (Ling, 2003; Ling, 2004); whereas, adults moreover tend to emphasize mobile phone use to feel safe and secure (Ling, 2004). Regarding gender, the evidence points to mixed results (Bolton et al., 2013; Campbell, 2006; Ling & Haddon, 2003; Wu et al., 2013); and such mixed findings require continuous research in social media. Based on these findings, the following research questions were formulated:

Research Question 2

Research Q2a: How does self-esteem drive social media usage in young people?
Research Q2b: How does self-seeking status influence social media usage in young people?
Research Q2c: To what extent does age and gender affect social media usage?

Psychosocial Outcomes of Social Media Use

Current psychological research fronts have shifted from emergent use behaviour to the psychological consequences associated with social media use such as problematic, addictive or dependent use as a consequence of high usage (Bolton et al., 2013; Kuss & Griffiths, 2017; Walsh, 2009; Wu et al., 2013). Brown (1993) introduced technology addiction using indicators such as withdrawal, salience, loss of control and others. Based on the biomedical model of substance addiction, the behavioural addiction concept assumes that an individual dependent on a substance will exhibit withdrawal symptoms when they are denied that substance; and that can disrupt normal daily functioning. In the same way, when this is applied to behavioural addiction, a person can use a technological media to such an extent that lack of usage may lead to withdrawal symptoms and heavy usage can impact general wellbeing. It has been argued that the term addiction should be extended to include behavioural addictions such as excessive use of technology. According to Brown (1997), behavioural addictions entail usage without being able to control technology use. It is similarly difficult to abstain, and continuous use can be harmful to the user. Excessive, uncontrolled and impulsive usage can be described as an addiction problem (Billieux, 2012).

As social media use becomes prominent among young people, more findings are pointing to excessive and/or addictive use. Wu et al. (2013) reported that young people who spend more time on smartphones and social networking sites may be addicted to smartphones and social networking sites. This is supported by Kuss and Griffiths (2017) whose empirical review confirms that, due to the need for social connection, the main basis for social networking addiction is to sites such as Facebook, Instagram and Twitter. Furthermore, Fernandez-Lopez et al. (2017) in a multi-cultural study reported that social networking and social media may drive consumers into dependence and addiction.

Yet there are other studies suggesting that social media addiction may be culturally specific, may not be applicable to all use situations, and some young people can control the use of mobiles (Asante, 2018). According to Billieux et al. (2014), the biomedical model of addiction and dependence may not be applicable in all situations of excessive use and there is a need to offer alternative explanations. Ahmed, Qazi, and Perji (2011) found that young people in Pakistan use media technology within reasonable limits even if it is an integral aspect of daily life. Others see addiction as only a simplification of individual psychological functioning (Asante, 2018; Billieux, et al., 2015). However, Orford (2001) argued that excessive media usage behaviour might have negative outcomes but may not be described as an addiction. He however, suggests that high media use could be described as psychological attachment or involvement with the object. Hence, extensive usage of media technologies can only show high involvement or psychological attachment and not addiction. Walsh et al. (2009) used involvement in young people's mobile phone behaviour and reported that, although involvement was high, there was no connection between frequency of use and psychological involvement. Nonetheless little has been found on psychological attachment or involvement in social media. Hence, there is a need to put young people's heavy usage of social media into a different behavioral perspective for better understanding of emergent social media consumer behaviour. So for the purpose of this study, Orford's approach to explaining young people's psychological attachment or involvement is adopted in assessing behavioural effects. The study likewise adopted Walsh et al.'s (2009) psychological involvement and adapted it into three levels of psychological attachment, namely; emotional, cognitive and behavioral attachment. To this end, Research Question 3 was formulated.

Research Question 3

Research Q3a: How does emotional attachment to social media drive usage in young people?

Research Q3b: How does cognitive attachment to social media influence social media usage in young people?

Research Q3c: How does behavioral attachment to social media influence social media usage in young people?

Research Q3d: To what extent does age and gender affect psychological attachment to social media usage?

METHODS

The purpose of this section was to unfold the research methodology for answering the following research questions.

Research Q1: To what extent does social gratifications of relationship, entertainment and information influence social media usage in young people in a developing country?

Research Q2: How do individual factors of self-esteem and self-seeking status influence social media usage in young people in a developing country including moderation of age and gender?

Research Q3: How does emotional, cognitive, and behavioral attachment to social media influence social media usage in young people in a developing country including the moderating effects of age and gender?

To answer these questions the study adopted a quantitative approach in order to obtain better answers to the research questions and meet the objectives. A survey method, which is a widely used data collection method for measuring multiple variables, was used. The survey method allowed for a deductive approach based on a theoretical framework with empirical measurement through data analysis (Neuman, 2007).

The Study Context

The study was carried out in Ghana, an emerging economy in the West African sub-region with a considerable level of market potential for technology and digital media. With a population of 29.99 million people, Ghana has experienced high growth in technology as a result of market liberalization, privatization, technological advancement innovation and other benefits derived from using digital media (Atsu et al., 2013; Tobbin, 2012). According to ITU (2019), mobile subscription shows about 36,751 active users of smartphones in Ghana leading to high social media usage, social and economic growth in investment and GDP, improvement in micro trading and economic activities, and strengthening social ties.

Population and Sampling

The target population was young consumers from age 18-35 with a mean age of 28.4 currently pursuing tertiary education at various universities in Ghana. A survey was conducted in three main universities spread across Ghana. These universities were chosen because of their geographic location, large number of students, easy accessibility and young active users of social media on these campuses (Bian & Leung, 2015; Dlodlo, 2015). Also, the universities were used because the university campuses house predominantly young people and a number of studies in new media technologies have used such samples. The young students are considered to be the most active users of new media technologies because they are the generation who has been exposed widely to technology since they were born. They started playing with mobile phone toys and digital gadget so they may have more to share on mobile phones (Karikari et al., 2017; Walsh, 2007; Yan, 2017).

Cluster sampling, where geographic clusters are created and a random sample of individuals are selected, was used to sample universities and students from the various campuses (Wilson, 2012). This ensured that the majority of geographic areas were covered. The characteristics of respondents are described below in Table 1.

Three faculties were selected at random from each university and students were randomly selected for the survey from these faculties at lecture halls. Each member of the population had an equal chance of being selected for the survey. Students responded to the questionnaire by themselves under supervision after briefing them and obtaining their consent.

Measures and Scales Used for the Study

The survey questionnaire was made of three main sections - A, B and C. Questions assessing the social demographic data such as age, gender and type of social media frequently used were found in section A. Section B addressed mobile phone psychosocial gratifications, usage rate and individual factors. The questions here captured the social relationship, information and entertainment gratification and individual factors, self-esteem and self-seeking status. Section C was used to assess psychological attachment.

Table 1. Characteristics of respondents

Variables	Total Population	Sample Frequency	Percent of Sample
Institution: U.G. U.C.C. KNUST	29,754 31,229 31,189	201 222 182	33.3 36.8 30.0
Age: 20 years & below 21-25 years 26-30 years 31-35 years 36 years and above		210 252 115 25	34.8 41.7 19.0 4.2 0.3
Sex: Male Female		292 312	48.3 51.7
Frequently used social media: Facebook WhatsApp Twitter Instagram		211 158 116 72	34.9 26.2 19.2 11.9

Usage rate was measure based on the number of times or frequency of use in social media on a daily basis. From a range of 1-10 times, usage was described as low usage; 11-20 times was moderate usage; and above 20 times was considered to be extensive usage. This was further categorized into high users and low users.

Variables for psychosocial factors, individual factors and attachment were measured using a five-point Likert scale anchored from 1 to 5 and categorized into various responses ranging from (5) strongly agree to strongly disagree (1). Scores were then converted into high and low for the purpose of the analysis. Scales were adapted from related literature (Billiuex, 2012; Khan, 2017; Kuss et al., 2017; Walsh et al., 2009). However some were modified to suit the current research. Questions for the scales are described below in Table 2. The only validated scale available was the Rosenberg's (1965) self-esteem inventory, which was included in the current study. Table 3 presents the means, standard deviations and Cronbach's Alpha for all variables. All variables were with the acceptable range for Cronbach's Alpha .75 -.899 suggesting a good reliability level.

DATA ANALYSIS

The logistic regression, also referred to as Logit regression, was used in analyzing the data in both SPSS 21 and Stata/SE 14. In this type of regression the aim was to predict the relationship between two variables; where the dependent variable(s) is/are binary. This allowed for the assessment of the extent of the relationship between high users and low users of social media and its connection to various gratifications, individual factors and levels of psychological attachment. It also made it possible to measure the extent to which age and gender relates to gratifications, psychological attachment influences and the frequency of use in social media.

Table 2. Scales of measurement used

Information Seeking Gratification	Entertainment Gratification
Information gratification was assess based statements such as: To get information about things that interest you, To learn how to do things, To find out what is new out there, and To keep up with current issues and events	Information gratification was assess based statement such as: To be entertained, To play, To enjoy, To relax; and To pass time
Social and Relationship Gratification	**Self-Esteem**
To connect with friends and family To stay connected to those I care about To meet new people To belong to a community	On the whole I am satisfied with myself, At times I think I am no good at all, I feel I have a number of good qualities, I am able to do things as well as most other people, I feel that am a person of worth equal to other, In all I am inclined to feel that am a failure, I take a positive attitude towards myself
Self-Seeking Status	**Emotional Attachment**
To impress other users To feel important To make myself look cool To gain respect To establish personal identity	I am in love with my phone so much, I give my phone my first priority above anything else, Am always absorbed with my phone, I cannot live without my mobile phone
Cognitive Attachment	**Behavioural Attachment**
I cannot put my phone out of my mind The thought of losing my phone scares me Am always mentally conscious of my phone	I always have a drive to use my phone. My phone is the first thing I look at when I wake up Am always anxious to check my phone I cannot control my phone use behavior

Table 3. Construct reliability, means and standard deviations of scales

Constructs Used	Cronbach's Alpha	No. of Items	Mean	Standard Deviation
Information Gratification	.857	4 items	3.39	1.4
Self-Seeking Status	.868	5 items	3.13	1.37
Social Rel. Gratification	.871	4 items	3.16	1.03
Self-Esteem Gratification	.899	9 items	3.20	1.31
Entertainment Gratification	.784	5 items	3.14	1.31
Emotional Attachment	.700	5 items	1.33	0.72
Cognitive Attachment	.687	3 items	3.30	0.92
Behavioural Attachment	.780	4 items	1.08	0.72

RESULTS AND DISCUSSION

Social Media Gratifications in Young People

This chapter examined the psychosocial factors influencing social media behaviour including psychosocial gratifications and other personal factors driving social media usage behavior. It also assessed the extent to which these factors, social relationship, entertainment and information gratification, individual factors including self-esteem and self-seeking status and other factors such as age and gender drive usage behaviour. The findings are described in Table 4.

Table 4. Gratifications driving social media usage results

Predictor of Social Media Usage Rate	Odds Ratio	Standard Error	Z	P>Z	Confidence Interval (95%)
Social Relationship	3.72	0.06	-6.13	0.000	0.19; 0.42
Entertainment	3.56	0.83	6.00	0.000	2.44; 5.81
Information	2.49	1.91	4.94	0.000	2.80; 10.87
Self-seeking Status	1.01	0.28	0.02	0.983	0.58; 1.74
Self-esteem	3.77	0.83	6.00	0.000	2.44; 5.81
Gender	0.32	0.06	-6.52	0.000	0.23; 0.45
Age	0.64	0.10	-2.85	0.004	0.47; 0.87

Log likelihood = -441.66774

The results show that there is a significant positive relationship between social relationship gratification for using social media (with odds ratio of OR=3.72, p<0.000), entertainment (OR=3.56, p<0.000) and information gratification (OR=2.49, p<0.001). This shows that high users of social media are three times more likely to be driven by the need to bond through social interactions and the need to relate with other people including family, friends and other loved ones. Those driven by entertainment gratification are three times likely to use social media more and users who have a need for information are twice as likely to use social media at a higher rate.

It was observed that, for personal psychological variables, users with high self-esteem are more than three times more likely (OR=3.76, p<0.001) to use social media. The satisfactions that users pursue for social usage surprisingly include social relationship, information and entertainment gratifications, but interestingly self-seeking status, age and gender were not significant in relation to social media use.

These findings suggest that young people's drive for information and entertainment is high and that can make them vulnerable to high technology involvement and addictive tendencies. It also shows that young people are driven by the need to satisfy social relationships and interactions with friends and family members while seeking pleasure as well. Findings from several studies (Carter & Yeo, 2016; Khan, 2017; Rubin, 2002; Sundar & Limperos, 2014; Whiting & William, 2013; Wu et al., 2013) support the argument that emergent gratifications are tilting toward these psychosocial gratifications. This confirms a report by Lawlor and Rowley (2010) that gratifications for using social networking sites include personal identity and social relationships and another report by Leung (2013) which suggests that socio-psychological needs such as entertainment and cognitive needs are crucial predictors of social media behaviour. The motivations or satisfactions driving Facebook include relationship maintenance, companionship, passing time and entertainment. These satisfactions drive people into excessive usage leading to addiction. It appears that gratifications drive user behaviour into psychological attachments addictions; which is consistent with Kuss and Griffiths (2017) who confirm the need for social connection, identifying this as the main basis for social networking and why people can be addicted to such sites including Facebook, Instagram and Twitter. This is also supported by Khan (2017) and Whiting and Williams (2013) who reported predominant gratifications for using social media as entertainment, social interactions, information seeking and information sharing, relaxation, communication utility, convenience utility and others. Wilson et al. (2010) also confirms social media usage with high self-esteem. Several other findings have likewise been consistent with the current finding (Carter & Yeo, 2016; Khan, 2017; Rubin, 2002; Seidman, 2012; Steinfield et al., 2008; Sundar & Limperos, 2014; Wood & Scott 2016Wu et al., 2013).

It could therefore be concluded that, to a large extent, social psychological gratification and individual factors drive the continuous usage of social media by young people, similarly in developing and developed countries.

Social Media Psychological Attachment

The current study sought to examine the extent to which young people are psychologically attached to social media and how that attachment relates to social media. Adapting from Walsh et al. (2009), three main levels of attachment were assessed - cognitive, emotional and behavioral. The findings are detailed in Table 5.

Table 5. Social media psychological attachments

Predictor of Social Media Usage Rate	Odds Ratio	Standard Error	Z	P>Z	Confidence Interval (95%)
Emotional Attachment	2.62	0.51	4.90	0.000	1.78; 3.85
Cognitive Attachment	2.00	0.64	2.17	0.030	1.07; 3.73
Behavioral Attachment	0.30	0.06	-6.22	0.000	0.21; 0.44
Gender	0.52	0.09	-3.88	0.000	0.37; 0.72
Age	0.87	0.12	-0.99	0.323	0.66; 1.15

Log likelihood = -463.53888

The findings show that users of social media are influenced significantly by emotional attachment (OR=2.61; $p < .000$) and are likely to be preoccupied mentally, although not very strongly (OR=1.998, $p < 0.03$). In other words, those who use social media more are almost three times more likely to become emotionally attached or have strong emotional feelings towards social media. They are furthermore almost two times more likely to be attached at the cognitive or mental level to social media usage. This shows that young people are emotionally attached to social media as a behavioural consequence. This could be due to the human to human interactions on social media as emotional bonds develop with social interactions. Moreover, when people interact with others the words stay as impressions on the mind before bonds could develop. As could be observed through the gratifications that drive usage, it suggests that social relationships, entertainment and information are strong connections driving young users into high usage and hence towards emotional attachment. This confirms Wu et al. (2013) who report that young people who spend more time on smartphones and social network sites were more likely to be addicted to smartphones and social networking sites. Several other findings support either dependence or addiction of some sort (Fernandez-Lopez et al., 2017; Kuss & Griffiths, 2017). Although addiction could be too strong, the findings from this study suggest that young people are actually in love with the use of social media or it actually resonates well with them and makes them feel good, hence they cannot get it off their minds.

However, they do not show significant behavioural compulsion to use social media: this means they are conscious to use social media within acceptable limits and might not show withdrawal symptoms as proposed by behavioral addiction proponents. Moreover, age and gender did not influence social media usage behaviour significantly.

CONCLUSION AND IMPLICATIONS

The study was carried out to explore the extent to which social media gratifications and individual factors influence usage behaviour and whether the extent of psychological attachment contributes in driving continuous usage of social media. The findings suggest that social media frequency of use is driven by psychosocial gratifications such as information, entertainment, social relationships, and individual factor of self-esteem; nonetheless self-seeking status, age and gender were not significant in influencing social media behaviour. Social media psychosocial consequences were observed to show emotional attachment with slight cognitive attachment however behavioural attachment was not a strong predictor of psychosocial attachment in social media as well as age and gender. It could be concluded that social and psychological needs have replaced basic needs as far as new digital technologies such as social media is concerned. Due to the level of drive from these satisfactions there is a higher need to satisfy such needs by businesses in a way that will lead to positive psychosocial attachment for brands.

Although physiological gratifications may be important to consumers, it appears that new digital media has moved beyond meeting physiological needs to more psychosocial needs of information, entertainment, belongingness, and individual differences, which have become crucial in ensuring continuous usage and could, create resonance for brands online.

Findings from this study authenticate that technology gratifications have evolved, and for the current generation of millennials in a developing country, it is social relationship, information, and entertainment gratifications that drive their usage behavior. The findings strengthen the existence of emergent psychosocial gratifications and individual factors as the drivers of usage behaviour in social media. The findings strengthen the importance of media uses and behavioural effects, which in turn, drives continuous usage.

The finding extends the Uses and Gratification Theory that social media is strongly connected to psychosocial satisfactions and personal factors driving the extent to which young people use the media. It is the gratification obtained that predicts the continuous usage. Again, there are behavioural effects (such as psychological attachments) due to the gratifications obtained but these may not be strong enough to be referred to as an addiction.

These findings imply that businesses can influence young consumers' behaviour by engaging them through social media usage behavior. It implies that young consumers can be engaged through information, relationship, entertainment and activities that enhance their self-esteem. Considering the upsurge of information, entertainment and relationship gratifications driving young people's usage behaviour in social media, this could be used to facilitate policy information to communities, schools and other places by government and other policy formulators.

LIMITATIONS AND FUTURE RESEARCH

The study is limited to only students in a developing country; accordingly other researches can focus on young people in general. Further, the selection of three universities and a particular age cohort could affect the generalization of the results. Different age groups could present different usage behaviour that could have improved the understanding of consumer behaviour in social media. Also, the study is limited by the use of self-reports and scales used to gather information from respondents on their social usage behaviour and psychological attachment. For instance the number of times it is used in a day may not be wholly reliable. Future studies could add open-ended and qualitative sections to enrich the data. Finally, future research should compare more media uses and gratifications as well as dependence and psychological attachment.

REFERENCES

Babadi-Akashe, Z., Zamami, B. E., Abedini, Y., & Akbari, N. (2014). The relationship between mental health and addiction to mobile phones among university students of Shahrekord. *Addiction & Health*, 6(3-4), 93–94. PMID:25984275

Billieux, J., Philippot, P., Schmid, C., Maurage, J., & Linden, V. D. (2015). Is Dysfunctional Use of the Mobile Phone a Behavioural Addiction? Confronting Symptom-Based Versus Process-Based Approaches. *Clinical Psychology & Psychotherapy*, 22(5), 460–468. doi:10.1002/cpp.1910 PMID:24947201

Blumler, J. G., & Katz, E. (1974). *The Uses of Mass Communications: Current Perspectives on Gratifications Research*. Beverly Hills, CA: Sage Publications.

Bolton, R. N., Parasuraman, A., Hoefnagels, A., Migchels, N., Kabadayi, S., Gruber, T., ... Solnet, D. (2013). Understanding Generation Y and their use of social media: A review and research agenda. *Journal of Service Management*, 24(3), 245–267. doi:10.1108/09564231311326987

Bulduklu, Y. (2017). Mobile games on the basis of uses and gratifications approach: A comparison of the mobile game habits of university and high school students. *The International Journal of Research into New Media Technologies*, 1–17. doi:10.1177/1354856517748159

Carter, S., & Yao, A. (2016). Mobile apps usage by Malaysian business undergraduates and postgraduates: Implications for consumer behaviour theory and marketing practice. *Internet Research*, 26(3), 733–757. doi:10.1108/IntR-10-2014-0273

Chiu, S. I., Hong, F. Y., & Chiu, S. L. (2013). An analysis on the correlation and gender difference college students Internet addiction and mobilephone addiction in Taiwan (Vol. 2013). London, UK: Hindawi Publishing Corporation ISRN Addiction.

Choi, Y. K., Kim, J., & Mcmillan, S. J. (2009). Motivators for the intention to use mobile TV: A comparison of South Korean males and females. *International Journal of Advertising*, 28(1), 147–167. doi:10.2501/S0265048709090477

Choliz, M. (2012). Mobile-phone addiction in adolescence: The Test of Mobile Phone Dependence (TMD). *Prog Health Sci, 2*(1), 33-44.

Chuma, W. (2014). The social meanings of mobile phones among South Africa's 'digital natives': A case study. *Media Culture & Society, 36*(3), 398–408. doi:10.1177/0163443713517482

Dlodlo, N. (2015). Salient indicators of mobile instant messaging addiction with selected socio-demographic attributes among tertiary students in South Africa. *South African Journal of Psychology. Suid-Afrikaanse Tydskrif vir Sielkunde, 45*(2), 207–222. doi:10.1177/0081246314566022

Jenaro, C., Flores, N., Gomez-Vela, M., Gonzalez-Gil, F., & Caballo, C. (2007). Problematic internet and cell-phone use: Psychological, behavioral, and health correlates. *Addiction Research and Theory, 15*(3), 309–320. doi:10.1080/16066350701350247

Kaplan, A. M., & Haenlein, M. (2010). Users of the world, unite. The challenges and lucre of social media. *Business Horizons, 53*(1), 59–68. doi:10.1016/j.bushor.2009.09.003

Karikari, S., Osei-Frimpong, K., & Owusu-Frimpong, N. (2017). Evaluating individual level antecedents and consequences on Social Media use in Ghana. *Technological Forecasting and Social Change, 123*, 68–78. doi:10.1016/j.techfore.2017.06.023

Khan, M. L. (2017). Social Media engagement; what motivates user participation and consumption on Youtube. *Computers in Human Behavior, 66*, 236–247. doi:10.1016/j.chb.2016.09.024

Kuss, D. J., & Griffiths, M. D. (2017). Social networking sites and addiction: Ten lessons learned. *International Journal of Environmental Research and Public Health, 14*(3), 311. doi:10.3390/ijerph14030311 PMID:28304359

Kuss, D. J., Harkin, L., Kanjo, E., & Billieux, J. (2018). Problematic smartphone use: Investigation contemporary experiences using a convergent design. *International Journal of Environmental Research and Public Health, 15*(1), 142. doi:10.3390/ijerph15010142 PMID:29337883

Leung, L., & Wei, R. (1998). The Gratifications of Pager Use: Sociability, Information- Seeking, Entertainment, Utility, Fashion, and Status. *Telematics and Informatics, 15*(4), 253–264. doi:10.1016/S0736-5853(98)00016-1

Leung, L., & Wei, R. (2000). More than Just Talk on the Move: Uses and Gratification of Cellular Phones. *Journalism & Mass Communication Quarterly, 77*(2), 308–320. doi:10.1177/107769900007700206

Luo, X. (2002). Uses and gratifications theory and e-commerce behaviors: A structural equation modeling study. *Journal of Interactive Advertising, 2*, 34–41. doi:10.1080/15252019.2002.10722060

McCasland, M. (2005). Mobile marketing to millennials. *Young Consumers, 6*(3), 8–13. doi:10.1108/17473610510701133

Rubin, A. M. (2009). Uses and gratifications: An evolving perspective of media effects. In R. L. Nabi, & M. B. Oliver (Eds.), *The Sage handbook of media processes and effects* (pp. 147–160). Thousand Oaks, CA: Sage.

Seidman, G. (2013). Self-presentation and belonging on Facebook: How personality influences social media use and motivations. *Personality and Individual Differences, 54*(3), 402–407. doi:10.1016/j.paid.2012.10.009

Sheldon, P., & Bryant, K. (2016). Instagram: Motives for its use and relationship to narcissism and contextual age. *Computers in Human Behavior, 58*, 89–97. doi:10.1016/j.chb.2015.12.059

Steinfield, C., Ellison, N. B., & Lampe, C. (2008). Social capital, self-esteem, and use of online social network sites: A longitudinal analysis. *Journal of Applied Developmental Psychology, 29*(6), 434–445. doi:10.1016/j.appdev.2008.07.002

Sundar, S., & Limperos, A. (2013). Uses and Grats2.0: New Gratifications for New Media. *Journal of Broadcasting & Electronic Media, 57*(4), 504–525. doi:10.1080/08838151.2013.845827

Walsh, S. P., White, K. M., & Young, R. M. (2007). Young and connected: Psychological influences of mobile phone use amongst Australian youth. In G. Goggin,, & L. Hjorth (Eds.), *Mobile Media 2007: Proceedings of an international conference on social and cultural aspects of mobile phones, media and wireless technologies* (pp. 125-134). Sydney, Australia: University of Sydney.

Walsh, S. P., White, K. M., & Young, R. M. (2008a). *Needing to connect: The impact of self and others on young people's involvement with their mobile phone.* Manuscript submitted for publication.

Walsh, S. P., White, K. M., & Young, R. M. (2008c). The phone connection: A qualitative exploration of how belongingness and social identification relate to mobile phone use amongst Australian youth. *Journal of Community & Applied Social Psychology.*

Whiting, A., & Williams, D. (2013). Why people use social media: A uses and gratifications approach. *Qualitative Market Research, 16*(4), 362–369. doi:10.1108/QMR-06-2013-0041

Woods, H. C., & Scott, H. (2016). Sleepyteens: Social media use in adolescence is associated with poor sleep quality, anxiety, depression and low self-esteem. *Journal of Adolescence, 51*, 41–49. doi:10.1016/j.adolescence.2016.05.008 PMID:27294324

Yan, Z. (2017). *Mobile Phone behaviour.* New York, NY: Cambridge University Press. doi:10.1017/9781316417584

ADDITIONAL READING

Barker, V. (2009). Older adolescents' motivations for social network site use: The influence of gender, group identity, and collective self-esteem. *Cyberpsychology & Behavior, 12*(2), 209–213. doi:10.1089/cpb.2008.0228 PMID:19250021

Blumler, J. G., & Katz, E. (1974). *The Uses of Mass Communications: Current Perspectives on Gratifications Research.* Beverly Hills, CA, USA: Sage Publications.

Bolton, R. N., Parasuraman, A., Hoefnagels, A., Migchels, N., Kabadayi, S., Gruber, T., ... Solnet, D. (2013). Understanding Generation Y and their use of social media: A review and research agenda. *Journal of Service Management, 24*(3), 245–267. doi:10.1108/09564231311326987

Boyd, D. (2015). *It's complicated: The Social Lives of Networked Teens.* New Haven: Yale University Press.

Kaplan, A. M., & Haenlein, M. (2010). Users of the world, unite. The challenges and Opportunities of social media. *Business Horizons*, *53*(1), 59–68. doi:10.1016/j.bushor.2009.09.003

Karikari, S., Osei-Frimpong, K., & Owusu-Frimpong, N. (2017). Evaluating individual level antecedents and consequences on Social Media use in Ghana. *Technological Forecasting and Social Change*, *123*, 68–78. doi:10.1016/j.techfore.2017.06.023

Kuru, O., Bayer, J., Pasek, J., & Campbell, S. W. (2017). Understanding and measuring mobile Facebook use: Who, why & how. *Mobile Media and Communication*, *5*(1), 102–120. doi:10.1177/2050157916678269

Lievrouw, L. A., & Livingstone, S. (2002). *Handbook of New Media: Social Shaping and Consequences of ICTs*. London: Sage Publication Ltd.

KEY TERMS AND DEFINITIONS

Behavior: The actions and activities of a person or how a person's conduct.

Gratification: Satisfaction or pleasure obtained for engaging in behavior to fulfil a specific desire. Common gratification for using social media include: relationships, to relieve boredom and loneliness, for entertainment, etc.

Millennials/Second Digital Generation Users (2DG): Young consumers born in the 1990s, considered to be natives to digital media and distinct from the older segments of the population.

Outcome: A consequence or the way something turns out.

Psychological Attachment: A deep and enduring emotional bond which connects one person to another or an object.

Psychosocial: The interrelation of social factors, individual thought patterns, behavior, and how these influence interrelationships with others in a social setting.

Social Media: This is a Web 2.0-based social interactive plat form that allows users to generate and share ideas, pictures, videos, information, interests, and other expressions.

Uses and Gratification Theory (U&G): A theoretical perspective that examines why and how users engage with media to fulfil specific needs or achieve specific goals, based upon their psychological characteristics, social factors, and motives.

This research was previously published in The Psychology and Dynamics Behind Social Media Interactions; pages 368-389, copyright year 2020 by Information Science Reference (an imprint of IGI Global).

Chapter 57
My Little Joy in Life:
Posting Food on Instagram

Wan Chi Leung
University of Canterbury, New Zealand

Anan Wan
Georgia College & State University, USA

ABSTRACT

To post food on social media has become a frequent source of fun and joy in life for many mobile users. In investigating such a common scene on Instagram among its young users, the authors of this chapter investigated the relationship between social activity, personal traits like narcissism and shyness, and uses and gratifications from posting food photos on Instagram. Uses of Instagram for posting selfies were also examined for comparison. Results showed that while posting food photos were associated with social activity, posting selfies were associated with shyness. Narcissists were more likely to involve in posting both food photos and selfies. Implications of the results in explaining the generation of visual contents on social media are discussed.

INTRODUCTION

Food, as an important part of daily life, is likely to be universally welcomed by everyone. The joy from food not only comes with its taste, but with its visual appeal as well. With the development of technology in recent years, the joy from the appearance of food can be visually recorded and shared anytime, anywhere. One of the important apps for photo sharing is Instagram, which was launched in October 2010, and has become popular since then for its visual components and the hands-on creative features. Instagram is particularly popular among young adults. As of October 2018, 31% of the global Instagram users were aged 18-24, compared with 27% of the global Facebook users in the same age group (Statista, 2018). The gender distribution of young adult Instagram users aged 18-24 was more balanced than Facebook: 15% of the global Instagram users were female and 16% were male, versus 11% of the

DOI: 10.4018/978-1-6684-6307-9.ch057

global Facebook users were female and 16% were male. It shows that Instagram were popular among both female and male young adults.

Among various categories of photos on Instagram, food was identified as one of the top eight popular photo categories (Hu, Manikonda, & Kambhampati, 2014). Over 30% of the users in Hu et al.'s (2014) study posted more than two photos about food in their accounts. As of November 2018, there have been more than 300 million posts using the hashtag #food on Instagram, and more than 180 million posts using the hashtag #foodporn, indicating the popularity of sharing food photos on Instagram.

Instagram's focus on visual arts and the App-embedded filters makes it a suitable and convenient platform for photo sharing. Comparing to other social media platforms such as Twitter and Facebook, Instagram has lowered the requirements in artistic and photography skills, so almost anyone can enjoy producing attractive photos via Instagram. Verbal descriptions on how visual and gustatory attractive the food is might be difficult, but showing a photo of the food is a more convenient way to convey the same messages.

Although posting food photos has been popular for years (Hu et al., 2014), little is known about how people could gratify from posting food and why they would especially like to post food on social media. In view of the popularity of Instagram among young adults, the purpose of this exploratory study is to investigate young adults' gratifications from posting food photos (photos with food as the main theme) on Instagram, and how these gratifications are related to the use of Instagram for posting food photos. Also, how young adults' social activity and personal traits including narcissism and shyness are associated with posting food photos on Instagram is examined.

This study provides significant findings in indicating how the ubiquitous use of visual images of food for communication can satisfy young adult users. In other words, food consumption, is no longer only about nutritional needs, but the visual aspects of food can serve as a communication tool with Instagram as a platform. A number of studies have been conducted about Instagram selfie uploaders, (e.g., Al-Kandari, Melkote & Sharif, 2016; Williams & Marquez, 2015; Dhir et al., 2016; Kim et al., 2016), but not much have been done studying the motives of a large amount of Instagram users who have posted food photos. This study fills the research gap by investigating how young Instagram users satisfy their needs through posting food, an important aspect of everyday life.

Past research suggested that common Instagram users who focus more on posting food photos still like to post other categories of photos as well, which is quite different from the "selfies-lovers" who prefer posting self-portraits on Instagram exclusively (Hu, Manikonda, & Kambhampati, 2014). While both food photos and selfies can be easily posted anytime, anywhere, the two types of visual contents differ greatly by their levels of self-disclosure. In view of this, we also investigate young adults' use of Instagram for posting selfies (a self-portrait photo taken by oneself, which can include an individual alone or an individual with any other persons) on Instagram to see how the differences in visual appeals lead to different Instagram use. By comparing the use of Instagram in posting food photos and selfies among narcissistic and shy individuals, this study provides important implications on the relationship between the visual contents and individual characteristics.

LITERATURE REVIEW

Gratifications of Posting Food on Instagram

The uses and gratifications approach has been employed by researchers to study audiences' active consumption of mass media contents for more than half a century. It assumes the audiences actively select the media to meet their social and psychological needs and expectations (Katz et al., 1973). The term "gratifications set" refers to multiple possibilities for audiences to form and re-form the basis of their media-related interests, needs or preferences (McQuail, 2005). As Lindlof and Schatzer (1998) suggests, the difference between computer-mediated communication and other media use is that the former is more transient and multimodal, with fewer codes of conduct governing use, and allows for a higher degree of "end-user manipulation of content." Nowadays, the uses and gratifications approach has been applied to study the users of social media to generate contents. Leung's (2009) study indicates the motives of online user-generated contents include recognition needs, cognitive needs, social needs and entertainment needs, and their civic engagement.

Today, a smart phone is both a personal medium and a multipurpose device converging with the internet (Humphreys, Von Pape, & Karnowski, 2013). Wei's (2008) study found that the use of the mobile phone for news-seeking and web-surfing was driven by instrumental use motives, while playing video games via the mobile phone was driven by the motive of passing time. Gerlich et al. (2015) conducted an exploratory analysis of the uses and gratifications sought of mobile apps. Findings suggested that reasons for using mobile apps included engagement/disengagement, passing time, gaining knowledge and education, and social uses. In this study, we focus on Instagram, a popular mobile social media app which relies largely on photos as a visual component for information sharing. Lee, Lee, Moon, and Sung (2015) suggest that Instagram users have five social and psychological motives to share and review photos on Instagram: social interaction, archiving, self-expression escapism, and peeking. The activity of food blogging involves the creation and production of photos, and the processes of selecting and editing images, which make food blogging time consuming but very enjoyable (Cox & Blake, 2011).

In view of the literature using the uses and gratifications approach, the following hypothesis is proposed:

H1: The more gratifying the Instagram users find from posting food photos, the higher their personal involvement in posting food photos.

Social Activity

Rubin and Rubin (1982) associated television use and the concept of "contextual age", measured by various factors including social activity, as an important indicator for assessing life-position and communication behavior. While motives for posting photos on Instagram can be very different from television usage, social activity can be an important factor associated with Instagram use. Social activity indicates to what extent a person is socially active. A socially active person displays little affinity with the media and feels more comfortable with interpersonal interaction than a less mobile person. Instagram allows users to share photos and network with other users via visually-attractive photos, and the online visual expression can be a self-disclosure of social activity in their real lives (Rubin & Rubin, 1982; Sheldon & Bryant, 2016). A research question is proposed to examine how social activity is associated with the food photo posting behaviors:

RQ1.1: How is social activity associated with the personal involvement in posting food photos?

Previous visual studies have shown that human faces are powerful ways to communicate non-verbally (Takeuchi & Nagao, 1993). In online social media contexts, visuals with human faces also have more power in engaging and interacting with other users, for example, photos with faces are more likely to receive likes and comments (Bakhshi, Shamma & Gilbert, 2014). A study has shown that self-portraits were the most popular photo category on Instagram (Hu, Manikonda, & Kambhampati, 2014). Al-Kandari et al.'s (2016) survey found that the need for visual self-expression was the strongest predictor of the self-disclosure use of Instagram. As posting food photos and selfies involve different kinds of self-disclosure in social activity, a research question is proposed to compare the different behaviors:

RQ1.2: How is social activity associated with the personal involvement in posting selfies?

Narcissism

In recent years, a number of researchers have studied the role of narcissism in predicting social media use. According to Campbell and Foster (2007), "Individuals with narcissistic personality possess highly inflated, unrealistically positive views of the self. Often-times, this includes strong self-focus, feelings of entitlement, and lack of regard for others. Narcissists focus on what benefits them personally, with less regard for how their actions may benefit (or harm) others" (p.115). Social media are different from the traditional media, in a sense that they allow users to generate the contents on their own accounts – meaning that narcissists now have their platform to build up their images of the narcissistic self, which can be "positive, inflated, agentic, special, selfish, and oriented toward success" (Campbell and Foster, 2007, p.118).

Poon and Leung (2011) have found that narcissistic individuals reported more frequent online content production. Davenport et al.'s (2014) study indicated that narcissism was a stronger predictor of Facebook friends than Twitter followers. Ong et al.'s (2011) study found that narcissistic people are more likely to engage in features presenting self-generated content such as profile picture rating, status update frequency. Sheldon and Bryant (2016) surveyed college students and found a positive relationship between narcissism and using Instagram for the purposes of surveillance and being cool. The authors argued that Instagram appeared to be cool, accommodating narcissists' wish to be perceived in a positive light. Therefore, the following hypothesis is proposed:

H2.1: The higher the level of narcissism of the Instagram users, the higher their personal involvement in posting food photos.

Paramboukis, Skues and Wise's (2016) online survey suggested that uploading photos of one's physical appearance was associated with grandiose narcissism (traits such as exhibitionism and aggression). The following hypothesis is proposed:

H2.2: The higher the level of narcissism of the Instagram users, the higher their personal involvement in posting selfies.

Shyness

Shyness is defined as "one's reaction to being with strangers or casual acquaintance's: tension, concern, feelings or awkwardness and discomfort, and both gaze aversion and inhibition of normally expected social behavior." (Cheek & Buss, 1981, p.330; Buss, 1980). To shy individuals, the development of asynchronous computer-mediated communication such as social media has been important - Asynchronous computer-mediated communication not only reduces the need to interpret peripheral communicative behaviors such as body languages and tones of voice, but also gives shy individuals more control of the interaction and reduces the effects of situation-specific cues such as unexpected interruptions (Chan, 2011).

Past research has shown that social media remove the divide between shy and non-shy individuals. Baker and Oswald's (2010) survey found that among relatively shy individuals, greater Facebook use predicted satisfaction, importance, and closeness with Facebook friends, and increased social support received from friends. Stritzk, Nyugen and Durkin's (2004) experiment indicated that shy individuals differed from non-shy individuals in terms of rejection sensitivity, initiating relationships, and self-disclosure in an offline context, but they were not significantly different on these three domains in the online context. Sheldon's (2013) study suggested that while shyness was negatively correlated with self-disclosure to a face-to-face friend, it was not correlated with time spent on Facebook and self-disclosure to a Facebook friend. The following hypotheses are proposed:

H3.1: The higher the level of shyness of the Instagram users, the higher their personal involvement in posting food photos in posting food photos.
H3.2: The higher the level of shyness of the Instagram users, the higher their personal involvement in posting selfies.

Finally, in order to explore the uses of Instagram in posting food photos, the following research question is proposed:

RQ2: How do demographics, narcissism, shyness, social activity, general Instagram use, and gratifications sought predict a) personal involvement in posting food photos on Instagram; b) frequency of posting food photos on Instagram?

METHOD

Data Collection

To investigate Instagram use by young adults, a survey was administered to undergraduate students who had posted food photos on Instagram in the past. Following approvals by the Institutional Review Board in the U.S. and the Human Ethics Committee in New Zealand, a focus group of undergraduate students and a pilot test of the questionnaire, data were gathered through an online survey on Qualtrics and the distribution of paper questionnaires in 2016 in two public universities in the United States and in New Zealand respectively. The online survey link was snowballed from the undergraduate students, and the paper questionnaires were distributed to undergraduate students in class. A total of 373 respondents took part in the survey. After eliminating responses who indicated no experience in posting food photos on Instagram and incomplete responses, 223 responses (59.8%) were eligible for further analysis.

Among the analyzed responses, 136 (61.0%) were from the United States, and 87 (39.0%) were from New Zealand. 151 (67.7%) respondents were female, 53 (23.8%) were male, and 19 (8.5%) had their gender not revealed or undefined. The majority of the respondents were White/Caucasian (n = 181, 81.2%). The mean age of the respondents was 21.6, with 189 (84.8%) respondents aged 25 or below.

MEASUREMENTS OF MAJOR VARIABLES

Gratifications for Posting Food Photos on Instagram

To assess the gratifications sought from posting food photos on Instagram, respondents were asked to indicate their opinion for 34 items, on a 7-point Likert scale ranging from 1 (strongly disagree) to 7 (strongly agree). The items were adapted from previous studies on Instagram uses and social media use in general (Sheldon & Bryant, 2016; Lee et al., 2016; Whiting & Williams, 2013; Malik, Dhir & Nieminen, 2016). A pilot test with 15 Instagram users was conducted to eliminate the ambiguous and irrelevant items. The final survey instrument consists of 34 statements about gratifications sought from posting food photos.

An exploratory factor analysis of 34 items, with principal components and Varimax rotation, was conducted. Six factors were yielded using following criteria: eigenvalue greater than 1.0, and all factor loadings greater than 0.4. Six factors emerged, which explained 79.76% of the total variance. Eleven items were deleted due to low factor loadings.

Factor 1 was labeled "self-promotion," containing six items (Cronbach's alpha = .94). Factor 2, "escapism", contained four items (Cronbach's alpha = .94). Factor 3 was named "information sharing" (Cronbach's alpha = .93). Factor 4, "archiving," has a Cronbach's alpha at .80. Factor 5 was named as "creativity" (Cronbach's alpha = .90). Factor 6 was "self-disclosure" (Cronbach's alpha = .86). The items of all factors can be found in Table 1. The scores of the items under each factor were summated and averaged to become a single variable.

Personal Involvement in Posting Food Photos and Selfies on Instagram

Respondents' level of personal involvement in posting food photos on Instagram was assessed by their perceived importance of posting food photos on Instagram. Respondents indicated their opinion toward three items taken and adapted from the five items in Mittal's (1995) Product Category Involvement Scale (PCIS), which captures people's involvement in products. In this study the measurement used is a 7-point Likert scale, ranging from 1 (strongly disagree) to 7 (strongly agree), with three items: 1) Posting food photo on Instagram is important to me; 2) Posting food photo on Instagram means a lot to me; 3) Posting food photo on Instagram is valuable to me. The three items gave a high reliability (Cronbach's alpha = .957), and the scores of the three items were summated and divided by three to give the final score of the variable (M = 3.19, SD = 1.65).

Table 1. Factor analysis of gratifications sought from posting food photos on Instagram

I post food photos on Instagram...	Component						Mean	S.D.
	1	2	3	4	5	6		
Factor 1: Self-promotion								
1. To gain attention	.863						3.66	1.79
2. To be more popular	.857						4.10	1.76
3. To get more likes	.845						4.14	1.85
4. To get more comments	.844						3.69	1.79
5. To be noticed by others	.724						3.76	1.77
6. Because sharing food photos on Instagram is trendy	.612						4.07	1.74
Factor 2: Escapism								
7. To forget about troubles		.903					2.61	1.67
8. To avoid loneliness		.878					2.52	1.67
9. To escape from reality		.847					2.65	1.68
10. To relax		.780					3.19	1.90
Factor 3: Information sharing								
11. To share something useful about food			.861				3.46	1.72
12. To share something informative about food			.860				3.59	1.77
13. To share something important about food			.823				3.49	1.77
Factor 4: Archiving								
14. To record my traces (e.g., trip) via photomap				.796			3.92	1.94
15. To remember special events				.743			5.25	1.51
16. To take fancy food photos and save them online				.675			4.09	1.82
17. To depict my life through photos				.587			4.58	1.74
Factor 5: Creativity								
18. To create visual art					.798		4.41	1.86
19. To show off my photography skills					.793		4.12	1.78
20. To produce attractive visual content					.770		4.70	1.76
Factor 6: Self-disclosure								
21. To express my actual self (who I really am)						.778	4.15	1.78
22. To disclose happenings around me						.695	4.41	1.70
23. To share my personal information with others						.695	3.64	1.78
Eigenvalues	10.47	2.52	2.10	1.23	1.03	1.00		
Variances explained	45.53	10.94	9.13	5.34	4.46	4.36		
Cronbach's Alpha	.94	.94	.93	.80	.90	.86		
Extraction Method: Principal Component Analysis. Rotation Method: Varimax with Kaiser Normalization.								
a. Rotation converged in 6 iterations.								

N = 223.

Three similar items were used to measure the personal involvement in posting selfies on Instagram. The three items also gave a high reliability (Cronbach's alpha = .941), and the scores of the three items were summated and divided by three to give the final score of the variable (M = 2.77, SD = 1.65). The difference between the personal involvement in posting selfies and food photos were then computed.

Frequency in Posting Food Photos on Instagram

Respondents were asked to indicate their frequency of posting food photos by a 7-point Likert scale, ranging from 1 (Almost never), 2 (Rarely), 3 (Sometimes), 4 (Quite often), to 5 (Very often) (M = 2.60, SD = .776). Respondents also answered the question "On average, how long do you spend on taking and editing a food photo before posting it for others to see on Instagram?" by indicating a number in minutes (M = 6.36, SD = 7.62).

General Instagram Use

Respondents' general Instagram use were measured by the number of followers they had on Instagram (M = 5.19, SD = 461), and the number of Instagram accounts they were following (M = 4.51, SD = 328).

Social Activity

The items of social activity, modified from Rubin and Rubin (1982), were measured by three items on a 7-point scale: 1) I often travel, vacation, or take trips with others; 2) I often visit friends, relatives, or neighbors in their homes; 3) I often participate in games, sports, or activities with others. The three items give an acceptable reliability (Cronbach's alpha = .763), and they were summated and divided into the final score (M = 5.11 SD = 1.25).

Narcissism

Narcissism was measured by four items on a 7-point Likert scale, adapted from the Hypersensitive Narcissism Scale (HSNS) (Hendin & Cheek, 1997): 1) I can become entirely absorbed in thinking about my personal affairs, my health, my cares or my relations to others; 2) I dislike sharing the credit of an achievement with others; 3) I feel that I have enough on my hands without worrying about other people's troubles; 4) I feel that I am temperamentally different from most people. The Cronbach's alpha of the four items was .741, showing they were fairly reliable. The scores of the four items were summated and divided by four to become the final score of narcissism (M = 3.86, SD = 1.21).

Shyness

Four items, adapted from the shyness scale by Cheek and Buss (1981), were set up to measure shyness: 1) I am socially somewhat awkward; 2) I don't find it hard to talk to strangers; 3) I feel tense when I'm with people I don't know; 4) I am often uncomfortable at parties and other social functions. Respondents were asked for their opinion toward the four items, on the 7-point scale ranging from 1 (strongly disagree) to 7 (strongly agree). The four items gave a very high reliability (Cronbach's alpha = .911). The scores were summated and divided by four as the final score of the variable (M = 3.49, SD = 1.61).

Demographics

Respondents were asked to indicate their age, gender, and ethnicity. Age was indicated by a number in years. Options for gender were Male; Female; and Others (please specify). Options for ethnicity were Hispanic or Latino; American Indian or Alaska Native; Asian; Black or African or African American; Native Hawaiian or Other Pacific Islander; White or Caucasian or European; Maori; Arab or Middle Eastern; Others (please specify).

RESULTS

H1 proposed that the more gratifying the Instagram users find from posting food photos, the higher personal involvement in posting food photos on Instagram. To test the hypothesis, a hierarchical regression was run. The first block of predictors were users' demographic variables, including age, race and nation of residence. Race and nation of residence were entered as dummy variables, with 0 = White or Caucasian or European, 1 = Others, and 0 = the U.S., 1 = New Zealand respectively. The six gratifications were entered as the second block of the predictors (F = 21.71, $p < .001$, adjusted R square = .509). The multicollinearlity was acceptable (VIF < 2.30). Escapism ($\beta = .154$, $p < .05$), information sharing ($\beta = .310$, $p < .001$), archiving ($\beta = .164$, $p < .05$) were found to be significant predictors of personal involvement in posting food photos on Instagram. H1 was supported.

RQ1.1 asked how social activity is associated with the personal involvement in posting food photos. To answer a research question, a hierarchical regression with demographics controlled as the first block and the social activity as the second-block predictor was run (F = 3.22, $p < .01$, adjusted R^2 = .052). Social activity was found to be a significant predictor ($\beta = .154$, p < .05) of the personal involvement in posting food photos on Instagram. The result of the regression was shown in the first column of Table 2.

Table 2. Hierarchical regressions of personal involvement in posting food photos on Instagram

DV	Personal Involvement in Posting Food Photos	
Predictors	**β**	**β**
Block 1: Demographics		
Age	.085	.095
Race	.025	.068
Gender	-.062	-.074
Nation	-.151*	-.175*
Adjusted R²	.036	.036
Block 2: Narcissism and shyness		
Social activity	.154*	
Narcissism		.224***
Incremental R²	.016	.046
Total adjusted *R²*	.052	.082

Note: * p < .05, ** p < .01, *** p < .001; N = 223.

RQ1.2 asked how social activity is associated with the personal involvement in posting selfies. A similar hierarchical regression was run, with demographics controlled. The regression equation was insignificant.

H2.1 proposed that the higher the level of narcissism of the Instagram users, the higher their personal involvement in posting food photos on Instagram. A hierarchical regression with demographics controlled ($F = 4.62$, $p < .001$, adjusted $R^2 = .082$) indicated that narcissism was a significant predictor of the personal involvement in posting food photos ($\beta = .224$, $p < .001$). H2.1 was supported. The result of the regression was shown in the second column of Table 2.

H2.2 proposed that the higher the level of narcissism of the Instagram users, the higher their personal involvement in posting selfies on Instagram. A hierarchical regression with demographics controlled ($F = 3.81$, $p < .001$, adjusted $R^2 = .077$) indicated that narcissism significantly predicted personal involvement in posting selfies ($\beta = .266$, $p < .001$). H2.2 was supported. The result of the regression was shown in the first column of Table 3.

Table 3. Hierarchical regressions of personal involvement in posting selfies on Instagram

DV	Personal Involvement in Posting Selfies	
Predictors	β	β
Block 1: Demographics		
Age	-.025	-.036
Race	.035	.035
Gender	-.194*	-.180*
Nation	.011	-.017
Adjusted R^2	.011	.011
Block 2: Narcissism and shyness		
Narcissism	.266***	
Shyness		.160*
Incremental R^2	.066	.20
Total adjusted R^2	.077	.031

Note: * p < .05, ** p < .01, *** p < .001; N = 223.

H3.1 proposed that the higher the level of shyness of the Instagram users, the higher their personal involvement in posting food photos on Instagram. A hierarchical regression with demographics controlled ($F = 3.03$, $p < .05$, Adjusted $R^2 = .048$) indicated that shyness was insignificant in predicting of the personal involvement in posting food photos. H3.1 was not supported.

H3.2 proposed that the higher the level of shyness of the Instagram users, the higher their personal involvement in posting selfies on Instagram. A hierarchical regression with demographics controlled ($F = 2.06$, $p < .05$, Adjusted $R^2 = .031$) indicated that shyness was a significant predictor of personal involvement in posting selfies ($\beta = .160$, $p < .05$). H3.2 was supported. The result of the regression was shown in the second column of Table 3.

RQ2a asked for demographics, narcissism, shyness, social activity, general Instagram use, and gratifications sought predicted personal involvement in posting food photos on Instagram. To answer this research question, a hierarchical regression was performed. The first block of predictors were users' demographic variables. The second block of predictors were narcissism and shyness, followed by the number of followers on Instagram and the number of following Instagram accounts as the third block of predictors. The six factors of gratifications sought from posting food photos on Instagram were entered as the fourth block of predictors. Personal involvement in posting food photos on Instagram was entered as the dependent variable. The regression equation was significant (F = 13.670, $p < .001$), with an adjusted R square at .495. Results showed that significant predictors included nation of residence (β = -.164, $p < .01$), escapism (β = .16, $p < .05$), information sharing (β = .277, $p < .001$), and archiving (β = .174, $p < .01$). Detailed results are shown in Table 4.

Table 4. Hierarchical regressions of personal involvement in posting, frequency of posting, and time spent editing food photos on Instagram

DV - Predictors	Personal involvement (β)	Frequency (β)
Block 1: Demographics		
Age	.022	.000
Race	.004	-.097
Gender	-.035	-.161*
Nation	-.164**	-.167*
Adjusted R^2	.034	.027
Block 2: Narcissism and shyness		
Narcissism	.005	.099
Shyness	.025	-.168
Incremental R^2	.086	.057
Block 3: Social activity		
Social activity	.005	.033
Incremental R^2	.012	.003
Block 4: General Instagram use		
Followers	.042	-.123
Following a/c	-.024	-.052
Incremental R^2	.014	-.07
Block 5: Gratifications sought		
Social interaction	.119	-.043
Escapism	.160*	.226**
Information sharing	.277***	.296***
Archiving	.174**	.121
Creativity	.102	.089
Self-disclosure	.079	.034
Incremental R^2	.383	.0253
Total adjusted R^2	.495	.333

Note: * p < .05, ** p < .01, *** p < .001; N = 223.

RQ2b was proposed to examine how demographics, narcissism, shyness, social activity, general Instagram use, and gratifications sought predicted the frequency of posting food photos on Instagram. Predictors were entered into the hierarchical regression equation with the same order as before, with the frequency of posting food photos as the dependent variable (F = 7.445, $p < .001$, adjusted $R^2 = .333$). Results showed that significant predictors included gender ($\beta = -.161$, $p < .05$), nation of residence ($\beta = -.167$, $p < .05$), escapism ($\beta = .226$, $p < .01$), and information sharing ($\beta = .296$, $p < .001$). Detailed results are also shown in Table 4.

DISCUSSION

Findings in this study offer meaningful implications for the theoretical approaches in uses and gratifications. In this exploratory study, six gratifications sought from posting food photos on Instagram by young adults were found. They were self-promotion, escapism, information sharing, archiving, creativity and self-disclosure. Among the six gratifications, escapism, information sharing, and archiving were found to be significant predictors of personal involvement in posting food photos on Instagram. Motives including self-promotion and self-disclosure were not significant predictors of personal involvement and frequency of posting food photos on Instagram. Al-Kandari et al.'s (2016) survey showed the need for visual self-expression was the strongest predictor of the self-disclosure use of Instagram. Sharing food photos without human faces reduces the extent of self-disclosure, which may not satisfy the need for self-expression on social media as other types of photos, such as selfies.

However, posting food photos does satisfy Instagram users' psychological needs by escapism. Unlike selfies that may lead to criticisms on the uploader's appearance, taking photos of food allows the individual to reduce the stress caused by criticisms, by showing the gustatory attractive food without any engagement of a personal appeal. Distress may also be eased physiologically with the consumption of food after taking the food photo. Sharing food photos on Instagram brings ordinary joy that can be shared by everyone, regardless of physical appearances and physical conditions.

Food photos are also informative, as shown by the gratifications of information sharing and archiving. Food photos contain important information about eating, which is always an important aspect of human life. The information on a food photo can include a person's lifestyle, a recipe, a restaurant, and so on, and is worth sharing. Archiving did not predict the frequency of posting food photos, but significantly predicted the personal involvement of posting food. While food is something that appears in everyone's life frequently, it seems everyday food does not need to be archived. Archiving with food photos may only be needed under special circumstances such as remembering an event, celebrating important dates, visiting a famous restaurant, traveling to another place, etc.

Many of the past studies treated content generation on social media as a single, holistic behavior, but our analysis suggests the underlying psychological mechanism behind posting different types of contents can be different. Our findings explore young adults' uses of social media in different ways, by comparing different psychological factors' associations with personal involvement of posting food photos and posting selfies. The comparison enriches our understanding of the content generation behavior on social media.

Social activity significantly predicted the personal involvement in posting food photos, but not selfies. In other words, more socially active people involve more in posting food photos. It can be because posting food photos is a "non-invasive" type of self-disclosure. Food involved in social activity, such as food during gatherings and travels, are usually more visually appealing and can initiate the motives of sharing them online. The mobile nature of Instagram allows food photos to be shared in these social activities easily, but keeping the privacy of the users at the same time because their own appearances are not shown in these photos. On the contrary, posting selfie is a kind of self-disclosure closely related to self-expression (Al-Kandari et al., 2016). The act of taking and posting selfies may not involve any types of social interactions, and thus it does not necessarily associate with social activity.

This study also disclosed the relationships between narcissism and the involvements of Instagram users in posting food photos and selfies among young adults. The more narcissistic the Instagram user, the more involved they were in posting both food photos and selfies on Instagram. Such a finding is in line with previous research (e.g., Poon & Leung, 2011; Kim et al., 2016). Posting either food or selfies on Instagram can be a way to satisfy the narcissists' needs to promote themselves, attract attentions from others, and share personal information with others. After all, regardless of food or selfies, posting photos on Instagram is a form of self-disclosure. In addition to sharing something with others, Instagram is a perfect platform to equip normal social media users with hands-on mobile photography skills to produce and share visually-attractive creative works with others. To narcissistic individuals, food can be visual extension of themselves, that serves a similar communication function with their selfies.

Shy individuals were found to be more involved in posting selfies. For shy individuals, face-to-face interactions with strangers or casual acquaintances can be a source of awkwardness and discomfort (Cheek & Buss, 1981), so expressing themselves by posting selfies on the social media may reduce the stress caused by self-expressions in real life. On the contrary, posting food photos is less associated with self-expressions and is not associated with tensions built up in face-to-face interactions among shy individuals. This piece of finding shows clearly that the nature of the visual content posted on social media is an important factor influencing users' communication patterns. Food, without any visual self-disclosure, is a more universal way of communication across people with different levels of shyness.

Our sample covers college students from both U.S. and New Zealand, and findings indicated that Instagram users in the U.S. were more involved in posting food photos. One reason may be the differences in eating habits between the two countries. For example, the per capita food expenditure away from home in 2014 in the U.S. was USD 2,293, while the per capita expenditure eating out in New Zealand was much lower at NZD 1,688 (approximately USD 1,182); The share of consumer expenditures on food that were consumed at home in 2015 was much higher in New Zealand (14.9%) than in the U.S. (6.4%) (United States Department of Agriculture, 2016). Food that are non-homemade (offered by restaurants, cafes, etc.) are usually visually more appealing, initiating greater desires to share on Instagram, which may explain the national difference.

In addition, results showed that women involved more than men in posting selfies on Instagram, but there was no gender difference in posting food photos. This is consistent with previous research findings, for example, Dhir et al. (2016) found that women were more likely to take personal and group selfies and post compared to men. Food photos, without showing any physical appearances, on the other hand, engaged men and women equally. Women significantly posted food photos more frequently than men, but both genders involved in posting food photos similarly.

While race was not a significant predictor in the personal involvement in posting selfies, Williams and Marquez's (2015) semi-structured interviews suggested White social media users had an aversion to selfies, whereas Black and Latino users generally approved of selfies. Contrary to selfies, food photos do not disclose the uploaders' race. As we argued before, the joy of posting food photos on Instagram can be shared by everyone, regardless of their gender and race. While selfies involve the visual appeal of the photographer and are more popular among people with good appearances, food photos can be uploaded by all demographics, because literally, everyone consumes food every day.

LIMITATIONS AND FUTURE STUDY

Although this exploratory study provides several promising insights for understanding young adult Instagram users' behaviors of posting food and selfies, it does have several limitations. First, all participants were recruited from college campuses through snowball sampling. Future study should use a more diverse and representative sample outside the university. Then, differences were discovered from comparing the sample from different countries of residence, the United States and New Zealand, but both countries are dominated by western cultures. Future study can explore young adults' use of Instagram in countries with other cultures, and investigate whether and how culture influences their mobile photography preferences and behaviors. Finally, this study only examined food-and-selfie-posting behaviors on Instagram, so future study would investigate similar topic on other social media platforms such as Facebook, Twitter, Snapchat etc. to understand more about users' self-disclosure of visual contents under the specific characteristics

REFERENCES

Al-Kandari, A., Melkote, S. R., & Sharif, A. (2016). Needs and Motives of Instagram Users that Predict Self-disclosure Use: A Case Study of Young Adults in Kuwait. *Journal of Creative Communications*.

Baker, L. R., & Oswald, D. L. (2010). Shyness and online social networking services. *Journal of Social and Personal Relationships*, *27*(7), 873–889. doi:10.1177/0265407510375261

Bakhshi, S., Shamma, D. A., & Gilbert, E. (2014, April). Faces engage us: Photos with faces attract more likes and comments on Instagram. In *Proceedings of the 32nd annual ACM conference on Human factors in computing systems* (pp. 965-974). ACM. 10.1145/2556288.2557403

Buss, A. H. (1980). Shyness and sociability. *Journal of Personality and Social Psychology*, *41*, 330–339.

Campbell, W. K., & Foster, J. D. (2007). The narcissistic self: Background, an extended agency model, and ongoing controversies. *Self*, 115–138.

Chan, M. (2011). Shyness, sociability, and the role of media synchronicity in the use of computer-mediated communication for interpersonal communication. *Asian Journal of Social Psychology*, *14*(1), 84–90.

Cheek, J. M., & Buss, A. H. (1981). Shyness and sociability. *Journal of Personality and Social Psychology*, *41*(2), 330–339. doi:10.1037/0022-3514.41.2.330

Cox, A. M., & Blake, M. K. (2011, March). Information and food blogging as serious leisure. In P. Willett (Ed.), ASLIB proceedings (Vol. 63, No. 2/3, pp. 204-220). Emerald Group Publishing Limited. doi:10.1108/00012531111135664

Davenport, S. W., Bergman, S. M., Bergman, J. Z., & Fearrington, M. E. (2014). Twitter versus Facebook: Exploring the role of narcissism in the motives and usage of different social media platforms. *Computers in Human Behavior*, *32*, 212–220. doi:10.1016/j.chb.2013.12.011

Dhir, A., Pallesen, S., Torsheim, T., & Andreassen, C. S. (2016). Do age and gender differences exist in selfie-related behaviours? *Computers in Human Behavior*, *63*, 549–555. doi:10.1016/j.chb.2016.05.053

Gerlich, R. N., Drumheller, K., & Babb, J. (2015). App Consumption: An Exploratory Analysis of the Uses & Gratifications of Mobile Apps. *Academy of Marketing Studies Journal*, *19*(1), 69.

Hendin, H. M., & Cheek, J. M. (1997). Assessing Hypersensitive Narcissism: A Re-examination of Murray's Narcissism Scale. *Journal of Research in Personality*, *31*(4), 588–599. doi:10.1006/jrpe.1997.2204

Hu, Y., Manikonda, L., & Kambhampati, S. (2014, June). What We Instagram: A First Analysis of Instagram Photo Content and User Types. ICWSM.

Humphreys, L., Von Pape, T., & Karnowski, V. (2013). Evolving mobile media: Uses and conceptualizations of the mobile internet. *Journal of Computer-Mediated Communication*, *18*(4), 491–507. doi:10.1111/jcc4.12019

Katz, E., Blumler, J. G., & Gurevitch, M. (1973). Uses and gratifications research. *Public Opinion Quarterly*, *37*(4), 509–523. doi:10.1086/268109

Kim, E., Lee, J. A., Sung, Y., & Choi, S. M. (2016). Predicting selfie-posting behavior on social networking sites: An extension of theory of planned behavior. *Computers in Human Behavior*, *62*, 116–123. doi:10.1016/j.chb.2016.03.078

Lee, E., Lee, J. A., Moon, J. H., & Sung, Y. (2015). Pictures Speak Louder than Words: Motivations for Using Instagram. *Cyberpsychology, Behavior, and Social Networking*, *18*(9), 552–556. doi:10.1089/cyber.2015.0157 PMID:26348817

Leung, L. (2009). User-generated content on the internet: An examination of gratifications, civic engagement and psychological empowerment. *New Media & Society*, *11*(8), 1327–1347. doi:10.1177/1461444809341264

Lindlof, T. R., & Shatzer, M. J. (1998). Media ethnography in virtual space: Strategies, limits, and possibilities. *Journal of Broadcasting & Electronic Media*, *42*(2), 170–189. doi:10.1080/08838159809364442

Malik, A., Dhir, A., & Nieminen, M. (2016). Uses and Gratifications of digital photo sharing on Facebook. *Telematics and Informatics*, *33*(1), 129–138. doi:10.1016/j.tele.2015.06.009

McQuail, D. (2005). *Mass communication theory* (5th ed.). London: Sage.

Mittal, B. (1995). A comparative analysis of four scales of consumer involvement. *Psychology and Marketing*, *12*(7), 663–682. doi:10.1002/mar.4220120708

Ong, E. Y., Ang, R. P., Ho, J. C., Lim, J. C., Goh, D. H., Lee, C. S., & Chua, A. Y. (2011). Narcissism, extraversion and adolescents' self-presentation on Facebook. *Personality and Individual Differences*, *50*(2), 180–185. doi:10.1016/j.paid.2010.09.022

Paramboukis, O., Skues, J., & Wise, L. (2016). An Exploratory Study of the Relationships between Narcissism, Self-Esteem and Instagram Use. *Social Networking*, *5*(02), 82–92. doi:10.4236n.2016.52009

Poon, D. C. H., & Leung, L. (2011). *Effects of narcissism, leisure boredom, and gratifications sought on user-generated content among net-generation users*. Academic Press.

Rubin, A. M., & Rubin, R. B. (1982). Contextual age and television use. *Human Communication Research*, *8*(3), 228–244. doi:10.1111/j.1468-2958.1982.tb00666.x

Rubin, R. B., Rubin, A. M., Graham, E., Perse, E. M., & Seibold, D. (2010). *Communication research measures II: A sourcebook*. Routledge. doi:10.4324/9780203871539

Sheldon, P. (2013). Voices that cannot be heard: Can shyness explain how we communicate on Facebook versus face-to-face? *Computers in Human Behavior*, *29*(4), 1402–1407. doi:10.1016/j.chb.2013.01.016

Sheldon, P., & Bryant, K. (2016). Instagram: Motives for its use and relationship to narcissism and contextual age. *Computers in Human Behavior*, *58*, 89–97. doi:10.1016/j.chb.2015.12.059

Statista. (2018). *Statistics and Market Data on Social Media & User-Generated Content*. Accessed at https://www.statista.com/markets/424/topic/540/social-media-user-generated-content/

Stritzke, W. G., Nguyen, A., & Durkin, K. (2004). Shyness and computer-mediated communication: A self-presentational theory perspective. *Media Psychology*, *6*(1), 1–22. doi:10.12071532785xmep0601_1

Sung, Y., Lee, J. A., Kim, E., & Choi, S. M. (2016). Why we post selfies: Understanding motivations for posting pictures of oneself. *Personality and Individual Differences*, *97*, 260–265. doi:10.1016/j.paid.2016.03.032

Takeuchi, A., & Nagao, K. (1993, May). Communicative facial displays as a new conversational modality. In *Proceedings of the INTERACT'93 and CHI'93 Conference on Human Factors in Computing Systems* (pp. 187-193). ACM. 10.1145/169059.169156

United States Department of Agriculture. (2016). *Food expenditures*. Retrieved from https://www.ers.usda.gov/data-products/food-expenditures/food-expenditures/#Expenditures%20on%20food%20and%20alcoholic%20beverages%20that%20were%20consumed%20at%20home%20by%20selected%20countries

Whiting, A., & Williams, D. (2013). Why people use social media: A uses and gratifications approach. *Qualitative Market Research*, *16*(4), 362–369. doi:10.1108/QMR-06-2013-0041

Williams, A. A., & Marquez, B. A. (2015). Selfies| The Lonely Selfie King: Selfies and the Conspicuous Prosumption of Gender and Race. *International Journal of Communication*, *9*, 13.

This research was previously published in Impacts of Mobile Use and Experience on Contemporary Society; pages 70-85, copyright year 2019 by Information Science Reference (an imprint of IGI Global).

Chapter 58
The Impact of Similarity and Self–Esteem on Facebook Behaviors, Perceptions, and Attitudes

Bryon Balint
Belmont University, Nashville, USA

ABSTRACT

From their inception, electronic social networks (ESNs) have held the potential to either (1) expose individuals to a greater diversity of beliefs and interests by removing geographical barriers to communication; or (2) act as "feedback loops" by facilitating relationships and communication among like-minded individuals. In this survey study, the author will examine changes in communication behaviors and perceptions on Facebook from 2013 to 2017. The findings conclude that individuals with lower self-esteem have become less willing to share their views on Facebook, perceive a higher number of negative experiences, and spend less time communicating and more time passively consuming content. The same behavioral changes are found when individuals believe that fewer of their online "friends" have similar beliefs, and when individuals are more prone to "unfriending" others. General comfort in sharing views online is associated with a higher willingness to share views and communicate on Facebook, but also more negative experiences.

INTRODUCTION

In the 2016 U.S. presidential election Donald Trump narrowly lost the popular vote to Hillary Clinton, who captured about 51.1% of individual votes. However, Trump won the Electoral College by a wide margin, in part because both Republican and Democratic votes tend to be concentrated in specific geographic areas. Trump won approximately 2,600 counties to Clinton's 500, and about 2,200 of those were "landslide counties" in which Trump won by a margin of 20% or greater (Unruh, 2016). In 2016, 60% of Republican voters lived in landslide counties; by contrast, in 2008 this percentage was 48%, and

DOI: 10.4018/978-1-6684-6307-9.ch058

in 1992 it was 38% (Aisch et al., 2016). One conclusion that has been drawn from such statistics is that people tend to live near others who are similar to themselves. Within an economic range, people are likely to choose neighborhoods that provide easier access to their preferred activities, religious institutions, and schools. Stated more broadly, people tend to choose neighborhoods in which the inhabitants are culturally similar, and this phenomenon is often correlated with political and religious affiliation. Over time, a "feedback loop" results as individuals are continually exposed to the same political and religious viewpoints (Bishop, 2008).

Many of the geographic factors that limit exposure to a diversity of viewpoints are less relevant in an online setting. Electronic social networks (ESN's) such as Facebook, Instagram, and LinkedIn have made it easier to stay connected with many others (Claybaugh & Haried, 2014). People are connected in ESN's to many of the same people to whom they are connected in the physical world, but they are also likely to be connected to others who they seldom, if ever, encounter in real life. For example, on Facebook people may be "friends" with high school classmates whom they have not seen or spoken to verbally in decades, or with distant family friends and relatives who are typically seen every few years at events such as weddings and family reunions. To the extent that these distant connections live in different geographies, they are more likely to exhibit different economic and cultural characteristics. By interacting with distant connections through ESN's, people are more likely to be exposed to these different characteristics (Balint & Gustafson, 2015). However, ESN's can also facilitate the opposite effect in the form of online communities of interest. The same technology that enables people to connect with others in geographically dispersed locations can also be used to find like-minded individuals online. Thus, although ESN's such as Facebook have existed in consumers' lives since the early 2000's, evidence about ESN's ability to effectively create and spread new political, religious, or social ideas across groups is mixed (Furner, 2013). Some experts believe that ESN's are more successful than traditional, offline forms of communication in spreading new viewpoints, but others feel that ESN's are useless, or even detrimental, in the dissemination of diverse beliefs. For example, ESN's have been blamed for causing more apathy towards political and social causes by allowing people to simply broadcast their opinions without encouraging them to consider others' beliefs as well (Gladwell, 2010; Neil, 2013). Particularly in the U.S. religion is highly correlated with political affiliation, and online discourse of political, religious and social issues has become more divisive since the 2012 presidential election. In addition to current events, individuals may also turn to social media to learn new information about long-standing religious or political doctrine (Almobarraz, 2016). An increasing percentage of content that is posted and discussed online is from sources that are perceived as partial to one end of the political spectrum or the other, discouraging the presentation of diverse viewpoints (McHugh, 2016). Even more insidiously, there is evidence that terrorist groups such as Al-Qaeda and other radical activist groups use ESN's to recruit members and organize activities (Knibbs, 2017).

Adding to this tension is the fact that ESN's change over time. Like most technology companies, ESN providers periodically make changes to the user interface, security settings, or back-end algorithms that affect what content users see (Balint & Rau-Foster, 2014). Most ESN's use collaborative filtering and user feedback to determine the types of content users are most likely to click through. For example, if a Facebook user consistently clicks on articles from conservative sources and spends time reading them, Facebook is more likely to display conservative articles in the future. This gives users what they like, and also generates more revenue for Facebook (McHugh, 2016). However, it also means that the user is less likely to see articles presenting contradictory viewpoints. Individuals have become more likely to "second-screen" social media on mobile devices or tablets, making political messages more salient

(Barnidge, Gil de Zúñiga, & Diehl, 2017). Finally, individual attitudes towards particular ESN's evolve over time. Facebook users have started to spend less time micro-blogging and more time posting pictures and articles (McHugh, 2017). More individuals have started to turn to Twitter as a primary news source (Luckerson, 2017). Social norms and face-to-face friend networks may also influence how individuals choose to use ESN's.

In this paper, we examine changes in Facebook behaviors and perceptions over the past four years. We relate these changes to individual characteristics such as self-esteem, perceived similarity with online "friends", and general comfort in sharing views online. We investigate these issues through two surveys of Facebook users – one conducted in 2013, the other in 2017. The results may help to illuminate individuals' motivations for participating in ESN's, which should also be informative for ESN providers. Our paper also contributes to theory on the relationships between self-esteem, homophily, and communication in ESN's.

Other recent studies have examined individuals' motivations and propensity for engaging in political discourse online, and found that online political discourse is no more likely than face-to-face political discourse (Kruse, Norris, & Flinchum, 2018). In contrast, other studies have pointed out that the speed and dissemination of diverse information may actually make online political discussion and conflict resolution easier (Zeitzoff, 2017). In addition, recent evidence suggests that engaging in political discourse online may motivate individuals to join political organizations in real life (Zhang & Lin, 2018). Finally, other studies (e.g. Yang, Barnidge, & Rojas, 2017) have examined the relationship between political disagreement and "unfriending" or "unfollowing", as we do. However, our study differs in that we also examine discussion of religious and personal interests, and that we examine changes in those activities over time.

THEORETICAL BACKGROUND AND HYPOTHESES

Changes in ESN Behavior

Much academic research and anecdotal evidence suggests that in the physical world, people tend to associate with others who are similar to themselves. In many cases, this association is a result of geographical convenience. If a man belongs to a particular health club or attends a particular church, he is likely to live relatively near that club or church; otherwise he would choose one that is more convenient. Other people that go to the same club or church are also likely to live near their locations. In addition, people that live in the same geographic area are likely to have similar incomes, and income is often correlated with demographic characteristics such as education level, race, and political affiliation (Bishop, 2008).

In other cases, association in the physical world is a function of personal interests as well as geography. For example, out of necessity, a woman may be willing to travel a greater geographic distance to get to work than she would to go to a health club. But at work, she is likely to form relationships with others that have similar or related skills, suggesting similar levels of education and ability. Children are another facilitator of association. Many adults become acquainted because their children are friends and either go to the same school or participate in mutual activities such as athletic teams. These associations are based on both geography and personal interests. In addition, people with children who are of similar ages are naturally more likely to be similarly aged themselves.

Many people who form associations or friendships in the physical world maintain those same associations or friendships within ESN's. ESN's often facilitate communication and organization even for individuals who also connect with one another in the physical world; they have become ubiquitous in personal interaction (Special & Barber, 2012). Because ESN's are not constrained by geography, neither are the associations within them. However, evidence suggests that over the past several years, both the communication patterns on ESN's and the social networks themselves have come to resemble their face-to-face counterparts more closely. For example, in 2013 Facebook implemented an "Unfollow" function. This function allows a user to not see a friend's content without severing the tie to that friend or sending a notification (Ha, 2013). With the unfollow function, Facebook has made it easier for a user to filter undesired content without affecting the relationship directly. A good offline analogy might be ignoring someone's phone calls or invitations to activities without explicitly telling that person you no longer want to be friends. At the same time, evidence suggests that individuals have also become more likely to unfriend people on ESN's with whose viewpoints they disagree (McHugh, 2016). Since the beginning of 2016, people have become more likely to brag on ESN's about how many individuals they have blocked or unfriended. Because it is easier and less socially awkward to unfriend somebody online than in real life, it is reasonable to assume that a greater proportion of these "unfriended" individuals are online only and not encountered often face-to-face.

In summary, the associations that people maintain in the physical world – or the associations that people maintain within ESN's that are also maintained in the physical world – are more likely to arise between people that share similar characteristics. In comparison, associations that are maintained mostly or entirely within ESN's are more likely to arise between people that do not share similar characteristics. However, this distinction has eroded over the past several years due to changes in ESN's themselves and changes in user behavior. For this study, we examine three specific types of characteristics: political viewpoints, religious beliefs, and personal interests. People are often implicitly or explicitly discouraged from discussing political, religious, and personal matters in environments such as the workplace. However, individuals are more likely to share this type of information online, despite potential privacy or risk concerns (Wang, 2012).

ESN's and Self-Esteem

Previous studies have related personality traits such as self-esteem to ESN usage. An individual's level of comfort in presenting his or her own views in ESN's has been positively related to subjective well-being, perceived social support, and self-esteem (Park et al., 2011; Khare, 2012). Conversely, individuals with low self-esteem and social anxiety are generally less likely to disclose personal information (Ledbetter, Mazer, DeGroot, Meyer, Mao, & Swafford, 2011; Sousa, MacDonald, & Fougere, 2012). A possible exception may arise when individuals disclose information in an effort to bolster their own self-esteem; however, in this case, the information is not likely to be potentially stigmatizing (Nadkarni & Hoffman, 2012). Individuals who are willing to share potentially stigmatizing information such as political views, religious beliefs, or personal interests have been shown to have higher self-esteem and confidence in their views (Kim & Lee, 2011; Ledbetter et al., 2011). However, other individuals may divulge this information intentionally in order to project a higher level of confidence and self-esteem (Young, Dutta, & Dommety, 2009). An individual's level of comfort in sharing sensitive information publicly demonstrates confidence in his or her beliefs in the physical world as well.

Prior research has suggested that individuals lower in self-esteem may actively try to accumulate more friends on ESN's to compensate for a lack of confidence in themselves (Lee, Moore, Park, & Park, 2012). Additionally, there is evidence that a negative U-shaped relationship exists between the number of an individual's ESN acquaintances and perceived social support (Kim & Lee, 2011); while the initial effect of adding acquaintances is increased well-being and social support, this effect disappears as more acquaintances are added. Due to the time and effort involved in maintaining face-to-face relationships, individuals with more ESN relationships are more likely to have relationships based on interactions that occur primarily within the ESN. In other words, if a person has 120 "friends" on Facebook, it is reasonable that he would interact with 60 of them (50%) in the physical world over the course of a month. Alternatively, if a person has 2400 Facebook "friends", interacting with 1200 of them over the course of a month is not as feasible.

We relate self-esteem to three behaviors related to changes in ESN usage. The first measure is a switch from content creation and communication to content consumption. Previous studies have shown that individuals who are more comfortable creating their own content on ESN's are also more likely to spend time reading others' content (Vasalou et al., 2010; Attrill and Jalil, 2011). The second measure is a change in willingness to share one's own views on ESN's. Individuals with higher self-esteem are less likely to change their behavior regarding sharing their own views. Finally, we examine self-esteem in relation to changes in negative experiences online. Individuals who are more confident in expressing their views are expected to be less discouraged when receiving negative feedback (Kim & Lee, 2011; Ledbetter et al., 2011). Thus:

H1: Individuals with higher self-esteem *have not* become less likely to share their own views on ESN's.
H2: Individuals with higher self-esteem *have not* become less likely to communicate and more likely to consume content on ESN's.
H3: Individuals with higher self-esteem *have not* perceived an increase in negative experiences on ESN's.

A related indicator of self-esteem is an individual's comfort in sharing personal views specifically online. While an individual with high self-esteem might be more confident in expressing personal views, he or she may not be as willing to do so online. This could be for reasons such as unfamiliarity with technology, security concerns, or a desire not to have a permanent electronic record of comments. At the same time individuals that express they are more comfortable sharing views online may actually do so, regardless of self-esteem. This will lead to additional opportunities where individuals risk being exposed to negative feedback from others. Thus:

H4: Individuals that are generally more comfortable sharing their views online *have not* become less likely to share their own views on ESN's.
H5: Individuals that are generally more comfortable sharing their views online *have not* become less likely to communicate and more likely to consume content on ESN's.
H6: Individuals that are generally more comfortable sharing their views online *have* perceived an increase in negative experiences on ESN's.

Blocking behavior includes "unfriending" or "unfollowing" someone online, or blocking specific content or types of content that are deemed offensive. Individuals with higher levels of self-esteem are more likely to enjoy interacting with people on ESN's whose characteristics and views differ from their own (Kwon et al., 2010). This suggests that individuals who are higher in self-esteem are less likely to block others on ESN's. Thus:

H7: Individuals that are more likely to block others on ESN's *have* become less likely to share their own views on ESN's.

H8: Individuals that are more likely to block others on ESN's *have* become less likely to communicate and more likely to consume content on ESN's.

H9: Individuals that are that are more likely to block others on ESN's *have* perceived an increase in negative experiences on ESN's.

ESN's and Homophily

Homophily is the sociological principle that individuals are drawn to connect to others who are similar to themselves. This similarity may arise from sociodemographic, behavioral, or intrapersonal characteristics (McPherson et al., 2001). Over time homophily can become a contributor to the structure and dynamics of social networks through the dynamic sorting and filtering mechanisms described earlier. While research on homophily and social networks predates the existence of ESN's, its implications have proven surprisingly relevant and important. Not only do individuals intentionally include others in their ESN's who are similar to themselves, but the content filtering mechanisms present in ESN's actually promote and strengthen homophily, sometimes to the extent of excluding dissimilar others (McHugh, 2016).

Regardless of self-esteem or other personal characteristics, it would be natural for homophily to affect changes to one's ESN behavior over time. All else being equal, individuals who are less willing to share their own views or to communicate in general will probably be more willing to do so if more of their friends are similar to themselves. Likewise, an individual whose social network exhibits more homophily will probably be less likely to have negative experiences on ESN's. Further, the specific type of homophily may be important – for example, the fact that many of one's friends are Democrats may not affect one's propensity for sharing controversial views on sports. However, we expect homophily to affect changes in ESN behavior as follows:

H10: Individuals whose social networks contain more friends with similar interests *have not* become less likely to share their own views on ESN's.

H11: Individuals whose social networks contain more friends with similar interests *have not* become less likely to communicate and more likely to consume content on ESN's.

H12: Individuals whose social networks contain more friends with similar interests *have not* perceived an increase in negative experiences on ESN's.

Our research model is depicted in Figure 1. For simplicity, the perceptions of behavioral changes we examine – willingness to share views, communication vs. consumption, and negative experiences – are grouped together. The other personal and social characteristics we examine are expected to affect those behavioral changes in the same direction, with the exception of comfort in sharing views (H4 through H6).

Figure 1. Research Model

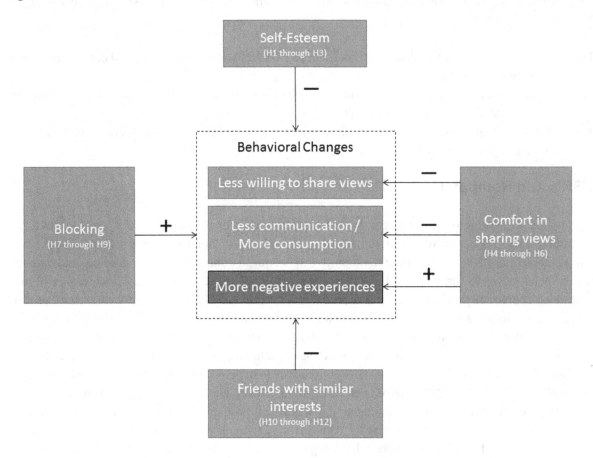

RESEARCH METHODS

The research questions were investigated using an online survey of Facebook users. Facebook is currently the leading ESN in terms of active monthly users, with over 2 billion users as of June 2017 (Flemming, 2017). The survey responses were collected in June 2017. Respondents (n=564) were recruited using Amazon's Mechanical Turk service, with two qualifications: first, that the respondent must be a Facebook user, and second, that the respondent must have a Mechanical Turk Worker satisfaction rating of 99% or higher. Respondents were compensated for completing the survey. After removing observations containing missing or incomplete values, 513 responses remained. A majority of the respondents were between the ages of 20 and 39 (n=350) and also college graduates (n=309). These characteristics are representative of the total population of Facebook users (Duggan & Brenner, 2013). The respondents also included a slightly larger than average number of females (n=301).

Respondents completed a 35-item survey (see Appendix A) that asked about their Facebook activity and their perceptions of the viewpoints of their Facebook "friends". Respondents were first asked how many Facebook "friends" they had, and then how many of those people the respondent talked with at least once per month outside of Facebook, i.e. face-to-face (FTF). They were then asked to estimate how many of those FTF friends shared the same political views as themselves, and then how many of their non-FTF Facebook "friends" shared the same political views as themselves. These questions were repeated for religious beliefs and personal interests. Next, the respondents were asked about the frequency with which they read or block content that is contrary to their own views. Next, respondents were asked to assess changes in their Facebook behavior over the past couple of years. These questions serve as the dependent variables in testing most of our hypotheses. Finally, respondents were asked about where (online or offline) they were most comfortable sharing political, religious and personal content. To measure self-esteem, respondents also completed the Rosenberg Self-Esteem Scale (Rosenberg, 1965). This scale is widely used and has been validated by numerous studies (e.g. Heatherton & Polivy, 1991).

The distinction between different groups of "friends" is an important one. Facebook "friends" with whom the respondent speaks at least once per month outside of Facebook (i.e., FTF) are assumed to be the closest and most important. Our survey is structured so that each respondent answers the same group of questions about political, religious and personal views for each of these different sets of "friends". Other questions such as those from the self-esteem scale are specific to the individual. All hypotheses were tested using ordered logit regressions. An ordered logit is appropriate for survey data such as this where the dependent variable has discrete outcomes that are ordered in a specific sequence (Kennedy, 2003).

RESULTS

Results for Hypotheses 1 through 3 are reported in Table 1. In this set of results self-esteem is the independent variable, used in regressions with the three dependent variables of interest. The results indicate that higher levels of self-esteem are associated with a lower likelihood of being less willing to share views on Facebook. Higher levels of self-esteem are also associated with a lower likelihood of communicating less and consuming more, and a lower likelihood of having more negative experiences. All of these results are statistically significant. Thus, Hypotheses 1 through 3 are all fully supported. Self-esteem is a significant predictor of changes in Facebook behavior over the past several years.

Table 1. Coefficients and Standard Errors for Ordered Logit Regressions on Self Esteem

	Less Willing to share views (H1)	Less communication (H2)	More negative experiences (H3)
self_esteem	0.056	0.045	0.032
	(0.015)***	(0.015)**	(0.008)***
X^2	14.78***	9.27**	14.42***

***$p < 0.001$, **$p < 0.01$, *$p < 0.05$

Regression results for Hypotheses 4 through 6 are in Table 2. In this set of results comfort in sharing views online is the independent variable, and it is separately evaluated for political, religious, and personal content. The results indicate that higher levels of comfort in sharing content online are associated with a lower likelihood of being less willing to share views on Facebook, as well as a lower likelihood of communicating less and consuming more. This is the case for political, religious and personal content. All of these results are statistically significant; thus, Hypotheses 4 and 5 are supported. The opposite is true with negative experiences. Individuals who are more comfortable sharing political, religious or personal content are significantly more likely to have had more negative experiences on Facebook. Therefore, Hypothesis 6 is also supported. In summary, individuals who are more comfortable sharing their views online have not changed their behavior over the past few years but are having more negative experiences. We will examine this further in a post-hoc analysis.

Table 2. Coefficients and Standard Errors for Ordered Logit Regressions on Comfort in Sharing Views Online

	Less Willing to share views (H4)	Less communication (H5)	More negative experiences (H6)
comfort_political	0.646	0.395	-0.444
	(0.113)***	(0.112)***	(0.112)***
X^2	33.72***	12.60***	16.10***
comfort_religious	0.415	0.395	-0.258
	(0.110)***	(0.111)***	(0.112)***
X^2	14.47***	12.69***	5.32*
comfort_personal	0.321	0.197	-0.421
	(0.110)**	(0.111)+	(0.113)***
X^2	8.52**	3.13+	14.04***

$***p < 0.001, **p < 0.01, *p < 0.05, +p < 0.10$

Regression results for Hypotheses 7 through 9 are in Table 3. In this set of results the frequency of blocking is the independent variable, and it is separately evaluated for political, religious, and personal content. The results indicate that individuals who have become less willing to share their views are associated with a higher frequency of blocking political and religious content, but not personal content. A change from communication to consumption is also associated with the likelihood of blocking political content, but not religious or personal content. Thus, Hypotheses 7 and 8 are partially supported. Individuals who are more likely to block political, religious and personal content also report that they have begun to encounter significantly more negative experiences on Facebook. Therefore, Hypothesis 9 is fully supported.

Regression results for Hypotheses 10 through 12 are in Table 4. In this set of results the percentage of friends with similar interests is the independent variable, and it is separately evaluated for political, religious, and personal content. The results indicate that higher percentages of online friends sharing similar interests are not associated with changes in willingness to share views, or in communication vs. consumption patterns. The exception is with personal interests; individuals with a higher percentage of friends with similar personal interests have not become less communicative on Facebook, to a significant extent. Thus, Hypotheses 10 is not supported while Hypothesis 11 is supported for personal content only. Individuals with more friends sharing similar political, religious or personal interests are significantly less likely to have had more negative experiences on Facebook. Therefore, Hypothesis 12 is fully supported.

Table 3. Coefficients and Standard Errors for Ordered Logit Regressions on Frequency of Blocking

	Less Willing to share views (H7)	Less communication (H8)	More negative experiences (H9)
blocking_political	-0.010	-0.017	-0.026
	(0.006)+	(0.007)*	(0.006)***
X²	3.16+	6.29*	18.62***
blocking_religious	-0.013	-0.009	-0.033
	(0.008)+	(0.009)	(0.009)***
X²	2.95+	1.11	16.74***
blocking_personal	-0.010	-0.006	-0.038
	(0.009)	(0.010)	(0.010)***
X²	1.25	0.310	15.80***

***p < 0.001, **p < 0.01, *p < 0.05, +p < 0.10

Table 4. Coefficients and standard errors for ordered logit regressions on friends with similar interests

	Less Willing to share views (H10)	Less communication (H11)	More negative experiences (H12)
homophily_political	-0.126	-0.058	0.577
	(0.254)	(0.255)	(0.264)*
X²	0.250	0.050	4.77*
homophily_religious	-0.330	0.178	0.562
	(0.253)	(0.256)	(0.257)*
X²	1.700	0.490	4.79*
homophily_personal	0.266	0.572	0.637
	(0.254)	(0.254)*	(0.256)*
X²	1.100	5.10*	6.21*

***p < 0.001, **p < 0.01, *p < 0.05, +p < 0.10

In total, 11 of 12 hypotheses were either fully or partially supported; Table 5 provides a summary of these results. As a robustness check, we also estimated the results for all hypotheses using ordered probit analyses. Ordered probit analysis is similar to ordered logit analysis but uses the normal distribution instead of the logistic distribution. Ordered probit analysis is preferred by some disciplines, most notably Economics (Kennedy, 2003). Using ordered probit analyses, all hypotheses were supported in the same manner as they were with the ordered logit analysis. These results are available upon request.

Post-Hoc Analysis

The results for Hypothesis 6 were somewhat surprising as they ran contrary to the results for the first 5 hypotheses. Our data show that self-esteem is positively correlated with fewer negative experiences and with comfort in sharing views, but that comfort in sharing views is correlated with more negative

Table 5. Results Summary

H1: Self-esteem and less willingness to share	Supported
H2: Self-esteem and less communication	Supported
H3: Self-esteem and negative experiences	Supported
H4: Comfort and less willingness to share	Supported
H5: Comfort and less communication	Supported
H6: Comfort and negative experiences	Supported
H7: Blocking and less willingness to share	Partially Supported
H8: Blocking and less communication	Partially Supported
H9: Blocking and negative experiences	Supported
H10: Homophily and less willingness to share	Not Supported
H11: Homophily and less communication	Partially Supported
H12: Homophily and negative experiences	Supported

experiences. One simple explanation for this is that individuals who are generally comfortable sharing their views online do share their views more often, and consequently have more negative experiences. If this is the case, then we might expect that online friends that have similar interests would moderate, or dampen, this effect.

To examine this proposition, we ran an additional set of analyses similar to the ones in Column 4 of Table 2, but with the inclusion of the variable for percentage of online friends with similar interests. The results are in Table 6, and they support this proposition. Negative experiences are more likely when individuals are comfortable sharing their political, religious and personal views, but this effect is moderated by homophily in ESN's.

DISCUSSION

The primary hypothesis put forth in this study – that individuals with higher self-esteem are less likely to have changed their behavior on ESN's – is strongly supported. While individuals have on average become less likely to share their views, less communicative, and more likely to report negative experiences, high self-esteem individuals are less likely to report these changes. An important implication of this finding is that if this trend continues over time, a greater share of the content and communication present on ESN's will come from high self-esteem individuals. High self-esteem is also positively correlated with comfort in sharing views. Consequently, there is an inherent tension between the results for H3 and H6: Individuals that are more comfortable in sharing views report more negative experiences, while those that have high self-esteem report fewer. Our post-hoc analysis reveals that the relationship depicted in H6 appears to be modified by the number of friends with similar interests. Taken together, these findings may support the conclusion that ESN's are likely to continue to become more divisive in terms of political, religious and social content (McHugh, 2016). Individuals with high self-esteem are more likely to communicate their views, are more comfortable with their views, and are less likely to be bothered by conflict, particularly when like-minded individuals are also present. This is somewhat

Table 6. Post-Hoc Analysis

	More negative experiences (H6)
comfort_political	-0.459
	(0.112)***
homophily_political	0.642
	(0.265)*
X^2	16.10***
comfort_religious	-0.271
	(0.112)*
homophily_religious	0.595
	(0.258)*
X^2	10.067***
comfort_personal	-0.431
	(0.114)***
homophily_personal	0.677
	(0.257)**
X^2	21.000***

***$p < 0.001$, **$p < 0.01$, *$p < 0.05$

incongruous with previous research demonstrating that ESN's present a greater diversity of viewpoints (e.g. Balint & Gustafson, 2015). However, differences in the political climate in the U.S. and abroad may explain these differences. ESN's and social media in general were just beginning to gain popularity leading up to the 2008 election. Barack Obama's campaign used these technologies sparsely, relying more on platforms such as official campaign websites and YouTube videos to communicate with voters and directly refute attacks by other candidates (Miller, 2008). Using the Internet as a communication platform was an important contributor to Obama's election. In 2012, Facebook and other ESN's played a larger role in political discourse. Obama's campaign expanded its use of ESN platforms such as Twitter and Facebook, and posted far more content than Mitt Romney, the Republican nominee for the presidency (Rosenstiel & Mitchell, 2012). By Election Day, Obama had twice as many Facebook likes and twenty times as many Twitter retweets as did the Romney campaign. Additionally, the Pew Internet Project found after the election that approximately thirty percent of social networking users were influenced to vote by their peers through social media, and that a record number of college-aged voters had showed up at the polls (Rutledge, 2013). An important difference between the Internet strategies of the 2008 and 2012 Obama campaigns was that less of the content was under the campaign's direct control. Instead, more of the discourse came between different users of the site rather than between the users and the candidates themselves (Rosenstiel & Mitchell, 2012).

Of course, giving people on ESN's the opportunity to see content relating to contrary viewpoints does not guarantee that they will read it. The results for Hypothesis 7 through 9 suggest that individuals who are more comfortable blocking users and content have become less likely to communicate and share views and more likely to report negative experiences. Taking these results together, these individuals appear to have the opposite profile of the high-esteem individuals described above. These individuals are more likely to block contrary content, but also less willing to engage with others and more likely to report negative experiences when they do. Communication research suggests that if a recipient's current beliefs are addressed before a contradictory one is introduced, the recipient will be more likely to consume them (Biocca, 1988). Reducing cognitive dissonance between current and contradictory beliefs may therefore be an effective strategy for organizations attempting to reach these users (Harmon-Jones & Mills, 1999). Perversely, these individuals may also be primary targets for terrorists and other radical activist groups which feed on negativity and close-mindedness (Knibbs, 2017).

Our analyses also show that greater homophily on ESN's is associated with a lower degree of behavioral change. Individuals with more friends with similar interests have not become less willing to communicate or share their views, and are less likely to have negative experiences. This is an important finding in terms of social influence. Marketers using social graphs often try to influence networks by identifying influential members, and in the ESN context, this would translate to finding individuals with a large number of "friends" (Gladwell, 2002). However, the current results of our study suggest that individuals with networks consisting of a higher percentage of like-minded friends are more likely to communicate with others. Perhaps political organizations or religious groups would have more success by targeting these individuals. More generally, activist organizations or internet marketers may be able to disseminate their messages to a larger audience by crafting separate messages for each demographic being addressed. Though we did not measure it explicitly, self-esteem has been shown to be positively correlated with extraversion. Therefore, extraversion may also play a role in this finding. Individuals who are more likely to share their own views are also more likely to engage in discussion of others' views, and to communicate more actively through ESN's in general (Gosling et al., 2011). While ESN's such as Facebook may make it easier for people to be exposed to a greater diversity of interests, ESN's may also provide a mechanism for political, religious, and focused interest groups to get organized and to foster communication exclusively about their own views. By joining or becoming a "fan" of an organization within an ESN, one is increasing the likelihood that he or she will become acquainted with other members who will in turn influence his or her viewpoints. This can create a feedback loop through which individuals are consistently given similar, like-minded messages (Bishop, 2008). On the other hand, exposure to a constant stream of diverse viewpoints may create cognitive overload and confusion. Openness to others' views may engender a lack of commitment to any one view, causing the openness to be counterproductive in the search for adoptable beliefs. This also represents an opportunity for further research.

Like any survey research, ours is not without limitations. We have asked individuals to self-report changes in Facebook behavior, but these reports may not strictly match actual changes in behavior. In addition, we have not measured homophily objectively; rather, we rely on subjects' perceptions of the similarity of their friends' interests. The ability to measure changes in behavior and objective measures of similarity and blocking may present an opportunity for further research.

CONCLUSION

This study has examined changes in behavior on Facebook, currently the most popular ESN. We examine willingness to share views, willingness to communicate, and lack of negative experiences. We find that high self-esteem and high homophily are associated with higher levels of changes in these behaviors. We also find that individuals who are more likely to block contrary content are less willing to exhibit these behaviors. Finally, individuals who are more comfortable sharing views general have not become less willing to share them on Facebook and have not started communicating less on Facebook, but also report more negative experiences on Facebook. Perceptions of negative experiences are moderated by homophily. In total, 11 of our 12 hypotheses were either fully or partially supported.

This study contributes to the existing literature on ESN's, homophily, and communication. To the best of our knowledge, this paper is among the first studies to measure and report on changes in Facebook behavior over the past several years. From a practitioner perspective, the results from this survey have the potential to influence how political, religious, and personal interest groups can reach new members and facilitate communication. This may help address recent calls for the promotion of civic engagement and digital citizenship within educational institutions (Gleason & Von Gillern, 2018). ESN providers may also use our results in helping to craft an environment that may foster different types of communication.

REFERENCES

Aisch, G., Pearce, A., & Yourish, K. (2016). The divide between red and blue America grew even deeper in 2016. *New York Times*. Retrieved from https://www.nytimes. com/interactive/2016/11/10/us/politics/red-blue-divide-grew-stronger-in-2016.html

Almobarraz, A. (2016). Investigating the seeking behavior for religious information in social media. *International Journal of Information Systems and Social Change*, 7(4), 67–79. doi:10.4018/IJISSC.2016100104

Attrill, A., & Jalil, R. (2011). Revealing only the superficial me: Exploring categorical self-disclosure online. *Computers in Human Behavior*, 27(5), 1634–1642. doi:10.1016/j.chb.2011.02.001

Balint, B., & Gustafson, J. (2015). Nobody knows you're a dog but everybody knows you're a Republican: Finding diversity in political, religious and personal association on Facebook. *International Journal of Information Systems and Social Change*, 6(4), 1–16. doi:10.4018/IJISSC.2015100101

Balint, B., & Rau-Foster, M. (2014). Cybersnooping: I see what you did there. *Journal of Organizational Culture. Communications and Conflict*, 19(1), 72–81.

Barnidge, M., Gil de Zúñiga, H., & Diehl, T. (2017). Second screening and political persuasion on social media. *Journal of Broadcasting & Electronic Media*, 61(2), 309–331. doi:10.1080/08838151.2 017.1309416

Biocca, F. A. (1988). Opposing conceptions of the audience: The active and passive hemispheres of mass communication theory. *Communication Yearbook*, 11(648), 51–80.

Bishop, B. (2008). *The big sort: Why the clustering of like-minded America is tearing us apart*. New York, NY: Houghton Mifflin Company.

Claybaugh, C., & Haried, P. (2014). Professional social network participation of business school graduates: Effects of university, degree type, and gender. *International Journal of Information Systems and Social Change*, 5(1), 1–15. doi:10.4018/ijissc.2014010101

Duggan, M., & Brenner, J. (2013). The demographics of social media users – 2012. *Pew Internet*. Retrieved from http://pewinternet.org/reports/2013/social-media-users.aspx

Flemming, J. (2017). Facebook reaches 2 billion users. *LA Times*. Retrieved from http://www.latimes.com/business/la-fi-tn-facebook-hate-speech-20170627-story.html

Furner, C. (2013). Cultural determinants of information processing shortcuts in computer supported groups: A review, research agenda and instrument validation. *International Journal of Information Systems and Social Change*, 4(3), 17–32. doi:10.4018/jissc.2013070102

Gladwell, M. (2002). *The tipping point: How little things can make a big difference*. New York, NY: Bay Back Books.

Gladwell, M. (2010, October 4). Annals of innovation: Small change. *The New Yorker*, 42-50.

Gleason, B., & Von Gillern, S. (2018). Digital citizenship with social media: Participatory practices of teaching and learning in secondary education. *Journal of Educational Technology & Society*, 21(1), 200–212.

Gosling, S. D., Augustine, A. A., Vazire, S., Holtzman, N., & Gaddis, S. (2011). Manifestations of personality in online social networks: Self-reported Facebook-related behaviors and observable profile information. *Cyberpsychology, Behavior, and Social Networking*, 14(9), 483–488. doi:10.1089/cyber.2010.0087 PMID:21254929

Ha, A. (2013). Facebook is replacing its "hide all" button with "unfollow." *TechCrunch*. Retrieved from https://techcrunch.com/2013/12/02/facebook-unfollow/

Harmon-Jones, E., & Mills, J. (1999). *An introduction to cognitive dissonance theory and an overview of current perspectives on the theory*. Washington, DC: American Psychological Association. doi:10.1037/10318-001

Heatherton, T. F., & Polivy, J. (1991). Development and validation of a scale for measuring self-esteem. *Journal of Personality and Social Psychology*, 60(6), 895–910. doi:10.1037/0022-3514.60.6.895

Kennedy, P. (2003). *A guide to econometrics* (5th ed.). Cambridge, MA: The MIT Press.

Khare, A. (2012). Antecedents to evaluating the brand image of Orkut as a social networking society: An exploratory study on Indian youth. *International Journal of Information Systems and Social Change*, 3(2), 60–72. doi:10.4018/jissc.2012040104

Kim, J., & Lee, J. R. (2011). The Facebook paths to happiness: Effects of the number of Facebook friends and self-presentation on subjective well-being. *Cyberpsychology, Behavior, and Social Networking*, 14(6), 359–364. doi:10.1089/cyber.2010.0374 PMID:21117983

Knibbs, K. (2017). Extreme moderation. *The Ringer*. Retrieved July 28, 2017 from https://theringer.com/curbing-terrorist-social-media-activity-facebook-twitter-google-601ff9684068

Kruse, L. M., Norris, D. R., & Flinchum, J. R. (2018). Social media as a public sphere? Politics on social media. *The Sociological Quarterly*, 59(1), 62–84. doi:10.1080/00380253.2017.1383143

Kwon, O., & Wen, Y. (2010). An empirical study of the factors affecting social network service use. *Computers in Human Behavior*, 26(2), 254–263. doi:10.1016/j.chb.2009.04.011

Ledbetter, A. M., Mazer, J. P., DeGroot, J. M., Meyer, K. R., Mao, Y., & Swafford, B. (2011). Attitudes toward online social connection and self-disclosure as predictors of Facebook communication and relational closeness. *Communication Research*, *38*(1), 27–53. doi:10.1177/0093650210365537

Lee, J. R., Moore, D. C., Park, E., & Park, S. G. (2012). Who wants to be 'friend-rich'? Social compensatory friending on Facebook and the moderating role of public self-consciousness. *Computers in Human Behavior*, *28*(3), 1036–1043. doi:10.1016/j.chb.2012.01.006

Luckerson, V. (2017). Twitter finds meaning (and madness) under Donald Trump. *The Ringer*. Retrieved from https://theringer.com/twitter-social-media-politics-donald-trump-6fe4b60f91f9

McHugh, M. (2016). How we built our bubble. *The Ringer*. Retrieved from https://theringer.com/social-media-echo-chamber-2016-election-facebook-twitter-b433df38a4cb

McHugh, M. (2017). Where Facebook's going, we don't need words. *The Ringer*. Retrieved from https://theringer.com/facebook-status-updates-visuals-over-text-ac4d6dd6dfc1

McPherson, M., Smith-Lovin, L., & Cook, J. M. (2001). Birds of a feather: Homophily in social networks. *Annual Review of Sociology*, *27*(1), 415–444. doi:10.1146/annurev.soc.27.1.415

Miller, C. C. (2008, November 7). How Obama's internet campaign changed politics. *The New York Times*.

Nadkarni, A., & Hofmann, S. G. (2012). Why do people use Facebook. *Personality and Individual Differences*, *52*(3), 243–249. doi:10.1016/j.paid.2011.11.007 PMID:22544987

Neil, S. P. (2013). Trayvon Martin, social media and inactive activism. *Huffington Post*. Retrieved from http://www.huffingtonpost.com/shane-paul-neil/trayvon-martin-social-med_b_3596261.html

Park, N., Jin, B., & Jin, S. A. (2011). Effects of self-disclosure on relational intimacy in Facebook. *Computers in Human Behavior*, *27*(5), 1974–1983. doi:10.1016/j.chb.2011.05.004

Political Segregation: The big sort. (2008, June 19). *The Economist*.

Rosenberg, M. (1965). *Society and the adolescent self-image*. Princeton, NJ: Princeton University Press. doi:10.1515/9781400876136

Rosenstiel, T., & Mitchell, A. (2012). How the presidential candidates use the web and social media. Pew Research Center. Retrieved from http://www.journalism.org/files/legacy/direct_access_final.pdf

Rutledge, P. (2013). How Obama won the social media battle in the 2012 presidential campaign. *MPR Center*. Retrieved from http://mprcenter.org/blog/2013/01/how-obama-won-the-social-media-battle-in-the-2012-presidential-campaign/

Sousa, K. J., MacDonald, L. E., & Fougere, K. T. (2012). Internet privacy concerns versus behavior: A protection motivation approach. *International Journal of Information Systems and Social Change*, *3*(4), 53–64.

Special, W. P., & Barber, K. T. (2012). Self-disclosure and student Satisfaction with Facebook. *Computers in Human Behavior*, *28*(2), 624–630. doi:10.1016/j.chb.2011.11.008

Unruh, B. (2016). Trump's "landslide": 2,623 to 489 among U.S. counties. *WorldNetDaily*. Retrieved from http://www.wnd.com/2016/12/trumps-landslide-2623-to-489-among-u-s-counties/

Vasalou, A., Joinson, A. J., & Courvoisier, D. (2010). Cultural differences, experience with social networks and the nature of 'true commitment' in Facebook. *International Journal of Human-Computer Studies*, *68*(10), 719–728. doi:10.1016/j.ijhcs.2010.06.002

Wang, J. (2012). The face-off between user privacy and information exploitation in online social Networking. *International Journal of Information Systems and Social Change*, *3*(3), 19–36. doi:10.4018/jissc.2012070102

Yang, J., Barnidge, M., & Rojas, H. (2017). The politics of "unfriending": User filtration in response to political disagreement on social media. *Computers in Human Behavior*, *70*, 22–29. doi:10.1016/j.chb.2016.12.079

Young, S., Dutta, D., & Dommety, G. (2009). Extrapolating insight from Facebook profiles: A study of religion and relationship status. *Cyberpsychology & Behavior*, *12*(3), 347–350. doi:10.1089/cpb.2008.0165 PMID:19366321

Zeitzoff, T. (2017). How social media is changing conflict. *The Journal of Conflict Resolution*, *61*(9), 1970–1991. doi:10.1177/0022002717721392

Zhang, X., & Lin, W. (2018). Hanging together or not? Impacts of social media use and organizational membership on individual and collective political actions. *International Political Science Review*, *39*(2), 273–289. doi:10.1177/0192512116641842

This research was previously published in the International Journal of Information Systems and Social Change (IJISSC), 10(1); pages 37-53, copyright year 2019 by IGI Publishing (an imprint of IGI Global).

APPENDIX

Survey Questions

	Mean	S.D.
How many Facebook friends do you have?	418.485	606.487
In the past month, about how many of your Facebook friends have you spoken with through offline methods (i.e., face-to-face or with your phone)?		
	20.027	32.163
About how many of those Facebook friends (with whom you HAVE spoken offline in the past month) share the same beliefs, values, and interests as you?		
Political beliefs or values	60.838	31.910
Religious beliefs / values	52.994	35.503
Personal interests	51.672	34.083
About how many of your other Facebook friends (with whom you HAVE NOT spoken offline in the past month) share the same beliefs, values, and interests as you?		
Political beliefs or values	47.722	31.939
Religious beliefs / values	40.001	31.972
Personal interests	36.988	32.158
When you see or hear beliefs or values that are contrary to your own through offline media such as billboards, television advertisements, and face-to-face conversations, how likely are you to read or listen to this content? (1=Very likely, 2 = Likely, 3 = Unlikely, 4 = Very Unlikely)		
Content contrary to my political beliefs or values	2.386	0.829
Content contrary to my religious beliefs or values	2.571	0.901
Content contrary to my personal interests	2.347	0.902
On Facebook, you will sometimes encounter content such as posts, comments, or links to other websites that are contrary to your own beliefs and values. How many times have you blocked a Facebook friend or hidden his / her posts because he / she has posted this content?		
Political beliefs or values	2.784	10.091
Religious beliefs / values	1.994	9.001
Personal interests	4.895	13.660
How likely are you to read such content? (1=Very likely, 2 = Likely, 3 = Unlikely, 4 = Very Unlikely)		
Content contrary to my political beliefs or values	2.388	0.805
Content contrary to my religious beliefs or values	2.606	0.869
Content contrary to my personal interests	2.442	0.888
How strongly do you agree or disagree with the following statements about yourself? (1 = Strongly agree, 2 = Agree, 3 = Disagree, 4 = Strongly disagree) * indicates questions that are reverse-coded		
On the whole, I am satisfied with myself.*	1.869	0.679
At times, I think I am no good at all.	2.891	0.855
I feel that I have a number of good qualities. *	1.653	0.610
I am able to do things as well as most other people. *	1.678	0.622

continues on following page

	Mean	S.D.
I feel I do not have much to be proud of.	3.162	0.773
I certainly feel useless at times.	2.698	0.899
I feel that I am a person of worth, at least on an equal plane with others. *	1.747	0.639
I wish I could have more respect for myself.	2.538	0.907
All in all, I am inclined to feel that I am a failure.	3.150	0.787
I take a positive attitude towards myself. *	1.924	0.724
How strongly do you agree or disagree with the following statements about yourself? (1 = Strongly agree, 2 = Agree, 3 = Disagree, 4 = Strongly disagree)		
In the past couple of years, I have had more negative experiences communicating with others on Facebook.	2.528	0.852
In the past couple of years, I have become less willing to share my viewpoints on Facebook.	2.109	0.946
In the past couple of years, I have started to spend less time communicating with others on Facebook and more time reading content on Facebook.	2.018	0.858
Where do you feel most comfortable sharing the following types of information? (1 = Only offline, 2 = Mostly offline, 3 = Mostly through online social networks, 4 = Only through online social networks)		
Personal information, such as your phone number and birth date.	1.811	0.626
The reasons that you support a particular political party over others.	2.006	0.741
Information about the religious activities in which you engage.	1.813	0.742
Your romantic feelings toward another person.	1.791	0.720
The social causes you support.	2.465	0.747

Chapter 59
Remaining Facebook versus Face-to-Face Friends after a Romantic Breakup:
Factors that Distinguish Those Who Do from Those Who Do Not

Dylan T Medeiros
University of Arkansas, Fayetteville, USA

Lynne M Webb
Florida International University, Miami, USA

ABSTRACT

The study queried whether the relational characteristics that influence individuals to remain face-to-face friends with former romantic partners following a break up also impact the decisions to remain Facebook "friends" with former romantic partners. The sample included over 300 young adults who met two criteria: They maintained an active Facebook account and reported a pre-marital, romantic break-up. The results revealed that the variables that impact post-dissolution friendship decisions of former romantic partners in the face-to-face context (quantity of relational investments, relational satisfaction, and relational disengagement strategies) do not impact former romantic partners' decisions to maintain or dissolve Facebook friendships. These results provide evidence that romantic partners may experience different relational motivations and dynamics in online versus off-line venues.

DOI: 10.4018/978-1-6684-6307-9.ch059

REMAINING FACEBOOK VERSUS FACE-TO-FACE FRIENDS AFTER A ROMANTIC BREAKUP

Researchers continue to examine factors associated with former romantic partners remaining face-to-face friends following their breakup (e.g., Griffith, Gillath, Zhao, & Martinez, 2017; Hadden, Harvey, Settensten, & Agrew, 2018; Mogilski & Welling, 2017); however, very few studies have examined friendships between former romantic partners on social media venues such as Facebook. We could locate no previous study that examined whether the same factors (that distinguish former romantic partners who elect to remain face-to-face friends from those who do not elect to remain friends) were equally effective in distinguishing those who remain Facebook friends versus those who do not.

Given the prevalence of social media in contemporary life, our study endeavored to discover the extent to which the research findings concerning face-to-face friendship between former romantic partners apply to social media friendships. To that end, we examined factors that might distinguish college students' who remain Facebook friends with former romantic partners versus those who elect to "unfriend" former partners. The term "unfriend" comes from Facebook's friend-managing features that allow a user to "delete" a fellow user from his/her list of Facebook friends and thus prevent the former friend from directly viewing the user's profile and status updates.

Existing literature examining face-to-face relationships suggests that the quantity of relational investments (Stanley, Rhoades & Markman, 2006), disengagement behaviors used in the breakup process (Banks, Altendorf, Greene, & Cody, 1987), and relational quality prior to the breakup (Rhoades, Kamp Dush, Atkins, Stanley, & Markman, 2011) influence the decision to (or not to) remain face-to-face friends with former romantic relationship partners. We directly examined whether these three factors differ significantly across two groups: former romantic partners who elect to remain Facebook friends versus those who do not.

Originally intended to connect college students at one U. S. university, Facebook now serves 1.47 billion daily active users worldwide (Facebook, 2018) and is widely considered the most used social media outlet on the planet. Research on Facebook primarily focuses on two topics: privacy/self-disclosure (e.g., Bazarova, 2012; Kanter, Afifi, & Robbins, 2012) and, more relevant to the current study, social networking (e.g., Craig & Wright, 2012; Crosier, Webster, & Dillon, 2012). For a detailed review of this literature, see Caers et al. (2013).

SOCIAL NETWORKING ON FACEBOOK

Crosier et al. (2012) argues that humans have a genetic predisposition to desire connection and that online social networks provide venues for satisfying that desire. Facebook creates an environment where sharing and connecting with others is easier in many ways than traditional forms of face-to face interaction. Indeed, Facebook "friendships" involve extremely low commitment. Users can elect to (a) post (or not to post) updates on their thoughts and activities for friends to read as well as (b) read (or not read) friends' posts. Activity leads to a sense of "keeping up with" people but Facebook allows users' to maintain "friend" status whether or not they actively engage on the website. Similarly, friendship status does not change if users spend a few minutes a day on the website or a few hours per day. Such a disassociation between investment and relationship status stands in sharp contrast to face-to-face relationships that seem to fade away if friends do not stay in regular contact as well as regularly share information and/ or experiences together.

Researchers argue that, in addition to creating connections, Facebook also plays a vital role in the maintenance of personal relationships (Craig & Wright, 2012; Ledbetter & Mazer, 2014) and the enactment of relational closeness (Ledbetter et al., 2011). Perceptions of similarity and attraction may be heightened in text-based online interactions due to lack of nonverbal feedback, thereby creating an atmosphere conducive to more sharing (Walther, 2011). Furthermore, the prevalence of social media can intensify the quantity of information being shared, resulting in greater access to personal information--meaning the sheer number of Facebook users creates an environment in which users share massive amounts of information. Additionally, some aspects of the quality of shared information can facilitate network growth and perceived closeness. One such piece of information is "relationship status." Here the user indicates whether he/she is in a romantic relationship, and, if so, names that partner. Every member of both relational partners' networks receives a notice when a relationship status is announced or altered. Thus, social networking has evolved from making connections based on "likes" and "comments" to an on-going part of romantic relationships where partners declare they are "in a relationship with" each other, integrate their social networks, and connect with each other (Fox, Osborn, & Warber, 2014). Indeed, romantic partners may "struggle to maintain privacy and independence" on Facebook (Fox et al., 2014, p. 527).

FACEBOOK ROMANCE

In 2010 alone, 43,869,800 people changed their Facebook relationship status from "In a Relationship" to "Single" (Wasserman, 2010). In one interview study, many college students characterized Facebook as "a threat to their romantic relationships" (Gershon, 2011) for multiple reasons including inducing feelings of anxiety and jealousy. Indeed, Facebook permits users to stay in touch with former romantic partners as well as the social networks that supported those past relationships—easy fodder for the jealousy impulse.

A fledgling line of research examines the role of Facebook in romantic relationships (Bowe, 2010; Fox & Warber, 2013; Yang, Brown, & Braun, 2014). Because social media allow users to widen their networks via groups based on schools attended, religion, political affiliations, hobbies, fandom, and other common interests, many users encounter former relational partners in the online world. Users may experience social pressure to friend and to stay friends with their former partners. In one documentary, CNN reported that the number of individuals saying they would be likely to "unfriend" a partner post-breakup at a mere 22 percent (Bartz & Ehrlich, 2010).

Although the decision to unfriend relational partners post dissolution has been extensively researched in face-to-face relationships (e.g., Bullock, 2011; Emery & Dillon, 1994; Rhoades et al., 2011), it remains largely unexplored in online venues. We could locate only two published studies (Marshall, 2012; Tran & Joormann, 2015) that examined remaining Facebook friends with former romantic partners; both studies examined the psychological repercussions of such decisions. Marshall (2012) documented an association between Facebook surveillance of a former romantic partner and increased stress/negative feelings about the break-up as well as increased longing/sexual desire for the former partner. Tran and Joormann (2015) reported "particularly negative emotional consequences" for former partners who remain Facebook friends and ruminate about the ex's profile. In contrast to these studies of the psychological after effects of remaining Facebook friends, our study explored factors that might contribute to the decision itself to unfriend or remain Facebook friends with a former relational partner.

UNFRIENDING ON FACEBOOK

Deleting a Facebook friend serves as "a form of relationship termination" (Bevan, Pfyl, & Barclay, 2012, p. 1458). This process cannot be undone once the "unfriend" button is pressed without resending a "friend request" to the "unfriended" user. Facebook does not send an automatic notice of unfriending but, if the unfriended user checks the status of the relationship, they can learn of the unfriending. Additionally, Facebook regularly sends users a list of "people you may know" based on mutual friendships to encourage networking. When a user sees the name of a former romantic partner in his/her newsfeed among a list of "people you may know," this sighting serves as the official notification that of the unfriending.

A growing body of research examines unfriending on Facebook. Some studies examine how users respond to being unfriended. Users often experience being unfriended as expectancy violation (Bevan, Ang, & Fearns, 2014)—as something unexpected that violates perceived relational and/or societal norms—and are more likely to ruminate about the unfriending if the unfriender was a close partner (Bevan et al., 2012). However, most research on unfriending focuses on identifying the prompts to or motivations for unfriending. For example, some scholars argue that unfriending is a means of enacting perceived Facebook norms (LeFebvre, Blackburn, & Brody, 2015); some users describe as normal the Facebook behaviors of "modifying online relationship statuses, 'unfriending' previous partners, and limiting profile access to manage relationship termination" (LeFebvre et al., 2015, p. 78).

Other scholars link unfriending to users' individual characteristics or behaviors rather than the viewing unfriending as simply a response to ever evolving norms governing Facebook (McLaughlin & Vital, 2012). For example, Quercia, Bodaghi, and Crowcroft (2012) documented that Facebook friendships are more likely to dissolve when they are "not embedded in the same social circle, between people whose ages differ, and if one of the two is neurotic or introverted" (p. 251). In contrast, Pena and Brody (2014) linked unfriending to status updates that made the unfriender look bad. For example, a user posting a status update that contains a critical or snarky remark about a Facebook friend, especially if that person is tagged, may become a prime candidate for unfriending (e.g., "Here's Kim Smith TRYING to look good but, yeah, not so much!" with an unflattering picture of Kim). Our study followed in this tradition of discovering motivations or prompts to unfriending by attempting to identify the relational preconditions that might motivate a user to unfriend a romantic partner following a break up.

The term "break up" is typically used in everyday discourse to reference Gottman's (1993) notion of relational dissolution. However, as one form of the relationship ends, a new relational form can emerge; relationships can experience metamorphoses and romantic relationships can transform into friendships. If the former relationship was merely an acquaintanceship, the users may not particularly care about the unfriending. However, unfriending from long-term relationships with multiple investments, as is typically of relationships with romantic partners, might be more unsettling.

RELATIONAL INVESTMENTS

Previous research indicates that shared lifestyles and the quantity of "relational investments" influence the decision to remain face-to-face friends after a breakup (Emery & Dillon, 1994; Rhoades et al., 2011). Stanley et al. (2006) defined "relational investments" as shared aspects of relationships; they may include tangible items such as joint physical property and children as well as less tangible but nonetheless meaningful shared aspects of the relationship such as insider jokes, relational history, and daily dependency on relational partners for social support. In the face-to-face world, a breakup often means a complete separation in physical space, allowing individuals to terminate future contact. However, the extent to which former partners can remain separate is inhibited by factors such as shared lifestyles and elements such as common children, friends, and physical possessions (Emery & Dillon, 1994; Rhoades et al., 2011).

In a study of cohabiting couples, Stanley et al. (2006) noted that staying friends with former partners proves particularly difficult in relationships with large quantities of relational investments. Quantity of investments directly correlates with duration of relationship, meaning, the longer the individuals were together, the more relational investments they are likely to share. In addition, the number of pre-breakup relational investments correlates with the difficulty former partners experience renegotiating the relationship to "friends" in the post-breakup period; the more investments, the more complicated the negotiation process, and the more distant the possibility of friendship with a former romantic partner (Stanley et al., 2006). Given the above described findings, we wondered if investments would similarly influence online connections; thus, we posed the first research question:

RQ1: Do former romantic partners who elect to remain Facebook friends post dissolution (versus those who do not elect to remain Facebook friends) report differences in *quantity of investments* prior to the breakup?

DISENGAGEMENT STRATEGIES

The decision to maintain face-to-face friendships post-dissolution can be directly influenced by the disengagement strategies employed during the breakup process (Banks et al., 1987; Cody, 1982). These strategies range from providing a full explanation of the reason(s) for dissolving the romantic relationship to neglecting the partner and avoiding of future contact. Individuals who engaged in tactics viewed as "de-escalating" (i.e., explaining the reason for the disengagement) were more likely to maintain some level of closeness post-breakup than those who did not (Banks et al., 1987). Behaviors seen as "de-escalating" included expressing interest in and emphasizing the benefits of changing the relationship dynamic while maintaining the possibility of a modified future relationship of a different sort as opposed to complete termination of the relationship on every level, including friendship (Banks et al., 1987). In their study of non-marital relationship dissolution, Lambert and Hughes (2010) found that positively toned de-escalating behaviors that express goodwill were more likely to generate friendships between former romantic partners. These findings raise the question of whether, similarly, disengagement strategies may play a role in the decision to remain online friends with a former romantic relationship partner.

RQ2: Do former romantic partners who elect to remain Facebook friends post dissolution (versus those who do not elect to remain Facebook friends) report differences in disengagement strategies used during the breakup?

RELATIONAL SATISFACTION

The term "relationship satisfaction" is here used to describe an individual's perception of a relationship as enjoyable, rewarding, and high quality. Since the 1983 publication of Norton's "marital quality" instrument, assessing relational satisfaction has become a common practice in relationship studies, especially studies of romantic relationships. Not surprisingly, previous scholars have examined relational satisfaction before, during, and after break-ups.

As the tactics employed during the breakup process may influence the viability of face-to-face friendship post-breakup, so too does the quality of the relationship prior to the breakup (Bullock, 2011; Rhoades et al., 2011). Rhoades et al. (2011) found that a relational breakup can cause psychological distress and reduced life satisfaction; however, a relational breakup also can bring partners relief and peace, especially when both partners experience mutual dissatisfaction during the relationship. Furthermore, the more satisfied individuals are with their partners during the relationship, the more likely they are to engage in friendship maintenance after the romantic aspect of the relationship has ended (Bullock, 2011; Rhoades et al., 2011); it is notable that this association was documented across two points in time: Perceptions of relational satisfaction during the relationship were assessed prior to the breakup (Rhoades et al., 2011) as well as assessed after the breakup (Bullock, 2011). These findings support the notion that a satisfying romantic relationship is more likely to produce a satisfying face-to-face friendship after the romantic relationship ends. Conversely, if the relationship was unsatisfying, a relational transformation to being "just friends" is less likely to occur. Given these finding, we posed our third and final research question:

RQ3: Do former romantic partners who elect to remain Facebook friends post dissolution (versus those who do not elect to remain Facebook friends) report differences in relational satisfaction prior to the breakup?

Given the prevalence of social media in contemporary life, our study endeavored to identify factors that may motivate Facebook users who remain friends with their romantic partner after the dissolution of the romantic relationship. Existing literature examining face-to-face relationships suggests that quantity of investments (Stanley et al., 2006), disengagement behaviors used in the breakup process (Banks et al., 1987), and relational quality prior to the breakup (Rhoades et al., 2011) may influence the decision to remain (or not to remain) friends with a former romantic partner. Our study directly tested whether these three factors differ significantly across the two groups: former romantic partners who elected to remain Facebook friends versus those who did not.

METHODS

Participants

We recruited over 300 undergraduate students from the basic communication course at a public, flagship university in the southeastern United States who met two criteria: They maintained an active Facebook account and experienced the breakup of a premarital, romantic relationship. Students received extra credit for participation in the study. We asked participants to recruit additional qualified individuals to the study, thus "snowballing" the sample, but they did not receive additional extra credit for doing so.

Participants included 114 males and 219 females ($N=323$) between the ages of 18 and 24 ($M=19.71$; $SD=2.87$). They self-reported as primarily freshmen ($N=148$) but the sample also included 116 sophomores, 39 juniors, 19 seniors, and one graduate student. Participants reported five ethnicities: 273 Caucasian, 17 African American, 17 Hispanic, 9 Native American, and 8 Asian/Pacific Islander. Participants described breakups that occurred "last week" to "5 years ago" ($M = 16.84$ months, $SD = 17.29$ months). Participants reported on both long-distance ($N = 74$; 23%) and proximal former relationships with daily face-to-face interaction ($N = 248$; 77%). These numbers appear consistent with previous reports that between 25 and 40 percent of U. S. college students report being in long-distance relationships (Aylor, 2014). The majority of our participants remained Facebook friends with their former romantic partner (241; 74.61%), but many did not (82; 25.39%).

Instruments

Relational Investments were assessed using Rusbult's (1980) investment-model scale. Previous communication researchers (e.g., Bullock, 2011; Ferrara & Levine, 2009; Vanderdrift, Lehmiller, & Kelly, 2012; Wieselquist, 2009) successfully employing the instrument (reporting Cronbach alpha scores of .90, .83, .84, and .70 respectively). The instrument contains 10 Likert-scale items to measure sharing possessions and resources (i.e., money, transportation) as well as the quantity of mutual friends, clubs, and organizational memberships. For example, one item stated: "When we were in a romantic relationship, I invested a great deal of time in our relationship." Participants responded on a 5-point scale from "strongly agree" to "strongly disagree." We asked participants to evaluate each statement in the time frame of "when we were in a romantic relationship." For our sample, the Cronbach alpha score was .88 ($Mdn = 29.00$, $M = 28.31$, $SD = 6.19$).

Disengagement Strategies were assessed using Cody's (1982) Relational Disengagement Strategies. We asked participants to evaluate each of the 15 statements in the time frame of "during the breakup process." The instrument assesses perceptions of behaviors during the breakup, specifically five disengagement strategies:

- Behavioral de-escalation: contact avoidance without explanation,
- Negative identity management: ending relationship without explanation and typically citing the other as the source of the breakup,
- Justification: explanation of reasons for breakup,
- Positive tone: attending to the feelings of the partner to avoid an unpleasant end.
- De-escalation: discussing the benefits of changing the relationship dynamic with possibility of resuming in the future, and

We employed measures of this final factor, de-escalation, in our analyses. A sample item for this factor was "When we were breaking up, my romantic partner told me that he/she was very, very sorry about breaking off the relationship." Participants responded on a 5-point scale from "strongly agree" to "strongly disagree." We asked participants to evaluate each statement in the time frame of "when we were breaking up." Previous researchers (Cupach & Metts, 1986; Starks, 2007) linked these strategies to relational outcomes. Additionally, multiple previous researchers offered evidence of the instrument's reliability, reporting the following Cronbach alpha scores for de-escalation: Banks et al. (1987) = .74; Cody (1982) =.86; and Lambert & Hughes (2010) = .84. Analysis with our data yielded a Cronbach alpha score of .79 for de-escalation strategies (Mdn= 12.0, M= 11.02, SD= 3.95).

Relational Satisfaction was assessed using a modified, four-item version of the Dyadic Adjustment Scale (Spanier, 1976) developed by Sabourin, Valois, and Lussier (2005). Previous researchers (Rhoades et al., 2011) correlated scores from the modified scale with desire to maintain relationships post-breakup, suggesting predictive validity. The four Likert-scale items measure attitudes about the relationship overall, the breakup, and the frequency of confiding/intimate conversation. For example, one item stated "In general, while you were involved with your romantic partner, how often did you think that things between you and your partner were going well?" Participants responded on a six point scale from "all the time" to "never." We asked participants to evaluate the four statements in the time frame of "while you and your romantic partner were in a romantic relationship." Sabourin et al. (2005) offered evidence of convergent validity between the original and refined instruments assessing relational satisfaction as well as reliability of the modified version (Cronbach's Alpha = .84). Similarly, Bullock (2011) reported a Cronbach alpha score of .90. Unfortunately, as described in detail below, the four items failed to cohere into a single factor in our factor analysis. The two items that factored together had a low Cronbach alpha score of .67. Therefore, each item was treated as a separate indicator of relationship satisfaction in the subsequent analyses: degree of happiness (*Mdn*=3.0, *M*=3.28, *SD*= 1.40) and frequency of discussion of termination (*Mdn*=5.0, *M*=4.59, *SD*= 1.15).

Demographics and Relational Status were assessed with the final questionnaire in the survey. Using primarily checklists, we asked participants for the personal information we used to describe the sample (i.e., age, year in school, and so forth). Additionally, we asked participants to indicate their "current Facebook relationship status" by selecting for a checklist of options drawn from the Facebook venue. Finally, we asked participants to…

Please think about the last romantic relationship you were involved in that ended. In other words, if you are currently in a relationship – not that relationship – but instead the previous relationship. Please estimate when your previous romantic relationship ended. (Example: 6 months ago)

Are you currently Facebook friends with the person with whom you had the romantic relationship?
_____*Yes* _____ *No*

Procedures

Students were emailed a message explaining the project and inviting them to participate. The message included a link that directed them to one of three versions of the on-line survey. To ameliorate order effects, the three versions offered counter-balanced orders of the major instruments. Approximately equal numbers of participants complete each version of the survey.

The online survey began with the informed-consent form and a cover letter. Next, participants were prompted to recall their most recent romantic breakup and to complete the survey with this relationship in mind. The three major instruments followed; then, a brief demographic survey gathered data to describe the sample.

Prior to the primary data-collection, a group of 55 participants drawn from the research population who met the criterion for inclusion in the study participated in a pretest version of the survey. The pretest version included the above described questionnaires and comment boxes for feedback. Based on feedback from the pretest, we slightly reworded a few questions, slightly modified the structure of the survey, and added a question concerning geographical distance from partner.[1] We used the resulting, modified version of the survey to collect our data.

RESULTS

Preliminary Analysis [2]

Scores for items across all instruments assessing the variables of interest (quantity of relational investments, preference for de-escalatory disengagement strategies, and relational satisfaction) were factor analyzed to identify patterns of response. A principle-axis factor analysis with Varimax rotation across 100 iterations revealed three principle factors. The emergent factors generally aligned with the three variables of interest. However, we dropped the items that double-loaded on multiple principle factors or emerged as individual items comprising unique minor factors. Only one (preference for use of de-escalatory disengagement strategies) of the five disengagement strategies (negative identity management, positive tone, justification, behavioral de-escalation, and de-escalation) loaded appropriately and yielded a Cronbach's alpha greater than .70. Recall that de-escalatory strategies involve discussing the benefits of changing the relationship dynamic with possibility of resuming in the future. Measures of other strategies were abandoned.

Relational Investments

Eight of the ten items from the Investment Model Scale (Rusbult, 1980) loaded on the same factor and thus were used to calculate quantity of relational investments. The Cronbach's alpha across these eight items was .88.

Disengagement Strategies

Items from Cody's (1982) disengagement strategies instrument (based on the Relational Disengagement Strategies model) loaded together into one factor. Originally comprised of 15 items, in this sample, only six items loaded together on the factor of preference for de-escalatory disengagement strategies. Items from each of the five dimensions of disengagement (negative identity management, de-escalation, justification, behavioral de-escalation, and positive tone) loaded cleanly and separately, but only preference for de-escalatory disengagement strategies yielded a Cronbach's alpha greater than .70. Its Cronbach's alpha score was .79.

Relational Satisfaction

Items assessing relational satisfaction were adapted from Spanier's (1976) Dyadic Adjustment Scale and loaded together on one factor. Originally comprised of 4 items, only two items (degree of happiness during the relationship and frequency of discussion of termination) loaded on the factor of relational satisfaction. The remaining items were abandoned (confided in the partner; thoughts of things going well). Given a low Cronbach's alpha across the two items (.67), each item was treated as a separate indicator of relational satisfaction in subsequent analyses: degree of happiness (M=3.28, SD= 1.40) and frequency of discussion of termination (M=4.59, SD= 1.15).

Concern for Normalcy

Next, descriptive statistics and histograms of each variable of interest were examined to determine skewness. Two variables appeared normally distributed (i.e., investments and de-escalatory disengagement strategies), whereas the other two variables appeared non-normal (i.e., degree of happiness and frequency of discussion of termination). The skew and kurtosis scores were respectively -.36 and -.12 for investments, -.48 and -.61 for de-escalatory disengagement strategies, .08 and -.86 for degree of happiness, as well as -.09 and -.73 for discussion of termination.

Based on these results, we employed non-parametric analyses in the subsequent analyses, specifically Mann-Whitney U tests. Spiegel described the Mann-Whitney U test as "one of the most powerful of the nonparametric tests and it is a useful alternative to the parametric t" (1956, p. 116). The Mann-Whitney U test is appropriate in situations where the data are ranked, where the data deviate from normalcy, and where there are noticeable differences between the number of cases in the two groups being compared (MacFarland & Yates, 2016); our data set met all three of these criteria.

Sex Differences

The sample contained an unequal ratio of male (N=114) to female (N=219) participants. Previous studies involving college students reported a similarly unequal distribution, perhaps indicating that such a distribution frequently occurs in research when sampling college students (Clayton, Osborne, Miller, & Oberle, 2013; Junco, 2013; Tazghini, & Siedlecki, 2013).

Scholars have noted sex and gender differences in the use of Facebook (for a review of this research, see Webb & Temple, 2015). Therefore, we conducted a chi-square analysis to discover if males versus females were more likely to report remaining Facebook friends with a former romantic partner. Results revealed that, in this sample, females were significantly more likely to remain Facebook friends than males (X^2=367.56, df=9, p=.001, 77.29% of female participants versus 69.37% of the male participants). Similarly, males were more likely than females to *not* remain Facebook friends with former romantic partners (30.63% of the male participants versus 22.71% of the female participants).

Additionally, we conducted a series of relevant Mann-Whitney U tests and discovered no significant differences between the sexes across the variables of interest. Therefore, all data was combined for subsequent analyses and treated as one sample.

Relational Type

Participants reported involvement in long distance relationships 23% (N=74) as well as in proximal relationships 77% (N=248). A series of Mann-Whitney U tests revealed no significant differences between the scores of participants from proximal versus long-distance relationships across the variables of interest. Therefore, all data was combined for subsequent analyses and treated as one sample.

Primary Analysis

Like previous researchers (Marshall, 2012; Tran & Joormann, 2015), we divided our respondents' scores into to two groups (i.e., users who unfriended former romantic partners and those who did not). A series of Mann-Whitney *U* tests were conducted to test for differences between the groups across the variables of interest (quantity of investments, preference for de-escalatory disengagement strategies, relational satisfaction). The analyses yielded no significant differences (see Table 1). The results answer the research questions in the negative. The variables of interest fail to distinguish former romantic partners who remain Facebook friends from those who do not.

Table 1. Differences by Friendship Maintenance

Relational Characteristics	Facebook Friends With Former Partner	Mean Rank	Sum of Ranks	Mann-Whitney U	Z	2-tailed alpha
Relational	Yes	149.62	34411.50	7846.50	-1.655	.09
Investments	No	168.90	13174.50			
De-escalation	**Yes**	**160.10**	**37144.00**	**8444.00**	**-1.20**	**.22**
Strategies	**No**	**146.05**	**11684.00**			
Degree	Yes	160.38	38330.00	9470.00	-.129	.89
of Happiness	No	158.88	12710.00			
Discussion of	**Yes**	**163.95**	**39183.00**	**8856.00**	**-1.184**	**.23**
Termination	**No**	**150.33**	**12177.00**			

DISCUSSION

Interpretation of Results

The results of the present study provide relational scholars with a new perspective on friendships with former romantic partners. Our results document that, at least in one sample of college students, the factors that distinguish former romantic partners who remain face-to-face friends (quantity of relational investments, relational satisfaction, and relational disengagement strategies) from those who do not may not distinguish former romantic partners who maintain versus those who dissolve Facebook friendships.

Quality of Investments

The results indicate that the quantity of investments made during a romantic relationship do not influence decisions regarding Facebook friendships after the romantic relationship was terminated. In contrast, Stanley et al. (2006) found that larger quantities of relational investments directly influence face-to-face friendship outcomes after dissolution of romantic relationships. Thus, it appears investments may impact face-to face versus Facebook friendships differently.

However, a trend toward significance emerged in the analyses relevant to quantity of relational investments. Retesting with a larger sample could result in significant findings. Participants who reported remaining Facebook friends in the post-dissolution period tended to have fewer investments. One potential explanation for this finding is that individuals who make fewer investments have less to lose from a change in the relationship status than those with larger quantities of investments; therefore, lowering the quantity of relational investments makes the relationship less costly to both partners. Individuals who reported larger quantities of investments may suffer a greater loss when relationship dynamics change and therefore have more difficulty adjusting to the modified relationship making Facebook friendships challenging.

Relationship Disengagement Strategies.

The results indicate no significant difference in the disengagement strategy of de-escalation between former romantic partners who chose to terminate Facebook friendships versus those who chose to remain Facebook friends. Cody's (1982) findings suggest that engaging in de-escalatory disengagement strategies (i.e., fully explaining feelings and attitudes about the relationship to the partner, tending to the emotional needs of the partner, and indicating a desire for modified relationship in the future) results in more positive friendship outcomes than any of the other four relational disengagement strategies (negative identity management, positive tone, behavioral de-escalation, justification). However, Cody examined face-to-face friendships and not online friendships.

We offer the following explanation for our findings: Regardless of the disengagement strategy employed prior to the relationship dissolution, former romantic partners may avoid terminating Facebook friendships to save face in front of their social networks both on and offline (Wang, 2015). Instead, a user can elect to no longer see a former partner's posts simply by unfollowing that Facebook friend; thus, the user remains "friends" with the former romantic partners but simply never learns new information about the person via Facebook.

A second possible explanation for the findings involves measurement. Please recall that the results of our factor analyses limited our analyses to only one disengagement strategy, specifically de-escalation. In contrast, Cody's (1982) instrument assesses four additional disengagement strategies: contact avoidance, negative identity management (ending relationship without explanation), explaining the reasons for the breakup, and taking a positive tone (attending to the partner's feelings). It is entirely possible that one or more of these factors contribute to former romantic partners' decisions to unfriend each other on Facebook after the dissolution of their relationship. Unfortunately, in this study, we were unable to assess the potential influence of these four additional strategies. Regardless of the explanation, our results indicate that using de-escalation strategies during the dissolution phase of the romantic relationship may have no impact on whether former romantic partners elect to remain Facebook friends.

Relational Satisfaction During the Romantic Phase of the Relationship

Our findings revealed no significant differences in two aspects of relational satisfaction (degree of happiness and frequency of discussion of termination) between former romantic partners who decided to terminate Facebook friendships versus those who do not. This result is not consistent with the findings of Rhoads et al. (2011) who reported that relational satisfaction during a relationship has significant impact on the decision to retain or terminate face-to-face friends with former romantic partners. The inconsistencies between the results of the two studies may be simply a matter of differences in measurement. Although we used the same 4-item version of the Dyadic Adjustment Scale (Sabourin et al., 2005; Spanier, 1976), Rhoades et al. (2011) measured relationship quality prior to the breakup whereas we retrospectively assessed perceptions of relational satisfaction during the romantic phase of the relationships. Perceptions can change over time and our differing results may reflect such changes.

Alternatively, perhaps expressed happiness during the romantic relationship becomes irrelevant to any continuing online relationship post-breakup and thus does not impact the decision to remain or terminate Facebook friendships. Perhaps the decision to remain Facebook friends is fueled by other factors such as the desire to publicly present the breakup as amicable or the desire to publicly present an online identity as someone who gets along with everyone.

Overall Findings

Taken as a whole, this study indicates no significant differences in the quantity of relational investments, de-escalation strategies, or relational satisfaction (degree of happiness and frequency of discussion of termination) between former romantic partners who terminate Facebook friendships versus those who chose to remain Facebook friends. These findings directly contradict previous findings regarding face-to-face friendships post breakup. Thus, our results provide further evidence that online relationships may operate differently than face-to-face relationships.

Facebook friendships may have different meanings and values than those occurring face-to-face. It can be a casual matter to be someone's Facebook friend. Indeed, the activity is associated with the early stages of relationship development (Yang et al., 2014) and young adults accept friendship requests from stranger (Caer et al., 2013). Thus, being Facebook friends can be viewed as a casual, low commitment activity. If a user no longer wishes to see posts from a given friend, the user can hide that friend's posts from his/her news feed as well as not allow that friend to see the user's posts. Facebook privacy settings allow users complete control over information sent to and received from any given "friend," including a former romantic partner. Indeed, Facebook friendship is such a low-involvement enterprise, that a user may seem small or petty to joint friends in their Facebook social network for not allowing the Facebook friendship to continue.

Alternative factors not investigated in the present study may influence the decision to remain or terminate Facebook friendships. Such factors may include the size and scope of the shared Facebook social network (Lampe, Ellison, & Steinfield, 2006), the desire to remain a part of former romantic partner's life, the perceived benefits of changing the relationship dynamic to friendship with the possibility of resuming a romantic components in the future, emotional reactions to the breakup (Cole, 2014), and the desire to "keep tabs" or engage in on-going surveillance of a former romantic partners sometimes called Facebook stalking (LeFebvre et al., 2015; Blackburn, & Brody, 2014; Marshall, 2012; Tong, 2013).

LIMITATIONS AND SUGGESTIONS FOR FUTURE RESEARCH

Multiple limitations of this research are worth noting, perhaps most notably its sample. Given that our sample only included U. S. college students ages 18 to 24, our findings should not be generalized to a wider population of Facebook users. Furthermore, replicating our study with a larger, national, and more diverse sample may yield somewhat different findings. Such future research could explore additional and multiple factors that may influence former romantic partners' decisions to remain or not remain Facebook friends.

We used counter-balancing in our survey design to ameliorate order effects. Nonetheless, while participants completed the survey, they may have provided answers on the second and third instruments influenced by their thinking about the previous scale. For example, participants who completed the disengagement strategies instrument either first or second may have experienced negative feelings and thoughts about the break-up that lead to lower scores on the relational satisfaction scale as well as the relational investment scales. Future studies may desire to place the disengagement strategies instrument after any other relational assessment.

At least four factors may have limited the reliability of our test instruments: (a) We slightly reworded questionnaire items to address concerns raised by our pretest participants. (b) We tailored the instruments to assess relationships after they ended. (c) The breadth of time since the breakup reflected in the sample (from "last week" to "5 years ago") allowed for diversity in the sample but also may have limited the accuracy of recall regarding disengagement strategies. (d) Our survey assessed only one-side or version of the break-up as only one partner provided answers to the instrument.

Future research could recruit both former relational partners to participate in surveys and thus gauge perceptions of communication behavior during the dissolution process from two perspectives. Given that this study sought to apply face-to-face findings to online relationships, and that the reliability of the survey was limited, future researchers may desire to employ instruments that better address the idiosyncrasies of online behaviors to more accurately assess Facebook behavior.

CONCLUSION

Despite these limitations, the study offers new information to social media and relational scholars: This study represents a necessary first step toward identifying the factors that influence and/or motivate former romantic partners to remain connected via social media. Second, the study offers further documentation that the variables of importance in face-to-face relational decisions and behaviors may not be equally influential in online venues. Third, the study identified two variables that appear to clearly *not* distinguish former romantic partners who remain Facebook friends from those who do not among at least one sample of college students: de-escalation strategies used in the breakup process (i.e., discussing the benefits of changing the relationship dynamic with possibility of resuming in the future) as well as measures of relational satisfaction prior to the breakup (i.e., degree of happiness and frequency of discussion of termination). Fourth, the study identified a variable that may be worthy of further study, given the statistical trend that emerged in the data; perhaps quantity of relational investments provides the basis for a valid distinction between the former romantic partners who remain FaceBook friends versus those who do not. Fifth, the study is heuristic in that it provides meaningful directions for future research, most especially encouraging researchers to engage in exploratory research to determine directly from users the key factors that drive their desires and decisions regarding unfriending versus remaining Facebook friends with former romantic partners. Finally, the results here reported provide a warrant for future studies examining whether findings from face-to-face studies examining romantic relationships apply in the world of online relationships.

REFERENCES

Aylor, B. A. (2014). Maintaining long-distance relationships. In D. J. Canary & M. Dainton (Eds.), Maintaining relationships through communication: Relational, contextual, and cultural variations. East Sussex, UK: Psychology Press.

Banks, S. P., Altendorf, D. M., Greene, J. O., & Cody, M. J. (1987). An examination of relationship disengagement: Perceptions break up strategies and outcomes. *Western Journal of Speech Communication*, *51*(1), 19–41. doi:10.1080/10570318709374250

Bartz, A., & Ehrlich, B. (2010, September 1). To defriend or not to defriend: That is the question. *CNN.com*. Retrieved from http://articles.cnn.com/2010-09-01/tech/netiquette.defriending_1_friend-request-facebook-jug-band/2?_s=PM:TECH

Bazarova, N. N. (2012). Public intimacy: Disclosure interpretation and social judgments on Facebook. *Journal of Communication*, *62*(5), 815–832. doi:10.1111/j.1460-2466.2012.01664.x

Bevan, J. L., Ang, P. C., & Fearns, J. B. (2014). Being unfriended on Facebook: An application of expectancy violation theory. *Computers in Human Behavior*, *33*, 171–178. doi:10.1016/j.chb.2014.01.029

Bevan, J. L., Pfyl, J., & Barclay, B. (2012). Negative emotional and cognitive responses to being unfreinded on facebook: An exploratory study. *Computers in Human Behavior*, *28*(4), 1458–1464. doi:10.1016/j.chb.2012.03.008

Bowe, G. (2010). Reading romance: The impact Facebook rituals can have on a romantic relationship. *Journal of Comparative Research in Anthropology & Sociology*, *1*, 61–77. Retrieved from https://pdfs.semanticscholar.org/3361/4896eca88aebbceef2d4ee0ee2de59e088f4.pdf

Bullock, M. H., Hackathorn, J., Clark, E. M., & Mattingly, B. A. (2011). Can we be (and stay) friends? Remaining friends after dissolution of a romantic relationship. *The Journal of Social Psychology*, *151*(5), 662–665. doi:10.1080/00224545.2010.522624 PMID:22017080

Caers, R., De Feyter, T., De Couck, M., Stough, T., Vigna, C., & Du Bois, C. (2013). Facebook: A literature review. *New Media & Society*, *15*(6), 982–1002. doi:10.1177/1461444813488061

Clayton, R. B., Osborne, R. E., Miller, B. K., & Oberle, C. D. (2013). Loneliness, anxiousness, and substance use as predictors of Facebook use. *Computers in Human Behavior*, *29*(3), 687–693. doi:10.1016/j.chb.2012.12.002

Cody, M. J. (1982). A typology of disengagement strategies and an examination of the role intimacy, reactions to inequity and relational problems play in strategy selection. *Communication Monographs*, *49*(3), 148–170. doi:10.1080/03637758209376079

Cole, M. (2014). *Post-breakup emotion and obsessive relational intrusion in the mediated world (Unpublished dissertation)*. Tempe: Arizona State University. Retrieved from http://repository.asu.edu/attachments/135109/content/Cole_asu_0010E_14026.pdf

Craig, E., & Wright, K. B. (2012). Computer-mediated relational development and maintenance on Facebook. *Communication Research Reports*, *29*(2), 119–129. doi:10.1080/08824096.2012.667777

Crosier, B. S., Webster, G. D., & Dillon, H. M. (2012). Wired to connect: Evolutionary psychology and social networks. *Review of General Psychology, 16*(2), 230–239. doi:10.1037/a0027919

Cupach, W. R., & Metts, S. (1986). Accounts of relational dissolution: A comparison of marital and non-marital relationships. *Communication Monographs, 53*(4), 311–334. doi:10.1080/03637758609376146

Emery, R. E., & Dillon, P. (1994). Conceptualizing the divorce process: Renegotiating boundaries of intimacy and power in the divorced family system. *Family Relations, 43*(4), 374–379. doi:10.2307/585367

Facebook. (2018). Company information: Stats. Retrieved from https://newsroom.fb.com/company-info/

Ferrara, M. H., & Levine, T. R. (2009). Can't live with them or can't live without them?: The effects of betrayal on relational outcomes in college dating relationships. *Communication Quarterly, 57*(2), 187–204. doi:10.1080/01463370902881734

Fox, J., Osborn, J. L., & Warber, K. M. (2014). Relational dialectics and social networking sites: The role of Facebook in romantic relationship escalation, maintenance, conflict, and dissolution. *Computers in Human Behavior, 35*, 527–534. doi:10.1016/j.chb.2014.02.031

Fox, J., & Warber, K. M. (2013). Romantic relationship development in the age of Facebook: An exploratory study of emerging adults' perceptions, motives, and behaviors. *Cyberpsychology, Behavior, and Social Networking, 16*(1), 3–7. doi:10.1089/cyber.2012.0288 PMID:23098273

Gershon, I. (2011). Un-friend my heart: Facebook, promiscuity, and heartbreak in a neoliberal age. *Anthropological Quarterly, 84*(4), 865–894. doi:10.1353/anq.2011.0048

Gottman, J. M. (1993). A theory of marital dissolution and stability. *Journal of Family Psychology, 7*(1), 57–75. Retrieved from https://pdfs.semanticscholar.org/f27c/a9a4012e77c1abe317f111b4aed34662c766.pdf doi:10.1037/0893-3200.7.1.57

Griffith, R., Gillath, O., Zhao, X., & Martinez, R. (2017). Staying friends with ex-romantic partners: Predictors, reasons, and outcomes. *Personal Relationships, 24*(3), 550–584. doi:10.1111/pere.12197

Hadden, B. W., Harvey, S. M., Settensten, R. A., & Agrew, C. R. (2018). What do I call us? The investment model of commitment processes and changes in relationship categorization. *Social Psychology and Personality Science.* doi:10.1177/1948550617745115

Junco, R. (2013). Comparing actual and self-reported measures of Facebook use. *Computers in Human Behavior, 29*(3), 626–631. doi:10.1016/j.chb.2012.11.007

Kanter, M., Afifi, T., & Robbins, S. (2012). The impact of parents 'friending" their young adult child on Facebook on perceptions of parental privacy invasions and parent-child relationship quality. *Journal of Communication, 62*(5), 900–917. doi:10.1111/j.1460-2466.2012.01669.x

Lambert, A. N., & Hughes, P. C. (2010). The influence of goodwill, secure attachment, and positively toned disengagement strategy on reports of communication satisfaction in non-marital post-dissolution relationships. *Communication Research Reports, 27*(2), 171–183. doi:10.1080/08824091003738123

Lampe, C., Ellison, N., & Steinfield, C. (2006, November). A Face (book) in the crowd: Social searching vs. social browsing. In *Proceedings of the 2006 20th anniversary conference on Computer supported cooperative work* (pp. 167-170). 10.1145/1180875.1180901

Ledbetter, A. M., & Mazer, J. P. (2014). Do online communication attitudes mitigate the association between Facebook use and relational interdependence? An extension of media multiplexity theory. *New Media & Society*, *16*(5), 806–822. doi:10.1177/1461444813495159

Ledbetter, A. M., Mazer, J. P., DeGroot, J. M., Meyer, K. R., Yuping, M., & Swafford, B. (2011). Attitudes toward online social connection and self-disclosure as predictors of Facebook communication and relational closeness. *Communication Research*, *38*(1), 27–53. doi:10.1177/0093650210365537

LeFebvre, L., Blackburn, K., & Brody, N. (2015). Navigating romantic relationships on Facebook: Extending the relationship dissolution model to social networking environments. *Journal of Social and Personal Relationships*, *32*(1), 78–98. doi:10.1177/0265407514524848

MacFarland, T. W., & Yates, J. M. (2016). *Introduction to nonparametric statistics for the biological sciences using R*. Geneva: Springer. doi:10.1007/978-3-319-30634-6

Marshall, T. C. (2012). Facebook surveillance of former romantic partners: Associations with postbreakup recovery and personal growth. *Cyberpsychology, Behavior, and Social Networking*, *15*(10), 521–526. doi:10.1089/cyber.2012.0125 PMID:22946958

Mc Laughlin, C., & Vitak, J. (2012). Norm evolution and violation on Facebook. *New Media & Society*, *14*(2), 299–315. doi:10.1177/1461444811412712

Mogilski, J. K., & Welling, L. M. (2017). Staying friends with an ex: Sex and dark personality traits predict motivations for post-relationship friendship. *Personality and Individual Differences*, *115*, 114–119. doi:10.1016/j.paid.2016.04.016

Norton, R. (1983). Measuring marital quality: A critical look at the dependent variable. *Journal of Marriage and the Family*, *45*(1), 141–151. doi:10.2307/351302

Pena, J., & Brody, N. (2014). Intentions to hide and unfriend Facebook connections based on perceptions of sender attractiveness and status updates. *Computers in Human Behavior*, *31*, 143–150. doi:10.1016/j.chb.2013.10.004

Quercia, D., Bodaghi, M., & Crowcroft, J. (2012). Loosing "friends" on Facebook. In *Proceedings of the 4th Annual ACM Web Science Conference* (pp. 251-254). doi:10.1145/2380718.2380751

Rhoades, G. K., & Kamp Dush, C. M. Atkins, D. C., Stanley, S. M., & Markman, H. J., (2011). Breaking up is hard to do: The impact of unmarried relationship dissolution on mental health and life satisfaction. *Journal of Family Psychology, 25*, 366-374. Retrieved from http://psycnet.apa.org/buy/2011-08238-001

Rusbult, C. E. (1980). Commitment and satisfaction in romantic associations: A test of the investment model. *Journal of Experimental Social Psychology*, *16*(2), 172–186. doi:10.1016/0022-1031(80)90007-4

Sabourin, S., Valois, P., & Lussier, Y. (2005). Development and validation of a brief version of the dyadic adjustment scale with a nonparametric item analysis model. *Psychological Assessment*, *17*(1), 15–27. doi:10.1037/1040-3590.17.1.15 PMID:15769225

Spanier, G. B. (1976). Measuring dyadic adjustment: New scales for assessing the quality of marriage and similar dyads. *Journal of Marriage and the Family*, *38*(1), 15–28. Retrieved from http://trieft.org/wp-content/uploads/2010/09/DAS%2BArticle.pdf doi:10.2307/350547

Spiegel, S. (1956). *Nonparametric statistics for the behavioral sciences*. New York, NY: McGraw-Hill.

Stanley, S. M., Rhoades, G. K., & Markman, H. J. (2006). Sliding vs. deciding: Inertia and the premarital cohabitation effect. *Family Relations*, *55*(4), 499–509. doi:10.1111/j.1741-3729.2006.00418.x

Starks, K. M. (2007). Bye bye love: Computer-mediated communication and relational dissolution. *Texas Speech Communication Journal, 32*, 11-20. Retrieved from https://web.a.ebscohost.com/abstract?direct=true&profile=ehost&scope=site&authtype=crawler&jrnl=03638782&AN=27713769&h=gAb%2b5DwWPWO6q5Mt1hK5q%2bFKCR8lfGYt6lv6bA4ebr572jN%2fHNCHisUpBbipajqm2CHd8V2bLxms7Te7ceKzpA%3d%3d&crl=c&resultNs=AdminWebAuth&resultLocal=ErrCrlNotAuth&crlhashurl=login.aspx%3fdirect%3dtrue%26profile%3dehost%26scope%3dsite%26authtype%3dcrawler%26jrnl%3d03638782%26AN%3d27713769

Tazghini, S., & Siedlecki, K. L. (2013). A mixed method approach to examining Facebook use and its relationship to self-esteem. *Computers in Human Behavior*, *29*(3), 827–832. doi:10.1016/j.chb.2012.11.010

Tong, S. T. (2013). Facebook use during relationship termination: Uncertainty reduction and surveillance. *Cyberpsychology, Behavior, and Social Networking*, *16*(11), 788–793. doi:10.1089/cyber.2012.0549 PMID:23786171

Tran, T. B., & Joormann, J. (2015). The role of Facebook use in mediating the relation between rumination and adjustment after a relationship breakup. *Computers in Human Behavior*, *49*, 56–61. doi:10.1016/j.chb.2015.02.050

Vanderdrift, L. E., Lehmiller, J. J., & Kelly, J. R. (2012). Commitment in friends with benefits relationships: Implications for relational and safe-sex outcomes. *Personal Relationships*, *19*(1), 1–13. doi:10.1111/j.1475-6811.2010.01324.x

Walther, J. B. (2011). Theories of computer-mediated communication and interpersonal relations. In M. L. Knapp & J. A. Daly (Eds.), *Sage handbook of interpersonal communication* (4th ed., pp. 443–480). Thousand Oaks, CA: Sage.

Wang, S. S. (2015). To unfriend or not: Exploring factors affecting users in keeping friends on Facebook and the implications on mediated voyeurism. *Asian Journal of Communication*, *25*(5), 465–485. doi:10.1080/01292986.2014.990469

Wasserman, T. (2010, December 31). Facebook by the numbers in 2010 [STATS]. Mashable. Retrieved from http://mashable.com/2010/12/31/facebook-by-the-numbers-in-2010-stats/

Webb, L. M., & Temple, N. (2015). Gender issues and digital technology: The challenges and opportunities for empowerment and enactment. In B. Guzzetti & M. Lesley (Eds.), *Handbook of Research on the Social Impact of Digital Media* (pp. 638–669). Hershey, PA: IGI Global. doi:10.4018/978-1-4666-8310-5.ch025

Wieselquist, J. (2009). Interpersonal forgiveness, trust, and the investment model of commitment. *Journal of Social and Personal Relationships*, *26*(4), 531–548. doi:10.1177/0265407509347931

Yang, C. C., Brown, B. B., & Braun, M. T. (2014). From Facebook to cell calls: Layers of electronic intimacy in college students' interpersonal relationships. *New Media & Society*, *16*(1), 5–23. doi:10.1177/1461444812472486

ENDNOTES

[1]   A copy of the survey instruments is available upon request from the first author at dylmed@gmail.com.

[2]   Detailed results on our preliminary analyses are available upon request from the first author at dylmed@gmail.com.

This research was previously published in the International Journal of Interactive Communication Systems and Technologies (IJICST), 9(1); pages 1-16, copyright year 2019 by IGI Publishing (an imprint of IGI Global).

Chapter 60
Today Is Your Birthday!
Analysing Digital Celebration and Social Culture of Young People on Facebook

Doris Ngozi Morah

(iD) https://orcid.org/0000-0002-7854-3238
Madonna University, Nigeria

Chinwe Elizabeth Uzochukwu
Nnamdi Azikiwe University, Awka, Nigeria

ABSTRACT

Facebook birthdays have become increasingly trendy among young people globally and in Africa since the arrival of smart technologies. The study investigates the idea of celebrating birthdays on Facebook among selected Nigerian university students and reactions to this new trend. Using the diffusion of innovations theory and mixed research methods, in-depth interviews were conducted on six respondents, and profile activities of 300 Facebook users' content was analysed to investigate the research objectives. Findings demonstrate that most users found it convenient and economical to celebrate birthdays on Facebook. Online celebrations offer more global online visibility than offline parties leading to the formation of digital cultures and connections. The result led to a proposal for the bicultural convergence model that explains user experiences to social media effect. Poor network and high-cost data tariff, among others, posed challenges. The study recommends the provision of cheap or free internet access in Nigeria and Africa to enable increased growth of the digital social culture.

INTRODUCTION

Social media use initiated a new culture in human sociology and communication ecology. Carr & Hayes as cited in Ajhabash & Ma (2017, p.1) defined social media as "Internet-based, disentrained, and persistent channels of mass personal communication facilitating perceptions of interactions among users, deriving value primarily from user-generated content." The interactivity and participatory features of social media draw the attraction of many people globally, particularly the younger generation called millen-

DOI: 10.4018/978-1-6684-6307-9.ch060

nial, who exploit it for various purpose. Social media is also useful in many areas of human endeavour, including health, communication, development, economic, commerce, education, agriculture, political, socio-cultural rationale, among others. A subdomain of social media is known as social networking sites under which Facebook, Twitter, and Instagram, among other categories.

Young people have broadly embraced the use of social media, especially in Africa and Nigeria, probably as an easy means of education, communication and socialisation. Globally, Facebook is the most popular social network (Alhabash & Ma, 2017; Farahbakhsh, Han, Cuevas & Crespi, 2017) with a usage statistics of 74.58% as of September 2020 (https://gs.statcounter.com/social-media-stats). Alhabash and Ma (2017, p.2) corroborate Duggan's findings that "about three-quarters of Internet users report having a Facebook account, and 7 in 10 users report accessing the site daily, highlighting the habitual and ritualised nature of Facebook use." Duggan's findings indicate that people mostly visit Facebook sites whenever they access the internet.

Presently, the role of social media has become diversified to such an extent that some human activities are now executed online on web communities. In the past, though celebrating one's birthday was fun provoking, tasking and involved excellent preparation whenever a person's birthday comes up. In Nigeria, birthdays are celebrated as a significant event depending on the financial status of the celebrant. It requires sending invitations to family and friends; organising musicals; and preparing foods and drinks. Young people usually celebrate birthday parties with their peers and friends at home or on campuses. Presently, in Nigeria, there seems to be a paradigm shift in social celebrations as social networking sites(SNS) such as Facebook, has become an attractive hub for birthdays parties in this age of smartphone pervasiveness.

Facebook is the most popular social media platform among youths in Nigeria (Morah, Udeze & Ekwenchi, 2019; Mbanaso, Dandaura, Ezeh & Iwuchukwu, 2015) and presently has a usage rate of 55.94% as of September 2019-September 2020 (https://gs.statcounter.com/social-media-stats/all/nigeria). The surge in usage is likely to contribute to increased interest in Facebook birthdays, especially among young people. Its potentialities of allowing people to bond with family members, friends and acquaintances; and its capacity to provide users with the opportunity to post and share contents such as photos and status updates (Stec as cited in Alhabash & Ma, 2017, p.2), makes Facebook ideal for birthday celebrations leading to cultural formation among young people.

The relevance of Facebook in social-cultural development and integration of society also help motivate young people to maintain such accounts. The individual's use of social media, however, is often based on perceived expectation and gratification and is often personalised by different motivational factors. Some research further highlighted some of those motivational factors as the ability: to gain social capital by initiating and maintaining friendships (Alhabash & Ma, 2017; Lenhart, 2009; Valenzuela, Park, & Kee, 2009) and; to create and enhance a self-image (Utz, 2010; Zhang, 2010). Deuze (2015, p.1) succinctly surmises "all people use social media a lot, for all kinds of purposes—but mostly to be in touch with family and friends, to be present and seen in the lives of people they care about." Deuze's mindset underscores the position of Facebook in cultural formation and socialisation.

Expectedly, in the Nigerian Facebook sphere, celebrations of online birthday are also booming, especially among young people on campus who spend most of their time online (Pew Internet Research, 2018). Mbanaso, Dandaura, Ezeh & Iwuchukwu (2015) found that Facebook ranked highest as the most commonly used social media platform among young people with 91%, followed by WhatsApp (87%) in a study of five tertiary institutions in Central Nigeria. The widespread adoption of the Facebook sphere for birthdays is now synonymous to a cultural carnival arena where people from different backgrounds that are multiethnic, and multicultural gather, advertises and celebrates their birthdays; posting photographs, cakes, gifts items, wishes, among others. Though novel, it introduced a new norm among the Nigerian Facebook users and their online community/friends. Under this dispensation, users celebrate birthdays of their friends, families, spouses, loved ones, colleagues, classmates, role models, among others. The new Facebook birthday norm likewise affects user's level of communicativeness and mutuality even as there is evidence that the new media has somehow become the message justifying McLuhan's technological determinism theory (Morah, 2012). It has helped brought people tighter as a family and broken geographical barriers, thereby advancing relationship which aligns with Farahbakhsh, Han, Cuevas, & Crespi (2017) mindset. However, there might be some challenges emanating with such celebration that are peculiar to different users to be investigated in the study.

The Facebook birthday trend is also enhanced and mediated by technology and social networks which keep evolving with the society as described as network sociability. Network sociability culminates to an individual-centred network which is specific to the individual and peer-group formation when the network becomes the context of behaviour for its participants (Castells, Fernandez-Ardevol, Linchuan Qiu & Sey, 2004). It drives relational activities on social media, such as birthday celebrations. Hinged on Jenkins et al. (2007) mindsets that there will be a better understanding of technology-supported social relations when an accurate knowledge of specific platform integrates with an ecological perspective, this study is apt and current. Each social-mediated platform possesses particular potentialities that contribute to building exclusive communication environments (Farahbakhsh, Han, Cuevas & Crespi, 2017; Alhabash & Ma, 2017). The buildup of such environment helps to nurture and create cultures which support Baran (2008) views that media literacy and use has a strong correlation with culture. This study, therefore, investigates user's perceptions of the idea of celebrating birthdays on Facebook among selected Nigerian university students and its link with the formation of digital culture.

The Problem and Research Significance

The dearth of literature about the bonds of Facebook birthdays and formation of digital culture in Nigeria is a significant concern because policymakers do not have the facts as the basis of their decisions. Considering the pervasiveness of Facebook and smartphone usage in Nigeria plus their contributions towards developing technology-mediated social relations in the new public sphere; an empirical examination into the extent of youth behaviour on Facebook towards birthday celebrations is apt. It should provide incisive insights into user perceptions of the significance of Facebook birthday celebrations in digital culture formation.

The Facebook celebration often requires a change in the profile and wall pictures. The profile photograph is generally an essential element of online self-presentation that is significant for relational success. Research (Young & Quan-Haase, 2009) found that 98.7% of college students post their photos on Facebook. Mbanaso, Dandaura, Ezeh & Iwuchukwu (2015) found that Facebook has widespread popularity(91%) because of its interactive features like wall post, chat, call, video, gaming, like and share capabilities. The authors believe that Facebook's easy registration process, multiple connection avenues and user-friendly web interfaces also facilitate its wide adoption among young people in Nigeria. Deuze (2015, p.2) research on how people use social media also found "that when doing so, people tend to approximate their normal selves." Such an attitude might be the real motive given by some people who spend most of their time on social media, communicating to real (yet imagined, in as much invisible) others (friends). Such actions are often regarded as numerous endeavours to "project and live up to one or more versions of ourselves that we create and get co-created in media" (Deuze, 2015, p.2).

Despite the prevalence and importance of this viral communication, little known research has analysed users perceptions of Facebook birthdays and its connections with the formation of digital cultures (which might develop into mutual connections and communities), particularly in Nigerian and among young people in tertiary institutions. The study, therefore, examines the celebration of birthdays on Facebook among selected Nigerian university students and how these users react to the new trend of online self- presentation and digital culture formation. Doing so will expand on the existing knowledge surrounding social media and its limits. . The study will also educate and guide owners of Facebook on essential features to include in the app for users benefit. It also concerns how and why different online populations of young adults use and perceive the benefits of Facebook birthdays.

Research Objective and Questions

The primary aim of this study was to analyse the celebration of birthdays on Facebook among selected Nigerian youths and how these users perceive the digital culture formation. To this end, these research questions guided the study:

RQ1: What is the frequency of Facebook birthday celebrations among selected users within the study period?
RQ2: How do users react to the use of Facebook as a platform for birthday celebrations?
RQ3: To what extent does use of Facebook for birthdays influence formation of digital culture among selected users?
RQ4: What are the inherent challenges of celebrating birthdays on Facebook?

Facebook and Birthday Celebrations

The new culture of celebrating birthdays on Facebook is overwhelmingly fascinating, especially, among young people who also, advertise their celebration date weeks and days before the actual date as done in local real-life communities. Fiebert, Tilmont & Warren (2013) argue that the cultural involvement with social networking sites, with regards to the global online visibility of Facebook, is dramatic as over 845 million Facebook users spent approximately 10 billion minutes a day on the platform in February 2012. The statistic skyrocketed in 2020 to a whopping 2.7 billion active user as of the second quarter (www.statista.com). Domingo (2015) on his part, posits that "social media is an intriguing stage for social interactions." This assertion captures the present position of Facebook in celebrations of birthday, especially among young people as everyone wants to get noticed.

Widespread use of Facebook in Nigeria accelerated by the introduction of GSM phone and presently adopted in many areas of human endeavour (Morah, 2012). Having a Facebook account seems to be more synonymous with providing the basic needs of many Nigerians. The country has a subscription rate of 27120000 facebook subscribers and 61.2% internet penetration as of December 31, 2019 (internetworldstats.com). The high adoption rate undermines the role of media in socialisation and evident in the widespread use of Facebook for birthdays. It falls in line with Uzochukwu, Morah & Okafor (2015, p.284) view that the media is powerful and play a significant role in forming and influencing people's attitudes and behaviour. Probably, this might be one factor that propels users to celebrate themselves and their friends on Facebook.

Digital Culture and Social Media

Social media use is firmly rooted in the daily practices of people, just like standard cultural practices. Domingo (2015) believes online conversations shape the offline activities; and "their offline personas are selectively (re)presented online." This assumption implies that people are influenced by their online activities which they might act-out while offline and vice visa. The difference in an online and offline context does not mean much for digital citizens as their online life is "always on, and available in their pockets" (Domingo, 2015, p.1).

The use of Facebook for birthday celebrations is positively associated with higher levels of self-satisfaction and social trust (Valenzuela et al., 2009). The above view means that people who have online identities feel more connected with their peers and are generally happier with increased social contentment. Ellison, Steinfield, and Lampe (2007) collaborate that perceptions of being connected to others result from the convenience and free-of-cost services provided by Facebook, such as daily reminders of friends' birthdays. For Domingo (2015), the central irony in social environments is that users can control almost what they share of themselves and as well be "more prone to show their backstage to a much wider audience than in face-to-face interactions" (p.2).

Pempek, Yermolayeva & Calvert (2009) argue that creating social connections is equally positively linked with building a social identity. Facebook users successfully do this by indicating membership of specific subgroups (race, gender, sexuality, among others) and subcultures (such as music and movies). Pempek, Yermolayeva & Calvert (2009) findings indicate that Facebook was also mostly used to acquire information about others, as well as in reconnecting with real-life friends. Waldman (2016, p.202) believes that Facebook helps to nurture communities because of its potentialities. He notes that its "design makes us think that we're talking to specific other people in controlled spaces. We see others' faces and are taken to others' personal profile pages to interact with them; this creates a perception of safety" (p.202). Based on these premises, it is, therefore, evident that Facebook has the great potentiality of expanding and strengthening people's social networking and trust, which makes it a promising avenue for cultural formation.

Diffusion of Innovation Theory (DOI)

Underlying the usage of Facebook in celebrating birthdays is the theoretical work of pioneering social science scholar Everett M. Rogers, who researched the adoption and diffusion of innovations. This leading theory for analysing technology characteristics concerning technological consumption is called diffusion of innovation theory (Pavlik & Bridges, 2013, p.11). Essentially, this theory suggests that when a concept is perceived as new, an individual utilises communication tactics within their social systems to arrive at a decision point of either adoption or rejection of the innovation. Peter and Olson (2010) indicate that innovation's characteristics serve as a significant influence on an individual's adoption decision. Diffusion of innovation theory, besides, predicts that the media and other interpersonal contacts provide information and influence audience behaviour towards the adoption of innovations.

Specific personal characteristics also influence innovation adoption; demographic indicators such as sex, age and educational and social backgrounds become vital markers. In the social or cultural organisation; however, Rogers stated there are various levels at which different people react to and adopt change. People chose to adopt technology at multiple stages. A person's decision to adopt or reject an innovation is often determined by such innovation itself (Rogers, 2003). In this context, Facebook birthday is an innovation that is penetrating the global public sphere, and young people are responding to and adopting it at a different phase. The adoption pattern should conform to Roger's principle of five stages of adoption- (innovators, early adopters, early majority, late majority, and laggards).

Methodology, Population and Sampling

The research adopted the mixed research methods of In-depth Interview (IDI) and online content analysis to provide answers to the articulated research question. Indepth interview was chosen to deeply investigate how celebrants perceive the concept of Facebook birthdays and its influence on them; while online content analysis was used to actually map the rate and nature of Facebook celebrations by the selected respondents within the study period. The fear from respondents of falling victims to Nigeria's proposed Social Media bill constrained the researchers to interview only six respondents out of the selected Facebook users. The researchers purposively selected and interviewed six respondents through In-depth Interview (IDI) and content analysed activities of 300 Facebook users for three months from August 20- October 20, 2018. The aim was to investigate information concerning the number of birthday wishes and notice received; the relational patterns; the appropriateness of using a social media platform for birthday celebrations and the inherent challenges. All potential participants were current university students selected at random from the researchers' list of active Facebook friends by utilising a table of random numbers. The researcher sought their consent through direct chat before the study.

Certain conditions were also considered in the purposive selection of participants. If a prospective participant was chosen and found not to be a Nigerian undergraduate student, the researchers proceeded to the next eligible person on their list of Facebook friends, and continue to purposively select individuals from there. The researcher's personal Facebook friends were, however, exclusively deployed for this study for two reasons. (a) Facebook policies and; (b) only active Facebook friends can access the user timelines, profile page, stories, broadcast and updates which we needed to view when coding the total number of birthday requests and celebrations.

In-depth Interview IDI of six Facebook users also formed part of the mixed methods. It provided answers to research questions two and four. The six respondents were selected from six account owners of the chosen purposively 300 Facebook accounts that were content analysed. The selected respondents were students in third and final years of tertiary education who maintained active accounts on Facebook for five years and above.

The data collection method used for this was some open-ended questions administered using *aide-memoire* in an unstructured form to each of the six respondents purposively selected online at different points during the study. Facebook Messenger utilised for the Interview done from August 20 to October 20, 2018. The researcher sent a message to the respondents via chat box to seek consent and book appointments with them before the actual study period. The chats and audio calls are stored during the interviews, and the responses transcribed later.

Unit of Analysis

The unit of analysis comprised all posts on birthday celebrations on Facebook in the form of request, updates, photos, broadcast, reminders, comments, among others. With the use of simple descriptive statistics; the manifest data were examined for frequency, prominence of birthdays and level of celebrations. The outcomes of the Interview were given and analysed using thematic analysis. The researcher tried to assure confidentiality during the Interview. The respondents were assigned acronyms in the following order: User AF- female user 1; User AM- male user 1; User BF- female user 2; User BM- male user 2; User CF- female user 3; and User CM- male user 3.

FINDINGS AND DISCUSSIONS

The data analysed was obtained from the result of 300 Facebook accounts content analysed for three months, and six respondents studied through in-depth Interview from among the selected sample of young Nigerian undergraduates on Facebook.

Demographic Data

Out of the three hundred Facebook account studied, 154 (51.33%) belong to male respondents, while the remaining 146 accounts (48.66%) belong to females. This result implies that more male accounts were studied more than female. It also indicates that there is a gender disparity in social media use among young people and might be a pointer to gender gaps in access to digital technology. For the Interview, however, there was an equal ratio of three males and three female interviewed using Facebook Messenger. The research findings present below:

RQ1: What is the frequency of Facebook birthday celebrations among selected users within the study period?

Table 1. Extent to which selected users receive birthday wishes

Variable	Frequency	Percentage
always	194	64.7%
often	78	26%
sometimes	22	7.3%
rarely	6	2%
never	-	-
total	300	100%

The result on Table 1 from the 300 Facebook profile visited shows that majority of the users 64.7% always receive birthday wishes regularly whenever their birthday comes up, followed by 78(28%) users who often receive such message in the form of text, pictures, video, audio and comments. A minimal outcome observed among six users who rarely received any such communications. The finding implies that Facebook birthday are regularly celebrated among the selected users, and most people are currently celebrating their birthdays online, especially among Nigeria students. This result corroborates Ekwenchi, Morah & Adum (2015) that Nigeria students are significantly using social media on campus.

Table 2. How selected users celebrate their birthday on Facebook

Variables	Frequency	Percentage
Actively	163	54.3
Moderately	65	21.7
Low key	48	16
No celebration at all	24	8
Total	300	100

Findings on Table 2 shows that majority (54.3%) of the selected users actively celebrate their birthdays on Facebook while; 21.7% celebrate moderately with reduced participation, and 16% does theirs on a very low- key. Only 24 accounts representing 8% did not celebrate their birthday at all. This result shows a high interest among young people in celebrating their birthday with assistance from Facebook. It also underscores the point that there is a high rate in adoption of social media among young people and falls in line with Mbanaso, Dandaura, Ezeh & Iwuchukwu (2015) and Morah & Omojola (2018) findings. The result also correlates with Table 1 result as the selected users also have an interest in celebrating their birthdays online even as they celebrated other people.

RQ2: How do users React to the use of Facebook as a Platform for Birthday Celebrations?

Table 3. Users reactions to Facebook birthdays

Variables	Frequency	Percentage
Very Important	256	85%
Less Important	33	11%
Not Important	11	4%
Total	300	100%

Data on Table 3 shows that a majority(85%) of the selected users regard the celebration of birthdays on Facebook as very important, while 11% consider it not so important. Only a minimal 4% of the user regarded the celebration as unimportant. The findings indicate the importance of birthday among university students and corroborate Morah & Omojola (2018) stand on the usefulness of social media to young people.

Interview Result for RQ2

Responses from the IDI corroborate the finding of the online content analysis in Table 3. It shows that the majority of users found it more convenient and economical to celebrate their birthday online, and it also offers them more global online visibility than offline parties. With regards to research question 2, USER AF opines that:

I think it is good celebrating my birthday on Facebook. As a student, it will save time and money. I no longer need to suspend my educational activities to hold parties. I will no longer spend money on feasting friends. I can say that the celebration of birthdays on Facebook is a perfect development, especially for students.

In contrast, USER BF argues that:

I think Facebook birthdays are not real. It doesn't make sense to me. You don't get any present, and you don't see your friend. The only gain will be the photos, wishes, beautiful words from friends and so on. Even some of the wishes might be a pretence. It gives me more joy to stay with friends and celebrates.

For USER CF, however, the above is good a reason as celebrating "my birthday on Facebook is good shaa, but for me, it is better to have offline, with family and friends. It adds life to the celebration offline. If you are well-off as a student, it will be livelier and adds more fun." There is a divergent opinion from USER AM who expresses the view that:

Yes, I prefer celebrating on Facebook as it will reduce cost. As a student in this country, you must huzzal to eat; buy books; keep fit and move on. When you hold the party online, you don't spend much shaa, and you will not be afraid of any harm from the village or friend. For me, it is better done on Facebook and then forgotten.

USER BM also recognised Facebook birthday as necessary on the point that:

It is perfect, especially for we students. It will enable you to reach out to all your friends without wasting money and time. It is better to combine the two if you have some money. You can buy a small cake and wine, call a friend on campus and celebrate your birthday. In some cases, someone might surprise a celebrant with a cake and drinks. You take photos and video, dance around and upload to Facebook. It is cheaper that way and easier for me as a student in this country.

The above findings imply that one can merge the online and offline celebration for more visibility and enjoyment. The above instance is a kind of media convergence that bothers on cultures where the online culture will merge with real-life culture during the celebration. The experiences will be different and unique. Such birthdays usually celebrated at the same time with people doing the party at home and broadcasting it live on a social platform. There will be responses from friends from every culture; who will join the party online and send wishes and comments.

Proposal for a Bicultural Convergence Model

The phenomenon as described and emanating from the finding here could be regarded as *Bicultural Convergence Model*. The concept of *Bicultural Convergence model* assumes that media technology could be used to share and promote culture online and in real life the same time. Under this dispensation, the individual and communal effect are heightened; leading to acceptance and increased use of such technology in future. It implies that users experiencing this effect are more likely to accept and use Facebook for birthdays, as found in the study.

Similarly, responses show that USER CM regarded such Facebook celebration as useful and economical:

The use of Facebook for celebrating a birthday is useful to enable friends that were absent because of proximity and engagements to enjoy with you. I feel happy doing it online, for instance; I am not with my family now. So how will I have celebrated my day if not for the videos, chats, chats and wishes on Facebook? This online revolution has simplified human and social communication and is quite beautiful and impressive (USER CM).

In summary, findings show that majority 5(83%) respondents found it very important, more convenient and economical to celebrate their birthday online; and it also offers them more global online visibility than offline parties. The tendency to find more youth on social media celebrating birthdays is therefore prevalent among university students as Facebook is widely used by most Nigerians (Morah, Udeze & Ekwenchi, 2019; Mbanaso, Dandaura, Ezeh & Iwuchukwu, 2015).

RQ3: To what extent does use of Facebook for birthdays influence formation of digital culture among selected users?

Table 4. The nature of the relationship existing among celebrant

Variables	Frequency	Percentage
Family	46	15.33%
Relationship	68	22.67%
Direct friends	40	13.33%
Students/course mates	70	23.33%
Online friends	34	11.33%
Friends of friends	29	9.67%
Others	13	4.33%
Total	300	100%

Data on Table 4 show results of analyses on the relationship between the chief celebrant and their friends. Findings show that most users 23.33% are celebrated by their fellow students and course mates; followed by people they have a close relationship with 22.7% and online friends with a total 21% of the respondent's family members (15.33%) and direct friends (13.33%) got a moderate point. This finding implies that there is an extension of social culture to the online space with loved ones still celebrating birthdays for their beloved, which falls in line with Domingo (2015) arguments.

Data on Table 5 sought to examine the users that have their birthdays celebrated by friend independently even as those users celebrated on their own. Results on Table 5 shows that majority 46.3% of the selected users are celebrated by friends always; while friends often celebrate 28.7% and sometimes 15%. No friend celebrated about eleven accounts representing 3.7% of users during their birthdays. The result shows that if someone was not online for some time, one's birthdays are still remembered by a loved one as done in real life. This finding is an indication that users have become part of a community that will always celebrate the users birthday whenever. Such a community usually is bond by a communal culture preexisting among them and controlling their activities.

RQ4: What are The Inherent Challenges of Celebrating Birthdays on Facebook?

Table 5. How often are users celebrated on Facebook?

Variable	Frequency	Percentage
Always	139	46.3
Often	86	28.7
Sometimes	45	15
Rarely	19	6.3
Never	11	3.7
Total	300	100%

This research question 4 sought to investigate the challenges of celebrating birthdays on Facebook. For USER AF, there are some challenges:

Yes, there are so many of them in this country. One challenge is network failure and money for data. The data doesn't last and even on chats, it is always going fast fast. The networks centres should reduce their tariff. I use two networks for data, especially the ones with more bonuses that is Glo Nigeria or Airtel Nigeria.

USER BF believes that finance is also a significant challenge for offline parties which she prefers as her "major challenge will be financing the party. If I am given money for the celebration, facebook celebration will be for my distance friends. So after the celebration, I will upload the video and photos for my absent friends and family."

On the same vein, USER CF insists that Facebook birthdays are unnatural despite the obstacles:

It is not real at all and has many challenges; one is network failure, low battery and data. If you want to reply a comment, you might encounter problems of low battery. The worst will be that EDDC might not bring light in time. Also, your data might finish, and you might not have money for a top-up. However, this cannot happen if you organise a party (USER CF).

Respondent USER AM on his part pointed out the hindrances: "the problems are mainly network, battery and data. Once these three are there, you can comfortably relate with friends and have a grand birthday online. That is the in-thing now, especially for students. It actually saves a lot of money."

Similarly, USER BM agrees that his "only problem with using Facebook is the cost of data and battery life. My network provider is always on, and my phone is very sharp. So the celebration continues." The respondent USER CM expressed a similar view with most respondents that:

The challenge I have is poor network to chat, upload pictures and videos to loved ones. I prefer online birthdays because the excerpt will remain viral forever, for easier retrieval. If it is an offline celebration, you might lose the images or videos to a photographer. It is cheaper and trendy to do it on Facebook. I can buy a small cake, cut with my friends with drinks and show the world. It's lovely and fun. It will even motivate others to start celebrating theirs.

This result implies that Facebook birthday celebrations can as well set agenda for other users and even serve as gratification for some media users. The finding corroborates with the tenets of the agenda-setting and diffusion of innovations theories. Business outfits that deal on gifts items will thereby get advertised as people post updates of birth parties online. This fall in with Morah, Ekwenchi & Chiaha (2019) views that social media fosters economic development in Nigeria because of its affordability and ease of access.

In summary, Internet access, poor network and high data tariff were identified by a majority of the respondents to be significant challenges to using Facebook for birthday celebrations among young people. The above result implies that though Facebook celebrations of birthdays are novel and cheaper, the underpinned challenges might hinder their full acceptance, especially in rural areas where there might be inadequate electric supply and inadequate network/data coverage.

CONCLUSION AND RECOMMENDATIONS

The finding has demonstrated that young Nigerians are celebrating their birthdays on Facebook, although there are some inherent challenges. The study also indicated the presence of a new culture among young Nigerian online celebrants on Facebook. The Facebook birthday culture has excellent resemblance with offline parties except for physical touch. However, some respondents complained bitterly about this which shows that people are persuaded by certain factors like the evolving technology to celebrate because; others are doing so which validates the diffusion of innovations theory that happens in stages and the *Bicultural Convergence model* that believes that users experiencing this effect are more likely to accept a particular technology. The result further demonstrates that the concept of shared usage norms appears as a dynamic and continuously negotiated process. This media use patterns vary not only among different groups but also diachronically: as what respondents used to perceive as appropriate behaviour in the past (e.g. birthday celebrations offline/ real life) is no longer widely accepted as trendy. Therefore, we can recognise that specific birthday remembrance norms do exist and are deployed by users, but we cannot highlight stable and universally shared usage patterns as perceived online.

The study recommends the provision of free internet access in Nigeria and Africa to enable the development of digital social culture in the continent. Further study should be conducted on the proposed *Bicultural Convergence model* further to strengthen its propositions with regards to digital culture. There should also be further studies on the celebration of birthdays on other social media platforms to find the most widely acceptable and useful platform for online birthdays.

REFERENCES

Alhabash, S., & Ma, M. (2017). A tale of four platforms: Motivations and uses of facebook, twitter, instagram, and snapchat among college students? *Social Media + Society*, *3*(January-March), 1–13. doi:10.1177/2056305117691544

Baran, S. J. (2008). Introduction to mass communication: Media literacy and culture (5th ed.). New York: McGraw-Hill.

Castells, M., Fernandez-Ardevol, M., Qiu, J., & Sey, A. (2004). *The mobile communication society: A cross-cultural analysis of available evidence on the social use of wireless communication technology.* Annenberg Research Network on International Communication.

Deuze, M. (2015). A call for compassion in social media studies. *Social Media + Society*, *1–2*(1). Advance online publication. doi:10.1177/2056305115580333

Domingo, D. (2013). Follow them closely. *Social Media + Society*, *1–2*. Advance online publication. doi:10.1177/2056305115578134

Ekwenchi, O. C., Morah, D. N., & Adum, A. N. (2015). Smartphone usage on nigerian campuses: Who is doing what on whatsapp? *International Journal of Advanced Multidisciplinary Research Report*, *1*(1). http://rex.commpan.com/index.php/ijamrr/article/view/49/48

Ellison, N. B., Steinfield, C., & Lampe, C. (2007). The benefits of Facebook "friends:" Social capital and college students' use of online social network sites. *Journal of Computer-Mediated Communication*, *12*(4), 1143–1168. doi:10.1111/j.1083-6101.2007.00367.x

Facebook: Active users worldwide. (n.d.). Retrieved from www.statista.com

Farahbakhsh, R., Han, X., Cuevas, A., & Crespi, N. (2017). Analysis of publicly disclosed information in facebook profiles. arXiv:1705.00515v1.

Fiebert, M. S., Tilmont, L., & Warren, C. R. (2013). It's your birthday! Greetings as a function of gender and relationship status on facebook. *International Review of Social Sciences and Humanities*, *4*(2), 206–208. www.irssh.com

Internet world stats: Usage and population statistics. (n.d.). Retrieved from https://www.internetworld-stats.com/stats1.htm

Jenkins, H., Clinton, K., Purushotma, R., Robinson, A. J., & Weigel, M. (2007). *Confronting the challenges of participatory culture: Media education for the 21st Century*. The MacArthur Foundation.

Lenhart, A. (2009). Pew internet project data memo. *Pew Internet & American Life Project*, *2*, 17.

Mbanaso, U. M., Dandaura, E. S., Ezeh, G. N., & Iwuchukwu, U. C. (2015). *The use of social networking service among Nigerian youths between ages 16 and 25 years*. Retrieved from https://www.researchgate.net/publication/283726255 doi:10.1109/CYBER-Abuja.2015.7360513

Morah, D. N. (2012). Web 2.0 and nigerian press: Opportunities on facebook and twitter. *Journal of Communication and Media Research*, *4*(1), 153–167.

Morah, D. N., Ekwenchi C. O. & Chiaha A. I. (2019). Fears and realities: Investigating social media use for sustainable economic development in nigeria. *Transdisciplinary Agora for Future Discussions Journal, 1*(1), 22-33. Retrieved from https://www.magzter.com/US/TAFFDS,-Inc./Transdisciplinary-Agora-for-Future-Discussions-Journal/Education/

Morah, D. N., & Omojola, O. (2018). Social media use and entrepreneurship development in nigeria: Lagos and onitsha in focus. *International Journal of Advance Study and Research Work, 1*(5), 15–26.

Morah, D. N., Udeze, S. E., & Ekwenchi, O. C. (2019). Online engagements and nigerian polity: Exploring users reactions to election results on facebook. *International Journal of Advance Study and Research Work, 2*(5), 1–11.

Pempek, T. A., Yermolayeva, Y. A., & Calvert, S. L. (2009). College students' social networking experiences. *Journal of Applied Developmental Psychology, 30*(3), 227–238. doi:10.1016/j.appdev.2008.12.010

Social media stats Nigeria: September 2019-September 2020. (n.d.). Retrieved from https://gs.statcounter.com/social-media-stats/all/nigeria

Social media stats worldwide: September 2019-September 2020. (n.d.). Retrieved from https://gs.statcounter.com/social-media-stats

Utz, S. (2010). Show me your friends, and I will tell you what type of person you are: How one's profile, number of friends, and type of friends influence impression formation on social network sites. *Journal of Computer-Mediated Communication, 15*(2), 314–335. doi:10.1111/j.1083-6101.2010.01522.x

Uzochukwu, C. E., Morah, D. N., & Okafor, E. G. (2015). Coverage of child rights and protection issues: Analysis of selected broadcast media in Nigeria. *Nigerian Journal of Communication, 12*(1), 272–297.

Valenzuela, S., Park, N., & Kee, K. F. (2009). Is there social capital in a social network site? Facebook use and college students' life satisfaction, trust, and participation. *Journal of Computer-Mediated Communication, 14*(4), 875–901. doi:10.1111/j.1083-6101.2009.01474.x

Waldman, A. E. (2016). Privacy, sharing, and trust: The facebook study. *Case W. Res. L. Rev. 67*(193). Retrieved from https://scholarlycommons.law.case.edu/caselrev/vol67/iss1/10

Young, A. L., & Quan-Haase, A. (2009). Information revelation and internet privacy concerns on social network sites: A case study of facebook. In *Proceedings of the 4th international conference on communities and technologies* (pp. 265–274). New York: ACM. 10.1145/1556460.1556499

Zhang, J. (2010). Self-enhancement on a self-categorisation leash: Evidence for a dual-process model of first- and third-person perceptions. *Human Communication Research, 36*(2), 190–215. doi:10.1111/j.1468-2958.2010.01373.x

This research was previously published in the International Journal of Social Media and Online Communities (IJSMOC), 12(1); pages 40-52, copyright year 2020 by IGI Publishing (an imprint of IGI Global).

Chapter 61
#Childathlete:
Examining the Ways in Which Children are Being Presented and Perceived on Instagram

Fallon R. Mitchell
University of Windsor, Canada

Sarah J. Woodruff
University of Windsor, Canada

Paula M. van Wyk
University of Windsor, Canada

Sara Santarossa
University of Windsor, Canada

ABSTRACT

The present study aimed to examine the tone and focus of the conversation associated with #childathlete on Instagram. Additionally, the visual content of five child athlete Instagram accounts were analyzed to determine if fitspiration (e.g., exercise, healthy eating, inspiration, showcase strength, and empowerment) or objectification (e.g., emphasis of specific body parts, suggestive posing, or emphasis on appearance) were promoted. Using Netlytic, a text analysis was conducted to analyze the conversation surrounding #childathlete and the top five child athlete accounts (based on likes) that were managed by parents were selected for visual content analysis. The text analysis revealed that the conversation was positive in tone and focused on sport/exercise. Analysis of the visual content indicated that the child athlete accounts focused athleticism, activity, and fitness, with little presence of objectification. Future research should further explore social media as a strategy for promoting and improving physical activity among users.

DOI: 10.4018/978-1-6684-6307-9.ch061

INTRODUCTION

Social comparison theory (Festinger, 1954) suggests that one may engage in comparison with others to fulfill the basic human need for self-evaluation (Engeln-Maddox, 2005). Comparison to media ideals is often prominent among children (Harrison, 2001), as media ideals may be perceived as a goal against which one can evaluate their own appearance (Engeln-Maddox, 2005). However, engaging in (social) comparison with ideal images, such as *fitspiration* imagery (Tiggemann & Zaccardo, 2015), often results in individuals criticizing themselves, rather than the unrealistic ideal characteristics (Harrison, 2001). Thus, children who use Instagram may perceive the individuals depicted in *fitspiration* imagery as ideals, prompting children to engage in comparison, potentially leading to a host of negative outcomes (e.g., internalization of ideals, body dissatisfaction, eating pathology, and preoccupations with physical appearance; Engeln-Maddox, 2005; Fredrickson & Roberts, 1997; Mills et al., 2002). Furthermore, as children encounter the challenges and changes of puberty, such as increased fat deposition in women, the value placed on thin and toned bodies becomes more salient, as prior to puberty children are only in the process of internalizing ideals (Harrison & Hefner, 2006). Consequently, as children develop their adult bodies, they may become at an increased risk of problematic eating, depressive symptoms, and body dissatisfaction, among other negative mental health outcomes (Fredrickson & Roberts, 1997).

It has been suggested that girls, as young as five years of age, who compete in sports may be at a greater risk for unhealthy weight loss behaviours and eating disorders (Davison et al., 2002). The prevalence of weight concerns may be especially elevated among girls who participate in aesthetic sports (i.e., sports that promote leanness), such as cheerleading and gymnastics, as these activities often suggest or imply that appearance is important for success (Davison et al., 2002; Kong & Harris, 2015). Thus, aesthetic sports may place greater emphasis on achieving the ideal body (i.e., thin and toned; Davison et al., 2002; Kong & Harris, 2015). Weight concerns may also result from appearance based comments made by parents, coaches, and peers (Davison et al., 2002). The impact appearance based comments may have on health behaviours could be particularly important to consider within the context of child athletes on Instagram, as this social media site enables users to view, like, and comment on visual posts (Instagram, 2019). Thus, children's use of Instagram and exposure to *fitspiration,* in combination with participation in (aesthetic) sports, may place them at a greater risk for negative health consequences.

Although research has examined the presentation of children in traditional media (e.g., magazines, television), a paucity of literature has examined the ways in which children are being presented and perceived on social media, specifically Instagram. Therefore, the purpose of this study was:

1. To determine the tone of the conversation surrounding *#childathlete* (e.g., positive or negative), and the conversation focus (e.g., on appearance or athletics/healthy behaviour); and
2. To investigate if visual content from five child athlete Instagram accounts, managed by parents, were promoting *fitspiration* (depict exercise, healthy eating, inspiration, showcase strength and empowerment) or objectification (emphasizes specific body parts or features, depicts suggestive posing, or emphasizes appearance and the 'ideal' body).

BACKGROUND

Currently, literature has focused on social media's role in establishing body ideals that suggest women should be thin and toned (Tiggemann & Zaccardo, 2016) and men should be muscular (Carrotte et al., 2017). One trend that has contributed to the establishment of body ideals for women and men is *fitspiration* (Tiggemann & Zaccardo, 2016). On social media, *fitspiration* is often expressed using the hashtags *#fitspiration* (Tiggemann & Zaccardo, 2016) and/or *#fitspo* (Carrotte et al., 2017; Santarossa et al., 2016). As of May 29, 2019, *#fitspiration* had 17.7 million posts and *#fitspo* had 65.9 million posts, thus, indicating that these trends have widespread popularity (on July 5, 2020 there were 18.6 million posts and 70.5 million posts, respectively). *Fitspiration* (and its shortened counterpart *fitspo*) is an amalgamation of the words fitness and inspiration. As such, it may be defined as visual content (i.e., images and videos) that aims to motivate social media users to pursue healthier lifestyles (Abena, 2013). More specifically, *fitspiration* promotes healthy eating, exercise, self-care, strength, and empowerment (Santarossa et al., 2016; Tiggemann & Zaccardo, 2016). Tiggemann and Zaccardo (2016) and Santarossa et al. (2016) conducted content analyses of images collected from Instagram that were tagged with *#fitspiration* and *#fitspo*, respectively. Additionally, Santarossa et al. (2016) conducted network and text analyses to examine popular themes/text surrounding *#fitspo*. The authors of the two studies suggest that *fitspiration* tends to promote unrealistic and often unattainable body ideals, rather than fitness and healthy lifestyles (Santarossa et al., 2016; Tiggemann & Zaccardo, 2016). Through social comparison, users exposed to unrealistic and unattainable ideals promoted by *fitspiration* imagery may experience body dissatisfaction (Santarossa et al., 2016; Tiggemann & Zaccardo, 2016).

Further, *fitspiration* may indirectly promote objectification (e.g., content that emphasizes appearance, specific body parts, and suggestive posing; Santarossa et al., 2016; Tiggemann et al., 2009), and it may contribute to many negative outcomes, such as distorted body image (Tiggemann & Zaccardo, 2016) and disordered eating (Holland & Tiggemann, 2016). As suggested by objectification theory (Fredrickson & Roberts, 1997), objectification may be harmful as it treats an individual as a collection of body parts contributing to many potentially negative psychological consequences, such as reduced motivation, shame, anxiety, diminished bodily awareness, and depression (Fredrickson & Roberts, 1997), eating disorders (Fredrickson & Roberts, 1997; Mills et al., 2002), and body dissatisfaction (Harper & Tiggemann, 2008; Santarossa et al., 2016). Thus, the widespread use of *fitspiration* on social media (e.g., Instagram; Santarossa et al., 2016) combined with the rising popularity of social media among children may be problematic (boyd et al., 2011) and may result in various negative health consequences (Fredrickson & Roberts, 1997; Harper & Tiggemann, 2008; Mills et al., 2002; Santarossa et al., 2016). Consequently, social media companies have banned children younger than 13 years of age in response to the Children's Online Privacy Protection Act (COPPA), which regulates the information that commercial websites can collect and use about children (Federal Trade Commission [FTC], 1998). However, children continue to gain access to social media (boyd et al., 2011).

Often parents help their children falsify their age to circumvent the age restrictions put in place by social media companies (i.e., younger than 13 years of age), as they equate the age restrictions to a maturity rating, rather than a legal restriction (boyd et al., 2011). As parenthood consists of personal and social identities, parents may also confirm their identities and influence other's perceptions of them by managing their children's appearances, which may serve as a reflection of the parent rather than the child (Collett, 2005). Thus, posting about their children in a positive, aesthetically pleasing manner on social media may provide parents with the ability to use their child as a commodity to elicit positive perceptions of their parenting abilities. To help contextualize, among 27,534 participants, 70% reported using social networking sites (i.e., a subgroup of social media platforms); 96% of whom were 15-24 years old (Coyne et al., 2018). Additionally, the PEW Research Center found that 72% of adolescents (13-17 years) used Instagram (Anderson & Jiang, 2018). Granted, these findings are for individuals older than 13 years of age, and thus beyond the age restrictions listed for social media sites, it is still important to note the young age of users and the plausibility that they began having an online presence prior to when permitted. By circumventing age restrictions parents may be exposing their children to multiple risks (e.g., exposure to inappropriate content and cyberbullying; O'Keeffe & Clarke-Pearson, 2011), extending beyond the aforementioned use of their information by commercial websites. Individuals, including children, may process visual content as reality (Li et al., 2015) as they are unaware of how the image was actually constructed. Consequently, social media (e.g., Instagram), which shares visual content (Instagram, 2019) may become problematic when combined with certain types of imagery (e.g., *fitspiration*).

PRESENTATION OF CHILDREN IN THE MEDIA

Issues, Controversies, Problems

While it is important to outline the risks associated with children's exposure to *fitspiration,* examining how children are being presented in the media is another important perspective. Children being sexualized is of growing concern with media and commercial marketing playing a significant role (Bragg et al., 2011). Girls, in particular, have been subjected to immense sexualization by the media, as girls are frequently depicted in revealing clothing and provocative poses (Egan & Hawkes, 2008). Exposure to sexualized content may result in girls engaging in self-objectification, whereby they evaluate their bodies in an attempt to conform to society's standards for attractiveness (Zurbriggen et al., 2007). Consequently, self-objectification may teach girls to view their bodies in terms of sexual desirability, rather than health, wellness, or achievements (Zurbriggen et al., 2007).

METHODS

Using Netlytic (Gruzd, 2016), a text analysis was conducted to analyze the conversation surrounding *#childathlete*. To determine which child athlete Instagram accounts were to be included for further analysis, the output file created by Netlytic (Gruzd, 2016) was organized by likes, and the top five child athlete accounts (based on likes) that indicated they were managed by a parent (i.e., stated in the user's Instagram biography) were selected. A coding scheme was developed and implemented to analyze visual content from the five aforementioned Instagram accounts. Each method will be further discussed below.

Data Collection and Netlytic Analysis

All publicly available media on Instagram tagged with *#childathlete* were downloaded using Netlytic (Gruzd, 2016). Beginning on April 23rd, 2018 the data were collected for one month (31 days). Once data collection was complete, Netlytic (Gruzd, 2016) created an output file that recorded the link to the visual content, publication date, author of the post (who made the post), description of the post (containing

#childathlete), number of likes the post received, if an Instagram filter was used, and the geographical location of the author. Netlytic (Gruzd, 2016) collected, organized (by frequency), and filtered (removed filler words, such as 'of' or 'too') words/hashtags found within the *#childathlete* dataset to produce a list of meaningful words/hashtags. Furthermore, Netlytic (Gruzd, 2016) was used to analyze categories of words that represented broader concepts within the conversation surrounding *#childathlete*. The authors modified two of the existing Netlytic (Gruzd, 2016) categories: 'feelings (good)' and 'feelings (bad)'. 'Feelings (good)' was modified by adding the synonyms "inspire" and "empower" to represent the positive elements associated with the *fitspiration* (e.g., inspiration and empowerment; Santarossa et al., 2016; Tiggemann & Zaccardo, 2016). Additionally, the authors created four categories (i.e., 'sport/exercise', 'qualities', 'appearance', and 'food/eating behaviour') each containing 18 synonyms (see Table 1), which reflected key elements of *fitspiration* (e.g., physical activity, healthy eating, and strength; Santarossa et al., 2016; Tiggemann & Zaccardo, 2016) and objectification theory (e.g., emphasis on appearance; Santarossa et al., 2016). Depending on the author created categories, several synonyms were moved from the Netlytic (Gruzd, 2016) categories into the author created categories, according to relevance. For example, "courageous" was moved from 'feelings (good)' to 'qualities'. Based on the pre-determined synonyms, Netlytic (Gruzd, 2016) identified and counted which records (i.e., the number of captions and comments *#childathlete* appeared in) in the dataset belonged to each category.

Table 1. Description of text analysis categories

Category	Synonyms
Sport/Exercise	Gymnast***, crossfit, soccer, track, run***, cheer***, yoga, baseball, train***, workout, physical activity, exercise, practice, fitness, gym, competition***, perform***, active
Qualities	Flexible, strong, strength, smart, health***, unhealthy, aggressi***, daring, athlet***, determin***, energ***, skill***, competitive***, dedicate***, talent***, confid***, courage***, brav***
Appearance	Beaut***, chub***, cute, fat, fit, gorgeous, musc***, pretty, skinny, small, thin, tone, ugly, young***, short***, tall***, attractive, handsome
Food/Eating behaviour	Food, supplement, processed, junk, treat, diet, eating disorder, fruit, veg***, protein, carb***, restrict***, binge eating, electrolyte, macro***, cal***, snack, meal
Feelings (good)	Agreeable, amused, calm, charming, cheerful, comfortable, cooperative, delightful, eager, elated, empower, empowered, enchanted, encouraged, energetic, enthusiastic, excited, exuberant, fair, faithful, fantastic, fine, friendly, funny, gentle, glorious, good, great, happy, helpful, hilarious, inspire, jolly, joyous, kind, lively, lovely, lucky, nice, obedient, perfect, pleasant, proud, relieved, silly, smiling, splendid, successful, thankful, thoughtful, victorious, vivacious, witty, wonderful, zany, zealous
Feelings (bad)	Angry, annoyed, anxious, arrogant, ashamed, awful, bad, bewildered, bored, clumsy, creep, cruel, dangerous, defeated, defiant, depressed, disgusted, disturbed, dizzy, dull, embarrassed, envious, evil, fierce, flipped-out, foolish, frantic, frightened, grieving, grumpy, helpless, hungry, hurt, ill, itchy, jealous, jittery, lazy, lonely, mean, nasty, nervous, obnoxious, panicky, scary, selfish, sore, tense, terrible, testy, thoughtless, tired, troubled, upset, uptight, weary, worried

Note. *** Indicates truncation.

Image Selection and Coding of Visual Content

The output file produced by Netlytic (Gruzd, 2016) was sorted by likes, as likes may serve as quantitative evidence of popularity (Chae, 2017), and the top five child athletes (based on number of likes) who indicated their Instagram accounts were managed by a parent were selected for further analyses. The last

50 posts from each athlete's account ($N = 250$), beginning at the most popular post (based on likes) that was collected by Netlytic, were analyzed using the visual content coding scheme (Geurin-Eagleman & Burch, 2016; Gruzd, 2016); this number was deemed reasonably manageable by the authors.

A coding scheme similar to those used by Tiggemann and Zaccardo (2016) and Santarossa et al. (2016) was implemented for this study (Table 2). Visual content ($N = 250$) was coded according to content categories (i.e., 'action', 'food', 'objectification', or 'other'). The variables within the content categories were developed based on key elements of *fitspiration* (e.g., physical activity, healthy eating, inspiration, strength, and empowerment; Santarossa et al., 2016; Tiggemann & Zaccardo, 2016) and objectification theory (e.g., emphasis on appearance, specific body parts, and suggestive posing; Santarossa et al., 2016); the same visual content could be coded for multiple content categories. Visual content coded for 'action' was further coded for the presence of physical activity or posing (e.g., posed in fitness clothes), while visual content coded for 'objectification' was further coded for body size, suggestive posing, emphasis on specific body parts, or the absence of an individual's face/head. If the visual content depicted 'food', it was further coded as food (e.g., sandwich), supplement (e.g., protein bar), or health (i.e., healthy or unhealthy). Finally, posts were coded for 'other', which accounted for interactivity (e.g., the post prompted Instagram users to like the photo or follow the author), inspiration (e.g., the post encouraged users to improve their lives and make positive choices), focus of the visual content, type of shot, and size of the visual content.

Table 2. Description of coded variables

Content Category	Variable	Description	Intraclass Correlation Coefficient
Action	Overall Photo Type	Posing (fitness related, e.g., in fitness clothes or at the gym), posing (fitness unrelated), athletic action, food	0.98
	Body Function	Visual content focused on the ability to perform	1.00
	Active/Passive	The action the individual is carrying out in the visual content	0.93
Food	Type of Food	Supplement, processed foods, mixed (processed and not processed)	1.00
	Food Health	Food was healthy or unhealthy	1.00
Objectification	Muscularity	Presence or absence of muscle definition	1.00
	Body Size	Individual was rated as underweight, normal weight, overweight, or obese based on the body image assessment for obesity (BIA-O)	1.00
	Objectification	Presence or absence of elements of objectification	1.00
	Touch	Self-touching, touching others, being touched	0.84
	Genitals/buttocks	Focus of content	1.00
	Clothing	Presence or absence of clothes (e.g., unrevealing, bathing suit)	1.00
Other	Focus of Photo	Who/what the visual content emphasized (e.g., athlete, scenery)	1.00
	Type of Shot	The amount of the individual depicted (e.g., selfie, head shot, half body, full body)	0.88
	Size	The distance at which the visual content was taken (e.g., further from view, normal, close up)	1.00
	Interactivity	Visual content and/or caption cuing Instagram users to interact	1.00
	Inspiration	Presence of inspiration in the visual content and/or caption	1.00

Coding Reliability

A code book, with instructions and examples, was created and utilized by two coders to assess all visual content ($N = 250$). All coding was completed independently. Based on intraclass correlation coefficients (ICC), acceptable levels of agreement are generally between 0.40 and 0.75 (Fleiss, 1986). Specifically, for this study, the minimum acceptable value of an ICC was 0.70. Any variable with an ICC of less than 0.70 required the coders to meet with a moderator to discuss, and agree upon a final code. Table 2 indicates levels of agreement after all codes were fully agreed upon.

RESULTS

Text Analysis

Among the 254 records downloaded, there were 5,133 unique words. Of the 15 most frequently used words/hashtags, *#childathlete* was the most popular. However, *#childathlete* was excluded from analysis as it was the topic of this study. Consequently, *#gymnast* became the top word/hashtag with 54 messages (the number of messages the word/hashtag appeared in) and 54 instances (the number of times the word/hashtag appeared; see Table 3). Additionally, Netlytic (Gruzd, 2016) distributed words/phrases into the categories: 'sport/exercise', 'qualities', 'appearance', 'food/eating behaviour', 'feelings (good)', and 'feelings (bad)'. 'Sport/exercise' was the largest category accounting for 44.6% ($n = 242$) of words/phrases (Figure 1).

Table 3. Most frequently used words associated with #childathlete (N = 254)

Term	Number of Messages	Percentage of Total Records	Number of Instances	Percentage of Total Records
#gymnast	54	21.3%	54	21.3%
#gymnastics	52	20.5%	52	20.5%
#athlete	42	16.5%	42	16.5%
#strong	37	14.6%	37	14.6%
#fitkids	29	11.4%	29	11.4%
#flexible	27	10.6%	28	11.0%
#fun	26	10.2%	27	10.6%
#kidsofinstagram	24	9.4%	24	9.4%
#instagood	24	9.4%	24	9.4%
today	23	9.1%	24	9.4%
#trainhard	23	9.1%	24	9.4%
#littlegymnast	22	8.7%	22	8.7%
#gymnasticgirl	22	8.7%	37	14.6%
#gymnastlife	22	8.7%	22	8.7%
#igkids	21	8.3%	21	8.3%

Figure 1. Categories of words/phrases associated with #childathlete posts (N = 254)

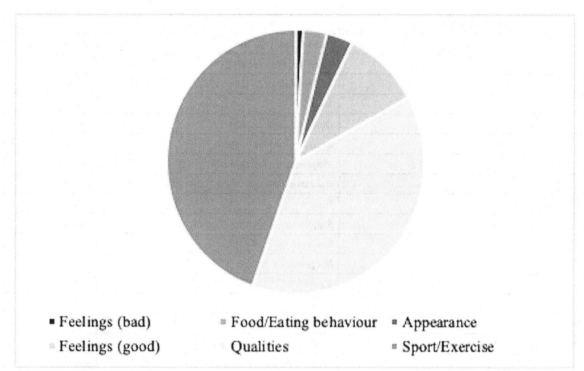

- Feelings (bad)   Food/Eating behaviour   Appearance
- Feelings (good)   Qualities   Sport/Exercise

Coding of Visual Content

Of the total visual content ($N = 250$), the majority ($n = 170$; 68.0%) depicted the athlete as the focus of the photo, in a posed position ($n = 136$; 54.4%), containing athletic markers ($n = 73$; 53.7%). Refer to Table 4 for further details regarding the visual content.

CONCLUSION

This study examined the conversation associated with *#childathlete* to determine the associated tone and focus of the conversation. Additionally, visual content from the top five child athlete Instagram accounts were analyzed to determine if *fitspiration* (e.g., exercise, healthy eating, inspiration, showcase strength and empowerment) or objectification (e.g., emphasis of specific body parts or features, suggestive posing, or appearance) was being promoted. Using the 254 downloaded records and 250 visual content items, the results were broken into text and visual content analyses.

Interpretation of the text analysis indicates a positive conversation surrounded *#childathlete*, which focused on athletics, suggesting those using the hashtag may have been promoting healthy lifestyles. As appearance comprised a small portion of the conversation and sport/exercise accounted for a much larger portion it is suggested that individuals using *#childathlete* were not focused on promoting ideal bodies. Thus, the findings of this study suggest that *#childathlete* may encourage healthy lifestyles (Abena, 2013), as 'sport/exercise' and 'qualities' were the largest categories and the majority of the most

Table 4. Content analysis/coding scheme of visual content (N = 250)

Variable (N = 250; 100%)	Details	n (%)
Photo type (N = 250; 100.0%)	Posed (fitness related)	73 (53.7)
	Posed (not fitness related)	63 (46.3)
	Athletic action	92 (36.8)
	Food	1 (0.4)
	Other (e.g., animals, scenery)	21 (8.4)
	Image depicted the full body	187 (74.8)
	Image depicted half the body	57 (22.8)
	Head shot/selfie	6 (2.4)
Food (n = 10; 4.0%)	Food	7 (70.0)
	Supplement	3 (30.0)
	Processed	7 (70.0)
	Not processed	1 (10.0)
	Mixed	2 (20.0)
	Healthy	2 (20.0)
	Unhealthy	8 (80.0)
Body function (n = 103; 41.2%)	Aerobic and anaerobic endurance	11 (10.7)
	Muscle strength and endurance	30 (29.1)
	Joint flexibility	16 (15.5)
	Energy efficiency and power	46 (44.7)
Active/Passive (N = 250; 100.0%)	Active in sport	87 (34.8)
	Passive in sport	20 (8.0)
	Active non-sport	15 (6.0)
	Passive non-sport	128 (51.2)
Muscularity (N = 250; 100.0%)	Little to no definition	179 (71.6)
	Visible definition	71 (28.4)
	High level of definition	0 (0.0)
Objectification (N = 250; 100.0%)	Posed in a sexy manner	9 (3.6)
	A specific body part is the main focus	0 (0.0)
	Face/head is not clearly visible	0 (0.0)
Interactivity (n = 108; 43.2%)	Cue to like photo	2 (1.9)
	Cue to follow author page/company	6 (5.6)
	Cue to tag friends	1 (0.9)
	Cue to comment	85 (78.7)
	Cue to purchase/use a coupon	6 (5.6)
	Other (e.g., cue to vote)	8 (7.4)
Inspiration (n = 56; 22.4%)	Inspiration related to fitness	34 (60.7)
	Inspiration not related to fitness	22 (39.3)

frequently used terms (e.g., *#gymnast*, *#strong*, and *#flexible*) emulated these categories. The promotion of exercise and healthy lifestyles on a global platform, such as Instagram, may be beneficial considering 23% of adults and 81% of children (11-17 years) do not achieve recommendations for physical activity worldwide (WHO, 2019). Social media allows users to engage in social comparison, which may act as a social incentive for users to increase physical activity (Zhang et al., 2016). Future research should examine using *fitspiration* imagery in physical activity/exercise interventions to determine if this type of imagery may result in behaviour change. Despite a more in-depth analysis being needed to determine if changes in physical activity levels occurred, the possibility that social media influences its users' behaviours (Zhang et al., 2016), combined with its potential to reach large audiences (Guo & Saxton, 2014; Pegoraro, 2010), may create an effective medium for promoting physical activity on a global scale due to increased social support (Rote et al., 2015; Zhang et al., 2015). However, research that examines the effectiveness of social media based physical activity interventions is inconclusive and should be further explored to determine if social media interventions result in sustained behaviour changes (Maher et al., 2014; Rote et al., 2015).

The analysis of the most frequently used terms demonstrated that *#childathlete* was primarily associated with other hashtags, which may be used on Instagram to foster online communities (Saxton et al., 2015) by connecting users who share common interests and similar characteristics (Bruns & Burgess, 2011; Veale et al., 2015). Within the text analysis, children and gymnastics emerged as common themes through the use of hashtags, such as *#fitkids, #kidsofinstgram, #gymnast, and #gymnastics*. By utilizing multiple hashtags to engage with different online communities, in this case communities of/for children and gymnasts, users may have been able to interact with accounts that extended beyond those who followed them, subsequently expanding their reach and possibly enticing other users to follow their account (Bruns & Burgess, 2011). A resultant would be increasing their perceived popularity and influence on users who follow hashtags, such as *#childathlete*.

The creation of a community specific to children may be cause for some concern, as Instagram requires users to be at least 13 years of age (Instagram, 2019). Instagram and COPPA have age restrictions in place to protect children's privacy (FTC, 1998) among other potential dangers, such as exposure to inappropriate content and cyberbullying (O'Keeffe & Clarke-Pearson, 2011). Regardless of such age restrictions, parents may be creating and managing accounts dedicated to their children, as was demonstrated by all accounts analyzed in this study. As children are already considered a vulnerable population, sharing information about them may further increase their vulnerability by exposing them to unknown users in a public setting (Minkus et al., 2015). When parents post about their children, they may be indirectly impacting their children's lives (Minkus et al., 2015). Posting about children makes their information publicly available, potentially compromising their privacy, exposing them to predators, and inhibiting their ability to hide their online presence later in life (Minkus et al., 2015). Future research should consider interviewing parents to gain a better understanding of their knowledge regarding social media and why they fabricate the age of their children.

It is unlikely that parents were intentionally exposing their children to the dangers of social media; rather parents were likely attempting to market their children to gain popularity and endorsement deals, mimicking the marketing of children that has been demonstrated within promotions, advertisements, and media (Cook, 2004). Often when children are used in marketing, they are used in a manner that either exploits or empowers them (Cook, 2004). Traditionally news media emphasize exploitation, while marketers emphasize empowerment (Cook, 2004). However, parents use of children varies between exploitation and empowerment (Cook, 2004). As 'sport/exercise' and 'qualities' were the largest categories and the majority of the most frequently used terms (e.g., *#gymnast*, *#strong*, and *#flexible*) were related to these categories, it may be suggested that parents were portraying their children in a mostly empowering manner. Associating young athletes, especially girls who may not be considered strong or athletic, with qualities such as strength may encourage sport participation by suggesting they can be powerful (Heinecken, 2016). Future research should specifically investigate this dichotomy.

Furthermore, by using hashtags, parents are able to engage with and promote their children in various online communities, subsequently expanding the reach of their child's Instagram account and potentially gaining new followers (Bruns & Burgess, 2011). Often Instagram accounts that have numerous followers may be perceived as popular and as having significant influence (De Veirman et al., 2017). Thus, increasing the number of followers could lead to the child becoming a social media influencer (i.e., someone with a sizeable network of users following them; De Veirman et al., 2017). As a result of having widespread reach, social media influencers may receive endorsement deals from a variety of brands (De Veirman et al., 2017). Thus, using multiple hashtags may be a strategic approach on behalf of the parents to gain influencer status for their child(ren) and the potential benefits that accompany such status. Although this study was able to support that parents may be creating and managing Instagram accounts for their children, future research should conduct a more in-depth analysis to better understand the parents' intentions for creating accounts dedicated to their children. According to impression management research, parents may use their children in two ways: as a prop (i.e., the child is used as a display and contributes to a mother's appearance), and as an associate (i.e., the child's behaviour is used as a reflection of the mother's ability and self-presentation; Collett, 2005). By using their children as props or associates, parents are able to establish and verify their roles as good parents (Collett, 2005). Additionally, a more in-depth text analysis could provide a more comprehensive understanding of the context of the conversation within these communities, as this study viewed the words out of context. Thus, determining if the communities aimed to share information about children, acting as an informational source, or if they were communities of children with Instagram accounts.

Another theme that emerged from the most frequently used terms was gymnastics (e.g., *#gymnast* and *#gymnastics*), which is often referred to as an aesthetic sport (i.e., a sport that emphasizes appearance and thinness; Slater & Tiggemann, 2011). As the athletes who participate in aesthetic sports, such as gymnastics, are predominantly girls, the prevalence of gymnastics within the most frequently used terms may indicate that the *#childathlete* community consisted predominantly of girls. However, due to being beyond the scope of this study, the gender of the users participating in the conversation surrounding *#childathlete* was not analyzed. Future research should consider conducting a gendered analysis of the users involved with hashtags, such as *#childathlete*, on Instagram and other social media (e.g., Twitter) to determine if the prevalence of aesthetic sports is specific to *#childathlete* and/or Instagram.

Another potential explanation for the emergence of gymnastics, rather than other sport, is that Instagram and gymnastics both emphasize aesthetics (concern with appearance). Aesthetic sports have been linked with negative health consequences (e.g., self-objectification, body image disturbance, disordered eating) due to the emphasis they place on appearance (Davison et al., 2002; Kong & Harris, 2015; Slater & Tiggemann, 2011). The paucity of appearance-centered conversation may suggest that within the *#childathlete* community, gymnastics was being promoted for its athletic endeavours rather than aesthetics. Shifting away from a focus on aesthetic-based success may be beneficial for many athletes, as focusing on athletics may promote healthy behaviours (e.g., physical activity/exercise), while discouraging unhealthy behaviours (e.g., body dissatisfaction, eating disorders). Thus, the conversation associated with *#childathlete* seems to suggest *fitspiration* promotes healthy lifestyles.

Although high levels of objectification have been associated with aesthetic sports and linked with increased internalization of thin ideals and self-objectification among athletes (Varnes et al., 2014), the majority of visual content did not promote objectification. Rather, in line with the text analysis, the visual content more strongly aligned with the promotion of positive attributes, such as activity, athleticism, and fitness. Overall, the indications from this study were that appearance and objectification were not prevalent within the text and visual analyses, rather there was a greater focus on athletics.

However, even the small presence of objectification may be of concern, as this study examined accounts that were dedicated to children. According to Instagram, visual content that depicts children as nude or partially nude may be removed for safety purposes, as this content could be used in unforeseen ways (Instagram, 2019). Allowing visual content that depicts children in an objectified manner to be posted on Instagram may indirectly and unknowingly expose children to predators, commercial exploitation, and/or surveillance, among other dangers (Minkus et al., 2015). As the results of this study indicate that some of the visual content was perceived as objectifying, it may be suggested that Instagram's screening of visual content should be improved to better protect children. However, it is also possible that images that were perceived, and thus reported, by other users or were flagged by Instagram, were already removed. Thus, our findings may be conservative. Furthermore, this study utilized two coders to analyze the visual content. Thus, the results reflect only two perspectives. Future research should consider conducting focus groups to gather more diverse and comprehensive perceptions of the visual content, as perceptions of objectification may vary by individual.

Nonetheless this study was able to identify that the text and visual content promoted healthy behaviours, such as physical activity, more than objectification. However, it is unknown if changes in behaviour occurred among users. Additionally, while this study may provide evidence that children were a topic of interest on Instagram, it remains unknown why children emerged as a theme, as this study was unable to determine the true valence of the words, as the words were viewed out of context. However, with the recent changes made to Instagram, Netlytic (Gruzd, 2016) is no longer able to collect data from Instagram making data collection for a more in-depth analysis difficult to complete using this method. Thus, this study was able to obtain and analyze data that are no longer easily accessible. Although more complex analyses could be conducted, the analyses selected for this study are a common approach within social media research and best addressed the research questions. Furthermore, while it was demonstrated within our sample selection that parents may manage Instagram accounts for their children, this study was unable to determine if those parents were knowledgeable about COPPA (FTC, 1998) and age restrictions for social media and/or if the account was truly managed by the parent.

As the popularity of social media continues to rise, additional research regarding children may be important. For example, investigating the impacts social media may have on children's development, in addition to better understanding the ways in which children are being presented and perceived online. *#childathlete* contradicted past findings regarding *fitspiration* by demonstrating low objectification and higher prevalence of athleticism, activity, and fitness focused content. Further, the dissociation of aesthetic sports from objectification and aesthetic-based success through the promotion of athletic endeavours may enhance the athletes' health by reducing the importance of body ideals in aesthetic sports. Due to its widespread reach, social media may be a strategy for the promotion of physical activity, which could lead to increased physical activity levels and overall improved health and well-being.

REFERENCES

Abena, C. (2013). *From thinspo to fitspiration: How social media could be affecting your body image.* College Fashion. https://www.collegefashion.net/college-life/from-thinspo-to-fitspiration-how-social-media-could-be-affecting-your-body-image/

Anderson, M., & Jiang, J. (2018). *Teens, social media & technology 2018.* Pew Research Center. http://publicservicesalliance.org/wp-content/uploads/2018/06/Teens-Social-Media-Technology-2018-PEW.pdf

boyd, D., Hargittai, E., Schultz, J., & Palfrey, J. (2011). Why parents help their children lie to Facebook about age: Unintended consequences of the 'Children's Online Privacy Protection Act'. *First Monday, 16*(11). https://journals.uic.edu/ojs/index.php/fm/article/view/3850/3075

Bragg, S., Buckingham, D., Russell, R., & Willett, R. (2011). Too much, too soon? Children, 'sexualization' and consumer culture. *Sex Education, 11*(3), 279–292. doi:10.1080/14681811.2011.590085

Bruns, A., & Burgess, J. E. (2011). The use of Twitter hashtags in the formation of ad hoc publics. In *Proceedings of the 6th European Consortium for Political Research (ECPR) General Conference.* University of Iceland. https://eprints.qut.edu.au/46515/1/The_Use_of_Twitter_Hashtags_in_the_Formation_of_Ad_Hoc_Publics_%28final%29.pdf

Carrotte, E. R., Prichard, I., & Lim, M. S. C. (2017). "Fitspiration" on social media: A content analysis of gendered images. *Journal of Medical Internet Research, 19*(3), e95. doi:10.2196/jmir.6368 PMID:28356239

Chae, J. (2017). Virtual makeover: Selfie-taking and social media use increase selfie-editing frequency through social comparison. *Computers in Human Behavior, 66*, 370–376. doi:10.1016/j.chb.2016.10.007

Collett, J. L. (2005). What kind of mother am I? Impression management and the social construction of motherhood. *Symbolic Interaction, 28*(3), 327–347. doi:10.1525i.2005.28.3.327

Cook, D. T. (2004). *The commodification of childhood: The children's clothing industry and the rise of the child consumer.* Duke University Press. doi:10.1215/9780822385431

Coyne, P., Santarossa, S., Polumbo, N., & Woodruff, S. J. (2018). The associations of social networking site use and self-reported general health, mental health, and well-being among Canadians. *Digital Health, 4*. Advance online publication. doi:10.1177/2055207618812532

Davison, K. K., Earnest, M. B., & Birch, L. L. (2002). Participation in aesthetic sports and girls' weight concerns at ages 5 and 7 years. *International Journal of Eating Disorders, 31*(3), 312–317. doi:10.1002/eat.10043 PMID:11920993

De Veirman, M., Cauberghe, V., & Hudders, L. (2017). Marketing through Instagram influencers: The impact of number of followers and product divergence on brand attitude. *International Journal of Advertising, 36*(5), 798–828. doi:10.1080/02650487.2017.1348035

Egan, R. D., & Hawkes, G. L. (2008). Endangered girls and incendiary objects: Unpacking the discourse on sexualization. *Sexuality & Culture, 12*(4), 291–311. doi:10.100712119-008-9036-8

Engeln–Maddox, R. (2005). Cognitive responses to idealized media images of women: The relationship of social comparison and critical processing to body image disturbance in college women. *Journal of Social and Clinical Psychology*, *24*(8), 1114–1138. doi:10.1521/jscp.2005.24.8.1114

Federal Trade Commission (FTC). (1998). *Children's Online Privacy Protection Rule ("COPPA")*. Federal Trade Commission. https://www.ftc.gov/enforcement/rules/rulemaking-regulatory-reform-proceedings/childrens-online-privacy-protection-rule

Festinger, L. (1954). A theory of social comparison processes. *Human Relations*, *7*(2), 117–140. doi:10.1177/001872675400700202

Fredrickson, B. L., & Roberts, T. A. (1997). Objectification theory: Toward understanding women's lived experiences and mental health risks. *Psychology of Women Quarterly*, *21*(2), 173–206. doi:10.1111/j.1471-6402.1997.tb00108.x

Geurin-Eagleman, A. N., & Burch, L. M. (2016). Communicating via photographs: A gendered analysis of Olympic athletes' visual self-presentation on Instagram. *Sport Management Review*, *19*(2), 133–145. doi:10.1016/j.smr.2015.03.002

Gruzd, A. (2016). *Netlytic: Software for automated text and social network analysis*. Netlytic. http://Netlytic.org

Guo, C., & Saxton, G. D. (2014). Tweeting social change: How social media are changing nonprofit advocacy. *Nonprofit and Voluntary Sector Quarterly*, *43*(1), 57–79. doi:10.1177/0899764012471585

Harper, B., & Tiggemann, M. (2008). The effect of thin ideal media images on women's self-objectification, mood, and body image. *Sex Roles*, *58*(9-10), 649–657. doi:10.100711199-007-9379-x

Harrison, K. (2001). Ourselves, our bodies: Thin-ideal media, self-discrepancies, and eating disorder symptomatology in adolescents. *Journal of Social and Clinical Psychology*, *20*(3), 289–323. doi:10.1521/jscp.20.3.289.22303

Harrison, K., & Hefner, V. (2006). Media exposure, current and future body ideals, and disordered eating among preadolescent girls: A longitudinal panel study. *Journal of Youth and Adolescence*, *35*(2), 146–156. doi:10.100710964-005-9008-3

Heinecken, D. (2016). Empowering Girls Through Sport? Sports Advice Books for Young Female Readers. *Children's Literature in Education*, *47*(4), 325–342. doi:10.100710583-016-9281-7

Holland, G., & Tiggemann, M. (2016). A systematic review of the impact of the use of social networking sites on body image and disordered eating outcomes. *Body Image*, *17*, 100–110. doi:10.1016/j.bodyim.2016.02.008 PMID:26995158

Instagram. (2019). *Help Center*. Instagram. https://help.instagram.com

Kong, P., & Harris, L. (2015). The sporting body: Body image and eating disorder symptomatology among female athletes from leanness focused and nonleanness focused sports. *The Journal of Psychology*, *149*(2), 141–160. doi:10.1080/00223980.2013.846291 PMID:25511202

Li, H., Boguszewski, K., & Lillard, A. S. (2015). Can that really happen? Children's knowledge about the reality status of fantastical events in television. *Journal of Experimental Child Psychology, 139*, 99–114. doi:10.1016/j.jecp.2015.05.007 PMID:26094241

Maher, C. A., Lewis, L. K., Ferrar, K., Marshall, S., De Bourdeaudhuij, I., & Vandelanotte, C. (2014). Are health behavior change interventions that use online social networks effective? A systematic review. *Journal of Medical Internet Research, 16*(2), e40. Advance online publication. doi:10.2196/jmir.2952 PMID:24550083

Mills, J. S., Polivy, J., Herman, C. P., & Tiggemann, M. (2002). Effects of exposure to thin media images: Evidence of self-enhancement among restrained eaters. *Personality and Social Psychology Bulletin, 28*(12), 1687–1699. doi:10.1177/014616702237650

Minkus, T., Liu, K., & Ross, K. W. (2015). Children seen but not heard: When parents compromise children's online privacy. In *Proceedings of the 24th International Conference on World Wide Web* (pp. 776-786). International World Wide Web Conferences Steering Committee. 10.1145/2736277.2741124

O'Keeffe, G. S., & Clarke-Pearson, K. (2011). The impact of social media on children, adolescents, and families. *Pediatrics, 127*(4), 800–804. doi:10.1542/peds.2011-0054 PMID:21444588

Pegoraro, A. (2010). Look who's talking—athletes on Twitter: A case study. *International Journal of Sport Communication, 3*(4), 501–514. doi:10.1123/ijsc.3.4.501

Rote, A. E., Klos, L. A., Brondino, M. J., Harley, A. E., & Swartz, A. M. (2015). The efficacy of a walking intervention using social media to increase physical activity: A randomized trial. *Journal of Physical Activity & Health, 12*(6), S18–S25. doi:10.1123/jpah.2014-0279 PMID:25599378

Santarossa, S., Coyne, P., Lisinski, C., & Woodruff, S. J. (2016). #fitspo on Instagram: A mixed-methods approach using Netlytic and photo analysis, uncovering the online discussion and author/image characteristics. *Journal of Health Psychology*, 1–10. doi:10.1177/1359105316676334 PMID:27852889

Saxton, G. D., Niyirora, J., Guo, C., & Waters, R. (2015). #AdvocatingForChange: The strategic use of hashtags in social media advocacy. *Advances in Social Work, 16*(1), 154–169. doi:10.18060/17952

Slater, A., & Tiggemann, M. (2011). Gender differences in adolescent sport participation, teasing, self-objectification and body image concerns. *Journal of Adolescence, 34*(3), 455–463. doi:10.1016/j.adolescence.2010.06.007 PMID:20643477

Taveras, E. M., Rifas-Shiman, S. L., Field, A. E., Frazier, A. L., Colditz, G. A., & Gillman, M. W. (2004). The influence of wanting to look like media figures on adolescent physical activity. *The Journal of Adolescent Health, 35*(1), 41–50. doi:10.1016/S1054-139X(03)00370-7 PMID:15193573

Tiggemann, M., Polivy, J., & Hargreaves, D. (2009). The processing of thin ideals in fashion magazines: A source of social comparison or fantasy? *Journal of Social and Clinical Psychology, 28*(1), 73–93. doi:10.1521/jscp.2009.28.1.73

Tiggemann, M., & Zaccardo, M. (2015). "Exercise to be fit, not skinny": The effect of fitspiration imagery on women's body image. *Body Image, 15*, 61–67. doi:10.1016/j.bodyim.2015.06.003 PMID:26176993

Tiggemann, M., & Zaccardo, M. (2016). 'Strong is the new skinny': A content analysis of #fitspiration images on Instagram. *Journal of Health Psychology, 23*(8), 1003–1011. doi:10.1177/1359105316639436 PMID:27611630

Varnes, J. R., Stellefson, M. L., Miller, M. D., Janelle, C. M., Dodd, V., & Pigg, R. M. (2014). Body esteem and self-objectification among collegiate female athletes: Does societal objectification make a difference? *Psychology of Women Quarterly, 39*(1), 95–108. doi:10.1177/0361684314531097

Veale, H. J., Sacks-Davis, R., Weaver, E. R., Pedrana, A. E., Stoové, M. A., & Hellard, M. E. (2015). The use of social networking platforms for sexual health promotion: Identifying key strategies for successful user engagement. *BMC Public Health, 15*(1), 85. doi:10.118612889-015-1396-z PMID:25884461

World Health Organization (WHO). (2019). *Physical Inactivity: A Global Public Health Problem.* World Health Organization. https://www.who.int/dietphysicalactivity/factsheet_inactivity/en/

Zhang, J., Brackbill, D., Yang, S., Becker, J., Herbert, N., & Centola, D. (2016). Support or competition? How online social networks increase physical activity: A randomized controlled trial. *Preventive Medicine Reports, 4*, 453–458. doi:10.1016/j.pmedr.2016.08.008 PMID:27617191

Zhang, J., Brackbill, D., Yang, S., & Centola, D. (2015). Efficacy and causal mechanism of an online social media intervention to increase physical activity: Results of a randomized controlled trial. *Preventive Medicine Reports, 2*, 651–657. doi:10.1016/j.pmedr.2015.08.005 PMID:26844132

Zurbriggen, E. L., Collins, R. L., Lamb, S., Roberts, T. A., Tolman, D. L., & Ward, L. M. (2007). *Report of the APA Task Force on the Sexualization of Girls.* American Psychological Association. https://www.apa.org/pi/women/programs/girls/report-full.pdf

This research was previously published in the International Journal of Social Media and Online Communities (IJSMOC), 11(1); pages 1-14, copyright year 2019 by IGI Publishing (an imprint of IGI Global).

Chapter 62

Does Using Social Network Sites Reduce Depression and Promote Happiness?
An Example of Facebook–Based Positive Interventions

Sen-Chi Yu

National Taichung University of Education, Taichung City, Taiwan

ABSTRACT

Positive interventions based on theories in positive psychology have proven effective in contributing to well-being. Although college students frequently use social networking sites, few studies have investigated the use of these sites to facilitate positive interventions. For this research, two positive interventions, photo diaries and the expression of gratitude, were developed and implemented in Facebook using a randomized controlled trial. 136 college students were recruited and randomly assigned them to one of two experimental groups or a control group. Results indicated that photo diary reduced depression during the posttest stage, and these effects continued during the follow up stage. Concerning happiness, the photo diary presented no significant effects in the posttest but did present significant effects in the follow up. Expression of gratitude showed no significant effects on happiness in the posttest but did show significant effects in the follow up. The results of the study demonstrate that social networking sites can be used to implement positive interventions.

1. INTRODUCTION

In the last half century, psychology researchers have made significant progress in the treatment of negative emotions and mental illnesses. However, excessive focus on negative psychological factors can only mitigate symptoms; it cannot help patients foster positive psychological factors (Seligman et al., 2005). Suppose we consider where an individual's psychological state falls on a normal distribution. Psycholo-

DOI: 10.4018/978-1-6684-6307-9.ch062

gists generally concentrate on moving patients from the left (negative) side of the normal distribution to the middle mean; they have rarely explored techniques to move patients from the mean to the right (positive) side. Psychologists should not simply focus on treating mental illnesses; they should also strive to improve the mental well-being of patients and aid them in building more meaningful lives (Yu & Chou, 2009).

In view of this, Seligman promoted positive psychology during his term as president of the American Psychological Association and collated various past studies associated with positive emotions and happiness. Positive psychology can be roughly divided into three areas: positive emotions, positive characters, and positive institutions. These areas are associated with three corresponding lifestyles: the pleasant life, engaged life, and meaningful life (Seligman et al., 2005).

Research involving positive psychology has made progress in domains such as psychology, education, and business administration (Seligman et al., 2006). Methods that teach individuals how to enhance their positive thinking, emotions, and behaviors based on positive psychology are called positive interventions (PIs) or positive activity interventions (PAIs). A number of studies (Duckworth et al., 2005; Lyubomirsky, Sheldon & Schkade, 2005; Seligman et al., 2005) have established that PIs can effectively enhance happiness or reduce depression as well as improve internal locus of control and willingness to participate. One advantage of PI methods is that individuals can practice them independently. Moreover, PIs are less costly and time-consuming than psychotherapy and can swiftly improve moods while decreasing the degree of stigmatization, all without adverse effects. Nonetheless, although PIs have proven effective in laboratory scenarios, researchers have advised that understanding contextual factors associated with PIs, such as continued practice, motivations, and person-activity fit, is likely to further enhance the effectiveness of these methods (Biswas-Diener, 2011). Sheldon and Lyubomirsky (2004) also emphasized the importance of person-activity fit in PIs, which increases the personal motivation of individuals to participate in PIs and prevents hedonic adaption from impairing PI effectiveness.

In recent years, the proportion of college students with mental health issues has remained high and even continued to increase. Thirty percent of college students reported having felt depressed in the last year (Wickham, 2016). Another survey in Taiwan revealed that almost a quarter of college students had experienced depression (Yu & Hsu, 2013). Finally, a survey conducted by the Center for Collegiate Mental Health found almost half of college students attended co-counseling for mental health concerns, and 30.3% of college students who sought mental health services in 2013 reported having seriously considered a suicide attempt at some point in their life; this was up from 23.8% in 2010 (Novotney, 2014). These surveys show that mental health issues of college students cannot be ignored. Studies have showed that positive and negative emotions are in fact independent dimensions rather than opposite poles. That is, the present of one do not indicate the absence of the other (Lucas et al., 2003). In view of this, the absence of depression does not guarantee happiness. PIs are likely to be an effective tool in improving the mental health of college students, as they use positive psychology to promote mental health and develop resistance against negative life events.

Although that gratitude is a universal characteristic that transcends cultural, little research has focused on cross-cultural influences on gratitude (Wang et al., 2015). Parks & Biswas-Diner (2013) pointed that expressing gratitude have sometimes adverse effect when used by collectivism culture students. For collectivism culture (e.g. Taiwan, Singapore, China, and Japan) expressing gratitude publicly can make individuals discomfited, particularly if their cultural norm is to avoid attracting attention. Traditional gratitude intervention demands the thanker express their gratitude face-to-face, which may make the thanker embarrassment. Previous research has found that computer mediated communication, such as

Facebook or Twitter, can reduce the anxiety of face-to-face communication (Yu, 2015). However, little attention has been given to the use SNS for gratitude intervention.

We also believe that in terms of the person-activity fit for college student, social network sites (SNSs) such as Facebook are an effective medium for implementing PIs. The internet has become an integral part of modern life, and many PIs and psychological experiments have already been conducted over the internet (Mitchell et al., 2009; Seligman et al., 2005; Yu & Hsu, 2013). Visiting an SNS is one of the most common reasons for internet use, and Facebook is currently the most popular SNS (Hew, 2011). For college students, Facebook is an essential means of communication. On average, a college student uses Facebook for 2.70 hours a day and has 365.16 Facebook friends (Yu, 2015). At present, few studies have used Facebook to perform PI research.

We posit that the multiple functions of SNSs facilitate PI implementation for the following reasons. First, SNSs are a part of everyday life for college students; thus, using SNSs to perform PIs will minimize interference with student lifestyle and should also increase student willingness to participate in the study. Second, although some PIs are effective, they must be performed deliberately and may be challenging to implement in everyday life. In contrast, if SNS-based PIs are effective, they can exert more extensive and lasting influence since SNSs are already being used by college students. Third, the built-in functions of SNSs (such as wall posting and the like button) can record the frequency of interactions and the amount of feedback, which expedites data collection. Lastly, by using a preexisting SNS the researchers avoid the need to set up a separate website, which reduces costs and also interferes with participants to a lesser degree.

For this study, we developed two PIs using Facebook and adopted a quasi-experimental design to explore whether Facebook-based PIs can increase happiness and reduce depression.

2. LITERATURE REVIEW

2.1. A Brief Introduction to Positive Psychology

The field of positive psychology explores three domains: the pleasant life, the engaged life, and the meaningful life (Seligman et al., 2005). The pleasant life pertains to positive emotions experienced by an individual in their past, present, and future (Duckworth et al., 2005). Positive emotions are indicative of well-being and have been shown to be associated with strong work performance, higher productivity, greater marriage satisfaction, better social relationships, and better physical health (Layous et al., 2011).

The engaged life involves the use of positive traits in life, such as strengths and virtues. In their book, "Character Strengths and Virtues: A Handbook and Classification," Peterson and Seligman categorized the 24 character strengths (i.e. curiosity, love of learning, judgment, originality, emotional intelligence, perspective, bravery, diligence, genuineness, kindness, loving and being loved, loyalty, fairness, leadership, self-control, prudence, modesty, appreciation of beauty and excellence, gratitude, hope, sense of purpose, mercy, humor, and zest) that are universal and across all aspects of life (Peterson & Seligman, 2004). Specifically, they categorized the 24-character strengths into 6 major virtues: wisdom and knowledge, courage, love, justice, temperance, and transcendence.

The third domain, meaningful life, refers to a person whose lifestyle is devoted to serving positive institutions bigger than him or herself, from which the individual can utilize positive traits. Devoting time and energy to matters greater than oneself often brings increased meaning to life (Duckworth et al., 2005). However, there are a wide range of institutions that individuals can choose to serve, and different individuals generally choose to serve different positive institutions such as family, community, a religious organization, or work (Seligman, 2002).

2.2. A Brief Introduction to Positive Interventions

Based on positive psychology, positive interventions (PIs) are designed to teach individuals how to increase positive thinking, behaviors, and emotions. Duckworth et al. (2005) reported that techniques of cultivating positive psychology can be used to rebuff depression, anxiety, and anger. Below, we explain several PI-related studies, which are also summarized in Table 1.

Research has already shown that PIs can reduce depression. For example, Grant, Salcedo, Hynan, Frisch, and Puster (1995) conducted a reading therapy PI with 16 clinically depressed patients and no control group. Upon completion of the PI, 13 of the participating patients displayed significantly reduced depression. Seligman had individuals with severe depression participate in a PI called Three Good Things, which required the participants to keep a journal and explain three good things that happened each day. After 15 days, the CES-D score of participants decreased by 16.7, and 94% of participants felt more relieved (Seligman, 2002). In a week-long randomized controlled trial (RCT), Seligman et al. (2005) randomly assigned 411 subjects with mild depression to one of six groups, including a control group and five different PI groups. The PIs included 1. gratitude visit, 2. three good things in life, 3. you at your best, 4. using signature strengths, and 5. identifying signature strengths. Results from this experiment indicated a greater sense of well-being and reduced depression in PI groups, the effects of which remained even after the completion of PI activities. Gratitude visit contributed to greater well-being for a month, whereas the effects of three good things in life and using signature strengths in a new way lasted for as long as six months. The results of this study revealed that even simple self-guided activities can have long-term benefits for individuals with mild depression.

Some Internet-based PIs were also proposed. Redzic et al. (2014) conducted an Internet-delivered health promotion, named organic programming (OP), on seven classes of ninth-grade student participants over two semesters. OP is a psycho-educational program designed to teach skills related to positive psychology and depression prevention. The participants evaluated OP was helpful, interesting, fun, and reduced risk for depression. However, no empirical statistical data was provided in this study. Besides, Cohn, Pietrucha, Saslow, Hult, and Moskowitz (2014) developed Affective Health to Improve Adherence (DAHLIA), a self-paced online intervention for type 2 diabetes that teaches positive affect skills such as savoring, gratitude, and acts of kindness. Forth-nine participants were randomized to the five-week DAHLIA course or an emotion-reporting wait-list control. The results showed that DAHLIA participants showed a significantly greater decrease in depression than controls. With regard to the use of PIs to foster a sense of well-being, Emmons and McCullough conducted an RCT with a gratitude intervention. Results showed that the participants in the gratitude group felt better about their overall life, regarded the coming week more optimistically, and perceived better connections to other people. In addition, those participants displayed more positive emotions and fewer negative emotions (Emmons & McCullough, 2003).

Lyubomirsky, Sheldon, and Schkade performed two PIs, *count your blessings* and *kindness,* to investigate the effect of intervention duration and frequency. The results showed that the participants that had counted their blessings once a week felt happier, which led the researchers to conclude that less frequent interventions are probably more able to prevent habituation. For the *kindness* intervention, the results revealed that participants who performed all acts of kindness within a single day were happier (Lyubomirsky et al., 2005). Mitchell et al. (2009) conducted a study over the internet, in which participants were asked to practice a six-step procedure for problem solving. Results demonstrated that the continuous promotion of well-being is feasible and that interventions related to well-being can be effectively introduced via the internet.

In conclusion, PIs can reduce depression and contribute to well-being. However, for college students, the aforementioned interventions can be modified for SNS implementation in order to improve person-activity fit. For example, the brief writing intervention used by Burton and King (2004) can be modified to internet writing in order to better conform to daily habits of college students. That is to say, nowadays college students rarely keep diaries on paper; they prefer to keep them online (e.g. on Facebook or a blog). For the expression of gratitude intervention, past research required participants to write a letter of gratitude then visit their benefactor in person and read their letter to them. However, expressing gratitude online is easier, and not having to speak in person could reduce anxiety and thus increase the willingness of students to participate in the intervention activity. Furthermore, expressing gratitude face to face may be less suitable in some cultures, such as collectivist cultures, the norms of which are to avoid attention (Parks & Biswas-Diener, 2013).

Thus, using the internet to show gratitude may be more appropriate in some contexts. Moreover, using Facebook to facilitate PIs can cut down on research costs related to the maintenance of an external website, such as that used in the study by Mitchell el al (2009). In addition, college students already use Facebook often, thus this platform will present less interference with daily life and will increase student willingness to participate. In view of the aforementioned reasons, this study proposed and investigated the use of SNS-based PIs.

2.3. The Relationships Between Internet, SNS Use and Well-Being

Prior research has shown that the use of internet may detract from face-to-face relationships and reduce well-being (Kraut et al., 1998). But some skeptics have argued that perhaps people with lower well-being are more likely to use internet, rather than internet causing lower well-being (Yu & Chou, 2015). The Internet has many social applications (e.g., Facebook, Instagram) that encourage users to build and maintain on-line social networks. Through these SNS people could fulfill their social needs. Studies have found that Facebook use has a positive impact on subjective well-being and adjustment of college students (Ellison et al., 2007; Steinfield et al., 2008).

2.4. Person–Activity Fit of Positive Intervention

No single intervention is effective for everybody. A proper fit between a person and a particular happiness-increasing activity is likely to influence the effectiveness of an intervention (Sin, Della Porta, & Lyubomirsky, 2011). The preference, interests, values, motivation, and strengths of an individual might influence the participation and duration of intervention. Therefore, contextual factors such as personal lifestyle, interests and values should be considered when designing positive intervention (Biswas-Diener, 2011). For example, a college student may find it more rewarding to keep a journal on social network sites (such as blogs, Facebook, Instagram) than on traditional paper-based journal when performing the "Three good thing" intervention.

Although person-activity fit influences the effectiveness of positive intervention, research on person-activity fit are rarely investigated. Sin et al., (2011) found expressing gratitude may be a difficult and disadvantageous for depressed individuals, in contrast with non-depressed general population. Sheldon & Lyubomirsky (2004) also pointed that the effectiveness of positive intervention varied hugely from one individual to another and be influenced by each participant's needs and interests. Judging from these, positive interventions using SNSs should be feasible for college students since they were accustomed to use SNSs. Using SNSs to perform PIs will minimize disturbance with student daily life and should also increase student willingness to participate and maintain the activity.

From what has been discussed above, the hypotheses of this study are as follows:

1. Facebook -based PIs can reduce depression;
2. Facebook -based PIs can increase happiness.

Table 1. Summary of positive interventions

Author	Research Design	Results
Grant et al. Reading therapy	No control group	The depression of participants was reduced, and continued to display effects of intervention one week following the completion of intervention activities.
Seligman Three good things	No control group	The CES-D scores of the participants decreased by 16.7, and 94% of the participants felt more relieved.
Emmons & McCullough Gratitude intervention	RCT	The gratitude group felt better about their overall life, was more optimistic about the coming week, perceived better connections to other people, and displayed more positive emotions and fewer negative emotions.
Lyubomirsky et al. a. Count your blessings b. Kindness	RCT	a. Only the participants that counted their blessings once a week felt happier. b. Only the participants that performed all the acts of kindness within a single day felt happier.
Seligman et al. Five PIs	RCT	The PI participants experienced an increased sense of well-being and reduction of depression, the effects of which continued after the completion of the PIs.
Mitchell et al. Three stages in learning and practicing a for problem solving	RCT	The results demonstrated that the continuous promotion of well-being is feasible and that the well-being intervention can be effectively introduced via the internet.
Redzic et al. OP	No control group	The participants evaluated OP was helpful, interesting, fun, and reduced risk for depression
Cohn et al. DAHLIA	RCT	DAHLIA reduced depression

3. METHODS

3.1. Participants

The participants of this study were recruited from a university in Central Taiwan. After receiving consent from teachers, we explained experimental procedures and terms of confidentiality during breaks between classes, and students who were willing to participate filled out a consent form.

We recruited a total of 151 participants and randomly assigned them to one of two experimental groups or a control group. Of these, 136 completed the pretest, 128 completed the posttest, and 115 completed the follow-up test. Attrition rate of post-test and follow up stages were 5.88% and 15.44%, respectively. A coupon raffle was organized to encourage participation. Our study population included 34 male (25%), and 102 female (75%) students. The number of first-, second-, third-, and fourth-year students were 45 (33.1%), 35 (25.7%), 50 (36.7%), and 6 (4%), respectively. A survey that was administered prior to the start of the experiment indicated that all participants had used Facebook before prior to induction into the study.

3.2. Instruments

The instruments of this study included the General Happiness Scale and the Center for Epidemiologic Studies Depression Scale.

3.2.1. Center for Epidemiologic Studies Depression Scale (CES-D)

Currently one of the most widely adopted depression scales in the world, the CES-D scale (Radloff, 1977) has been translated and verified for reliability and validity in a number of languages. This study used the Chinese version (Yu & Yu, 2007), which contains 20 question items scored on a four-point Likert scale. The analytical results revealed that CES-D Cronbach's alpha equals .891, indicating good reliability.

3.2.2. General Happiness Scale

This study used the Chinese version of the General Happiness Scale (GHS) employed by Yu and Hsu (2013), which was translated from the GHS developed by Lyubomirsky and Lepper (1999). The original scale contains four question items scored on a seven-point Likert scale. We conducted item analysis based on results of the pretest. The analytical results revealed that the fourth question item used reverse wording showed poor psychometric properties. Eliminating this item would increase the reliability of the scale from 0.80 to 0.87. Therefore, we eliminated the fourth question item and kept the remaining three for research analysis.

3.3. Experimental Procedure

We adopted a randomized controlled trial (RCT) for this study. The experimental groups took a pretest prior to the start of the experiment and were then required to complete a Facebook-based PI over the course of two weeks. Immediately following completion of the PI, participants took a posttest, and four weeks following completion of the PI, participants completed a follow-up test. The control group also took pretest, posttest, and follow-up test, but did not undergo any type of intervention. Figure 1 illustrates the procedure of the experiment. The PIs were designed based on theories in positive psychology; the details of PIs are in Figure 1.

Figure 1. Participant flow through the study

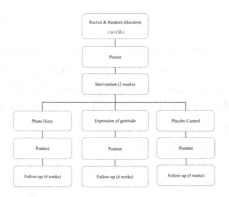

3.3.1. Experimental Group 1: Photo Diary

We designed this PI based on Character Strength and Virtues theory (Perterson & Seligman, 2004), "Three Good Thing" intervention (Seligman et al., 2005), and Savoring theory (Bryant & Veroff, 2007). We supposed that taking meaningful pictures is related to exercising some strengths and virtues such as creativity, spirituality, and the appreciation of beauty. Moreover, Facebook facilitates responses from friends and sharing with others, likely reduced negative emotions and promoting positive emotions.

Using the photo album function of Facebook, the participants were asked to post photos or videos that they felt were worth sharing and that made them happy in a personal album. Content could be related to department events, traveling, dates, cuisine, or shopping, and the participants were asked to record their reasons for choosing each photo or video, similar to a record of their lives, and to invite friends to respond with a "like". The purpose of this psychological assignment was to promote emotional sharing, social support, and happiness using self-disclosure.

3.3.2. Experimental Group 2: Expression of Gratitude

We designed this PI based on Character Strength and Virtues theory (Perterson & Seligman, 2004), "Gratitude visiting" intervention (Seligman et al., 2005), and Cultural concerns on gratitude (Parks & Biswas-Diner, 2013; Wang et al., 2015).

Participants in this group were asked to write a declaration of gratitude to someone on their Facebook wall, such as "I would like to thank...for the past two days because..." or "Something good happened today, and it was probably caused by..." The participants had to change this declaration every two to three days and invite their friends to respond with a "like". The purpose of this psychological assignment was to promote the expression of gratitude, which is a virtue mentioned in positive psychology, and to improve the positive emotional status of participants through this perception and expression of gratitude.

3.4. Statistical Analysis

We employed ANCOVA using the pretest scores as a covariate and the posttest and follow-up test scores as dependent variables.

4. RESULTS

To checks on the PI manipulations, we surveyed participants' number of photo diary post and expression of gratitude on post-test and follow-up stages. According to participants' self-report, for the photo diary part, the average number of shares in the experiment groups per week was 0.75 (SD =1.18) before the experiment and 6.00 (SD = 5.78) during the experiment. The results of the paired-t test indicate that the number of photo diary shares during the post-test stage was significantly higher than that in the pre-test stage (p<.05). This means that the subjects were indeed participating in the PI. During the follow-up stage, the subjects were not required to continue the PI. However, they shared an average of 1.40 (SD = 2.75) times per week, which is significantly higher than the average weekly number of shares during the pre-test stage (p < .05). This indicates that the subjects proactively integrated photo diaries into their daily lives.

With regard to the expression of gratitude, the subjects in the experiment groups expressed their gratitude 1.32 (SD = 2.23) times a week on average. During the experiment, this number increased to 6.93 (SD = 5.78). The results of the paired-t test show that the subjects expressed their gratitude more frequently during the post-test than during the pre-test stage (p < .05), which means that the subjects were indeed engaging in PI. During the follow-up stage, the subjects were not required to continue the PI. However, they expressed their gratitude an average of 1.41 (SD = 2.78) times per week, which is higher than the average weekly number of shares during the pre-test stage, but the difference was not significant (p > .05).

In contrast, during the experiment, the subjects in the control group shared their photo diaries an average of 0.60 times per week and expressed their gratitude an average of 1.18 (SD = 3.54) times per week.

Table 2 and 3 summarizes the results in terms of outcome scores and treatment effect. The details of the analytical results were as follows.

4.1. Depression

Experimental group 1 (the Photo diary) displayed reduced depression in the posttests, and this reduction continued through to the follow up as shown in Figure 2 and Table 2.

Concerning the homogeneity of variance between the experimental group 1 and control groups, the Levene test results found homogeneity held for both posttest and follow-up stage (p > .05). For the posttest stage, ANCOVA results revealed a significant difference between the two groups (F (1, 81) = 10.542, p =< .05) and a medium effect size (eta squared = .115 > .059). For the follow up stage ANCOVA results also revealed a significant difference between the two groups ((F (1, 81) = 6.892p = 0.05) and a medium effect size (eta squared = 0.077 > 0.059).

Experimental group 2 (expression of gratitude) did not present significant effects on depression in the posttest (F(1, 74 = 3.326, p > .05) and in the follow up (F(1, 74 = 3.086, p > .05) as shown in Figure 2 and Table 3.

Figure 2. CESD means by group

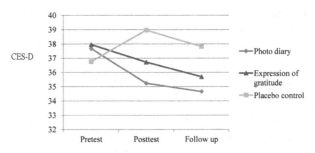

Table 2. CES-D treatment effect of Experimental Group 1

	Contrast Group	**Experimental Group 1**	**Treatment Effect**
Pretest	36.76	37.67	
Posttest	38.96	35.23	F(1,81) = 10.542 p = .002**
Follow up	37.36	34.65	F(1,81) = 6.892 p =.010*

*p < .05 **p < .01

Table 3. CES-D treatment effect of Experimental Group 2

	Contrast Group	**Experimental Group 2**	**Treatment Effect**
Pretest	36.76	37.95	
Posttest	38.96	37.29	F(1,74) = 3.326 p = .072
Follow up	37.36	36.19	F(1,74) = 3.080 p = .083

*p < .05

4.2. Happiness

With regard to happiness, Experimental Group 1 presented no significant effects in the posttest but displayed significant effects in the follow up, as shown in Figure 3 and Table 4. Concerning the homogeneity of variance between the experimental group 1 and control groups, the Levene test results found homogeneity held for both posttest and follow-up stage (p >.05). For the posttest stage,

For the posttest stage, ANCOVA results did not reach the level of significance (F (1, 80) = 0.198, p > .05). In the follow up stage, ANCOVA results revealed a significant difference between the two groups (F(1,80) = 5.353, p < .05) and a medium effect size (eta squared=0.062>0.059).

Expression of gratitude showed no significant effects on happiness in the posttest but did show significant effects in the follow up, as shown in Figure 3 and Table 4. Concerning the homogeneity of variance between the experimental group 2 and control groups, the Levene test results found homogeneity held for both posttest and follow-up stage (p >.05). For the posttest stage, ANCOVA results did not reach the level of significance (F (1, 74) = 3.174, p > .05). In the delayed follow up stage, ANCOVA results revealed a significant difference between the two groups ($F(1, 74) = 3.174$, $p < 0.05$) and a low effect size (eta square $= .051 > .010$).

Figure 3. GHS means by group

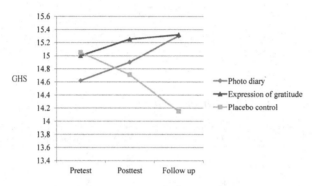

Table 4. GHS treatment effect of Experimental Group 1

	Contrast Group	**Experimental Group 1**	**Treatment Effect**
Pretest	15.05	14.62	
Posttest	14.71	14.90	$F(1, 80) = .198$ $p = .657$
Follow up	14.15	15.30	$F(1, 80) = 5.353$ $p = .023*$

*$p < .05$

Table 5. GHS treatment effect of Experimental Group 2

	Contrast Group	**Experimental Group 2**	**Treatment Effect**
Pretest	15.05	15.00	
Posttest	14.71	15.25	$F(1, 74) = 3.174$ $p = .406$
Follow up	14.15	15.32	$F(1, 74) = 4.289$ $p = .042*$

*$p < .05$

5. DISCUSSION

On the whole, the experimental photo diary intervention proved significant effect in relieving depression. Positive interventions rely on the participant's voluntary completion of intervention tasks; therefore, it's vital that the acceptance and daily habits of the participants are taken into consideration when designing a positive intervention. College students are already in the habit of using SNSs every day, so incorporating SNSs interfered with their daily lives the least, which made them more willing to complete the interventions. The results of this study indicate that merging positive interventions with the SNSs that college students were already accustomed to using on a daily basis is an effective approach. Sin, Della, and Lyubomirsky (2011) stated that positive intervention experiments are generally more effective when the participants are accepting of them. Biswas-Diner (2011) also indicated that the contextual factors (personal and situational) of positive interventions influence experiment effectiveness. Moreover, Sin et al. (2011) suggested that factors such as duration of intervention, continued practice, person-activity fit, and motivation can affect the overall effectiveness of interventions for individuals. In summary, positive interventions must consider contextual factors such as personal interests and values to be effective. Therefore, positive interventions that integrate SNSs are found to be suitable for college students.

Experimental Group 1 displayed significantly reduced depression in both the posttest and the follow up. We infer that sharing photos can instantly reduce loneliness, increase the frequency of interpersonal interactions, and reduce depression with lasting effects. As the CES-D scale covers a wide range of aspects, including happiness, loneliness, and interpersonal relationships, it was able to reveal effects in all areas. This result is similar to those obtained by Grant et al. (1995), Seligman (2002), and Seligman et al. (2005) indicates that the depression-relieving effects of positive interventions not only apply to individuals suffering from depression but can also apply to their non-depressed counterparts. Mitchell et al. (2009) also found that positive interventions utilizing the internet as a medium could relieve depression. Unlike the website that Mitchell et al. (2009) specifically designed for their experiment, the results of this study show that SNSs are also effective.

Seligman proposed that positive psychology includes three major domains: the pleasant life, the engaged life, and the meaningful life. The pleasant life encompasses life satisfaction, positive emotions, and optimism; the engaged life emphasizes the display of strengths and virtues, and the meaningful life involves dedication to positive organizations. We believe that sharing photos can increase positive emotions, which is a sub-factor of the pleasant life. Furthermore, completing the photo sharing assignment is associated with the display of strengths and virtues such as creativity, spirituality, and the appreciation of beauty. Many of the participants' photos were of themselves with family members, classmates, or club members or contained a visual record of their activities, which can also be considered dedication to a positive organization (Yu & Chou, 2009).

In this study, the PI for Experimental Group 1, photo diary, required participants to share bits of their life on Facebook in the form of photos or videos of themselves interacting with classmates or friends. Without the internet, sharing diaries and photos would have required face-to-face invitations, thereby limiting the number of invitations. However, the photo album and chat functions of Facebook enable subjects to actively remind their friends to look at updates, which increases the frequency of sharing. Furthermore, sharing conventional paper photos is static, whereas sharing photos on SNSs can be a dynamic and continual process. For example, after an individual views photos on Facebook, they can use the Like button or leave a message, which may induce further communication. This can lead to continual discussions that last for several days, which may explain why the PI for Experiment Group 1 presented lasting effects on depression and happiness.

The PI used by Experimental Group 1 in this study did not present significant effects on happiness until the follow up. We thus infer that photo sharing activities may require some time in order to initiate changes. For example, after participants posted their photos, the number of responses was sometimes low initially; however, as the number of responses grew steadily, effects on happiness became more apparent. Furthermore, the GHS covers peer comparison (e.g. "Compared with most of my peers, I consider myself happy?") as well as one's own happiness (e.g. "In general, I consider myself a very happy person?"). For this reason, the assessment of happiness does not only include one's own status. As the numbers of likes and responses grow, participants may feel that their happiness is gradually surpassing that of their peers.

The expressions of gratitude generated by experimental group 2 also showed a significant influence on promoting happiness at follow up stage. This indicates that the expression of gratitude on an SNS is effective for from collectivist-culture individuals (such as Chinese culture). Parks and Biswas-Diener (2013) indicated that public face-to-face expressions of gratitude are less desirable in collectivist cultures, which tend to emphasize group harmony rather than individual uniqueness. In such cultures, emotions are restrained and not directly expressed, and abasement and humility are required with regard to positive events. Chinese culture considers abasement to be an expression of modesty, humbleness, and politeness. Modesty and self-effacement are important virtues (Noronha, 2002). Face-to-face expressions of gratitude require the thanker to loudly recite their gratitude in front of the subject of gratitude (Seligman et al., 2005). In collectivist cultures, this can create embarrassment and discomfort for both the thanker and the subject of gratitude. It also violates the life principle of abasement and can therefore have the opposite effect and significantly reduce the willingness of participants to complete the intervention. In contrast, expressing gratitude via SNS is less direct and less discomforting.

6. RESEARCH LIMITATIONS

The use of the internet to perform psychological experiments is limited by the popularity of internet use and the participants' ability to use the internet. Facebook users are mostly teenagers and middle-aged-and-under adults. The PIs used by this study are less suitable for individuals that do not have previous Facebook experience, such as older adults.

Neither of the PIs used in this study displayed significant effects in the GHS posttest. We believe that this result is associated with the item properties of the GHS, which emphasize personal happiness compared to that of peers but do not include many other aspects of happiness. Researchers may wish to consider other instruments to measure happiness or positive emotions in future studies, such as the Positive and Negative Affect Schedule.

Concerning the length of intervention procedures, the length of this experiment was two weeks, which may be too short to estimate long term effects. We suggest that the experiment period be extended in future research. Researchers can also encourage participants to make sharing or gratitude assignments a habit, which may prolong the effects of the experiment.

Next, applying two or more interventions may increase the beneficial effects observed in this experiment. However, when exploring the advantages of using two or more types of interventions, the order of the interventions and the interaction effects of the interventions must be taken into account.

REFERENCES

American College Health Association. (2012). *American college health association-national college health assessment II: Reference group executive summary fall 2011*. Hanover, MD: American College Health Association.

Biswas-Diener, R. (2011). Applied positive psychology: Progress and challenges. *The European Health Psychologist, 13,* 24–26.

Bryant, F. B., & Veroff, J. (2007). *Savoring: A new model of positive experience.* New Jersey, NJ: Lawrence Erlbaum Associations.

Burton, C. M., & King, L. A. (2004). The health benefits of writing about intensely positive experiences. *Journal of Research in Personality, 38*(2), 150–163. doi:10.1016/S0092-6566(03)00058-8

Cohn, M. A., Pietrucha, M. E., Saslow, L. R., Hult, J. R., & Moskowitz, J. T. (2014). An online positive affect skills intervention reduces depression in adults with type 2 diabetes. *The Journal of Positive Psychology, 9*(6), 523–534. doi:10.1080/17439760.2014.920410 PMID:25214877

Duckworth, A. L., Steen, T. A., & Seligman, M. E. P. (2005). Positive psychology in clinical practice. *Annual Review of Clinical Psychology, 1*(1), 629–651. doi:10.1146/annurev.clinpsy.1.102803.144154 PMID:17716102

Ellison, N. B., Steinfield, C., & Lampe, C. (2007). The benefits of Facebook "friends": Social Capital and College Students' Use of Online Social Network Sites. *Journal of Computer-Mediated Communication, 12*(4), 1143–1168. doi:10.1111/j.1083-6101.2007.00367.x

Emmons, R. A., & McCullough, M. E. (2003). Counting blessings versus burdens: An experimental investigation of gratitude and subject well-being in daily life. *Journal of Personality and Social Psychology, 84*(2), 377–389. doi:10.1037/0022-3514.84.2.377 PMID:12585811

Grant, G. M., Salcedo, V., Hynan, L. S., Frisch, M. B., & Puster, K. (1995). Effectiveness of quality of life therapy for depression. *Psychological Reports, 76*(3), 1203–1208. doi:10.2466/pr0.1995.76.3c.1203 PMID:7480486

Hew, F. K. (2011). Students' and teachers' use of Facebook. *Computers in Human Behavior, 27*(2), 662–676. doi:10.1016/j.chb.2010.11.020

Kraut, R., Lundmark, V., Patterson, M., Kiesler, S., Mukopadhyay, T., & Scherlis, W. (1998). Internet paradox: A social technology that reduces social involvement and psychological well-being? *The American Psychologist, 53*(9), 1017–1031. doi:10.1037/0003-066X.53.9.1017 PMID:9841579

Layous, K., Chancellor, J., Lyubomirsky, S., Wang, L., & Doraiswamy, M. (2011). Delivering happiness: Translating positive psychology intervention research for treating major and minor depressive disorders. *Journal of Alternative and Complementary Medicine (New York, N.Y.), 17*(8), 675–683. doi:10.1089/acm.2011.0139 PMID:21721928

Lucas, R. E., Diener, E., & Larsen, R. J. (2003). Measuring positive emotions. In S. J. Lopez & C. R. Snyder (Eds.), *Positive psychological assessment: A handbook of models and measures* (pp. 201–218). Washington, DC: American Psychological Association. doi:10.1037/10612-013

Lyubomirsky, S., & Lepper, H. (1999). A measure of subjective happiness: Preliminary reliability and construct validation. *Social Indicators Research, 46*(2), 137–155. doi:10.1023/A:1006824100041

Lyubomirsky, S., Sheldon, K. M., & Schkade, D. (2005). Pursuing happiness: The architecture of sustainable change. *Review of General Psychology, 9*(2), 111–131. doi:10.1037/1089-2680.9.2.111

Mitchell, J., Stanimirovic, R., Klein, B., & Vella-Brodrick, D. (2009). A randomised controlled trial of a self-guided internet intervention promoting well-being. *Computers in Human Behavior*, *25*(3), 749–760. doi:10.1016/j.chb.2009.02.003

Noronha, C. (2002). *The theory of culture-specific total quality management: Quality management in Chinese regions*. Great Britain, England: Palgrave Macmillan. doi:10.1057/9780230512351

Novotney, A. (2014). Students under pressure. *Monitor on Psychology*, *45*(8), 36–41.

Parks, A., & Biswas-Diener, R. (2013). Positive Interventions: Past, present and future. In T. Kashdan & J. Ciarrochi (Eds.), *Bridging acceptance and commitment therapy and positive psychology: A practitioner's guide to a unifying framework* (pp. 140–165). Oakland, CA: New Harbinger.

Peterson, C., & Seligman, M. E. P. (2004). *Character strengths and virtues: A handbook and classification*. Washington, DC: American Psychological Association.

Radloff, L. S. (1977). The CES-D scale: A self-report depression scale for research in the general population. *Applied Psychological Measurement*, *1*(3), 385–401. doi:10.1177/014662167700100306

Redzic, N. M., Taylor, K., Chang, V., Trockel, M., Shorter, A., & Taylor, C. B. (2014). An Internet-based positive psychology program: Strategies to improve effectiveness and Engagement. *The Journal of Positive Psychology*, *9*(6), 494–501. doi:10.1080/17439760.2014.936966

Seligman, M. E. P. (2002). *Authentic happiness: Using the new positive psychology to realize your potential for lasting fulfillment*. New York, NY: Free Press.

Seligman, M. E. P., Rashid, T., & Parks, A. C. (2006). Positive psychotherapy. *The American Psychologist*, *61*(8), 774–788. doi:10.1037/0003-066X.61.8.774 PMID:17115810

Seligman, M. E. P., Steen, T. A., Park, N., & Peterson, C. (2005). Positive psychology progress: Empirical validation of Intervention. *The American Psychologist*, *60*(5), 410–421. doi:10.1037/0003-066X.60.5.410 PMID:16045394

Sheldon, K. M., & Lyubomirsky, S. (2004). Achieving sustainable new happiness: Prospects, practices, and prescriptions. In A. Linley & S. Joseph (Eds.), *Positive psychology in practice* (pp. 127–145). Hoboken, NJ: John Wiley & Sons. doi:10.1002/9780470939338.ch8

Sin, N. L., Della Porta, M. D., & Lyubomirsky, S. (2011). Tailoring positive psychology interventions to treat depressed individuals. In S. I. Donaldson & M. J. N. Csikzentmihalyi (Eds.), *Applied positive psychology: Improving everyday life, health, schools, work, and society* (pp. 79–96). New York, NY: Routledge.

Steinfield, C., Ellison, N. B., & Lampe, C. (2008). Social capital, self-esteem, and use of online social network sites: A longitudinal analysis. *Journal of Applied Developmental Psychology*, *29*(6), 434–445. doi:10.1016/j.appdev.2008.07.002

Wang, D., Wang, Y. C., & Tudge, J. R. H. (2015). Expressions of Gratitude in Children and Adolescents. *Journal of Cross-Cultural Psychology*, *46*(8), 1039–1058. doi:10.1177/0022022115594140

Wickham, J. (2016). College students and depression. Mayo Clinic. Retrieval from http://mayoclinichealthsystem.org/hometown-health/speaking-of-health/college-students-and-depression

Yu, S. C. (2015). Happiness or addiction: An example of Taiwanese college students' use of Facebook. *International Journal of Technology and Human Interaction, 11*(4), 26–40. doi:10.4018/IJTHI.2015100102

Yu, S. C., & Chou, C. (2009). Does authentic happiness exist in cyberspace? Implications for understanding and guiding college students' Internet attitudes and behaviors. *British Journal of Educational Technology, 40*(6), 1135–1138. doi:10.1111/j.1467-8535.2008.00880.x

Yu, S. C., & Hsu, W. H. (2013). Applying structural equation modeling methodology to test validation: An example of cyberspace positive psychology scale. *Quality & Quantity, 47*(6), 3423–3434. doi:10.100711135-012-9730-3

Yu, S. C., & Yu, M. M. (2007). Comparison of Internet-based and paper-based questionnaires in Taiwan using multi-sample invariance approach. *Cyberpsychology & Behavior, 10*(4), 501–507. doi:10.1089/cpb.2007.9998 PMID:17711357

This research was previously published in the International Journal of Technology and Human Interaction (IJTHI), 16(3); pages 56-69, copyright year 2020 by IGI Publishing (an imprint of IGI Global).

Chapter 63
Profiling the Users of High Influence on Social Media in the Context of Public Events

Lu An

Center for Studies of Information Resources, Wuhan University, China & School of Information Management, Wuhan University, China

Junyang Hu

School of Information Management, Wuhan University, China

Manting Xu

School of Information Management, Wuhan University, China

Gang Li

Center for Studies of Information Resources, Wuhan University, China

Chuanming Yu

Zhongnan University of Economics and Law, China

ABSTRACT

The highly influential users on social media platforms may lead the public opinion about public events and have positive or negative effects on the later evolution of events. Identifying highly influential users on social media is of great significance for the management of public opinion in the context of public events. In this study, the highly influential users of social media are divided into three types (i.e., topic initiator, opinion leader, and opinion reverser). A method of profiling highly influential users is proposed based on topic consistency and emotional support. The event of "Jiankui He Editing the Infants' Genes" was investigated. The three types of users were identified, and their opinion differences and dynamic evolution were revealed. The comprehensive profiles of highly influential users were constructed. The findings can help emergency management departments master the focus of attention and emotional attitudes of the key users and provide the method and data support for opinion management and decision-making of public events.

DOI: 10.4018/978-1-6684-6307-9.ch063

INTRODUCTION

Public events often trigger a lot of reports and online discussions. Many users express their opinions on social media (Sharma & Lbansal, 2015). High influential users play an important role in guiding the online public opinion of events and can be divided into three types. The first type of users frequently expresses their opinions on an event. The posts that they generate often receive a lot of likes, retweets and comments and are marked as "popular posts" by Sina Weibo, a well-known microblogging platform in China. The "popular posts" is a function of the Sina Weibo platform. The platform calculates the heat value of each microblog post on the topic, and sorts the posts according to the heat value. "Popular posts" are those at the top of the list, which can be obtained directly from the platform (Sina Weibo, 2014). In this study, this type of users is called "topic initiators".

The second type of users obtains much attention from netizens, thus forming a high influence and leading the public opinion, namely the "opinion leaders". The posts published by the "topic initiators" often trigger a lot of discussion, but their views may not necessarily be approved. However, the posts by "opinion leaders" are more likely to be supported by others (Bamakan et al., 2019). Opinion leaders are identified based on the topic initiators. According to the spiral of silence theory, the formation of public opinion is a spiral process in which one side is more and more vocal while the other side is more and more silent (Noelle-Neumann, 1974). With the passage of time, some netizens do not agree with the "mainstream opinion" and dare to express their different opinions. Then the "silent majority" may respond positively, and their new opinions may gain more support. Users who express the new opinion "reverse" the mainstream opinion on the event, and are also high influential users. This type of users is named as "opinion reverser".

The three types of high influential microblog users shape the public opinion in different manners, i.e., to attract, lead or reverse the attention of the public. To identify and profile the three types of high influential users can help the event management departments understand the evolution patterns of the public opinion and discover the key nodes in the social network. It is also of significance to reveal the relationship between the users' basic attributes and their influence and whether users' behaviors are associated with their support. Thus, the research questions of this study are (1) to divide the high influential microblog users into three roles, i.e., topic initiators, opinion leaders and opinion reversers and to propose their identification methods; (2) to profile the three kinds of high influential users; and (3) to reveal the correlations among the users' basic attributes and microblog attributes. As the event of Dr. Jiankui He editing infants' genes aroused a tsunami of public opinion, this study took the event as the investigated case.

The opinion initiators launch salient topics and the opinion leaders promote the consistency of public opinion, which facilitates the formation of the spiral of silence. The opinion reversers break the consistent opinion and bring about anti-spiral of silence. The contribution of this study is to propose the quantitative methods of identifying the key nodes in the process of the spiral of silence and anti-spiral of silence. The research findings can help the emergency management departments guide the public opinion in a timely manner.

BACKGROUND

The Identification of High Influential Users on Social Media

High influential users are also known as opinion leaders, innovators, prestigious or authoritative actors (Bouguessa & Romdhane, 2015). They are often seen as experts in a field (Liu et al., 2014). Finding opinion leaders is an important task in many fields (Aleahmad et al., 2016). Some scholars distinguished opinion leaders, influencers, and discussants according to the types of user behaviors and their influence (Jabeur, Tamine, & Boughanem, 2012). High influential users were also divided into creators and communicators of emerging topics (Li et al., 2014), or classified according to the content that they communicate and their rights (Xiao et al., 2014). Quercia et al. (2011) differentiated popular, influential, listener, highly-read and star users based on users' cognition and psychological behaviors. Wu (et al., 2011) used the Twitter Lists to divide high influential users into organizations, media, celebrities, and blogs.

Although existing studies have considered the degree of support of users when identifying high influential users of social media, they rarely examine the topic consistency of microblog posts and comments. There is a phenomenon that the comment content of commenters is emotionally supportive, but the comment content is not related to the original post. In this study, when identifying high influential users of social media, the comments that are not related to the topics of the original posts are removed to ensure the topic consistency between posts and their comments.

Existing studies on the indicator system of identifying high influential users usually consider retweets, mentions (@), the number of fans/original posts/replies and the total number of posts (Cha et al., 2010). Jin and Wang (2013) also measured user influence through the closeness and intermediary of the user network structure. The characteristic indicators varied in different studies. Bigonha et al. (2011) used betweenness centrality, eigenvector centrality, in-degree, the Twitter follower–followee ratio, mentions, replies, retweets and other indicators to determine user influence. Räbiger et al. (2015) adopted following, retweets, comments, mentions, user centrality and quality of tweets to measure user influence.

The existing studies on the characteristic indicators of identifying high influential users usually consider many characteristics of high influential users. This study combines the user's own influence with the effect of comments, and explores the influence of commenters.

Profiling the Users of Social Media

User profiling is to obtain the users' attributes and behaviors to understand the users' interests, needs, rules, settings, and other information (Araniti et al., 2003). Farnadi et al. (2016) used the machine learning model to infer the user's age, gender, and personality characteristics according to the content of the posts and various behavior dynamics. Lee et al. (2014) built user profiles based on their twitter timeline and activities at different time. Lakiotaki et al. (2011) constructed and improved the user profiles through the user's feedback results.

In the process of profiling social media users, the existing studies seldom focus on the special situation of public events, and do not divide the identified high influential users into different levels. In this study, the users' personal attributes are first obtained from their microblog homepage, and the users' profiles are constructed and improved according to the users' opinions on the event and the subsequent influence, i.e., the users' focus on the topics and the degree of support that they receive.

Topical and Sentiment Analyses of Microblogging

Topic models are widely used to identify topics of microblogging. It is found that the combination of a topic model and context information can achieve better results in topic extraction (Zhou and Zhang, 2018). The Biterm topic model proposed by Yan et al. (2013) transforms the document into co-occurrence word pairs, and directly simulates the generation process of the co-occurrence mode of all the words in the corpus to learn the topics in the short text. It overcomes the problem of information sparseness of microblogging and considers the semantic relationship between words. The model can better explain the content of microblogging than traditional topic models and can effectively adapt to the short text. Thus, this study uses the Biterm topic model to identify the topics of microblog posts and comments.

Sentiment analysis was proposed by Pang et al. (2002). The common method mainly includes machine learning methods (such as decision tree, support vector machine, neural network, and Bayesian network) and dictionary-based methods (Hu et al., 2013). Support vector machine (SVM) was first proposed by Vapnik (2000). It aims to improve the generalization ability of the learning machine by seeking the minimum structural risk, and to obtain good statistical patterns in the case of a small number of samples. It is found that the SVM has better performance than other methods in the task of sentiment analysis (Hajmohammadi, 2013; Karanasou et al., 2015; Huang et al.,2015). Thus, this study adopts the SVM technique to perform sentiment analysis of microblogging.

THEORIES AND METHODS

The Spiral of Silence Theory

According to the spiral of silence theory (Noelle-Neumann, 1974), with the passage of time, individuals with majority opinions are more and more active in expressing their opinions, while individuals with minority opinions tend to be silent under the pressure of public opinion. However, social media platforms support anonymous activities. People do not necessarily hide their true thoughts on the Internet, but may freely express their opinions and support the minority. Finally, the opinion of the minority can even reverse the opinion of the majority, forming the "anti-spiral of silence" (Zhu et al., 2018). One of the research tasks of this study is to identify high influential users. Based on the concept of anti-spiral of silence, users with different viewpoints but great influence as events develop are to be identified and are named as "opinion reversers".

Data Collection and Preprocessing

Taking the event of "Jiankui He editing the infants' genes" as an example, this study used "gene editing infant" as the keyword to obtain the content and comments of 154 popular microblog posts between November 1, 2018 and February 28, 2019 on the Sina Weibo platform. Generally speaking, only users who receive enough comments are likely to become high influential users. Thus, the posts with fewer than 100 comments were removed, and finally 42,959 comments of 138 microblog posts were obtained.

The jiebaR package was used for word segmentation. The original dictionary was expanded with *Sogou Daily Vocabulary, Sogou Online Popular New Words, Sogou Gene Vocabulary, Sogou Cell Biology Vocabulary, and Sogou Ethics Lexicon* (Sogou Dictionary, 2019) as well as145 high-frequency words generated by the online word frequency analysis tool Tuyue (Tuyue, 2019). In this study, 1893 stop words from the stop word dictionaries by the Harbin Institute of Technology, Machine Intelligence Laboratory of Sichuan University, and Baidu (Baidu Stop Words, 2019) were used to remove stop words.

Sentiment Analysis of Microblogging

The method based on the emotion dictionary is adopted to construct the training set. The words in the National Taiwan University Sentiment Dictionary (NTUSD) and the Chinese microblog emotion dictionary constructed by An et al. (2017) are selected as the basic emotional polarity words. Then, we calculate the chi square statistics (χ^2) of the remaining words. The words with high χ^2 values are selected as the feature words of the microblog posts or comments. The weight of feature words is calculated based on the Term Frequency-Inverse Document Frequency (TF-IDF) technique.

The emotion values of microblog posts are calculated and sorted. A certain proportion of posts with high emotion values and low emotion values is selected as the positive and negative training set respectively. They are trained by the SVM technique and an emotion classifier is to obtained to classify the comments. There are three types of emotional tendencies, i.e., 1, - 1, and 0. Here 1 indicates that the comment is of positive emotion; 0 indicates that the comment is rational discussion; and - 1 indicates that the comment is of negative emotion. Finally, the sum of the emotional tendencies of all the feature words in each comment is calculated to determine the emotional support of the comment to the post, and judge whether the user who publishes the post is a positive or negative high influential user.

Identifying and Profiling High Influential Users

This study proposes the methods of identifying three types of high influential users, i.e., topic initiator, opinion leader and opinion reverser. The user who publishes a popular microblog post is a topic initiator. An opinion leader is defined as the user who has a high explicit influence (such as having many followers, fans and so forth) and a high implicit influence (e.g., his or her posts receive many related and supportive comments). In previous studies, a user's explicit influence is often considered, such as the number of retweets, the number of fans, the number of posts, the number of comments (Cha, 2010), personal profile, account authentication, the number of followers (Mei et al., 2015), the number of likes, the account level, and the average length of replies (Riquelme & González-Cantergiani, 2016). However, a user's implicit influence is hard to measure and usually ignored.

In this study, both explicit and implicit influence of a user are considered. An indicator system of high influential user identification is constructed to calculate a user's influence index, and to identify opinion leaders and opinion reversers. See Table 1. The indicators of high influential users include basic information of users and basic attributes of microblogging. The user's influence index is obtained by the weighted sum of all the indicators. Two novel indicators are added, i.e., support and topic consistency between microblog posts and their comments. The calculation method of support is shown in Equation (1), where Degree(S_d) indicates the support degree of microblog post d. Count(support) represents the number of supportive comments of post d, and $Count\left(\overline{support}\right)$ represents the number of negative comments of post d:

$$Degree\left(S_d\right) = Count\left(support\right) - Count\left(\overline{support}\right) \tag{1}$$

Table 1. The indicators of high influential users

Category	Indicators
Basic information of users	Account level
	Number of followers
	Number of fans
	Number of posts
	Account authentication
	Personal profile
Basic attributes of microblogging	Number of likes
	Number of comments
	Number of retweets
	Average length of replies
	Support
	Topic consistency

Sentiment analysis is conducted for all the comments of each popular post. To identify opinion leaders, the posts that are supported by their comments are retained. The biterm topic model is used to extract the topics of posts and comments and determine the topic consistency between a post and its comments. The comments that are inconsistent with the topics of the original post is removed. The standard deviation method (Al-Anzi et al., 2017) is adopted to determine the weight of each indicator. Finally, the opinion leader value of each user is calculated to determine opinion leaders.

The identification of opinion reversers is based on opinion leaders. We examine the publishing time of posts, and divide the evolution of public opinion into different time periods. The viewpoint composition of opinion leaders during each time period is explored. The users whose viewpoints are obviously different from the mainstream opinion at the late stage of the event are opinion reversers. They are a kind of special opinion leaders.

The static information of a microblog user's homepage is combined with her or his dynamic behavior data. Firstly, we obtain the account authentication, personal profile, and other information on a user's microblog homepage and construct a user's basic profile. Each user is labelled with some tags according to her or his basic information. For example, the account of Guoke is labelled with "Science, Technology". Then, according to the basic information of users and the basic attributes of microblogging, the role type of each user is identified and labeled. Finally, combining with the basic attributes and the influence of users, the characteristics and roles of different types in the event are analyzed.

DATA ANALYSIS AND RESULTS

Topic Identification and Sentiment Analysis

The Biterm topic model was used to determine the feature word pairs of each topic. The number of topics was determined by the minimum perplexity. Experiments show that the optimal number of topics was 20. They can be divided into five categories. See Table 2.

Table 2. The categories and keywords of the topics

Topic Categories	Topic No.	Keywords
I Contents related to the experiment of project team	V1	genes, CCR5, risk, HIV, discovery, virus, infection
	V2	ethics, committee, Shenzhen, innovation, hospital, experiment
	V3	projects, universities, technology, South, informed
	V5	Jiankui He, gene editing infants, gene editing, humans, research
	V18	Jiankui He, team, couple, content, platform
II Attitudes and statements from various organizations	V4	human, statement, clinical, link, web page
	V8	scientists, the world, condemnation, influence, life, union
	V15	science, ethics, research, regulations, China, law, morality
	V20	gene editing infants, AIDS, immunization, first cases, initiation, modification
III Relevant departments began to investigate	V6	national, violations, health commission, related
	V9	Ministry of Science and Technology, China, research, attention
	V10	gene editing infants, volunteer, Guangdong Province, implementation, investigation team
	V16	research, technology, reproduction, regulation, science and technology
	V19	related, regulatory, purpose, country, investigation, safety
IV Jiankui He introduced the content of the experiment	V7	video, response, Beijing News, controversy, immunization, future
	V11	health, birth, baby, Lulu, Nana, associate professor
	V13	Summit, editing, international, Genome, 2nd Session
V Opinions of experts on the experiment	V12	gene editing, testing, genetics, clinical, CRISPR, USA
	V14	gene editing infants, events, journalists, firsts, professors, experts, scholars
	V17	Jiankui He, speech, data, publicity, appearance, publication

After preprocessing, 138 popular posts were left, and then the topic consistency between the comments and the posts in question was examined. A total of 4,391 comments were found to be inconsistent with the topics of the corresponding posts and removed. Then 38,568 comments remained.

The sentiment analysis was conducted to classify the comments associated with all the popular posts on each topic. For all the 138 posts, only one post regarding Jiankuai He's remarks was generally opposed by the commenters. Jiankui He did not realize that his behavior trampled on the bottom line of morality and ethics and violated relevant laws and regulations. His comments intensified netizens' anger. The publishers of the remaining 137 posts were considered as the candidate opinion leaders.

Identification and Feature Analysis of Opinion Leaders

This study used the indicator system of high influential user identification that was constructed to identify opinion leaders. The weight of each indicator was determined by the standard deviation method and the sum of the weight values of each indicator was 1. See Table 3.

Table 3. Indicators and their weight values of high influential user identification

Indicator	Weight	Indicator	Weight	Indicator	Weight
Account level	0.061	Number of followers	0.144	Number of fans	0.162
Number of posts	0.153	Number of likes	0.078	Number of comments	0.084
Number of retweets	0.080	Average length of replies	0.095	Support	0.143

The influence indices of some users are shown in Table 4. It is seen that the influence indices of No.22 blogger "The People's Daily" and No.6 blogger "CCTV news" are higher than other bloggers. "The People's Daily" ranks the first. It has the largest number of fans among all the candidate opinion leaders, and its number of followers ranks the second. CCTV news has the second largest number of fans among all the candidate opinion leaders with its number of followers ranking fifth and the number of posts ranking sixth. They are considered as opinion leaders.

Table 4. Bloggers' basic attributes and influence indices (partial data)

Blogger	BLogger No.	Account Level	Number of Followers	Number of Fans	Number of Posts	Number of Likes	Number of Comments	Number of Retweets	Average Length of Replies	Support	Influence Index
The People's Daily	22	48	3034	88169306	98172	58331	33456	35321	32.869	148	0.754
CCTV news	6	48	2645	83791861	108756	19830	11840	8877	41.395	194	0.625
China News Network	4	48	1251	45335328	115106	30827	14930	12387	28.571	297	0.530
The Beijing News	8	48	2344	35805026	96211	23240	9356	8977	39.175	238	0.519
Xinhua viewpoint	19	48	2968	64079985	106623	9703	3077	3829	17.618	124	0.498

To reveal the correlation between the indicators of opinion leaders and the influence index, a Spearman's test was conducted as shown in Table 5.

Table 5. The correlation between the users' basic attributes and the influence index

			Account Level	Number of Followers	Number of Fans	Number of Posts	Influence Index
Spearman's rho	Account level	correlation coefficient	1.000	.534**	.597**	.646**	.501**
		Significance (bilateral)	.	.000	.000	.000	.000
		N	138	138	138	138	138
	Number of followers	correlation coefficient	.534**	1.000	.456**	.289**	.645**
		Significance (bilateral)	.000	.	.000	.001	.000
		N	138	138	138	138	138
	Number of fans	correlation coefficient	.597**	.456**	1.000	.818**	.811**
		Significance (bilateral)	.000	.000	.	.000	.000
		N	138	138	138	138	138
	Number of posts	correlation coefficient	.646**	.289**	.818**	1.000	.698**
		Significance (bilateral)	.000	.001	.000	.	.000
		N	138	138	138	138	138
	Influence index	correlation coefficient	.501**	.645**	.811**	.698**	1.000
		Significance (bilateral)	.000	.000	.000	.000	.
		N	138	138	138	138	138

**. The correlation was significant at 0.01 level (bilateral)

Table 6. The correlation between basic attributes of microblogging and the influence index

			Support	Number of Likes	Number of Comments	Number of Retweets	Influence Index
Spearman's rho	Support	correlation coefficient	1.000	.606**	.571**	.546**	.082
		Significance (bilateral)	.	.000	.000	.000	.337
		N	138	138	138	138	138
	Number of likes	correlation coefficient	.606**	1.000	.902**	.915**	.324**
		Significance (bilateral)	.000	.	.000	.000	.000
		N	138	138	138	138	138
	Number of comments	correlation coefficient	.571**	.902**	1.000	.853**	.434**
		Significance (bilateral)	.000	.000	.	.000	.000
		N	138	138	138	138	138
	Number of retweets	correlation coefficient	.546**	.915**	.853**	1.000	.305**
		Significance (bilateral)	.000	.000	.000	.	.000
		N	138	138	138	138	138
	Influence index	correlation coefficient	.082	.324**	.434**	.305**	1.000
		Significance (bilateral)	.337	.000	.000	.000	.
		N	138	138	138	138	138

**. The correlation was significant at 0.01 level (bilateral)

Table 5 shows that when the confidence level is 0.01, there are significant strong correlations between the influence index and the number of followers/the number of fans/the number of posts, and between the account level/the number of fans and the number of posts. Significant medium correlations exist between the account level and the number of followers/the number of fans/the influence index, and between the number of fans and the number of followers. In addition, there are significant weak correlations between the number of followers and the number of posts.

Table 6 reveals the correlation between basic attributes of microblogging and the influence index. When the confidence is 0.01, there are significant strong correlations between support/the number of comments/the number of retweets and the number of likes, and between the number of comments and the number of retweets. Significant medium correlations exist between support and the number of comments/the number of retweets, and between the number of comments and the influence index. Significant weak correlations exist between the number of likes/the number of retweets and the influence index. It is notable that there is no significant correlation between support and the influence index, which indicates that the two indicators measure different dimensions of users.

Identification and Feature Analysis of Opinion Reversers

The birth of the HIV/AIDS gene-edited infants triggered a huge discussion. In the following month, all the professors from the Biology Department of Southern University of Science and Technology and lawyers issued a statement on the incident. Subsequently, the discussion on the incident gradually weakened. On January 21, 2019, the investigation results of the Guangdong Provincial "gene-edited infant incident" investigation team showed that Jiankui He's team deliberately evaded supervision and implemented the human embryo gene editing activities for reproductive purposes which was prohibited by the nation. The Chinese Academy of Engineering also said that the relevant departments should improve relevant laws and regulations dynamically, which caused a heated discussion on Sina Weibo. In the next ten days, the discussion on the microblogging platform gradually weakened again.

Since the incident clearly involved ethical issues and the survey results showed that the team's experimental project violated relevant regulations, there was no large-scale opinion reversal phenomenon on the microblogging platform. However, the No.31 blogger "Intellectuals" published a post worthy of attention. The content was about the views of Professor George Church, a professor of genetics at Harvard University and the director of the Genome Research Center of Harvard Medical School. Before Jiankui He announced the birth of gene-edited infants, Professor Church knew about the clinical trial conducted by Jiankui He and held a neutral attitude towards the experiment. There were different voices in the comments on this post. Some netizens thought that while criticizing Jiankui He and pursuing his responsibility, people should also treat gene editing objectively and think about how to deal with the current results and similar situations in the future. After all, since it was invented, improving the technology was also the current goal of scientists. The emergence of this kind of view broke the absolute dominance of the condemnation view before November 29, 2018. Thus, the blogger "Intellectuals" who published the post was considered as an opinion reverser.

Construction of High Influential User Profiles

The high influential users were profiled from the perspectives of microblog authentication, the number of popular posts, influence index ranking, topics, and the role type. According to the information of microblog users' homepages, combined with the performance of users in this event, we determined the role type of each high influential user and profiled them as shown in Table 7.

Table 7. Profiles of high influential microblogging users (partial data)

Blogger	Microblog Authentication	Number of Popular Posts	Influence Index Ranking	Topics	Role Type
CCTV news	Official microblog of CCTV News Center	7	2	V2, V5, V6, V7, V8, V9, V10, V12, V13, V14, V15, V17, V18, V19, V20	opinion leader
People's Daily	Legal person micro blog of people's daily	5	1	V2, V3, V5, V8, V9, V10, V14, V15, V16, V17, V18, V19	opinion leader
Intellectuals	Decai Jiebei (Beijing) Technology Co., LTD	6	90	V3, V4, V5, V7, V8, V12, V13, V14, V15, V16, V17, V18, V20	opinion reverser
This is America	Global network U.S. press station	2	121	V7, V8, V9, V14, V15, V20	topic initiators
Phoenix video	Ifeng.com video official microblog	1	72	V7, V12, V13, V14	topic initiators

DISCUSSION

In the context of public events, it is very important to identify high influential users of social media for the management of online public opinion. First, identifying the topic initiators can help the emergency management departments timely grasp the salient topics of public opinion that appear at the early stage of the event. Second, opinion leaders not only voice their opinions, but also can lead others' thoughts and have influence on the general public (Nunes et al., 2018). Finding opinion leaders can help emergency management departments grasp the focus and emotional attitudes of core users of social media. Third, the identification of topic reversers can help the emergency management departments discover the changes of public opinion at the later stages of the event, find the key users of opinion reversal, and explore the factors that induce the public opinion to reverse. At the same time, the management departments can also master the diversity of public opinions.

In general, the findings of this study can help the emergency management departments understand and guide the online public opinion at different stages of the event, and provide support for the follow-up emergency management. Through constructing the profiles of high influential users on the social media, the management departments can leverage the information to guide public opinion according to the characteristics of users. For example, scientific and technological microblog users can be encouraged to publish popular scientific information about the event. Media users can be encouraged to report real-time tracking information about the event. Public security users can release event processing information and so forth.

CONCLUSION

This study proposes a method of identifying high influential microblog users based on topic consistency and emotional support. Taking the event of "Jiankui He editing the infants' genes" as an example, the topics of microblogging were extracted and the comments were screened for topical consistency. The indicator system of high influential user identification has been built upon the sentiment classification of comments and used to identify opinion leaders on social media. On the basis of opinion leaders, the time of publishing posts was introduced to identify users with different opinions but high influence, namely opinion reversers. Finally, the user profiles were constructed, combining the information of microblog users' homepages and the performance of the users during the event. The topic initiators and opinion leaders tend to promote the formation of the spiral of silence to some extent and may potentially inhibit different opinions, which are proposed by opinion reversers. The contribution of this study is to propose the quantitative methods of identifying the key nodes in the process of the spiral of silence and anti-spiral of silence.

The results outline the characteristics and classification of high influential users of social media in the context of public events and can help related departments guide the public opinions according to the users' characteristics, such as encouraging high influential scientific microblog accounts to publish popular scientific information, encouraging media accounts to publish real-time tracking reports of events, and using the public security accounts to publish the processing results of events. The limitation of the research is the lack of in-depth research on satirical comments. Another limitation is to identify microblog posts with different viewpoints by human judgment, which may be subjective. Natural language processing is developing rapidly in the field of emotion recognition and has great potential (Wang et al., 2019). In future, the authors will try to introduce the ironic calculation and other methods to improve the accuracy of sentiment classification of online comments, and explore the automatic recognition method of opinion reversal.

ACKNOWLEDGMENT

This work was supported by the Major Project of the Ministry of Education of China (Grant No. 17JZD034) and the National Natural Science Foundation of China (Grant No. 71921002, 71603189, 71790612, 71974202).

REFERENCES

Al-Anzi, AbuZeina, & Hasan. (2017). Utilizing standard deviation in text classification weighting schemes. *International Journal of Innovative Computing, Information, & Control, 13*(4), 1385–1398.

Aleahmad, A., Karisani, P., Rahgozar, M., & Oroumchian, F. (2016). OLFinder: Finding opinion leaders in online social networks. *Journal of Information Science, 42*(5), 659–674. doi:10.1177/0165551515605217

Araniti, G., De Meo, P., Iera, A., & Ursino, D. (2003). Adaptively controlling the QoS of multimedia wireless applications through "user profiling" techniques. *IEEE Journal on Selected Areas in Communications, 21*(10), 1546–1556. doi:10.1109/JSAC.2003.815226

Au, L., & Ou, M. (2017). Social Network Sentiment Map of the Stakeholders in Public Health Emergencies. *Library and Information Service*, *61*(20), 120–130.

Baidu Stop Words. (2019). *Baidu stop word library*. https://shurufa.baidu.com/dict

Bamakan, S. M. H., Nurgaliev, I., & Qu, Q. (2019). Opinion Leader Detection: A Methodological Review. *Expert Systems with Applications*, *115*, 200–222. doi:10.1016/j.eswa.2018.07.069

Bigonha, C., Cardoso, T. N., Moro, M. M., Gonçalves, M. A., & Almeida, V. A. (2011). Sentiment-based Influence Detection on Twitter. *Journal of the Brazilian Computer Society*, *18*(3), 169–183. doi:10.100713173-011-0051-5

Bouguessa, M., & Romdhane, L. B. (2015). Identifying Authorities in Online Communities. *ACM Transactions on Intelligent Systems and Technology*, *18*(3), 169–183.

Cha, M. (2010). Measuring User Influence in Twitter: The Million Follower Fallacy. *The International Conference on Weblogs & Social Media*.

Dictionary, S. (2019). *Sogou Input Word Library*. http://pinyin.sougou.com/dict/

Farnadi, G., Sitaraman, G., Sushmita, S., Celli, F., Kosinski, M., Stillwell, D., & De Cock, M. (2016). Computational Personality Recognition in Social Media. *User Modeling and User-Adapted Interaction*, *26*(2-3), 109–142. doi:10.100711257-016-9171-0

Hajmohammadi, M. S. (2013). A SVM-based Method for Sentiment Analysis in Persian Language. *The International Conference on Graphic and Image Processing*. 10.1117/12.2010940

Hu, X., Tang, J., & Gao, H. (2013). Unsupervised Sentiment Analysis with Emotional Signals. In *Proceedings of the 22nd International Conference on World Wide Web*. ACM. 10.1145/2488388.2488442

Huang, J., Tong, R., & Jiang, R. (2015). Sentiment Analysis in Financial Domain Based On SVM with Dependency Syntax. *Computer Engineering & Applications*, *51*(23), 230–235.

Jabeur, L. B., Tamine, L., & Boughanem, M. (2012). *Active Microbloggers: Identifying Influencers, Leaders and Discussers in Microblogging Networks. In String Processing and Information Retrieval (SPIRE 2012)* (Vol. 7608). Springer.

Jin, X., & Wang, Y. (2013). Research on Social Network Structure and Public Opinions Dissemination of Micro-blog Based on Complex Network Analysis. *Journal of Networks*, *8*(7), 1543–1550. doi:10.4304/jnw.8.7.1543-1550

Karanasou, M., Doulkeridis, C., & Halkidi, M. (2015). DsUniPi: An SVM-based Approach for Sentiment Analysis of Figurative Language on Twitter. *The International Workshop on Semantic Evaluation*. 10.18653/v1/S15-2120

Lakiotaki, K., Matsatsinis, N. F., & Tsoukia, S. A. (2011). Multicriteria User Modeling in Recommender Systems. *IEEE Intelligent Systems*, *26*(2), 64–76. doi:10.1109/MIS.2011.33

Lee, W. J., Oh, K. J., Lim, C. G., & Choi, H. J. (2014). User Profile Extraction from Twitter for Personalized News Recommendation. *The International Conference on Advanced Communication Technology*. 10.1109/ICACT.2014.6779068

Li, J., Peng, W., Li, T., Li, Q., & Xu, J. (2014). Social network user influence sense-making and dynamics prediction. *Expert Systems with Applications*, *41*(11), 5115–5124. doi:10.1016/j.eswa.2014.02.038

Liu, N., Li, L., Xu, G., & Yang, Z. (2014). Identifying domain-dependent influential microblog users: A post-feature based approach. *Twenty-eighth AAAI Conference on Artificial Intelligence.*

Mei, Y., Zhong, Y., & Yang, J. (2015). Finding and analyzing principal features for measuring user influence on Twitter. *2015 IEEE First International Conference on Big Data Computing Service & Applications*. 10.1109/BigDataService.2015.36

Noelle-Neumann, E. (1974). The Spiral of Silence: A Theory of Public Opinion. *Journal of Communication*, *24*(2), 43–51. doi:10.1111/j.1460-2466.1974.tb00367.x

Nunes, R. H., Ferreira, J. B., de Freitas, A. S., & Ramos, F. L. (2018). The Effects of Social Media Opinion Leaders' Recommendations on Followers' Intention to Buy. *RBGN-Revista Brasileira de Gestao de Negocios*, *20*(1), 57–73.

Pang, B., Lee, L., & Vaithyanathan, S. (2002). Thumbs up? Sentiment Classification Using Machine Learning Techniques. In *Proceedings of the ACL-02 Conference on Empirical Methods in Natural Language Processing*. Stroudsburg: Association for Computational Linguistics.

Quercia, D., Ellis, J., Capra, L., & Crowcroft, J. (2011). In the Mood for Being Influential on Twitter. *2011 IEEE Third International Conference on Social Computing, Privacy, Security, Risk and Trust (Passat).*

Räbiger, S., & Spiliopoulou, M. (2015). A Framework for Validating the Merit of Properties that Predict the Influence of a Twitter User. *Expert Systems with Applications*, *42*(5), 2824–2834. doi:10.1016/j.eswa.2014.11.006

Riquelme, F., & González-Cantergiani, P. (2016). Measuring user influence on Twitter: A survey. *Information Processing & Management*, *52*(5), 949–975. doi:10.1016/j.ipm.2016.04.003

Sharma, N., & Lbansal, K. (2015). Comparative Study of Data Mining Tools. *Journal of Database Management*, *2*(2), 35–41.

Tuyue. (2019). *Tuyue - hot word analysis tool.* http://www.picdata.cn/ci_b.php

Vapnik, V. (2000). SVM method of Estimating Density, Conditional Probability, and Conditional Density. *The IEEE International Symposium on Circuits & Systems*. 10.1109/ISCAS.2000.856437

Wang, W., & Siau, K. (2019). Artificial Intelligence, Machine Learning, Automation, Robotics, Future of Work and Future of Humanity: A Review and Research Agenda. *Journal of Database Management*, *30*(1), 61–79. doi:10.4018/JDM.2019010104

Weibo, S. (2014). *Popular Microblog Management Specification (Trial Version)*. https://weibo.com/p/1001603766710724380562

Wu, S., Hofman, J. M., Mason, W. A., & Watts, D. J. (2011). Who says what to whom on Twitter. *Proceedings of the 20th International Conference on World Wide Web*. 10.1145/1963405.1963504

Xiao, F., Noro, T., & Tokuda, T. (2014). Finding News-topic Oriented Influential Twitter Users Based on Topic Related Hashtag Community Detection. *Journal of Web Engineering*, *13*(5&6), 405–429.

Zhou, Q., & Zhang, C. (2018). Detecting Users' Dietary Preferences and Their Evolutions via Chinese Social Media. *Journal of Database Management*, *29*(3), 89–110. doi:10.4018/JDM.2018070105

Zhu, Y., Huang, Z., Wang, Z., Luo, L., & Shuang, W. (2018). Influence and Extension of the Spiral of Silence in Social Networks: A Data-Driven Approach. *The 8th IEEE/ACM International Conference on Advances in Social Networks Analysis and Mining*.

This research was previously published in the Journal of Database Management (JDM), 32(2); pages 36-49, copyright year 2021 by IGI Publishing (an imprint of IGI Global).

Chapter 64
Social Networks and Cultural Differences:
Adidas's Case on Twitter and Sina Weibo

José Duarte Santos

https://orcid.org/0000-0001-5815-4983
Polytechnic of Porto, Portugal

Steffen Mayer
Aschaffenburg University of Applied Sciences, Germany

ABSTRACT

The purpose of this chapter is the comparison of social media strategy on Twitter and Sina Weibo by the German company Adidas. A successful social media campaign is pushing brand awareness and companies improve their focus on that. Due to the internet censorship of the Chinese government, the social media landscape in China differs from the Western world. Therefore, companies need cultural and linguistic know how to be successful on Chinese platforms like Sina Weibo. The chapter compares how Adidas uses Twitter and Sina Weibo for their marketing purpose. Cultural differences and the local adaption of their social media appearance will be presented.

INTRODUCTION

Marketing is a well-developed method and is constantly changing its rules according to the needs and developments being held in and around it. To establish itself, it has begun adopting new paradigms of business (Saravanakumar & SuganthaLakshmi, 2012). The rapid development of the Internet is producing new ways to connect with the customer. One of the new forms of advertisement is Social Media. Bonnie Sainsbury, who is a Canadian influencer says: "Social media will help you build up loyalty of your current customers to the point that they will willingly, and for free, tell others about you" (e-Clincher, 2015). A blog, post or tweet can be twisted and viewed by millions almost for free and enables companies to make their own interest content that viewers will follow.

DOI: 10.4018/978-1-6684-6307-9.ch064

With the help of the Internet, social media campaigns can be launched globally. As a result, companies are able to increase their brand awareness around the world. Whereas famous social media platforms like Twitter, Facebook or Instagram are famous in most of the countries, it can not be used in one of the most important markets in the world. China has draconian internet restrictions and is blocking most of the western social media platforms. As a result, western marketing campaigns are stopping right at the Chinese border. However, the restriction has supported the development of Chinese social media platforms like Sina Weibo. This platform varies much from their western counterparts. Logically, they need specific advertisement approaches to be successful in the Chinese market. So, this work is based on one central research question: the presence of a brand on the social network Sina Weibo implies adjustments compared to the presence on the Twitter network?

The terms Social Media, Web 2.0, Social Media Marketing and Microblog will be described to set the framework of the article. Second, social media platforms Twitter and Sina Weibo will be described and differences will be exposed. Besides technical differences on the platform, the article also shows cultural differences by analyzing the United States of America, Germany, and China. Communication is always a matter of culture and needs to be adapted according to the target market. Furthermore, the paper introduces the company Adidas with its most important business categories. One of the main parts of the article is the usage analyzation of Twitter and Sina Weibo. Part of the analysis is the structure, frequency of posts, the use of mediums, content, design, language, and the use of models and celebrities.

BACKGROUND

Social Media and Web 2.0

The term Web 2.0 was introduced by Tim O´Reilly and defines the business revolution in the computer industry. The change is due to the movement of the internet as a platform and the attempt to understand the rules of success for this platform. The aim is to build applications that harness network effects to get better the more people use them. Internet users are no longer limited to a one-sided communication flow in which companies only inform through websites. Web 2.0 effects online users by how many things they can do, interact, combine, remix, upload and customize for themselves (Shuen, 2018).

The term social media refers to all posts in the form of text, pictures, videos or audio which are created in order to get an interaction. Therefore, social media is connecting technology, content, and creativity to achieve a communicational exchange on a virtual platform (Hettler, 2012). Besides the information exchange, Weinberg, Ladwig and Pahrmann (2012) focus on the fact that social media enables communication without geographical boundaries and at every time. The values of social media sites are their users and the content which users are sharing. This term of information is referred as user-generated content.

Social media platforms can be divided into three groups (Kreutzer, 2018):

1. Communication: blogs, micro-blogs, private and business social networks, Messenger;
2. Cooperation between user: wiki, rating portal;
3. Content-sharing: text-sharing, foto-sharing, video-sharing, audio-sharing.

Social Media Marketing

In the today's world, companies change their marketing strategy from being product-centric to being customer-centric and relationship-driven (Sheth, Sisodia, & Sharma, 2000). Social Media Marketing (SMM) is a tool that supports that trend.

SMM is used to describe the use of social media platforms for the purpose of marketing. Akar and Topçu (2011) has defined SMM as the promotion of the company and its products through social media. On the other hand, Drury (2008) describes the increase of brand awareness among consumers through the word of mouth principle as a purpose of SMM. For Tuten and Soloman (2017), SMM is the utilization of social media platforms to create, communicate, deliver, and exchange offerings that has value for an organization's stakeholder. While the first definitions have a concentrated focus on the classical promotion of the company, Assaad and Gómez (2011) sees SMM as a great opportunity to talk with the customer on a personal level. Therefore, those social networking sites should be considered as an additional channel with unique characteristic and not like a traditional marketing tool. For them, SMM is an effective means of getting vital information that is essential to the success of the business.

Microblogs

This paper will focus on the use of Microblogs. Therefore, it is important in order to describe the term in detail. Microblogs are an established form in the group of social media platforms with a broad interest in consumers and companies. They differ from traditional blogs in that its content is typically smaller in file size. Mostly, the length of a text message is limited to less than 200 characters and focusses on the exchange of short sentences, individual images or video links (Kaplan & Haenlein, 2011). The limitation is also the main factor of their success story and they are are typically used for crisis management, journalism, or politics (Aichner & Jacob, 2015; Mendoza, Poblete & Castillo, 2010). The biggest and most famous microblogging provider in Western countries is Twitter, whereas in China Sina Weibo is the most popular platform (Kreutzer, 2018).

What Is the Success Story of Microblogs?

First, microblogs create a concept called ambient awareness. The theory describes the feeling of closeness and intimacy a person gets by reading through various several small tweets of one blogger. Due to that ambient awareness, microblogs result in a relatively high level of social presence, that can be achieved between two individuals, and media richness, defined as the amount of information that can be transmitted in a given time interval (Daft & Lengel, 1986).

The second reason behind the popularity of microblogs is the unique type of communication. When a person decides that a tweet of another person is relevant, he can become a follower of that person. Following means, the user is getting all new posts of the person he decides to follow (Cha, Haddadi, Benevenuto & Gummadi, 2010). In many cases, the content of tweet may be read and immediately forgotten, but in other cases the post might be seen so relevant that the user chooses to retweet the post. Tweet is a message that the user receives from a person he follows and directly forward to his own followers (Weinberg et al., 2012). The initial tweet can be forwarded from one user to another and can transform from a simple piece of information to a word-of-mouth phenomenon (Kaplan & Haenlein, 2011).

The third reason for its popularity is the motivation of a user to get additional information about the tweeted subject because the tweet with its limited characters can not fully describe the topic. By using short URL´s, microblogging messages become similar to traditional ads, which motivate users to click on it (Kaplan & Haenlein, 2011). The "click-through" can positively affect consumer behaviour (Manchanda, Dubé, Goh & Chintagunta, 2006).

Marketing Strategies of Companies Based on Microblog

Microblogs have a huge potential for companies to get the customer brand opinion, improve the relationship and communication with the customer and solve customers problems. Therefore, companies can use microblogs as a brand promotional tool. The brand image has a significant influence on customers buying decisions (Malik et al., 2013). Microblog messages contain much information about brands including brand sentiment, product experience and customer satisfaction (Sui & Yang, 2010).

The companies can use that information flow to increase their brand awareness, creating an official microblog account and publishes news and information about their product and activities via it. It is important that a company follows a clear strategy on how to present itself on a microblog platform (Kreutzer, 2018). The published information can impress the customers and engage them to receive more relevant information and intensify the brand image (Sui & Yang, 2010). For the right communication, companies have to safe all rights of their brand name (Kreutzer, 2018).

The content of a post is very important and has to be attractive to the customer. Therefore, companies should provide exclusive information about their products, their company or their industry. Moreover, they should attract customers by exclusive offers (limited and attractive in terms of price) and exclusive services (preview for new offers or new products). Those exclusive contents will bind customers closer to the company. The reason for that is, that customer will check the postings on the microblog frequently if they believe they will only receive the information through that channel (Kreutzer, 2018).

Microblogs are very suitable for big companies in order to start a community with their fans. In such a community, the company can directly or indirectly talk with its clients about the company or new offers. Moreover, companies can use those platforms to launch customer service and answer customer questions or complaints. The answers will be posted publicly and force the customer service to work quickly, respectful and solution-oriented and will result to a better customer service level (Kreutzer, 2018; Sui & Yang, 2010).

Twitter

Twitter can be categorized as a microblog and was founded in 2006 in San Francisco (Arceneaux & Weiss, 2010). It enables the user to post short messages to individuals who have chosen to follow the sender. Retweeting the post engages the follower to participate in the conversation (Burton, Dadich & Soboleva, 2013). A post is limited by Twitter to 280 characters (Geier & Gottschling, 2019). The platform is not just limited to text messages. Moreover, Twitter enables its users to use pictures, videos or quoting other posts. Through the use of "@" in their own post, users can refer to other accounts like a company or a private person (Hettler, 2012). The use of hashtags is also very popular on Twitter. It serves to refer to certain topics without the need to explain them. Hashtags are linked to posts with the same hashtag to help to connect a variety of different posts about the same topic. Users who have an interest in a topic can use the search function of Twitter for looking up a hashtag. (Weinberg et al., 2012). The importance of Twitter has increased tremendously in our society based on the use of celebrities. The best example is the sitting US president Donald Trump who announces his political agenda on a daily basis on Twitter (Stolee & Caton, 2018).

In the first quarter of 2019, Twitter had 330 million active monthly users (Twitter, 2019). Moreover, Twitter generated 4.17 billion visitors on their webpage (SimilarWeb, 2019). 27 percent of all users are from the US, followed by Japan with 14 percent (SimilarWeb, 2019). In comparison to other social media platforms, Twitter is not used from a specific age group. The difference in the daily use of a 16-year-old person compared to a 49-year-old varies by only 4 percent (Brown, 2017). Besides Twitter, other microblogs exist but they play a niche role and are mostly in financial difficulties (Hettler, 2012). Therefore, Twitter can be described as the most important microblogging platform for the western world.

Social Media in China and Sina Weibo

China is by far the number one of internet users. In 2018, 828.51 million people in China used the Internet (Statista, 2020). Moreover, China has the world´s most active environment for social media. Almost every Internet user in China uses social media. The Chinese internet is also a unique place. Western social media is not taking place in China. The country has blocked the world´s four most visited websites: Google, Facebook, Youtube and Twitter and also denied other western social media platforms access to the Chinese market (Wang, 2016). In reality, most Chinese internet users do not really notice the absence of western social media because the country has accustomed themselves to indigenous websites. Today, China has a grown and unique social media landscape. Social media in China is experiencing a massive growth without copying the western equivalents. Instead, they are new creations customized for the Chinese culture, habits, and behaviour (He & Pedraza, 2015). Some of the social media innovations are even leading the global trend of media development. Chinese platforms live in a complicated and competitive environment and face quick changes. All in all, the Chinese social media platforms can be defined as unique, complex fragmented and local (He & Pedraza, 2015).

Sina Weibo is one of the most famous social network sites in China and has become a crucial medium to share information like breaking news, social events and products (Lei et al., 2018). The microblogging platform was launched in 2009 and has grown rapidly to influence millions of internet users in China. It can be described as the Chinese version of Twitter (Nooruddin & Zhang, 2012). In July 2019, almost 600 million unique devices have visited Sina Weibo (Statista, 2019), which is nearly two times more visitors than Twitter (330 million).

Chinese use microblogging platforms like Sina Weibo to get credible information about current events or news. The reason for that is, that microblogging sites allow to spread informations quickly (Liu, 2016). As already mentioned, Weibo is often compared to Twitter. Besides that, Weibo might be more social in terms of openness of network, applications and multimedia choices (Chen & Zhang, 2011). In the early days, Weibo had a limit of 140 characters but has removed this limit in January 2016 by by allowing users to post up to 2.000 characters (Hlee, Cheng, Koo & Kim, 2017). Weibo allows their users to follow others, comment on other´s weibos and click the "zan" button which is similar to a "like" button in western social media, and add weibos to the personal gallery (Hlee et al., 2017). Moreover, users can integrate graphical emoticons, pictures, music, and videos to their weibos (Guan et al., 2014). Comparable to Twitter is the use of hashtags which enable users to find weibos and news (Hlee et al., 2017).

An advantage of Sina Weibo is their cooperation with the big online market place Alibaba. Sina Weibo has connectivity to Alibaba which enables companies to sell their products through the microblogging page. They also invented their own payment system "Weibo Payment" in order to make the purchasing progress quicker and more efficient (Havinga, Hoving & Swagemakers, 2016).

Each social media platform in China attracts specific users with different characteristics (Sullivan, 2012). Consumers who favour Sina Weibo tend to be in higher income brackets, earning more than 1.300$ a month, and they are much more likely to live in big cities (Chiu, Lin & Silverman, 2012). Very interesting for companies is the Enterprise-Version of Sina Weibo. It enables companies to analyze their followers (age, gender, regional differences). Those data can be used for further marketing strategies. Furthermore, Sina Weibo offers marketing tools which enable organisations to get in conversations with their follower and start online surveys (Liu, 2016). Companies can send private messages to either a specific percentage of followers or to all of them. The messages can be used to get customer attention, send them prize competitions, or interesting news in order to increase the interest to follow the company (Liu, 2016). Like Twitter, Weibo also requires a specific strategy of how to operate on the platform. In general, the plan is relatively similar. Companies should use hashtags cleverly, create a fan base, post relevant and interesting topics, take the respond of the followers serious. Weibo has to be seen as an influential marketing tool with all the different aspects it offers(Chen & Zhang, 2011).

A great challenge for using Sina Weibo is the cultural difference entrepreneurs have to face. A European or American company can not post or interact with their follower in the same way they are used in their home market. The Chinese culture has different rules and defines different taboo on topics like humour, erotic, politics and religion. This cultural framework can deviate extremely to the western usage. To be successful in the Chinese social media world, companies have to hire social media workers with explicit cultural competence about the Chinese culture. Companies should also consider to post in mandarin and therefore hire a Chinese speaking employee (Svensson, 2014).

Cultural Diferences

While the explosive growth of social media is a phenomenon across many countries, the way people use the platform and their reason for doing so may vary according to their social and cultural milieu (Kim, Sohn & Choi, 2011). Therefore, it is necessary to adopt a deeper look at the cultural differences of China compared to the United States and Germany as a benchmark.

Hofstede, which is a leading expert on cultural studies, defines culture as a collective programming of the mind that distinguished the members of one group or category of people from others (Hofstede, 2011). Moreover, Hofstede (2011) is dividing culture into six dimensions which are: Power Distance, Uncertainty Avoidance, Individualism vs. Collectivism, Masculinity vs Feminity, Long Term vs Short Term Orientation, Indulgence vs Restraint. The chapter will focus only on two of the six Hofstede dimensions which are power distance and individualism vs collectivism.

According to Hofstede, power distance explains how societies deal with inequalities and hierarchies in terms of social status, wealth and power. In a culture with a high-power distance, less powerful members of an organization accept and expect that power is made available unequally (Hofstede, 2011). In a society with low power distance, equality is treasured and authorities are often challenged (Fi & McNeal, 2001). In terms of marketing, consumer in a high-power distance country has a tendency to use expensive, luxurious symbols and high-status appeals such as celebrity endorsement to highlight power, wealth, and elitism. In contrast, low power distance countries prefer down-to-earth appearances with normal persons (Albers-Miller & Gelb, 1996). It is noted, that China has a very high score of 80, whereas Germany and the US only score 35 and 40 points. That illustrates that Chinese culture extreme values power distance.

Individualism describes a society in which everyone is only looking after himself and his family. Independence, individuality, and self-realization have a great importance. Moreover, actions are determined by personal goals and individual welfare. In comparison, a collectivistic side is a culture in which people are integrated into a robust, family-extended group which stays loyal and oppose other groups. The goals of a community and collectivistic welfare take precedence over personal achievement. Furthermore, they live in a "we" society in which interdependence with others is valued. (Hofstede, 2011). A collectivistic society is more likely to share content within its group (Ji et al., 2010). Social media appearances should respect the difference between individualism and collectivism. A collectivistic country appreciates collectivistic appeals like popularity, collective benefits, and group achievement, and less individualistic approaches like uniqueness or the promotion of adventures (Cheong, Kim & Zheng, 2010). According to the graph, China can be categorized as a collectivistic culture. Germany is tending to be more individualistic, whereas the United States can be characterized as strongly individualistic.

Another factor which is not described in the six dimensions model of Hofstede is the difference in communication. Hall (1973) states, that human communication always follows cultural and contextual patterns. Furthermore, Hall (1989) divides cultures into high context and low context depending on the amount of information transmitted at the moment of communication. The general term of context can be described as the information that surrounds an event and must be known in order to understand the meaning of an event or subject. A high context message is one in which most of the information is already in the person, while very little is explicitly transmitted in the message. Those cultures do not require or expect in-depth background information because they keep themselves informed about everything having to do with the people who play a significant role in their life. In contrast, in a low context message, the mass of the information is vested in the explicit code. For our article it is important to know that China is clarified as a high context culture whereas Germany and the United States are a low context culture. Low context people compartmentalize their personal relationships and many other aspects of day-to-day life. As a consequence, each time they interact with others they need detailed background information (Hall & Hall, 2001). In other words, low context communication tends to be more direct, is less focussing on context, and contains more factual information (Gudykunst, 2004; Kim, Cole & Gould, 2009). In comparison, high context communication is more indirect and ambiguous, favouring metaphors and symbols and is less understandable to persons who are outside the group (Kim et al., 2009). Societies which favour a low context communication style use rational cues such as product features, the functional value of a product or references to competing brands to promote a product. On the other side, high context cultures talking in a more direct and implicit way about a product or a brand (Gudykunst, 2004). They use a persuasive communication style which is more likely to use emotional appeals and symbolic association with a celebrity or lifestyle (Tsai & Men, 2012). For example, Chinese advertisements feature values that are symbolic and suggestive of human emotions. Moreover, web sites are more likely to offer information about consumers connection to their community (Lee, Geistfeld & Stoel, 2007). In high context cultures, the news are transmitted colourful, inspirational and in an interesting way. Pathos and entertainment are preferred (Corduan, 2018). Furthermore, high-context cultures prefer special graphics, design elements, and colourful background design. Users in those cultures place more emphasis on the appearance of posts, are less focused, and therefore prefer a variety of content types.

Companies operating in a high context should focus on building a relationship with the customer through the soft-sell approach (Pollay, 1983). Consumers in China focus on the intangible aspects of advertising messages. Of great importance is the aesthetic and entertainment values, rather than product features and benefits (Mooij, 2018). A successful way to transport good feelings and create a happy atmosphere is the use of celebrities and the approach of an emotional appealing (Johansson, 1994).

METHODOLOGY

The data analysis in this chapter is based on a quantitative approach, whereby the researcher obtained the data from observing the last 40 social media posts posted by Adidas company on Twitter and Sina Weibo. The observation of the posts was made during the month of November 2019. By counting specific characteristic the author was able to put the observation into a quantitative perspective and present the results. The variables analyzed were structure of account network, topic of the post, design of the post, language of the post, diversity of the post and cooperation with celebrities.

ADIDAS BACKGROUND

Adidas was founded in 1949 by Adi Dassler in the small German city Herzogenaurach. Today, it is a multinational corporation that designs and manufactures shoes, clothing, and accessories. It is the largest sportswear manufacturer in Europe and the second-largest in the world (Kreutzer, 2018). The brand has a long history and deep-rooted sports connection with a diverse portfolio of major global sports. Today, Adidas is one of the most recognized and iconic global brands. The company's mission is to be the best sports brand in the world by designing, building and selling the best sport products in the world, with the best service and experience and in a sustainable way (Adidas, 2018). In 2018, Adidas generated worldwide sales of 21.915 billion Euros (increase of 3.3% to 2017), 7.1 billion Euros were generated in China (increase of 14.9% to 2017) (Adidas, 2018).

Brand Adidas is divided into the following sub-brands (Adidas, 2019):

- Adidas Sport: sportswear for professionals
- Adidas Original: A lifestyle brand marked by the iconic Trefoil logo.
- Adidas Core: sportswear for everyone
- Reebok Running: innovative technologies for high-performance runners
- Reebok Training: specialized products of fitness
- Reebok Classics: sportive fitness clothes for the daily life

In 2019, Adidas has over 57000 employees and produced over 900 million sports and sports lifestyle products. Sales of 21.015 billion Euros were generated in 2018 by Adidas.

RESULTS

Network Presence of Adidas

Adidas Original has established themselves successfully in the western and Chinese microblogging platform. They have a structured and successful social media strategy by adapting to both regions. While addressing a wide customer range on Twitter, they focus especially on the Chinese culture on Sina Weibo. Language, colours, celebrities, and models are customized for Chinese preferences. Furthermore, Adidas is able to maintain its core values and recognition in both markets. They do adapt but do not change their branding. This is noticeable by having the same profile picture and the slogan "Three Stripes. Past. Present. Future" on both platforms.

Adidas states that their Original sub-brand is a main driver of their global success. The sub-brand has verified accounts on Twitter and Sina Weibo with millions of followers and will be used for the following comparison. Adidas Original´s Twitter account is addressing the users globally, whereas the Sina Weibo account is posting specifically for the Chinese market. This must be taken into consideration for the following analysis. According to the 2018s annual report, Adidas believes that possible changes in customer demands might be high. One reason is the quick changes in demand for fashion. Therefore, it is necessary to identify fashion trends. Social media interaction with the customer helps to spot changing fashion preferences (Adidas, 2018).

Today, the Twitter Account of Adidas Original has 4.07 million followers and cumulative 17,500 tweets. Retweets are included. The account was founded in February 2009 and has a global focus. In comparison, the Adidas Original Account of Sina Weibo has currently 2.46 million followers and 4,600 posts. Adidas posts regularly on Twitter and Sina Weibo. In this article, the last recent 40 posts of both platforms were analysed. Adidas needed 105 days for 40 posts on Twitter, whereas they needed only 73 days on Sina Weibo. Adidas is posting more frequently on Sina Weibo (1.8 days/post) than on Twitter (2.6 days/post). Table 1 presents the variables compared.

Table 1. Comparison of adidas on Twitter and Sina Weibo

Variable	Twitter	Sina Weibo
Followers	4.07 million	2.46 million
Posts	17500	4600
Number of days to make 40 publications	105	73
Range of days per post	2.6	1.8

Source: authors

Structure of Account Network

The structure of their Twitter and Sina Weibo account is relatively similar. Both platforms use the same Adidas Original logo as their profile picture and the slogan "Three Stripes. Past. Present. Future" in their profile description. Furthermore, both websites use their cover picture to promote the newest fashion advertisements. Currently, both sides are presenting the new shoe collection on their cover picture. In the profile description of Sina Weibo, Adidas connects the user to other Adidas communities at Sina Weibo and to the external social network Douban. In contradiction, Adidas is not using links on their Twitter profile.

A visible contrast is the use of colours. The cover picture of Twitter is kept mainly white and makes a subtle but classy impression. In contrast, Adidas Original uses for Sina Weibo a very colourful background to promote their shoes. For using a cover picture at Sina Weibo Adidas needs to be a verified company.

Topic of the Post

One of the most important aspects of analysing a post is the topic which it is addressing. Every post is establishedof a different purpose. Promoting a product, a new collection, presenting new information about the company or just telling a story. Interesting content is bounding the customer closer to the company´s profile. Big differences in the online topics were noticeable during the last 40 posts on both platforms. On Twitter, Adidas Original is focussing primarily on their shoe collection. More than 70% of their posts present the newest footwear and only 10% of the posts are promoting the street wear collections. The missing 20% are dealing with presenting the latest cooperation, telling a story, or dealing with diverse topics.

In contradiction, Adidas Original diversificate the topics on Sina Weibo. 43% of their posts are presenting the newest footwear and 38% promote the street wear collection. Likewise to Twitter, the final 20% is presenting the latest cooperation, telling a story or presenting diverse topics.

Design of the Post

By addressing the follower on social media, the design of the post is an important factor. Especially the used colour have to attract the users and reflect cultural standards. It is noted, that Adidas Original uses more colour for their posts on Sina Weibo than on Twitter. Most of the posts on Twitter are comparable to the left picture. The shoe is in front of a white and simple background. No colours that might distract the consumer from the product is visible. In contrast, Adidas uses colourful pictures on Sina Weibo. Most of the pictures offer a full range of different colours. The product is not part of the main focus. More than 80% of all pictures on Twitter show a subtle background, while Adidas posts more than 60% with a colourful one.

Language of the Post

The language on both platforms is different and adapted to the target market. On Twitter, Adidas is communicating for a global performance in english, whereas on Sina Weibo the used language is mandarin. However, the name of the shoes are not translated and remains in English. In order to compare the text messages, the post has to concern a similar topic. One good example is the promotion of the "YEEZY" collections that are also optically very similar. Adidas is keeping their messages on Twitter very short. They only introduce the shoe model and the date for the sales launch. The writing style is direct, offers factual information and therefore focus on a low-context culture.

On Sina Weibo, Adidas is using more text to interact with with their customer. They start the conversation with the question "What´s the matter, let´s talk outside the clouds Ù" After that, they introduce the name of the shoe collection and present details about the used materials or the weight. The date of sales launch is presented with the information that the collection is limited. Furthermore, they describe the shoe with the statement: "The iconic mid sole makes you feel like walking through the clouds" which refers to the first sentence of the post.

Diversity of the Post

When looking at the posts on Sina Weibo, it is noticeable that the majority of the models and beauty bloggers are from Asia. In contradiction, Adidas uses ethnically diverse models on Twitter. However, this result is understandable, and it makes sense that the Chinese market to select models with which the target group can identify with. Twitter is used globally. Therefore, Adidas hoes to have to address all different ethnicities with the goal that no one feels excluded.

Cooperation With Celebrities

As an outfitter to numerous famous athletes, sport teams and sports organizers, Adidas has gained international significance. According to their own annual report, they focus on promotional partnerships and brand marketing activities (digital advertising, point of sales) (Adidas, 2018).

Adidas´s brand awareness was achieved mainly through promotional partnerships. Adidas is sponsoring sporting events and equipping major football teams or athletes such as Lionel Messi or Aaron Rodgers. Marketing through promotional partnerships with famous athletes has been a tradition since the company´s foundation and is, therefore, an important factor in increasing Adidas brand awareness (Heiden, 2015). Moreover, Adidas also focus on non-sports celebrities such as American musician Kanye West and Pharrell Williams to expand the brand reach. In collaboration with Kanye West, Adidas Original created the "YEEZY" collection, which is very successful internationally (Yang, 2019). In October 2019, Adidas Original advertised the New "YEEZY BOOST 700" shoe and the Pharrell Williams collection on Twitter. Each of both posts has more than 1.400 likes which are a significant difference in other Twitter posts from Adidas Original. But, Adidas is not promoting the campaign with pictures or mentions of Kanye West and Pharell Williams. The collection "YEEZY" stands for itself. One exception is the announced collaboration of Pharrel William´s Human Race with Nigo´s Human Made. For that advertisement, they used pictures of both designers to promote the new campaign. These types of cooperation are also suitable for the Chinese market. However, it is necessary to work with personalities who have a high reputation in China. As a result, Adidas is partnering with Chinese celebrities and public figures. One of the newest campaigns on Sina Weibo is promoting the shoe "Adidas Continental 80" in cooperation with the Chinese actress and singer Yang Mi. She can be considered as a superstar on Sina Weibo with more than 105,6 million followers. The post was liked 107.900 times and reposted more than 77.000 times. The figures are ten times higher than normal Adidas Original posts. Adidas is working closely together with celebrities. Almost every post is linked with a famous person like Lu Han (musician) with 60 Mio followers or Angela Yeung Wing (model) with 101 Mio followers. The "YEEZY" collection was the only posts that were not linked with a star.

The following table summarizes for the variables analyzed the differences between the two social networks.

Table 2. Major differences in Adidas' presence on social networks Twitter and Sina Weibo

Variable	Twitter	Sina Weibo
Structure of account network	Cover picture essentialy white	Cover picture colourful background
Topic of the post	Focussing primarily on their shoe collection	Diversificating the topics
Design of the post	Few colors	Full range of different colours.
Language of the post	English	Mandarin, but the name of the shoes are not translated; more text
Diversity of the post	Ethnically diverse models	Beauty bloggers from Asia
Cooperation with celebrities	Partnering with famous athletes and non-sports celebrities	Partnering with chinese celebrities and public figures

Source: authors

DISCUSSION

The symbolism of color and the importance that people give varies between countries and is an element that marketing and in particular marketing on social networks can not belittle, to achieve go against the culture of the country. This situation is explored by Adidas on the cover of social networks and also in the number of colors used in the creation of posts.

Adidas Original is implementing the recommendations from the literature. By keeping their posts simple on Twitter they use the method that is favouring low context cultures. Sina Weibo is used in China which is categorized as a high-context culture. Consequently, they utilize colourful pictures, and special graphics and design elements in order to be adapted to the taste of the culture.

The theme of the post is more concentrated on the social network Twitter, than on the social network Sina Weibo. By using an inspirational and symbolic writing style, the post appeals perfectly to high-context cultures. Moreover, the aesthetic of a post is really important for a high-context culture. Therefore, Adidas uses the symbol of a cloud as an additional design element to increase the optical impression. The writing language used on Twitter - English - goes against a more global presence, but that in the case of China, the company felt the need to go against the local culture, using Mandarin, bearing in mind that language is one of the maximum expressions of a culture.

Also the use of personalities, incorporating in its communication Chinese celebrities and public figures, reveals that in the social network Sina Weibo, the company seeks to meet a local communication. On Twitter the diversity of nationalities is a reality, as well as the area of activity of these people, which demonstrates that there is a preference to be as comprehensive as possible, which fits into the transversality of various cultures. The difference in the diversity of the post, which in the social network Sino Weibo bet on beauty bloggers from Asia reinforces the focus of the Adidas brand on Asian culture.

CONCLUSION

Since introducing Web 2.0, Social media has become an effective tool for communication without geographical boundaries at every time. Companies benefit from that development by using social media marketing. This form of marketing contributes to interact with the customer on a personal level, increase brand awareness and push the success of the company. Microblogs are a form of social media platform which is limiting the length of text messages. Their success story is built on several aspects. By creating ambient awareness the users feel a closeness and intimacy between themselves. Moreover, the unique type of communication through the function of resending posts can create a mass word-of-mouth phenomenon and motivate a user to get additional information on a specific topic. Companies have discovered the potential of microblogs and developed them as a brand promotional tool. Increasing communication with their customers, creating a community, inform about the newest products are some of the information a company shares on microblogs. The most famous microblog in the western world is Twitter with 330 million active monthly users.

Companies face difficulties when entering the Chinese social media markets. Famous western platforms like Facebook or Twitter are blocked by the government. As a result, China has developed its own unique social media landscape customized to the local culture. The most famous equivalent to Twitter is Sina Weibo with almost 600 million visitors per month. For a successful social media performance in China, companies need to understand the culture. Therefore, the article showed the differences between China, Germany, and the United States by using Hofstede´s six dimension models. The main differences were noticeable in the categories "Power Distance", "Individualism" and Hall´s division in "High context" and "Low context".

Company Adidas Original uses both social media platforms successfully. The analyse of their social media usage showed similarities and differences in both platforms. The structure, company profile and profile picture is relatively similar. Furthermore, both platforms use their cover picture for the newest product promotions. Commonly, the use of pictures or videos is also spread. However, social media team of the company is adapting its online presence on the market. In general, Adidas is posting more frequently on Sina Weibo (1,8 posts/day) than on Twitter (2,6 posts/day). By focussing on street wear on Twitter the focus of the microblogging platform is set differently to Sina Weibo which also concentrates on the street wear collection. Another adaption that both platforms do is on the design and the used language. On Twitter, Adidas provides only the main product information and focus on the design of the post on the product, whereas they do a different approach on Sina Weibo. By focussing on the use of a high-context culture, the language is more inspirational and provides more information. Moreover, the design can be described as more colourful.

Adidas uses the cooperation with celebrities differently on Twitter and Sina Weibo. With the help of celebrities, Adidas creates its own collections which they promote on Twitter. One of the famous product lines is called "YEEZY" that is promoted by models and not by the celebrities themselves. The promotional strategy on Sina Weibo is differently. First, Adidas collaborates only with celebrities known in China. Secondly, they use the reputation of the star by putting them in the main focus of their post. In Summary, Adidas is able to present the company on both platforms successfully. By adapting to the cultural standards they ensure that the followers can identify with the brand without losing their core values and brand recognition.

The study is positioned as exploratory and we consider that it provides some indications for the development of more structured and in-depth studies, namely on the elements that were analyzed in the two social networks and which contribute to check for differences in content and presentation, including graphics. It has several limitations, such as the mode used for the selection of posts, the number of posts used and the criteria used in the choice of the elements considered to analyze the post.

REFERENCES

Adidas. (2018). *Adidas annual report, 2018*. Retrieved from https://report.adidas-group.com/fileadmin/user_upload/adidas_Annual_Report_GB-2018-EN.pdf

Adidas. (2019). *Company brands*. Retrieved from https://www.adidas-group.com/en/brands/adidas/

Aichner, T., & Jacob, F. (2015). Measuring the degree of corporate social media use. *International Journal of Market Research*, *57*(2), 257–276. doi:10.2501/IJMR-2015-018

Akar, E., & Topçu, B. (2011). An examination of the factors influencing consumers' attitudes toward social media marketing. *Journal of Internet Commerce*, *10*(1), 35–67. doi:10.1080/15332861.2011.558456

Albers-Miller, N. D., & Gelb, B. D. (1996). Business advertising appeals as a mirror of cultural dimensions: A study of eleven countries. *Journal of Advertising*, *25*(4), 57–70. doi:10.1080/00913367.1996.10673512

Arceneaux, N., & Weiss, A. S. (2010). Seems stupid until you try it: Press coverage of Twitter, 2006-9. *New Media & Society*, *12*(8), 1262–1279. doi:10.1177/1461444809360773

Assaad, W., & Gómez, J. M. (2011). Social network in marketing (social media marketing) opportunities and risks. *International Journal of Managing Public Sector Information and Communication Technologies*, *2*(1), 13.

Brown, K. M. (2017). *Anteil der mehrmals täglichen Nutzer von ausgewählten soizalen Netzwerken nach Altersgruppen weltweit im Jahr 2016*. Retrieved from https://de.statista.com/statistik/daten/studie/680253/umfrage/mehrmals-taegliche-nutzung-von-sozialen-netzwerken-nach-altersgruppen/

Burton, S., Dadich, A., & Soboleva, A. (2013). Competing voices: Marketing and counter-marketing alcohol on Twitter. *Journal of Nonprofit & Public Sector Marketing*, *25*(2), 186–209. doi:10.1080/10495142.2013.787836

Cha, M., Haddadi, H., Benevenuto, F., & Gummadi, K. P. (Eds.). (2010). Measuring user influence in twitter: The million follower fallacy. *Fourth international AAAI conference on weblogs and social media*.

Chen, S., Zhang, H., Lin, M., & Lv, S. (2011, December). Comparision of microblogging service between Sina Weibo and Twitter. In *Proceedings of 2011 International Conference on Computer Science and Network Technology* (Vol. 4, pp. 2259-2263). IEEE. 10.1109/ICCSNT.2011.6182424

Cheong, Y., Kim, K., & Zheng, L. (2010). Advertising appeals as a reflection of culture: A cross-cultural analysis of food advertising appeals in China and the US. *Asian Journal of Communication*, *20*(1), 1–16. doi:10.1080/01292980903440848

Chiu, C., Lin, D., & Silverman, A. (2012). *China's social-media boom*. McKinsey & Company.

Corduan, A. (2018). *Social media als instrument der kundenkommunikation*. Springer. doi:10.1007/978-3-658-22317-5

Daft, R. L., & Lengel, R. H. (1986). Organizational information requirements, media richness and structural design. *Management Science*, *32*(5), 554–571. doi:10.1287/mnsc.32.5.554

Drury, G. (2008). Opinion piece: Social media: Should marketers engage and how can it be done effectively? *Journal of Direct, Data and Digital Marketing Practice*, 9(3), 274–277. doi:10.1057/palgrave. dddmp.4350096

e-Clincher. (2015). *43 Of The Best Social Media Marketing Quotes*. Retrieved from https://eclincher. com/blog/43-of-the-best-social-media-quotes/

Geier, A., & Gottschling, M. (2019). Wissenschaftskommunikation auf Twitter? Eine Chance für die Geisteswissenschaften! *Mitteilungen des Deutschen Germanistenverbandes, 66*(3), 282–291. doi:10.14220/ mdge.2019.66.3.282

Guan, W., Gao, H., Yang, M., Li, Y., Ma, H., Qian, W., Cao, Z., & Yang, X. (2014). Analyzing user behavior of the micro-blogging website Sina Weibo during hot social events. *Physica A*, *395*, 340–351. doi:10.1016/j.physa.2013.09.059

Gudykunst, W. B. (2004). Bridging differences: *Effective intergroup communication. Sage (Atlanta, Ga.).*

Hall, E. T. (1973). *The slient language*. Anchor.

Hall, E. T. (1989). *Beyond culture*. Anchor.

Hall, E. T., & Hall, M. R. (2001). Key concepts: Underlying structures of culture. *International HRM: Managing diversity in the workplace*, 24-40.

Havinga, M., Hoving, M., & Swagemakers, V. (2016). Alibaba: a case study on building an international imperium on information and E-Commerce. In R. T. Eden (Ed.), *Multinational Management: a casebook ons Asis's global market leaders* (pp. 13–32). Springer. doi:10.1007/978-3-319-23012-2_2

He, X., & Pedraza, R. (2015). Chinese social media strategies: Communication key features from a business perspective. *El Profesional de la Información*, *24*(2), 200–209. doi:10.3145/epi.2015.mar.14

Heiden, A. (2015). *Sponsoring im Profifußball: Das Beispiel adidas*. Bacherol Master Publishing.

Hettler, U. (2012). *Social media marketing: Marketing mit Blogs, sozialen Netzwerken und weiteren Anwendungen des Web 2.0*. Gebundenes Buch.

Hlee, S., Cheng, A., Koo, C., & Kim, T. (2017). The difference of information diffusion for Seoul tourism destination according to user certification on Sina Weibo: Through data crawling method. *International Journal of Tourism Sciences*, *17*(4), 262–275. doi:10.1080/15980634.2017.1384131

Hofstede, G. (2011). Dimensionalizing cultures: The Hofstede model in context. *Online Readings in Psychology and Culture*, *2*(1), 8. doi:10.9707/2307-0919.1014

Ji, M. F., & McNeal, J. U. (2001). How Chinese children's commercials differ from those of the United States: A content analysis. *Journal of Advertising*, *30*(3), 79–92. doi:10.1080/00913367.2001.10673647

Ji, Y. G., Hwangbo, H., Yi, J. S., Rau, P. P., Fang, X., & Ling, C. (2010). The influence of cultural differences on the use of social network services and the formation of social capital. *International Journal of Human-Computer Interaction*, *26*(11-12), 1100–1121. doi:10.1080/10447318.2010.516727

Johansson, J. K. (1994). The sense of "nonsense": Japanese TV advertising. *Journal of Advertising*, *23*(1), 17–26. doi:10.1080/00913367.1994.10673428

Kaplan, A. M., & Haenlein, M. (2011). The early bird catches the news: Nine things you should know about micro-blogging. *Business Horizons*, *54*(2), 105–113. doi:10.1016/j.bushor.2010.09.004

Kim, H., Coyle, J. R., & Gould, S. J. (2009). Collectivist and individualist influences on website design in South Korea and the US: A cross-cultural content analysis. *Journal of Computer-Mediated Communication*, *14*(3), 581–601. doi:10.1111/j.1083-6101.2009.01454.x

Kim, Y., Sohn, D., & Choi, S. M. (2011). Cultural difference in motivations for using social network sites: A comparative study of American and Korean college students. *Computers in Human Behavior*, *27*(1), 365–372. doi:10.1016/j.chb.2010.08.015

Kreutzer, R. T. (2018). *Social-Media-Marketing kompakt: Ausgestalten, Plattformen finden, messen, organisatorisch verankern*. Springer Gabler. doi:10.1007/978-3-658-21147-9

Lee, M. S., Geistfeld, L. V., & Stoel, L. (2007). Cultural differences between Korean and American apparel web sites. *Journal of Fashion Marketing and Management*, *11*(4), 511–528. doi:10.1108/13612020710824571

Lei, K., Liu, Y., Zhong, S., Liu, Y., Xu, K., Shen, Y., & Yang, M. (2018). Understanding user behavior in sina weibo online social network: A community approach. *IEEE Access: Practical Innovations, Open Solutions*, *6*, 13302–13316. doi:10.1109/ACCESS.2018.2808158

Liu, Y. (2016). *Social Media in China*. Springer Gabler. doi:10.1007/978-3-658-11231-8

Malik, M. E., Ghafoor, M. M., Iqbal, H. K., Ali, Q., Hunbal, H., Noman, M., & Ahmad, B. (2013). Impact of brand image and advertisement on consumer buying behavior. *World Applied Sciences Journal*, *23*(1), 117–122.

Manchanda, P., Dubé, J.-P., Goh, K. Y., & Chintagunta, P. K. (2006). The effect of banner advertising on internet purchasing. *JMR, Journal of Marketing Research*, *43*(1), 98–108. doi:10.1509/jmkr.43.1.98

Mendoza, M., Poblete, B., & Castillo, C. (2010, July). Twitter under crisis: Can we trust what we RT? In *Proceedings of the first workshop on social media analytics* (pp. 71-79). 10.1145/1964858.1964869

Mooij, M. (2018). *Global marketing and advertising: Understanding cultural paradoxes* (5th ed.). SAGE Publications Limited.

Nooruddin, Z., & Zhang, L. (2012). *7 Steps to Weibo Success*. Retrieved from https://www.chinabusinessreview.com/7-steps-to-weibo-success/

Pollay, R. W. (1983). Measuring the cultural values manifest in advertising. *Current Issues and Research in Advertising*, *6*(1), 71-92.

Saravanakumar, M., & SuganthaLakshmi, T. (2012). Social media marketing. *Life Science Journal*, *9*(4), 4444–4451.

Sheth, J. N., Sisodia, R. S., & Sharma, A. (2000). The antecedents and consequences of customer-centric marketing. *Journal of the Academy of Marketing Science*, *28*(1), 55–66. doi:10.1177/0092070300281006

Shuen, A. (2018). *Web 2.0: A Strategy Guide: Business thinking and strategies behind successful Web 2.0 implementations*. O'Reilly Media.

SimilarWeb. (2019). *Twitter.com - Visits weltweit 2019 | Statista*. Retrieved from https://de.statista.com/statistik/daten/studie/1021439/umfrage/anzahl-der-visits-pro-monat-von-twittercom/

Statista. (2019). *Apps - Top 20 nach Anzahl der Unique Devices in China 2019 | Statista*. Retrieved from https://de.statista.com/statistik/daten/studie/894126/umfrage/beliebteste-apps-nach-anzahl-der-unique-visitors-in-china/

Statista. (2020). *Number of internet users in China from December 2008 to December 2018*. Retrieved from http:// https://www.statista.com/statistics/265140/number-of-internet-users-in-china/

Stolee, G., & Caton, S. (2018). Twitter, Trump, and the Base: A Shift to a New Form of Presidential Talk? *Signs and Society (Chicago, Ill.)*, *6*(1), 147–165. doi:10.1086/694755

Sui, Y., & Yang, X. (2010, June). Article. In *Second International Conference on Communication Systems, Networks and Applications* (*Vol. 1*, pp. 164-167). IEEE.

Sullivan, J. (2012). A tale of two microblogs in China. *Media Culture & Society*, *34*(6), 773–783. doi:10.1177/0163443712448951

Svensson, M. (2014). Voice, power and connectivity in China's microblogosphere: Digital divides on SinaWeibo. *China Information*, *28*(2), 168–188. doi:10.1177/0920203X14540082

Tsai, W.-H., & Men, L. R. (2012). Cultural values reflected in corporate pages on popular social network sites in China and the United States. *Journal of Research in Interactive Marketing*, *6*(1), 42–58. doi:10.1108/17505931211241369

Tuten, T. L., & Solomon, M. R. (2017). Social media marketing. *Sage (Atlanta, Ga.)*.

Twitter. (2019). *Anzahl der monatlich aktiven Nutzer von Twitter weltweit vom 1. Quartal 2010 bis zum 1. Quartal 2019 (in Millionen)*. Retrieved from https://de.statista.com/statistik/daten/studie/232401/umfrage/monatlich-aktive-nutzer-von-twitter-weltweit-zeitreihe/

Wang, X. (2016). *Social media in industrial China*. UCL Press. doi:10.2307/j.ctt1g69xtj

Weinberg, T., Ladwig, W., & Pahrmann, C. (2012). *Social Media Marketing: Strategien für Twitter, Facebook & Co*. O'Reilly.

Yang, J. (2019). Cheap Wheat Adidas-apmkingstrack. com. *American Journal of Industrial and Business Management*, *9*(3), 720–726.

This research was previously published in Analyzing Global Social Media Consumption; pages 121-137, copyright year 2021 by Information Science Reference (an imprint of IGI Global).

Chapter 65

Communication on Social Network Sites:
Assessing Cyberbullying Among Young Women in Nairobi, Kenya – Case of Facebook Platform

Denish Ouko Otieno
Moi University, Kenya

Faith Halima Kirigha
Kenya Institute of Mass Communication, Kenya

Alfred Okoth Akwala
Technical University of Kenya, Kenya

ABSTRACT

Facebook is regarded as a popular social network in Kenya more so among the youth besides other sites like Instagram and Twitter. A study conducted by World Wide Web Foundation revealed that more than one in every five women in Kenya have experienced cyberbulling. Such study results justifies that the internet is rife with harassment with more women bearing the brunt as compared to men. The main objective of the study was to establish forms of cyber-bullying among young women between 25 to 35 years old on Facebook platform. It was established that unwanted trolls, doxing, and sexual harassment were the dominant cyberbullying trends on Facebook among young women in Kenya with men being the highest perpetrators of cyberbullying than women. It was also established that there is lack of awareness among young women on Facebook Safety, which is a resource developed by Facebook for reporting inappropriate content and help protect people who may be feeling self-injury due to cyberbullying on Facebook.

DOI: 10.4018/978-1-6684-6307-9.ch065

INTRODUCTION

Mathews et al. (2000) define social media as any medium of communication that allows interaction and network of relationships. While social network sites (hence forth referred to as SNS) are platforms or sites that facilitate communication, interaction and social relations, Aggarwal and Charu (2011) state that SNS are more about the tools used to make that content available to others and to allow users to connect, to engage with it and to build online communities. SNS can as well be defined as internet based social spaces designed to facilitate communication, interaction, collaboration and content sharing across network of contacts. Furthermore, Aggarwal and Charu (2011) state that sites which are used for sharing online media content such as Flickr, Youtube, and Instagram can also be considered as indirect forms of social networks because they allow an extensive level of user interaction. Boyd and Ellison (2007) concludes that SNS are web-based services that allow individuals to construct a public or semi-public profiles within a bounded system, articulate a list of others with whom they share a connection.

It is with the advent of the 21st Century - the information age - that the explosion of social network took place. Impressive growth of social network tendency was recorded when Facebook was launched in February 2004. Facebook is considered as the largest network across the globe. Before the historical diffusion of SNS, with the launch of Facebook, other SNS were launched as well. According to Boyd and Ellison (2007), the first recorgnisable social network site launched was SixDegress.com in 1997. It allowed users to create profiles, list their friends and beginning in 1998, they were able to surf the friend lists.

Preceding this historical diffusion of Facebook, SNSs like AsianAvenue, BlackPlanet, MiGente, LiveJournal and Friendster were launched and re-launched. This process of adding features and innovating the platforms, supplied as an advantage for the development of Facebook, as well as for the progress of the large number of SNSs used actually, such as Twitter, Skype, E-mail, YouTube and Flicker. In the beginning of 2005, as pointed by Boyd and Ellison (2007), with the large attendance of SNS platforms, SNS became a global phenomenon. In addition, SNS have changed the way people interact and communicate. Furthermore, these Web platforms provide tools, with open services, that facilitate the interaction, information sharing and online communication.

Moreover, in the digital age, with the advent of internet, people are becoming more and more dependent on SNS to interact and create social relations in addition to communication. This dependence is due to the tools that SNS provide that allow users to have social relations easily without any kind of constraints or fears created when it comes to a direct interaction and social relations with the society.

Kaplan and Haenlein (2014) define social media as a group of internet based applications that build on the ideological foundations of Web 2.0 and that allow the creation and exchange of user generated content. The advent of social media has presented a unique opportunity for communication. Social media platforms like Facebook and Twitter over the years have attracted a number of young people, especially the youth. These interactive platforms have made the world become a global village and what happens in Europe is business in Africa and vice versa. People are spending more time on SNS, which has grown at a rapid pace and has become more popular than any other interaction platform in history (Parvez et al., 2019). The SNS has since enabled social relations and networks between individuals, virtually connecting those with similar interests, experiences and/or real-life connections (Cheung et al., 2015). Just as social media platforms present opportunities for interaction, users are also faced with challenges of abuse from other online users.

In social media it is made compulsory for users to create digital identities which may include some personal information such as name, physical address, e-mail address, phone number, date of birth, e.t.c. Even though individuals disclose their personal information to the SNS providers, that same information can easily be accessed by social media users who learn more about your personal preferences, lifestyle, relationship status, e.t.c. (Krasnova et al., 2010).

Merchant (2006) posits that wider-reaching changes in the economic, political and social order which have had both global and local impact have produced the necessity and the desire to create and maintain new kinds of social networks which have led to the emergence of new social identities, identities that are more accurately defined by lifestyle, and media consumption. Scare stories tend to focus on the internet as constructed by popular media of being a place inhibited by weird and scary people, in which weird and scary things take place. Current trends of sexual, psychological violence that have been recorded on different social media platforms link our online identity to increased cyberbullying threats and scare stories, such as your virtual property is never secured - it can be stolen or maliciously corrupted by virus; your personal details are easy to locate - so easy that internet criminals can steal and use your identity; you are constantly under surveillance - where you go, what you do and what you say is always tracked; your personal safety is at risk - children and young people in particular are at risk from sexual predators; and, finally, you should not trust who you meet - people are not who (or even where) they say they are. The benchmarks of these fears are fuelled by the thought that engaging in internet based communication can actually pose a threat to a persons' identity. It is against this background that the study focused on the overall objective to establish forms of cyberbullying among young women on Facebook platform. The specific study objective is to establish ways in which young women protect themselves from cyberbullying on Facebook platform and to establish the motivation behind young women using Facebook as a social network platform.

STUDY BACKGROUND

According to a survey conducted by Communication Authority of Kenya (CA,2018), the use and access to information technology equipments (IT) was more prevalent among the youth between 20 to 35 years. This prevalence in IT use is further supported by statistics from International Telecommunication Union (ITU, 2018), which recorded that the number of internet users in Kenya grew from 21 percent in 2016 to 26 percent in 2017. Such steady rise in IT use also translates to exacerbate online vices such as cyberbullying.

As online communication is developing at such a fast pace that new ways of targeting and abusing individuals online are constantly emerging (Barrett, 2016). This is not limited to phony profiles for nonexistent people which neither social media companies nor technological innovations provide effective ways of identifying and deleting such accounts (Vishwanath, 2018). Although divulging personal information may provide a virtual safe space to victims of violence (where the victims report the abuser), digital identities can be misused by others, possibly resulting in serious negative results i.e. humiliation, destroying careers, reputations, and relationships, and drive victims to suicide, while presenting "honor" violence in societies. Phony profiles created to hide individuals' identities presents the 'dark side' i.e. cyberbullying, addictive use, trolling, fake news, online witch hunts, and privacy abuse. Regardless of the many opportunities offered by social media, there are a number of incidents indicating that social media undeniably has a "dark side" (Baccarella et al., 2018).

In the context of this study, cyberbullying can be defined as any online behaviour that constitutes assault of the well-being of the target individual or group. This form of harassment takes many forms that include unwanted trolls, unwelcome contact, sexual harassment, threats of rape or death, and cyberstalking. It can affect a persons' emotional and psychological well-being. In addition, cyberstalking also involves intimidation or explicit threats. Once a person realises that they are being stalked, they are likely to become paranoid, scared, and withdraw from social spaces.

Research and practice have mostly focused on the "bright side" of social media by highlighting opportunities offered by this technology (Baccarrela et al., 2018). However, it is increasingly observable that social media presents enormous risk to individuals. Phony profiles, digital identities, cyberstalking and trolling have aided these risks. Former Facebook executive Chamath Palihapitiya, stated that he regrets that some of the tools he has helped to create "are ripping apart the social fabric of how society works" (Wong, 2017). This quote vividly underscores how the qualities of enormous presence of social media platforms are also undermining the freedoms and well being of individuals and community they serve. Communication Authority of Kenya (CA) in 2018 reported that cases of cyberbullying and general cyber security were on the rise among the youth and children, yet they are the fastest online growing demography. In the wake of new challenges in the digital space, the government of Kenya established Computer Misuse and Cybercrime Act, 2018 that provides for offences relating to computer systems to enable timely and effective detection, prohibition, prevention, response, investigation and prosecution of computer, cybercrimes; to facilitate international co-operation in dealing with computer and cybercrime matters; and for connected purpose (Government of Kenya, 2018). Despite the enactment of this law several forms of cybercrime have been on the rise, more so among women in Kenya.

A study conducted by World Wide Web Foundation (2016) revealed that more than one in every five women in Kenya have experienced cyberbullying. Such study results reveal that the internet is rife with harassment with more women bearing the brunt as compared to men. For example, in Kenya, a 29 year old female Facebook user is reported to have committed suicide after her appeal for help on a certain group was met with ridicule. In a Facebook post " the young woman alleged that her ex-boyfriend had defiled her daughter and while she had recorded a statement with the police, the culprit was still free". The young woman threw herself and her daughter in front of a moving car and she was pronounced dead on the spot while her daughter survived the incident. (https://nairobinews.nation.co.ke/life/cyber-bullying-womans-suicide/).

Indeed cases of cyberbullying continue to thrive among women, not leaving behind those in the public eye. More recently in April 2020 Kenyas' first CoronaVirus recovery patient was heavily bullied by Kenyans online after coming forward to speak to Kenyans on her recovery journey. A section of Kenyans took to online to discredit and question the truth in her story. To further escalate the scenario, her personal conversations and nude photos were leaked online which led to her being heavily trolled and bullied. In the wake of this, Kenyas' Health Cabinet Secretatry, Mutahi Kagwe, was angered by Kenyans' behaviour, calling them out for trivialising government efforts to combat the disease. The cabinet secretary called on police to arrest social media abusers. (https://www.ifree.co.ke/2020/04/brenda-ivy-cherotich-and-yvonne-okwara-victims-of-cyberbullying-in-recent-times/)

Sharing of nudes and sex tapes as revenge tool or form of shamming and bullying women has become the norm in Kenyas' social media platforms. Men are said to send photos of their private parts to women who accept their friend request on Facebook. Such men feel invisible when they are on the internet hence do things they can hardly do face to face (https:www.nation.co.ke/lifestyle/sartuday/leaking-nudes-is-the-new-form-of-sexual-violence/1216-5527196-y8mh5t/index.html)

The surge on cyberbullying on Facebook platform prompted the social media site to developed tools with sets of options that help one to determine who can read your posts including other security options one needs to adhere to while on the platform. "With the help of these new tools, if someone posts something on Facebook that makes you concerned about their well-being, you can reach out to them directly — and you also can also report the post to us. We have teams working around the world, 24/7, who review reports that come in. They prioritise the most serious reports like self-injury" (Facebook, 2016).

This study will therefore add knowledge on the risks social media present to its users, more so focusing on forms of cyberbullying and experiences among young women in Nairobi, Kenya. In addition, by highlighting the 'dark side' of social media use, young women will become more conscious of the potential risks they are likely to face while on social network platforms like Facebook.

PROBLEM STATEMENT

Facebook as a Social Network Site (SNS) is popular among the youth in Kenya. SNS have brought a number of opportunities since their advent; however, there are several indicators on their dark side. Baccarella et al. (2018) posit that research and practice have mostly focused on the 'bright side' of social media by exploring opportunities afforded by this technology, however, it is a reality that social media present enormous risks to individuals and even society as a whole. The dark side of SNS presents risks such as cyberbullying, and platform for proliferation of fake news. Communication Authority of Kenya (CA, 2018) reported that there were increasing cases of cyberbullying among the youth in Kenya. In the wake of this challenge the government of Kenya established Computer Misuse and Cybercrime Act, 2018 that provides for offences relating to computer systems, however, cyberbullying continue to thrive among young women in Kenya with recent case of Kenyas' COVID-19 recovery patient bullied online (Daily Nation, April, 2020). According to a study on cyberbullying among university students, it was established that there is high prevalence of cyberbullying in universities where male students are more likely to commit acts of cyberbullying more than their female counterparts (Ndiege et al., 2020). It is, therefore, evident that cyberbullying continues to escalate on several SNS and if left unchecked then digital platform safety cannot be guaranteed. Therefore, the gist of the study is that despite laws being in place to protect online community where the youth forms a larger demography and exposure of the group on the online platforms, cyberbullying continues to take a worring trend, more so among young women in Kenya. It is, therefore, a study interest to investigate forms of cyberbullying among young women in Kenya.

THEORETICAL FRAMEWORK

Theory in qualitative research presents a systematic way of understanding events or situations. It is a set of concepts, definitions, and propositions that explain or predict these events or situations by illustrating the relationships between variables (U.S Department of Health and Human Services, 2005).

Communication Theory of Identity (CTI) was used in the study to help establish the motivation for young women in using Facebook as a social network platform. CTI was developed by Michael Hecht and colleagues. The theory emerged in the 1980s as part of shift from identity being considered as central element of human existence to identity as a social phenomenon. (Littlejohn & Foss, 2009). The proponents of the theory argue that humans are inherently social beings whose lives revolve around communication, relationships and communities who operate from multiple and shifting identities, just like the online community which is characterised by mixed identities of users, that is, from use of pseudo accounts, to use of nick names and exhibition of different behaviours during interactions. As a result, identities and identification are key processes through which people and groups orient themselves to each other and the world around them. This argument supports the reason why people join SNS, among them, to connect with others, and make new friends which in turn help to satisfy peoples' sense of belonging; to communicate and share, thereby connecting with online audience in deeper ways through interaction.

Muted Group theory was used in the study to help establish forms of cyberbullying among young women. As Littlejohn and Foss (2009) posit, the theory focuses on the ways that communication practices of dorminant groups suppress, mute, or devalue the words, ideas, and discourses of surbordinate groups. The theory is concerened with what and how much people with differing social status speak, when and where they speak, with what words and concepts, in what modes or channels and with what repercussions. The proponents of Muted Theory argue that members of the surbordinate groups do speak and may have a lot to say, but in mixed situations they may have little power to say it without getting in trouble. Empirical studies done by Communication Authority (CA, 2018) and World Wide Web Foundation (2016) indeed indicate that women are the most targeted group when it comes to cyberbullying. The studies further reveal that men treat women as surbordinate groups in most discussion forums, hence in cases where women would assert their ideas in public discourse they always find themselves on the receiving end by their male counterparts who devalue their opinions. While Facebook as a social network platform creates an environment for interactive communication among men and women, in most cases women are unfairly targeted and bullied when they give their contributions on these platforms and as a result they become victims to cyberbullying. This theory therefore helps us to understand various forms of cyberbullying among young women on Facebook platform.

METHODOLOGY

Qualitative research approach was used based on the type of data and method of data collection used which included informal conversations, and semi-structured interviews. Informal conversations were done on face to face basis with study participants to help follow up issues that arose during interaction with the study participants. For example, study participants were engaged to reveal wether all cyberbullying experiences were from the people whom they are connected to via Facebook or not. Narrative as a technique in qualitative approach was used to generate data, where study participants shared their experiences in regard to forms of cyberbullying they have been subjected to on Facebook platform, how they protect themselves against cyberbulying on Facebook and what motivates them to prefer Facebook as their social network site of choice. Jwan and Ong'ondo (2011) posit that narrative research is the study of how different human experience the world around them and involves methodology that allows people to tell the stories of their lives. It involves collecting data about the participants experience and the meanings they attribute to those experience.

Sample Size

A population is the group that research focuses on (Cooper & Schindler, 2003). The study targeted young women in Nairobi between the ages of 22 years and 35 years who were active on Facebook platform. The study participants were all accessing Facebook via their smartphones. Participants were asked to voluntarily state their age before data was collected. All study participants were willing to state their age which was between 22 and 35 years old. 50 percent of the study participants were university students while another 50 percent were working class. The target population was chosen because they were most vulnerable to cyberbullying according to a report by Communication Authority of Kenya (CA, 2018) and at the same time the demography registered an increase in use of information based technology services in Kenya.

Purposive sampling was used to select 20 study participants. 50 perecent of the study participants were purposively sampled because research done by Ndiege et al. (2020) on cyberbullying among university students in Kenya revealed that cyberbullying in universities was indeed rampant among female students. Another 50 percent of the study participants were also purposively sampled based on report by World Wide Web Foundation which found out that in Kenya more than one in every five women have experienced cyberbullying. Qualitative research tends to work with relatively small number of cases/participants, therefore, qualitative researchers sacrifice quantity for detail. This means that scope in qualitative research is more considered in terms of detail of what we get from the case(s) than the number of cases (Silverman, 2005).

Data Analysis and Presentation

Thematic analysis as qualitative data analysis strategy was used, hence an inductive approach where themes emerged from data. Thematic analysis is the search for themes of relevance to the research topic under which reasonably large amounts of data from different sources such as observations, interviews and documents can be organised (Hammersley et al., 2001). During data analysis, the following stages were followed: transcribing data - here 10 study participants narratives were translated from Kiswahili to English language; re-familiarising with the data; first phase coding; second phase coding; third phase coding; and product report. Data was presented in form of narratives.

Study Trustworthiness/Credibility

Qualitative validity means that the researcher checks for the accuracy of the findings by employing certain procedures, while qualitative reliability indicates that the researcher's approach is consistent across different researchers and different projects (Gibbs, 2007). The research adopted multiple approach validity strategies to check on accuracy of the findings (Creswell, 2014). Strategies used were: data triangulation, use member checking to determine the accuracy of the qualitative findings through taking final report or specific descriptions or themes back to participants and determining whether these participants feel that they are accurate; clarification of the bias researcher brings to the study; use peer debriefing to enhance the accuracy of the account; and use external auditor to review the entire study.

SUMMARY OF FINDINGS

Forms of Cyberbullying Among Young Women on Facebook Platform

During semi-structured interviews the study established that most young women were experiencing sexual harassment from their male connections on Facebook platform. All the 20 study respondents interviewed said they had encountered sexual harassment. A study participant narrated her experience thus:

A male friend whom we connected with via Facebook stated asking about my nude photos. He persisted for so long that I had to block him from my connections list.

During informal conversations it was further established that it does not matter if you are connected to a person since there are people who go to your profile with intention of obtaining information such as mobile number, email address then they use the contacts to reach you and start requesting for sex. Young women also faced cases of doxing while on Facebook platform where their male connections have revealed personal information without their consent solely for the purpose of embarrassing them. All the 20 study participants responded to have experienced doxing of Facebook platform.

In one of the semi-structured interviews *dissing* was also noted to be another form of cyberbullying that young women faces on Facebook platform. This is an act where a bully spreads cruel information about their target through public posts or private messages to either ruin their reputation or relationship with other people. In these situations the bully tends to have a personal relationship with the victim either as an acquaintance or a friend. During informal conversation it was established that young women experience *dissing* mostly from male counterparts whom either they were in a relationship with or have shown interest in them but they were not interested. Another interesting thing is that dissing was also established to occur among young women as witnessed during observation where a study participant volunteered to reveal some of the alarming private messages she received from a male friend with intention of ruining her reputation.

Unwanted trolls where a bully seeks to intentionally upset others by posting inflammatory comments online with malicious and harmful intent. Trolling can also be an act of creating discord on the internet by starting quarrels or upsetting people by posting inflammatory or off topic messages in an online community. All the 20 study respondents said to have experienced unwanted trolls. This was established during informal conservations, semi-structured interviews and observations. These occur when a person post a comment online that shows their particular standpoint on an issue. A study participant during informal conversation opined that men still are uncomfortable when women comment issues on politics. In Kenya since politics is male a dominated field there is still some public expectation that women should not be active participants in political debates. Most young women admitted to have received unwanted trolls when they contributed on some emotive political debates on Facebook. In fact a study respondent said that at one point she was told by a male with whom she had been friends on Facebook for a long time that her place is in the kitchen and she had no moral authority to contribute in matters politics.

Masquerading was also noted as a form of cyberbullying experience, more so by young women who are public figures and are on Facebook platform. Masquerading happens when a bully creates a made up profile such as creating fake email account, fake social media profile, and selecting new identity and photos to fool the victim and the bully tends to be someone the victim knows very well. In one of the interviews a participant opined that she had been threatened online to pay out money so that her private information is not revealed to the public by masquerading accounts on Facebook platform.

The Muted Group Theory has helped us to answer the research question on forms of cyberbullying amaong young women. The theory posits that communication practices of the dorminant groups do suppress, mute or devalue words and ideas of the surbodinate groups. As revealed during informal conversation young women experienced '*dissing*' from their male counterparts where their ideas were devalued so as to scare them from participating in debates.

Ways in Which Young Women Protect Themselves from Cyberbullying on Facebook Platform

From the results of both informal conversation and semi-structured interviews, study participants who have experienced cyberbullying have become paranoid on active interaction on Facebook platform and opted to become passive consumers of Facebook content by making a decision not to contribute in any discussion to avoid further bullies from their connections. Other ways young women stated to deal with cyberbullying include leaving Facebook platform by deleting their accounts, blocking those who bully them from their connections, and un-friending. Out of the 20 study participants only one person said to have reported case of cyberbulling to the police but none had flagged any content of cyberbullying as inappropriate through Facebook-Safety or visited Facebook Help Centre (https://www.facebook.com/help/594991777257121/)

Motivation of Young Women In Using Facebook as a Social Network Platform

The study established that most young women were on Facebook platform because it is a popular platform in Kenya hence they can connect with a number of their friends. Another reason was that the platform is user friendly and most enjoyed the recently added new feature where you can engage *Data Mode* to use Facebook when bundles are used or in case you are running low on data bundles you can use Free Data Mode, *Go to Free*, which allows you to only read texts. Another reason study participants gave is that Facebook is the first social network site they joined and for the past 10 years they had been on the platform, hence it gave them their first online experience of creating content, sharing information, connecting to new friends, getting informed in happenings around the world. Communication Theory of Identity used in the study posits that human beings are inherently social beings whose lives revolved around communication and relationships. As revealed in the study what motivated young women to use Facebook platform is the sense of belonging to a group so that they can communicate and create bonds.

CONCLUSION

The study concludes that sexual harassment, unwanted trolls and doxing are the dominant types of cyberbullying that young women in Nairobi, Kenya, face on Facebook platform. There are also other forms of cyberbullying such as dissing, and masquerading experienced by young women on Facebook platform. Forms of cyberbullying experiences were similar among study participants who were college students and the working class.

Young women experiencing cyberbullying on Facebook platform have not taken advantage of the new security features developed by Facebook platform to curb rising cases of online harassment i.e Facebook Safety platform developed in June, 14th, 2016. No single study participant noted to have reported any case of cyberbullying through Facebook Safety platform. Despite the enactment of the Computer Misuse and Cybercrime Act, 2018 by the Kenya Government to enable timely and effective detection, prohibition, prevention, response, investigation and prosecution of computer and cybercrimes; young women still haven't taken advantage of the new law in place to protect themselves from cyberbullying by reporting perpetrators to the authority, instead they suffer in private as they are bullied by their connections and those whom they are not connected to on Facebook platform.

RECOMMENDATION

The study recommends that there is need for sensitisation on how women in Kenya can protect themselves on social network platforms so as to reduce cases of cyberbullying.Communication Authority of Kenya (CA) and other stake holders should roll out campaigns to create awareness among young women on the need to actively report cases of cyberbullying on social network platforms. Facebook as a social network platform should as well sensitise its users through automatic prompts to be aware of the new safety measures it has developed to ensure safe online use.

REFERENCES

Aggarwal & Charu. (2011).*Social Network Data Analytics*. Kluwer Academic Publishers. Available at: http://charuaggarwal.net/socialtoc.pdf

Authority of Kenya. (2018, March 1). *Publications*. Retrieved from www.ca.go.ke/images//downloads/universal_access/survey/National%20ICT%20Survey.pdf

Baccarella, C., Wagner, T., Kietzmann, J., & McCarthy, I. (2018). Social media? It's serious! Understanding the dark side of social media. *European Management Journal, Elsevier., 36*(4), 431–438. doi:10.1016/j.emj.2018.07.002

Barrett, D. (2016). *Faking social media accounts could lead to criminal charges*. Available at: https://www.telegraph.co.uk/news/uknews/crime/12180782/Faking-social-media-accounts-could-lead-to-criminal-charges.html

Boyd, D., & Ellison, N. (2007). Social Network Sites: Definition, History, and Scholarship. *Journal of Computer-Mediated Communication, 13*(1), 210–230. doi:10.1111/j.1083-6101.2007.00393.x

Cheung, C., Lee, Z., & Chan, T. (2015). Self-disclosure in social networking sites. *Internet Research, 25*(2), 279–299. doi:10.1108/IntR-09-2013-0192

Communication Authority of Kenya. (2017). *First quarter sector statistics report for the financial year 2017/2018*. Nairobi: Communication Authority of Kenya. Retrieved from https://ca.go.ke/wp-content/uploads/2018/02/Sector-Statistics-Report-Q1-2017-18.pdfCommunication

Cooper, D. R., & Schindler, P. S. (2003). *Business Research Methods* (8th ed.). McGraw-Hill.

Creswell, J. W. (2014). *Research Design: Qualitative, Quantitative and Mixed Methods Approaches* (4th ed.). Sage.

Gibbs, G. R. (2007). Analyzing Qualitative Data. In U. Flick (Ed.), *The Sage Qualitative Research Kit*. Sage. doi:10.4135/9781849208574

Government of Kenya. (2018). *The Computer Misuse and Cybercrime Act*. Kenya Gazette Supplement No 60 (Acts No.5). Nairobi: Government Printer.

Guy, M. (2006). Identity, Social Networks and Online Communications. *E-learning*, *3*(2). Advance online publication. doi:10.2304/elea.2006.3.2.235

Hammerseley, M., Gomm, R., & Woods, P. (2001). *Research Methods in Education: Handbook*. Open University.

ITU. (2018, January 1). *Publications: ICT Development Index*. Retrieved from https://www.itu.int/net4/ITU-D/idi/2017/

Jeniffer, G., & Antigone, D. (2016). *Facebook Safety*. https://www.facebook.com/safe.../youth/facebook-basics/privacy

Jwan, J., & Ong'ondo, C. (2011). *Qualitative Research. An Introduction to Principles and Techniques*. Moi University Press.

Kaplan, A. M., & Haenlein, M. (2014). Collaborative projects (social media application): About Wikipedia, the free encyclopedia. *Business Horizons*, *57*(5), 617–626. doi:10.1016/j.bushor.2014.05.004

Krasnova, H., Spiekermann, S., Koroleva, K., & Hildebrand, T. (2010). Online Social Networks: Why We Disclose. *Journal of Information Technology*, *25*(2), 109–125. doi:10.1057/jit.2010.6

Littlejohn, S., & Foss. K. (2019). *Encyclopedia of Communication Theory*. Sage.

Matthews, H., Limb, M., & Taylor, M. (2000). The street as thirdspace: class, gender and public space. In S. Holloway & G. Valentine (Eds.), *Children's Geographies: Living, Playing, Learning and Transforming Everyday Worlds* (pp. 63–79). Routledge.

Merchant, G. (2006). Identity, Social Networks and Online Communication. *E-Learning and Digital Media*, *3*(2), 235–244. doi:10.2304/elea.2006.3.2.235

Nation, D. (2020). *Leaking Nudes is the New Form of Sexual Violence*. https://www.nation.co.ke/lifestyle/saturday/Leaking-nudes-is-the-new-form-of-sexual-violence/1216-5527196-y8mh5t/index.html

Ndiege, J. R. A., Okello, G., & Wamuyu, P. K. (2020). Cyberbullying among University Students: The Kenyan Experience. *The African Journal of Information Systems*, *12*(1), 2. https://digitalcommons.kennesaw.edu/ajis/vol12/iss1/2

Parvez, S., Rahaman, A., Fatema, K. & Rani Mondal, D. (2019). Impact of Social Networking Sites on Interpersonal Relationship among Teenager: A Sociological Analysis in the District of Bagerhat. *British Journal of Arts and Humanities*, 14-27. doi:10.34104/bjah.019.1427

Silverman, D. (2005). *Doing Qualitative Research* (2nd ed.). Sage Publications.

U.S Department of Health and Human Services, National Institute of Health. (2005). *Theory at a Glance. A Guide for Health Promotion Practice* (2nd ed.). National Cancer Institute.

Vishwanath, A. (2018). Why do so many people fall for fake profiles online? *The Conversation.* Available at: https://theconversation.com/why-do-so-many-people-fall-for-fake-profiles-online-102754

Wong, J. C. (2017). Former Facebook executive: Social media is ripping society apart. *The Guardian.* Retrieved from https://www.theguardian.com/technology/2017/

World Wide Web Foundation. (2016). *Womens' Rights Online.* Report Card, Measuring Progress, Drviving Action. https://webfoundation.org/wro-network/

This research was previously published in Dialectical Perspectives on Media, Health, and Culture in Modern Africa; pages 224-238, copyright year 2021 by Information Science Reference (an imprint of IGI Global).

Chapter 66
Rise of Facebook in the USA and WeChat in China:
Commodification of Users

Naziat Choudhury

Department of Mass Communication and Journalism, University of Rajshahi, Bangladesh

ABSTRACT

The owners of Facebook and WeChat repeatedly promote their media as the preferred platform for people to connect. Improving social relationships was marketed as the reason for their innovation. But users' urge to unite on these OSN services alone cannot explain the success of these media in the US and China. There is a different or rather new business approach underpinning these OSN services that contribute to their success. The author argues that there is an implication of owners' profit-based interest in ensuring the popularity of their online platforms. Audience commodity analysis as discussed by Dallas W. Smythe and Christian Fuchs is employed in the contexts of the US and China to comprehend the complex factors related to online social media owners' interest and their negotiation with the government in online media's prosperity. Through archival research including examination of newspapers, policy documents from OSN-based companies, and survey results from 2015 to mid-2018, this chapter demonstrates the political economy of Facebook and WeChat.

INTRODUCTION

Facebook in the US and WeChat in China are two of the most popular online social networking (OSN) services in the world. Both are trying to win the top place in the OSN market. This paper tries to understand the political economy aspect of these popular online social media. Facebook has been in the news in recent times with the way they deal with their users' data (BBC, 2018). The latest report suggests that Facebook has accumulated "… millions of user passwords in plain text files" (Cuthbertson, 2019, para. 1). This raised questions about how the other social media deal with their user base. In a world where commodification processes demand that companies look for new forms of consumer dependency, the

DOI: 10.4018/978-1-6684-6307-9.ch066

rise of OSN platforms and the power of these media to actively engage users has become a new frontier. Whilst users have been engrossed in communicating within their online social networks, company owners have been busy designing the online platforms in a way that helped to harvest these communication contents for profit. Facebook (owned by Facebook) and WeChat (owned by Tencent) have used sophisticated algorithms to transform these online platforms into automatic personal data-collecting apparatus. Some of these OSN services have spread out from their originating country to other countries in the world and are not confined to specific geographic locations. The political economy factors that were associated with the success of these online services are analysed here in the context of the US and China. It is argued that there is an implication of owners' profit-based interest in ensuring the popularity of their online social platforms.

BACKGROUND

Audience commodity analysis as discussed by Dallas W. Smythe (1981) and Christian Fuchs (2016) is employed in the contexts of the US and China to comprehend the complex factors related to online social media owners' interest as well as their negotiation with the government in online media's prosperity. It is important to focus on the influence of government regulation and surveillance of OSN services. These companies function within laws and regulations set by the government of a country. Governments design and create a market economy which structures the way a company will run. Examples of these can be the structure of taxation and private data ownership and control in the case of OSN-based companies.

The limited inquiry on the political economy perspective of OSN services in China (in the English language) was evident while conducting this research. The central focus of the majority of research papers was censorship or use practices. The Chinese Internet scenario poses unique characteristics that separate it from others; namely, the obvious state control over the Internet activities. In the case of OSN services, Benney (2014) argues that the Internet in China was another tool for state control. He further argued that the Internet interfaces were designed in a way that the users were unconsciously led to use the technology in a certain manner conformed to the Chinese state and market. This, he showed, was congruent with Sina Weibo (Benney, 2014).

This article demonstrates how the companies of OSN services are monetising and commodifying the "attention economy" of media users (Goldhaber, 1997, para. 3; Christophers, 2010; Trottier, 2016). The greater the number of users of an online platform, the greater the potential for possible revenue. Following the work of Dallas Smythe (1981) on the audience commodity, this paper explores the way advertising has driven the development of OSN features. In turn, the advertising market is the basis for financial success with OSN services across China and the US. Christian Fuchs (2016) demonstrates that online social platforms have two forms of economies: the advertising economy and the finance economy. In the advertising economy, owners earn revenues from advertisement sales. In the finance economy, these owners of OSN services raise stock prices by "sell[ing] shares to investors" (Fuchs, 2016, p. 35).

Audience power is used by these OSN industries to gain revenue, in which audience time is referred to as a "commodity" (Smythe, 1981, p. 234). Smythe (1981) shows that audiences play the roles of being both a worker and buyer. He explains that, in the context of commercial television industry, audience's attention is sold to the advertisers and commercials are sold back to the audiences. These audiences participate in the consumption process of commercials, but in this process of buying and selling, they do not gain financial profit (Smythe, 1981). Smythe (1981) argues that audiences work to produce commodities and all the hours spent not working and not sleeping are purchased by advertisers which he describes them as audience commodity.

As key artefacts for understanding the political economy of OSN services, the policy documents of Facebook and WeChat are brought into the article for analysis purposes. Archival research is needed to analyse the OSNs' policy-related reports as well as newspaper articles. In this paper, archival research consisted of the examination of newspapers, policy documents from OSN-based companies and their miscellaneous reports and survey results. These sources provided information to document the ways OSN companies use users' contents, companies' relationships with advertisers, the companies' profit-making and government's relationships to these companies.

Archival research has treated the policy documents of the OSN companies as texts, the investigation of which reveals the curious mechanisms of the political economy of OSN services. For audience commodity-related factors, research materials from 2015 to mid-2018 were collected. Archival materials such as statistical data are collected from Facebook.com, WeChat.com, Tencent.com, Alexa.com, Socialbakers.com, Statista and the Pew Research Center. Additionally, Factiva was used to search for newspaper articles.

AUDIENCE COMMODIFICATION AND OSN SERVICES

Fuchs (2012b, 2016) discusses how the commodification process takes place on commercial OSN services. He points out three main areas of concern related to this. First, basing his discussion on Marx's analysis of capitalism, Fuchs (2012b) argues that commercial OSN services like Facebook only offer their users a platform to communicate by commodifying their personal data. There exists no financial exchange between the owners and users for such activity, despite the owners gaining profit through this commodification process. So, for Fuchs (2012b), Facebook is a place for "consumption" and "production" (p. 714).

The second area for concern for Fuchs (2012b) is the emphasis on the advertisers' interest in the content created by the users. Within this process, the argument of Smythe (1981) is evident where "the audience itself – its subjectivity and the results of its subjective creative activity – is sold as a commodity" (Fuchs, 2012b, p. 704). Fuchs (2012b) claims that in the case of OSN platforms, work is outsourced to users who provide services without any financial gain. This helps the companies to invest less, save labour costs and "exploit" the workers (Fuchs, 2012b, p. 711). By content, Smythe (1981) was referring to television programs and radio broadcasts. But in this research content will be understood as the materials produced by the users. Most of the content on these OSN services is produced by users.

Despite the various online platforms and whether a user is using mobile or computer technologies, users provide free labour while creating content online. Beverungen et al. (2015) argue that Facebook provides not simply a space where people can communicate "freely" but actually contributes to a new form of free labour (p. 480). The workers of Facebook offer dual services: mapping out the website to allow for the creation of more content by the users and hence the production of more data; and building algorithms for collecting those data. Facebook's popularity is based on its power to retain its users through the search option and the inclusion of other popular OSN platforms, thus ensuring "compulsory friendship" (Gregg, 2011, p. 96).

It is important to note that users' data not only concerns the number of them using OSN services; advertising companies also build profiles of users with details including hobbies and interests as well as their online use patterns (Fuchs, 2012c). The commercials are tailored accordingly to meet the demand of the target audiences. The equation is simple: more user engagement with an online platform means better returns for the owners of that network as the company will make a bigger profit. For example, the existence of Facebook might be jeopardised if its users do not share or create content or communicate information with other that the advertising companies can collect and then direct advertisements to the users (Fuchs, 2012b). In simple terms, the political economy perspective argues that the more free labour is available on Facebook, the greater its chance for profitability as well as the promise of future profitability. The political economy perspective is not only limited to this form of economic surveillance but also the political surveillance (Fuchs, 2012a; Sandoval, 2012). This leads to the third point of focus.

As Fuchs (2012a, 2012b) highlights, the government has an interest in the commodification process. Along with these advertising companies, the state also has an interest in the users' data. OSN users and the contents they create are of great interest to both governments and the owners of OSN services.

THE COMMODIFICATION OF USERS

Source of Revenue

In order to understand the commodification of users' process, first the source of revenue needs to be discussed, followed by the users' role in the process. Facebook's (2014) Annual Report began with two clear statements in the overview section:

Our mission is to give people the power to share and make the world more open and connected.

Our business focuses on creating value for people, marketers, and developers. (p. 5)

The second statement quoted above clearly defines the business aspect of Facebook. Facebook, which is a commercial company, makes their revenue and profit mainly through advertising, a fact which is not clearly declared within the two quoted statements. Although Facebook does not mention its reliance on advertising for profit in its overview statement, it is explained in the section on how Facebook creates value for marketers:

We generate the substantial majority of our revenue from selling advertising placements to marketers. Our ads let marketers reach people on Facebook based on a variety of factors including age, gender, location, and interests. Marketers purchase ads that can appear in multiple places including in News Feed on mobile devices and personal computers, and on the right-hand side of personal computers. (Facebook, 2014, p. 5)

Small companies found Facebook a cheaper and more convenient place to advertise than other media. Initially, it was mainly small and medium-sized businesses that used Facebook space to advertise their products (Deagon, 2015; Swartz, 2015). These advertisements on Facebook's mobile devices are strategically placed within the News Feed, while advertisements on the desktop version are on the right-hand side of the profile. Although Facebook do not release details about the companies that have advertised on the site, they do mention that large portion of the revenue comes from such small companies (Swartz, 2015). Understanding the lack of technical expertise of these small businesses, Facebook offers training regarding online advertisements. Also to support small businesses, Facebook has introduced tools such as Local Awareness ads that can lead these companies towards their targeted audiences. Through this feature, businesses can identify potential customers in a specific area belonging to particular age group and gender with specific interests (Swartz, 2015). This enables a much easier process of targeting online users with advertisement and companies are now more knowledgeable about their potential customers.

Additionally, to further support this, Facebook launched a mobile ad manager service (IOS apps) through which advertising companies can create, manage and monitor commercials from around the globe. Facebook frequently opens new avenues for advertising companies to create and reach suitable online users. All these business-boosting approaches relate to users being hit with more advertisements. Such initiatives have proven effective for Facebook, as the advertising revenue grew from US$ 4,279 million in 2012 to US$ 11,492 million in 2014 (Facebook, 2014).

Facebook's decision to focus on small and medium-size businesses by providing them with technical support encourages other companies to join. Hence, more and more companies are investing in advertising on Facebook. Facebook (2016d) reports that in 2016, the OSN service had three million companies advertising on their site, out of which 70 percent were from outside the US. Facebook might soon challenge Google's top position, as these are the only two leading companies for online advertisements. Google's online advertising market share fell from 32 percent in 2013 to 31 percent in 2014, while Facebook's share increased from 5.8 percent in 2013 to 7.8 percent in 2014 (Deagon, 2015). In terms of digital display advertising revenue, Facebook has overtaken Google. In the US market, this form of revenue for Google dropped from 13.7 percent in 2014 to 13.0 percent in 2015 (Sullivan, 2015). These figures reflect the strength of Facebook as a company. Increasing revenue provides a positive and strong image of the company to the advertisers and, due to growth in both revenue and the number of users on Facebook, the company earned trust and satisfaction in the market that led to rise in share prices by 33 percent in 2015 (Chaykowski, 2015). This in turn encourages more companies to invest in advertising on the site. It is interesting to note that although the price of each ad increased 285 percent in the first quarter of 2015, the viewership of advertisements fell 62 percent (Goel, 2015). So, either the advertisement viewership or the prices of it did not have an impact on the number of advertisements the company received; rather, the number of users and their activities on the site did, as discussed in the next section on the commodification of users' content.

Tencent, the owner of popular OSN service WeChat in China, relies on Value Added Services (VAS) for revenue (Tencent, 2016b). The Chinese OSN services' advertising environment is dominated by two main Internet companies, Tencent and Sina Weibo. Among the two, Tencent has the bigger market, as Tencent's advertising business increased 110 per cent in year-on-year revenue in 2016 from 2015, in comparison to Sina Weibo, which saw a rise of 52 percent (Perez, 2016). Tencent's revenue in 2016 from VAS rose by 34 percent to RMB 24,964 million. VAS includes online games, content subscription services, QQ membership and sales of virtual items. The company's second highest revenue came from online advertisements, which increased 73 percent (RMB 4, 701 million), as seen in Table 1 (Tencent, 2016b). It is interesting to note here that, just like Facebook, WeChat began its journey as an ad-free destination. However, in August, 2015 the company began to roll out advertisements on its "Moments" section.

Table 1: Revenue of tencent

Revenues (Unaudited)	1Q 2016 (RMB in millions)	4Q 2015 (RMB in millions)
VAS	31, 995	30, 441
Online advertising	4, 701	5, 733
Others	2, 330	1, 640

Source: (Tencent, 2016b)

Based on the sources of revenue discussion of Facebook and Tencent, two points stand out: the dependence on advertisement for revenue and also the dependence on advertisement for survival in the online social media market. These two perspectives also indicate that marketers and advertisers are inclined to select those OSN platforms that harness more membership, based on Facebook and WeChat's large user base. This will be explained in the following section.

Users' Relationship to the Revenue-Making Process

Users' contribution to the revenue-making process aspect can be seen through the relationship between the number of users and the profit earned. As the number of Facebook users continue to increase, so does its revenue. It makes sense that advertising companies would not be interested in advertising on websites that have a limited number of users or that are losing their users. There is a clear business motivation behind Facebook's reluctance to publish details on deactivating accounts. Another significant matter missing in their data is the number of people who have multiple accounts and also details of false accounts. Fear of losing advertisers may drive the company to publish only general data on the total number of users. In doing this, Facebook is maximising the market economy approach.

Figure 1. Revenue and net income of Facebook from 2007 to 2015

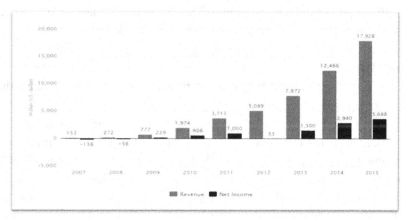

Source: Statista, 2016a

Figure 2. Number of Facebook users in millions from 2008 to 2015

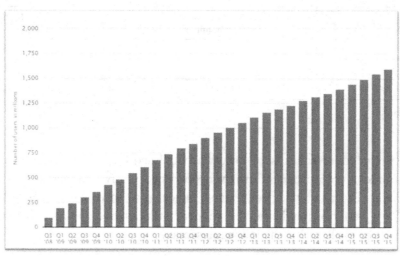

Source: Statista, 2016b

Figure 1 shows Facebook's annual revenue and net income from 2007 to 2015. The figure clearly illustrates the increase of the company's revenue every year. In parallel to that, Figure 2 shows a constant rise in the number of Facebook users. The concept of "more users meant more advertisements" appears to be demonstrated here. Figures 1 and 2 are a clear indication of such a trend.

Figure 1 shows that Facebook as a company lost net income from US$ 1 billion in 2011 to US$ 53 million in 2012; however, the total revenue continued to increase in those years. In connection with the total revenue is the number of users, which continued to grow in 2012 (as seen in Figure 2). This is the time when Facebook gradually lost its stronghold position to other OSN services. During that period, new OSN apps began to emerge and online users were looking for online media that offered new and innovative features. Facebook realised that this new online media could potentially create an impediment to the success of Facebook. For instance, Instagram is one such OSN service which continued to attract new users, so Facebook purchased the company for US $1 billion dollars in 2012. This merger proved to be a successful business deal, as in consecutive years Facebook had a rise in net income. Whenever Facebook faces a threat of extinction, the company quickly purchases popular mobile apps, often above their market value. The company has understood that Internet users are constantly shifting from one platform to another. From Friendster, MySpace and then Facebook, history shows that Internet users are always on the move.

WeChat's popularity also plays a role in Tencent's business revenue from advertisements. WeChat's monthly users' number is clearly correlated to revenue from advertisements, as can be seen in Table 2.

Despite being able to earn revenue successfully from advertising, Tencent's WeChat has ventured into payment services where purchases can be paid for with the app instead of using cards or cash. The mobile payment option has witnessed an incredible growth rate of 253.69 percent (2014) and 194.86 percent (2013). 90 percent of this "Code Scanning Group" is dominated by only two companies, Alipay and WeChat Payment (Chen, 2016, para. 1). In introducing this feature, WeChat appears to have taken control of the method of financial payment. In both the financial and communication sector, WeChat has retained their users. The app is designed so that users can use the one app to conduct their personal as

Table 2. Number of monthly users and revenue collection of WeChat

Year	Number of Monthly Users (WeChat) (in millions)	Revenue from Advertisements (in millions in RMB)
2013	355	5,034
2014	500	8,308
2015	697	17,468
2016	762	4,701 (First Quarter)

Source: Statista, 2016c; Tencent, 2015, 2016a, 2016b

well as financial activities. Stores also offer special discounts and promotions through the app payment option. Therefore, the retail stores as well as Tencent are being benefiting here while also providing convenience to the users. In 2015, WeChat Payment could be used at more than 300,000 retail stores, and approximately 200 million WeChat users conjoined their ATM cards with the WeChat Payment service (China Internet Watch, 2016). Part of this payment option is WeChat's successful initiative of digital red envelopes (known as *hongbao*), which could be sent through WeChat. During the Spring Festival holiday, 3.27 billion cash-filled virtual envelopes were sent in 2015 and this number jumped to 32.1 billion in 2016 (Meng, 2016b). The introduction of this feature was another attempt on the part of WeChat to retain its users and encourage more users to join.

In addition to the mobile payment option, Tencent has begun to target specific groups with WeChat. For instance, it has introduced a work-based app, known as Enterprise WeChat or Qiye Weixin, which can be used by big and small companies. This chatting option in WeChat allows users to do word-based activities including clocking in and out as well as seeking leave from the office (Meng, 2016a).

Mobile advertising is an example of how a larger user base attracts advertisers. Following the introduction of mobile apps, Facebook's number of daily active users rose to 894 million in September 2015, which was a 27 percent increase from 2014 (Facebook, 2015a). There seems to be a clear relationship between number of users and revenue collection. In the third quarter of 2015, mobile advertising revenue was around 78 per cent of total advertising revenue. This form of revenue was up from 66 percent in the third quarter of 2014 (Facebook, 2015a). This growth continued in the fourth quarter of 2015 as well. Mobile advertising revenue grew by 80 percent of the total advertisement revenue, which was also an increase from 69 percent in the fourth quarter of 2014 (Facebook, 2016a).

Tencent has also sensed the current pulse of the Internet users' reliance on mobile devices and has benefited from mobile advertising. Around 80 percent of Tencent's total advertising revenues came through mobile platforms. Tencent company's report proclaims that greater traffic on mobile-based apps and development in monetisation of advertising inventories led to this growth (Tencent, 2016b). Mobile advertising is a key area for revenue collection for these OSN services.

Facebook and Tencent embody the commercial entity in its full form and are similar to that of other conglomerates in the mass media industries around the world such as Time Warner and Disney. For instance, the Time Warner company owns businesses in different areas such as publishing (Time Inc., Little Brown and Co.), film (Warner Bros., New Line Cinema) and television production and distribution (Warner Television, WB Network) (Wasko, 2005). Disney also owns the American Broadcasting Company (ABC) television network and is a partial owner of ESPN, A & E and Lifetime channels along with its own home video, music and theme parks and resorts. Facebook and Tencent are taking the same route. Facebook owns several companies such as Instagram, WhatsApp and Onavo, Tencent holds QQ, Tencent Weibo and WeChat. Facebook and Tencent are the leading Internet-based companies along with Amazon, Alibaba and Google. Wasko (2005) argues that companies that purchase other businesses belonging to a similar group are regarded as being horizontally integrated, using Time Warner, who owns more than 140 magazines, as an example (Wasko, 2005). Thus Facebook and Tencent belong to this form of conglomerate, as their businesses concentrate mainly on information and communication technologies.

In the first phase of understanding the role that users play in the revenue process and how users are being commodified, it is important to note that Facebook and Tencent are commercial Internet-based institutions whose aim is profit-making. In this process, both users and advertisements are correlated and are crucial for the companies' survival. By capitalising on the users, the owners of these online social media, especially Facebook and Tencent, are constantly presenting new features to attract more users. These users are used as data for advertisers who can target ads to users, based on their preferences. This process clearly resonates with Smythe's (1981) concept of a "free lunch," where users are encouraged to use online social media and then these users and their contents are sold to advertisers for profit. Users are part of the profit-making process but not part of the profit-sharing.

THE COMMODIFICATION OF USERS' CONTENT

Data Collection and Management

According to data published by STRATA in 2015, advertising agencies prefer to use OSN services to advertise on and Facebook was the predominant choice (93 percent chose Facebook) (Whitman, 2015). Similarly, another survey conducted by RBC Capital Markets found that ad buyers were more interested in spending money advertising on Facebook (61 percent) in comparison to Google (53 percent) and YouTube (43 percent) (Ray, 2015). In the current Internet era, advertisements are mainly targeted. On average, Internet users use Facebook and other sites owned by the company for over 46 minutes per day. In 2015, Facebook users performed 1.5 billion searches a day and the company "indexed" around two trillion posts, according to the owner of Facebook, Mark Zuckerberg (Seetharaman, 2015). In connection with that, advertising revenue is also escalating. The average revenue per user on Facebook in 2015 was US$ 3.73, which is a 33 percent year-over-year increase (Gottfried, 2016).

In order to provide users with Internet-based advertisements, marketers or concerned companies need information about users. Marketers mainly target the young (8 to 24 years old), knowing that they hold the purchasing power of about US$ 211 billion (Montgomery, 2015). Facebook discloses its interest behind collecting data on users. One such reason is for marketing communications (Facebook, 2015b). Although what is involved in these communications is not clear, Facebook explains that personal information such as names and emails that could identify individuals is not provided to third parties (Facebook, 2015b). Without users' consent, identifiable personal information is not disclosed to advertising or Facebook's analytics partners. Instead of identifiable information, they provide them with aggregated information (Facebook, 2015b). Within that aggregated information, what type of data are collected and shared with the companies are not clear. Additionally, how in-depth the data collection processes are remains void within the company's published documents. This is an ambiguous area regarding the type of information Facebook collects.

The more information collected means that companies can better target advertisements. Facebook uses a complex tracking system to monitor and monetise users' behaviours. Facebook not only collects information but also stores it for an indefinite period. Even after user's accounts have been deleted, Facebook retains their data. Once it has information on users, the information never goes away. In other words, the data collected are recycled and reused according to the needs of the company and the advertisers. In its data policy, Facebook affirms that data would be erased if the account did not exist anymore and when they "no longer need the data to provide products and services" (Facebook, 2015b). Therefore, removing accounts from the site does not mean the complete elimination of data. The company also warns that "information that others have shared about you is not part of your account and will not be deleted when you delete your account" (Facebook, 2015b). For profit accumulation, Facebook uses invisible tracking, data monitoring and data monetising processes.

In order to efficiently collect users' information, Facebook invested in an online advertising providing company and bought the e-commerce search engine company "The Find" in 2015 to provide target-oriented advertisements to the users. This company "connects people to products" (Sloane, 2015, para. 2). "The Find" incorporated its activities within Facebook's advertising services, so that online retail stores could target shoppers more efficiently.

Chinese OSN companies are also following Facebook in the matter of purchasing new apps and adding new features to its already existing OSN service. The Chinese economy is primarily focused on exports and investments but now it has shifted to innovation and consumption (Fu, 2016). The giant success of the Internet in China has led to constant innovation, introducing new elements that would encourage more consumption and consumption-created demand for advertisements and, in turn assist, both Internet-based company owners and marketers in profit-making.

The extraordinary buying capacity and the propensity of the brand shopping of Chinese Internet users means that online media in China is a fertile land for advertisers. In 2015, there were 659 million online media users in China, which was more than in the US and Europe combined (Kemp, 2015). Along with this, the number of online shoppers in China increased from 301.89 million in 2013 to 413.25 million in 2015 (Statista, 2016c). Advertising companies would clearly like to reach this large numbers of users. Targeted advertising requires information on users which has been revealed already. Tencent's policy related to users' data collection and management is similar to Facebook, and the company has similar policies concerning collecting data for the purpose of targeted advertisements. Although WeChat has announced that users' content is not provided to third parties, the terms of use state that users' content is shared with other organisations in the name of service developments:

… in using Your Content for these purposes, we and our affiliate companies may copy, reproduce, host, store, process, adapt, modify, translate, perform, distribute and publish Your Content worldwide in all media and by all distribution methods, including those that are developed in the future;

we may share Your Content with third parties that we work with to help provide, promote, develop and improve WeChat, but these third parties (other than our affiliate companies) will not make any separate use of Your Content for their own purposes (i.e. for any purposes that are not related to WeChat). (WeChat, 2016a, para. 23)

Such claims are broad enough to encapsulate advertising companies' interest in collecting users' personal information. Although Facebook and WeChat provide targeted advertisements on users' pages, they do not clarify the type and amount of users' data collected for advertisers to provide targeted advertising. Socio-cultural or political differences have no control over how users' data are being used by these online OSN companies.

The Complex Process of Privacy Settings

The features of Facebook are designed to encourage users to provide more information about themselves. This structural design creates more involvement with the site, meaning more information for advertisers. Previously, this information about users was collected without their consent. European countries have investigated Facebook's use of personal data on the Facebook site as well as on external sites through "like" and "share" buttons. Belgium's Privacy Commission declared that, "Facebook processes the personal data of its members as well as other Internet users 'in secret,' without asking for consent or adequately explaining how the data would be used" (Fleisher and Fairless, 2015, para. 3). Due to allegations such as these, Facebook recently launched advertising preferences through which users could control the advertisements they saw. Under "Ad Choices" on Facebook, the company explained the process. Interestingly, users have to opt out from each device separately; in other words, opting out through mobile devices do not mean automatically removing advertisements from the other devices that a user uses. Introducing these options indicates that Facebook is aware of users' fear that personal data may be collected. Facebook also mentions that the users need to visit specific advertising companies to opt out i.e., Digital Advertising Alliance in the US, the Digital Advertising Alliance of Canada in Canada and the European Interactive Digital Advertising Alliance in Europe (Facebook, 2019). The association with these companies reflects Facebook's collaboration with powerful data analysis and research centres around the world to collect data on users in most effective manners.

The process for users to change their Facebook privacy settings is notoriously complex. Although the option to opt-out from advertisements and public views exists, several levels of approval automatically discourage the users from it. By default, users agree to share personal data with Facebook. When signing in to be a member of Facebook, users are inevitably roped into their tracking system. Content is posted as "public" by default. Not all Facebook users are familiar with privacy settings. In general, Internet users avoid the process of disabling tracking mechanisms due to its complexity. A survey showed that 91 percent of respondents in the US made no adjustments to their Internet or cell phone use to evade monitoring (Madden and Rainie, 2015).

Users' data are not only being shared with marketers and advertising companies but also with publishers. Facebook wants the site to become a one-stop destination where news, entertainment and communication are provided and the company is achieving this aim at the expense of users' personal data. The site allows certain news-based media houses to publish their news straight on the site and these houses "will keep all of the revenue on ads they sell directly; when the ads are sold by Facebook, revenue will be shared. Publishers will also get lots of data about how their stories are faring on Facebook" (Stelter, 2015, para. 6). Facebook has data on billions of users, which these media companies could easily access to gain insight into their audiences or readers. As Stelter (2015) mentions, no news-based companies in the USA or in other countries have such a vast array of audiences alone as Facebook does. Interestingly, the newsfeed algorithm through which Facebook controls what users see has generated controversy. News items with various perspectives usually seen on websites may not be viewed by the users. For instance, when the protests in Ferguson, Missouri in the United States were widely covered by all media and became a major domestic issue, the proof of the incident on Facebook was limited (Miller, 2015). This raises the issue of who has control over news items that are made visible to the users on Facebook.

Users in WeChat also need to undertake several levels of tasks to opt out from receiving targeted advertisements. In their privacy policy, the company declares that a privacy officer or marketing communication page should be contacted for shielding personal information from advertising companies. Guaranteed protection through such a process is not ensured, as the users may continue to receive "advertisements that are not direct marketing" (WeChat, 2016b). WeChat seems to have followed Facebook's footstep in users' information protection to pay heed to advertisers. Despite this growth, users are skeptical about storing information on the site due to fear of privacy leaks. Although 80 percent of WeChat users used their real names to register, the Internet Society of China found that around 78 percent of Chinese Internet users complained about stolen personal information including names and addresses (Ma and Cao, 2015). Due to the number of complaints such as these, Facebook and WeChat changed their privacy policies and introduced new options which involved layers of adjustments.

Surveillance by Governments

This section explores the political strategies and policies of online media, including the influence of state control on the owners of these online social media sites. The vested interests of online social media owners are linked to state interest as well. In the case of Facebook, the company's policy towards government requests for users' data states:

We may access, preserve and share your information in response to a legal request (like a search warrant, court order or subpoena) if we have a good faith belief that the law requires us to do so. This may include responding to legal requests from jurisdictions outside of the United States where we have a good faith belief that the response is required by law in that jurisdiction, affects users in that jurisdiction, and is consistent with internationally recognized standards. We may also access, preserve and share information when we have a good faith belief it is necessary to: detect, prevent and address fraud and other illegal activity; to protect ourselves, you and others, including as part of investigations; or to prevent death or imminent bodily harm. (Facebook, 2015c, para. 35)

This rather ambiguous policy has led the company to face legal battles many times within and outside of the US. A major legal action the company faced was related to users' data transfer from European Union (EU) to the US. EU was concerned about the US's data surveillance, especially as, unlike the US, they have a protection law for personal data (Fox-Brewster, 2015). EU countries have ensured their citizens have a fundamental right to know the information that companies have on them.

Through Facebook, some companies in the US were able to access European users' data through the Safe Harbour Framework (agreement between US and EU where US could transfer EU citizens' data). Due to concerns over the safety of personal information, the European Court of Justice ordered the Safe Harbour as invalid in 2015 (Fox-Brewster, 2015). Edward Snowden, the whistleblower, revealed that the US National Security Agency (NSA) was involved in online surveillance in 2013. According to him, the NSA in the US and the Government Communications Headquarter (GCHQ) in the UK collected Internet users' information by using programs such as PRISM and XKeyScore (Fuchs, 2016, p. 31). These programs allowed NSA and GCHQ to gather detailed browsing and content data on Internet users including online social media content (Fuchs, 2016). Facebook publishes a record of countries whose governments have requested users' details and the restriction to certain contents. These requests covered all Facebook services including WhatsApp. Regarding these requests, Facebook clarifies:

Every request we receive is checked for legal sufficiency. We required officials to provide a detailed description of the legal and factual basis for their request, and we push back when we find legal deficiencies or overly broad or vague demands for information. We frequently share only basic subscriber information ... We have included instances in which we have removed content that governments have identified as illegal, as well as instances that may have been brought to our attention by non-government entities, such as NGOs, charities, and members of the Facebook community. (Facebook, 2016c, para. 37)

Data published by Facebook shows that the US government made more requests than any other country, which supports the view that the US government intends to have some form of control over users' data (Facebook, 2016b).

That the government of China carries out surveillance on Internet users, Internet-based companies and the content created by users is well known. In order to monitor online activities, China imposed three forms of censorship: the Great Firewall (restrictions on foreign websites), the Golden Shield (monitoring local online activities) and the keyword blocking (online content with prohibited words or phrases) (Monggilo, 2016). Moreover, each website installed up to 1,000 censors and the government has employed around 20 to 50 thousand Internet police (*wang jing*) and Internet monitors (*wang guanban*) (King et al., 2013). China has engaged hundreds of thousands of people who are known as "fifty cent party" (*wumao dang*), based on their fees per post, to write positive notes on the government (Gunitsky, 2015). In the name of security, profiles are blocked, content is deleted and access to international websites such as Facebook, Twitter and YouTube are barred by the government.

For obvious reasons, WeChat follows the Chinese government's Internet surveillance rules. As with all of the Internet companies in China, WeChat is also held liable for all the information shared through the app. This implies that WeChat has to censor the users' content that is circulated within China. Hence, the company has different terms of services for those residents (in Chinese language) and non-residents of China (in English). The Chinese privacy policy provides more detail regarding the acceptability of users' content than the English version. For instance, section 8 in the Chinese language terms of services provides a detailed guideline of the subject matters that are prohibited "in violation of state laws and regulations" (WeChat, 2016c). Hence, it can be assumed that Internet surveillance exists in similar pattern for all OSN services in China. Ng (2015) shows that political issues that are most censored in public accounts of WeChat are Bo Xilai, Hu Yaobang, Hu Jintao, the freedom of the press, demolitions and the maintenance of stability. Nevertheless, WeChat is a more favourable tool for the government of China than other micro-blogging sites and social networking sites as the design of the messenger apps matches the interests of the government. As Ng (2015) points out, other forms of online social media's capability of convenient mass reach worried the government and WeChat is far more personal. Hence, the design of WeChat is appreciated by the government of China for two reasons: it avoids clashing with the government's strict censorship policy on collective action; and it makes a profit. This was also reflected in Monggilo's (2016) statement, who writes, "the Chinese government does not want the state and its citizens into the democratic activists, but activists on liberalism or capitalism with the Internet." (p. 948). So, the Chinese government allows the expansion of its market with a strict vigilance on online activities which perform against the party's interest. Micro-blogging site Weibo was seen as a threat to the stability of the regime, as it was increasingly becoming a place of protest for many Internet users. This led to government to make requests to the site to block content. Due to such pressure, researchers such as Ng (2015) assume that WeChat's popularity might be the result of strict control on Weibo. He argues:

Whether government officials intentionally set out to attack Weibo to push users to the less viral-enabling WeChat or whether this was an unintended consequence is unclear, but intention aside, the net result was a boon to regulators and policy makers who were concerned about Weibo's role in facilitating nationwide conversations and organizing capacities. (Ng, 2015, para. 14)

Since the 1990s the number of state-owned enterprises has decreased while the number of private institutions has increased. Nearly 12 million private companies were in business by 2013 (Tse, 2015). During Mao's regime, party members were mainly farmers and labourers but now they are more likely to be businesspeople. The composition of party workers in CCP related to business has increased over the years from 13 percent in 1993 to 34 percent in 2004 (Li, 2009). The following table shows the top wealthiest businesspeople and their membership to the state party.

Table 3. Businessmen's membership to state party in China

Name	Company	Wealth (in US$ trillion)
Robin Li	Baidu	14.7
Ma Huateng	Tencent Holdings Ltd.	14.4
Lei Jun	Xiaomi	13.5

Source: (Shabrina and Winarsih, 2016)

In the case of China, the online media owners appear to have some form of affiliation with the government party. Data in Table 3 show that Baidu and Tencent owners have membership in state party which directs towards their connections with the authorities of China. For example, by 2012, Tencent developed Party committee and the owner of Tencent became part of the 25 vice-presidents of the Internet Society of China, "an intermediary organization under CCP guidance" (Creemers, 2016, p. 4). Moreover, Ma Huateng was also one of the delegates in the Chinese People's Political Consultative Conference (CP-PCC) and the National People's Congress (NPC) in 2015 (AFP, 2015). Ma Huateng was also part of the team of businessmen who accompanied Xi Jinping on his first formal state visit to the United States.

The discussion in this section indicates that both the governments in the US and China conduct surveillance on users. The broad context of political culture in both contexts is different, as the US is democratic while China practices socialism. Despite the contrast in political culture, the government and owners share a mutual interest in users' data and their online content, which is also pointed out by Fuchs (2016).

CONCLUSION

Facebook and Tencent share certain commonalities between them in terms of audience commodity. OSN sites and messenger app companies such as these rely on advertisements for their revenue and Facebook and WeChat are the biggest revenue earners in this respect. The more users an OSN service has, the larger number of users, marketers and advertising companies can reach with minimum investments.

The next resemblance among these companies is sharing users' information and user-created content with advertising companies. These companies share such information with the advertisers in order to generate financial revenue. Companies like Facebook and Tencent need to survive in the ever-competitive market of OSN services. Without the state's direct or indirect support, these companies may not be able to continue with their businesses. Hence, these companies share users' information with the government.

The main findings of this research supports the existence of the commodification process on OSN services. Owners of these OSN companies are making profits by commodifying the users of these services. Facebook and Tencent gain profit from selling users' data to advertising and marketing companies. But, their main intention is to provide more support to advertisers than to users. To benefit the advertisers, these companies design and incorporate many features that would force users to create more content and thus allow the company to gain more information on users, while users have been provided with only one or two options to protect their information from advertisers (i.e., an opt-out option). Moreover, how the protection of personal data works is not clear. On the one hand, for monetary gains, users' data are shared with advertisers and marketers. And on the other hand, information is not delivered to the government in the name of protecting users' privacy. It is also not clear if information is provided to the government without the users' consent. Therefore, economic and government surveillance is being conducted simultaneously on these OSN services where users are being taken advantage of on both accounts. OSN sites and messenger apps in both the US and China depend on two powerful institutions for their existence: advertising companies and the government. The substantial growth of their user base reflects not only the interest of the users to build social capital on online social media but also the sites' increasing dependence on advertising that has shifted from mainstream media to online social platforms.

REFERENCES

Abutaleb, Y. & Bhattacharjee, N. (2015, Aug. 13). Facebook Struggles to Sell Advertising in India. *Reuters*. Retrieved from http://in.reuters.com/article/facebook-india-ads-idINKCN0QH0DY20150812

AFP. (2015, March 2). 5 of China's 10 wealthiest to take part in key political meetings. *Business Insider*. Retrieved from http://www.businessinsider.com/afp-chinas-wealthiest-to-take-part-in-key-political-meetings-2015-3?IR=T&

BBC. (2018, Dec. 19). Facebook's data-sharing deals exposed. Retrieved from https://www.bbc.com/news/technology-46618582

Benney, J. (2014). The Aesthetics of Chinese Microblogging: State and Market Control of Weibo. *Asiascape: Digital Asia*, *1*(3), 169–200. doi:10.1163/22142312-12340011

Beverungen, A., Böhm, S., & Land, C. (2015). Free Labour, Social Media, Management: Challenging Marxist Organization Studies. *Organization Studies*, *36*(4), 473–489. doi:10.1177/0170840614561568

Chaykowski, K. (2015, Nov. 4). Facebook Beats Third-Quarter Earnings, Revenue Estimates, Shares Rise. *Forbes*. Retrieved from https://www.forbes.com/sites/kathleenchaykowski/2015/11/04/facebook-beats-third-quarter-earnings-revenue-estimates-shares-rise/#37a0771a37a0

Chen, G. (2016). Quick Pass Churns Payment Market. Retrieved from http://en.ce.cn/Insight/201604/18/t20160418_10589502.shtml

China Internet Watch. (2016). WeChat Payment Reached over 300K Retail Stores. Retrieved from http://www.chinainternetwatch.com/17437/wechat-payment-reached-over-300k-retail-stores

Christophers, B. (2010). *Envisioning Media Power: On Capital and Geographies of Television*. Lanham, MD: Lexington Books.

Creemers, R. (2016, May 24-25). Disrupting the Chinese State: New Actors and New Factors. Paper Presented at the *Conference on Digital Disruption in Asia: Methods and Issues*, University of Leiden, The Netherlands.

Cuthbertson, A. (2019, March 22). Facebook Admits Storing Millions of User Passwords in Plain Text Files for Years. *Independent*. Retrieved from https://www.independent.co.uk/life-style/gadgets-and-tech/news/facebook-passwords-plain-text-instagram-admission-a8833941.html?utm_medium=Social&utm_source=Facebook&fbclid=IwAR35iRRkYT9ezasULRIaY0YrWdJqUicx9TEWmKvUiBD8KKwS_Ws2dgL58XQ#Echobox=1553185822

Deagon, B. (2015, March 9). Facebook Making Progress with Major Brand Advertisers. *Investor's Business Daily*. Retrieved from http://www.investors.com/facebook-targets-national-brand-advertisers/

Facebook. (2014). *Facebook Annual Report*. Retrieved from https://materials.proxyvote.com/Approved/30303M/20150413/AR_245461/#/8/

Facebook. (2015a). Facebook Reports Third Quarter 2015 Results. Retrieved from http://investor.fb.com/releasedetail.cfm?ReleaseID=940609

Facebook. (2015b). Data Policy. Retrieved from https://www.facebook.com/full_data_use_policy

Facebook. (2015c). Data Policy. Retrieved from https://www.facebook.com/privacy/explanation

Facebook. (2016a). Facebook Reports Fourth Quarter and Full Year 2015 Results. Retrieved from http://investor.fb.com/releasedetail.cfm?ReleaseID=952040

Facebook. (2016b). Government request report. Retrieved from https://govtrequests.facebook.com/#

Facebook. (2016c). Publishing Information about Government Requests to Facebook. Retrieved from https://govtrequests.facebook.com/about/

Facebook. (2016d). Three Million Business Stories. What's Yours? Retrieved from https://www.facebook.com/business/news/3-million-advertisers

Facebook. (2019). AdChoices. Retrieved from https://www.facebook.com/help/568137493302217

Fleisher, L. & Fairless, T. (2015, May 15). Belgian Watchdog Raps Facebook for Treating Personal Data 'With Contempt'. *The Wall Street Journal*. Retrieved from https://www.wsj.com/articles/belgian-watchdog-slams-facebooks-privacy-controls-1431685985

Fox-Brewster, T. (2015, Oct. 6). 'Landmark' Decision Threatens Facebook Use Of European Personal Data. *Forbes.com*. Retrieved from https://www.forbes.com/sites/thomasbrewster/2015/10/06/safe-harbour-invalid/#1d98763a1d98

Fu, J. (2016, Jan. 26). Optimism Over China's Economy Won Out at Davos. *China Daily*. Retrieved from http://europe.chinadaily.com.cn/opinion/2016-01-26/content_23244212.htm

Fuchs, C. (2012a). Critique of the Political Economy of Web 2.0 Surveillance. In C. Fuchs, K. Boersma, A. Albrechtslund, & M. Sandoval (Eds.), *Internet and Surveillance: The Challenges of Web 2.0 and Social Media* (pp. 31–70). New York, NY: Routledge.

Fuchs, C. (2012b). Dallas Smythe Today - The Audience Commodity, the Digital Labour Debate, Marxist Political Economy and Critical Theory. Prolegomena to a Digital Labour Theory of Value. *TripleC*, *10*(2), 692–740. doi:10.31269/triplec.v10i2.443

Fuchs, C. (2012c). The Political Economy of Privacy on Facebook. *Television & New Media*, *13*(2), 139–159. doi:10.1177/1527476411415699

Fuchs, C. (2016). Baidu, Weibo and Renren: The Global Political Economy of Social Media in China. *Asian Journal of Communication*, *26*(1), 14–41. doi:10.1080/01292986.2015.1041537

Goel, V. (2015, April 23). Facebook Reports Quarterly Results Dominated by Shift to Mobile and Video. *The New York Times*. Retrieved from http://www.nytimes.com/2015/04/23/technology/facebook-q1-earnings.html?_r=0

Goldhaber, M. H. (1997). The Attention Economy and the Net. *First Monday*, *2*(4). Retrieved from http://journals.uic.edu/ojs/index.php/fm/article/view/519/440

Gottfried, M. (2016, Jan. 27). Facebook: It's Hard to Argue with Results Like These; The Social Network's Results Show it Hasn't Missed a Step. *The Wall Street Journal Online*. Retrieved from https://www.wsj.com/articles/facebook-its-hard-to-argue-with-results-like-these-1453936786

Gregg, M. (2011). *Work's Intimacy*. Cambridge, UK: Polity.

Gunitsky, S. (2015). Corrupting the Cyber-Commons: Social Media as a Tool of Autocratic Stability. *Perspectives on Politics*, *13*(1), 42–54. Retrieved from http://individual.utoronto.ca/seva/corrupting_cybercommons.pdf doi:10.1017/S1537592714003120

Kemp, S. (2015). *Digital, Social and Mobile in 2015*. Retrieved from http://wearesocial.com/uk/special-reports/digital-social-mobile-worldwide-2015

King, G., Pan, J., & Roberts, M. E. (2013). How Censorship in China Allows Government Criticism but Silences Collective Expression. *The American Political Science Review*, *107*(2), 326–343. doi:10.1017/S0003055413000014

Li, C. (2009). The Chinese Communist Party: Recruiting and Controlling the New Elites. *Journal of Current Chinese Affairs*, *38*(3), 13–33. doi:10.1177/186810260903800302

Ma, S. & Cao, Y. (2015, Dec. 18). Experts Call to Keep Data Safe. *China Daily*. Retrieved from http://www.chinadaily.com.cn/business/tech/2015-12/18/content_22741317

Madden, M. & Rainie, L. (2015). *Americans' Attitudes about Privacy, Security and Surveillance*. Retrieved from http://www.pewinternet.org/files/2015/05/Privacy-and-Security-Attitudes-5.19.15_FINAL.pdf

Meng, J. (2016a, April 19). Tencent's WeChat Launches New App for Enterprises. *China Daily*. Retrieved from http://www.chinadaily.com.cn/business/tech/2016-04/19/content_24649488.htm

Meng, J. (2016b, Feb. 16). Tencent Claims Surge in Digital Red Envelopes over New Year. *China Daily*. Retrieved from http://www.chinadaily.com.cn/business/tech/2016-02/16/content_23496768.htm

Miller, C. C. (2015, May 15). How Facebook's Experiment Changes the News (and How It Doesn't). *The New York Times*. Retrieved from http://www.nytimes.com/2015/05/15/upshot/how-facebooks-experiment-changes-the-news-and-how-it-doesnt.html

Monggilo, Z. M. Z. (2016, Jan. 26-28). Internet Freedom in Asia: Case of Internet Censorship in China. Paper Presented at the *International Conference on Social Politics, Universitas Muhammadiyah Yogyakarta*, Indonesia. 10.18196/jgp.2016.0026

Montgomery, K. C. (2015). Youth and Surveillance in the Facebook Era: Policy Interventions and Social Implications. *Telecommunications Policy*, *39*(9), 771–786. doi:10.1016/j.telpol.2014.12.006

Ng, J. Q. (2015). Politics, Rumors, and Ambiguity: Tracking Censorship on WeChat's Public Accounts Platform. Retrieved from https://citizenlab.org/2015/07/tracking-censorship-on-wechat-public-accounts-platform/

Perez, B. (2016, April 4). China's Social Networks Set for Boom, As Advertising Spending Forecast to Jump 56 Per Cent to Us$5.33b This Year. *South China Morning Post*. Retrieved from http://www.scmp.com/tech/enterprises/article/1933558/chinas-social-networks-set-boom-advertising-spending-forecast-jump

Ray, T. (2015, Oct. 3). Rich Get Richer as Google and Facebook Dominate Web Ads. *Barron's Asia*. Retrieved from http://www.barrons.com/articles/rich-get-richer-as-google-and-facebook-dominate-web-ads-1443851396

Sandoval, M. (2012). A Critical Empirical Case Study of Consumer Surveillance on Web 2.0. In C. Fuchs, K. Boersma, A. Albrechtslund, & M. Sandoval (Eds.), *Internet and Surveillance: The Challenges of Web 2.0 and Social Media* (pp. 147–169). New York, NY: Routledge.

Seetharaman, D. (2015, July 30). Facebook, Google Tighten Grip on Mobile Ads; Facebook's Quarterly Revenue Jumps 39% as it Lures Big Brand Advertisers and Smartphone Users. *The Wall Street Journal Online*. Retrieved from https://www.wsj.com/articles/facebook-revenue-rises-39-1438200350

Shabrina, F., & Winarsih, A. S. (2016, Jan. 26-28). Businesspeople Co-Optation In China's Communist Party Adaption. Paper Presented at the *International Conference on Social Politics, Universitas Muhammadiyah Yogyakarta*, Indonesia.

Sloane, G. (2015, March 13). Facebook Buys a Company That Could Solve an Annoying Online Ad Problem. *Adweek*. Retrieved from http://www.adweek.com/news/technology/facebook-buys-company-could-solve-annoying-ad-problem-163475

Smythe, D. W. (1981). *Dependency Road: Communications, Capitalism, Consciousness, and Canada*. Norwood, NJ: Ablex.

Statista. (2016a). Facebook's Revenue and Net Income from 2007 to 2015 (in Million U.S. Dollars). Retrieved from http://www.statista.com/statistics/277229/facebooks-annual-revenue-and-net-income/

Statista. (2016b). Number of Monthly Active Facebook Users Worldwide as of 4th quarter 2015 (in Millions). Retrieved from http://www.statista.com/statistics/264810/number-of-monthly-active-facebook-users worldwide/

Statista. (2016c). Number of Monthly Active WeChat Users from 2nd Quarter 2010 to 4th Quarter 2015 (in Millions). Retrieved from http://www.statista.com/statistics/255778/number-of-active-wechat-messenger-accounts/

Stelter, B. (2015, May 13). Why Facebook is Starting a New Partnership with 9 News Publishers. *CNN*. Retrieved from http://money.cnn.com/2015/05/13/media/facebook-instant-articles-news-industry/

Sullivan, L. (2015, March 26). Google Takes Backseat to Facebook's Digital Display Ad Revenue. *MediaPost.com*. Retrieved from http://www.mediapost.com/publications/article/246520/google-takes-backseat-to-facebooks-digital-displa.html?utm_source=newsletter&utm_medium=email&utm_content=headline&utm_campaign=81438

Swartz, A. (2015, March 25). How Facebook is Courting Small Businesses and Their Advertising Dollars. *Silicon Valley/San Jose Business Journal Online*. Retrieved from http://www.bizjournals.com/sanjose/news/2015/03/25/how-facebook-is-courting-small-businesses-and.html

Tencent. (2015). Tencent Announces 2014 Fourth Quarter and Annual Results. Retrieved from http://www.tencent.com/en- us/content/ir/news/2015/attachments/20150318.pdf

Tencent. (2016a). Tencent Announces 2015 Fourth Quarter and Annual Results. Retrieved from http://www.tencent.com/en-us/content/ir/news/2016/attachments/20160317.pdf

Tencent. (2016b). *Tencent Announces 2016 First Quarter Results*. Retrieved from http://www.tencent.com/en-us/content/ir/news/2016/attachments/20160518.pdf

Trottier, D. (2016). *Social Media as Surveillance: Rethinking Visibility in a Convergence World*. New York, NY: Routledge. doi:10.4324/9781315609508

Tse, E. (2015). *China's Disruptors*. New York, NY: Penguin.

Wasko, J. (2005). Studying the Political Economy of Media and Information. *Comunicação e Sociedade*, 7(0), 25–48. doi:10.17231/comsoc.7(2005).1208

WeChat. (2016a). Terms of Service. Retrieved from http://www.wechat.com/en/service_terms.html

WeChat. (2016b). Privacy policy. Retrieved from http://www.wechat.com/en/privacy_policy.html

WeChat. (2016c). Terms of Use and Privacy Policy (Chinese language versions). Retrieved from http://weixin.qq.com/cgi-bin/readtemplate?uin=&stype=&promote=&fr=wechat.com&lang=zh_CN&ADTAG=&check=false&nav=faq&t=weixin_agreement&s=default

Whitman, R. (2015, Aug. 26). Study Finds Social Media Claiming Larger Share of Ad Budgets. *MediaPost.com*. Retrieved from http://www.mediapost.com/publications/article/257029/study-finds-social-media-claiming-larger-share-of.html

ADDITIONAL READING

Smythe, D. W. (1977). Communications: Blindspot of Western Marxism. *Canadian Journal of Political and Social Theory*, *1*(3), 1–27.

Svec, H. A. (2015). On Dallas Smythe's "Audience Commodity": An Interview with Lee McGuigan and Vincent Manzerolle. *TripleC*, *13*(1), 270–273.

van Dijck, J. (2013). *The Culture of Connectivity: A Critical History of Social Media.* Oxford: Oxford University Press. doi:10.1093/acprof:oso/9780199970773.001.0001

Yang, K., Zhang, C., & Tang, J. (2012). Internet Use and Governance in China. In Y. Chen & P. Chu (Eds.), *Governance and Cross-boundary Collaboration: Innovations and Advancing Tools* (pp. 305–324). Hershey, PA: IGI Global Publications. doi:10.4018/978-1-60960-753-1.ch017

Zhang, H., Lu, Y., Gupta, S., & Zhao, L. (2014). What Motivates Customers to Participate in Social Commerce? The Impact of Technological Environments and Virtual Customer Experiences. *Information & Management*, *51*(8), 1017–1030. doi:10.1016/j.im.2014.07.005

KEY TERMS AND DEFINITIONS

Attention Economy: A concept where media, in a modern competitive market, tries to gain and keep the attention of the audience to its channel, newspaper or online service.

Audience Commodification: A political economy concept related to media. Audiences contribute to media companies' profit-making process both as worker and buyer. But they gain no financial profit.

Government surveillance: A situation where the government observes the activities of an individual and group to collect information on them and in some cases it may affect their privacy.

Online Social Networking Services: Social platforms on the Internet that are created by building online profiles with valid email address. These are used to communicate and share contents with others.

Political Economy: The interdisciplinary study of the relationship between economy and politics.

Social Media Policies: Policies created and followed by the social media companies to conduct their activities and business.

User Data: All information and content collected and stored about a social media user by the government and/or companies of social media.

This research was previously published in New Media and Visual Communication in Social Networks; pages 233-254, copyright year 2020 by Information Science Reference (an imprint of IGI Global).

Chapter 67
Loneliness, Disclosure, and Facebook Usage:
Results From a Hong Kong Survey

Fung Yin Lee
Hong Kong Baptist University, China

Lynne M. Webb
Florida International University, USA

ABSTRACT

The authors conducted an online survey of 241 emerging adults in Hong Kong, China to assess potential associations between loneliness, Facebook usage, and self-disclosure on Facebook. Loneliness was not associated with Facebook usage, but rather inversely related with negative disclosure; the lonelier the Facebook user, the less he/she disclosed negative information. The pattern of associations between Facebook usage and self-disclosure indicted that the more time users spent on Facebook, the more they revealed positive disclosures and the less they revealed negative disclosures. The authors argue that these findings may provide evidence of a "remain positive" norm among emerging adult Facebook users in Hong Kong. They note that their findings may be unique to their cultural context.

INTRODUCTION

Emerging Adult Theory argues that a distinct life stage exists between adolescence and adulthood, a time when individuals "have not yet settled into the long-term choices and life-paths that make up adulthood" (Bigham, 2012, p. 533). As originally conceived by Arnett (2015), this life stage extended from late teens through the 20s when individuals address the challenging tasks that typically accompany the transition into adulthood. Munsey (2006) identified five features of emerging adulthood:

- Identity exploration concerning lifestyles and believe systems (e.g., religion, politics)

DOI: 10.4018/978-1-6684-6307-9.ch067

- Instability. Individuals may change residents frequently, moving frequently for education, work, and/or family reasons. They may change intimate partners and friends frequently as well. The challenge for emerging adults is to find stability including negotiating on-going, positive inter-personal relationships and moving along a chosen career path that allows life in primarily one location.

- Self-focus. Given the above described instability and focus on identity exploration, emerging adults remain self-focused until they begin making commitments to specific career paths and to significant others—commitments that lead to adulthood.

- Feeling in between. Individuals know they are not children or teenagers anymore, but often do not see themselves as adults yet.

- Endless possibilities. This time of exploration and confusion leaves emerging adults with a sense of incompleteness but also with a sense of wonder and endless possibilities. The experience of endless possibilities can lead to a sense of empowerment or feeling overwhelming by too many options.

The Theory of Emerging Adulthood is not without its critics (Hendry & Kloep, 2007). Some adherents have argued that tying the definition of emerging adulthood to its challenges rather than specific ages is more sensible, given that individuals complete development tasks at differing paces (Bigham, 2012). Additionally, researchers argue that ethnicity (Munsey, 2006) and culture (e.g., Arseth, Kroger, Martinussen, & Bakken, 2009) may influence how individuals experience this life stage. Despite these concerns, an on-going line of research has emerged that examines the online behavior of emerging adults (e.g., Wu & Webb, 2016).

This chapter reports the findings of an original research study that continues an exploration of emerging adulthood among these newer concerns (i.e., extended age-frame, cultural differences, and online behaviors). We examined Facebook usage and its relationship to emerging adult users' perceived loneliness and self-disclosure on Facebook in a Hong Kong sample. This study fills a gap in the current body of research in two ways: (a) by examining the inter-relationships among this specific combination of three variables (i.e., loneliness, self-disclosure on Facebook, and Facebook usage per se) as well as (b) collecting data from a culturally unique sample, emerging adults in Hong Kong.

BACKGROUND

Motivations for users to join and use social networking websites (SNS) vary (boyd, 2006; Bryant, Marmo, & Ramirez, 2011; Chen, 2015), but the primary motivation is to communicate and maintain relationships with other users (Dwyer, Hiltz & Passerini, 2007). Individuals can form online communities around shared interests with others outside their pre-existing social group or location (Webb & Lee, 2011). However, many participants in large SNSs like Facebook primary search for and communicate with their offline connections rather than looking for new people to meet (Lampe, Ellison, & Steinfield, 2006; Miller & Mundey, 2015). Nonetheless, the more users want to maintain relationships on social media, the more likely they are to spend time in self-disclosing activities, such as updating Facebook profile information, posting status updates, and uploading photos and videos.

One of the largest, well known, and well-studied SNS in the world is Facebook (Rains & Brunner, 2015). On February 4, 2019, Facebook turned 15 years old and reported 1.5 billion daily, active users world-wide in May 2019 (Facebook, 2019). Indeed, Facebook is big business with offices in 20 U. S. cities and 47 overseas cities, including an office in Hong Kong (Facebook, 2019).

Facebook provides multiple opportunities for self-disclosure, here defined as consciously communicating messages about the self to others. For example, users can reveal personal information on their personal profiles including birthdate, education background, hobbies, sexual orientation, and relationship status. Additionally, users can upload photos and videos of their activities as well as reveal their thoughts and feelings via status updates; this information in turn appears on their friends' news feed. Therefore, it is not surprising that self-disclosure on Facebook is a well-researched topic (Caers et al., 2013). A google-scholar search using the two keywords Facebook and self-disclosure yielded over 30,600 results in May 2019.

This extensive line of research examines users' self-disclosure on Facebook in Argentina (Linne, 2014), Australia (Saling, Cohen, & Cooper, 2019), Germany (Utz, 2015), Japan (Omori & Allen, 2014), Korea (e.g., Kwak, Choi, & Lee, 2014), Mainland China (e.g., Liu & Brown, 2014), Poland (e.g., Blachnio, Przepiorka, & Rudnicka, 2016), Slovenia (e.g., Zlatolas, Welzer, Hericko, & Holbl, 2015), the United Kingdom (e.g., Green, Wilhelmsen, Wilmots, Dodd, & Quin, 2016), and the United States (e.g., Crabtree & Pillow, 2018). However, very little of this research was completed Hong Kong (i.e., Cheung, Lee, & Chan, 2015). Given the unique cultural aspects of Hong Kong, with its 99 years history of British occupation mingled with its ethnically Chinese roots, it is reasonable to question whether Hong Kong Facebook users would follow the same norms of self-disclosure documented in other cultures.

Indeed, perhaps in acknowledgement of its uniqueness, a growing body of over 25 published studies examines various Facebook behaviors of Hong Kong residents, including peer network characteristics (Chan, 2018), talk among colleagues (Nam, Chun, & Hin, 2014), and one specific type of self-disclosure, sharing sex stories (Yeo & Chu, 2017). However, only one previous research has examined Hong Kong Facebook users' self-disclosure as a general matter (Chenug et al., 2015). That study assessed perceived costs and benefits of self-disclosure on Facebook but failed to directly assess the relationship between Hong Kong users' self-disclosure on Facebook with their reported loneliness. This is concerning, given that previous studies linked loneliness and self-disclosure on Facebook among users in Australia (Al-Saggaf & Nielsen, 2014) and Korea (Jin, 2013; Lee, Noh, & Koo, 2013). Our study expands this fledgling line of research by testing whether such a relationship can be similarly documented among Facebook users in a Hong Kong sample.

Many studies have examined the relationship between loneliness and Facebook use (see Song et al, 2014 for a meta-analysis of this research). However, we could locate no previous work that examined this association in Hong Kong users. To address this gap in the literature, we elected to focus our study on Facebook use, loneliness, and self-disclosure among a Hong Kong sample of emerging adults.

Facebook

Facebook is the most popular SNS on Earth (Ahmad, 2019). Users can search for other registered users and initiate requests to become friends. Facebook friends range from established intimate relationships to acquaintances. While the research on self-disclosure and Facebook is extensive, as is the research on loneliness and Facebook use, nonetheless, much of the existing academic research on Facebook has focused on interpersonal processes more indirectly related to loneliness and/or self-disclosure. They include boundary tending (Miller & Mundey, 2015), privacy concerns (Tsay-Vogel, Shanahan, & Signorielli, 2018), feeling connected (Utz, 2015), social anxiety (e.g., Burke & Ruppel, 2015), social cohesion (Hollenbaugh, & Ferris, 2014), general interpersonal relations (Kwak et al., 2014), and the overarching concern of acquiring and maintained social capital (Liu & Brown, 2014). Additionally, recent studies report mixed outcomes associated with frequent Facebook usage including (a) lower depressive symptoms in females with high neuroticism (Simoncic, Kuhlman, Vargas, Houchins, & Lopez-Duran, 2014) but (b) higher stress and lower quality of life among college students (Bevan, Gomez, and Sparks, 2014) as well as associations with narcissism (Blachnio et al., 2016) among emerging and middle-aged adults. In sum, loneliness and self-disclosure remain common targets of both direct and indirect investigation by Facebook researchers.

Loneliness and Facebook Use

We view loneliness as an uncomfortable psychological state associated with a desire for increased human interaction. Loneliness has been linked to reduced social support and reduced life satisfaction (Kong & You, 2013). For lonely individuals, online social media, such as Facebook, may offer a less demanding communication medium than face-to-face (FtF) interaction. Facebook makes connecting with others easy by facilitating connections in the following manner: Its customized features allow users with common interests to easily discover each other and converse.

In their meta-analysis of the research on loneliness and Facebook usage, Song et al. (2014) report that, early on, many studies documented an association between loneliness and Facebook use. Following recognition of this documentation, researchers focused on the question of whether Facebook usage decreased or increased loneliness. While the previous evidence was mixed, Song and associates (2014) presented definitive evidence that loneliness, driven by shyness and low self-esteem, leads to increased Facebook usage. Rather than retest the directionality of the association, our study tested whether loneliness and Facebook usage remain correlated with a Hong Kong sample.

Like Song et al. (2014), we located many studies of loneliness and Facebook use. These studies employed samples of emerging adults in diverse locations including Australia (e.g., Al-Saggaf & Nielsen, 2014), Belgium (e.g., Frison & Eggermont, 2015), Germany (Utz, 2015), Korea (Jin, 2013), Poland (Balachnio, Przepiorka, Boruch, & Balakier, 2016), Scotland (Phu & Gow, 2019), Turkey (Satici, 2019), and the United States (e.g., Wohn & LaRose, 2014). However, this association remain undocumented in a Hong Kong sample. Therefore, we posed the following research question:

RQ1: Is there an association between loneliness and Facebook usage?

Self-Disclosure and Facebook Use

In addition to testing whether Facebook usage is related to loneliness in a Hong Kong sample, we questioned whether either users' loneliness or Facebook usage is associated with their self-disclosure on Facebook. Self-disclosure (here defined as revealing information about the self to others) is widely considered an important factor in the development and maintenance of relationships in FtF and well as social media contexts (Bazarova & Choi, 2014). It has positive effects on online dating (Gibbs, Ellison, & Heino, 2006), online support communities (Turner, Grube, & Myers, 2001), virtual work teams (Walther, Slovacek, & Tidwell, 2001), and online interpersonal relationships (Kwak et al., 2014).

Relationship maintenance, often manifest as self-disclosure, is among the most prominent motivation for using Facebook (Dwyer et al., 2007; Ellison, Vitak, Gray, & Lampe, 2014; Lampe et al., 2006; Park & Lee, 2014). Users stay in touch with their offline relational partners via Facebook, (Miller & Mundey, 2015), including both geographically distant and close friends (Waters & Ackerman, 2011) as well as current and previous romantic partners (Medeiros & Webb, 2019). In addition to relationship maintenance, users may employ Facebook to satisfy engagement and affiliation needs—and both are associated with self-disclosure (Chen, 2015). Furthermore, Ledbetter et al. (2011) reported a link between self-disclosure on Facebook and relational closeness.

Many researches argue for a direct relationship between Facebook use and self-disclosure (Webb & Temple, 2015). For example, Linne identified "interchanging personal information between friends" (in other words, self-disclosure) as one of adolescents' the common uses of Facebook (2014, para. 1). Similarly, Park and Lee (2014) report that college students have four motivations for using Facebook, including self-expression and communication (in other words, self-disclosure). Finally, Hollenbaugh and Ferris (2014) documented an association between the breadth of self-disclosure on Facebook and relational maintenance per se as well as one of its specific components, openness.

A wave of recent studies documented a positive relationship between Facebook use and self-disclosure (Chang & Heo, 2014; Chen & Sharma, 2015; Crabtree & Pillow, 2018; Lee et al., 2013; Park & Baek, 2016; Tsay-Vogel et al., 2018). However, our study is the first to test this relationship using a Hong Kong sample. Such a sample-specific test appears relevant in light of increasing evidence that Facebook usage is influenced by cultural values such as individualism (Shneor & Efrat, 2014). Particularly relevant to our research, two studies reported cultural differences in self-disclosure on Facebook: Lee-Won, Shim, Joo, and Park (2014) documented cultural differences in self-presentation on Facebook between South Korean versus U. S. emerging adults; given that self-disclosure is the primary means through which users present their online identity, these cultural differences provide a warrant for our culturally-specific sample. Similarly, Omori and Allen documented differences in the willingness of emerging adult Facebook users in Japan versus the United States to post pictures of themselves "partying" and drinking (in other words, self-disclosing questionable recreational activities).

Valence of Disclosure

Given the extensive documentation of self-disclosure on Facebook, researchers recently turned their attention to examining the influence of the valence of self-disclosures on Facebook usage and other pertinent variables (e.g., Saling et al., 2019). As early as 1973, researchers noted that the valence of a disclosure (disclosing positive versus negative information) in FtF interactions influenced the receiver's perception of the discloser (Pearce & Sharp, 1973). More recent findings indicate that valence of disclosure also can prove salient in online interactions. We could locate seven previously published studies that examined positive versus negative disclosures on Facebook; their results indicate that salience of Facebook disclosures may be a variable worthy of observation.

- Qiu, Lin, Leung, and Tov (2012) documented that, among a sample of Singapore college students, Facebook users were more likely to disclose positive versus negative emotions.
- Lee-Won et al. (2014) documented that U. S. versus Korean college-student Facebook users engaged in more positive self-presentation (in other words, self-disclosure).

- Liu and Brown (2014) examined self-disclosure among first-year college students at three universities in Beijing in mainland China on Renren, the Chinese version of Facebook. Their results revealed that social skills were positively associated with self-disclosure, which in turn was associated with receiving positive feedback from friends.
- Jin (2013) reported that, among a Korean sample of emerging adults, lonely users were more likely to engage in negative self-disclosure and less likely to engage in positive self-disclosure.
- Bevan et al. (2015) reported that, in a sample of emerging adults in the United States, users preferred to disclose negative life events directly (e.g., status updates) whereas they preferred to disclose positive life events indirectly (e.g., posting pictures).
- Utz (2015) reported that positive (not negative) Facebook disclosures were associated with feelings of connection among a sample of German university students.
- Saling et al., (2019) reported that Australian Facebook users of many ages preferred receiving negative disclosures off-line rather than online.

We extended this exploration of positive versus negative valence of disclosures on Facebook to examine their potential relationships between loneliness, Facebook usage, and positive versus negative self-disclosure on Facebook. We believed that emerging adult Facebook users were likely to disclose positive (versus negative) information about the self to shape desirable online images. Therefore, we posed the following research question:

RQ2: Is there an association between positive or negative self-disclosure on Facebook and Facebook usage?

Loneliness and Self-Disclosure on Facebook

The relationship between the use of Facebook and self-disclosure might be more profound for lonely people who desire social relationships but lack opportunities for self-disclosure in FtF interaction. It is possible that, because of the impersonality and participation equality of online communication, lonely people may be more willing to disclose in greater breadth and depth. Also, Facebook may be a more comfortable place for the lonely to disclose than less interactive online venues such as Instagram and Twitter. If Facebook serves as a comfortable place for lonely people to self-disclose, lonely Facebook users and/or high disclosing users may use Facebook more frequently than less lonely users.

We could locate only three previous studies (Al-Saggaf & Nielsen, 2014; Jin, 2013; Lee et al., 2013) that tested for such associations. Among a sample of Australian users, Al-Saggaf and Nielsen (2014) reported that lonely Facebook users disclosed more personal and more relational information but fewer viewpoints. Lee et al. (2013) reported that loneliness increased self-disclosure on Facebook among their sample of Korean college students. Jin (2013) reported that, among a Korean sample of emerging adults, users' amount of time on Facebook was not associated with loneliness; however, lonely users were more likely to engage in negative self-disclosure and less likely to engage in positive self-disclosure. To explore if this set of previously examined relationships existed in a Hong Kong sample, we posted the following research question:

RQ3: Is there an association between loneliness and positive or negative self-disclosure on Facebook?

It is noteworthy that we could locate no previous study that examined possible associations between the particular array of variables examined in this study (i.e., loneliness, self-disclosure by valence, and Facebook use). Thus, in addition to retesting previously documented associations with a Hong Kong sample of emerging adults, our study fills this additional gap in the research on Facebook.

METHOD

Sample

We recruited 251 Facebook users ages 16 or older residing in Hong Kong, China to complete our on-line survey. For many reasons explained below, a Hong Kong sample presents an almost ideal sample for studying Facebook behavior generally and an appropriate sample to test the queried associations:

- Hong Kong residents engage in the Chinese cultural practice of "guanxi"; they prize networking and place high value on having and maintaining connections. Thus, they may visit Facebook often and work diligently to maintain their Facebook connections.
- The vast majority of Hong Kong residents culturally identify as Chinese and thus feel an affinity with their immediate neighbor to the north, Mainland China. However, the government of Mainland China forbids the use of Facebook and affirmatively takes step to block its citizen's Facebook usage. Because of this policy, Hong Kong residents prize their access to Facebook and find it useful for maintaining ties with intercity friends in Hong Kong as well as ethnically Chinese friends living in countries other than Mainland China such as Malaysia, Singapore, and Taiwan.
- Because Hong Kong serves as an international hub for law, business, fashion and so forth, native Hong Kong residents often become acquainted with people from multiple countries and cultures. Thus, Hong Kong residents, more than residents of most locations, have the opportunity to communicate with intercultural relational partners around the world via Facebook.
- Because Hong Kong serves as an international hub for law, business, fashion and so forth, many Hong Kong residents are citizens of outside countries and territories. Thus, our sample, collected in Hong Kong, accurately represented a wider variety of foreign nationals than typically seen in most locations.
- Hong Kong is a densely populated urban area and thus residents experience frequent close physical proximity to one another; they often fail to engage in eye contact or interaction as a way to maintain personal space in one of the most densely populated cities in the world. Thus, a fair number of residents may experience loneliness.

Furthermore, recent articles reported on Facebook behavior in Japan (e.g., Omori & Allen, 2014), Korea (e.g., Ha, Kim, Labaque-Saena, Chang, & Park, 2015), Malaysia (e.g., Abdulahi, Samadi, & Gharleghi, 2014), and Singapore (e.g., Qiu et al., 2012). Our study adds to this growing body of knowledge concerning Facebook usage in Asia.

Our sample size of 251 was (a) consistent with recently research reports on the same topic such as Satici's 2019 article examining the relationship between loneliness and Facebook use among 280 Turkish university students and (b) almost identical to the sample size of 264 reported in the only previously published study of self-disclosure on a SNS that substitutes for Facebook among emerging adults in Mainland China (Liu & Brown, 2014).

Typical of survey research of emerging adult Facebook users (e.g., Phu & Gow, 2019), we employed convenience sampling. Our sample included 95 (37.8%) males and 156 (62.2%) females. Most of the respondents ($n = 157$; 62.5%) were ages 20-24. However, the sample also contained younger emerging adults ages 16-19 (14.3%) and older emerging adults ages 25-29 (15.1%). Only 4% of our sample were over age 29. Thus, our Hong Kong sample was almost exclusively comprised of emerging adults.

Respondents reported diverse educational experiences ranging from completing secondary level (13.6%) to holding a certificate or associate degree (11.6%) to an earned baccalaureate degree (61.8%) to a graduate degree (12.8%). The majority reported having a monthly income of HK$10,000 or below (69.7%), followed by HK$10,000-$20,000 (23.5%). The respondents hailed from various walks of life, but were mostly students (60.6%). The second largest group provided social services (8.4%), a typical "starter job" for emerging adults in Hong Kong.

One advantage of collecting data in an international city is the sample's diversity. Our convenience sample contained citizens of seven countries including France, Mainland China, Malaysia, Taiwan, United Kingdom, and the United States—but the majority of respondents claimed Hong Kong citizenship ($n =231$, 92.00%). Similarly, the vast majority of our respondents self-identified as Asian ($n =247$, 98.40%), with the remaining identifying as Caucasian.

Instruments

Because we recruited respondents in Hong Kong, a multi-national city, the survey displayed 64 questions in the city's two dominant languages: English and traditional Chinese characters. We discovered existing instruments in English and then translated them into Chinese. Next, the questions were back translated by graduate students in Communication to ensure consistency and accuracy across the two language versions.

- **Loneliness.** The revised UCLA Loneliness Scale developed by (Russell, Peplau, & Cutrona, 1980) contains 20-items rated on 4-point Likert scales that range from 1 (never) to 4 (often). The scale included items such as "I am outgoing and friendly." The scale proved reliable with our sample, yielding a Cronbach alpha of 0.90.
- **Self-disclosure on Facebook.** The Revised Self Disclosure Scale (RSDS) developed by Wheeless and Grotz (1976) is a self-report instrument of 31 items scored on 5-point Likert scales ranging from 5 (strongly agree) to 1 (strongly disagree). We reworded the items to address self-disclosure on Facebook. For example, one item stated, "I usually disclose positive things about myself on Facebook".

A factor analysis of our respondents' scores using principal components analysis with Varimax rotation yielded two self-disclosure factors, namely negative self-disclosure and positive self-disclosure.[1] Negative self-disclosure was comprised of two items with a Cronbach's alpha of 0.80. Positive self-disclosure was comprised of 13 items identified in previous studies across four dimensions of self-disclosure (i.e., accuracy, depth, breath, intention) with a Cronbach's alpha of 0.81.

- **Facebook Usage.** Following Leung (2002), we employed three measures to assess Facebook usage. We asked (a) how many days a week they visited Facebook, (b) how many hours a day they spent on Facebook, and (c) how much time they typically spent per visit.

Procedures

We pretested our survey with 21 users drawn from the research sample. Based on their feedback, we made minor word changes to the questionnaires to increase clarity; for example, we rewrote instructions using more specific terms.

We posted three versions of the revised survey, each at its own URL. Each version contained the same instruments but in differing, counter-balanced orders to ameliorate order effects. Based on their birth months, we directed approximately a third of the respondents to each of the three URLs.

Typical of survey sampling of Facebook users (e.g., Phu & Gow, 2019), we employed multiple methods of recruitment to increase the size and diversity of our convenience sample. Specifically, the authors each posted an invitation to the survey on their Facebook pages and urged their Facebook friends to *not* take the survey but to repost the recruitment invitation. Thus, members of the researchers' social network served as recruiters but not as respondents in the study, minimizing the introduction of researcher bias. Additionally, the survey's URLs were sent via an invitational email to undergraduate students in Communication classes at a large, state-sponsored university in Hong Kong. The URLs remained live for 14 consecutive days and thus allowed for the collection of 251 completed surveys.

RESULTS

Preliminary Analyses

We factor analyzed the scores from the items on the loneliness and self-disclosure instruments using principal components analysis with Varimax rotation.[1] The loneliness scale factored cleanly and, as mentioned above, the self-disclosure scale reduced to two factors: positive disclosure and negative disclosure.

Next, we examined the frequency distributions for the variables. Three indicators of Facebook usage (days per week, hours per day, and time per visit) were not normally distributed. Therefore, we conducted nonparametric tests for the analyses involving these measures. We conducted parametric tests to assess the potential relationships between loneliness and positive versus negative self-disclosure.

Primary Analyses

We computed Spearman's correlation coefficients to assess (a) the potential association between loneliness and Facebook usage and (b) the potential association between self-disclosure and Facebook usage. Facebook usage was not significantly associated with loneliness (see Table 1), suggesting that Facebook users' loneliness was not associated with increased or decreased Facebook usage. Conversely, both positive and negative self-disclosure were associated with Facebook usage (see Table 1). Positive self-disclosure was positively correlated with two measures of Facebook usage, indicating that the more days per week users visited Facebook as well as the more hours per day they spent on Facebook, the more they engaged on positive self-disclosure on Facebook. Conversely, negative self-disclosure was negatively correlated with hours per day on Facebook, suggesting that the more hours per day users spent on Facebook, the less they self-disclosed negatively on Facebook. In all three significant results, increased Facebook usage was associated with either more positive or less negative self-disclosure.

Finally, we calculated Pearson's correlation coefficients to assess the potential correlation between loneliness and self-disclosure on Facebook. Loneliness was not correlated with positive self-disclosure ($r = -0.05$, $p = $ NS). However, loneliness was negatively correlated with negative self-disclosure ($r = -0.22$, $p = 0.01$). The lonelier the Facebook user, the less he/she disclosed negative information.

Table 1. Correlations between loneliness, self-disclosure, and facebook usage

	Facebook Usage Pattern		
	Days per Week	**Hours per Day**	**Time per Visit**
Loneliness	-0.01 (n.s.)	0.08 (n.s.)	-0.01 (n.s.)
Self-disclosure on Facebook			
Positive self-disclosure	0.18**	0.18**	-0.01 (n.s.)
Negative self-disclosure (R)	-0.08 (n.s.)	-0.17**	-0.01 (n.s.)

Notes: **$p<0.01$, n=251

DISCUSSION

Loneliness and Facebook Usage

Our results answer RQ1 in the negative. Loneliness was not significantly associated with Facebook usage. Our results are consistent with a few previous studies (i.e., Baker & Oswasld, 2010; Wohn & LaRose, 2014) conducted with U.S. freshmen, but inconsistent with the conclusion of Song et al.'s (2014) meta-analysis and with the vast majority of previous studies testing for such an association.

We offer three explanations for our findings: (a) We may be observing cultural differences. Given that Facebook is very popular in Hong Kong, it may be too cool to be on Facebook for anyone to ignore its draw; thus, differences across loneliness scores could not be documented. (b) We assessed positive and negative self-disclosure rather than using overall self-disclosure scores as was typical for the earlier researched that documents a positive correlation. Thus, both measurement and sample differences may explain our results. (c) Previous research indicates that factors other than loneliness influence Facebook usage; such factors include shyness (Baker & Oswald, 2010), self-esteem (e.g., Leighton, Legate, LePine, Anderson, & Grahe, 2018; Varnali & Toker, 2015), self-inferiority (Hong, Huang, Lin, & Chiu, 2014), and stress (Bevan et al., 2014). Thus, loneliness was not associated with Facebook usage across samples in two locations: the United States and now Hong Kong.

For at least two reasons, Facebook may offer limited appeal to lonely users looking for new relational partners online: (a) Facebook users primarily search for and communicate with existing, offline connections rather than looking for new people to meet (Lampe et al., 2006; Miller & Mundey, 2015). (b) Facebook users primarily reveal their profile information to existing, offline connections (Lampe et al., 2006). Attempts to befriend users unknown in the FtF world are typically ignored or rejected.

Instead of Facebook, lonely people may turn to SNS that focus on connecting strangers based on shared interests, political views, or activities like dating websites, blogs, forums, and chatrooms where they can present themselves as more extroverted, less shy, more intelligent, more fun loving, and generally more favorable. In such alternative forums, they can enjoy a greater sense of safety and perceived ability to control anonymity as well as communicate with multiple fellow users in real time.

Loneliness and Facebook Usage

Our results revealed associations between self-disclosure and Facebook usage, thus, answering RQ2 in the affirmative. These results are consistent with previously published findings (Chang & Heo, 2014; Chen & Sharma, 2015; Crabtree & Pillow, 2018; Lee et al., 2013; Park & Baek, 2016; Tsay-Vogel et al., 2018). However, our results are the first to document this association in a Hong Kong sample.

An association between self-disclosure and Facebook usage may be the result of the reciprocity norm of self-disclosure (Pearce & Sharp, 1973). Users' Facebook pages, posts, and comments contain self-information that functions as self-disclosure. Therefore, the more time a user spends on Facebook, the more he/she is exposed to the self-disclosures of others and then may disclose reciprocally, perhaps disclosing in greater depth and breadth to further prompt the disclosure of others.

Additionally, social exchange theories argue that people develop and maintain relationships based on reciprocal exchange of rewards (Dunbar, 2015). Applying this principle to self-disclosure, online interactants may reveal themselves to people who self-disclose to them. Facebook seems an ideal medium for such exchanges.

Valence of Disclosure and Facebook Usage

Perhaps the most interesting findings of the study surround the valence of Facebook self-disclosure. We report three significant findings that add to the growing understanding of how the valence of self-disclosure functions on Facebook.

- First, we adapted our self-disclosure instrument by add the words "on Facebook" to each item. Recall that its factor analysis yielded two factors divided by valence (positive versus negative) rather than the expected four factors found in previous studies (i.e., accuracy, depth, breath, intention). This result was our first indication that valence of disclosure may be a salient factor for our respondents.
- Second, our analyses revealed the significant negative correlation between hours per day on Facebook and negative self-disclosure. The more hours spent per day on Facebook, the less the respondents tended to self-disclosure negatively on Facebook.
- Third, two measures of Facebook usage (number of days per week and hours per day) were positively correlated with positive self-disclosure. The more Facebook usage, the more positive self-disclosure.

Our results, consistent with previously reported findings (Qiu et al., 2012; Lee et al., 2014), indicate that disclosure on Facebook tends to be positive. In fact, our results indicate that the more time spent on Facebook, the less negative self-disclosure. We believe our results provide evidence for the existence of a "stay positive" Facebook norm. As users learn the norms of Facebook, including the norm of posting primarily positive status updates, they might desire to obey the "stay positive" norm as well as to interact in a positive manner to maintain their relationships.

We are not the first researchers to discuss Facebook norms. McLaughlin and Vitak (2012) documented ways users enforce Facebook norms. Miller and Munday (2015) identified three Facebook norms. Our data results may identify a fourth norm: Stay positive in posts and status updates. The notion of a "stay positive" Facebook norm is consistent with the findings of two recent studies: Toma and Carlson (2015) report that college students' perception that they portray a positive version of the self in their Facebook profiles as well as Burke and Ruppel's (2015) finding that users report greater interaction success on Facebook on days when they report more positive self-presentation.

Loneliness and Self-Disclosure on Facebook

Our RQ3 analyses yielded mixed results. Negative self-disclosure correlated negatively with loneliness, whereas positive self-disclosure did not correlate with loneliness. The lonelier the user, the less he/she revealed negative information. Conversely, the less lonely the user, the more he/she revealed negative information. This finding was *not* consistent with previous research findings including Lee et al's (2013) report that that loneliness increased self-disclosure on Facebook among their sample of Korean college students. Also, these results are inconsistent with Jin's (2013) report that, among a Korean sample of emerging adults, lonely users were more likely to engage in negative self-disclosure and less likely to engage in positive self-disclosure. Our results are the first to document this exact relationship: Negative self-disclosure correlated negatively with loneliness, whereas positive self-disclosure did not correlate with loneliness.

Our findings are consistent with recent results documenting that Facebook users prefer receiving negative disclosures offline (Saling et al., 2019). Perhaps lonely users are especially sensitive to communication norms and endeavor to follow them conscientiously. Indeed, lonely users might be attempting to maintain and develop Facebook relationships—and might avoid negative disclosure to do so. Less lonely users may feel sufficiently secure in their relationships to be comfortable revealing negative information.

Loneliness and Facebook Usage

In sum, based on data from our sample and a few previously published studies, loneliness appears to be unrelated to Facebook usage, at least among certain populations. Perhaps previously identified user characteristics such as shyness (Baker & Oswald, 2010), self-esteem (e.g., Varnali & Toker, 2015), self-inferiority (Hong et al., 2014), and stress (Bevan et al., 2014) exercise more influence over Facebook usage than loneliness.

However, loneliness may prompt cautiousness, as loneliness appears to be associated with less negative self-disclosure on Facebook. In general, the more time the emerging adults in our sample spent on Facebook, the more likely they were to engage in positive self-disclosure and the less likely they are to reveal negative information. This pattern of self-disclosure seems reasonable, given that the primary way to interact on Facebook is to post a comment or status update, thus revealing information about the self, and given the potential existence of a Facebook norm of "staying positive."

Given the inconsistences between our findings and previous results with alternative populations, our outcomes may indicate that culture may play a role in Facebook users' communication patterns. Such a conclusion would be consistent with previously published results that emerging adult behavior can differ from culture to culture (Arseth et al., 2009). Additionally, examining valence of self-disclosure may allow more nuanced understandings of the norms governing Facebook disclosures.

LIMITATIONS AND FUTURE RESEARCH DIRECTIONS

We acknowledge multiple limitations to our study. Our sample was gathered in one location, Hong Kong. The sample proved fruitful for a study of Facebook usage, given the many significant findings of the study. However, the generalizability of the findings to other locations awaits testing. Furthermore, multiple Chinese cultural norms (i.e., social hierarchy, monitoring displays of strong emotion, face concerns, and emphasis on group harmony) can influence respondents' replies in research (Kwan, Chun, & Chesla, 2011).

Furthermore, because there is no directory of Facebook users, probability sampling was impossible. Thus, the representativeness of our convenience sample remains unknown. Additionally, because this was a one-time survey, causality could not be established. Future research could examine the causal relationships between loneliness, self-disclosure, and Facebook use, perhaps employing experimental interventions and longitudinal methods. Finally, the limitations of self-report data include recall problems and social-desirability biases.

Although beyond the score of our study, future research might examine further the link between self-disclosure and users' motivations for disclosure on Facebook (Bazarova & Choi, 2014). Certain motivations may account for the amount and valence of disclosures. Additionally, future studies of disclosure could move beyond survey data to examine actual Facebook profiles, as such examinations have proved fruitful in previous studies of Facebook behavior of emerging adults (e.g., Boupha, Grisso, Morris, Webb, & Zakeri, 2013; Taraszow, Aristodemou, Shitta, Laouris, & Arsoy, 2010; Webb, Wilson, Hodges, Smith, & Zakeri, 2012).

CONCLUSION

Despite these limitations, our study contributes to scholarly understanding of user-interactions on SNS. We offer the first examination of the relationships between loneliness, self-disclosure on Facebook, and Facebook usage among a Hong Kong sample of emerging adults. We now know that, at least among one sample of Facebook users, the more time spent on Facebook, the more users engage in positive self-disclosure on Facebook. The more hours per day users spent on Facebook, the less negative self-disclosure they reveal on Facebook. However, two measures of Facebook usage (days per week on Facebook and time spent on Facebook per visit) were not significantly correlated with negative self-disclosure. The higher the loneliness score, the less users reveal negative self-information on Facebook. We offered two logical explanations for our results: the reciprocity norm of self-disclosure and the proposed Facebook norm of remaining positive. Finally, our study offers evidence that Facebook norms may be culture specific and measuring self-discourse valence may provide a more nuanced understanding for those norms.

REFERENCES

Abdulahi, A., Samadi, B., & Gharleghi, B. (2014). A Study on the negative effects of social networking sites such as Facebook among Asia Pacific University scholars in Malaysia. *International Journal of Business and Social Science*, *5*(1), 133–145. Retrieved from http://www.ijbssnet.com/journals/Vol_5_No_10_September_2014/18.pdf

Al-Saggaf, Y., & Nielsen, S. (2014). Self-disclosure on Facebook among female users and its relationship to feelings of loneliness. *Computers in Human Behavior*, *36*, 460–468. doi:10.1016/j.chb.2014.04.014

Arnett, J. J. (2015). *Emerging adulthood: The winding road from the late teens through the twenties* (2nd ed.). New York: Oxford University Press. doi:10.1093/oxfordhb/9780199795574.013.9

Arseth, A. K., Kroger, J., Martinussen, M., & Bakken, G. (2009). Intimacy status, attachment, separation-individuation patterns, and identity status in female university students. *Journal of Social and Personal Relationships*, *26*(5), 697–712. doi:10.1177/0265407509347927

Baker, L. R., & Oswald, D. L. (2010). Shyness and online networking services. *Journal of Social and Personal Relationships*, *27*(7), 873–889. doi:10.1177/0265407510375261

Bazarova, N. N., & Choi, Y. H. (2014). Self-disclosure in social media: Extending the functional approach to disclosure motivations and chacteristics on social network sites. *Journal of Communication*, *64*(4), 635–657. doi:10.1111/jcom.12106

Bevan, J. L., Cummings, M. B., Kubiniec, A., Mogannam, M., Price, M., & Todd, R. (2015). How are important life events disclosed on Facebook? Relationships with likelihood of sharing and privacy. *Cyberpsychology, Behavior, and Social Networking*, *18*(1), 8–12. doi:10.1089/cyber.2014.0373 PMID:25584725

Bevan, J. L., Gomez, R., & Sparks, L. (2014). Disclosures about important life events on Facebook: Relationships with stress and quality of life. *Computers in Human Behavior*, *39*, 246–253. doi:10.1016/j.chb.2014.07.021

Bigham, D. S. (2012). Emerging adulthood in sociolinguists. *Language and Linguistics Compass*, *6*(8), 533–544. doi:10.1002/lnc3.350

Blachnio, A., Przepiorka, A., & Rudnicka, P. (2016). Narcissism and self-esteem as predictors of dimensions of Facebook use. *Personality and Individual Differences*, *90*, 296–301. doi:10.1016/j.paid.2015.11.018

Boupha, S., Grisso, A. D., Morris, J., Webb, L. M., & Zakeri, M. (2013). How college students display ethnic identity on Facebook. In R. A. Lind (Ed.), *Race/Gender/Media: Considering diversity across audiences, content, and producers* (3rd ed.; pp. 107-112). Boston, MA: Pearson. Retrieved on June 10, 2019 from https://www.researchgate.net/publication/225271141_How_college_students_display_ethnic_identity_on_Facebook

boyd, d. m. (2006). Friends, Friendsters, and MySpace Top8: Writing community into being on social network sties. *First Monday, 11*(12). Retrieved Jan 23, 2010 from http://www.firstmonday.org/issues/issue11_12/boyd/

Bryant, E. M., Marmo, J., & Ramirez, A. (2011). A functional approach to social networking sites. In K. B. Wright & L. M. Webb (Eds.), *Computer mediated communication in personal relationships* (pp. 3–20). New York: Peter Lang Publishers.

Burke, T. J., & Ruppel, E. K. (2015). Facebook self-presentation motives: Daily effects on social anxiety and interaction success. *Communication Studies*, *66*(2), 204–217. doi:10.1080/10510974.2014.884014

Caers, R., De Feyter, T., De Couck, M., Stough, T., Vigna, C., & Du Bois, C. (2013). Facebook: A literature review. *New Media & Society*, *15*(6), 982–1002. doi:10.1177/1461444813488061

Chan, M. (2018). Reluctance to talk about politics in Face-to-face and Facebook settings: Examining the impact of fear of isolation, willingness to self-censor, and peer network characteristics. *Mass Communication & Society*, *21*(1), 1–23. doi:10.1080/15205436.2017.1358819

Chang, C. W., & Heo, J. (2014). Visiting theories that predict college students' self-disclosure on Facebook. *Computers in Human Behavior*, *36*, 79–86. doi:10.1016/j.chb.2013.07.059

Chen, G. M. (2015). Why do women bloggers use social media? Recreation and information motivations outweigh engagement motivations. *New Media & Society*, *17*(1), 24–40. doi:10.1177/1461444813504269

Chen, R., & Sharma, S. K. (2015). Learning and self-disclosure behavior on social networking sites: The case of Facebook users. *European Journal of Information Systems*, *24*(1), 93–106. doi:10.1057/ejis.2013.31

Cheung, C. M. K., Lee, Z. W. Y., & Chan, T. K. H. (2015). Self-disclosure in social networking sites: The role of perceived cost, perceived benefits and social influence. *Internet Research*, *2*(2), 279–299. doi:10.1108/IntR-09-2013-0192

Crabtree, M. A., & Pillow, D. R. (2018). Extending the dual factor of Facebook use: Social motives and network density predict Facebook use through impression management and open self-disclosure. *Personality and Individual Differences*, *133*, 34–40. doi:10.1016/j.paid.2017.06.017

Dunbar, N. E. (2015). A review of theoretical approaches to interpersonal power. *Review of Communication*, *15*(1), 1–18. doi:10.1080/15358593.2015.1016310

Dwyer, C., Hiltz, S. R., & Passerini, K. (2007). Trust and privacy concern within social networking sites: A comparison of Facebook and MySpace. *Proceedings of Thirteenth Americas Conference on Information Systems*. Retrieved June 10, 2019 from http://csis.pace.edu/dwyer/research/DwyerAMCIS2007.pdf

Ellison, N. B., Vitak, J., Gray, R., & Lampe, C. (2014). Cultivating social resources on social network sites: Facebook relationship maintenance behaviors and their role in social capital processes. *Journal of Computer-Mediated Communication*, *19*(4), 855–870. doi:10.1111/jcc4.12078

Facebook. (2019). *Stats.* Retrieved May 30, 2019 from https://newsroom.fb.com/company-info/

Frison, E., & Eggermont, S. (2015). Toward an integrated and differential approach to the relationships between loneliness, different types of Facebook use, and adolescents' depressed mood. *Communication Research*, *43*, 279–282. doi:10.1177/0093650215617506

Gibbs, J. L., Ellison, N. B., & Heino, R. D. (2006). Self-presentation in online personals: The role of anticipated future interaction, self-disclosure, and perceived success in Internet dating. *Communication Research, 33*(2), 1–26. doi:10.1177/0093650205285368

Green, T., Wilhelmsen, T., Wilmots, E., Dood, B., & Quinn, S. (2016). Social anxiety, attributes of online communication and self-disclosure across private and public Facebook communication. *Computers in Human Behavior, 58*, 206–213. doi:10.1016/j.chb.2015.12.066

Ha, Y. W., Kim, J., Libaque-Saenz, C. F., Chang, Y. H., & Park, M. C. (2015). Use and gratifications of mobile SNSs: Facebook and KakaoTalk in Korea. *Telematics and Informatics, 32*(3), 425–438. doi:10.1016/j.tele.2014.10.006

Hendry, L. B., & Kloep, M. (2007). Conceptualizing emerging adulthood: Inspecting the emperor's new clothes? *Child Development Perspectives, 1*(2), 74–79. doi:10.1111/j.1750-8606.2007.00017.x

Hollenbaugh, E. E., & Ferris, A. L. (2014). Facebook and self-disclosure: Examining the role of traits, social cohesion, and motives. *Computers in Human Behavior, 30*, 50–58. doi:10.1016/j.chb.2013.07.055

Hong, F. Y., Huang, D. H., Lin, H. Y., & Chiu, S. L. (2014). Analysis of the psychological traits, Facebook usage, and Facebook addition model of Taiwanese university students. *Telematics and Informatics, 31*(4), 597–606. doi:10.1016/j.tele.2014.01.001

Jin, B. (2013). How lonely people use and perceive Facebook. *Computers in Human Behavior, 29*(6), 2463–2470. doi:10.1016/j.chb.2013.05.034

Kong, F., & You, X. Q. (2013). Loneliness and self-esteem as mediators between social support and life satisfaction in late adolescence. *Social Indicators Research, 110*(1), 271–279. doi:10.100711205-011-9930-6

Kwak, K. T., Choi, S. K., & Lee, B. G. (2014). SNS flow, SNS self-disclosure and post hoc interpersonal relations change: Focused on Korean Facebook user. *Computers in Human Behavior, 31*, 294–304. doi:10.1016/j.chb.2013.10.046

Kwan, C. M. L., Chun, K. M., & Chesla, C. A. (2011). Cultural norms shaping research group interviews with Chinese American immigrants. *Asian American Journal of Psychology, 2*(2), 115–127. doi:10.1037/a0024184 PMID:21760974

Lampe, C., Ellison, N., & Steinfield, C. (2006). A Face(book) in the crowd: Social searching vs. social browsing. In *Proceedings of the 2006 20th Anniversary Conference on Computer Supported Cooperative Work* (pp. 167-170). New York: ACM Press. 10.1145/1180875.1180901

Ledbetter, A. M., Mazer, J. P., DeGroot, J. M., Meyer, K. R., Yuping, M., & Swafford, B. (2011). Attitudes toward online social connection and self-disclosure as predictors of Facebook communication and relational closeness. *Communication Research, 38*(1), 27–53. doi:10.1177/0093650210365537

Lee, K. T., Noh, M. J., & Koo, D. M. (2013). Lonely people are no longer lonely on social networking sites: The mediating role of self-disclosure and social support. *Cyberpsychology, Behavior, and Social Networking, 16*(6), 413–418. doi:10.1089/cyber.2012.0553 PMID:23621716

Lee-Won, R. J., Shim, M. S., Joo, Y. K., & Park, S. G. (2014). Who puts the best "face" in Facebook?: Positive self-presentation in online social networking and the role of self-consciousness, actual-to-total friends ratio, and culture. *Computers in Human Behavior*, *39*, 413–423. doi:10.1016/j.chb.2014.08.007

Leighton, D. C., Legate, N., LePine, S., Anderson, S. F., & Grahe, J. E. (2018, January 1). *Self-Esteem, self-disclosure, self-expression, and connection on Facebook: A collaborative replication meta-analysis.* doi:10.31234/osf.io/sx742

Leung, L. (2002). Loneliness, self-disclosure, and ICQ use. *Cyberpsychology & Behavior*, *5*(3), 241–251. doi:10.1089/109493102760147240 PMID:12123247

Linne, J. (2014). Common uses of Facebook among adolescents from different social sectors in Buenos Aires City. *Media Education Research Journal, 43,* 189-197. Retrieved June 10, 2019 from dialnet. unirioja.es/descarga/articulo/4738318/2.pdf

Liu, D., & Brown, B. B. (2014). Self-disclosure on social networking sites, positive feedback, and social capital among Chinese college students. *Computers in Human Behavior*, *38*, 213–219. doi:10.1016/j. chb.2014.06.003

McLaughlin, C., & Vitak, J. (2012). Norm evolution and violation on Facebook. *New Media & Society*, *14*(2), 299–315. doi:10.1177/1461444811412712

Medeiros, D. T., & Webb, L. M. (2019). Remaining Facebook versus face-to-face friends after a romantic breakup. *International Journal of Interactive Communication Systems and Technologies*, *9*(1), 1–16. doi:10.4018/IJICST.2019010101

Miller, B., & Mundey, P. (2015). Follow the rules and no one will get hurt: Performing boudary work to avoid negative interactions when using social network sites. *Information Communication and Society*, *18*(2), 187–201. doi:10.1080/1369118X.2014.946433

Munsey, C. (2006). Emerging adults: The in-between age. *Monitor (Charlottetown)*, *37*, 68. Retrieved from http://www.apa.org/monitor/jun06/emerging.aspx

Nam, M., Chun, B., & Hin, L. C. (2014). Impoliteness in Facebook Status updates: Stategic talk among colleagues "outside" the workplace. *Text & Talk, 34*, 165–188. doi:10.1515/text-2013-0042

Omori, K., & Allen, M. (2014). Cultural differences between American and Japanese self-presentation on SNSs. *International Journal of Interactive Communication Systems and Technologies*, *4*(1), 47–60. doi:10.4018/ijicst.2014010104

Park, N., & Baek, K. (2016). Effects of Facebook users' self-disclosure, Facebook use intensity, privacy concern and trust on continuous use intention of Facebook: Focusing on moderating effect of privacy protection skill. *Journal of Korean Content Association*, *16*(11), 53–62. doi:10.5392/JKCA.2016.16.11.053

Park, N. K., & Lee, S. Y. (2014). College students' motivations for facebook use and psychological outcomes. *Journal of Broadcasting & Electronic Media*, *58*(4), 601–620. doi:10.1080/08838151.2014.966355

Pearce, W. B., & Sharp, S. M. (1973). Self-disclosing communication. *Journal of Communication*, *23*(4), 409–425. doi:10.1111/j.1460-2466.1973.tb00958.x PMID:4589176

Phu, B., & Gow, A. J. (2019). Facebook use and its association with subjective happiness and loneliness. *Computers in Human Behavior*, *92*, 151–159. doi:10.1016/j.chb.2018.11.020

Qiu, L., Lin, H., Leung, A. K., & Tov, W. (2012). Putting their best foot forward: Emotional disclosure on Facebook. *Cyberpsychology, Behavior, and Social Networking*, *15*(10), 569–572. doi:10.1089/cyber.2012.0200 PMID:22924675

Rains, S. A., & Brunner, S. R. (2015). What can we learn about social network sites by studying Facebook? A call and recommendations for research on social network sites. *New Media & Society*, *17*(1), 114–131. doi:10.1177/1461444814546481

Russell, D., Peplau, L. A., & Cutrona, C. E. (1980). The revised UCLA Loneliness Scale: Concurrent and discriminant validity evidence. *Journal of Personality Assessment*, *42*, 290–294. doi:10.120715327752jpa4203_11 PMID:660402

Saling, L. L., Cohen, D. B., & Cooper, D. (2019). Not close enough for comfort: Facebook users eschew high intimacy negative disclosures. *Personality and Individual Differences*, *142*, 103–109. doi:10.1016/j.paid.2019.01.028

Satici, S. A. (2019). Facebook addiction and subjective well-being: A study of the mediating role of shyness and loneliness. *International Journal of Mental Health and Addiction*, *17*(1), 41–55. doi:10.100711469-017-9862-8

Shneor, R., & Efrat, K. (2014). Analyzing the impact of culture on average time spent on special media networking sites. *Journal of Promotion Management*, *20*(4), 413–435. doi:10.1080/10496491.2014.930281

Simoncic, T. E., Kuhlman, K. R., Vargas, I., Houchins, S., & Lopez-Duran, N. L. (2014). Facebook use and depressive symptomatology: Investigating the role of neuroticism and extraversion in youth. *Computers in Human Behavior*, *40*, 1–5. doi:10.1016/j.chb.2014.07.039 PMID:25861155

Song, H., Zmyslinski-Seeling, A., Kim, J. Y., Drent, A., Victor, A., Omori, K., & Allen, M. (2014). Does Facebook make you lonely? A meta-analysis. *Computers in Human Behavior*, *36*, 446–452. doi:10.1016/j.chb.2014.04.011

Taraszow, T., Aristodemou, E., Shitta, G., Laouris, Y., & Arsoy, A. (2010). Disclosure of personal contact information by young people in social networking sites: An analysis using Facebook as an example. *International Journal of Media and Cultural Politics*, *6*(1), 81–102. doi:10.1386/macp.6.1.81/1

Toma, C. L., & Carlson, C. L. (2015). How do Facebook users believe they come across in their profiles?: A meta-perception approach to investigating Facebook self-presentation. *Communication Research Reports*, *32*(1), 93–101. doi:10.1080/08824096.2014.990557

Tsay-Vogel, M., Shanahan, J., & Signorielli, N. (2018). Social media cultivating perceptions of privacy: A 5-year analysis of privacy attitudes and self-disclosure behavior among Facebook users. *New Media & Society*, 1–21. doi:10.1177/1461444816660731

Turner, J. W., Grube, J. A., & Myers, J. (2001). Developing an optimal match within online communities: An exploration of CMC support communities and traditional support. *Journal of Communication*, *51*(2), 231–251. doi:10.1111/j.1460-2466.2001.tb02879.x

Utz, S. (2015). The function of self-disclosure on social networking sites: Not only intimate, but also positive and entertaining self-disclosures increase feelings of connection. *Computers in Human Behavior*, *45*, 1–10. doi:10.1016/j.chb.2014.11.076

Varnali, K., & Toker, A. (2015). Self-disclosure on social networking sites. *Social Behavior and Personality*, *43*(1), 1–13. doi:10.2224bp.2015.43.1.1

Walther, J. B., Slovacek, C. L., & Tidwell, L. C. (2001). Is a picture worth a thousand words? Photographic images in long-term and short-term computer-mediated communication. *Communication Research*, *28*(1), 105–134. doi:10.1177/009365001028001004

Waters, S., & Ackerman, J. (2011). Exploring privacy management on Facebook: Motivations and perceived consequences of voluntary disclosure. *Journal of Computer-Mediated Communication*, *17*(1), 101–115. doi:10.1111/j.1083-6101.2011.01559.x

Webb, L. M., & Lee, B. S. (2011). Mommy blogs: The centrality of community in the performance of online maternity. In M. Moravec (Ed.), *Motherhood online: How online communities shape modern motherhood* (pp. 244-257). Newcastle upon Tyne, UK: Cambridge Scholars Publishing. Retrieved June 10, 2019 from https://www.researchgate.net/profile/Lynne_Webb/publication/225271136_Mommy_blogs_The_centrality_of_community_in_the_performance_of_online_maternity/links/0fcfd4fcffab5514ca000000.pdf

Webb, L. M., & Temple, N. (2015). Social media and gender issues. In B. Guzzetti & M. Lesley (Eds.), *Handbook of research on the societal impact of digital media* (pp. 638–669). Hershey, PA: IGI Global. doi:10.4018/978-1-4666-8310-5.ch025

Webb, L. M., Wilson, M. L., Hodges, M., Smith, P. A., & Zakeri, M. (2012). Facebook: How college students work it. In H. S. Noor Al-Deen & J. A. Hendricks (Eds.), *Social media: Usage and impact* (pp. 3–22). Lanham, MD: Lexington Books.

Wheeless, L. R., & Grotz, J. (1976). Conceptualization and measurement of reported self-disclosure. *Human Communication Research*, *2*(4), 338–346. doi:10.1111/j.1468-2958.1976.tb00494.x

Wohn, D. Y., & LaRose, R. (2014). Effects of loneliness and differential usage of Facebook on college adjustment of first-year students. *Computers & Education*, *76*, 158–167. doi:10.1016/j.compedu.2014.03.018

Wu, C. W., & Webb, L. M. (2016). Chinese international students' messages on the Family Forum: Topics, goals, and types of assistance. In M. F. Wright (Ed.), *Identity, sexuality, and relationships among emerging adults in the digital age* (pp. 128–149). Hershey, PA: IGI Global. doi:10.4018/978-1-5225-1856-3.ch009

Yeo, T. E. D., & Chu, T. H. (2017). Sharing "sex secrets" on Facebook: A content analysis of youth peer communication and advice exchange on social media about sexual health and intimate relations. *Journal of Health Communication*, *22*(9), 753–762. doi:10.1080/10810730.2017.1347217 PMID:28796578

Zlatolas, L. N., Welzer, T., Hericko, M., & Holbl, M. (2015). Privacy antecedents for SNS self-disclosure: The case of Facebook. *Computers in Human Behavior, 45*, 158-167. doi:10.1016/j.chb.2014.12.012

KEY TERMS AND DEFINITIONS

Emerging Adulthood: A distinct life stage exists between adolescence and full adulthood when individuals are exploring long-term choices.

Facebook Use (or Usage): Active engagement on Facebook across time operationalized as the amount of time the individual spends reading or writing in the social medium platform located at Facebook.com.

Hong Kong, China: A semi-autonomous city-state in the south-eastern corner of China, located on the South China sea. It is a densely populated urban center comprised of one main island and a small part of the mainland territory. Its native language is Mandarin, although English is widely spoken.

Loneliness: The individual experiences an uncomfortable psychological state associated with a desire for increased human interaction.

Self-Disclosure: An individual reveals information about the self to others.

Valence of a Disclosure: The perception of revealed information as either positive versus negative by either the sender, the receiver, or an observer.

This research was previously published in Recent Advances in Digital Media Impacts on Identity, Sexuality, and Relationships; pages 170-189, copyright year 2020 by Information Science Reference (an imprint of IGI Global).

Chapter 68
Transformation of China's Most Popular Dating App, Momo, and Its Impact on Young Adult Sexuality:
A Critical Social Construction of Technology Analysis

Weishan Miao
Chinese Academy of Social Sciences, China

Jian Xu
iD https://orcid.org/0000-0003-2798-0996
Deakin University, Australia

ABSTRACT

This chapter explores China's most popular dating app 'Momo' and its impact on young adult sexuality. It examines three interrelated questions at three different levels: First, at the macro level, in what social situations and institutions were mobile dating apps such as Momo invented in China? Second, at the meso level, if we consider Momo as a constantly changing social process, what are the transformations it has experienced, and, during this process, what societal forces have impacted the trajectory of changes and in what ways? Third, at the micro level, how the transformation of Momo's 'intimate infrastructures' at different developmental stages has impacted the sexuality and intimate relationships of its young adult users? It argues that mobile dating apps have to timely transform their design, functions, and market positions to adapt to the changing market competition and governmental regulations in China. The transformation of the intimate infrastructures of the mobile dating apps has also shaped the young adult users' intimate practices and sexuality.

DOI: 10.4018/978-1-6684-6307-9.ch068

INTRODUCTION

Technology has significantly transformed our emotional practices and intimate relationships – from love letters to telephone calls, from the use of the internet to the popularization of mobile phones. In China's increasingly digitized society, digital media becomes an important avenue for encountering, practicing and experimenting intimacy and love (Pei, 2010). The internet has been coded into Chinese people's intimate practices since China officially came online in 1994. In the early years of internet popularization, Chinese people used online forums, chat rooms and QQ (instant messaging) to experience intimate interactions. From 2000, dating websites, such as Jiayuan, Zhenai and Baihe, became more popular and professionalized and from 2010, the exponential growth of smartphone use, geolocation technologies and mobile apps encouraged the rapid emergence of mobile dating apps. These apps, such as Momo, Tantan and Blued, have significantly transformed young people's sexuality as well as China's traditional sexual culture and ideology.

In recent years, mobile dating apps have received increasing attention in everyday life and academic research around the world. In the US, 15% of adults have used online dating sites or mobile dating apps (Smith, 2016). In 2014, Momo, the Chinese version of Tinder, was listed on the Nasdaq, and by March 2019, had attracted 114 million active monthly users (Sina Finance, 2019). According to statistics released by iiMedia Research Group in June 2018, 55.82% of Momo users are male and 44.18% are female. Users under 24 years old, 25–30, 31–35, and 36–40 account for 38.34%, 31.34%, 14.22% and 7.41%, respectively of the total users (iiMedia, 2018). If we adopt the age range 18–35 to classify young adults (Petry, 2002), we can see that up to 70% of Momo users fall into this category. As China's most popular mobile dating app, the 'intimate infrastructures' (Liu 2016) Momo provides, and the transformation of the app, have greatly impacted the sexuality of Chinese young adults.

Existing research on mobile dating apps, mainly in the Western contexts, either studies the functions, features and formats of mobile dating apps (David & Cambre, 2016; Timmermans & Courtois, 2018), or explores how mobile dating apps are used by consumers, examining motives and self-representation (Chan, 2017; Wotipka & High, 2016). This body of research overemphasizes the 'intimate infrastructures' but neglects 'how these intimate infrastructures are produced and/or allowed and accepted' (Liu, 2016, p. 559). Therefore, it is timely and important to go beyond the dominant 'technology-consumption' framework to further study mobile dating apps from a production perspective and examine how the evolving product design of mobile dating apps has impacted the sexuality of their users.

To fill the gap, this chapter studies Momo with a production perspective, drawing upon the theoretical resources of social construction of technology (SCOT) that we will detail in the next section. More specifically, it explores three interrelated questions. First, at the macro level, in what social situations and institutions were mobile dating apps such as Momo invented? Second, at the meso level, if we consider Momo as a constantly changing social process, what are the transformations it has experienced, and, during this process, what societal forces have impacted the trajectory of changes and in what ways? Third, at the micro level, how has the transformation of Momo's 'intimate infrastructures' at different developmental stages impacted the sexuality of its young adult users?

Social Construction of Technology (SCOT): An Analytical Framework

Technological determinism has impacted the discussion of relations between technologies and societies in different historical periods. Neither technological utopianism nor pessimism has sufficiently considered technology as a 'sociotechnical phenomenon' (Bijker, 1995; Suchman, 1996). Even theories that treat technology as neutral, objective and natural, such as technological instrumentalism, have simplified technology as material infrastructure and neglected the related cognition, practices and the wider social situations and institutional arrangements (Dierkes & Hoffmann, 1992; MacKenzie & Wajcman, 1999).

As a notable theory that challenges technological determinism, science and technology studies (STS) conceptualize technology as a relational and interactional social process. It emphasizes that no technology is invented in a vacuum, but is a result of a variety of social forces (Mackay & Gillespie, 1992, p. 688). Therefore, in contrast to technological determinist claims that assume the relationship between technology and society is a one-way or linear process, STS foregrounds mutual impacts that are more complex, dynamic and intricate.

As an extension of the STS theory, SCOT aligns with these perspectives and assumptions. For example, it regards the development of technology as 'an alternation of variation and selection' (Pinch & Bijker, 1987, p. 135). More importantly, SCOT has developed a set of core concepts and a comprehensive interpretative framework. Specifically, SCOT starts from the identification of a series of relevant social groups. These groups have differing imaginaries and expectations of technologies because of their divergent demands of interests and cultural values. Moreover, these different interpretations of technology compete with each other and exemplify a form of 'interpretive flexibility', which 'suggests that technology design is an open process that can produce different outcomes depending on the social circumstances of development' (Klein & Kleinman, 2002, p. 29). Consequently, the trajectory of technological development does not follow a pre-determined direction, but is situated in varied possibilities brought about by the interpretive flexibility. During this process of intense conflict, a particular explanation and understanding of technology gradually prevails; thus, the design of technology becomes stabilized and finalized. However, what should be noted is that this stable condition is temporary because new themes keep emerging.

The theoretical approaches of STS and SCOT have received significant attention from media and communication studies. Researchers have started to adopt this frame for analyzing the development and changes of media technologies in areas such as broadcasting (Slotten, 1995), personal computers (Bardini & Horvath, 1995), blogs (Siles, 2012) and augmented reality technology (Liao, 2018). Nevertheless, few have employed this framework for exploring mobile dating apps. A recent study of China's gay social network app Blued closely examined the political and market environments and the company's visions that have shaped the platform's development (Miao & Chan, 2019). But no research has been conducted on heterosexual dating apps in China or elsewhere adopting this frame.

Despite the strengths of SCOT, it does face various challenges and has received criticism. One of the most notable criticisms argues that SCOT lacks attention to macro structural factors. Such criticisms (Klein & Kleinman, 2002) highlight the importance of considering the political economy, social structures and histories and cultures of different regions and countries. Bearing the promises and limitations of SCOT in mind, we adopt SCOT as an analytical framework while simultaneously considering China's political, social and cultural contexts to study Momo's transformation and the impact of this transformation on young adult sexuality.

METHODS

This study adopts a mixed-methods research design. First, we collected news coverage of Momo published between 2011 and 2018 by searching the Chinese characters for 'Momo' on Baidu, China's largest Internet search engine. More than 500 news reports were collected and read. In addition, we also examined Chinese academic publications on Momo, including journal articles and conference proceedings on China National Knowledge Infrastructure (CNKI), to understand both the popular and academic discourses on the popular mobile dating app.

To more reveal the functions and structures of the app and observe users' interactions on this platform, we adopted the popular 'walkthrough method' (Light, Burgess, & Duguay, 2018) used in app studies. We downloaded Momo onto our mobile devices and registered as a Momo user. In this way, we managed to acquire observational data through watching continued live streaming on Momo, reading Momo users' profiles, self-presentations and real-time posts and interacting with nearby users. In addition, we also conducted in-depth interviews with six young adult users of Momo between 18 and 30 years old.

Based on our close reading of the collected news coverage of Momo, we observed three stages of Momo's changing product positioning since its invention, from its initial position as a 'stranger-oriented' social network, to an 'interest-based' social network, to its current role of live-streaming social network. In the following sections, we will examine each of the three stages to understand what societal forces have impacted Momo's changing product positioning. We also examine how the transformation of Momo's 'intimate infrastructures' reflects and incorporates trends in sexuality of Chinese young adults but also enables and shapes new trends.

THE 'SUPER HOOK-UP' APP: A STRANGER-ORIENTED SOCIAL NETWORK

The most important thing is that when you are on a business trip and you are alone in the hotel, you can use the location-based service (LBS) of your mobile phone to find out that there is a young woman next door who is experiencing the same thing with you. (Tang Yan, Founder of Momo, cited from Fu, 2019)

Momo was established in 2011 as a stranger-oriented social networking app. Why did the founder position Momo as a 'stranger-oriented' social networking app? And why did it gain such great popularity among young people in so short a period of time? Tang Yan, the founder of Momo, believes that the emergence of LBS laid the most important technological foundation for Momo and other similar apps. However, it has been argued that the application of technologies is determined by their social meanings – that is, the particular social groups that use the technology, in what social contexts, and with what social implications and consequences (Yang, 2012). However, to Tang Yan, a profit-driven entrepreneur, the complex social meanings have been simplified into a 'motivation–demand' relationship. According to to the relevant media interviews with Tang Yan, he developed a strong interest in the potential of LBS before founding Momo. As Tang reflected:

Why do people check in online? Is it really that they are keen to let themselves know where they are? There must be a very strong motivation for them to do this. Otherwise there is no point sharing their location. (Sina Technology, 2012)

Wang Li, chief operations officer of Momo, gave a more detailed explanation:

We aim to explore the biggest value of LBS. We believe it has great potentials. It can make a lot of changes. Many LBS products were in a wrong direction from the very beginning. They think it's meaningless to check in. They believe that no one cares about where people are. But if you place LBS in a social networking and the local contexts, it becomes an opportunity for the transformation from online to offline connections. (Huxiu.com, 2012)

Clearly, we can see that Momo has emphasized the association between technology and social relations to promote offline interactions, but what social relations does Momo create? What are the motivations of looking for strangers nearby? As Liao (2018) argues, visions of the functional orientations of an emerging technology can shape, contest and stabilize the development of the technology. What is equally important is its leaders' understanding and imagination of the future of technological development (Borup, Brown, Konrad, & van Lente, 2006). From the very beginning, Tang Yan positioned LBS in the context of sexual networking. His assumption is confirmed by recent research that showed 'sex' as the only expected motivation of Momo users' requests to meet offline (Solis & Wong, 2019).

Therefore, meeting people's dating and sexual desires has become a key component of Momo's self-imaginary of its products. To argue for the importance of this imaginary, Tang constantly highlights 'inelastic demand'. Tang believes that it is human nature to socialize, and this is a need that must be fulfilled. More specifically, the inelastic demand here is sexual networking (Sohu, 2018). As Chen Zhilin, Momo's product manager, put it: 'Besides drug taking, sex should be the most irresistible desire for human beings' (China Venture, 2014). To prove the naturalness and legitimacy of this demand, Tang Yan, in many of his interviews, referred to the popularity of QQ's virtual floating bottle, same-city chatroom and WeChat's 'People Nearby' service (Douban, 2014). In so doing, Tang essentializes sexual networking as a crucial constituent of human behavior, creating continuous energy for the support of Momo's imagination of its expansive market share. Similar to how the general public imagine and practice the 'rigid demand' for Chinese real estate properties (Wang, 2018), the demand for sexual networking exemplifies a mechanism designed and maneuvered by particular social groups.

However, Tang's personal imaginary of technology should not be taken as an individual effort. Rather, it must be interpreted as a negotiation of the social, political and cultural environments, as well as industry competition and technological affordance. Clearly, the exploration of sex and new intimate relationships is the core of Tang's imaginary of Momo. Nevertheless, profiting from the operation of sex or advocating for sexual freedom cannot be done explicitly in China's restrained political atmosphere. Therefore, 'stranger-oriented networking' has become a euphemism for Momo to avoid political risk and negative self-branding.

The blurry and fluid boundaries between stranger-oriented networking and sexual relationships also create opportunities for public imagination. Stranger-oriented apps provide safe spaces for users to evade social bias. As noted in recent studies, Momo was developed in the context of China's urbanization, individualization and transformation of sexual culture (Xu & Wu, 2019). In this context, the general public enjoy the freedom of independence and mobility but also face the challenge of integrating into a new structure (Sun & Lei, 2017). The rise of Momo, therefore, is contextualized in a series of cultural politics between the traditional and the modern, the conservative and the progressive, loyalty and pleasure, stability and mobility. China thus becomes a laboratory for the Chinese to experiment with new intimate practices. This experimentation is, at the same time, subject to the influence of Chinese society's traditional values. The expression and practice of sex has long been reserved in China. Accordingly, in the name of stranger-oriented networking, Momo has turned the exploration of sexual relationships from a serious and traditional cultural experience into a new, pan-networking digital practice that is relaxing and entertaining.

At the user level, how has Momo's initial positioning as a stranger-networking app influenced its users' sexuality? We interviewed six young adult users of Momo who have been using the app for more than five years and asked them to talk about their understanding of dating, love and sex since using Momo. All six interviewees said that Momo had made dating easier and had created more opportunities to develop intimate relationships with strangers. As Interviewee A (male) said:

Momo is a convenient and costless platform for dating. I can search suitable dating partners on Momo whenever I have time and wherever I am. Before using Momo, I had to rely on my friends, colleagues and relatives to introduce dating partners to me and the opportunities to meet new dating partners are limited. It looks that I have unlimited opportunities on Momo as long as I'd like to spend time. Dating is not a serious thing as before but is more like eating fast food. However, I am still single. I found that the more I date the harder I can find the right person. I always think that the next one is better.

As a super-hook-up app, Momo has also become a popular platform for sexually active young people to look for one-night stands, though this was not the initial positioning of the platform. The use of Momo for one-night stands, to some extent, has promoted casual sex among young adults, which has been widely criticized by media and the government. As Interviewee B (male) described: 'Don't be serious. Just be happy! Most people are just playing around. No one should be responsible for anyone or feel guilty on Momo as we are all adults and know what we are doing'. Interviewees C and E (female) told us that they found it is hard to find a suitable dating partner to develop a serious relationship as many men were just looking for fun on Momo. But these interviewees still use Momo as they don't want to miss out on potential good partners. Both interviewees said they have to be careful when selecting dating partners to meet offline. Interviewee F (male) said that he doesn't want people around him to know he is on Momo because of the platform's stigma as a one-night stand app.

We can see that different users have their own interpretive flexibility towards Momo. Momo is like a digital supermarket of 'intimate relationships', in which different users can look for one or more types of intimate relationships, including dating, flirting, a serious relationship or casual sex. The speed, low-cost and unlimited possibilities for achieving intimacy with strangers enabled by the technological structure, and the functions and affordances of Momo to some extent have transformed young adult users' imaginations and practices of intimacy and sexuality in the digital era.

INTEREST-BASED SOCIAL NETWORKING: REBRANDING, PROFIT AND TRANSFORMATION

On 11 December 2014, Momo went public on the NASDAQ. The company's market value increased to US$3.151 billion (Sina Technology, 2014). Three years after Momo's August 2011 launch, Momo had become the second largest social networking app in China. However, it was increasingly being seen as a 'one-night stand' app and was accused of compromising family cohesion by the media and public alike. Media coverage of prostitution, sexual and other crimes conducted using Momo also proliferated (Alltechasia.com, 2017).

Momo's reported negative social impacts soon caught the attention of the Chinese government. In March 2015, Momo was fined CNY 60,000 (People.cn, 2015). To survive in the state-controlled internet industry, Momo had to adjust its service to stay within government regulations. In the 4.0 version, launched in April 2015, its once foremost service, 'People Nearby', was downgraded to the secondary menu. The 'groups' function, used to specify places where people were looking for sex partners or sexual fantasies, was removed. However, if we see the Momo case as an example of how governmental forces shape technology products, we then must admit that in the Chinese context, politics often only play a role of guiding a company's direction. It sets the bottom lines for technology companies, with directives such as no discussion of politically sensitive topics and no challenge to mainstream ideologies, values and social morality. The market more substantially influences the trajectory of technological development (Miao, 2019). As pointed out in some comments, since its initial public offering, Momo is no longer a start-up company, but a for-profit company that should be responsible to its investors (Alltechasia. com, 2017). Momo experienced setbacks on its second trading day, the share price dropped 11% on 12 December 2014. In the following six months, the share price dropped a further 40%. The response from investors was: 'Momo has still got no sophisticated business mode that can bring profit' (Guancha.cn, 2015). During this new stage, the founder's control of the company gave way to, or more accurately, became subject to the influence of market forces. Driven by capital, various types of technology firms have become standardized after they went public. New and existing users and the profit model become the decisive forces in technological development (Miao, 2019).

As a dating app that is dedicated to meeting users' particular needs, Momo is faced with a difficult dilemma under the influence of capital: when users' demands are satisfied – that is, when they find a stranger around them on Momo – they will soon leave the platform and switch to other social media such as WeChat for further conversation. But if their demand is not satisfied, they will want to leave the platform as it is not meeting their needs. The first situation is a common challenge faced by all dating services (Fiore & Donath, 2004). Fundamentally, this is because users cannot be constantly exposed to strangers.

Momo's transformation to an interest-based social networking app exemplifies an alternative imagination of how technology reshapes social relations. This is reflected directly in the changes of its product functions and design. In Momo version 6.0, the 'People Nearby' function was hidden in the secondary menu. It was replaced by a newsfeed function similar to that in WeChat, showing updates of people nearby or chosen by platform algorithms. The weakening of the 'People Nearby' function aims to highlight 'interest' functions. Now, when users log in to the latest version of Momo, they need to fill in personal details as well as six of their interests. In other words, Momo started to experiment with other dimensions of social networking aside from geolocation. Moreover, Momo has added a new function called 'chatroom'. Users can enter chatrooms with different themes any time to chat with people on topics in which they are interested. Momo has also created groups based on different themes, such as Karaoke, place of origin, board games and hiking. Users can choose to join groups according to their location, interests and ages. At the same time, Momo has added a new function of 'Offline Gathering' for group members. Users can send group messages or initiate gatherings by using web links embedded in these virtual groups.

Just like the role of sex in stranger-oriented networking, interest is merely a tool through which Momo promotes social networking. The focus of Momo has always been 'networking'. As Tang pointed out (Ifeng, 2014): 'Pure interest-based social networking is a false proposition. Interest must be related to a different dimension (such as geolocation) in order to become the foundation for social networking.' Clearly, we can see that although Momo has transformed from sex-oriented to interest-based, what remains unchanged are the intersection of geolocation and the conversion of online connections to offline interactions.

A few interviewees expressed that Momo's transition to interest-based networking could help them find people with the same interests as them. Moreover, they said it was easier to sustain online conversations with people who share the same interests. Interviewee D (female) likes the new 'Offline Gathering' function based on interests. She said:

I feel a bit awkward when meeting a dating partner offline, as sometimes we don't have much in common to talk about. The group gathering offline allows me to meet more people at one time. I can do my interested things and hunt for the right person at the same time.

Admittedly, Momo's transition to interest-based social networking mainly aims to dilute its stigma as a one-night stand app. It also began to promote 'interest' as an important element in intimate relationships, suggesting young adults should consider this more when pursuing relationships. This can be seen in a popular personalized signature available on Momo and adopted by thousands of users after this transition, that is, 'good-looking faces are invariably monotonic whereas interesting soul is truly one in a million'. As pointed out by Liu (2017), digital genres are increasingly converging. In her research on a popular Chinese dancing video game, QQ Dazzling Dance, she found that many players use the video game as a space for dating based on their common interest in the game, demonstrating that 'interest' can be used as an effective agency to build up intimate relationships among young adults in the digital space. Momo's transition to interest-based networking, to some extent, has pushed this trend forward.

LIVE-STREAMING SOCIAL NETWORKING: BECOMING A PAN-ENTERTAINMENT PLATFORM

Momo's transformation to interest-based social networking was pragmatic and strategic, but not very successful in market competition. The 6.0 version did not, in fact, cultivate user loyalty but slowed down the growth of user numbers. As mentioned by Tang in an interview, the changes brought about by interest-based social networking were in many ways too reckless (Sina, 2019). This failure provided a timely opportunity for Momo to ride China's live-streaming wave and complete its second strategic product adjustment. Since 2016, China has experienced exponential growth in the live video-streaming industry, with an estimated market value of CNY ¥20.8 billion (Xiang, 2017). It was not long before this emerging service became Momo's main source of revenue.

Some people might think that Momo was 'waiting for the wave'. However, a SCOT perspective helps us unpack the rationale behind Momo's shift, to see the complex transformation trajectory. As Tang explained, before the introduction of live streaming to Momo, the company had internal discussions about potential new services. Some options included ride sharing, e-commerce and even internet financing. But Tang insisted on maintaining the company's positioning, as he believed that these services were beyond

Momo's scope and it was impossible to make profit with such diverse offerings. After much exploration, Tang selected live streaming as Momo's newest service. Although this decision was opposed by the whole management team, Tang claims he insisted on it (Sohu, 2017a). In the second half of 2015, Momo launched a new service, 'Momo Live'. The aim of this new service was to cultivate 'concert-level' live streaming of famous entertainment stars. This attempt failed because of the high maintenance cost and low user interest. In early 2016, Momo entered the field of mobile live streaming. In April, it launched the live streaming service for ordinary users. The transformation of Momo's position has also encouraged changes in its functions. In April 2016, Momo launched its 6.7 version. The previous 'Discover' function became the 'Live streaming' function. In September that year, it added a new function for making micro videos called 'Moment'. These changes indicated that videos had become an important strategy for Momo's development.

Live streaming soon brought Momo enormous profits. In 2016, Momo's annual net revenue was three times higher than the previous year. The net profit of the fourth quarter of 2016 was 674% above 2015, of this, live streaming contributed to 80% of the profit (Xinhua, 2017). Therefore, the positioning of Momo has experienced tremendous change. It has evolved from stranger-oriented networking to interest-based networking, and later to a pan-entertainment platform. To explain this, Tang made an interesting comparison: 'Momo used to be like the dating corner in Shanghai People's Park. People come and people go. But now, Momo is like the Disneyland with all the fun facilities. People can come to meet strangers, but also experience other things' (36Kr, 2017). The introduction of live streaming has amplified the app's entertainment function but has weakened its networking function. 'More on entertainment and less on networking' thus becomes an alternative market positioning.

However, although live streaming has become the new engine for Momo's revenue and a pan-entertainment platform has become its new positioning strategy, Momo has declared and insisted on many occasions that it is still focused on social networking. Tang clarified: 'We still believe that Momo is more like a social networking platform, rather than a live streaming site. Social networking is still the foundation. Live streaming is more of an important part of our platform, or a strategy through which we make money, but it's not the foundation' (Sohu, 2017b). Live streaming could be understood as an alternative form of social networking, at least when compared with traditional mass media such as television. Users can directly interact with hosts and hostesses; such interaction normally takes place through watching, liking, following, commenting, gifting and sharing. Therefore, we can see that although the scenarios in which users consume are different, Momo has always focused on social networking, despite its transformation from interest-based social networking to live streaming networking.

Undoubtedly, Momo's transition into a live-streaming app has been successful. This is evident in its huge revenue. What has also been successful is Tang Yan's positioning of Momo as a pan-entertainment live-streaming platform. All of our interviewees agreed that 'using Momo now is so much more fun than before'. However, the questions remain, what has led so many users to join Momo's live-streaming services, including both viewers and performers? What types of live-streaming styles and content have they created? And how does this form of live streaming contribute to the formation of youth culture?

We identified three forms of live streaming in our online fieldwork: everyday life (e.g. family life, pets and cooking), entertainment (e.g. singing, dancing, gaming and travelling) and social interactions (e.g. networking, talk shows and chatting). Among all automated recommendations by the platform, female, particularly young and good-looking, casters are always on top of the list. From our observation, most of the viewers of these live streamers are male. Although Tang Yan has claimed that Momo live streaming is an example of transition into pan-entertainment, users' gendered practices, as we have identified, reveal that Momo's newly introduced entertainment functions are still imbedded in sexual relationships. This is evident in the fact that a large number of female live streamers display gendered content, deliver sexual messages and establish intimate relationships with their viewers. Indeed, such a gender performance is widely observed in the emerging live-streaming industry in China (Zhang & Hjorth, 2017).

What is worth noting is that the recent wave of user growth brought by Momo live streaming highlights the commodification, monetization and datafication of sexual relationships. Audience admiration and support of these performers can be monetized through virtual gifts on the platform, and Momo shares a proportion of performers' income from these virtual gifts. In China's mass media, topics such as 'female internet celebrities' and 'monthly income of over one million' have become common. For the users, practices such as liking, commenting, reposting or even gifting have become the means through which they express their admiration of casters, or even attain their personal contact details. Studies have found that live streaming in dating apps has produced a body of data that is based on sex and emotion. The flow of views and visits embedded in these data has become important assets for app companies to attract investment (Wang, 2019).

CONCLUSION

This chapter uses Momo as a case study to investigate how the digital infrastructure for intimate relationships is produced, transformed and developed, as well as how the transformation of the infrastructures has impacted young adult sexuality. Three conclusions can be drawn based on our case study.

First, mobile dating apps emerged in the context of China's rapid modernization, privatization and digitization. To some extent, the popularity of mobile dating apps represented by Momo has challenged the traditional values, cultural norms and sexual culture. Such apps are always subject to governmental regulation while also having to explore innovative business models to attract market capital. The sustainable profits of these businesses are dependent on finding a balance between the Party and the market.

Second, as demonstrated in the case of Momo, mobile dating apps have to transform their design, function and market positioning to increase their competitiveness in the market. The transformation has to consider a series of factors, including changing preferences of users, new technologies, and changing government regulations.

Last but not least, as a platform for intimate relationships, mobile dating apps have not only reflected and satisfied the intimate and sexual desires of Chinese young adults but also have created and shaped new sexual and intimate relationships between them. This chapter on Momo has shed light on the interrelations between the transformation of the intimate infrastructures and the transformation of young adult intimacy and sexuality enabled by mobile dating apps.

REFERENCES

Alltechasia.com. (2017). *How China's top dating app Momo turned from disruptor to conformist*. Retrieved from https://alltechasia.com/how-chinas-top-dating-app-momo-turn-from-disruptors-conformists/

Bardini, T., & Horvath, A. T. (1995). The Social Construction of the Personal Computer User. *Journal of Communication*, *45*(3), 40–66. doi:10.1111/j.1460-2466.1995.tb00743.x

Bijker, W. E. (1995). *Of Bicycles, Bakelites, and Bulbs: Toward a Theory of Sociotechnical Change.* Cambridge, MA: MIT Press.

Borup, M., Brown, N., Konrad, K., & van Lente, H. (2006). The sociology of expectations in science and technology. *Technology Analysis and Strategic Management*, *18*(3–4), 285–298. doi:10.1080/09537320600777002

Chan, L. S. (2017). Who uses dating apps? Exploring the relationships among trust, sensation-seeking, smartphone use, and the intent to use dating apps based on the Integrative Model. *Computers in Human Behavior*, *72*, 246–258. doi:10.1016/j.chb.2017.02.053

China Venture. (2014). *Momo yuanzui yu lixiangguo. Tang Yan: zhiyao zuo seqing jiu duoshou* [Momo's sins and goals. Tang Yan: Will never relate the app to pornography]. Retrieved from https://www.chinaventure.com.cn/cmsmodel/news/detail/260390.html

David, G., & Cambre, C. (2016). Screened Intimacies: Tinder and the Swipe Logic. *Social Media and Society*, *2*(2), 1–11. doi:10.1177/2056305116641976

Dierkes, M., & Hoffmann, U. (Eds.). (1992). *New Technology at the Outset: Social Forces in the Shaping of Technological Innovations.* Frankfurt: Campus Verlag.

Douban. (2014). *Tang Yan jiangshu ziji wei "yuepao shenqi" de xibai zhilu. Momo nasi dake shangshi* [Tang Yan told how he washed away the stigma of Momo as "one-night stand" app. Momo went public on the NASDAQ]. Retrieved from https://site.douban.com/249066/widget/notes/18138972/note/475276108/

Fiore, A. T., & Donath, J. S. (2004). Online personals: an overview. CHI '04 Extended Abstracts on Human Factors in Computing Systems, 1395–1398.

Fu, Y. (2019). *Tantan zheyu seqing, momo shuaibudiao yuepao* [Tantan declined because of 'pornography'. Momo can't get rid of its 'one-night stand stigma] Retrieved from https://www.sohu.com/a/311115285_649045

Guancha.cn. (2015). *Momo cong "liang"* [Momo turning 'good']. Retrieved from https://www.guancha.cn/Science/2015_04_13_315677.shtml

Huxiu.com. (2012). *Momo zenme zai yinian nei yunying chu qianwan yonghu* [How Momo attracted millions of users within a year]. Retrieved from https://www.huxiu.com/article/3450.html

Ifeng. (2014). *Momo CEO Tang Yan: Chun xingqu shejiao shige weimingti* [Momo's CEO Tang Yan: Pure interest-based social networking is a false proposition]. Retrieved from http://tech.ifeng.com/vc/detail_2014_03/03/34358584_0.shtml

iiMedia. (2018). *Naxieren zui xihuan moshengren shejiao? Momo nanxing yonghu juduo* [Who likes stranger networking most? Most Momo users are male]. Retrieved from https://www.iimedia.cn/c900/62037.html

Klein, H. K., & Kleinman, D. L. (2002). The social construction of technology: Structural considerations. *Science, Technology & Human Values*, *27*(1), 28–52. doi:10.1177/016224390202700102

Kr. (2017). *Zhuanqian hou de Momo weihe haozhi shuyi toufang guanggao? Xiangzuo Disini, buzuo shanghai renmin gongyuan* [Why did Momo spend millions on advertisements after making profits? It's because it wants to become the Disneyland, not the Shanghai People's Park]. Retrieved from https://36kr.com/p/5072398

Liao, T. (2018). Mobile versus headworn augmented reality: How visions of the future shape, contest, and stabilize an emerging technology. *New Media & Society*, *20*(2), 796–814. doi:10.1177/1461444816672019

Light, B., Burgess, J., & Duguay, S. (2018). The walkthrough method: An approach to the study of apps. *New Media & Society*, *20*(3), 881–900. doi:10.1177/1461444816675438

Liu, T. (2016). Neoliberal ethos, state censorship and sexual culture: A Chinese dating/hook-up app. *Continuum*, *30*(5), 557–566. doi:10.1080/10304312.2016.1210794

Mackay, H., & Gillespie, G. (1992). Extending the Social Shaping of Technology Approach: Ideology and Appropriation. *Social Studies of Science*, *22*(4), 685–716. doi:10.1177/030631292022004006

MacKenzie, D., & Wajcman, J. (Eds.). (1999). *The Social Shaping of Technology* (2nd ed.). Buckingham, UK: Open University Press.

Miao, W. (2019). *Behind the App: Understanding the development of technology from the perspective of media production*. Unpublished manuscript.

Miao, W., & Chan, L. S. (2019). *The Rise of Blued, China's World Largest Gay Social App: How Politics, Visions, and Capital Construct an Emerging Technology*. Paper presented at the annual conference of the International Communication Association, Washington DC.

Pei, Y. (2010). *Shengyu qishi niandai: Shanghai nianqing nvxing de xing yu shenghuo zhengzhi* [Born in the 1970s: Young women's sex and life politics in Shanghai]. Beijing: Social Sciences Academic Press.

People.cn. (2015). *"Jingwang 2015" qude chuzhan chengguo* [The "Jingwang" campaign in 2015 has been successful]. Retrieved from http://paper.people.com.cn/rmrbhwb/html/2015-04/03/content_1550072.htm

Petry, N. M. (2002). A comparision of young, middle-aged, and older adult treatment-seeking pathological gamblers. *The Gerontologist*, *42*(1), 92–99. doi:10.1093/geront/42.1.92 PMID:11815703

Pinch, T. J., & Bijker, W. E. (1987). The Social Construction of Facts and Artefacts: Or How the Sociology of Science and the Sociology of Technology Might Benefit Each Other. In W. E. Bijker, T. P. Hughes, & T. Pinch (Eds.), *The Social Construction of Technological Systems: New Directions in the Sociology and History of Technology* (pp. 17–50). Cambridge, MA: MIT Press.

Siles, I. (2012). The rise of blogging: Articulation as a dynamic of technological stabilization. *New Media & Society*, *14*(5), 781–797. doi:10.1177/1461444811425222

Sina. (2019). *Huikan Momo 6.0, Tang Yan shuo wo gaide tai lumang le* [Looking back at Momo 6.0, Tang said I was too reckless]. Retrieved from https://tech.sina.com.cn/csj/2019-03-25/doc-ihsxncvh5280046.shtml

Sina Finance. (2019). *17 Ji lianxu yingli, gujia yaozhan de Momo neng shangche le ma?* [Can we now invest in Momo after a consecutive rise in share price for 17 quarters?]. Retrieved from https://finance.sina.com.cn/other/hsnews/2019-05-29/doc-ihvhiqay2147435.shtml

Sina Technology. (2012). *Momo Tang Yan: Wo meiyou daode jiepi* [Momo's Tang Yan: I don't moral mysophobia]. Retrieved from https://tech.sina.com.cn/i/2012-01-31/18306670156.shtml

Sina Technology. (2014). *Momo qidong fumei shangshi* [Momo went public in the US]. Retrieved from http://tech.sina.com.cn/z/momoipo/

Slotten, H. R. (1995). Radio Engineers, the Federal Radio Commission, and the Social Shaping of Broadcast Technology: Creating "Radio Paradise.". *Technology and Culture, 36*(4), 950–986. doi:10.2307/3106920

Smith, A. (2016). *15% of American Adults Have Used Online Dating Sites or Mobile Dating Apps.* Retrieved from https://www.pewinternet.org/2016/02/11/15-percent-of-american-adults-have-used-online-dating-sites-or-mobile-dating-apps/

Sohu. (2017a). *Tang Yan: "Zuo zhibo yiyi guxing. Jingti biandi rengong zhineng"* [Take my own course to explore live-streaming. Be on guard agianst AI expansion]. Retrieved from https://www.sohu.com/a/126495997_118918

Sohu. (2017b). *Tang Yan: "Momo gengxiang shejiao pingtai, er bushi zhbo pingtai"* [Tang Yan: 'Momo is more like a social networking platform, rather than a live streaming platform']. Retrieved from https://www.sohu.com/a/130652781_628084

Sohu. (2018). *Momo CEO Tang Yan: "zheme haokande guniang, you shenme banfa keyi rangwo dingwei ta?"* [Momo CEO Tang Yan: What a beautiful girl! How can I find her location?]. Retrieved from https://www.sohu.com/a/253457870_100068454

Solis, R. J. C., & Wong, K. Y. J. (2019). To meet or not to meet? Measuring motivations and risks as predictors of outcomes in the use of mobile dating applications in China. *Chinese Journal of Communication, 12*(2), 206–225. doi:10.1080/17544750.2018.1498006

Suchman, L. (1996). Supporting Articulation Work. In R. Kling (Ed.), *Computerization and Controversy: Value Conflicts and Social Choices* (2nd ed., pp. 407–423). San Diego, CA: Academic Press. doi:10.1016/B978-0-12-415040-9.50118-4

Sun, W., & Lei, W. (2017). In Search of Intimacy in China: The Emergence of Advice Media for the Privatized Self. *Communication, Culture & Critique, 10*(1), 20–38. doi:10.1111/cccr.12150

Timmermans, E., & Courtois, C. (2018). From swiping to casual sex and/or committed relationships: Exploring the experiences of Tinder users. *The Information Society, 34*(2), 59–70. doi:10.1080/01972243.2017.1414093

Wang, M. (2018). 'Rigid demand': Economic imagination and practice in China's urban housing market. *Urban Studies (Edinburgh, Scotland), 55*(7), 1579–1594. doi:10.1177/0042098017747511

Wang, S. (2019). Chinese affective platform economies: Dating, live streaming, and performative labor on Blued. *Media Culture & Society*. doi:10.1177/0163443719867283

Wotipka, C. D., & High, A. C. (2016). An idealized self or the real me? Predicting attraction to online dating profiles using selective self-presentation and warranting. *Communication Monographs, 83*(3), 281–302. doi:10.1080/03637751.2016.1198041

Xiang, T. (2017). *Report: China's live streaming market grew 180% in 2016.* Retrieved from https://technode.com/2017/03/31/chinas-live-video-streaming-market-grew-180-2016-report/

Xinhua. (2017). *Momo sijidu jinglirun tongbi zhang 674%, yue huoyue yonghu da 8100 wan* [The net profit of the fourth quarter of 2016 was 674% above 2015. Monthly active users reached 81 million]. Retrieved from http://www.xinhuanet.com//info/ttgg/2017-03-08/c_136111191.htm

Xu, D., & Wu, F. (2019). Exploring the cosmopolitanism in China: Examining mosheng ren ("the stranger") communication through Momo. *Critical Studies in Media Communication, 36*(2), 122–139. doi:10.1080/15295036.2019.1566629

Yang, G. (2012). A Chinese Internet? History, practice, and globalization. *Chinese Journal of Communication, 5*(1), 49–54. doi:10.1080/17544750.2011.647744

Section 6
Critical Issues and Challenges

Chapter 69
Positive vs. Negative Emotions and Network Size:
An Exploratory Study of Twitter Users

Yeslam Al-Saggaf
Charles Sturt University, Australia

ABSTRACT

This chapter looks at the relationship between the expression of positive and negative emotions in Twitter and users' network size. The questions that guided this study are: Do users who tweet twice or more "I am bored," "I am excited," "I feel lonely," "I feel loved," "I feel sad," and "I feel happy" gain more followers and friends or lose them? Do users who express positive emotions twice or more have more followers and friends compared to users who express negative emotions or less? Do users who express boredom, excitement, loneliness, feeling loved, sadness, and happiness twice or more interact more with their networks or less? To address these questions, the study collected 35,096 English tweets in 2016. The findings indicate that users who tweeted these emotions, their number of followers and number of friends have increased, not decreased and that only users who expressed excitement had more followers and friends than users who expressed boredom. The study contributes to the literature on the benefits that lonely, sad, and bored users can reap from expressing emotions in Twitter.

INTRODUCTION

Self-expression is one of the main motivators for sharing content in social media (Shao 2009). Self-expression is not only a way of presenting the self, but it can also be used to control the impressions of viewers and foster supportive relationships (Shao 2009). However, emotions expressed in status updates can have an impact on a user's network size (Lin and Qiu 2012). Hutto et al. (2013), for example, found that negative emotions expressed in tweets reduce, while positive emotions facilitate, network growth. In a similar vein, Al-Saggaf & Ceric (2016), who explored the relationship between the expression of boredom and excitement on Twitter and network size, i.e. the number of followers and number of friends,

DOI: 10.4018/978-1-6684-6307-9.ch069

found that generally speaking users who expressed boredom had smaller network sizes compared to users who expressed excitement. Similarly, Al-Saggaf, Utz, & Lin (2016), who explored the relationship between the expression of loneliness, emotion loved, sadness and happiness on Twitter and network size, found that users who expressed loneliness had smaller network sizes compared to users who expressed emotion loved and users who expressed sadness had less friends than users who expressed happiness. Al-Saggaf, Utz, & Lin's (2016) findings are consistent with Dunder's et al. (2016) findings. The explanation given by Al-Saggaf, Utz, & Lin (2016) was that it could be because expressing negative emotions is less attractive to a user's network (Utz 2015) or that loneliness might lead to personality attributions, i.e. the assumption that something is wrong with the lonely person. Regardless, these findings suggest not all users reap the benefits of self-expression; especially when they don't address others in their status updates. Both Al-Saggaf & Ceric and Al-Saggaf, Utz, & Lin (2016) studies compared users who tweeted a negative emotion with users who tweeted a positive emotion using a single tweet. While these studies contributed to the limited literature on the relationship between emotions and network size, the fact that they made inferences about the relationship between expression of emotions and network size based on a single tweet weakened the strength of their inferences. This study looked at network size for each group of users, i.e. 'bored', 'excited', 'lonely', loved', 'sad' and 'happy,' separately at Time 1 when they expressed these emotions and at Time 2 when they expressed these emotions again later. Comparing network sizes for each group of users at Time 1 and Time 2 allowed within group comparisons. The study also compared the network sizes of each negative emotion with its opposite emotion. The study collected 35,096 tweets posted in English to Twitter between 16 December 2016 and 24 December 2016 and performed several statistical tests to address the following research questions:

- Do users who express excitement, happiness and being loved twice or more in their tweets gain more followers and friends than users who express boredom, loneliness and sadness twice or more in their tweets or less?
- Do users who express positive emotions twice or more have more followers and friends compared to users who express negative emotions or less?
- Do users who express boredom, excitement, loneliness, emotion loved, sadness and happiness twice or more interact more with their networks or less?

METHOD

Process of Collecting and Preparing Data for Analysis

35,096 tweets posted in English were collected from Twitter between 16 December 2016 and 24 December 2016. The tweets were retrieved using the Digital Methods Initiative Twitter Capture and Analysis Toolset (DMI-TCAT)[1]. For the TCAT to work, an App was developed in Twitter to automatically authorise TCAT to retrieve data from Twitter on behalf of the author. To retrieve the tweets of users who explicitly expressed the above mentioned emotions, i.e. boredom, excitement, loneliness, emotion loved, sadness and happiness, the phrases "I am bored", "I am excited", "I feel lonely", "I feel loved", "I feel sad" and "I feel happy", in double quotations marks, were used. After downloading the data of interest, it was queried using SQLite for users who expressed these emotions one, twice or more and three times or more. Only tweets for users who expressed these emotions with these criteria were stored in datasets and imported for analysis after the process of data preparation. Table 1 shows the breakdown of users who tweeted these emotions twice or more during the data collection period.

The datasets were imported into SQLite, R 3.3.1 and SPSS (IBM SPSS Statistics Version 20) for analysis. Along with the tweets, TCAT also returned the from_user_id, from_user_name, to_user_name, the date and time the tweet was created, the user's language, the source of the tweet, the user's profile image url, the number of user's followers and the number of the user's friends. The retweets (RTs) were not removed during analysis as retweeting these tweets was considered an expression of such emotion.

The following attributes were used to prepare data for analysis: from_user_id, created_at (date and time tweet created), to_user_name, from_user_followercount and from_user_friendcount. Twitter does not use the term "friend", but tools that retrieve tweets from Twitter, such as TCAT call users who follow each other 'friends' (Al-Saggaf & Ceric, 2016). It is not possible, however, to know if TCAT actually checks a Twitter user's followers to see if the user also follows them before deciding the number of friends a user has (Al-Saggaf & Ceric, 2016). The reason for using 'numbers of friends' in this paper is because TCAT uses this term.

To compare the users network sizes the first time (in the dataset) they expressed one of the above six emotions and the last time, SQLite was used to query the dataset, using created_at, from_user_followercount and from_user_friendcount, for the number of followers and number of friends at the earliest time in the dataset a user's first tweet was posted (Time 1) and also at the last time (Time 2). Table 2 shows an example of such data for a de-identified user.

Table 1. The breakdown of users who tweeted these emotions twice or more

Emotion	Term used to refer to groups	N
"I feel lonely"	Lonely	2186
"I feel loved"	Loved	4144
"I feel sad"	Sad	8405
"I feel happy"	Happy	3201
"I feel bored"	Bored	5540
"I feel excited"	Excited	11620

Table 2. Example of data used in the statistical analysis

From_user_id	from_user_followercount at T1	from_user_friendcount at Time 1	Time 1	from_user_followercount at Time 2	from_user_friendcount at T2	Time 2
XXXXXXXXXXXX	263	3	16/12/2016 10:35	272	3	24/12/2016 7:31

Statistical Analysis

The number of followers variable at Time 1 and the number of followers variable at Time 2 were both of type metric or continuous. Both variables did not display a normal distribution. A log-transformation, using LN(variable + 1), did not bring these variables to normality. In a similar vein the difference between the variables, i.e. the number of followers variable at Time 1 - the number of followers variable at Time 2 also did not display a normal distribution and a log transformation also did not bring the difference between these two variables to normality. For these reasons the Wilcoxon procedure, which corresponds with the paired t-test, was performed on the two variables to compare their means. This process was followed for all users who tweeted twice or more or three times or more "I am bored", "I am excited", "I feel lonely", "I feel loved", "I feel sad" and "I feel happy".

The number of friends variable at Time 1 and the number of friends variable at Time 2 were both of type metric or continuous and both variables as well as the difference between them did not display a normal distribution and a log transformation also did not bring them to normality. For these reasons, the Wilcoxon procedure was performed on the number of friends variable at Time 1 and the number of friends variable at Time 2 to compare their means. This process was followed for all users who tweeted twice or more or three times or more "I am bored", "I am excited", "I feel lonely", "I feel loved", "I feel sad" and "I feel happy".

To compare the means of the number of followers and the number of friends of users who expressed a negative emotion and users who expressed the opposite positive emotion, i.e. "I am bored" vs. "I am excited", "I feel lonely" vs. "I feel loved" and "I feel sad" vs. "I feel happy", a series of Mann-Whitney tests were performed. This was done for all users who tweeted twice or more "I am bored", "I am excited", "I feel lonely", "I feel loved", "I feel sad" and "I feel happy." Mann-Whitney tests were also performed to compare the means of the number of followers and the number of friends variables for users who tweeted "I am bored" at Time 2 (last time) three times or more vs. users who tweeted "I am bored" only once.

FINDINGS

Network Size of Users Who Tweeted an Emotion
Twice or More at Time 1 vs. Time 2

Wilcoxon signed-rank tests on the number of followers variable at Time 2 and the number of followers variable at Time 1 for users who tweeted twice or more "I am bored", "I am excited", "I feel lonely", "I feel loved", "I feel sad" and "I feel happy" were significant. Table 3 shows the results of the Wilcoxon tests. Table 4 shows the means of the difference, i.e. no. of followers at T2 - no. of followers at T1, the median and the standard deviations for all user groups. It appears that users who expressed these emotions twice or more in their tweets their number of followers has increased, not decreased. This suggests that these users gained more followers, not lost them. This may mean that either users who express negative emotions are reaping the benefits of having online connections (Lee et al. 2013) or that expressing negative emotions is not as costly as earlier studies have found. Similarly, Wilcoxon signed-rank tests on the number of friends variable at Time 2 and the number of friends variable at Time 1 for users who tweeted twice or more "I am bored", "I am excited", "I feel lonely", "I feel loved", "I feel sad" and "I feel happy" were significant. Table 3 shows the results of the Wilcoxon tests. Table 4 shows the means of the difference, i.e. no. of friends at T2 - no. of friends at T1, the median and the standard deviations for all user groups. It appears that users who expressed these emotions twice or more in their tweets their number of friends has increased, not decreased. This suggests that these users added more friends, not unfriended the users they followed.

Table 3. The results of the Wilcoxon tests

No. of followers at T2 - no. of followers at T1					No. of friends at T2 - no. of friends at T1				
Users	**N**	**Z**	**p**	**Scores: +ve vs. -ve**	**Users**	**N**	**Z**	**p**	**Scores: +ve vs. -ve**
Lonely	67	-2.99	.003	23 vs.8	Lonely	67	-3.1	.002	21 vs.6
Loved	80	-4.97	0.000	42 vs.5	Loved	80	-4.37	0.000	30 vs.5
Sad	242	-4.72	0.000	68 vs.28	Sad	242	-3.16	0.002	56 vs.24
Happy	107	-2.94	0.003	34 vs.12	Happy	107	-3.37	0.001	28 vs.7
Bored	278	-7.42	0.000	117 vs.41	Bored	278	-4.67	0.000	84 vs.39
Excited	390	-6.34	0.000	143 vs.59	Excited	390	-5.94	0.000	130 vs.40

Table 4. The means of the difference, i.e. No. of followers at T1 - no. of followers at T2, the median and the standard deviations

Dif = No. of followers at T1-no. of followers at T2					Dif=no. of friends at T1-no. of friends at T2			
Users	**N**	**Mean (Dif)**	**Median**	**SD**	**N**	**Mean (Dif)**	**Median**	**SD**
Lonely	67	-46.99	0	246.8	67	-30.66	0	173.23
Loved	80	-4.44	-1	10.02	80	-2.96	0	9.057
Sad	242	-12.88	0	140.37	242	-7.52	0	149.53
Happy	107	-20.72	0	169.23	107	-12.63	0	95.00
Bored	278	-14.98	0	80.29	278	-9.83	0	59.22
Excited	390	-1.31	0	52.38	390	2.18	0	55.87

Network Size of Users Who Tweeted a Positive Emotion Twice or More vs. Users Who Expressed a Negative Emotion

To compare the means of the number of followers and the number of friends of users who expressed a negative emotion and users who expressed the opposite positive emotion, i.e. "I am bored" vs. "I am excited", "I feel lonely" vs. "I feel loved" and "I feel sad" vs. "I feel happy", a series of Mann-Whitney tests were performed. This was done for all users who tweeted twice or more "I am bored", "I am excited", "I feel lonely", "I feel loved", "I feel sad" and "I feel happy." The Mann-Whitney tests revealed a significant difference in scores between users who expressed excitement and users who expressed boredom with users who expressed excitement having more followers and friends than users who expressed boredom. There were no significant differences in the means of the number of followers and the number of friends for users who expressed emotion loved vs. emotion lonely and those who expressed emotion happy and emotion sad. It is not clear why bored users had smaller network sizes than excited users but this is a question for future research. Table 5 shows the significant results of the Mann-Whitney tests.

Table 5. The results of the Mann-Whitney tests

Users	No. of followers				No. of friends			
	N	U	p	Mean Rank: Excited vs. Bored	N	U	p	Mean Rank: Excited vs.Bored
Excited vs.Bored	668	49229	0.043	347.3 vs.316.6	668	40099	0.000	370.7 vs. 283.7

Network Size of Users Who Tweeted Twice or More "I Am Bored" vs. Users Who Tweeted This Emotion Three Times or More

The smaller network size of the bored group compared to the excited group raised another question: Do users who expressed boredom three times or more ended up with smaller or larger network sizes? To compare the means of the number of followers and the number of friends variables at Time 2 and the number of followers and the number of friends variables at Time 1 for users who tweeted twice or more "I am bored" vs. users who tweeted "I am bored" three times or more Wilcoxon signed-rank tests were performed. The results were significant. Table 6 shows the results of the Wilcoxon tests. Table 7 shows the means of the difference, i.e. no. of followers/friends at T2 - no. of followers/friends at T1, the median and the standard deviations for these two user groups. (For users who tweeted twice or more "I am bored", this information was obtained from the earlier analysis). It appears that users who expressed "I am bored" three times or more in their tweets their number of followers has increased more compared to users who tweeted "I am bored" twice or more (Mean difference: -30.6 vs.-14.9). Similarly, it appears that users who expressed "I am bored" three times or more in their tweets their number of friends has increased more compared to users who tweeted "I am bored" twice or more (Mean difference: -17.42 vs.-9.82). However, these observations are only indicative as some users are present in both groups i.e. those who tweeted twice or more and those who tweeted tree times or more.

Table 6. The results of the Wilcoxon tests

Users	No. of followers at T2 - no. of followers at T1				Users	No. of friends at T2 - no. of friends at T1			
	N	Z	p	Scores: +ve vs. -ve		N	Z	p	Scores: +ve vs. -ve
Bored (twice or more)	278	-7.42	0.000	117 vs.41	Bored (twice or more)	278	-4.67	0.000	84 vs.39
Bored (three times or more)	65	-3.79	0.000	33 vs.15	Bored (three times or more)	65	-3.99	0.000	28 vs.9

Table 7. The means of the difference, i.e. no. of followers at T1 - no. of followers at T2, the median and the standard deviations

Users	No. of followers at T1 - no. of followers at T2				No. of friends at T1 - no. of friends at T2			
	N	Mean (Diff)	Median	SD	N	Mean (Diff)	Median	SD
Bored (twice or more)	278	-14.98	0	80.29	278	-9.83	0	59.22
Bored (three times or more)	65	-30.6	-1	148.53	65	-17.42	0	84.31

Network Size of Users Who Tweeted "I Am Bored" Three Times or More vs. Users Who Tweeted this Emotion Once

To compare the means of the number of followers and the number of friends variables for users who tweeted "I am bored" at Time 2 (last time) three times or more vs. users who tweeted "I am bored" only once, a random sample of 65 tweets were selected from the 4831 single tweet dataset (to match the number of users who tweeted three times or more). Using a Mann-Whitney the means of the number of followers and the number of friends for the two groups of users were compared. The results were only significant for the number of friends of these two groups with those who tweeted "I am bored" three times or more ending up with fewer friends compared to those who tweeted "I am bored" once. There was no significant difference in scores between the number of followers for users who expressed boredom three times or more and users who expressed boredom once. Table 8 shows the results of the Mann-Whitney test.

Table 8. The results of the Mann-Whitney test

Users	No. of friends			
	N	U	p	Mean Rank once vs.3 times or more
Bored once vs. Bored three times or more)	130	1479	0.003	75.25 vs.55.75

The Presence of @Replies for Users Who Tweeted an Emotion Twice or More

The presence of @replies is a more meaningful indicator of interaction between two users than the size of their networks (Ackland, 2013). When @replies are included at the beginning of a tweet, it become a direct message to a user. When it is included in the middle of a tweet, it is simply a mention of another user (Ackland, 2013). To compare the percentage of @replies across the six groups SQLite was used to query the dataset with the help of the to_user_name attribute of a tweet, which contains the name of the user after the @ sign at the beginning of a tweet. A chi-square test $\chi^2(5, N=4249) = 12.69, p = 0.026$ indicated interesting differences between one group and the other five. While the percentage of @replies within the tweets of five of the groups ranged between 18% and 21.3%, only 9.42% of the "I feel lonely" tweets included @replies. While the percentage of @replies within the tweets of the five groups is relatively low, it appears the lonely users interacted with their networks the least. This is in line with Al-Saggaf & Ceric's (2016) finding. Table 9 shows the percentage of @replies across the six groups.

Table 9. The percentage of @replies across the six groups

Group	Percentage of @replies
Lonely	9.42%
Loved	19.3%
Sad	21.3%
Happy	18%
Bored	18.5%
Excited	20.5%

DISCUSSION AND CONCLUSION

Al-Saggaf & Ceric (2016) and Al-Saggaf, Utz, & Lin (2016) studies compared users who tweeted a negative emotion with users who tweeted a positive emotion using a single tweet. While these studies contributed to the limited literature on the relationship between emotions and network size, the fact that they drew conclusions about the relationship between expression of emotions and network size based on a single tweet limited the value of their conclusions. This study looked at network sizes for each group of users, i.e. 'bored', 'excited', 'lonely', loved', 'sad' and 'happy' separately, at the time of expressing these emotions and using two or more tweets posted later and three or more tweets posted later to find out if the expression of these emotions affects network size. The study also compared the network sizes of each negative emotion with its opposite emotion. The study collected 35,096 tweets posted in English to Twitter between 16 December 2016 and 24 December 2016 and performed several statistical tests to address the research questions listed above.

The preliminary findings of this study indicate that users who tweeted "I am bored", "I am excited", "I feel lonely", "I feel loved", "I feel sad" and "I feel happy" twice or more at different times their number of followers has increased, not decreased. It appears that these users gained more followers, not lost them. Similarly, these users number of friends has increased, not decreased which suggests that they must have added more friends, not unfriended the users they followed. However, when the means of the number of followers and the number of friends of users who expressed a negative emotion and users who expressed the opposite positive emotion, i.e. "I am bored" vs. "I am excited", "I feel lonely" vs. "I feel loved" and "I feel sad" vs. "I feel happy", were compared only users who expressed excitement had more followers and friends than users who expressed boredom. There were no significant differences in the means of the number of followers and the number of friends for users who expressed emotion loved vs. emotion lonely and those who expressed emotion happy and emotion sad.

This finding encouraged a closer look at the bored group. Users who expressed "I am bored" three times or more in their tweets their number of followers has increased more compared to users who tweeted "I am bored" twice or more. The same happened with their friends. That is, users who expressed "I am bored" three times or more in their tweets their number of friends has increased more compared to users who tweeted "I am bored" twice or more. This finding may suggests that users who tweet about boredom more often their number of followers and number friends increase. However, when the means of the number of followers and the number of friends variables for users who tweeted "I am bored" three times or more vs. users who tweeted "I am bored" only once were compared the results were only significant for the number of friends of these two groups with those who tweeted "I am bored" three times or more ending up with fewer friends compared to those who tweeted "I am bored" once. There was no significant difference in scores between the number of followers for users who expressed boredom three times or more and users who expressed boredom once. Further research is needed to shed light on these preliminary findings.

Al-Saggaf & Ceric (2016) and Al-Saggaf, Utz, & Lin (2016) found that Twitter users who expressed negative emotions had less followers and less friends compared to Twitter users who expressed positive emotions. The explanation given was that it could be because expressing negative emotions is less attractive to followers (Utz 2015). The preliminary findings of the current study suggest that users who tweeted negative emotions more often ended up having more followers and more friends. This suggests that either users who express negative emotions are reaping the benefits of having online connections (Lee et al. 2013) or that expressing these emotions is not as costly as earlier studies have found. But some groups, such as the 'bored' group behaved slightly differently when compared with the 'excited' group. Further research is needed to explore the relationships between these groups and their network sizes using more data collected over a longer period of time. Also, Kivran-swaine and Naaman (2011) found that users are more likely to express emotions of joy and sadness in larger and sparser networks. When their network is dense, users' posts seem to be less emotional. A future study could look at the relationship between these groups and their network sizes taking into account the size of their networks, i.e. the effects of emotions on users with smaller networks vs. users with larger networks.

Only 9.42% of the tweets expressing loneliness contained @replies, in contrast to 21.3% of the tweets expressing sadness, 18% of the tweets expressing happiness and 19.3% of the tweets expressing emotion loved. The interactivities for boredom and excitement were similar to the interactivities for sadness, happiness and emotion loved. Thus, while all these five emotions were expressed in direct interactions and non-direct interactions, loneliness was expressed mainly in a non-direct way. That lonely Twitter users express loneliness directly less frequently is in some way consistent with Al-Saggaf and Nielsen (2014) study findings that fewer lonely Facebook users revealed their status updates compared to those emotion connected and more lonely users did not disclose their wall compared to the few who did. As mentioned above, expressing loneliness might lead to personality attributions, i.e. the assumption that something is wrong with the lonely person. However, that sad and bored people are not less likely to share their emotions with a specific other person could be because sadness and boredom are often caused by external factors. For example, a person can become sad because of a loss of a loved person and this is not in the control of the person.

Lonely people have difficulties in receiving social support which can decrease their well-being and eventually lead to depression. They also disclose less about themselves both offline and online (Al-Saggaf and Nielsen 2014). According to self-disclosure is the mediating mechanism between use of online media and decreased loneliness. Their study investigated whether loneliness has a direct/indirect effect on well-being when mediated by self-disclosure. The findings of their study showed that loneliness positively influences self-disclosure in a way that lonely people rely on social network sites to compensate for their unsuccessful offline relations. On the other hand, their study also found that self-disclosure can reduce emotions of loneliness thereby enhancing well-being. Thus, if lonely Twitter users interact directly less frequently, then they do not fully reap the potential benefits of interacting with others online so as to reduce their emotions of loneliness.

There are a number of limitations that must be acknowledged. (1) Data collection occurred around Christmas time, this may have influence the findings. A future study should collect data during diffident periods of time to ensure the findings are not specific to a certain period of time. (2) The effects of other confounding factors, such as a user's total number of tweets, the number of favourites, the number of lists and the date an account was created, were not considered in this study. A future study should consider these variables as control variables to explore their effects. (3) Only tweets that expressed these emotions using the phrases "I am bored", "I am excited", "I feel lonely", "I feel loved", "I feel sad" and "I feel happy", in double quotations marks were retrieved. Emotions expressed in tweets differently such as "very sad today" were not retrieved. This was done to achieve consistency when comparing the various emotion groups and also because it is difficult to think of all the possible ways to express such emotions. However, a future study should use data mining algorithms to first classify tweets into emotional categories and then conduct these analyses.

ACKNOWLEDGMENT

The author wishes to thank Ho Leung Ip from Charles Sturt University for his help with the statistical tests used in this study.

REFERENCES

Ackland, R. (2013). Web social science: Concepts, data and tools for social scientists in the digital age. *Sage (Atlanta, Ga.)*.

Al-Saggaf, Y., & Ceric, A. (2016). Boredom on Periscope and the number of Twitter followers: An exploratory study. In P. McIntyre & J.M. Fulton (Eds.), *Refereed proceedings of the Australian and New Zealand Communication Association conference: Creating Space in the Fifth Estate*. Available at: http://www.anzca.net/conferences/past-conferences/

Al-Saggaf, Y., & Nielsen, S. (2014). Self-disclosure on Facebook among female users and its relationship to emotions of loneliness. *Computers in Human Behavior*, *36*, 460–468. doi:10.1016/j.chb.2014.04.014

Al-Saggaf, Y., Utz, S., & Lin, R. (2016). Venting negative emotions on Twitter and the number of followers and followees. *International Journal of Sociotechnology and Knowledge Development*, *8*(1), 45–56. doi:10.4018/IJSKD.2016010103

Dunder, I., Horvat, M., & Lugovic, S. (2016). Word occurrences and emotions in social media: Case study on a Twitter corpus. *2016 39th International Convention on Information and Communication Technology, Electronics and Microelectronics, MIPRO 2016 - Proceedings*, 1284–1287. 10.1109/MIPRO.2016.7522337

Hutto, C. J., Yardi, S., & Gilbert, E. (2013). A longitudinal study of follow predictors on twitter. *Proceedings of the SIGCHI Conference on Human Factors in Computing Systems - CHI '13*, 821. 10.1145/2470654.2470771

Kivran-swaine, F., & Naaman, M. (2011). Network Properties and Social Sharing of Emotions in Social Awareness Streams. *Proceedings of the ACM 2011 conference on Computer supported cooperative work*, 379–382. 10.1145/1958824.1958882

Lee, K.-T., Noh, M.-J., & Koo, D.-M. (2013). Lonely people are no longer lonely on social networking sites: the mediating role of self-disclosure and social support. *Cyberpsychology, Behavior and Social Networking*, *16*(6), 413–8. doi:10.1089/cyber.2012.0553

Lin, H., & Qiu, L. (2012). Sharing emotion on Facebook. In *Proceedings of the 2012 ACM annual conference extended abstracts on Human Factors in Computing Systems Extended Abstracts - CHI EA '12*. New York: ACM Press. 10.1145/2212776.2223838

Shao, G. (2009). Understanding the appeal of user-generated media: a uses and gratification perspective. *Internet Research*, *19*(1), 7–25. doi:10.1108/10662240910927795

Utz, S. (2015). The function of self-disclosure on social network sites: Not only intimate, but also positive and entertaining self-disclosures increase the emotion of connection. *Computers in Human Behavior*, *45*, 1–10. doi:10.1016/j.chb.2014.11.076

ENDNOTE

[1]   http://www.intersect.org.au/research-tools/tcat

This research was previously published in Developments in Information Security and Cybernetic Wars; pages 284-297, copyright year 2019 by Information Science Reference (an imprint of IGI Global).

Chapter 70

Usage Behaviors on Snapchat, Instagram, and WhatsApp:
Between–Group Analyses

Abdullah J. Sultan

https://orcid.org/0000-0002-8853-3826

College of Business Administration, Kuwait University, Kuwait

ABSTRACT

The main objective of this research is to investigate usage behaviors of different age groups across popular social-media platforms and show what usage behavior is mostly utilized in each social media platform. A sample of 2,883 social media users was used to run a series of t-tests to support the research hypotheses. The findings show that young users (compared with old users) are more likely to use social media platforms for social and personal needs. In addition, across platform analyses indicate that users of WhatsApp (compared with Snapchat and Instagram) are more likely to use the platform for socially integrative needs (e.g., connecting with friends and family and talking), while Instagram and Snapchat users are more likely to use the platforms for affective needs (e.g., entertaining), personally integrative needs (e.g., enhancing self-expression and getting to know new people), tension release (e.g., escaping from boredom), and cognitive needs (e.g., seeking information). A more detailed analysis of age groups across the platforms are further discussed.

INTRODUCTION

Social media usage has grown exponentially over the last decade, especially with the vast development of mobile applications. Among the different social media platforms, Facebook is the leader of social media. Other popular social media applications are Snapchat, Instagram, Twitter, Pinterest, Tumblr, and Vine, while popular mobile-chat applications include WhatsApp, WeChat, and Facebook Messenger. There were an estimated 3.46 billion active social media users worldwide in 2019 (Statista, 2019). Although social media presence is dominating users daily activates, it is especially widespread among

DOI: 10.4018/978-1-6684-6307-9.ch070

teens and young adults. It has become an essential form of communications for young individuals and thus has drawn researchers' interests in several disciplines including social psychology, communications, sociology, and marketing. By large, marketing field covers an increasing number of researches and articles that have addressed social media issues (Alalwan et al., 2017). This growing stream of research provides strong evidence that social media and their implications should be the center of attention for both practitioners and researchers.

In 2020, marketers are expecting to spend over $102 billion on social media advertising (Statista, 2020) to engage their users and get them to convert to their brands. Social media has become an essential part of many marketing campaigns due to its influential effects. Despite the importance of social media as a communication channel for both business and individual users, little is understood about how and why users use new social media platforms and how these platforms affect users' lives. More importantly, most of the communication messages that have been directed toward users are randomly placed on social media platforms with very little knowledge about usage behaviors. The traditional paradigm of integrated marketing communications (IMC) suggests that marketers should send a unified customer-focused message using different promotion tools in order to intensify the message effectiveness on target segments and achieve organizational objectives (Boone and Kurtz, 2007). However, the tools and strategies for communicating with customers have changed considerably in the era of social media (Mangold and Faulds, 2009). Given the distinctive designs and features of social media platforms, one may argue that, in the new paradigm of social media communications, marketers should develop unique strategies for each social media platform in order to match the usage behaviors of platform users.

Overall, consumers are turning away from the traditional media and demand more control over their media consumption (Mangold and Faulds, 2009). These consumers use social media to create personalized profiles and engage with their friends and acquaintances with no time or space limitations. The majority of consumers depend on social media applications to share views, give opinions, and generate content (e.g., information, photos, and videos) in order to stay in contact with their friends and informed about trending news or events (Amichai-Hamburger and Vinitzky, 2010; Kuss and Griffiths, 2011). Past research has demonstrated different social motives of Internet-communication users such as user's need to belong and self-presentation (Nadkarni and Hofmann, 2012). In addition, group identification, collective self-esteem, and keeping in touch with friends are other types of social motives for a continuous user engagement on social media (Floros and Simos, 2013; Kuss and Griffiths, 2011). Researchers have also shown that social media is a prospering environment for consumers who have higher levels of shyness and anxiety in face-to-face interactions since it is easier to fulfill social needs online than via offline communications (Banjanin et al., 2015; Steinfield, Ellison, and Lampe, 2008).

For almost a decade, academic researchers and practitioners have given much attention to consumer participation on social media (Alalwan et al., 2017; Kamboj and Rahman, 2017; Zhang and Luo, 2016). In addition, the Marketing Science Institute (MSI) highlights researchers' interests in customer participation on social media (MSI, 2016). Most studies concerning customer participation on social media are mainly focusing on the conceptualization with little empirical evidence (Khan, 2017). The opportunity to strengthening the relationship with customers using social media has seen as a significant scholarly work (Kamboj et al., 2017). Marketers have emphasized their presence on social media to communicate directly with customers and increase customer involvement in the brand. Therefore, understanding customer involvement and usage behaviors on social media may assist academic researchers and marketers develop suitable communication strategies unique to social media platforms in order to effectively target customers.

The present research aims to describe usage patterns in three most popular and under-researched social media applications (i.e., Snapchat, Instagram, and WhatsApp). Specifically, the researcher will investigate how social media usage behaviors differ across age groups and social media platforms. In addition, the researcher will utilize the uses and gratifications theory to explain how social media fulfills different needs and wants. Although uses and gratifications theory has been researched extensively in the communications literature, it has received little attention in the marketing and social media literatures (Kamboj, 2020; Phua, Jin, and Kim, 2017). In fact, some researchers have argued that the "question why people use different features cannot truly be explained without the most prominent theoretical framework for active media use behavior: The uses-and-gratifications approach" (Leiner, et al., 2018, p. 195). Leiner et al. (2018) have argued that the implication of the uses and gratifications theory to explain social web usage is rather complicated due to the continuous development of platforms and their features. Social media has brought about a series of disruptive challenges to the marketing field. Therefore, the present research will contribute to research and practice on social media marketing by implicating the uses and gratifications theory in order to demonstrate the different usage behaviors of social media platforms and give directions for marketers who are interested in engaging users with their communication messages on Snapchat, Instagram, and WhatsApp. Furthermore, like Mangold and Faulds (2009), the present researcher advocates that the traditional IMC paradigm is no longer applicable in the new era of social media and hence marketers should design distinctive messages that match with the usage behaviors of each social media platform.

In the next sections, the researcher will provide an overview of the literatures pertaining to social media and uses and gratifications theory. Then, the researcher will explain the research methodology and discuss the research findings, theoretical contributions, practical implications, and future research directions.

COMMON SOCIAL MEDIA PLATFORMS

The last decade has seen a surge of mobile technologies, especially in the social media platforms. Social media is defined as "a group of internet-based applications that build on the ideological and technical foundations of Web 2.0, and that allow the creation and exchange of user generated content" (Kaplan and Haenlein, 2010, p. 61). Examples of popular social media platforms include Snapchat, Instagram, and WhatsApp. These social media platforms have become very common social networks among users. As of 2018, the average daily social media usage mounted to 136 minutes per day, up from 135 minutes in the previous year (Statista, 2019). Users access social media for a variety of reasons. They use social media to search for entertaining content, share photos and videos with friends, and mainly to stay close with friends. The next section describes the functions of Snapchat, Instagram, and WhatsApp.

SNAPCHAT

Snapchat is a multimedia sharing mobile platform. Although it has other sharing features, it has become famous for video sharing. Snaps is a popular feature for the creation of photos or videos. Users can edit Snaps with texts, filters, or stickers. Users specify a time limit for how long recipients can view their Snaps before they will be deleted. Snapchat is the most popular social media application among teens and young adults aged less than 25 years. Brands have used Snapchat as a strategic platform to target teens and millennials. The number of active users reached 186 million in 2018 (Statista, 2019).

INSTAGRAM

Instagram is one of the most popular photo-sharing platforms. It has over one billion monthly active users (Statista, 2019). The Instagram application allows users to edit and share photos with other users publicly or privately. Like Snapchat, Instagram users can apply shaded filters to their photos before posting them to their profiles. In 2019, photo sharing in Instagram alone reached 500 million daily active stories users worldwide (Statista, 2019). Stories is a popular feature in Instagram for posting photos and video sequences that disappear after 24 hours. Most users use Instagram to keep contact with friends and family, get entertainment, and follow brands.

WHATSAPP

WhatsApp is a cross-platform instant messaging application for mobile devices, which uses the Internet to transmit messages. As of 2019, WhatsApp reached 1.6 billion monthly active users, making it the most popular mobile messenger application (Statista, 2019). In fact, it is the third most popular social network after Facebook and YouTube. Most users access WhatsApp to stay in close contact with friends and family.

USES AND GRATIFICATIONS THEORY

Past researchers have adapted Maslow's theory to describe how individuals use mass communication channels to fulfill personal needs (Katz, Blumer, and Gurevitch, 1974). These researchers along with others (Rubin, 1994) have utilized uses and gratifications theory to understand individuals' social and psychological needs that influence media choice and engagement. Uses and gratifications theory is a theoretical model for explaining how and why individuals search for different media to fulfill specific needs and wants (Katz et al., 1974). One of the theory assumptions is that users are goal-oriented in their media selection to achieve optimal levels of gratifications (Rubin, 1986). The theory has been implicated in several media such as television (McQuail, Blumler, and Brown, 1972), radio (Mendelsohn, 1964), newspapers (Elliott and Rosenberg, 1987), and video games (Sherry et al., 2001). Recently, research has used the uses and gratifications theory to examine usage behaviors in the context of social media (e.g., Chi, 2011; Kwon et al., 2014; Taylor, Strutton, and Thompson, 2012). Human needs attained through media in general have been classified into five categories: cognitive, affective, personally integrative, socially integrative, and tension release (West and Turner, 2010). In addition, other researchers have explored social media needs by investigating users' psychological and behavioral characteristics (Ko, Cho, and Robert, 2005; Korgaonkar and Wolin, 1999; Par, Kee, and Valenzuela, 2009; Raacke and Bonds-Raacke, 2008; West and Turner, 2010). These researchers have argued that social media users not only search for information and entertainment content, but also socially interact with other users and engage with them using interactive tools (Korgaonkar and Wolin, 1999). Due to numerous designs and features of social media platforms, users obtain different gratifications. For example, Snapchat, Instagram, and WhatsApp offer interactive tools, such as Snaps, Stories, and Group Chatting, that are utilized by users to gratify their social needs. Park, Kee, and Valenzuela (2009) have found that socializing and self-presentation are social needs attained by young individuals through social media as well as personal needs such as entertainment and information seeking. In some occasions, users also discuss information about brands with other users. Sharing brand content is very common among brand communities on social media. This type of users is motivated to differentiate themselves by talking about their brand experiences with other users in order to create a group membership or brand community (Muniz and O'Guinn, 2001). Given the previous discussion, it has been argued that social media is a popular communication and socializing platform among teens and young adults and these users utilize the platform to fulfill their social and personal needs. Furthermore, Volkom, Stapley, and Malter (2013) show that there is a significant relationship between age and the perception of technologies. That is, compared to other age groups, older adults are less likely to use new technologies for new purposes such as communication and entertainment. In addition, Magsamen-Conrad et al. (2015) argue that different studies have shown how age groups have different motives for using technological devices, but current uses and gratifications research treats all effects the same regardless of age groups. Therefore, the present research argues that users of social media, in general, utilize these platforms to fulfill social (e.g., connecting with friends and family, getting to know new people, self-expression, and talking) and personal needs (e.g., entertaining, escaping from boredom, and seeking information); however these gratifications are more pronounced in younger individuals compared to older groups, leading to the following hypothesis:

Hypothesis 1a: Younger social media users (compared to older users) are more likely to use social media for connecting with friends and family.

Hypothesis 1b: Younger social media users (compared to older users) are more likely to use social media for getting to know new people.

Hypothesis 1c: Younger social media users (compared to older users) are more likely to use social media for talking.

Hypothesis 1d: Younger social media users (compared to older users) are more likely to use social media for entertaining.

Hypothesis 1e: Younger social media users (compared to older users) are more likely to use social media for escaping from boredom.

Hypothesis 1f: Younger social media users (compared to older users) are more likely to use social media for self-expressing.

Hypothesis 1g: Younger social media users (compared to older users) are more likely to use social media for seeking information.

Katz et al. (1974) claim that different media offer a unique blend of characteristics that distinguish their gratifications from each other. That is, each medium offers content that is characteristic of its format. Although social media is described as interactive, there are differences between each platform in terms of the nature of interactions they provide. Hence, users obtain different types of gratifications. Past research has shown that Facebook and Instant Messaging (IM) are used to pastime, have fun, relax, and escape from everyday pressures and responsibilities (Quan-Haase and Young, 2010). One thing that Quan-Haase and Young (2010) have found to be different is that Facebook is used to find out about social events and activities (i.e., social information). In the present research, the researcher argues that the three social media platforms (i.e., Snapchat, Instagram, and WhatsApp) are different in nature and have distinguishable attributes and thus users may utilize the platforms in different ways and obtain different gratifications. WhatsApp has Private and Group Chatting features that are focused toward socially integrative needs (e.g., connecting with friends and family and talking), while Snapchat and Instagram have sharing features such as Snaps and Stories that are more oriented toward affective needs (e.g., entertaining), personally integrative needs (e.g., enhancing self-expression and getting to know new people), tension release (e.g., escaping from boredom), and cognitive needs (e.g., seeking information). Since Snapchat and Instagram features are so similar, the present researcher believes that these platforms tab on the same users' gratifications. Whereas, WhatsApp is another platform that is more about private conversations with family and friends. To expand on the literature, the three social media platforms are compared in terms of the types of gratifications that they support. This comparison would offer insights into the motives that make users continue using each tool. Therefore, the present research argues that the three social media platforms fulfill different uses and gratifications, leading to the following hypothesis:

Hypothesis 2a: WhatsApp (compared with Snapchat and Instagram) is more likely to be used for connecting with friends and family.

Hypothesis 2b: WhatsApp (compared with Snapchat and Instagram) is more likely to be used for talking.

Hypothesis 2c: WhatsApp (compared with Snapchat and Instagram) is less likely to be used for entertaining.

Hypothesis 2d: WhatsApp (compared with Snapchat and Instagram) is less likely to be used for escaping from boredom.

Hypothesis 2e: WhatsApp (compared with Snapchat and Instagram) is less likely to be used for self-expressing.

Hypothesis 2f: WhatsApp (compared with Snapchat and Instagram) is less likely to be used for getting to know people.

Hypothesis 2g: WhatsApp (compared with Snapchat and Instagram) is less likely to be used for seeking information.

METHODOLOGY

Participants

The present research utilized a student-snowballing sampling procedure to distribute the research questionnaire using an online-survey platform. Students were given survey links and asked to distribute the links to their friends and family in their Snapchat, Instagram, and WhatsApp applications for extra class credits. The researcher used the ballot-box-stuffing option in the online-survey platform to prevent the submissions of multiple surveys. In addition, the users' IPs were checked and there were no redundancies. Generally speaking, students are a good population for this type of research because it is evident that the age distribution of active social media users worldwide is between the ages of 16 and 34 years old (Statista, 2019). Snapchat, Instagram, and WhatsApp are among the topmost popular social media platforms among these young individuals. Therefore, the current research focused on individuals who are active users of these three platforms as research participants. The sampling procedure resulted in a sample of 2,883 social media users. The sample consisted of 661 males and 2,224 females. The age was distributed as follows: <18 (5.3%), 18-25 (55.7%), 26-35 (20.1%), 36-45 (10.9%), 46-55 (6.1%), and >55 years of age (2%). The social media platforms were distributed as follow: Snapchat (35.6%), Instagram (45.3%), and WhatsApp (19.1%).

Measures

Due to the nature of this research, the researcher developed three online surveys that had identical measures and directed to different social media platforms (i.e., Snapchat, Instagram, and WhatsApp). All participants were asked to indicate whether they used the platform in a daily base. If they responded positively, then they were asked to rate the extent to which they used the platform to perform the following usage behaviors (adopted from Sultan, 2014): 1) connecting with friends and family members, 2) getting to know new people, 3) talking, 4) entertaining, 5) escaping from boredom, 6) expressing the self, and 7) seeking latest news and information, ranged from 1 (never) to 5 (always). At the end of the survey, participants were asked to indicate their gender and age group (<18, 18-25, 26-35, 36-45, 46-55, and >55 years of age).

Results

Before conducting the main analysis, the data set was screened for missing data in rows and found no missing data. Moreover, the researcher removed 11 cases due to being not engaged (they gave almost the same answer to every Likert scale item), resulting in a total of 2,872 social media users. The correlations among the examined usage-behavior variables were checked. The correlations ranged from 0.11 to 0.42, which showed no signs of multicollinearity, see Table 1. Moreover, convergent validity was demonstrated by showing that the usage-behavior variables were positively correlated, which proved that these variables were related. While discriminant validity was demonstrated by showing that the usage-behavior variables were correlated weakly (below 0.30), which proved that they measured different constructs.

In addition, the researcher utilized a principle component factor analysis using promax rotation to analyze the different factors emerging from the usage-behavior variables. The variables were suitable for factor analysis because the Kaiser-Meyer-Olkin (KMO) statistic indicated a value of 0.75, which is greater than 0.60, and communalities are greater than 0.30. Based on the analysis, the usage-behavior variables loaded on two unique factors: social needs (e.g., connecting with friends and family, getting to know new people, self-expression, and talking) and personal needs (e.g., entertaining, escaping from boredom, and seeking information), see Table 2. Furthermore, the reliability analysis indicated that the usage behavior had a Cronbach Alpha of 0.70, which is regarded to be good.

Before examining the research hypotheses, the usage-behavior variables, for each social media platform, were checked for normality using Kolmogorov-Smirnov test in SPSS. The results showed mixed findings, see Appendix. Due to the non-normality of some usage-behavior variables, the Wilcoxon-Mann-Whitney (WMW) test was utilized. The age predictor was first recoded using median split to divide users into two groups (younger and older groups). This resulted in aggregating the first two age groups to form the younger-user category (25 years and less) and the other three age groups to form the older-user category (26 years and more). When contrasting the recoded-age groups on usage-behavior variables using WMW test, the results demonstrated that age was statistically significant for connecting with friends and family ($M_{younger}$=3.69, M_{Older}=3.39, Z =-6.55, p<0.001; hypothesis 1a was supported), talking ($M_{younger}$=2.67, M_{Older}=2.22, Z =-10.26, p<0.001; hypothesis 1b was supported), getting to know new people ($M_{younger}$=2.50, M_{Older}=2.22, Z =-5.98, p<0.001; hypothesis 1c was supported), entertaining ($M_{younger}$=4.04, M_{Older}=3.76, Z =-6.79, p<0.001; hypothesis 1d was supported), escaping from boredom ($M_{younger}$=4.12, M_{Older}=3.73, Z =9.64, p<0.001; hypothesis 1e was supported), and self-expressing ($M_{younger}$=2.93, M_{Older}=2.65, Z =5.62, p<0.001; hypothesis 1f was supported). However, younger users did not differ from older users in using social media for seeking information ($M_{younger}$=3.82, M_{Older}=3.89, Z =-1.50, p=0.12; hypothesis 1g was not supported).

Table 1. Correlations among usage behaviors of social media platforms

	Connecting	Talking	Entertaining	Escaping	Self-expressing	Knowing people	Information
Connecting	1						
Talking	0.33**	1					
Entertaining	0.19**	0.11**	1				
Escaping	0.13**	0.16**	0.47**	1			
Self-expressing	0.39**	0.42**	0.19**	0.18**	1		
Knowing people	0.31*	0.41**	0.15**	0.12**	0.41**	1	
Information	0.18**	0.18**	0.29**	0.23**	0.22**	0.20**	1

**p<0.001

Table 2. Factor analysis of social media usage behaviors

Pattern Matrix[a]		
	Component	
	Social Need	Personal Need
Talking	.819	
Knowing People	.747	
Self-expressing	.724	
Connecting	.657	
Entertaining		.813
Escaping		.778
Information		.668
Extraction Method: Principal Component Analysis. Rotation Method: Promax with Kaiser Normalization.		
a. Rotation converged in 3 iterations.		

To test for the research hypothesis 2, the social media platform predictor was recoded by aggregating Snapchat and Instagram in a single group and WhatsApp in another group and used the WMW test to contrast both groups on the usage-behavior variables. The results indicated that WhatsApp (compared with Snapchat and Instagram) was more likely to be used for connecting with friends and family ($M_{WhatsApp}$=4.40, $M_{Snap+Inst}$=3.37, Z =-18.39, p<0.001; hypothesis 2a was supported) and talking

($M_{WhatsApp}$=3.01, $M_{Snap+Inst}$=2.37, Z =-12.41, p<0.001; hypothesis 2b was supported), while Snapchat and Instagram (compared with WhatsApp) were more likely to be used for entertaining ($M_{WhatsApp}$=3.82, $M_{Snap+Inst}$=3.96, Z =-3.15, p<0.001; hypothesis 2c was supported) and escaping from boredom ($M_{WhatsApp}$=3.82, $M_{Snap+Inst}$=4.01, Z =-4.48, p<0.001; hypothesis 2d was supported). However, contrary to the researcher's predictions, WhatsApp (compared to Snapchat and Instagram) was more likely to be used for self-expressing ($M_{WhatsApp}$=3.74, $M_{Snap+Inst}$=2.60, Z =-19.26, p<0.001), getting to know new people ($M_{WhatsApp}$=3.11, $M_{Snap+Inst}$=3.79, Z =-15.70, p<0.001), and seeking information ($M_{WhatsApp}$=4.10, $M_{Snap+Inst}$=3.79, Z =-5.58, p<0.001), hence hypothesis 2e, hypothesis 2f, and hypothesis 2g were not supported.

Based on the previous factor-analysis findings, the two factors that emerged were identified as social and personal needs. To further enhance the research findings, the researcher added another WMW test to show the significance of these needs among the social media platforms. The analysis indicated the WhatsApp (compared to Snapchat and Instagram) had significantly higher levels of social needs ($M_{WhatsApp}$=3.56, $M_{Snap+Inst}$=2.64, Z =-22.48, p<0.001), while the three platforms had similar levels of personal needs ($M_{WhatsApp}$=3.91, $M_{Snap+Inst}$=3.92, Z =-0.28, p=0.77). This finding indicated that WhatsApp had a unique characteristic when compared to Snapchat and Instagram and thus marketers should handle it exclusively.

A post-hoc analysis was conducted to examine the differences in usage behaviors for Snapchat and Instagram users. The WMW test indicated that Snapchat and Instagram users differed significantly in connecting with friends and family ($M_{Snapchat}$=3.70, $M_{Instagram}$=3.08, Z =-12.94, p<0.001), information seeking ($M_{Snapchat}$=3.56, $M_{Instagram}$=3.97, Z =-8.49, p<0.001), talking ($M_{Snapchat}$=2.62, $M_{Instagram}$=2.17, Z =-9.63, p<0.001) and self-expressing ($M_{Snapchat}$=2.70, $M_{Instagram}$=2.52, Z =-3.64, p<0.001), while the differences were not significant for getting to know new people ($M_{Snapchat}$=2.27, $M_{Instagram}$=2.19, Z =-1.45, p=0.147), entertaining ($M_{Snapchat}$=3.92, $M_{Instagram}$=3.98, Z =-1.77, p=0.076), and escaping from boredom ($M_{Snapchat}$=3.99, $M_{Instagram}$=4.02, Z =-0.77, p=0.438).

Further analyses were conducted using the WMW test to examine the differences in the recoded-age groups within the three social media platforms on usage-behavior variables. The results showed some interesting findings. When examining Snapchat users only, younger users were more likely to use Snapchat for connecting with family and friends ($M_{Younger}$=3.82, M_{Older}=3.61, Z =-2.76, p<0.01), talking ($M_{Younger}$=2.70, M_{Older}=2.46, Z =-2.91, p<0.01), entertaining ($M_{Younger}$=3.99, M_{Older}=3.80, Z =-3.18, p<0.001), and escaping from boredom ($M_{Younger}$=4.14, M_{Older}=3.71, Z =-6.25, p<0.001). However, the difference was not significant for getting to know new people, seeking information, and self-expressing (p>0.05), see Table 3. When examining Instagram users only, younger users were more likely to use Instagram for talking ($M_{Younger}$=2.37, M_{Older}=1.96, Z =-6.47, p<0.001), entertaining ($M_{Younger}$=4.08, M_{Older}=3.89, Z =-3.71, p<0.001), escaping ($M_{Younger}$=4.21, M_{Older}=3.81, Z =-7.35, p<0.001), and knowing people ($M_{Younger}$=2.31, M_{Older}=2.07, Z =-3.67, p<0.001). However, the difference was not significant for connecting with friends and family, seeking information, and self-expressing (p>0.05), see Table 4. When examining WhatsApp users only, younger users were more likely to use WhatsApp for talking ($M_{Younger}$=3.08, M_{Older}=2.78, Z =-3.11, p<0.01), entertaining ($M_{Younger}$=, M_{Older}=3.10, Z =-8.30, p<0.001), escaping ($M_{Younger}$=3.95, M_{Older}=3.42, Z=-4.60, p<0.001), and knowing people ($M_{Younger}$=3.17, M_{Older}=2.95, Z =-2.22, p<0.05). However, the difference was not significant for connecting with friends and family, seeking information, and self-expressing (p>0.05), see Table 5. Figure shows the plots for usage behaviors across the social media platforms and age groups.

Table 3. Results of the Wilcoxon-Mann-Whitney test between age groups for Snapchat users

Test variables	Age group	n	Average rank	Contrast significance
Connecting	Younger Older	672 349	529 477	Z =-2.76 p<0.01
Knowing people	Younger Older	672 349	516 502	Z =-0.74 Non-significant
Seeking information	Younger Older	672 349	512 508	Z =-0.21 Non-significant
Entertaining	Younger Older	672 349	531 472	Z =-3.18 p<0.001
Talking	Younger Older	672 349	530 475	Z =-2.91 p<0.01
Escaping	Younger Older	672 349	550 435	Z =-6.25 p<0.001
Self-expressing	Younger Older	672 349	516 501	Z =-0.82 Non-significant

Table 4. Results of the Wilcoxon-Mann-Whitney test between age groups for Instagram users

Test variables	Age group	n	Average rank	Contrast significance
Connecting	Younger Older	661 638	655 645	Z =-0.54 Non-significant
Knowing people	Younger Older	661 638	686 613	Z =-3.66 p<0.001
Seeking information	Younger Older	661 638	640 660	Z =-1.04 Non-significant
Entertaining	Younger Older	661 638	686 613	Z =-3.72 p<0.001
Talking	Younger Older	661 638	713 584	Z =-6.47 p<0.001
Escaping	Younger Older	661 638	721 577	Z =-7.35 p<0.001
Self-expressing	Younger Older	661 638	668 632	Z =-1.80 Non-significant

Last, the researcher ran a MANOVA, as a post-hoc analysis, to test for the interaction effect of re-coded age and social media platforms on usage behaviors as dependent variables, the interaction effect was statistically significant for entertaining only. The same interaction was non-significant for all other usage-behavior variables (p>0.05), see Figure for plots of age groups and social media platforms on usage-behavior variables.

Table 5. Results of the Wilcoxon-Mann-Whitney test between age groups for WhatsApp users

Test variables	Age group	n	Average rank	Contrast significance
Connecting	Younger Older	415 137	278 271	$\dot{Z}$ =-0.52 Non-significant
Knowing people	Younger Older	415 137	285 251	Z =-2.22 p<0.05
Seeking information	Younger Older	415 137	271 292	Z =-1.43 Non-significant
Entertaining	Younger Older	415 137	307 183	Z =-8.30 p<0.001
Talking	Younger Older	415 137	288 242	Z =-3.12 p<0.01
Escaping	Younger Older	415 137	294 225	Z =-4.60 p<0.001
Self-expressing	Younger Older	415 137	283 255	Z =-1.84 Non-significant

Figure 1. Usage behaviors between age groups across social media platforms

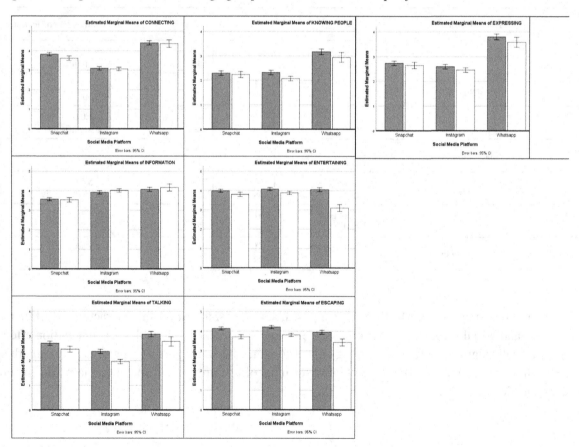

SUMMARY OF RESEARCH FINDINGS

The present research is based on one of the grounded works (i.e., uses and gratifications theory) in academic research that focuses on social media uses and gratifications. The researcher hypothesized that younger users are more likely to use social media platforms to fulfill social needs (e.g., connecting with friends and family, getting to know new people, and talking) and personal needs (e.g., seeking information, entertaining, escaping, self-expression). In addition, it was expected that users of Snapchat and Instagram turn to these platforms for affective needs (e.g., entertaining), personally integrative needs (e.g., enhancing self-expression and getting to know new people), tension release (e.g., escaping from boredom), and cognitive needs (e.g., seeking information), while users of WhatsApp focus on socially integrative needs (e.g., talking and connecting with friends and family). In general, the research findings partially supported the proposed hypotheses and provided several insights into how different social media users utilize Snapchat, Instagram, and WhatsApp.

It was determined that Snapchat, Instagram, and WhatsApp were more likely to be utilized by younger users (compared with older users) for talking, entertaining, escaping from boredom, self-expressing, and getting to know new people. With regards to seeking information, both younger and older users had similar tendencies to use the platforms. One explanation for not showing a statistical difference in the tendencies of seeking information across the age groups might be the fact that people, regardless of ages, have reasonable gratifications for knowledge and thus use different channels to gather as much information as possible in order to fulfill their basic need for knowledge. However, satisfying other types of gratifications mostly depend on convenience and lifestyles. For example, younger individuals might find it more convenient to use social media for entertainment, whereas older individuals may rely on different activities to get entertained. Moreover, older users have matured personality and their self-expression is well developed and do not rely on social media as much as younger users to express their opinions freely. In fact, older users do not spend long time on social media since they are busy with everyday activities and have other ways to obtain their gratifications. It was also shown that social media influenced younger generations more than older generations because the ages of 16 and 34 years old are, in general, the most active social media users.

The present research demonstrated that users fulfilled their gratifications at different levels in each platform. Users of WhatsApp (compared with Snapchat and Instagram) used the platform to connect and talk with friends and family, while users of Snapchat and Instagram used the platforms to entertain and escape from boredom. When examining the difference across the platforms with regards to self-expressing, getting to know new people, and seeking information, WhatsApp (compared with Snapchat and Instagram) users were less likely to depend on the platform to fulfill these gratifications. To explain these unexpected findings, one may argue that Snapchat and Instagram have important privacy features to which users may turn to stay anonymous as they are expressing themselves and getting to know new people. Once they feel conformable with other users, they may reveal their identities. These features are not fully available in WhatsApp platform because other users can still view mobile numbers and hence will be able to know their partners' identities. About the information seeking gratification, Snapchat and Instagram have features such as Snaps and Stories that promote a great amount of information about users, societal affairs, and businesses. However, WhatsApp has a limited capacity with its Status feature to share information with personal contacts only. Therefore, the features in Snapchat and Instagram (compared with WhatsApp) are more oriented toward making information available to the general public and hence users rely on these platforms as a main source of general information.

THEORETICAL CONTRIBUTIONS

The present research contributes to the existing literature in four ways. First, despite the increased interest that researchers have shown to study social media, most studies have focused on a single platform, overlooking the different natures of social media platforms. The present study fills this gap by comparing Snapchat, Instagram, and WhatsApp in order to highlight the different gratifications each platform offers to users. Second, the present research extends the uses and gratifications theory pertaining to new social media platforms. Most of the published research implicates the uses and gratifications theory on different communication-media platforms, including Facebook. However, new social media platforms such as Snapchat, Instagram, and WhatsApp have received little attention from social media researchers (Phua et al., 2017). In the present research, the researcher highlights important usage behaviors that users practice on these social media platforms in order to fulfil their gratifications. The results indicated that users who frequently used Snapchat, Instagram, and WhatsApp differed significantly on seven gratifications: connecting with friends and family, getting to know new people, talking, entertaining, escaping from boredom, self-expression, and seeking information. Third, the research provides insights into how different age groups use social media platforms. Considering the seven gratifications that different age groups obtain from new social media platforms may offer understanding of how to improve customer involvement particularly on Snapchat, Instagram, and WhatsApp. It has been shown in the present research that younger users (compared with older users) are more likely to utilize these platforms for talking, entertaining, escaping from boredom, self-expressing, and getting to know new people. These findings indicate that users' participations in these social media does have a positive effect on their daily life and hence is expected to increase their involvement with communication messages directed toward them. Last, the researcher puts forward an important argument about the applicability of the traditional IMC paradigm on social media platforms. Prior to social media, marketers believed that the control was predominately in their hands. This assumption is no longer valid with the introduction of social media platforms. Social media users have taken over the control and demanded more customized messages that fit their needs and wants. Past research has described these users as prosumer, which is the distinction between consumer and producer (Toffler, 1980). Considering new social media challenges, IMC seems to have some boundaries that limit its applicability in new media channels. Therefore, the present research advocates to revisit the IMC assumptions and consider the distinctiveness of social media platforms.

PRACTICAL IMPLICATIONS

In addition to the theoretical contributions, the research findings provide practical implications for marketers who utilize different social media platforms as marketing tools. Social media has been largely realized as an effective media to achieve marketing strategy goals. In order to increase the effectiveness of marketing campaigns, it is essential to design communication messages that match the usage behaviors of users in each platform and enhance a two-way communication. As it has been shown in the present research, users were more likely to turn to WhatsApp to connect and talk with friends and family. Thus, including WhatsApp as a tool in the marketing campaign requires a careful designing of communication messages that increase users' momentum for connecting and talking. For example, marketers might target WhatsApp users with contents that relate to the topics that bring conversations in their social circles such as announcing a long-awaited product launch or use WhatsApp as a customer-support service since it brings in conversations with customers. Furthermore, Snapchat and Instagram users use the platforms to entertain and escape from boredom. They are preferred platforms for humorous content due to their filters and custom effects. As such, it is possible to introduce creative messages that increase users' engagement with entertaining contents such as introducing a competition for creating filters/emojis, taking followers backstage inside the company, taking over the business account by a popular influencer, living a day in someone's shoes, and/or sharing favorite summer activities. All these campaigning ideas will spark interests and get the audience entertained and engaged with the communication messages. Therefore, social media marketers must infuse brands with personalities that match with users' gratifications on different social media platforms to effectively reach their target segments.

Furthermore, marketers have been utilizing the IMC model to communicate brand values to their target customers by designing consistent communication messages through different channels. The main goal of IMC is to have consistent and compelling messages in order to attract customers' attentions and intensify marketing effects. Although the IMC concept works well in traditional channels, it has some limitations on social media. The present research advocates to limit the usage of IMC on social media and adopt different communication strategies for each social media platforms due to the unique gratifications of platform users. These unique strategies will increase user engagement with brand messages.

LIMITATIONS AND FUTURE RESEARCH

Despite the theoretical and practical contributions of the present research, there are some limitations that deserve mentioning for future researchers. First, the research findings were mainly based on self-reported responses. It is possible that users evaluated their responses inaccurately due to telescoping bias. Future researchers should rely on behavioral data that are taken from social media analytics to improve the data accuracy and establish greater generalizability of the results. Second, the researcher utilized a student-snowball sampling procedure to collect the research data. Although a snowball sampling with students is convenient, it is a nonprobability sampling technique that leads to biased data because it depends on data coming from students' friends and family only. Third, the researcher used a median-split method to divide users into younger and older groups. Although, the median-split method is a well-accepted method in academic research to dichotomize research participants, it resulted in younger group aged 25 and less and older group aged 26 and older. One may argue that the data were skewed toward a young population and thus the older group included participants that could be considered young too. Future researchers should account for this issue by collecting data from a wider age range in order to get results applicable to the general social media population. Fourth, the measure of usage behaviors (i.e., uses and gratifications) was utilized from one prior study (Sultan, 2014). Future researchers should combine more measures and use factor analysis to validate the items of these measures. Fifth, the present research relied on the uses and gratifications theory to identify and compare usage behaviors of different social media platforms. Future researchers should utilize other theories such as the technology acceptance model (TAM) to show how users come to accept and use social media platforms. Perhaps, a comparison between uses and gratifications theory and other theories are useful to shed light on additional theoretical explanations. Last, the research provides early descriptive findings about the different uses and gratifications of new social media platforms. Future researchers should offer more theoretical explanations to elucidate processes and utilities of different usage behaviors particularly for new social media platforms and identify more implications for social media marketing.

REFERENCES

Alalwan, A. A., Rana, N. P., Dwivedi, Y. K., & Algharabat, R. (2017). Social media in marketing: A review and analysis of the existing literature. *Telematics and Informatics*, *34*(7), 1177–1190. doi:10.1016/j.tele.2017.05.008

Amichai-Hamburger, Y., & Vinitzky, G. (2010). Social network use and personality. *Computers in Human Behavior*, *26*(6), 1289–1295. doi:10.1016/j.chb.2010.03.018

Banjanin, N., Banjanin, N., Dimitrijevic, I., & Pantic, I. (2015). Relationship between internet use and depression: Focus on physiological mood oscillations, social networking and online addictive behavior. *Computers in Human Behavior*, *43*, 308–312. doi:10.1016/j.chb.2014.11.013

Boone, L. E., & Kurtz, D. L. (2007). *Contemporary marketing* (13th ed.). Thomson/South-Western.

Chi, H. H. (2011). Interactive digital advertising vs. virtual brand community: Exploratory study of user motivation and social media marketing responses in Taiwan. *Journal of Interactive Advertising*, *12*(1), 44–61. doi:10.1080/15252019.2011.10722190

Elliott, W. R., & Rosenberg, W. L. (1987). The 1985 Philadelphia newspaper strike: A uses and gratifications study. *The Journalism Quarterly*, *64*(4), 679–687. doi:10.1177/107769908706400401

Floros, G., & Siomos, K. (2013). The relationship between optimal parenting, Internet addiction and motives for social networking in adolescence. *Psychiatry Research*, *209*(3), 529–534. doi:10.1016/j.psychres.2013.01.010 PMID:23415042

Kamboj, S. (2020). Applying uses and gratifications theory to understand customer participation in social media brand communities. *Asia Pacific Journal of Marketing and Logistics*.

Kamboj, S., Kumar, V., & Rahman, Z. (2017). Social media usage and firm performance: The mediating role of social capital. *Social Network Analysis and Mining*, *7*(1), 51–56. doi:10.100713278-017-0468-8

Kamboj, S., & Rahman, Z. (2017). Customer participation in brand communities on social media: A systematic literature review. *International Journal of Web Based Communities*, *13*(4), 437–467. doi:10.1504/IJWBC.2017.089349

Kaplan, A. M., & Haenlein, M. (2010). Users of the world, unite! The challenges and opportunities of Social Media. *Business Horizons*, *53*(1), 59–68. doi:10.1016/j.bushor.2009.09.003

Katz, E., Blumler, J. G., & Gurevitch, M. (1974). The uses and gratifications approach to mass communication. Beverly Hills, Calif.: Sage Pubns. Ko H, Cho CH & Roberts, M. S. (1005). Internet uses and gratifications: A structural equation model of interactive advertising. *Journal of Advertising*, *34*(2), 57–70.

Khan, M. L. (2017). Social media engagement: What motivates user participation and consumption on YouTube? *Computers in Human Behavior*, *66*(1), 236–247. doi:10.1016/j.chb.2016.09.024

Korgaonkar, P. K., & Wolin, L. D. (1999). A multivariate analysis of web usage. *Journal of Advertising Research*, *39*(2), 53.

Kuss, D. J., & Griffiths, M. D. (2011). Online social networking and addiction—A review of the psychological literature. *International Journal of Environmental Research and Public Health, 8*(9), 3528–3552. doi:10.3390/ijerph8093528 PMID:22016701

Kwon, E. S., Kim, E., Sung, Y., & Yoo, C. Y. (2014). Brand followers: Consumer motivation and attitude towards brand communications on Twitter. *International Journal of Advertising, 33*(4), 657–680. doi:10.2501/IJA-33-4-657-680

Leiner, D. J., Kobilke, L., Rueß, C., & Brosius, H. B. (2018). Functional domains of social media platforms: Structuring the uses of Facebook to better understand its gratifications. *Computers in Human Behavior, 83*, 194–203. doi:10.1016/j.chb.2018.01.042

Magsamen-Conrad, K., Dowd, J., Abuljadail, M., Alsulaiman, S., & Shareefi, A. (2015). Life-span differences in the uses and gratifications of tablets: Implications for older adults. *Computers in Human Behavior, 52*, 96–106. doi:10.1016/j.chb.2015.05.024 PMID:26113769

Mangold, W. G., & Faulds, D. J. (2009). Social media: The new hybrid element of the promotion mix. *Business Horizons, 52*(4), 357–365. doi:10.1016/j.bushor.2009.03.002

Mcquail, D., Blumler, J., & Brown, J. R. (1972). *Sociology of the mass media*. Penguin Books.

Mendelsohn, H. (1964). Listening to radio. *People, society & mass communication*, 239-48.

MSI. (2016). *Marketing Science Institute Research Priorities 2016–2018*. MSI.

Muniz, A. M. Jr, & O'guinn, T. C. (2001). Brand community. *The Journal of Consumer Research, 27*(4), 412–432. doi:10.1086/319618

Nadkami, A., & Hofmann, S. G. (2012). Why do people use Facebook? Personality and individual differences. *Nafional Center for Biotechnology Informafion*. Retrieved from: http://www. ncbi. nlm. nih. gov/pmc/arficles/PMC3335399

Park, N., Kee, K. F., & Valenzuela, S. (2009). Being immersed in social networking environment: Facebook groups, uses and gratifications, and social outcomes. *Cyberpsychology & Behavior, 12*(6), 729–733. doi:10.1089/cpb.2009.0003 PMID:19619037

Phua, J., Jin, S. V., & Kim, J. J. (2017). Gratifications of using Facebook, Twitter, Instagram, or Snapchat to follow brands: The moderating effect of social comparison, trust, tie strength, and network homophily on brand identification, brand engagement, brand commitment, and membership intention. *Telematics and Informatics, 34*(1), 412–424. doi:10.1016/j.tele.2016.06.004

Quan-Haase, A., & Young, A. L. (2010). Uses and gratifications of social media: A comparison of Facebook and instant messaging. *Bulletin of Science, Technology & Society, 30*(5), 350–361. doi:10.1177/0270467610380009

Raacke, J., & Bonds-Raacke, J. (2008). MySpace and Facebook: Applying the uses and gratifications theory to exploring friend-networking sites. *Cyberpsychology & Behavior, 11*(2), 169–174. doi:10.1089/ cpb.2007.0056 PMID:18422409

Rubin, A. (1994). Media Uses and Effects: A Uses-and-Gratifications Perspective. In J. Bryant & D. Zillmann (Eds.), *Media Effects*. Lawrence Erlbaum Associates, Inc.

Sherry, J. L. (2001). The effects of violent video games on aggression: A meta-analysis. *Human Communication Research*, 27(3), 409–431. doi:10.1111/j.1468-2958.2001.tb00787.x

Statista. (2019). *Mobile social media - Statistics and facts*. Retrieved from: https://www.statista.com/topics/2478/mobile-social-networks/

Statista. (2020). *Social media advertising worldwide*. Retrieved from: https://www.statista.com/outlook/220/100/social media-advertising/worldwide

Steinfield, C., Ellison, N. B., & Lampe, C. (2008). Social capital, self-esteem, and use of online social network sites: A longitudinal analysis. *Journal of Applied Developmental Psychology*, 29(6), 434–445. doi:10.1016/j.appdev.2008.07.002

Sultan, A. J. (2014). Addiction to mobile text messaging applications is nothing to "lol" about. *The Social Science Journal*, 51(1), 57–69. doi:10.1016/j.soscij.2013.09.003

Taylor, D. G., Strutton, D., & Thompson, K. (2012). Self-enhancement as a motivation for sharing online advertising. *Journal of Interactive Advertising*, 12(2), 13–28. doi:10.1080/15252019.2012.10722193

Toffler, A. (1980). *The third wave*. Morrow.

Van Volkom, M., Stapley, J. C., & Malter, J. (2013). Use and perception of technology: Sex and generational differences in a community sample. *Educational Gerontology*, 39(10), 729–740. doi:10.1080/03601277.2012.756322

West, R. & Turner, L. H. (2010). *Understanding interpersonal communication: Making choices in changing times*. Cengage learning.

Zhang, M., & Luo, N. (2016). Understanding relationship benefits from harmonious brand community on social media. *Internet Research*, 26(4), 809–826. doi:10.1108/IntR-05-2015-0149

This research was previously published in the International Journal of E-Services and Mobile Applications (IJESMA), 13(1); pages 45-59, copyright year 2021 by IGI Publishing (an imprint of IGI Global).

Chapter 71
Hispanic Humor Styles on Facebook:
An Analytical Study

Valerie L Wang
West Chester University, West Chester, USA

Yi-Chia Wu
Tarleton State University, Stephenville, USA

Hao Lou
Ohio University, Athens, USA

ABSTRACT

To better understand how humor is used in today's multicultural virtual environment, this study investigates the humor styles of Hispanic Americans in a virtual community. Based on the four humor styles, the current study builds a theoretical framework to explain why cultural norms, gender role, acculturation, and education influence the humor styles of Hispanic Americans in computer-mediated communication. Two research questions and five hypotheses are developed in the research framework. The statistical analysis is based on content analysis of 400 Hispanic Facebook users, 93 of whom use humor in most recent News Feed. The results provide preliminary evidence of the influences of cultural norms, gender role, acculturation, and education on Hispanic humor styles.

INTRODUCTION

The excessive psychological benefits of humor have long been studied in research. Previous research found that humor not only can be used for relieving intrinsic stress (Dixon, 1980), but also helps build personal relationships and cope with interpersonal tension (Ziv, 1984). Wise usage of humor can elicit many positive signals, therefore lubricating personal appeal and interpersonal communications (Cann, Calhoun, & Banks, 1997; Martin, 2007). In particular, people appear to be creative and intelligent when

DOI: 10.4018/978-1-6684-6307-9.ch071

using humor in relationship building (Cann & Calhoun, 2001; Miller, 2000). People equipped with a good sense of humor are also viewed as sociable and self-confident (Chafe, 2007). Many past studies have highlighted the positive role of humor in effectively building and maintaining interpersonal relationships (Cann, Zapata, & Davis 2011; Li et al., 2002; McGee & Shevlin, 2009; Sprecher & Regan, 2002).

In advertising research, a general premise is that humor messages can create positive emotional reactions through delivering a "surprise" (Elpers, Mukherjee, & Hoyer, 2004). From this perspective, using humor in advertising and communications has been shown to have high effectiveness in stimulating consumers' positive psychological responses (Chung & Zhao, 2003; Cline, Altsech, & Kellaris, 2003; Lee & Mason, 1999). The positive impacts include some of the most important outcomes, such as viewers' positive attitudes toward the message and its sender, as well as attention to the message (Eisend, 2009). Given that our understanding of humor has been focused on traditional face-to-face and advertising contexts (Cann, Zapata, & Davis 2011; Galloway, 2010; Martin et al., 2003), it will be very interesting to examine how humor is used in the fast-growing virtual community.

Computer-mediated communication has fundamentally changed the way interpersonal interaction is carried out (Walther, 1996). In a virtual community, interpersonal communications are rather hyperpersonal because the members have a greater tendency to use an optimized presentation of self (Walther, 1996). Virtual community members also found it hard to make accurate impressions about others due to the absence of nonverbal cues (Okdie et al., 2011; Walther, 2007). Although humor can be strategically used to build emotional ties in the lack of nonverbal cues, previous research has not yet explored the determinant cultural and demographic factors that shape humor usage by virtual community members.

Thus, to bridge this research gap and better understand how humor is used in today's multicultural virtual environment, this study attempts to investigate the humor styles of Hispanic Facebook users. Based on the four humor styles conceptualized by Martin et al. (2003), we intend to find the percentage of Hispanic Americans using humor on Facebook and the popularity of the different humor styles used by Hispanic Americans. Furthermore, the current study builds a theoretical framework to explain why cultural norms, gender role, acculturation, and education may influence the humor styles of Hispanic Americans who are involved in computer-mediated communication. Further, the investigation on humor styles may provide further evidence on whether humor is significantly used by the Hispanic culture, and which humor styles are more popular than others in this culture. The findings also offer insights into understanding the communication styles of Hispanic Facebook users from psychological and sociological perspectives.

LITERATURE REVIEW

Humor Styles

In advertising research, Speck's (1991) typology of humorous advertising styles, which consists of incongruity-based, arousal-safety-based, and disparagement-based humor, has been used in many studies dealing with humorous advertising (Beard, 2008; Hatzithomas, Zotos, & Boutsouki, 2011; Lee & Lim, 2008; Spotts, Weinberger, & Parsons, 1997). By the same token, Martin et al. (2003) provided rich insights into humor styles, with a greater social discernment. The Humor Styles Questionnaire in Martin et al.'s (2003) study contains four humor styles with respect to individual use of humor from an intrapsychic standpoint. Follow-up studies have confirmed high reliability of the humor style measures reported in the original Humor Styles Questionnaire (Galloway, 2010; Kazarian & Martin, 2006).

Martin et al.'s (2003) Humor Styles Questionnaire specifies four humor styles: affiliative humor, self-enhancing humor, aggressive humor, and self-defeating humor. The *Affiliative Humor Style* portrays jokes and flirts in a group where the "entertainer" articulates humor and expects to charm others during this process. The *Aggressive Humor Style* is a harsher form of humor that typically implements humor as mockery, loss, and it also tends to omit others without considering the consequence. The *Self-Enhancing Humor Style* is described as an affirmative humor style that is closely aligned with coping and an optimistic viewpoint on life. Lastly, the *Self-Defeating Humor Style* is used by individuals who tend to present and accept a low self-efficacy through excessive self-downgrading and self-mockery.

Humor can be divided into positive (adaptive) and negative (maladaptive) kinds (Duncan, Smeltzer, and Leap, 1990; Zeigler-Hill and Besser, 2011). The affiliative humor style and the self-enhancing humor style are positive based on its effects, whereas the aggressive humor style and the self-defeating humor style result in negative disparagement (Martin et al., 2003). Martin et al.'s (2003) humor style framework is based on two dimensions: the direction of humor (positive versus negative) and the target of humor (on oneself versus on others). Martin et al.'s (2003) Humor Styles Questionnaire is provided in Table 1.

Table 1. Humor styles questionnaire by Martin et al. (2003)

Affiliative Humor Style
I usually don't laugh or joke around much with other people.*
I don't have to work very hard at making other people laugh—I seem to be a naturally humorous person.
I rarely make other people laugh by telling funny stories about myself.
I laugh and joke a lot with my closest friends.
I usually don't like to tell jokes or amuse people.*
I enjoy making people laugh.
I don't often joke around with my friends.*
I usually can't think of witty things to say when I'm with other people.*
Aggressive Humor Style
If someone makes a mistake, I will often tease them about it.
People are never offended or hurt by my sense of humor.*
When telling jokes or saying funny things, I am usually not very concerned about how other people are taking it.
I do not like it when people use humor as a way of criticizing or putting someone down.*
Sometimes I think of something that is so funny that I can't stop myself from saying it, even if it is not appropriate for the situation.
I never participate in laughing at others even if all my friends are doing it.*
If I don't like someone, I often use humor or teasing to put them down.
Even if something is really funny to me, I will not laugh or joke about it if someone will be offended.*
Self-Enhancing Humor Style
If I am feeling depressed, I can usually cheer myself up with humor.
Even when I'm by myself, I'm often amused by the absurdities of life.
If I am feeling upset or unhappy I usually try to think of something funny about the situation to make myself feel better.
My humorous outlook on life keeps me from getting overly upset or depressed about things.
If I'm by myself and I'm feeling unhappy, I make an effort to think of something funny to cheer myself up.
If I am feeling sad or upset, I usually lose my sense of humor.*
It is my experience that thinking about some amusing aspect of a situation is often a very effective way of coping with problems.
I don't need to be with other people to feel amused—I can usually find things to laugh about even when I'm by myself.
Self-Defeating Humor Style
I let people laugh at me or make fun at my expense more than I should.
I will often get carried away in putting myself down if it makes my family or friends laugh.
I often try to make people like or accept me more by saying something funny about my own weaknesses, blunders, or faults.
I don't often say funny things to put myself down.*
I often go overboard in putting myself down when I am making jokes or trying to be funny.
When I am with friends or family, I often seem to be the one that other people make fun of or joke about.
If I am having problems or feeling unhappy, I often cover it up by joking around, so that even my closest friends don't know how I really feel.
Letting others laugh at me is my way of keeping my friends and family in good spirits.

*Reverse-coded items.

Humor and Culture

Humor has been widely used across diverse cultures. Feinberg (1971) found that, in many well-known cultures, humor is manifested through criticism, sarcasm, irony, exaggeration, disguise, unforeseen changes of reasoning, and superiority over criticized victims. Based on the evidence collected from hundreds of ethnic groups, Apte (1985) stated that humor is widely used by all cultures in interpersonal communications. In empirical research, Ruch (1992) found that people from the U.S., Europe, and the Middle East use humor in similar ways. Other studies also found a great amount of likeness in the use of humor by people from Asia and North America (Chen & Martin, 2007; Nevo, Nevo, & Yin, 2001). Previous findings have also suggested that humorous advertising is popular across the world (Cruthirds et al., 2012; Laroche et al., 2011; Toncar, 2001).

However, cultural differences in the use and reaction to humor have been recognized in previous advertising research (Cruthirds et al., 2012; Hatzithomas, Zotos, & Boutsouki, 2011; Laroche et al., 2011; Lee & Lim, 2008; Toncar, 2001). Many differences found in cross-cultural humorous advertising reflect consumers' tradition and cultural preferences. For example, British advertising is found to use more subtle, understatement-type humor because its culture is more tolerant of ambiguity, while American advertising employs more straightforward, ludicrous humor because of the high uncertainty-avoidance culture (Toncar, 2001).

Kalliny, Cruthirds, and Minor (2006) found that it is common for Arab men to use aggressive humor in jokes with women because of the male-dominant culture, suggesting that interpersonal relationship characteristics in a culture silently influence how humor is used between individuals. The humor styles identified in the Humor Styles Questionnaire are said to be culturally bound because humor styles mirror the cultural environment people live in (Martin et al., 2003). It indicates that people's intended humor styles are culturally induced. Culture is defined as "the way of life of people, for the sum of their learned behavior patterns, attitudes, and material things" (Hall, 1976, p. 20). At the individual level, culture includes the social, ethical, and educational experiences a person accumulates (Arnould & Thompson, 2005). Overall, humor is a very important language beyond cultural boundaries. Based on the similarities and differences of humor, the extant literature reveals that every culture is prone to the use of humor and effective humor styles are culturally defined. It is critical to examine humor styles from a cultural perspective.

RESEARCH FRAMEWORK

In view of the positive role of humor in general, the intensity and types of humor used by Hispanic Americans in the virtual environment are still subject to exploratory investigation. Due to the lack of field data, this study starts the scientific inquiry by proposing two research questions below:

RQ1: What is the percentage of Hispanics who regularly use humor on Facebook?
RQ2: What are the most and least popular humor styles used by Hispanics on Facebook?

Following the two broad research questions assessing the usage of humor by Hispanics, we articulate a theoretical framework built upon cultural context (Hall, 1976), gender role and identity theory (Burke

& Tully, 1977; Tajfel & Turner, 1986), and acculturation theory (Padilla, 1980). The research framework consists of five hypotheses.

Unlike the mainstream Anglo-Saxon culture in the United States, the Hispanic culture rooted in Latin America tends to deliver high context messages (as compared to low context ones) in interpersonal communications (Copeland & Griggs, 1986; Hall, 1976). The high context communication style is an outcome of the high context Hispanic culture in which inferences and customs are well understood based on shared experiences of collectivistic members (Hall, 1976). On the contrary, people pertaining to the low context communication style, such as mainstream Americans, are considered more verbally explicit in interpersonal communications because of the individualistic low context culture (Hall, 1976). It has been highlighted that high and low context cultures have different patterns in computer-mediated communication (Wurtz, 2005).

It has been recognized that one of the drives determining the formation of a high context culture is the long-term, well-established relationship bonds among the members (Copeland & Griggs, 1986; Hall, 1976). As such, Hispanic individuals are more likely to exhibit a relationship orientation in the virtual community. By default, the cultural norms require Hispanics to keep a strong and stable social tie with others in the loop. According to Hofstede (1980), people from an individualistic culture tend to highlight self-interest, whereas people from a collectivistic culture such as Latin America consider the interests of the group over the individuals. Caucasian Americans belong to the individualistic culture and thus, are more likely to address personal wants and interests in their virtual interactions. In contrast, Hispanic Americans inherited their collectivistic culture from Latin America and thus, are more likely to put emphasis on group values and harmonious social behavior in the virtual community surroundings. Thus, the affiliative humor style can be a strategic match for Hispanics. The affiliative humor style reflects jokes and flirts in an interpersonal context where the humor initiator has the tendency to say funny things with the purpose of amusing and approaching others (Miczo, Averbeck, & Mariani, 2009). As such, Hispanics are more likely to express affiliative style jokes and flirts in a virtual context where they have the tendency to say funny things with the purpose of amusing and approaching others in the virtual community. It is also reasonable for Hispanics not to use aggressive humor in virtual communications because such humor messages are typically used to ridicule, defeat, or exclude others without regard for the negative effect.

H1: There are a higher percentage of Hispanics using the affiliative humor style than Hispanics using the aggressive humor style on Facebook.

For Hispanics, acculturation means the process of merging to a leading culture, the mainstream Anglo-Saxon Caucasian culture (Padilla, 1980). Although the acculturation process has been found to change Hispanic Americans' behaviors and lifestyles, Hispanic Americans are said to be loyal to their own culture (Wilson, 2007). Previous research found that Hispanic Americans are the most resistant to acculturation in the U.S., holding to their own norms, lifestyles, and behaviors (Alba, 1995; Livingston, 1992).

In a cultural context, social behavior is a function of in-group norms that members will conform to (Triandis, 1989). However, previous studies found that college students of different ethnic backgrounds have comparable behaviors and expectations (Duffy & Klingaman, 2009; Teng, Morgan, & Anderson, 2001). After going through higher education, students may not be bound to their own socio-cultural restrictions (Gushue & Whitson, 2006). College graduates from a collectivistic, Hispanic cultural background can experience a high level of acculturation, through many years of exposure to the individualistic, Caucasian style of culture.

Thus, the higher education experience can make tremendous impact on the use of certain humor styles commonly found in the mainstream culture. In many previous studies, educational level is said to be an important predictor of behavior (Grinstein & Nisan, 2009; Herpen, Nierop, & Sloot, 2012; Jansson, Marell, & Nordlund, 2011; Robb, Reynolds, & Abdel-Ghany, 2007). In a low context culture, people pay greater attention to self-interest and care more about own feelings (Hall, 1976). As such, the self-enhancing humor style and the aggressive humor style are more popular for Americans with a low context communication style. Hispanics, who are culturally sensitive to interpersonal conflict, tend to avoid the use of self-enhancing and aggressive humor styles. However, the educational learning experience will instill a sense of self into Hispanic individuals, making them act like Caucasians in social interactions. With learned manners, they are more likely to use the humor styles Caucasian Americans often use. Vice versa, those Hispanics lacking higher education are more likely to follow old demeanors and use their culturally bound humor styles.

H2: For Hispanics using the aggressive humor style, there is a higher percentage of those with university education than those with lower levels of education.

H3: For Hispanics using the self-enhancing humor style, there is a higher percentage of those with university education than those with lower levels of education.

Gender role expectation is a crucial component of cultural norms (Burke & Tully, 1977; Triandis, 1989). From a behavioral perspective, people abide by their expected gender role because gender is the primary identity (Burke & Tully, 1977). An individual's self-identity is usually constructed according to the cultural definitions of desirable male and female figures (Bem, 1981; Fritsche & Jonas, 2005; Triandis, 1989). A culturally bound individual encodes information about himself or herself according to the cultural definitions of desirable male and female attributes (Bem, 1981; Hoffman & Borders, 2001). High-context, collectivistic cultures tend to feature female gender roles as wives, maids, caregivers, and other service-oriented figures that show the subordinate status (Triandis, 1989; Kashima et al., 1995). Thus, Hispanic females, who conform to the collectivistic culture, have stronger gender role norms and tend to use the self-defeating humor style to reflect their perceived subservient status of self.

H4: For Hispanics using the self-defeating humor style, there is a higher percentage of women than men.

The high context Hispanic culture tends to have formed networks, long-term relationships, and strong boundaries (Hall, 1976). Besides, the high context culture shares a great deal of tacit knowledge within a community (Hall, 1976). Often, the communication patterns can only be fully understood by in-group individuals because they are hard to explain to people out of the culture (Copeland & Griggs, 1986; Hall, 1976).

Hispanics are usually bilingual individuals, and their unique code-switching communication style is a product of the socio-cultural environment (Bishop & Peterson, 2011; Luna & Peracchio, 2002). As a notable verbal behavior for Hispanic Americans, code-switching is a linguistic practice through the use of mixed expressions in English and Spanish (Luna & Peracchio 2002). Previous research found that less acculturated Hispanics are more prone to the use of Spanish language (Wilson, 2007). Less acculturated Hispanics may express a greater amount of humor using code-switching because the subtle meaning of many jokes can only be expressed and understood in the Hispanic context with the use of several Spanish words or expressions. On the flip side, acculturated Hispanics are less culturally bound, and are able to engage in interpersonal communication with explicit humor messages that can be understood by people outside the cultural context. Thus, it is expected that the educational experience can influence Hispanic individuals' code-switching behavior when humor is expressed.

H5: For Hispanics using code-switching in expressing humor, there is a lower percentage of those with university education than those with lower level of education.

METHODS

Media Selection

The objective of this study is to examine Hispanic humor styles in a virtual context. Data for this study is collected in a popular social networking website, Facebook.com. Facebook.com is selected as the target media based on the following four reasons. First, launched in 2004, Facebook.com is the largest online social networking website worldwide, with around 1.4 billion registered profiles. Thus, the virtual communities affiliated with Facebook.com can provide researchers a viable sampling frame as well as full access to the subjects of study. Second, user-submitted profiles on Facebook provide self-reported, detailed information about users' demographic information, such as age, gender, ethnicity, and educational level. Such demographic information is necessary for testing the hypotheses in this study using the content analysis approach. Third, Facebook offers a technologically advanced virtual community, allowing users to freely and quickly interact with friends and respond to received messages. Thus, the website creates an ideal condition for researchers to collect a sample of humor messages expressed in interpersonal two-way communication rather than human-computer interaction. Fourth, the humor styles of the users on Facebook are exhibited through News Feed updates. A content analysis on their self-supplied News Feed messages can help critically understand whether and how their humor styles are manifested.

Variables and Coding

In order to examine the two research questions and test the five hypotheses, the statistical analysis require a number of dependent and independent variables coded through content analysis. The required variables include two independent variables, gender and education level, and three dependent variables, humor usage, humor style, and code switching. Age is coded as a screening variable. Only users between 18 and 50 are selected.

Hispanic ethnicity is validated during data collection. Ethnicity is a culturally defined identity based on common characteristics shared by a cultural group, such as history, racial heritage, language, traditions, and religion (Camoroff & Camoroff, 2009). Americans usually self-report ethnicity as part of their demographic profiles. The U.S. Census Bureau (2012a, p. 2) defines Hispanic American as "a person of Cuban, Mexican, Puerto Rican, South or Central American, or other Spanish culture or origin regardless of race." Thus, as an ethnic group, Hispanic Americans share many common ethnic characteristics similar to those in Latin American cultures. In this study, ethnicity information is coded through self-reported

Facebook.com user profiles. To investigate the humor styles due to cultural heritage, the current study only examines profiles marked with self-reported full Hispanic ethnicity and excludes multi-cultural and multi-racial profiles.

Gender, educational level, and age are other demographic variables that are coded based on self-reported information. This study uses education as a proxy for acculturation. It is hypothesized that educated Hispanics tend to stress the use of the aggressive humor style more often than uneducated Hispanics do. The threshold set for the study is whether a Bachelor's degree is obtained or not reported in user profiles.

Humor usage and humor style are coded based on coder subjective evaluation on Facebook user's most recent News Feed update. The coders' job is three-fold: (1) to record the subjects' News Feed update, (2) to interpret the humor styles these messages carry, according to the Humor Styles Questionnaire (Martin et al., 2003), and (3) to transcribe code-switched humor messages. Specifically, based on Martin et al.'s (2003) humor style categories, the coder will judge if each update denotes any humor message, and what the primary humor style is if a humor message is identified. Following Mueller's (1992) suggestion for simplification, the coder only draws a single value from each message with one of the four humor styles. As such, only the dominant humor style is coded for each message. The coding sheet used in data collection is provided in Table 2.

Table 2. Coding sheet

Variable	Source	Categories
Gender	Self-reported	1 = Male 2 = Female
Education Level	Self-reported	1 = High school 2 = Associate degree 3 = Bachelor's degree 4 = Grad degree
Age	Self-reported	(Ratio variable, actual age is reported)
Humor Usage	Coder-interpreted	1 = Yes (Humor message is not found in the update) 2 = No (Humor message is found in the update)
Humor Style	Coder-interpreted	1 = Affiliative humor style (The individual uses jokes and flirts with others in order to please others during this process) 2 = Aggressive humor style (The individual uses sarcasm or mockery to omit others without considering the consequence) 3 = Self-enhancing humor style (The individual uses jokes in coping with adversity and showing an optimistic viewpoint on life) 4 = Self-defeating humor style (The individual uses jokes to reveal own weaknesses and flaws in exchange for others' understanding and sympathy)
Code-Switching	Coder-interpreted	If humor is found, then: 1 = No (Only English is used in the update) 2 = Yes (code-switching or Spanish is used in the update)

Sample and Reliability

The subjects of study are Hispanic Americans in general. The sample size is estimated following Voelker and Orton's (1993) sample size formula for binominal measures. With ±5% sampling error and 95% level of confidence, the study is desired to have 400 cases. To obtain an active group of Hispanic

American Facebook users, we attempt to seek Hispanic Americans affiliated with a Facebook group of a city in Texas. The city has approximately 150,000 residents, 85% of who are Hispanic Americans. The Facebook group has more than 5,000 self-reported Hispanic American users. Consequently, a sample containing 400 Hispanic Facebook user profiles that meet the criteria of this study is obtained via the convenience sampling approach.

Inter-coder reliability is an important aspect of the reliability for content analysis (Kassarjian, 1977). Three graduate students who are familiar with the Hispanic cultures are used as coders for this study. All the coders have previous content analysis experience. In addition, the three coders are trained to be proficient with the coding procedure in this study and the humor styles. The three coders independently determine the values in the coding sheet. Scott's Pi will be used as the measure for assessing inter-coder reliability of nominal data in content analysis (Scott, 1955). The inter-coder reliability is 100% for Humor Usage, 93.5% for Humor Style, and 96.7% for Code-Switching, reaching a 96.7% overall percentage of agreement.

Analytical Procedure

Using the coding sheet, the 400 Hispanic profiles collected from Facebook.com are examined through content analysis. The two research questions attempt to find (1) the percentage of Hispanics who regularly use humor on Facebook, and (2) the most and least popular humor styles used by Hispanics. Descriptive statistics will be used to illustrate the results.

RESULT

Answers for Research Questions

The two research questions respectively ask: "What is the percentage of Hispanics who regularly use humor on Facebook?" and "What are the most and least popular humor styles used by Hispanics on Facebook?" The result reveals that 93 out of 400 Hispanics use humor on Facebook. Thus, the corresponding percentage of humor usage by Hispanics is 23.3% on Facebook. To answer RQ1, approximately one out of four messages is a humorous message used by Hispanics. In addition, the result for RQ2 is summarized in Table 3. As it shows, being the most popular humor style, the affiliative humor style accounts for 62.4% of the total humor usage by Hispanics. The self-enhancing humor style is the least popular one for Hispanics, accounting for 7.5%.

TABLE 3. Hispanic humor styles on Facebook

	Number	**Percentage**
Affiliative Humor Style	58	62.4%
Aggressive Humor Style	20	21.5%
Self-Enhancing Humor Style	7	7.5%
Self-Deprecating Humor Style	8	8.6%
Humor Overall	93	100%

Hypotheses Testing

H1 argues that there are more Hispanics using the affiliative humor style than those using the aggressive humor style on Facebook. The Hispanic sample has 62.4% using affiliative humor style versus 21.5% using aggressive humor style. By comparing the percentages, H1 is supported with a clear difference seen in the sample ($\chi^2 = 7.31$, p = .00).

H2 argues that the aggressive humor style is more likely to be used by Hispanics with university education than Hispanics with lower level of education. In the sample, among the 20 Hispanics who use aggressive humor style on Facebook, 17 (85%) have received university education, while 3 (15%) have not. As seen, the aggressive humor style is mainly used by Hispanics with university education, more so than those with lower level of education ($\chi^2 = 3.11$, p = .08). Therefore, H2 is marginally supported (p < .10).

Similarly, H3 argues that the self-enhancing humor style is more likely to be used by Hispanics with university education than Hispanics with lower level of education. In the sample, among 7 Hispanics who use the self-enhancing humor style, 5 (71.4%) have received university education while 2 (28.6%) have not. The sample has a higher percentage of Hispanics with university education using the self-enhancing humor style. However, the result is not statistically significant to support H3 ($\chi^2 = .02$, p = .88) due to the small size of the users of this humor style.

H4 argues that the self-defeating humor style is more likely to be used by Hispanic women than Hispanic men. It shows that a total of 8 Hispanics use the self-defeating humor style in the sample, 5 women (62.5%) and 3 men (37.5%). The sample shows a higher percentage of women using the self-defeating humor style. However, the result is not statistically significant to support H4 ($\chi^2 = .63$, p = .43) due to the small size of the users of this humor style.

H5 argues that Hispanics with university education are less likely to use code-switching in expressing humor than Hispanics with lower level of education. It reveals that 75 out of 93 Hispanics in the sample use code-switching in expressing humor. Among them, 25 (33.3%) are university educated whereas 50 (66.7%) are not. The sample shows a smaller percentage of Hispanics with university education using code-switching in expressing humor than Hispanics with lower level of education, showing support for H5 ($\chi^2 = 7.10$, p = .00).

DISCUSSION

Through studying Hispanic users on Facebook, the results help to illustrate Hispanic humor styles in computer-mediated, virtual communications. RQ1 shows that humor messages accounts for approximately one quarter of all messages. This highlights the importance of understanding when and how humor is used by the Hispanic ethnic group in the virtual environment. In RQ2, it is found that the affiliative humor style is the most often used humor style by Hispanics. This is consistent with the cultural norm of the Hispanic culture, which is high context and relationship oriented. Furthermore, the self-enhancing humor style is least used by Hispanics. This is also logical from a cultural perspective. To maintain group harmony, Hispanics tend to avoid the expression of self-interest and the subsequent interpersonal conflict due to the emphasis on self-interest.

Based on the results of the five hypotheses, the findings provide preliminary evidence on how Hispanics are influenced by cultural norms, gender role, acculturation, and education in their use of humor. The humor styles of Hispanic Americans in computer-mediated communication are found to be congruent with their high context cultural norms. In the sample of 93 Hispanic Facebook users who use humor messages, 58, or approximately 60%, use the affiliative humor style in expressing humor interpersonal communications. The affiliative tendency implies that Hispanics enjoy use humor to make others laugh so that close relationship can be strengthened.

Education is seen to impact on Hispanic Americans on their interpersonal communication. With the sample collected, university education has made a difference in the humor styles of Hispanic Americans. Compared to their less educated counterparts, educated Hispanics tend to use the self-enhancing humor style and the aggressive humor style that are usually used in a low context culture. These humor styles are used to express self-interest and own feelings. The self-enhancing humor style and the aggressive humor style can be seen as outcomes of higher education in which a minority group learn to adopt the low context communication style of the majority group. On the contrary, when lacking university education experience, those Hispanics tend to follow culturally bound demeanors, which do not encourage the self-enhancing humor style and the aggressive humor style in interpersonal communications.

It is seen in the sample that the self-defeating humor style is more frequently used by Hispanic women than Hispanic men. The underlying reason is the impact of gender role on women in a collectivistic culture. It can be seen that Hispanic females tend to use the self-defeating humor style because of the subordinate status self-expected by them.

Lastly, it is found that code-switching is more frequently used by less educated Hispanics in the sample to express humor. University education helps Hispanics to become more acculturated and less culturally bound. Thus, those less educated/acculturated Hispanics rely on code-switching for the expression of humor because the message is best expressed in a intra-culturally understandable way using Spanish vocabularies. Overall, cultural norms, gender role, education, and acculturation are found to influence the way humor is expressed by Hispanics in a virtual community.

Theoretical Implications

Our findings extend important theoretical paradigms into the virtual environment. Combining cultural context (Hall, 1976), gender role and identity theory (Burke & Tully, 1977; Tajfel & Turner, 1986), and acculturation theory (Padilla, 1980), we illustrate humor usage patterns and humor styles in a virtual community based on gender and education. Theoretically speaking, this study provides a solid understanding of the relationship between humor styles and consumers' demographic differences. More importantly, culture shapes how humor is socially used. Our findings highlight that the choice of humor style is a learned behavior. Hispanic Americans increasingly use certain humor styles common to Caucasian Americans, indicating learned relational and social behavior. In a broader sense, globalization will increasingly make humor less culturally bound, eventually forming an individualistic, low context environment in the borderless virtual space.

Managerial Implications

Digital marketing managers usually aim to understand consumers' interpersonal communication styles before creating effective strategies for targeting. Linking humor styles to culture, gender, and education, the findings provide clear patterns guiding digital marketing managers in targeting specific segments. For example, when targeting less educated Hispanic consumers via electronic means, using both English and Spanish humor messages can be more intriguing for the audience. When crafting targeting strategies using humor messages, digital marketing managers should deliberately consider culture, gender, and education to create exceptional humor cues. Vice versa, the misuse of humor styles in communication with certain consumer segments may cause adverse effects. For example, it may not be wise to use aggressive humor style to start an electronic message to Hispanic consumers.

LIMITATION AND FUTURE RESEARCH RECOMMENDATIONS

A noteworthy limitation of the current study is the small sample size of humor usage. Although a total of 400 Hispanic Facebook users are coded, only 93 are actually in the sample to study humor usage. The small sample size limits the power of statistical testing. If there were sufficient number of cases collected and content analyzed for the comparison of different humor styles, compelling evidence can be provided to the five hypotheses. Thus, future research should collect a larger sample to validate and re-test the hypotheses.

The sample collected consists of ages between 18 and 50. The youth generation across cultures has a unique "young culture" that is not culturally bound (Kjeldgaard & Askegaard, 2006). In today's social environment in the U.S., Hispanic youth may share great similarity with Caucasian youth in interpersonal communications. However, the impact of age group is not taken into consideration. Future research should include the impact of young culture in the study of Hispanic humor styles.

The results of this study rely only on content analysis of a convenience sample of Facebook user profiles. Behavioral variables used to compare the consequences of different humor styles are not included. Future research should extend the findings in the current study to include the behavioral outcomes associated with humor usage. For example, are those individuals who use affiliate humor style more effective in virtual networking compared to those who use aggressive humor style, or those who do not use humor at all? Besides examining additional quantifiable information in the Facebook user profiles, interviews or surveys might offer much interesting other variables to be included in future analysis.

Our early attempt to investigate humor usage and humor styles of Hispanic Americans in the virtual environment may inspire cross-platform and cross-cultural studies in the future. Future research should collect additional data in face-to-face settings to compare the differences of humor usage between computer-mediated communication (e.g., Facebook) and face-to-face communication. Another approach is to collect multicultural data and make comparisons between Hispanic Americans and other cultures to gain insights on the differences of humor styles across cultures.

REFERENCES

Alba, R. D. (1995). Assimilation's quiet tide. *The Public Interest, 119*, 3–18.

Apte, M. L. (1985). *Humor and laughter: An anthropological approach*. Ithaca, NY: Cornell University Press.

Arnould, E. J., & Thompson, C. J. (2005). Consumer culture theory (CCT): Twenty years of research. *The Journal of Consumer Research, 31*(4), 868–882. doi:10.1086/426626

Beard, F. K. (2008). Advertising and audience offense: The role of intentional humor. *Journal of Marketing Communications*, *14*(1), 1–17. doi:10.1080/13527260701467760

Bem, S. L. (1981). Gender schema theory: A cognitive account of sex typing source. *Psychological Review*, *88*(4), 354–364. doi:10.1037/0033-295X.88.4.354

Bishop, M., & Peterson, M. (2011). Comprende code-switching? Young Mexican-Americans' attitudes and responses to language alternation in print advertising. *Journal of Advertising Research*, *51*(4), 650–659. doi:10.2501/JAR-51-4-648-659

Burke, P. J., & Tully, J. (1977). The measurement of role identity. *Social Forces*, *55*(4), 881–897. doi:10.2307/2577560

Camoroff, J. L., & Camoroff, J. (2009). *Ethnicity Inc*. Chicago, IL: Chicago Press. doi:10.7208/chicago/9780226114736.001.0001

Chen, G. H., & Martin, R. A. (2007). A comparison of humor styles, coping humor, and mental health between Chinese and Canadian university students. *Humor: International Journal of Humor Research*, *20*(3), 215–234. doi:10.1515/HUMOR.2007.011

Copeland, L., & Griggs, L. (1986). *Going International: How to make friends and deal effectively in the global marketplace*. New York: Random House.

Cruthirds, K., Wang, V., Wang, Y., & Wei, J. (2012). A comparison of humor styles in U.S. and Mexican television commercials. *Marketing Intelligence & Planning*, *30*(4), 1–15. doi:10.1108/02634501211231856

Duffy, R. D., & Klingaman, E. A. (2009). Ethnic identity and career development among first-year college students. *Journal of Career Assessment*, *17*(3), 286–297. doi:10.1177/1069072708330504

Feinberg, L. (1971). *Asian laughter: An anthology of oriental satire and humor*. New York: Weatherhill.

Fritsche, I., & Jonas, E. (2005). Gender conflict and worldview defense. *British Journal of Social Psychology*, *44*(4), 571–581. doi:10.1348/014466605X27423 PMID:16368020

Galloway, G. (2010). Individual differences in personal humor styles: Identification of prominent patterns and their associates. *Personality and Individual Differences*, *48*(5), 563–567. doi:10.1016/j.paid.2009.12.007

Grinstein, A., & Nisan, U. (2009). Demarketing, minorities, and national attachment. *Journal of Marketing*, *73*(2), 105–122. doi:10.1509/jmkg.73.2.105

Gushue, G. V., & Whitson, M. L. (2006). The relationship of ethnic identity and gender role attitudes to the development of career choice goals among Black and Latina girls. *Journal of Counseling Psychology*, *53*(3), 379–385. doi:10.1037/0022-0167.53.3.379

Hall, E. T. (1976). *Beyond cultures*. Garden City, NY: Anchor Press.

Hatzithomas, L., Zotos, Y., & Boutsouki, C. (2011). Humor and cultural values in print advertising: A cross-cultural study. *International Marketing Review*, *28*(1), 57–80. doi:10.1108/02651331111107107

Herpen, E., Nierop, E., & Sloot, L. (2012). The relationship between in-store marketing and observed sales for organic versus fair trade products. *Marketing Letters*, *23*(1), 293–308. doi:10.100711002-011-9154-1

Hoffman, R. M., & Borders, I. D. (2001). Twenty-five years after regarding classification variability. *Measurement & Evaluation in Counseling & Development*, *34*(1), 39–55. doi:10.1080/07481756.200 1.12069021

Hofstede, G. (1980). *Culture's consequences: International differences in work-related values*. Newbury Park, CA: Sage Publications.

Jansson, J., Marell, A., & Nordlund, A. (2011). Exploring consumer adoption of a high involvement eco-innovation using value-belief-norm theory. *Journal of Consumer Behaviour*, *10*(1), 51–60. doi:10.1002/cb.346

Kalliny, M., Cruthirds, K., & Minor, M. S. (2006). Differences between American, Egyptian and Lebanese humor styles: Implications for international management. *International Journal of Cross Cultural Management*, *6*(1), 121–134. doi:10.1177/1470595806062354

Kashima, Y., Yamaguchi, S., Kim, U., Choi, S. C., Gelfand, M. J., & Yuki, M. (1995). Culture, gender, and self: A perspective from individualism-collectivism research. *Journal of Personality and Social Psychology*, *69*(5), 925–937. doi:10.1037/0022-3514.69.5.925 PMID:7473038

Kassarjian, H. H. (1977). Content analysis in consumer research. *The Journal of Consumer Research*, *4*(1), 8–18. doi:10.1086/208674

Kazarian, S., & Martin, R. A. (2006). Humor styles, culture-related personality, well-being, and family adjustment among Armenians in Lebanon. *Humor: International Journal of Humor Research*, *19*(4), 405–423. doi:10.1515/HUMOR.2006.020

Kjeldgaard, D., & Askegaard, S. (2006). The glocalization of youth culture: The global youth segment as structures of common difference. *The Journal of Consumer Research*, *33*(2), 231–247. doi:10.1086/506304

Laroche, M., Nepomuceno, M., Huang, L., & Richard, M. (2011). What's so funny? The use of humor in magazine advertising in the United States, China, and France. *Journal of Advertising Research*, *51*(2), 404–416. doi:10.2501/JAR-51-2-404-416

Lee, Y. H., & Lim, E. A. (2008). What's funny and what's not: The moderating role of cultural orientation in ad humor. *Journal of Advertising*, *37*(2), 71–84. doi:10.2753/JOA0091-3367370206

Livingston, S. (1992). Marketing to the Hispanic-American community. *The Journal of Business Strategy*, *13*(2), 54–57. doi:10.1108/eb039483 PMID:10117144

Luna, D., & Peracchio, L. A. (2002). Uncovering the cognitive duality of bilinguals through word association. *Psychology and Marketing*, *19*(6), 457–475. doi:10.1002/mar.10020

Martin, R. A., Puhlik-Doris, P., Larsen, G., Gray, J., & Weir, K. (2003). Individual differences in uses of humor and their relation to psychological well-being: Development of the Humor Styles Questionnaire. *Journal of Research in Personality*, *37*(1), 48–75. doi:10.1016/S0092-6566(02)00534-2

Miczo, N., Averbeck, J. M., & Mariani, T. (2009). Affiliative and aggressive humor, attachment dimensions, and interaction goals. *Communication Studies, 60*(5), 443–459. doi:10.1080/10510970903260301

Mueller, B. (1992). Standardization vs. specification: An examination of westernization in Japanese advertising. *Journal of Advertising Research, 32*(1), 15–24.

Nevo, O., Nevo, B., & Yin, J. L. (2001). Singaporean humor: A cross-cultural cross-gender comparison. *The Journal of General Psychology, 128*(2), 143–156. doi:10.1080/00221300109598904 PMID:11506045

Padilla, A. M. (1980). The role of cultural awareness and ethnic loyalty in acculturation. In A. M. Padilla (Ed.), *Acculturation: Theory, Models, and Some New Findings* (pp. 47–84). Boulder, CO: Westview Press.

Robb, C. A., Reynolds, L. M., & Abdel-Ghany, M. (2007). Consumer preference among fluid milks: Low-fat vs. high-fat milk consumption in the United States. *International Journal of Consumer Studies, 31*(1), 90–94. doi:10.1111/j.1470-6431.2006.00492.x

Ruch, W. (1992). Assessment of appreciation of humor: Studies with the 3WD humor test. In C. D. Spielberger & J. N. Butcher (Eds.), *Advances in Personality Assessment* (Vol. 9). Hillsdale, NJ: Erlbaum.

Scott, W. (1955). Reliability of content analysis: The case of nominal scale coding. *Public Opinion Quarterly, 19*(3), 321–325. doi:10.1086/266577

Speck, P. S. (1991). The humorous message taxonomy: A framework for the study of humorous ads. *Journal of Current Issues and Research in Advertising, 13*(1/2), 1–44.

Spotts, H., Weinberger, M. G., & Parson, A. L. (1997). Assessing the use and impact of humor on advertising effectiveness: A contingency approach. *Journal of Advertising, 26*(3), 17–32. doi:10.1080/00913367.1997.10673526

Tajfel, H., & Turner, J. C. (1986). The social identity theory of intergroup behavior. In S. Worchel & W. G. Austin (Eds.), *Psychology of intergroup relations*. Chicago, IL: Nelson-Hall.

Teng, L. Y., Morgan, G. A., & Anderson, S. K. (2001). Career development among ethnic and age groups of community college students. *Journal of Career Development, 28*(2), 115–127. doi:10.1177/089484530102800203

Toncar, M. F. (2001). The use of humour in television advertising: Revisiting the US-UK comparison. *International Journal of Advertising, 20*(4), 521–539. doi:10.1080/02650487.2001.11104909

Triandis, H. C. (1989). The self and social behavior in differing cultural contexts. *Psychological Review, 96*(3), 506–520. doi:10.1037/0033-295X.96.3.506

U.S. Census Bureau. (2012a). Who's Hispanic in America? Retrieved from http://www.census.gov/newsroom/cspan/hispanic/2012.06.22_cspan_hispanics.pdf

Voelker, D. H., & Orton, P. Z. (1993). *Statistics*. Lincoln, NE: Cliffs Notes.

Wilson, R. T. (2007). Acculturation and discrimination in the global market place: The case of Hispanics in the U.S. *Journal of International Consumer Marketing, 20*(1), 67–78. doi:10.1300/J046v20n01_06

Wurtz, E. (2005). A cross-cultural analysis of websites from high-context cultures and low-context cultures. *Journal of Computer-Mediated Communication, 11*(1). doi:10.1111/j.1083-6101.2006.tb00313.x

Zeigler-Hill, V., & Besser, A. (2011). Humor style mediates the association between pathological narcissism and self-esteem. *Personality and Individual Differences, 50*(8), 1196–1201. doi:10.1016/j.paid.2011.02.006

This research was previously published in the International Journal of E-Business Research (IJEBR), 16(1); pages 60-73, copyright year 2020 by IGI Publishing (an imprint of IGI Global).

Chapter 72
The Tipping Point:
A Comparative Study of U.S. and Korean Users on Decisions to Switch Social Media Platforms

Soo Kwang Oh
Pepperdine University, USA

Seoyeon Hong
Rowan University, USA

Hee Sun Park
Korea University, South Korea

ABSTRACT

While previous researchers have addressed motivations to join and continue using social media, this paper focuses on why users quit certain social media and change their favorite platforms, such as the current shift from Facebook to Twitter to Instagram and Snapchat. Furthermore, this exploratory study seeks to build an understanding of social media usage and motivations for switching from a cross-cultural perspective by comparing findings from Korean and U.S. users. Findings from 19 focus group sessions (n = 118) highlight influences regarding modes of usage, user control, commitment, addiction, privacy, perceived relationships, self-construals, and social/cultural trends. Findings are further analyzed and compared in light of relevant theoretical frameworks and cultural differences.

INTRODUCTION

Popularity of social media platforms changes constantly, and there seems to be no infinite winner. For instance, MySpace was the most visited social networking site in 2008, attracting almost 80 million visitors a month (Robards, 2012); now its service has been discontinued. Cyworld used to be Korea's most popular social media site 15 years ago when it had 18 million members, which accounted for a third of

DOI: 10.4018/978-1-6684-6307-9.ch072

the nation's population (Han, 2017). Its user base declined drastically and has been replaced by other services. Likewise, KakaoStory once had monthly active users of 42 million (Sprinklr, 2017), only to lose a significant number recently.

The trend continues on: Facebook, the most active and popular social media site in the last decade, is undergoing a decrease in the number of daily active users for the first time, dropping by a million users compared to the previous year (Wagner & Molla, 2018). The social networking service is losing users in the younger demographic, who are increasingly abandoning it for other social media sites such as Snapchat and Instagram (Smith & Anderson, 2018). Twitter also reported losing one million monthly active users in the second quarter of 2018, resulting in a 21% one-day plunge in stock prices (Shaban & Timberg, 2018).

While motivations for using social media have been well-studied (Park & Lee, 2014; Ross et al., 2009; Ryan & Xenos, 2011), there is relatively limited understanding as to why users decide to reduce their use of one social media *and* start another. We believe different cultural norms could influence reasons for discontinuing use of an SNS platform. Therefore, examining the role culture plays in social media usage would be important for establishing scholarly and practical foundations regarding why some platforms retain users and others do not.

To address these questions, the present study attempts to identify why people shift to other platforms by examining motivators and deterrents for using social media, and also by incorporating cultural comparisons. In so doing, this study presents an exploratory look into how cultural background influences the motivation to switch among platforms, resting on the interface of new media research coupled with a cross-cultural approach.

LITERATURE REVIEW

As social media have evolved, users have engaged with the platform, the content and each other, establishing a way of life as it pertains to online—a digital culture (Miller, 2011). Digital culture is unique in that it is shaped and reshaped so quickly, highly participatory and unpredictable (Deuze, 2006), and also because it is highly influential (Enli, 2017). Scholars and practitioners examine social media culture to understand trends (Chae, Stephen, Bart, & Yao, 2017; Jiang, Luo, & Kulemeka, 2016).

Digital culture influences the platform on which they engage, and vice versa. Digital users form virtual communities and culture (Wu Song, 2009). Members determine desired ways to interact with each other, including community-specific practices on word usage and adequate behavior (Sherman, Payton, Hernandez, Greenfield, & Dapretto, 2016). At the same time, the very online space on which users interact influences the usage and culture. That is, specific features and characteristics of social media platforms also determine a collective set of attitudes, behaviors and trends among users (Robards, 2012).

We focus specifically on how these attitudes, behaviors and trends have changed, particularly to understand why people switch to new social media. We believe that the "switch" behavior occurs in two ways: *Switching from a platform* and *switching to a platform*. Users may decide to move away from a platform due to deterrents in their current usage, but also to move toward a new platform due to incentives that attract them to do so. Drawing from pertinent literature, theoretical frameworks for understanding the decision to switch from or to a social media platform can be explained in two levels: 1) at the individual level, associated with the user's own approval (or lack thereof) and 2) at the social level, having to do with communal interactions or pressure/appeal based on such.

Switching From Existing Platforms

An emerging line of research illustrates various factors regarding why users may elect to opt out of social media platforms. This is an important aspect to examine, since quitting one social media does not necessarily stop usage altogether; usage is reshaped in continuation because users still seek engagement through social media.

At the individual user level, studies have found that switching from/quitting a platform occurs due to decreased interest, information overload and concerns on addiction. Empirical findings indicate that users express dissatisfaction when they perceive content to be uninteresting, trivial or banal (Baker & White, 2011; Baumer et al., 2013). Another significant factor deterring usage of social media is information overload. In the age of multiple channels and an abundance of data, escalating amounts of content become too much for a user to handle (Maier, Laumer, & Eckhardt, 2015). This is also closely associated with users' discomfort regarding increased amounts of annoying content (e.g., too many/irrelevant posts, advertisements) (Rainie, Smith, & Duggan, 2013). Also, as users immerse themselves in social media, they become weary of their addiction (Young, Kuss, Griffiths, & Howard, 2017), which at times results in leaving as a countermeasure (Schoenebeck, 2014).

From a social point of view, privacy concerns are a significant factor for quitting a social media platform. This has particularly been prevalent in Facebook studies. For instance, Stieger and colleagues (2013) found that concerns for privacy were stronger among Facebook quitters than current users. Another study posted that violation of privacy may be a make-or-break factor for social media participation (Dindar & Akbulut, 2014).

Moreover, peer and social pressure is another significant factor: When close friends suggest that a certain platform is outdated or undesirable, one may decide to leave (Baumer et al., 2013). This is particularly notable because influences from a collective of users and their behavior shape users' decisions to move away from a social media platform. We believe this could be further explained through the role that culture plays in creating social pressure or diminishing one's satisfaction of a platform.

Switching to New Platforms

On the flipside, people may be motivated to move to new social media platforms because of some kind of appeal. At the individual level, users are enticed with desired features and content. A new service may become available with multimedia components, interactive functions (e.g., commenting, "like" or "share" buttons), or an attractive user interface (Nelson-Field, Riebe, & Sharp, 2012). Such features enhance the user experience and results in increased usage and popularity of a platform (Martin, 2012).

When it comes to social level factors, trends in society—often recognized through activities of social influencers (e.g., celebrities, politicians)—increase the willingness of a user to move to a new platform (Colapinto & Benecchi, 2014). If someone sees their favorite public figure on new social media, they are inclined to try the platform to engage with the mediated figures (Claessens & Van den Bulck, 2015; Colapinto & Benecchi, 2014). Increased media coverage and exposure also hint a new trend or perceived popularity, making the move appealing. As noted in the scarcity principle, the individual does not want to miss out on a trendy social media platform by not acting fast enough (Mittone & Savadori, 2009).

Moreover, a combination of the above increases the likelihood of content receiving more spotlight. This can be further explained with how new platforms become the go-to venue for viral content (Alhabash & McAlister, 2015; Yang & Wang, 2015).

Finally, attitudes and behaviors of other users influence the motivation to move to new platforms. When close friends move to new platforms, users will be inclined to move as well because they seek to interact with their companions (S. L. Lee, Kim, Golden, Kim, & Park, 2016). Credibility is another related factor, since close acquaintances are trusted more for decision making, even when online (Chae et al., 2017). In addition, this kind of user connection spreads through multiple networks at a rapid rate, significantly affecting how social trends are gauged.

Motives to leave current platforms or to move to new platforms are reciprocally associated with why people transition among platforms. However, we note that the literature is scarce when it comes to pinpointing influences that bring about the "switch." Therefore, this study integrated the two motives in addressing why users shift from one platform to another.

Cultural Considerations

Concurrently, this study explores how the aforementioned motives can be analyzed across cultures. This is especially important because social media usage is influenced by culture, and vice versa. Pertinent literature highlights a number of relevant theoretical frameworks.

Hofstede's Cultural Dimensions

Hofstede (1983) discussed various differences among cultures, particularly Eastern and Western, with the concept of cultural dimensions. Considering the abovementioned social-level factors for switching, a key concept for this study is that of collectivism vs. individualism: In Eastern culture an individual emphasizes the group needs over his/her own needs and the opposite in Western culture. The GLOBE study (Chhokar, Brodbeck, & House, 2007) of 25 cultures further divided collectivism into two sub-categories: Institutional collectivism (collectivism I), referring to the degree to which societal institutional practices encourage and reward the collective distribution of resources and collective action, and in-group collectivism (collectivism II) where individuals express pride, loyalty, and cohesiveness in their social institutions (Schlagwein & Prasarnphanich, 2014, p. 125).

In the context of social media, the differences between individualist and collectivist cultures and corresponding social media usage suggest that social media motivation differs across cultures. Choi and Im (2012) found that Korean users displayed collectivistic behaviors, posting more tweets promoting group harmony than their U.S. counterparts. Kang et al. (2015) also found that U.S. participants use multiple social media (individualistic characteristics) and Korean participants stick to a single one due to their collectivistic culture. We also believe that in the East, in-group collectivism will be especially stronger when it comes to social media use. This is also related to social influence theory (Kelman, 1958, p. 32), where an individual behaves to be more like others (conformity; p. 53). In a culture where in-group collectivism is strong, needs for belonging and esteem are sought through approval from others—we believe the same applies to social media behavior.

High vs. Low Context

Hall (1976, 1989) posits that societies can be categorized as high or low context. This refers to the amount of shared context within cultures that enable the meaning-making of communication messages. Eastern countries such as Korea, Japan, Taiwan, and China are considered high-context societies, where most of the information in a communication message is readily shared by members of society. Therefore, little information is needed in the coded message, and more implicit and indirect communication may occur. On the other hand, low-context societies such as the U.S., Germany and northern European countries (Hall & Hall, 1990, pp. 6-14) require an abundance of information to be explicitly embedded in communication messages. This is because a low context society lacks a common understanding that allows for facilitated decoding. Relating this differentiation to the abovementioned cultural dimensions, high-context communication is used predominantly in collectivist cultures and low-context in individualistic cultures (Chan, Li, Diehl, & Terlutter, 2007, p. 162).

Relating to the switching to/from discussion above, high vs. low context cultures pose theoretical grounds for understanding the switch motives at the social level. In a high context culture, an individual seemingly has a better understanding of others' ideas, attitudes and behaviors. Thus, motives such as peer pressure (switching from) and social trends (switching to) would have higher influence in these cultures. On the other hand, in low context cultures we may see that individual level motives are stronger, especially if a platform's features enhance or reduce the ability to express one's opinions.

Self-Construal

Self-construal is another noteworthy concept for understanding cultural differences in the social media context. It refers to how an individual construe themselves in light of how they are perceived by others. Markus and Kitayama (1991) argued that Eastern and Western individuals have "strikingly different construals of the self, of others, and of the interdependence of the two." (p. 224) The interdependence results in self-definition and how features of the self are influenced by relations with others. Individuals in many Asian cultures define the self closely based on the fundamental relatedness of individuals to each other—the emphasis is on harmony, "we-ness," and fitting in. On the other hand, Western culture values autonomy in social practice, fostering a more independent self-construal, where uniqueness is promoted and the individual is less conscious of how their own thoughts, feelings and actions will be perceived by others.

To elaborate, Yoo's (2012) analysis of why and how people use social network sites revealed that Korean participants focused on others, pursuing social/emotional support. Moreover, Koreans hesitated to publicly post their thoughts on social media because they were concerned with how others will judge them, whereas U.S. participants stated they freely post their ideas on Twitter and Facebook. Another study found that Asians used social media to maintain contacts and updates with friends rather than going in depth to view others' profiles or posts (S. L. Lee et al., 2016).

This is related to social bridging as well as the need to engage in self-construal by managing relationships based on how others will view the self. Kim and Papacharissi (2009) found that Korean web authors tended to use interlinks and photos of others, which allow for an indirect expression of social status and linking themselves to social groups and institutions (associated with interdependent self-construal in collectivistic cultures). On the contrary, U.S. virtual actors engaged more frequently in direct expression of the self, utilizing direct texts/photos and indicating their likes/dislikes, which is relevant to individualistic and low-context societies. In sum, primary self-construals may differ in individualistic and collectivist cultures, possibly influencing social media usage and discontinuance.

Incorporating theoretical frameworks on social media usage behavior and cultural contexts, we believe that the current study sheds light on understanding users' attitudes and behaviors related to switching social media. This inquiry is valuable as it extends our knowledge on how social media usage trigger changes in social trends from a cross-cultural perspective. Therefore, we pose the following research questions:

RQ1: What social media platforms do users in the U.S. and Korea use, and what aspects attract them to use those platforms?
RQ2: What do social media users in the U.S. and Korea dislike about social media?
RQ3: What makes U.S. and Korean social media users switch to another platform?

RQ1 and RQ2 seek to address the switching to/from factors—by understanding what social media platforms are being used and what users like/dislike about them, we are able to come up with possible causes that make a user abandon certain platforms or adopt new ones. The third question puts these potential factors in a continuum of social media usage by asking participants about what happened when they actually switched platforms. Synthesizing findings from the three questions will further help compare this phenomenon in the two cultures, U.S. and Korea.

METHOD

This study compared social media users in the U.S. and Korea. We conducted focus group interviews as they allow for a rich, in-depth look at topics through inter-participant interactions (Adams, 2000). We deemed the method appropriate for identification of key themes for exploratory inquiries and an elaboration of those findings through follow-up questions and group discussion (Morgan, 1996).

Sample

Total of 118 social media users were recruited for qualitative data collection. Specifically, nine sessions in Korea and ten in the U.S. were conducted with the goal of eliciting information about the respondents' uses of and motivations on social media, aspects they like or dislike, reasons for joining, reasons for quitting, and reasons for switching to a new social media platform (see table 1). Given the exploratory nature of the study, the sample size was considered adequate. In previous studies with similar approaches, Yoo (2012) interviewed 37 participants, Schoenebeck (2014) had 12 interviewees in a study about giving up Twitter, and Turan, Tinmaz and Goktaz (2013) recruited 20 participants for their social media motivation study.

These countries were selected because of salient differences noted in the literature regarding their communication styles based on cultural contexts. Both countries display high social media usage rates, but comparative studies have noted distinct differences regarding user preferences (H. Kang et al., 2015), modes of online interaction (S. L. Lee et al., 2016), responses to social/political issues (S. Y. Choi & Cho, 2017; S. Kang, Shim, & Kim, 2019), and trends (Oh & Choi, 2017).

Participants from both countries were undergraduate students between 19 and 25 years of age, which represents a key social media user demographic. They were recruited from undergraduate classes from universities in the U.S. and Korea. This recruiting method provided convenient access to the target population, and allowed for stronger social ties (i.e. affinity) as well as similarity in age, education, and social value. Therefore, the sample was a proper representation for addressing the research questions. Everyone in the sample had an experience of switching social media. Almost all participants from Korea had Facebook accounts ($n = 47$) and 75% of them used Instagram ($n = 42$). On the other hand, U.S. participants ($n = 65$) mainly comprised of Instagram and Snapchat, users, with about 30% of them no longer using Facebook.

Procedure

Each session lasted 45 to 60 minutes and was audiotaped. Sessions in each country were conducted in participants' native tongue (English and Korean respectively), and the translation of Korean materials to English was adequately executed as all authors are fluently bilingual in both languages. Transcripts of Korean and U.S. sessions were separately analyzed in order to examine cross-cultural differences.

Questions were drawn from existing literature (Baumer et al., 2013; Borowitz, 2013; Rainie et al., 2013; Robards, 2012) on motivations for quitting social media and further developed through a pilot session. In relation to motives regarding the switch to/from platforms, we asked about deterrents or incentives on using social media, and more specifically, how and why participants made the transition. Our questions included, "What was your first social media?" "Why did you stop using previous social media?" "What do you look for in social media?" "What prompted you to start a new one?" and "Why did you move from one to another?" Additional follow-up questions were posed in response to the group discussions.

Table 1. Focus group sessions in U.S. and Korea

	Number of Participants	
	Korea	**U.S.**
Session 1	6	7
Session 2	7	8
Session 3	8	8
Session 4	7	6
Session 5	7	7
Session 6	5	5
Session 7	5	7
Session 8	5	6
Session 9	4	6
Session 10	N/A	5
Total	53	65

Analysis

By listening to audio recordings and reading the transcripts, the researchers analyzed the data for any emerging ideas regarding motivational and behavioral elements associated with switching social media, and also contextual/cultural factors associated with these issues. Once an initial analysis of the data was complete, concepts were then grouped under larger categories to extract themes. These themes and their relationships were further analyzed and developed into theoretical constructs. Researchers also reviewed the themes and concepts for their consistency across each cultural context to ensure reliability of the data.

FINDINGS

RQ 1 asked what social media platforms participants in the U.S. and Korea use, and what aspects attract them to use those platforms. The following themes emerged.

Adopting Social Media: Breadth, Depth and Differences

Participants in the U.S. showed they adopted more new platforms and used them on a regular basis. U.S. participants mentioned more social media platforms that have used or are currently using (e.g., Facebook, Twitter, Instagram, Snapchat, Reddit, Tumblr, Pinterest, LinkedIn, YouTube, Tinder, and formerly Vine). Korean participants, with the exception of few, only spoke of Facebook and Instagram. U.S. participants in particular noted a more extensive history of adopting new platforms, and showed more depth and activeness in utilizing social media. For them, exploring new platforms and introductory features (e.g., filters on Snapchat, direct messaging on Twitter and Instagram, stories on Instagram) were attractive. On the other hand, Korean participants spoke of less variety in their social media activities, explaining that they are passive in usage, mostly to view content and kill time:

- "I started with Facebook, and then created a Twitter account, Instagram, and then Snapchat. I joined each service because of some new feature they had, like filters and stories. I stay in touch with all of those platforms still." (U.S. participant)
- "I do have a wide variety of social media I use on the daily … Before I go to sleep, there is like this ritual where I go around each one and perform specific tasks, like reacting to a story [on Instagram] or retweeting [on Twitter]." (U.S. Participant)
- "I actually deleted other social media apps. I just have Facebook and Instagram, and I only open them when I'm waiting for the subway or just to kill time, like for five minutes. I only scroll to see if there is something interesting, and that's it." (Korean participant)

Using Social Media: To Each Their Own

Over time, the participants reported they formed a specific purpose, usage pattern and liking for each platform. Responses differed for the two countries. Korean users for instance specifically pointed to a clear distinction on how each platform is used, citing "cultural norms." In several group discussions participants agreed that Facebook is normally used to post more significant events in life while Instagram serves as a place to document everyday life. According to the group conversations, Koreans treated Facebook as a "loud, open public space" while Instagram was regarded as a "quiet, private place." A notable finding related to this theme was that only Korean participants keen on sharing political ideas chose Facebook or Twitter as their favorite platform. All others preferred Instagram.

On the other hand, U.S. participants used Facebook mainly for networking, Twitter for information consumption and quick expression of ideas/opinions, and Instagram/Snapchat for entertainment. Unlike Korean participants who noted making distinctions for how to use the platforms based on what they perceived to be the social trend, U.S. participants reported establishing usage habits based on individual preferences:

- "I observed posts from others, and it looked like this is the way Instagram was supposed to be used, to post little things about life." (Korean participant)
- "I know that people don't use Twitter just to get news, but over time it's become like that. I don't interact with anybody on Twitter—for that I use Facebook or Instagram ... I try to figure out what works best for me." (U.S. Participant)

RQ 2 asked participants about things they did not like about social media, because negative perceptions or experiences on social media could arguably be key a key reason for a user's decision to leave the platform. From this discussion, the following themes were identified. In general, participants' current "dislikes" were focused largely on Facebook.

Leaving Social Media: No Control, No Friends, No More

This was a theme in both countries regarding Facebook. Because the platform does not allow for much control over what the user sees on the feed (i.e., in comparison to follower-based platforms such as Twitter and Instagram), participants discussed their dissatisfaction on both the content and layout.

Overall, we were able to conclude that this issue arose due to two main elements: 1) The Facebook network becomes overwhelming due to the fact that participants have had the longest history of using the platform and the massive network they had as a result; and 2) irrelevant content such as advertisements, posts from strangers, etc.

- "Some of us call Facebook a wrecked social media, because it shows you irrelevant content that one distant friend of yours may have 'liked' or commented on. It looks so ugly and when you see the comments from strangers, they are so mean and messy." (Korean participant)
- "I hate that Facebook has so many ads that don't even interest me. I think it's because it misunderstands my interests." (U.S. participant)

Related to the above, the kinds of relationships, or lack thereof, were possible turnoffs for participants. For instance, participants from both countries have had Facebook for a long time (five years or longer), and therefore the friends they have on the platform are not as relevant anymore. Also, because it is the most widely used platform, participants (more saliently in the U.S.) mentioned that they do not feel comfortable posting things on Facebook because there are too many eyes (e.g., parents, relatives, employers, distant friends).

A key difference was that Korean participants in particular raised concerns regarding what "friend" on social media really means. For many Korean participants, friendship required a sense of closeness and affection. Therefore, Korean participants showed a tendency to steer away from posting on Facebook, but only on Instagram to comment on close friends' posts. For them to continue being active on social media, relational values were key.

Leaving Social Media: The "Push Notification" Pushes You Away

Analogous the "lack of control" theme, participants stopped using Facebook because it pushed too much information (e.g., targeted/sponsored ads) to the participants, and they were overwhelmed or irritated by it. Korean participants also mentioned similar experiences when leaving blogging platforms due to over-commercialization.

U.S. participants also brought up privacy concerns regarding Facebook, Instagram (targeted advertisements) and Snapchat (unknowingly being featured on a stranger's snap post). Of those mentioning personal information-related issues, Facebook was the only platform they actually ended up quitting. Instagram and Snapchat's trendiness and gratifying factors seemed to outweigh potential concerns for privacy:

- "Fake news on Facebook is very irritating and agitating." (Korean participant)
- "Facebook distributes sponsored content that are no longer user-generated. They are posts from politicians, advertisers, and entertainers. I don't want to waste my time reading those." (Korean participant)
- "I deleted Facebook because all of a sudden I saw too many targeted ads. If I bought a pair of sneakers somewhere, Facebook would show me shoe ads every day. I got a little creeped out, to be honest … (when asked about whether Instagram ads aren't worrisome) … Instagram is creepy too sometimes, but it's too fun for me right now to quit." (U.S. participant)

With the final research question, we specifically examined why users left previous social media *and* moved to new platforms. The following were recognized as themes illustrating motives for moving to a new platform.

Switching To: Peer Pressure

Peer pressure was the most prominent reason for moving to a new platform. U.S. and Korean participants alike referred to "I moved because my best friend(s) did" as the most important reason why they moved to new platforms. In fact, this reason was brought up in each of the nineteen sessions that were conducted. This aspect was most salient in the switch from AIM or MySpace to Facebook (U.S.) and Cyworld to Facebook (Korea).

However, we note the stark contrast between the two groups regarding the motives behind switching because of friends. U.S. participants sought more to express and share their thoughts and stories with their friends. To them, "sharing life" was important across all platforms, regardless of which one they switched to (less so with Facebook, as discussed below). Korean participants, en masse, consistently mentioned that they wanted to read or view content from their peers. If content from familiar users weren't available, the platform was less appealing to them. One Korean participant summed up their perspective as follows:

- "Once my friends leave the platform, there is no one posting things that I want to read. Also, no matter what I post, there is no longer an interaction because no one reads it. So, the enjoyment disappears." (Korean participant)

Switching To: The In- and Out- of Social Media Trends

This theme highlights the fact that as technology evolves, so do people and the trends/culture they create. Ever since their first social media, participants could gauge how "in" or popular the platform is, and were quick to adapt. Participants in both countries said they tried to understand social media trends from their peer groups, celebrities, news, and by exploring new platforms. This was discernible in the mention of "cool" and "hip" with regard to social media usage among participants in both countries.

Participants from both countries seemed to be sensitive to the trends from their peer groups as all reported on how they took friends' suggestions by heart. Also, as mobile technologies advanced, participants noted that their taste for interface and appearance evolved. The appearance factor was a key reason mentioned for transitioning from MySpace (U.S. only), KakaoStory (Korea only) or Facebook to Instagram:

- "I made it a point to learn how to use Twitter and all the functionalities, since that was the one now. I didn't want to fall behind." (U.S. participant)
- "Instagram looked very clean and visually appealing. I am a visual person, so it looked more stylish than the old-fashioned KakaoStory." (Korean participant)

In addition, participants from both countries stated how their interests changed over time. As they grew older, they became more fixated on certain hobbies or topics; considering that users' social media usage patterns were compartmentalized by platform, some users saw themselves heavily using one platform over another. An example could be found with those who quit previous social media that served general functions (e.g., MySpace, Cyworld, Facebook) and took to Twitter (politics, celebrities, sports) or Pinterest (fashion, crafts) for their interests.

Leaving, Switching, Then Streamlining

Once switching (or newly adopting), users reported simplifying or limiting the various social media platforms at hand. Participants, more so in Korea, commented on the difficulty of committing to and maintaining several social media accounts. One participant questioned, "Why do I need another platform when I have this one?" Notably, this discussion was brought up in discussing why Korean participants stopped using Twitter—it was too cumbersome to actively use it, resulting in a number of participants who either dropped it or never got to use it regularly.

Another key external factor unique to the Korean group came up: Spare time. Korean participants agreed that in their teenage years, social media use just was not feasible due to the heavy workload in school. Many participants experienced a lapse in social media use during their high school years, which naturally led them to stop using existing platforms, and then start new ones that were available when they entered college. Such lapses were never mentioned in the U.S. groups.

With the U.S. participants, addiction was also notable factor for limiting social media use. For instance, three sessions had a discussion about being concerned with addiction to social media. Some mentioned that they intentionally stopped using a social media platform (e.g., deleted the app), but also recalled that they came back after a taking a temporary leave. Interestingly, being overly committed to social media was the reason for leaving, but at the same time a reason they decided to come back:

- "I was worried about how much time I spent on Facebook and Twitter, and so I decided to delete both apps. But that only lasted for a couple of weeks because I needed to stay in touch with my family on Facebook and I missed venting on Twitter." (U.S. Participant)

DISCUSSION

The purpose of this study was to understand why people choose to leave current social media platforms and also why they start different ones. To this end, we explored 1) how participants use social media and what aspects they like about social media, 2) what they dislike about social media platforms they are currently using, and 3) in relation to the above, what made them (or make them want to) switch. In addition, we sought to compare cultural differences between U.S. and Korea based on findings from the above inquiries. The current study illustrates a number of theoretical implications, including those associated with cross-cultural differences.

From the literature, motives to switch to/from social media can be discussed in two levels: individual and social. Our findings are congruent to those from pertinent studies. At the individual level, focus group participants cited reasons such as changing interests, information overload, perceived user control, and addiction for leaving a platform. They mentioned new forms of usage and features as a motive to start a new platform. At the social level, reasons for leaving included peer pressure, privacy concerns and declining popularity of a platform, whereas finding friends and emerging trends were reasons for joining a platform.

We further sought to pinpoint users' motives for actual switching behavior (leaving one *and* starting another). Our key finding here was that these factors are interlinked and work together to influence the switch, a set of circumstances that might be called the *tipping point*. At this juncture, participants lose interest in a platform due to decreased interest at the individual level, confirming this weakened affection through observing a decline in meaningful social interactions. At the same time, these users pay attention to social trends and platforms that are growing in popularity. Eventually they try the new platform, and find ways to adopt its features and enjoy it. For participants in this study, the tipping point was salient in their recent or current move from Facebook (partly Twitter as well) to Instagram. From accounts of many others, a surge of users and content on Snapchat could be explained similarly.

Our approach to look into the switch behavior rather than just quitting or newly adopting was adequate, as we found that social media usage was constantly a continuum for all users, regardless of gender, age or nationality. Leaving one platform did not necessarily mean a steep decline in social media usage overall, as participants migrated to another platform. We also note that the continuous leaving/adopting/switching still resulted in a balanced and consistent level of usage. This was evident in our findings on commitment and self-control regarding how many social media platforms are used, by how much.

This study also explored the influence of culture and how participants from two different countries explained their social media switch decisions. Our findings can be analyzed and discussed in light of a number of theoretical frameworks on cross-cultural comparisons.

Our finding on the diversification and amount of social media usage is applicable to what Luo (2014) calls "width and depth" across cultures (p. 13). Indeed, U.S. participants showed more width and depth, whereas Koreans displayed reservations with regard to self-disclosure and maintained only few platforms (H. Kang et al., 2015). Koreans inclined to use social media for monitoring those around them, rather than for interacting with others (J. Y. Lee, Park, Na, & Kim, 2016). This is also consistent with previous studies showing U.S. users value social interaction (Pentina, Basmanova, & Zhang, 2016) as opposed to Koreans who seek social recognition and acknowledgment from others in their activities (Y. Kim, Sohn, & Choi, 2011).

Our findings can also be discussed in light of Hofstede's (1983) individualism and collectivism. U.S. participants utilized social media based on individual preferences/needs whereas Koreans allocated their social media resources based on social media culture perceived to be dominant. Particularly, Korean participants' discontinuance can be discussed in light of collectivism. Korean responses hinted in-group collectivism (Schlagwein & Prasarnphanich, 2014), where harmony and uniformity within smaller and emotionally close-knit groups are valued. Koreans' dissatisfaction towards and eventual abandoning of Facebook and Twitter for extremist content (political, social) may have stemmed from feeling placed out of the in-group comfort zone—disruption of harmony was a strong deterrent for Korean participants, whereas U.S. participants only mentioned individual grievances for other users or features.

The contrast between U.S. and Korean participants are also related to Hall's (1976, 1989) notion of high- vs. low-context societies. In a high-context culture, common understanding of coded messages is key. Exemplifying this, a unique concept known as "*nun-chi*" (van Rjin, Bahk, & Stappers, 2007, p. 157) was mentioned a number of times in the Korean sessions. It refers to the need and effort to quickly grasp this common understanding and comply with it—as Korea falls under a high-context society, participants attempted to apply their culture's shared and implied contexts in their social media usage. On the flipside, findings from the U.S. can be interpreted with low-context culture: In low-context societies, individual's intended messages are rarely read in the same ways by others because they do not share similar contexts in decoding messages. Therefore, those in a low-context society need to be more explicit and direct. We posit that this characteristic is associated with U.S. participants' propensity to actively post one's ideas, and also for more tolerance toward highly opinionated posts from others.

Such cultural differences help us further understand why transitions among platforms looks different in the two countries. For example, in the U.S. group, higher levels of interaction and active posting on social media led to more frequent use of social media, and in turn resulted in concerns for addiction. Some participants "shut off" the platform for a while but came back to it later because they wanted the interaction. On the other hand, Korean participants tended to permanently leave a platform once they determined it wasn't for their taste. In other words, underlying motives for using social media influenced social media selection, how much they were used and what the switch behavior looked like in the long run (Stieger et al., 2013).

Both U.S. and Korean responses mentioned friends and peers were key factors for moving to new social media. However, influence from friends and peers resulted in opposite behaviors: Viewing oneself based on how one is construed by others (especially close others) elicited more outward activity for U.S. participants and more passivity and reservations among Korean participants (H. Kim & Papacharissi, 2009; S. L. Lee et al., 2016).

When U.S. participants were concerned about what others might think of them, they looked for additional platforms and more opportunities to communicate with others so as to maximize positive interactions (e.g., views, likes, comments). This was pertinently visible in how participants described their move to Instagram and Snapchat. When they first started these platforms, they knew that their close friends were already users and wanted to post the best selfies (Instagram) and funniest content (Snapchat) that guaranteed, to quote a participant, "at least five likes." In many cases, increased interaction on the platforms seemed to contribute to an improved self-esteem and self-confidence regarding their own portrayals (Thumim, 2012).

On the other hand, Koreans were more careful and passive, often times refraining from seeking out new platforms or actively expressing their ideas due to concerns about others passing negative judgment. An exemplary concept that came up in the Korean sessions is the notion of *"gwan-jong."* The term translates into "attention-seeker" and is used in a negative way. It was mentioned multiple times in the Korean groups, both as something they disliked about social media platforms (Facebook, Twitter) and a reason why they did not actively post content. Many participants stopped using a platform when they saw *"gwan-jong"* users, or when starting a new platform, chose not to be as active lest they might be labeled as such.

In Korea's case, a culture critical of the overly active (Tobin, Vanman, Verreynne, & Saeri, 2014) and modesty being a virtue (Hahm, 2004; Zhang, Lin, Nonaka, & Beom, 2005) impacted social media activity, both within and across platforms. Perhaps due to this reason, Korean participants generally downplayed the amount of their social media activity—through follow-up questions, we learned that many Korean participants were using social media more than what they had stated at the beginning. This may closely be associated with how self-representations and modes of participation are shaped by cultural formations and expectations that come as a result (Thumim, 2012, p. 62).

Such findings on awareness of others call for future research on self-construals at the individual level. Throughout the focus group interviews, concerns on how friends/peers would view the self were a key topic that influenced both switching to/from platforms. In addition to overall cultural differences, reasons for quitting and switching could depend on individuals' self-construal tendencies: Even in collectivist culture, those with strong independent self-construal may object to dominant collectivism on social media. Meanwhile, those with strong interdependent self-construal may choose to move to a new platform because their in-group members have switched, regardless of dominant cultural contexts.

Other findings on reasons for switching included commitment and trendiness. As for commitment, we noticed how external factors such as spare time during teenage years could be a key determinant for a participant's social media usage and habits in their twenties. This is not solely a cultural matter, as factors such as spare time and daily tasks are determined by many aspects of society and its cultural practices. Trendiness and popularity have to do with changing interests and preferences. Participants reported that these interests changed due to many different influences—some mentioned peers or influencers, and others mentioned one's own desired personal growth, which are all elements that differ largely based on culture (Martin, 2012).

This paper presents practical implications for the industry as well. Inquiries made in this study aid our understanding of users' dissatisfactions that drove them to seek other social media. In turn, findings suggest the industry could better adapt to meet user needs and preferences when it comes to their switch behavior—engaging users sufficiently in this regard would bring more users and activity, thereby fostering successful business operations.

Many users reported Twitter or Cyworld to be confusing to use, and MySpace, KakaoStory and Facebook to be unattractive in image/text presentation. Such firsthand accounts call upon the social media industry to better grasp the user experience (UX) aspect (Ferrucci & Tandoc, 2015; Hermida, Fletcher, Korell, & Logan, 2012).

Also, the practitioners ought to revisit approaches to personalized content on social media. In both cultures, abundance of targeted content was a significant turnoff; social media companies and advertisers should carefully review the effectiveness of such content and properly control them. Moreover, modes of personal interaction (e.g., "friending," "following") should also be reconsidered to better suit the needs of current users and their digital culture. Obtaining and utilizing information on how users feel about the content, interface, people, or features will enable companies to enhance people's motivation to use the platform.

Finally, the cross-cultural analysis from this study will be helpful for catering to different cultural groups or possibly in localization efforts. That is, social media companies ought to examine what their services are being used most for in different cultural contexts, and focus on developing/promoting functionalities tailored to such.

While this study explored important aspects of social media use and sought to provide meaningful cultural comparisons, it is not without limitations. First of all, the topic of social media is a moving target, and new trends as well as platforms may arise—with different features and content—and change the dynamics greatly. Therefore, findings from a study such as this may become outdated rather quickly. For example, changes implemented to a social media platform may quickly result in dissatisfaction, just as this study found that a recent Snapchat update was cause for grief. Future scholars should continue to pay attention to trends and engage in the most relevant and meaningful inquiry. Second, while we were able to conduct focus groups with 118 participants, the sample is still somewhat small and limited to students. We do believe these choices were adequate for an exploratory study of this nature, but we should be careful not to overgeneralize from the findings. Rather, we hope that the detailed, qualitative inquiry from this study would help future studies consider expanding on the scope of this paper. Lastly, we acknowledge that for a future study opportunity on the topic, a more comprehensive, mixed-method approach may help enrich findings. That is, by first conducting a quantitative study to discern generalities and trends of social media usage and then following it up with qualitative data, future studies could explore more profoundly the underlying motivations for making the switch to new social media platforms.

REFERENCES

Adams, W. J. (2000). How people watch television as investigated using focus group techniques. *Journal of Broadcasting & Electronic Media*, *44*(1), 78–93. doi:10.120715506878jobem4401_6

Alhabash, S., & McAlister, A. R. (2015). Redefining virality in less broad strokes: Predicting viral behavioral intentions from motivations and uses of Facebook and Twitter. *New Media & Society*, *17*(8), 1317–1339. doi:10.1177/1461444814523726

Baker, R., & White, K. (2011). In their own words: Why teenagers don't use social networking sites. *Cyberpsychology, Behavior, and Social Networking*, *14*(6), 395–398. doi:10.1089/cyber.2010.0016 PMID:21117974

Baumer, E. P. S., Adams, P., Khovanskaya, V. D., Liao, T. C., Smith, M. E., Sosik, V. S., & Williams, K. (2013). *Limiting, Leaving, and (re)Lapsing: An exploration of Facebook non-use practices and experiences*. Paper presented at the SIGCHI Conference on Human Factors in Computing Systems, New York, NY. 10.1145/2470654.2466446

Borowitz, A. (2013, April 7). Facebook unveils new waste of time. *The New Yorker*. Retrieved from https://www.newyorker.com/humor/borowitz-report/facebook-unveils-new-waste-of-time

Chae, I., Stephen, A. T., Bart, Y., & Yao, D. (2017). Spillover effects in seeded word-of-mouth marketing campaigns. *Marketing Science*, *36*(1), 89–104. doi:10.1287/mksc.2016.1001

Chan, K., Li, L., Diehl, S., & Terlutter, R. (2007). Consumers' response to offensive advertising: A cross-cultural study. *International Marketing Review, 24*(5), 606–628. doi:10.1108/02651330710828013

Chhokar, J. S., Brodbeck, F. C., & House, R. J. (2007). *Culture and leadership across the world: The GLOBE book of in-depth studies of 25 societies*. Lawrence Erlbaum. doi:10.4324/9780203936665

Choi, K., & Im, I. (2012). *Considering cultural differences with the use of Twitter on a mobile communication device under a dispersed group collaboration context*. Paper presented at the Americas Conference on Information Systems, Seattle, WA.

Choi, S. Y., & Cho, Y. (2017). Generating Counter-Public Spheres Through Social Media: Two Social Movements in Neoliberalised South Korea. *Javnost-The Public, 24*(1), 15–33. doi:10.1080/13183222.2017.1267155

Claessens, N., & Van den Bulck, H. (2015). Parasocial relationships with audiences' favorite celebrities: The role of audience and celebrity characteristics in a representative Flemish sample. *Communications: The European Journal of Communication Research, 40*(1), 43–65. doi:10.1515/commun-2014-0027

Colapinto, C., & Benecchi, E. (2014). The presentation of celebrity personas in everyday twittering: Managing online reputations throughout a communication crisis. *Media Culture & Society, 36*(2), 219–233. doi:10.1177/0163443714526550

Deuze, M. (2006). Participation, remediation, bricolage: Considering principal components of a digital culture. *The Information Society, 22*(2), 63–75. doi:10.1080/01972240600567170

Dindar, M., & Akbulut, Y. (2014). Why do pre-service teachers quit Facebook? An investigation on 'quitters forever' and 'quitters for a while'. *Computers in Human Behavior, 39*, 170–176. doi:10.1016/j.chb.2014.07.007

Enli, G. (2017). Twitter as arena for the authentic outsider: Exploring the social media campaigns of Trump and Clinton in the 2016 US Presidential election. *European Journal of Communication, 32*(1), 50–61. doi:10.1177/0267323116682802

Ferrucci, P., & Tandoc, E. C. Jr. (2015). The Facebook experience: A phenomenology of Facebook use. *Online Journal of Communication and Media Technologies, 5*(3), 176–197. doi:10.29333/ojcmt/2523

Hahm, C. (2004). The ironies of Confucianism. *Journal of Democracy, 15*(3), 93–107. doi:10.1353/jod.2004.0046

Hall, E. T. (1989). Beyond culture. New York, NY: Anchor Books.

Hall, E. T., & Hall, M. R. (1990). *Understanding cultural differences: Germans, French, and Americans*. Intercultural Press.

Han, E. (2017). *Cyworld*. Retrieved from https://medium.com/@eugyh/cyworld-homepage-used-to-be-one-of-koreas-most-popular-social-media-sites-330b0706e6e

Hermida, A., Fletcher, F., Korell, D., & Logan, D. (2012). Share, like, recommend. *Journalism Studies, 13*(5/6), 815–824. doi:10.1080/1461670X.2012.664430

Hofstede, G. (1983). National cultures in four dimensions: A research-based theory of cultural differences among nations. *International Studies of Management & Organization, 13*(1-2), 46–74. doi:10.1080/00208825.1983.11656358

Jiang, H., Luo, Y., & Kulemeka, O. (2016). Social media engagement as an evaluation barometer: Insights from communication executives. *Public Relations Review, 42*(4), 679–691. doi:10.1016/j.pubrev.2015.12.004

Kang, H., Pang, S. S., & Choi, S. M. (2015). Investigating the use of multiple social networking services: A cross-cultural perspective in the United States and Korea. *Transactions on Internet and Information Systems (Seoul), 9*(8), 3258–3275. doi:10.3837/tiis.2015.08.031

Kang, S., Shim, K., & Kim, J. (2019). Social media posts on Samsung Galaxy Note 7 explosion: A comparative analysis of crisis framing and sntiments in three nations. *Journal of International Crisis & Risk Communication, 2*(2), 259–290. doi:10.30658/jicrcr.2.2.5

Kelman, H. C. (1958). Compliance, identification, and internalization: Three processes of attitude change. *The Journal of Conflict Resolution, 2*(1), 51–60. doi:10.1177/002200275800200106

Kim, H., & Papacharissi, Z. (2009). Cross-cultural differences in online self-presentation: A content analysis of personal Korean and U.S. home pages. *Asian Journal of Communication, 13*(1), 100–119. doi:10.1080/01292980309364833

Kim, Y., Sohn, D., & Choi, S. M. (2011). Cultural difference in motivations for using social network sites: A comparative study of American and Korean college students. *Computers in Human Behavior, 27*(1), 365–372. doi:10.1016/j.chb.2010.08.015

Lee, J. Y., Park, S., Na, E. Y., & Kim, E. Y. (2016). A comparative study on the relationship between social networking site and social capital among Australian and Korean youth. *Journal of Youth Studies, 19*(9), 1164–1183. doi:10.1080/13676261.2016.1145637

Lee, S. L., Kim, J., Golden, K. J., Kim, J. H., & Park, M. S. A. (2016). A cross-cultural examination of SNS usage intensity and managing interpersonal relationships online: The role of culture and the autonomous-related self-construal. *Frontiers in Psychology, 7*, 376. doi:10.3389/fpsyg.2016.00376 PMID:27148100

Luo, S. (2014). Cross-cultural differences between American and Chinese college students on self-disclosure on social media (Ph.D.). Iowa State University, Ames, IA. doi:10.31274/etd-180810-3185

Maier, C., Laumer, S., Eckhardt, A., & Weitzel, T. (2015). Giving too much social support: Social overload on social networking sites. *European Journal of Information Systems, 24*(5), 447–464. doi:10.1057/ejis.2014.3

Markus, H. R., & Kitayama, S. (1991). Culture and the self: Implications for cognition, emotion, and motivation. *Psychological Review, 98*(2), 224–253. doi:10.1037/0033-295X.98.2.224

Martin, S. D. (2012). *Share, like, tweet and cheer: An examination of social media usage and the NFL* (Doctor of Philosophy Dissertation). University of Illinois at Urbana-Champaign, Urbana, IL.

Miller, V. (2011). *Understanding digital culture.* Sage.

Mittone, L., & Savadori, L. (2009). The scarcity bias. *Applied Psychology*, *58*(3), 453–468. doi:10.1111/j.1464-0597.2009.00401.x

Morgan, D. (1996). *Focus groups as qualitative research* (2nd ed.). Sage.

Nelson-Field, K., Riebe, E., & Sharp, B. (2012). What's not to "like?": Can Facebook fan base give a brand the advertising reach it needs? *Journal of Advertising Research*, *52*(2), 262–269. doi:10.2501/JAR-52-2-262-269

Oh, S.-K., & Choi, H. (2017). Broadcasting upon a shooting star: Investigating the success of Afreeca TV's livestream personal broadcast model. *International Journal of Web Based Communities*, *13*(2), 193–212. doi:10.1504/IJWBC.2017.084414

Park, N., & Lee, S. (2014). College students' motivations for Facebook use and psychological outcomes. *Journal of Broadcasting & Electronic Media*, *58*(4), 601–620. doi:10.1080/08838151.2014.966355

Pentina, I., Basmanova, O., & Zhang, L. (2016). A cross-national study of Twitter users' motivations and continuance intentions. *Journal of Marketing Communications*, *22*(1), 36–55. doi:10.1080/13527266.2013.841273

Rainie, L., Smith, A., & Duggan, M. (2013). *Coming and going on Facebook*. Pew Research Center's Internet and American Life Project.

Robards, B. (2012). Leaving MySpace, joining Facebook: 'Growing up' on social network sites. *Continuum (Perth)*, *26*(3), 385–398. doi:10.1080/10304312.2012.665836

Ross, C., Orr, E. S., Sisic, M., Arseneault, J. M., Simmerling, M. G., & Orr, R. R. (2009). Personality and motivations associated with Facebook use. *Computers in Human Behavior*, *25*(2), 578–586. doi:10.1016/j.chb.2008.12.024

Ryan, T., & Xenos, S. (2011). Who uses Facebook? An investigation into the relationship between the Big Five, shyness, narcissism, loneliness, and Facebook usage. *Computers in Human Behavior*, *27*(5), 1658–1664. doi:10.1016/j.chb.2011.02.004

Schlagwein, D., & Prasarnphanich, P. (2014). Social media around the GLOBE. *Journal of Organizational Computing and Electronic Commerce*, *24*(2-3), 122–137. doi:10.1080/10919392.2014.896713

Schoenebeck, S. Y. (2014). *Giving up Twitter for Lent: How and why we take breaks from social media*. Paper presented at the CHI 2014, Ontario, Canada.

Shaban, H., & Timberg, C. (2018). Twitter's stock plunges more than 19 percent after reporting drop in user numbers. *Washington Post*. Retrieved from https://www.washingtonpost.com/technology/2018/07/27/twitters-monthly-users-fell-by-million-second-quarter-following-purge-fake-suspicious-accounts

Sherman, L. E., Payton, A. A., Hernandez, L. M., Greenfield, P. M., & Dapretto, M. (2016). The power of the like in adolescnece: Effects of peer influence on neural and behavioral responses to social media. *Psychological Science*, *27*(7), 1027–1035. doi:10.1177/0956797616645673 PMID:27247125

Smith, A., & Anderson, M. (2018). *Social media use in 2018*. Retrieved from Pew Research Center: https://www.pewinternet.org/2018/03/01/social-media-use-in-2018/

Song, W. F. (2009). Virtual communities: Bowling alone, online together. New York: Peter Lang.

Sprinklr. (2017). *Sprinklr spotlight: KakaoTalk & KakaoStory.* Retrieved from https://blog.sprinklr.com/sprinklr-spotlight-kakaotalk-kakaostory/

Stieger, S., Burger, C., Bohn, M., & Voracek, M. (2013). Who Commits Virtual Identity Suicide? Differences in Privacy Concerns, Internet Addiction, and Personality Between Facebook Users and Quitters. *Cyberpsychology, Behavior, and Social Networking, 16*(9), 629–634. doi:10.1089/cyber.2012.0323 PMID:23374170

Thumim, N. (2012). *Self-representation and digital culture.* Palgrave Macmillan. doi:10.1057/9781137265135

Tobin, S. J., Vanman, E. J., Verreynne, M., & Saeri, A. K. (2014). Threats to belonging on Facebook: Lurking and ostracism. *Social Influence,* 1–12. doi:10.1080/15534510.2014.893924

Turan, Z., Tinmaz, H., & Goktas, Y. (2013). The reasons for non-use of social networking websites by university students. *Scientific Journal of Media Education, 21*(41), 137–145. doi:10.3916/C41-2013-13

Wagner, K., & Molla, R. (2018, January 31). Facebook lost daily users for the first time ever in the U.S. and Canada. *Recode.* Retrieved from https://www.recode.net/2018/1/31/16957122/facebook-daily-active-user-decline-us-canda-q4-earnings-2018

Yang, H. C., & Wang, Y. (2015). Social Sharing of Online Videos: Examining American Consumers' Video Sharing Attitudes, Intent, and Behavior. *Psychology and Marketing, 32*(9), 907–919. doi:10.1002/mar.20826

Yoo, J. (2012). A qualitative analysis of how and why people use social newtork sites: A cross-cultural comparison of Korea and the U.S. *Journalism and Mass Communication, 2*(6), 1–17.

Young, N. L., Kuss, D. J., Griffiths, M. D., & Howard, C. J. (2017). Passive Facebook use, Facebook addiction, and associations with escapism: An experimental vignette study. *Computers in Human Behavior, 71,* 24–31. doi:10.1016/j.chb.2017.01.039

Zhang, Y. B., Lin, M.-C., Nonaka, A., & Beom, K. (2005). Harmony, hierarchy and conservatism: A cross-cultural comparison of Confucian values in China, Korea, Japan, and Taiwan. *Communication Research Reports, 22*(2), 107–115. doi:10.1080/00036810500130539

This research was previously published in the International Journal of Social Media and Online Communities (IJSMOC), 12(1); pages 23-39, copyright year 2020 by IGI Publishing (an imprint of IGI Global).

Index

H

Half-Truth 591, 595

Happiness 10, 112-113, 137, 176, 350, 376, 416, 663, 755, 770, 924, 972, 997, 1009, 1037, 1048, 1052, 1054, 1056, 1062, 1067, 1116, 1128-1130, 1132-1134, 1170-1172, 1175-1177, 1179, 1181-1185, 1267, 1285-1286, 1293

Hashtag 771, 780, 867-871, 874, 878, 1087, 1160-1161, 1200, 1204-1205

hedonic motivation 286-289, 291, 293, 299, 301-302, 305-306, 320-322

High-Influence User 1186

Hispanic Americans 1313-1314, 1316-1321, 1323-1324

Homophily 240, 254-255, 272, 282, 719-720, 732, 930, 941, 1102, 1104, 1107, 1112, 1114-1115, 1117, 1311

humor styles 1313-1316, 1318-1326

Hybrid-Media Producer Journalist 595

hybrid-media producers 580-581, 584-585, 592

I

Identity Fraud 462, 465

Impact Of Social Media On Children 15, 24, 36, 54, 237, 634, 1025, 1168

Impression Management 41, 47, 53, 142-144, 146, 149-150, 155-156, 237, 327-328, 419, 423, 773, 910-912, 914, 924-925, 1061, 1164, 1166, 1264

improper use of social media 978-979, 982

Inciting Hatred 457, 462, 464

Independent Self-Construal 360, 362, 367, 371-372, 1333, 1342

Indigenous 879-892, 1205

informal organization 168, 193

information exchange factors 239, 241-242

Information Manipulation Theory 2 769, 774, 787, 789

Instagram 2, 7, 11, 39, 65-66, 101, 103, 108, 111-113, 115, 119-121, 134, 136, 165-166, 168, 171-172, 177, 180-181, 185, 230, 260-261, 324, 328, 330, 332-334, 336, 338, 348, 417-420, 425, 457, 459-460, 472, 495, 502, 509-510, 528, 568-569, 619-621, 623, 625, 699, 703, 708, 769, 771-772, 775, 777-780, 785-786, 790, 828-831, 833, 836-841, 850, 854-859, 862, 864, 882, 894-895, 897-901, 906-908, 910-911, 916, 918, 998-1001, 1008, 1019, 1021, 1024, 1035-1036, 1042, 1052, 1072, 1074, 1079, 1084, 1086-1101, 1103, 1141, 1152, 1154-1159, 1161, 1163-1169, 1174, 1202, 1218-1219, 1236, 1238, 1255, 1296, 1298-1305,

1307-1309, 1311, 1329-1330, 1335-1341

Interactivity 72, 74, 340, 346, 360, 375, 453, 493, 549, 620, 862, 951, 1140, 1159

Intercultural Connections 493

Interdependent Self-Construal 359-360, 362, 367, 369, 371-372, 376, 1333, 1342

Internet Use 26, 29, 38, 40-41, 45, 50-53, 55, 134-135, 142, 145, 154, 260, 490, 497, 501, 504-505, 507, 511-512, 635, 690, 695, 713, 824, 834, 924, 984-986, 988, 990-992, 1172, 1182, 1249, 1310

Intimacy 12, 56, 117, 134, 414, 495, 498, 503-505, 507-510, 513, 670-671, 674-675, 687, 690, 787, 908, 1010, 1013-1014, 1052-1055, 1062, 1065, 1117, 1135-1136, 1139, 1203, 1213, 1246, 1263, 1267, 1270-1271, 1275, 1279, 1282

Intimidation 143, 149, 457, 462, 465, 485, 914, 1221

intrinsic cognition 439-440, 442-443, 445-451

investment model 1057, 1064, 1067, 1121, 1129, 1136-1137, 1139

IP Address 3, 14

J

Jealousy 8-9, 44, 103, 114, 416, 502, 509, 689, 737, 1049, 1051-1056, 1058-1068, 1123

Journalism 23, 217, 376, 580-585, 588, 590-593, 595, 616-617, 725, 730, 829, 857-859, 923, 925, 934, 943, 947, 965, 1016, 1018, 1083, 1117, 1203, 1230, 1310, 1344, 1347

juror 515-519, 521-526

Jury Bias 515

K

knowledge collaboration system 439-440, 449

L

Le Nhat Phuong Hong 580-581, 587, 589-591

Likes 101-112, 114-115, 117-118, 160, 172, 229, 233-235, 404, 420, 423-426, 429-430, 459, 495, 500, 517, 530, 583-584, 586, 615, 626, 676, 678, 772, 787, 807, 812, 815, 833, 887, 899-900, 929, 973, 996, 1000-1001, 1072, 1089, 1099, 1113, 1123, 1154, 1157-1159, 1182, 1187, 1190, 1195, 1211, 1277, 1280, 1333, 1341

Linkedin 2, 7, 11, 15-16, 23, 39, 58, 65, 83, 154, 162, 166-168, 177, 199, 210-215, 224, 227, 247-248, 253, 259, 265, 287, 294, 308, 398, 401-405, 410, 482, 620, 638, 641, 722, 828-829, 831, 833, 836-840, 842, 851, 854-856, 1033, 1037, 1103, 1336

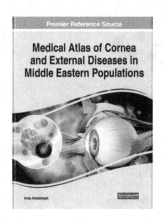
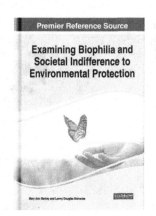
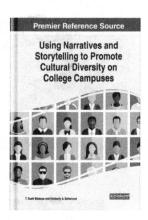

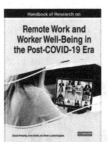

Printed in the United States
by Baker & Taylor Publisher Services